PUBLIC RELATIONS PRACTICES

Managerial Case Studies and Problems

PUBLIC RELATIONS PRACTICES

Managerial
Case Studies
and Problems

Fifth Edition

PATRICK JACKSON, Fellow PRSA

Editor, pr reporter
Senior Counsel, Jackson Jackson & Wagner
Former Adjunct Faculty, Boston University

ALLEN H. CENTER, Fellow PRSA

Former Resident Lecturer
San Diego State University
Former Vice President, Motorola, Inc.

Prentice Hall
Upper Saddle River, NJ 07458

Acquisitions Editor: Dave Borkowsky
Assistant Editor: Melissa Steffans
Production Editor: Lynne Breitfeller
Managing Editor: Fran Russello
Cover Designer: Jayne Conte
Design Director: Pat Wosczyk
Buyer: Marie MacNamara

 © 1995, 1990, 1985, 1981, 1975 by Prentice-Hall, Inc.
A Simon & Schuster Company
Upper Saddle River, New Jersey 07458

Printed in the United States of America

10   9   8

ISBN 0-13-098153-2

Prentice-Hall International (UK) Limited, *London*
Prentice-Hall of Australia Pty. Limited, *Sydney*
Prentice-Hall Canada Inc., *Toronto*
Prentice-Hall Hispanoamericana, S.A., *Mexico*
Prentice-Hall of India Private Limited, *New Delhi*
Prentice-Hall of Japan, Inc., *Tokyo*
Simon & Schuster Asia Pte. Ltd., *Singapore*
Editora Prentice-Hall do Brasil, Ltda., *Rio de Janeiro*

To all my students,
wherever, they are.   A.H.C.

To the teachers of public relations
who are giving us a new generation
of true professionals.   P.J.

Contents

CHAPTER 6   CONSUMER RELATIONS   192

CHAPTER 7   MEDIA RELATIONS   256

Preface

Twenty-two new cases have been added to this edition. So many major and rapid changes are occurring, affecting relationships, communications, and behavior that this additional material seemed essential.

On a grand scale, huge enterprises and wings of government are seeking to adjust beneficially to the global village of disparate cultures, values, and standards of behavior. At the local community level, life is strained, as jobs fall victim to technology or are moved to an area of lower wages and costs, with the tax base and public services such as education suffering. The function of public relations must be able to mediate in these changing circumstances, as they have in the past. Textbooks and courses must keep pace.

The practical purpose of this text remains the same. We seek, with case studies and problems, to help future practitioners develop agility in the principles and the application of effective two-way communications in a wide variety of situations likely to confront them and their employers.

- We have retained several timeless cases that involved turning-point issues or broke new ground in the maturing of the public relations function. These are identified as classics.
- Several cases with evolving subjects were updated.
- Some cases that have lost significance were dropped.

New cases are of such a nature that entry-level practitioners can readily identify with the topics. They deal with such broad matters of public concern as animal rights activism, the political correctness debate, corporate ethics and integrity, unsafe products, and financial takeovers.

HOW THE BOOK IS ORGANIZED

1. The first two chapters describe the purposes of public relations and the manner in which the function deals with problems and opportunities.
2. The bulk of the book contains real-life case studies in eight chapters organized according to primary publics such as employees and media or major problems such as public issues, crisis management, and standards or ethics.
3. Each chapter has a definitive introduction providing insights that come to life in the cases that follow. Introductions vary in size and substance, tailored to the assumed knowledge of students. Employee relations, for instance, reflects that most students have had work experience of some kind, whereas crisis management contains elements most students will not yet have encountered.
4. Each chapter closes with a case problem or two for class discussion closely related to the thrust of the chapter.
5. The last chapter deals candidly with career preparation.

We believe that there is enough variety to permit selectivity by educators, fitting the size of the class and the structure of the course—and enough provocation for lively classroom participation. For those interested in behavioral science research in depth, one case about the colossal effort to advance Beyond War (see Case 8–5) provides a clear application of diffusion theory in the real world of today and tomorrow. Another explains new research in risk communication.

THE AUTHORS AND THEIR APPROACH

Patrick Jackson has taught at several institutions, but is best known as editor of *pr reporter* and is a leading seminarian in professional development. He developed all the new case studies. He also amended and updated definitive passages to reflect the changes in the nature and emphasis of the calling and the roles and responsibilities of practitioners. Allen Center remains the book's originator and guiding spirit.

Patrick Jackson acknowledges help from colleagues Robin Schell, Lois Hogan, Stacey Smith, Isobel Parke, Robin Matchett, June Barber, Jim Beakey, Dick Dyer, and Jenna Wilson. Thanks additionally go out to the numerous student interns who contributed to the book in many ways: Marcy Resnick, Constance Chay, Andrea Proulx, Suzanne Canali, Tony Betke, Aimee Eliason, Kimberly Morris, and Kate Douglas.

Patrick Jackson and Allen Center mutually thank John Luecke, APR, who reviewed some of the new cases and provided valuable information to fine-tune them. Additional thanks go out to Frank Stansberry, APR, who, with the help of some of his students, provided some great case studies. They also thank the educators who reviewed the book and gave counsel on what worked in the classroom and what didn't.

The authors purposely chose to use a narrative description and avoided a set format for presenting each case. The real world does not come neatly packaged. The many teachers who regularly share their experiences with the text tell us they want students to gain experience in picking out the problem situation, delineating an environmental scan, and having to decide whether the solutions chosen were wise or flawed. Outlining the cases according to a formula denies them this most important learning from case studies.

Putting together a text of real-life case *studies*, contrasted with a collection of successful case *histories*, requires objective cooperation by the organizations represented, particularly when the subject, the scenario, or the conclusion is not laudatory. We are grateful for the information and illustrations supplied. We hope the cooperation pays off and this text enables instruction to be better attuned to the pressing needs of employers and the profession.

And finally, we would like to stress the importance and necessity of combining all public relations actions with both personal and professional ethics in behavior. This combination is outlined by the *Declaration of Principles* of PRSA's *Code of Ethics*. (see below). Other sections of the Code will be covered in further sections (see Case 5–1 for the interpretation of the code as it applies to financial relations and the introduction to Chapter 10 for the specific articles of the code of professional standards for the practice of public relations.)

CODE OF PROFESSIONAL STANDARDS FOR THE PRACTICE OF PUBLIC RELATIONS

This Code was adopted by the PRSA Assembly in 1988. It replaces a Code of Ethics in force since 1950 and revised in 1954, 1959, 1963, 1977, and 1983.

DECLARATION OF PRINCIPLES

Members of the Public Relations Society of America base their professional principles on the fundamental value and dignity of the individual, holding that the free exercise of human rights, especially freedom of speech, freedom of assembly, and freedom of the press, is essential to the practice of public relations.

In serving the interests of clients and employers, we dedicate ourselves to the goals of better communication, understanding and cooperation among the diverse individuals, groups, and institutions of society, and of equal opportunity of employment in the public relations profession.

We Pledge:

To conduct ourselves professionally, with truth, accuracy, fairness, and responsibility to the public;

To improve our individual competence and advance the knowledge and proficiency of the profession through continuing research and education;

And to adhere to the articles of the Code of Professional Standards for the Practice of Public Relations as adopted by the governing Assembly of the Society.

Chapter 1

The Purposes of Public Relations

PUBLIC RELATIONS IS AN APPLIED SCIENCE

However firm our grasp of the principles, the history, and the theories of any field, we must be able to apply them to actual cases. This statement is true for the entry-level recent graduate and for the seasoned professional. The proof of capability is in handling cases successfully for employers or clients.

- The bottom line of public relations practice is in the results that come from putting theories and principles to work—in a way that benefits the organization issuing the paycheck and the society of which that organization is a part.

For this reason, the case study method of learning about public relations is an essential part of a practitioner's education. Case studies accurately model situations that organizations, managers, and public relations practitioners routinely must face.

Though this book came into being primarily for use in the classroom—and includes practical exercises in each chapter suitable for students—it is also the major collection of carefully analyzed case studies for the field. Students can feel confident that they are using these cases right alongside seasoned veterans.

PUBLIC RELATIONS IS A RESPONSIBILITY OF MANAGEMENT

Although everyone in the organization can affect its relationships with various publics, establishing public relations policies, goals, and activities is clearly a managerial function. Public relations staffers are part of management.

The term *public relations* is often confusing because it is frequently used inaccurately. Used correctly, *public relations* describes the *processes* of practice—the techniques, strategies, structures, and tactics of the field. As such, the term is analogous to *law, medicine, nursing,* and so on. Too often, *public relations* is also used to describe the *outcomes* of effective practice—so we hear of "good public relations." The proper term for the desired outcomes of public relations practice is public *relationships.* An organization with effective public relations will attain positive public relationships.

In approaching the cases and problems presented in this book, an understanding of the meaning of management is essential. Here is a basic definition.

- Management is getting things done with people.

This statement means that managers work with and through others to carry out their assignments. Their job is not to do the work themselves but to guide and assist others in doing it. But there is another implication here that is related directly to public relations:

- Organizations must be able to get the cooperation of people both inside *and* outside the organization in order to achieve their objectives.

Thus, public relations managers must build capabilities in both the internal and external aspects of management. For this reason, they are usually selected as much for their managerial abilities in leading a staff and counseling others in the organization as for their public relations skills. The cases and problems in this book will help you practice both aspects.

THE FOCUS OF PUBLIC RELATIONS IS ON BEHAVIOR

When an organization invests resources in public relations, it expects that something will be different than before or than it would have been had the investment not been made. Examples of change might be:

- Improved purchases by and relationships with customers,
- Better community relationships,
- Active support on issues from opinion leaders,
- Reduced tension with watchdog agencies,
- Greater employee loyalty or productivity,
- More confidence in the value of a company's stock.

If all public relations does is maintain the status quo, it is being used ineffectually. In addition, if it changes only the way people feel or think about the organization—and vice versa—it has not realized its full potential. Effective public relations elicits mutually favorable *behavior* from both the organization and its publics.

Behavior may be of three types:

1. Getting people to do something,
2. Getting them not to do something,
3. Winning their consent to let the organization do something.

Looked at from another perspective, the type of change sought may be to

1. *Motivate* new behavior,
2. *Reinforce* existing positive behavior, or
3. *Modify* negative behavior.

In studying the cases we present, ask yourself what is different about behaviors after the public relations activities have been carried out. If the answer is nothing, you must consider whether public relations has failed.

ELEMENTS THAT MAKE UP THE FUNCTION

In general, public relations *is* what public relations *does* (which is true of every field). The employer, by formulating objectives, and practitioners, by accepting those objectives, define the function for that organization at that time.

Historically, the function has evolved from *one-way information transfer* to a *two-way concept* of sending messages and listening to feedback to the present idea of an organization's *adjusting harmoniously* with the publics on which it depends.[1] Underpinning this perspective, however, are at least six activities that are basic and endemic to practice:

Research. The first step in any project is to gather intelligence, in order to understand the variables in the case. What are key publics' opinions and attitudes? Who are the opinion leaders that matter? Which groups or persons are concerned enough to act?

Strategic planning. The situation and the data need to be formed into a strategy. Where are we now? How did we get here? Where do we want to be? How do we get there?

Counseling. Fellow managers must understand the plan and agree it should

---

[1]For thoughtful analysis of the evolving definition, see Scott M. Cutlip, Allen H. Center, and Glen M. Broom, *Effective Public Relations,* 7th ed. (Englewood Cliffs, N.J.: Prentice Hall, 1994), chapter 1.

be implemented. They may have a role in implementation and, at least, will need to explain it to their staffs.

Internal education. People in the organization need to be informed about the plan and their roles in it. Public relationships are not formed only by the executives or the public relations professionals, but by *everyone who interacts* with customers, employees, the community, stockholders, and all other publics.

Communication/action. The plan must be carried out. Messages or appeals are sent to the various publics involved; activities or actions are staged; feedback must be interpreted; and everyone must be kept informed as the project unfolds.

Evaluation. Another type of research, evaluation, charts effectiveness, or lack of it, and very likely will result in a new plan.

Chapter 2 reviews how this sequence is applied, in a four-step model.

PLANNING: MANAGEMENT BY OBJECTIVES

Effective organizations have a business plan made up of long-range *goals* far into the future and short-term *objectives* attainable soon. The name commonly given to this type of plan is *management by objectives,* or *MBO*.[2]

Within the statement of goals and objectives, the role expected of public relations is usually stated in general terms. Public relations activities tied to overall objectives constitutes what is called the **management concept** or **public relations strategy.**

Then, the public relations staff draws up a set of specific departmental goals and objectives. They devise programs or campaigns, hire talent, plan budgets, establish timetables, implement activities and communications, evaluate results—all, however, tied to the organization's overall business plan. This working process is called the **functional concept,** or **public relations tactics.**

One key to success in planning—observable in several cases in this book— is to anticipate problems and opportunities. This proactive, or preventive, approach is preferable to the reactive, after-the-fact, approach because it lets you take the lead, rather than being forced to respond to others. Increasingly, this **issue anticipation** approach is becoming one of the major values public relations is expected to provide.

---

[2]Courses in marketing and business methods are recommended for all students planning a career in public relations whether in profit or nonprofit enterprises. Readers who want a detailed understanding of management by objectives (MBO) should see Norman Nager and T. Harrell Allen, *Public Relations Management by Objectives* (New York: Longman, 1984).

WHAT COMES ACROSS IS VALUES

More than anything, what public relations activities communicate are the values and vision of the organization—for better or worse. These may be socially positive, acceptable values or questionable ones. But whatever the explicit message sent forth, with it goes an implicit message of whether the organization really cares about people, the community, the future, or is self-centered and concerned only with its immediate profits or success or possibly even antisocial.

The primary value public relations professionals promote inside organizations is the *open system*. An open system fosters the willingness to adjust and adapt to change, with management sensitive to all interactions in the environment. Such managers are available, listen well, and communicate forthrightly both within the organization and with external stakeholders.

In contrast is the *closed system* organization, where change is difficult. Managers cling to the status quo, sometimes desperately, and seek to change the environment that is unfavorable to the old ways. Usually they try to limit or tightly control the flow of information. In such organizations, public relations is often on the defensive, forced to put forth the view, "If only you knew us better, you'd agree with us." Private enterprise, as a system, is often accused of being closed. Often it seems to insist its ways are inviolate. "Everything, everybody else, must change to our ways" is the value that sometimes comes across. Needless to say, this attitude limits effectiveness.

For public relations practitioners, the conflict between closed and open systems of management poses a major issue. Must an organization always go along with public opinion? When is it acceptable to advocate change in public opinion? Many cases discussed here illuminate this conundrum.

THE COMMON DENOMINATORS

In almost all programs or campaigns, seven common characteristics prevail:

1. Concern about social norms, group attitudes, and individual behavior,
2. A strategy embodying specific objectives, selected audiences, careful timing, and cost controls,
3. Actions that are consistent with the policies, standards, and personality of the organization represented,
4. Emphasis on the use of **communications and participative activities to persuade,** rather than coercion,
5. Consideration of the ethical and legal implications and consequences,
6. A method of assessing the outcome in terms of benefits and costs, and

7. Translation of this assessment into decisions for continuation, alteration, or termination of the program.

THE PROVEN MAXIMS

As the library of case studies and the experience of scholars and practitioners have grown, the practice has accumulated an inventory of maxims with a high degree of reliability. Many of them derive from time-worn adages applied to persuasion and the formation of public opinion. Here are some examples of these maxims.[3]

1. An appeal to audience **self-interest** is most likely to be acceptable.
2. A **source of information** regarded as trustworthy, expert, or authoritative is most likely to be believed.
3. **Personal contact** is the most effective means of communication.
4. **Understanding a subject** is the first requisite for a communicator wishing to explain the subject to others.
5. **A suggested action,** as part of a message or coupled to it, is more likely to be accepted than a message by itself.
6. **Participation in, or awareness of, the decision process** increases the likelihood of acceptance.
7. **Personality needs and drives and peer group identity** affect the acceptance of messages and positions on issues.
8. **Degree of clarity, simplicity, and symbolism** have a direct and measurable effect on message acceptance by mass audiences.
9. **Explicitly stated messages** and appeals tend to produce more opinion change than explanations of concepts.
10. **Major issues and events** cause wide swings in public opinion for brief periods. The degree of lasting change tends to diminish with the passage of time.
11. **Self-imposed censorship** by the audience in not paying attention or not feeling involved can vary the degree of opinion change substantially.
12. **Subsequent events that reinforce the original stimulus** for opinion change will tend to increase the degree and durability of the change.
13. **Messages related to goals** are more readily acceptable than messages related to the steps and methods of attaining the goals.

[3]The "maxims" offered here are for the most part simple restatements of tenets advanced as "laws" of public opinion by Hadley Cantril, "barriers to communication" described by Walter Lippmann, Roper's "hypothesis," and Gallup's "regulators of the absorption rate of new ideas." Students can develop some of their own "maxims" or "precedential guidelines" by relating such concepts as the diffusion process, the concentric circle theory, and the two-step flow of information to situations with public relations overtones in their lives or in the news.

14. **When a public is friendly in a controversial situation,** presenting only one side of the issue tends to be effective. If the audience is not friendly, or is likely to be receptive to both sides, presenting both sides tends to be more effective.

15. In controversy, **opposing views seeking major change of opinion** tend to harden the positions held. Similarly, a strong threat to those positions tends to be less effective than a mild threat. A reliable assumption is that **people tend to resist change.**

16. When there is little to choose from between opposing views, a determining factor tends to be **the argument heard last.**

17. In a confusing situation involving opposing messages, people tend to **believe what they want to and hope for** rather than messages that strike discord.

18. **Sensitivity to public leadership** is heightened in times of crisis or controversy. At such times, people affirm or disapprove more forcefully and openly.

PROFESSIONALISM

Edward L. Bernays describes a **profession** as "an art applied to a science in a manner that puts public interest ahead of personal gain."[4] The practice of public relations lays claim to professionalism on six counts:

1. A codified body of knowledge[5] and a growing bank of precedents and case studies;

2. Insight into human behavior and the formation and movement of public opinion;

3. Skill in the use of communications tools, social science technology, and persuasion to affect opinions, attitudes, and behavior;

4. Mechanisms for academic training and professional development and for professional discipline through formal codes of ethics;[6]

5. A service that is essential in contemporary society; and

6. Nobility of purpose in harmonizing private and public interests—thus enabling individual self-determination and democratic societies to function.

---

[4]Bernays, Edward L. *The Later Years: Public Relations Insights 1956–1986.* Rhinebeck, N.Y.: H&M Publishers, pp. 138.

[5]See *The Public Relations Body of Knowledge,* updated annually by The Public Relations Society of America (PRSA) (available in computer disc and book form).

[6]See the uniform code of ethics as exemplified in PRSA's *Code of Professional Standards,* Chapter 10, p. 162.

In the cases presented in this book, observe whether the practitioners involved are meeting these tests of professionalism—and whether application of or failure to observe these guidelines has an impact on the practitioners' effectiveness.

SUCCESS

must be **CONFERRED** on us

like **OUTSIDERS**

customers
opinion leaders
neighbors
elected officials
vendors
voters
prospective employees
coalitions
stakeholders

Therefore, the bottom line for every organization is

BUILD RELATIONSHIPS

that **EARN TRUST**

and **MOTIVATE SUPPORTIVE BEHAVIORS**

REFERENCES AND ADDITIONAL READINGS

AWAD, JOSEPH F. *The Power of Public Relations.* New York: Praeger, 1985.

BASKIN, OTIS, and CRAIG ARONOFF. *Public Relations—The Profession and the Practice.* 3rd ed. Dubuque, Iowa: Wm. C. Brown, 1992.

BERNAYS, EDWARD L. *Crystallizing Public Opinion.* New York: Liveright, 1961. The first book on the field when it appeared in 1923—and still a good overview.

BUDD, JOHN F., JR. "When Less is More: Public Relations' Paradox of Growth," *Public Relations Quarterly* 35 (Spring 1990): 5–11.

BURSON, HAROLD. "Beyond PR: Redefining the Role of Public Relations." presented to the 29th Annual Distinguished Lecture of the Institute for Public Relations Research and Education, Inc., the Union League Club, New York, NY, October 2, 1990.

CUTLIP, SCOTT M., ALLEN H. CENTER, AND GLENN BROOM. *Effective Public Relations*, 7th ed. Englewood Cliffs, N.J.: Prentice Hall, 1994. Chapters 1, 2, 3, and 4.

GRUNIG, JAMES E., ED., *Excellence in Public Relations and Communications Management.* Hillsdale, N.J.: Lawrence Erlbaum Associates, 1992.

HAYNES, COLIN. *A Guide to Successful Public Relations.* Glenview, IL: Scott-Foresman, 1989.

HERBERT, RAY ELDON. *Precision Public Relations.* White Plains, N.Y.: Longman, 1988. Compendium of essays by public relations notables.

JACKSON, PATRICK. "Tomorrow's Public Relations." *Public Relations Journal* 41 (March 1985).

LESLY, PHILLIP. *Lesly's Public Relations Handbook.* Chicago, IL: Probus Publishing, 1991.

pr reporter 31 (September 26 1988). Deals editorially with acceptance yet insecurity of function, urges reenergizing through social compact and professional management awareness program.

WILCOX, DENNIS, AND PHILLIP AULT. *Public Relations Strategies and Tactics.* New York: Harper Collins, 1992.

See also *The Public Relations Body of Knowledge* compiled by The Public Relations Society of America (PRSA). This resource provides abstracts of articles, lectures, books, and book chapters relating to relevant areas of public relations. Available from PRSA 33 Irving Place, New York, NY 10003.

PROBLEM 1 BREAKING IN AN EMPLOYER

Although you have graduated with a major in public relations from Northern Illinois University, you have had no luck during the summer finding a job that will keep you in the Chicago loop area where your fiancee works. It seems as if the big firms and companies are downsizing and you have lost out to experienced people changing jobs.

You haven't given up. You have listed with a well-known employment agency specializing in communications and marketing jobs. You're living at home on the north side of Chicago, and you're making ends meet as a waiter in a large restaurant.

In mid-August the employment agency calls you. There's a growing catering service, Kitchens On Wheels Inc., headquartered in West Allis, Wisconsin, a suburb of Milwaukee on the interstate highway. They're looking for a young public relations person with some experience and interest in food services.

The fifteen-year-old business is run by its founder, George Workard. As a kid, he was a helper in his father's small restaurant; then he worked in the kitchen at a large, busy highway truck stop; and by age twenty-one he was a cook in a company that supplied airline meals. After two years of that, he bought one of their damaged food trucks, had it fixed up, rented a big old vacant building, borrowed money to equip it, and went into the catering business for himself. Today, he has a fleet of forty shiny, specially fitted kitchens on wheels with the slogan "We Bring Your Lunch Pail" painted on the side. It's another Horatio Alger, Jr., success story . . . only in America. Naturally, you want to look into it.

The employment agency sets up an appointment for you to be interviewed. The personnel manager in West Allis has you fill out an application, then says that anybody new in the office has to be approved by Mr. Workard. While you wait, the personnel manager shows you around. The office is small; the work area for cooking, sorting, packaging, and loading is huge and has some mechanization. Everybody handling food wears white and gloves. A few spotless trucks are in a separate building. You notice a few uniformed men and women who must be drivers or handle service at kitchen stops.

Finally, you go to Mr. Workard's office. It's a shambles of sample food cartons, utensils, cups, glasses, vending apparatus, menu lists, and other paraphernalia that suppliers have left behind. Mr. Workard, a small, rotund, continuous-talking and fast-acting bundle of energy and nerves, darts in. He waves the personnel man away and sits you down.

He tells you the business is getting too big for him to do everything. He wants a public relations person who will put out a newsletter "telling everybody what they should know" in order to get a better job done faster, who will work up an instruction manual to "help my people riding the trucks," who will "get our services written up in the local trade papers," and who will "get to know some of the important people around the area so they will appreciate how we do our part for the community."

After describing what he wants done, Mr. Workard adds what he doesn't want. He doesn't want to be bothered by reporters "aiming to write up how he came from nowhere and didn't get through grade school." He doesn't have time to waste sitting around on community committees that are "mostly talk." He'd rather give a little money after they've made up their minds. He also makes it clear that he will "sell the trucks and close the business" before he will sign a contract with a union. He doesn't say why he has such a deep grudge. He does say that he has a good personnel manager who hires only the "right kind of drivers and salesgirls." As for Wisconsin politics, he's "got a guy over in Madison who talks turkey to the politicians when they're off base." In running the business, he puts in his time "wherever the problem is, and that's not often in this room." Finally, in his staccato fashion, he tells you the PR job is a "one-year trial at $24,000. You get a secretary and an allowance of $20,000 for the newsletter and other expenses. Beyond that, ask for what you need." Finally, Mr. Workard says, "If the job sounds right to you, say so. If not, let's you and me not waste each other's time."

You ask him how long you have to think it over; there are the move from Chicago and other things to consider.

"What's to think over?" he says. "Either you want it, and can do it, or you don't and you can't. If you take it, and you do it right, you won't see or hear much from me. If you don't hear anything, or see me, that's good news. You're doing all right." Mr. Workard thinks that is really funny. He laughs heartily.

On the spur of the moment you decide to take the job, gambling that once you settle in, you'll be able to straighten Mr. Workard out as to what public relations is and isn't, what Kitchens On Wheels should or should not do in the name of public relations, and what his personal part in it should be.

Preparing to show up for work, you think about the purposes of public relations, the functional elements, the roles, tools, and media, the axioms or guidelines relevant to opinion formation and movement that you studied in school, and how to apply them here and now on the job. Specifically, in order for effective relationships to be a plus factor in the long-term growth and aspirations of Kitchens On Wheels, what modifications will you have to bring about in George Workard's notions about the function, his attitudes toward various public constituents and opposition groups, and, perhaps, his personal style? Put another way, what aspects of the situation do you see as problems requiring change or correction, and what do you see as opportunities to be seized, protected, and exploited?

Try converting the problems and opportunities on paper into a set of four or five personal and private goals that might take two or three years, and for each goal put down a specific objective to attain by six months and another to reach by the end of your trial year.

Looking at the objectives and the goals, write a proposal to Mr. Workard seeking his approval of a project or two that would get you started (consider, of course, whether it is a good or bad strategy at this point to reveal how your goals are related to him personally).

How Public Relations Deals with Problems and Opportunities

WHAT IS PUBLIC RELATIONS?

Here is a three-part definition of **public relations:**

1. Public relations is a condition common to every individual and corporate entity in the human environment—whether or not they recognize or act upon the fact—that refers to their reputation and relationship with all other members of the environment.
2. Public relations is the systematized function that evaluates public attitudes and behaviors; identifies the policies and procedures of an individual or organization, keeping in mind the public interest; and executes a program of action to earn public understanding and acceptance.
3. Public relations is the full flowering of the democratic principle, in which every member of society is valued for him– or herself and has both a right and a duty to express an opinion on public issues, and in which policies are made on the basis of free exchange of those opinions that results in public consent.

In other words,

- Public relations is something everyone has.
- Public relations fosters the improvement of public relationships through specific activities and policies.
- Public relations is the cornerstone of a democratic society.

PROACTIVE AND REACTIVE APPROACHES

An organization or corporation is a group of people working together for a specific purpose. That purpose invariably involves gaining the confidence of other people who will buy the product or use the service, invest in the organization's stock (or donate funds to nonprofit entities), and support its stands on issues. In short, every organization exists in a societal, or people, environment, first and foremost.

Because people form impressions and opinions of one another almost without thinking about it, every organization has a reputation, be it good or bad. Most likely, it will be good with some people, bad with others—depending on the perspective of those people and their particular interactions with the organization. As it does between persons, this reputation influences the ability of the organization to win friends, persuade others to do business with it, or be trusted in public matters.

The managerial challenge is whether something is consciously done to face the fact of reputation. When it is, the result is a public relations policy: recognition by management that positive relationships with key publics are essential to success. This management concept (see Chapter 1) is usually carried out as a functional concept by forming a public relations department and assigning it the responsibility for building and maintaining positive working relationships inside and outside the organization.

The approach the public relations department takes, however, is another challenge. Many companies—too many, some observers say—operate in a *reactive* mode. They wait for public criticism, for emergencies or bad publicity, before they act. They are usually likened to firefighters, who don't get going until there's a fire. Because reputations are formed and reformed in people's minds continuously, and because public issue debates are constantly taking shape, a more strategic approach is to be *proactive.* This approach is like fire prevention. In this approach, public relations practitioners are constantly looking for potential opportunities and problems. Thus, they will be ready to take advantage of opportunities when they arise and to prevent potential problems from flaring up.

STRATEGY AND PLANNING MAKE THE DIFFERENCE

Given the unpredictable nature of our world, there will always be unexpected situations that require reactive responses. But, just as luck comes to those who have prepared for it, so successful reactive responses are made by those who are prepared. The best preparation involves:

1. Understanding your organization or client's business, operations, and goals thoroughly;

2. Learning as much as possible about the publics on which it depends for success; and

3. Putting that understanding and knowledge together in a formal strategic plan.

With preparation, reactive responses are most likely to fit into the overall pattern of the public relations effort. Trouble comes when they do not fit—when what is put forward in response to, say, customer complaints, contradicts what the company has been saying in publicity, publications, or advertising. The company is not speaking with One Clear Voice, and this "double talk" raises questions of its accuracy and trustworthiness.

In analyzing the cases in this book, you will not know as much about the subjects or organizations as you would want to were you actually involved in the case. Never-theless, it should be apparent in most cases whether the public relations response was based on a strategic plan or just a hunch or gut feeling. More than anything else, planning makes the difference between success and failure.

PRELIMINARIES TO PLANNING

Many misunderstandings and poor public relationships occur because a legitimate inquiry is not promptly and properly answered by deed or word. Many others occur because responses are ill-timed, inaccurate, or altered by the interpretation given by a critic, or they are blown out of proportion by news media seeking sensational headlines.

Naturally, given a choice between spot reaction and time for a thoroughly considered response, public relations practitioners would opt for the latter. Sometimes there is no choice. Microphones are being thrust in your face, or a political figure is waiting impatiently in the reception area.

The substitute for a thoroughly considered response is a **strategic plan** that anticipates at least broad topics that are likely to arise. Specific problems that affect public opinion and relationships rarely exist in isolation. Each one is connected to larger matters of public concern. By considering these problems in a plan, in advance, one often can deal with a problem before it arises. Mastering the planning process is an essential and basic skill of public relations.

THE PUBLIC RELATIONS PROCESS

In devising a program or campaign, practitioners follow a series of logical steps that overlap so that they constitute a continuous **four-step process.** Here is the sequence:

1. **Fact-finding and data-gathering,** often including formal research, to define clearly the specific problem or opportunity.

2. **Planning and programming,** to devise and package a strategy.
3. **Action and communication,** to implement the strategy.
4. **Evaluation,** to determine reaction and to decide what, if anything, to do next, or differently.

A RUNNING EXAMPLE

A faulty valve at a nuclear reactor permits radioactive steam to escape. This defect raises questions about the functioning of the equipment, danger to employees and neighbors, the qualifications of the utility to operate the plant, and more.[1] That such an incident occurs is related to the larger questions of nuclear power safety, protection of public health, regulatory safeguards, the adequacy of various energy sources, and the appropriateness of the design and construction of present-day nuclear facilities. At still another level of public interest, such an incident brings into question the quality of the environment, the politics of energy, the economics of turning to alternative energy sources, and the influence on world affairs if the United States stops nuclear power development and other nations do not.

Audience Segmentation

On any public issue, and in any program to win allies or deal with opposition, the *variables* must be taken into account. Our example illustrates three major variables:

1. **The proximity of the audiences involved,** geographically and emotionally. In the radioactive emission at the nuclear plant,
   - **employees** on the job would be vitally involved,
   - so would the **neighbors;**
   - the next circle of proximity could be the **executives and engineers** of the utility,
   - the **inspectors** who had approved the equipment, including the leaking valve,
   - and the **supplier** of the valve.

---

[1]The example used is simulated. It benefits from the national attention focused by the Three Mile Island and Chernobyl incidents on the dangers of nuclear energy production. It is not, however, a replica. The risk of errors, mishaps, and accidents are inherent in the handling of flammable, toxic, and explosive substances. In the same time frame as Three Mile Island, an explosion at a California chemical plant killed two and injured eighty people; an explosion in Tennessee spewed toxic materials over a five-mile radius; and twenty persons were felled by chlorine fumes escaping at a mobile home park. Our technological society may face such problems.

2. The extent to which an audience can be helped or hurt, rewarded or penalized.

3. Timeliness.

There may be several important publics, but which ones need attention now, which a month from now, which next year? Because of proximity, but also because of *timeliness,* the employees and immediate neighbors of the nuclear plant are important publics for communications now. Once the emergency has passed, public relations efforts can target regulators and other government officials. Consumers of the nuclear-produced power may receive some information early regarding the availability of power, but a more extensive campaign may have to wait.

Both proximity and timeliness are examples of why *all publics are not created equal.* The importance of publics shifts with a change of events or because the campaign with one public has been completed. One of the important functions of the public relations professional is to counsel management about which publics should receive priority status. This counsel is based on the principle that public relations efforts generally are aimed at specific audiences or publics rather than at the general public or mass audiences. This principle raises the question of how to break the general public into smaller audiences that have particular importance for the organization. There are, however, even earlier questions to be answered.

FACT-FINDING AND DATA-GATHERING: THE FIRST STEP OF THE PROCESS

Much of what goes on in the name of public relations and persuasive communication is just plain busywork. Much more is wasted effort. Much is actually counterproductive, because it is unnecessary or because it is tactless, abrasive, immoral, or even unethical. Most of these problems can be avoided by making three preliminary determinations.

1. Do we really have a public relations problem?
2. If we do, is it a problem that can be
   a. alleviated,
   b. turned around in our favor, or
   c. countered by some sort of adjusting action or communication?
3. If it can be resolved, is action on our part indicated now or later?

Let us apply these questions to the problem of the radioactive steam emission at the nuclear plant. Suppose the backup valve had worked as it was supposed to. Suppose the contaminating steam had been promptly brought under control. Would we have had a problem of immediate public concern? What purpose would then have been served by announcing anything to anyone outside the plant?[2] Such an announcement might have forced a regulatory agency to shut down the plant, putting employees out of work. If that happened, how would the economics of the whole community be affected? Would news about the mechanical problem, and an averted emergency, actually be counterproductive if news media sensationalized it or if politicians opposed to nuclear power or to the party in power seized on it to make trouble for the administration and to further their own interests?

There is never a guarantee that practitioners can control any information that news media consider of public interest and within their prerogatives under the First Amendment. Nor is there any guarantee that one organization will not seize upon a competitor's problem to gain an advantage in the marketplace. There is often something to be gained and little to be risked, however, in refraining from the knee-jerk reaction to release information that helps one special interest at the expense of another—unless the greater interest of the whole public is at stake.

A great many isolated and insignificant situations are ballooned into problems of public proportion by the lack of real strategic thinking by management, by the miscalculation of overzealous communicators, and by the competitive efforts of news media.

In the on-going practice of public relations, remember the old adages, "Look before you leap," and "Don't go off half-cocked."[3]

PLANNING AND PROGRAMMING: THE SECOND STEP OF THE PROCESS

The process of handling public relations problems is so dynamic, with all four phases sometimes compressed into minutes, that hard lines dividing one phase from another cannot always be drawn. The lack of a clear separation between research and planning is a good example.

The drawing up of a plan of action implies that such matters as identifying target publics, setting specific objectives, figuring out a budget, and deciding on a timetable are all fixed in place like the numbered stops on an elevator. But they are not. All depend on an underlying strategy. Thus, there is a bridging that takes place in which the fact-finding and analysis of fact in the light of organizational goals and policies allow for choices to be made among the available alternatives.

---

[2]The rules for routine reports to the Nuclear Regulatory Commission would of course apply, raising the possibility that the news would get out from that source.

[3]A remarkable number of homely old adages applicable to public relations reappear in new words, sometimes as principles or maxims. Here are a few: "One false step can ruin the reputation of a lifetime," "One picture is worth a thousand words," "A stitch in time saves nine," "Methinks the lady doth protest too much," "Everybody loves a winner," "Once burned, twice shy."

RETURNING TO THE EXAMPLE

Continuing with the leaking valve problem at the nuclear plant and the concept of concentric circles of audience involvement, assume that (1) there is a public relations problem; (2) the problem can be alleviated by appropriate action or communication; and (3) the circles of involved publics are employees and neighbors, executives of the utility and of certain government agencies, the utility's shareholders, and the general public, in that sequence.[4]

Given these facts, what is the overriding *objective?* What are the desirable limits of responsive action? What form of response best attains the objective within the desired limits? What should be the content of the message and who the carrier? Or what should be the action and who the initiator?

Practitioners answer these questions by considering the pros and cons for each available alternative. For example, at the nuclear plant, assuming that news media will inquire, there are at least four available responses in the short term:

1. Deny that anything out of the ordinary has happened.
2. Admit a mechanical problem, but deny that there is any danger.
3. Admit a mechanical problem and indicate that it is being brought under control.
4. Admit a mechanical problem and indicate that it will be corrected as soon as possible.

Strategic thinking might conclude that the first response is deceitful or misleading. Lying to or misleading the public may be illegal. Even if this action is not illegal, getting caught would pose a threat to the future of local relationships, to the integrity of the utility, and to public acceptance of nuclear power. Obviously, that alternative would be rejected. Responses 2 and 3 run the same risks where credibility and public safety are concerned, if all does not turn out well. The fourth alternative is the truth *as the truth is known at the moment.* Thus, this response is acceptable, no matter what the outcome. (See Chapter 9 for details on effective programming in a crisis.)

Strategic thinking on a matter as grave as a nuclear accident, or the threat of one, would of course go to much greater depths than outlined in this example. It would involve top-level people in the utility, the energy industry, government, the community, and probably the employees, as a bare minimum. The point to remember is that strategic thinking encompasses research, analysis and a plan of action. This relationship is shown in Figure 2–1.

---

[4]The concentric circle concept derives from Elmo Roper's hypothesis that ideas penetrate to the whole public very slowly, moving from great thinkers to disciples, then to disseminators, next to the politically active, and finally to the politically inert.

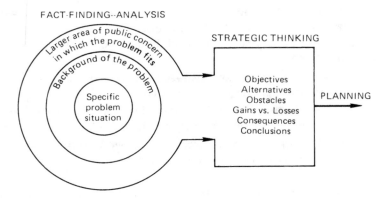

FACT-FINDING--ANALYSIS

STRATEGIC THINKING

Larger area of public concern in which the problem fits

Background of the problem

Specific problem situation

Objectives
Alternatives
Obstacles
Gains vs. Losses
Consequences
Conclusions

PLANNING

Figure 2–1   All the facts subjected to strategic considerations lead to a plan.

PLANNING

In much the same manner that fact-finding leads to and merges into **planning,** plans lead to and merge into **programs of action.** When a plan is set down on paper, it usually takes the form of a proposal. It may propose a public statement, a position paper, a detailed special event, a campaign, or an extended program to stimulate favorable reaction. It may propose as well that the organization take certain steps in its operations, or perhaps adopt or change a policy.

The actual submission or presentation of a plan of action must deal with more than long-term goals. It is expected to cover practical matters such as theme and appeal, budget, media, tools and vehicles, personnel and special talent, logistics, audience profiles, and the timetable. Above all, public relations plans must support an organization's particular objectives.

The specific response or message to be sent is sometimes determined by the situation confronted. If not, then it usually develops in the situation analysis or the strategic thinking. Decisions regarding the targeting of publics and the selection of message-carrying media may emerge as an aspect of strategic thinking. More often, they are determined as an aspect of the planning phase. We separate them here for emphasis.

SELECTION OF AUDIENCES: PRIMARY, INTERVENING, SPECIAL

One way to select priority audiences is to divide the whole public into primary, intervening, and special publics, and then to select a priority public from these groupings.

- A **primary public** is one that is directly affected by the actions or planned activities of an organization.

- An **intervening public** is a specific group that stands between a practitioner and a primary audience. For example, if parents are a primary audience, an intervening public can be their children. Such publics are often referred to as *gatekeepers*.
- A **special public** is an organized group generally with a set of bylaws and with regular meetings. There are two kinds of special publics:
  1. An *inward special public* is organized for the primary objective of serving its own members rather than nonmembers.
  2. An *outward special public* is organized for the primary reason of serving persons other than its own members.

If we apply these definitions to the nuclear plant example, employees, neighbors, and consumers of the electricity produced at the plant will be directly affected by the actions at the plant; they are the primary publics. Intervening publics include the media and some technical groups who may affect the primary audiences. Outward special publics for this example include environmentalists as well as the many groups that are organized to oppose nuclear energy publicly. Inward special publics would include national or regional associations that represent electrical producers or that represent manufacturers of electrical appliances.

Once such a listing of publics is made, the next step is to select those that warrant immediate attention and those that, although important, can wait. In this example, employees and neighbors, because of the safety factor, rate a high priority. Also very high, because of their long-range impact on the company, are consumers of the plant's nuclear-generated electricity and regulatory government officials. The media rate a high ranking also. Once the safety problem has lessened, the special publics opposing nuclear power would rank high. Electrical consumers in other areas, stockholders, and associations would rank further down the list.

The example of the nuclear plant accident explains why problem solving in public relations places great emphasis on the selection of target audiences preparatory to a planned public response.

SELECTION OF MESSENGERS

Information tools, the messengers, fall into several categories. The main criterion for choosing one over another is its credibility and thus its ability to motivate a receiving audience into an attitude or a behavioral action.

The term *media* is too often used to mean *news* media. For public relations practitioners, it means *any* medium of communication or feedback.

In the example of the incident at the nuclear plant, the audience motivation sought by the utility would be an attitude of calm confidence that all is well, or will turn out to be so. Contributing factors in media selection for each situation, crisis or not, can be (1) the importance and thus the priority of each audience, (2) the time allowed or required to get information to the audience, (3) the level of authority required for credibility, (4) the accuracy of a medium in hitting a target audience, and (5) the medium's ability to influence behavior efficiently in terms of cost and effort. For simplicity, we touch on six basic categories:

1. Individuals
2. Personalized message tools
3. Publications
4. Mass media
5. Advertising
6. Special events

Individuals

People are the most effective messengers. When a qualified person communicates, there can be emphasis, credibility, body language reinforcement, and the all-important opportunity for instant feedback. If the message is misunderstood, or only partially understood, questions can be asked. More details can be given until understanding is achieved. Action, too, can be immediate as in getting a donation, signatures on a petition, or volunteer workers.

Individuals can carry the message in the following ways, from most effective to least effective:

- **One-to-One**, ideally between peers, whether neighbors or corporate vice-presidents;
- **One-to-a-small group,** retaining the personalized aspect and offering opportunity for clarification, as in a meeting or open house, for example; and
- **One-to-a-large group**, providing the presence and credibility of a good speaker. There may be some sacrifice in the clarification process, however, because of the reluctance of some people to ask questions in this setting.

Personalized Message Tools

When face-to-face delivery by a person is not possible, there are media that allow personalization without serious sacrifice of credibility or control. Examples include:

- **Telephone calls** approximate the one-on-one ideal, providing opportunity for clarification, emphasis, and immediate reaction, losing only the face-to-face visual impression that gives notification by the attention span, facial expressions, and body language whether there is understanding and perhaps acceptance.

- **Letters or cards** run the gamut of good, bad, and indifferent, depending on whether personally written, addressed and signed, or the computer letter perceived as junk mail and consigned to the nearest wastebasket. There persists in our culture, however, a special psychological attachment to personal mail. It is controllable by the sender. Handled with skill and empathy, it can be credible and productive.
- **New computer, television, and other visual technology** is opening the way to extensive new approximations of "personalized" media. These include the picture phone, interactive computer dialoguing, teleconferencing, two-way television, and others.

Publications

Publications that are specialized and focused narrowly on a particular audience interest have appeal and utility for their readers—and therefore for public relations practitioners. This category does not embrace publications of a mass market or mass media nature and circulation. Among the kinds of specialized publications with a high efficiency ratio are:

- **Organizational or group newsletters** that go to individuals as members or as a special-interest group—assuring knowledge of and interest in the organization's doings and well-being. Examples are legion, such as dog lovers, conservationists, or chamber of commerce or church members.
- **Business or professional publications,** some of which have paid subscriptions and advertising, and others of which are free. Receivers of paid subscriptions tend to expect more than receivers of free publications. In public relations practice alone, there are several professional publications. The *Public Relations Journal* is one of the monthly magazines. *pr reporter* and *PR News* are among the weekly newsletters.
- **Employee publications** express a commonalty of membership and self-interest and provide specific significant information.

Mass Media

Newspapers, magazines, radio, and television offer the largest audiences and have the most demanding standards for usable messages. In these media, the sender forfeits control over the use of the information as to timing, emphasis, amount, or phraseology. Once material has been released, editorial values and judgment take over. As a rule, the closer a news item is to the competitive self-interests of a medium, the greater will be its value to the audience covered by that medium; and the more professionally the information is prepared and documented, the better are the chances it will be used. Awareness of demographics, each medium's set of priorities, and the philosophy and stance of media owners and editors, all have a bearing on whether an item will be accepted and on how it will be presented. Media selection is not an arena for amateurs.

Advertising

Advertising, in order to control the message, the timing, and the position in relation to other information carried by an outlet and to develop either a continuity or a complex message, has long been a tool of public relations. But the public's growing skepticism about advertising must be taken into account.

Special Events

Special events can combine the personalized touch of one-to-one or one-to-a-group encounters with the excitement of a rally, march, or convention. They can also be used to distribute publications, from leaflets to books. Question-and-answer forums are usual features. Exhibits or displays, films or audiovisuals can be used. There are several types of special events, ranging from a simple meeting or open house to an attempt to attract attention to an issue or cause by picketing. A basic question in using events is whether the target audience is the attendees or those not attending—or both.

PLANNING INVOLVES A TEAM

A public relations plan of action normally involves the participation of several groups in the organization. Usually the human resources department, financial department, legal counsel, and marketing or sales and operating or field staff are involved. Obviously, advance agreement on cooperation or collaboration is required. Finally, implementation of a plan of action requires the approval and commitment of top management. The current jargon for this aspect is "getting buy-in."

A classic example of commitment exists in the public posture of the oil industry. When the price of a gallon of gasoline began to rise rapidly in the 1970s, an official of one company made the statement publicly that the price would have to go to $1.50 a gallon, and then it would be practical to go out and explore for new oil resources. This statement set policy in the company. Consequently, it gave direction and management commitment to its communicators whether in news, advertising, or other forms of public contact. Another oil company's management committed itself to aggressive advocacy of the industry, the profit motive, and the private enterprise system. The communications programming to implement this stance proceeded with complete assurance.

When elaborate or bold public relations campaigns falter or are withdrawn midstream, it is often because they run into unexpected hurdles of adverse reaction, or some opposition within the organization, and the original conviction and commitment of top management was so marginal that it refused to follow through. When the winds of public opinion shift, organizations tend to react like a sensitive person. *Approvals based on conviction, and supported by management participation and adequate budget, are essential to effective public relations programming.*

The manner in which the planning phase of the problem-solving process moves into the action phase is shown in Figure 2–2.

ACTION AND COMMUNICATION: THE THIRD STEP OF THE PROCESS

When the problem is defined, audiences prioritized, and the strategic plan approved, action commences. It may take the form of a policy change, launching an internal or public campaign, redesigning a product, or countless other forms. Although the action is the *substance* of the plan, little benefit can be expected unless affected publics *know about it.* Therefore, communication with the hope of persuading and affecting behavior is built into almost all public relations activity. Even when the objective is to censor, to inhibit, to neutralize, or to ignore, some sort of communicative action can be required.

A bulletin at the nuclear plant warning employees that gossip, speculation, or exaggeration about the leaky valve problem could endanger their jobs would constitute communication, although designed in their own self-interest to inhibit it. Similarly, a telephone call to the inquiring reporter saying "off the record" that repair was imminent and asking whether release of the information could be delayed or the news value minimized to avoid risk of panic in the community would constitute

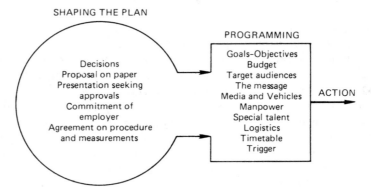

Figure 2–2   Formalized planning shapes into projects or programs of action.

a communicative action designed to edit or censor needlessly harmful public communication.

In practice, decisions on media, vehicles, talent, and budget concerning the implementation of a program usually are made during the planning phase rather than the action phase. These aspects of the process are shown in Figure 2–2 as independent activities simply for convenience. Usually, approvals granted by top managers allow latitude for alterations in media selection, timing or timetable, frequency of message, and other accommodations of changing circumstances.

There are a host of variables and unpredictables making this flexibility advisable. Among them are internal publication frequency; availability of news media contacts; competition for newsprint space or airtime; the differing level of public attention on a weekday versus a weekend; delays in copy composition, graphic art, filming, or printing of materials; delays caused by the illness or resignation of staff members; or interruptions caused by other tasks with higher priority or a greater immediacy.

SITUATION NORMAL, ALL FOULED UP (SNAFU)

Robert Burn's observation that the best laid schemes of mice and men often go wrong certainly applies to public relations programs seeking to capture or change the course of public opinion. Here's an example.

The naval forces based in San Diego were host to an offshore exercise called Valiant Heritage in which some ships and planes representing allies teamed up to deal with a simulated enemy invasion of San Diego. Elaborate preparations on a minute-by-minute basis were made for the handling of a one-day media visit to the aircraft carrier *Enterprise,* a central unit in the exercise.

The agenda read like clockwork, starting with the 8:00 A.M. time the press helicopter lifted off North Island base and headed 75 miles out to rendezvous with the *Enterprise.* Then, at precise times on the agenda, there were to be a press briefing with an admiral, observations of aircraft landings and takeoff, side trips by air to ships of allied nations or surveillance of an airstrike on a derelict ship, reassembly on the *Enterprise* for press debriefing, lunch, and flight return to North Island in time for dinner at home.

The first mishap was that some of the press arrived late at North Island. Next, about the time that all were in the helicopter, one photographer could not find some of his gear. The helicopter flight took longer than computed to reach the cruising *Enterprise.* At this point the detailed plans for handling the press were running twenty minutes behind the printed agenda in the hands of four or five hundred naval personnel who had something to do with the event one way or another.

Then, during the morning, there was an intercom invitation for members of the press to go up and visit the bridge. But the elevator had chosen this day to go on the blink. Traffic climbing up and down the narrow ship's stairway was crowded, to put it mildly.

All during the day, to the credit of the navy and the public affairs personnel involved, they stayed calm, kept the phones and intercom busy and improvised so that the news media got what they had come for and the collaboration of the allied nations appeared in a favorable light. In hindsight, the mishaps probably helped accept the impression of wartime activities; but the event wasn't planned that way.

Dedications, ground breakings, and anniversaries planned for sunshine sometimes have to be moved indoors midway because of rain. Messages calculated to win friends are sometimes found to be offensive to special audiences and have to be changed or scrapped. Financial reports requiring release on a specified day for legal reasons can run into a printer's mechanical problem the day before. A preplanned response to a reporter's unwanted and embarrassing question can be halted by the organization's lawyer after the organization's spokesperson has approved it.

So it goes in public relations. Snafus are normal, not unusual. The best plans therefore take this possibility into account by providing "fallback" or "safety net" actions in case snafus do occur.

- The ability to work under stress and improvise is a requisite in carrying out public relations programs. A talent for neutralizing what appears to be an adverse predicament, or turning adversity into a positive or favorable outcome, distinguishes the expert professional. "Making lemonade out of lemons" as practitioners like to say.

EVALUATION: THE FOURTH STEP OF THE PROCESS

Almost as important as the origination and activation of a program, and the running changes that may need to be made, is the follow-up (see Figure 2–3). Too many well-conceived and successful projects and programs are launched without any thought or commitment to continuity or encores.

As we have seen, public relations programs, like those in marketing, finance, or public administration, are subject to running changes to improve them. They are also subject to questions about their future: Should they continue? The tools for answering such questions are monitoring and measurement.

Monitoring

There are many ways to attain the benefits of monitoring. Clipping and broadcast services will monitor news media for their clients. They cut out newspaper and magazine articles mentioning the client's products, services, and viewpoints. They tabulate airtime mentions. But they do not see, hear, or clip all the news on any subject. Ten to fifteen percent of an organization's total publicity is a good estimate of what these services do deliver.

ACTION

Launching
Follow-up
Evaluation of
feedback
Decisions on what to
do next

Figure 2–3 Action involves two-way
communication, outbound and incoming.

Other methods of monitoring include surveys among employees, community, or special-interest audiences, whether members, donors, students, or investors. Advisory boards, test panels, and focus groups are used. Special events are gauged by feedback from participants or by exit interviews. There are specialized firms that monitor activities concerned with legislative or financial affairs and with fundraising or membership campaigns.

Perhaps the largest share of the vehicles set up to monitor the impact and progress of programs are tailor-made to an organization's particular needs. As hypothetical examples, a computer company wanting to be known as definitive in its field might monitor new books dealing with cybernetics. A food company might retain a prominent university nutritionist. The oil industry might lean heavily and regularly on its lobbyists for input. A local retailer might put coupons in advertisements or run a contest among the customers to see if its messages are getting through.

Measurement

There is a tendency in public relations practice to point at size of the audience at the linage or minutes of publicity, at the prestige of news outlets carrying material, and at the number of "friendly" newspeople or opinion leaders as meaningful indicators of a program's value or progress. There is the tendency to use these quantitative and qualitative features to predict success. To avoid such fallacious thinking, remember:

- Public appearance alone (circulation of a message) does not equal public reception (readership, listenership, viewership), nor does even a third-party news medium's impartiality (credibility) indicate or guarantee public acceptance (agreement or behaivor).

Efforts to quantify results are now often reported by practitioners as circulation attained per dollar of cost or as program cost as a percentage of gain in sales, funds raised, or members attracted. Or they might be reported in terms of coupons returned or inquiries per dollar of expenditure or as behaviors observed in key publics or individuals. Increasingly, the emphasis is on *behavioral measurement,* because it doesn't really matter whether a public received your message or attended your event *unless they did something about it.*

In the more sophisticated public relations operations, the degree of involvement of public relations with other organizational functions and the directness of the relationship of programs to organizational goals constitute the best measurements and the best indication of what lies ahead.

As the state of the art matures, computer technology is enabling measurement of the relative utility of the function, based on all the factors that go into programs and their impact individually and collectively on the behaviors of various audiences that make up an organization's constituency and opposition. The necessary information is accumulated and stored in computers for ultimate retrieval.[5] Such evaluation is the major emerging step in effective practice.

ASSESSMENT OPTIONS

From whatever feedback concerning a program is obtained for evaluation, one of five conclusions can be drawn.

1. Let's continue the program as is.
2. Let's continue the program with some changes.
3. Let's terminate the program; it has served its purpose.
4. Let's gradually wind down the program.
5. Let's start a new program to succeed this one.

THE NUCLEAR PLANT EXAMPLE AGAIN

Consider once more the problem posed by the leaking valve and the radioactive steam at the nuclear reactor. Had the backup valve worked, the faulty one been replaced quickly, the employees undisturbed, and no harm been done, the third choice might have been the best one: Terminate the program. But, if rumors had spread, making the community uneasy, then the fourth choice might have been made: Gradually wind down the program, with provisions for a calm and reassuring recap of the situation to employees and the hometowners.

If the situation at the nuclear plant had been such that communication could not be terminated or wound down, then public relations considerations would have

---

[5]For current research, see Glen Broom and David M. Dozier, *Using Research in Public Relations* (Englewood Cliffs, N.J.: Prentice Hall, 1990).

had to be recycled into one or another of the earlier basic steps: fact finding research, planning and programming, or action and communication. For example, assume that the utility's top management has decided, as a means of avoiding any conceivable possibility of another scare, that the company is going to set an example of maximum preventive maintenance for the whole industry to copy. As part of this decision, management wants public relations programming that will give its constituent publics and its critics, from employees to investors, from government regulatory bodies to competitors, good reason to appreciate what it is doing. With this turn of events, the role of public relations becomes that of public educator. Such a role calls for extensive research of factual and scientific information; strategic thinking addressed to the long haul, not to crisis; and planned programming on several levels of technology adapted to the ability of diverse audiences to comprehend.

Problem solving is a continuing process of adapting to changing circumstances. This process is shown in Figure 2–4.

PUTTING IT ALL TOGETHER

A step-by-step approach to problem solving as outlined on the preceding pages is not a panacea. It is not a surefire way to get the wanted result. It is not the only way to structure a sequential approach. Knowing how to proceed within a structure, however, is vastly better than having to operate on impulse. The process of responding to a public relations problem is like any other decision-making process by professionally trained managers. There is rarely only one absolutely right or best an-

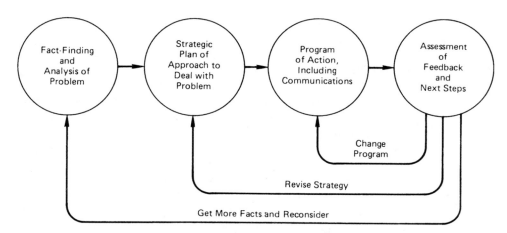

Figure 2–4 Problem solving portrayed as a continuous process.

swer to a public relations problem, or to one in marketing, fund-raising, or political campaigning.

This statement is easily put to a test. Gather together a few trained public relations consultants and present them with a communications problem, such as a rumor of a boycott, inevitably requiring some kind of reaction or response. The chances are that these experts, having a common training, will come up with different reactions and approaches. In each case, the reaction and approach will generally represent the honest conviction of the consultant. Effectiveness is enhanced by enthusiasm, personal conviction, and individual skills.

Suppose, however, that in the absence of a group of consultants, a resident practitioner was confronted with the fact that somebody had just thrown a brick through the window of the organization's headquarters. Assume that this action is a provocation calling for some kind of immediate response. The practitioner in seconds, or minutes, must decide whether to react by hurling the rock back at the attacker, ignoring the incident, or, perhaps, inviting the rock thrower to come in and talk things over and stay for dinner. Obviously, the circumstances here are extraordinary. Even though the decision process is compressed into seconds or minutes, the chances are that others in the organization—some junior to the practitioner, and some senior—would be involved. Whatever decision and response emerged would be the "right" one for that organization, at that moment, under the existing circumstances, and in consideration of whatever lay ahead.

Experience shows that a trained practitioner who knows how to apply a logical step-by-step analysis is always better able than an untrained person to deal with the unexpected. It is also in the nature of professional work that a practitioner is asked, on occasion, to follow a course of communication or action with which he or she does not fully agree, to assist a spokesperson or a cause for whom or which he or she has little enthusiasm, or to further a public interest that is felt to be at odds with his or her self-interest. The practitioner's acceptance or rejection of such requests is a personal matter.

WHAT TO LOOK FOR IN THE CASES

In the case studies and the problems that make up the balance of this textbook, it is not expected that all students or practitioners will agree on the controversial issues posed, such as gun control, birth control, smoking, product recalls, standards of ethics, or nuclear power. Disagreement does not mean that one is right and the other wrong. It means that all are reacting to the same stimuli. It is expected that individuals will differ in analysis of the campaigns and programs offered. They will favor a variety of solutions to the cases and to the job-related problems derived from actual situations. This is all as it should be, for a learning experience. It is hoped that differing views will hone professionalism.

Three tenets bear mention for their significance and relevance.

1. When there is a choice, a carefully considered and **structured approach** to public communication increases the odds of audience acceptance.
2. The measure of true professionalism can often be taken in terms of **objectivity,** as expressed in **empathy** toward the views of others and in the ability to set aside personal bias.
3. When the philosophy, convictions, and public posture of a practitioner and an employer are in **harmony,** the chances of **credibility** and **persuasion** are measurably enhanced.

Cases are presented in narrative form, rather than outline, because that most closely approximates the way information comes to practitioners working on a case. This presentation gives the reader responsibility for sorting the critical information from mere static—as in real life.

In making judgments about how well organizations and practitioners handled the situations outlined in the cases, perhaps the best guide is whether they demonstrated an awareness of the process of public relations—as shown in the illustrations in this chapter.

REFERENCES AND ADDITIONAL READINGS

BASKIN, OTIS, and CRAIG ARONOFF. *Public Relations–The Profession and the Practice.* 3rd ed. Dubuque, Iowa: William C. Brown, 1992.

BAUS, HERBERT, and PHILIP LESLY. "Preparation for Communicating." Chapter 20 in *Lesly's Public Relations Handbook.* 2nd ed. Chicago, IL: Probus, 1991.

BENNIS, WARREN G. *Organizational Development: Its Nature, Origins, and Prospects.* Reading, Mass: Addison-Wesley Publishing Company, 1969.

BRODY, E. W. *Communication Tomorrow: New Audiences, New Technologies, New Media.* New York: Praeger, 1990.

Brody, E. W. *Public Relations Programming and Production.* New York: Praeger, 1988.

BROOM, GLEN M., and DAVID M. DOZIER. *Using Research in Public Relations: Applications to Program Management.* Englewood Cliffs, N.J.: Prentice Hall, 1990. Definitive and up-to-date in this field.

CUTLIP, SCOTT M., ALLEN H. CENTER, and GLEN M. BROOM. *Effective Public Relations,* 7th ed. Englewood Cliffs, N.J.: Prentice Hall, 1994. See the four-step process. Chapters 10, 11, 12, and 13.

GOLDHABER, GERALD. *Organizational Communication.* 5th ed. Dubuque, Iowa: William C. Brown, 1990.

GRUNIG, JAMES E., and TODD HUNT. *Managing Public Relations.* New York: CBS College Publishing, 1984. See Chapters 6 and 7.

HABERMAN, DAVID A., and HARRY A. DOLPHIN. *Public Relations: The Necessary Art.* Ames, Iowa: Iowa State University Press, 1988.

HENDRIX, JERRY A. *Public Relations Cases.* 2nd ed. Belmont, Calif: Wadsworth, 1992. Case histories drawn from PRSA Silver Anvil Winner summaries.

KLEIN, GERHART L. *PR Law: The Basics.* Mt. Laurel, N.J.: Anne Klein & Associates, 1990.

LERBINGER, OTTO, AND NATHANIEL N. SPERBER. "Contingency Plans." Chapter 2 in *Manager's Public Relations Handbook.* Reading, Mass.: Addison-Wesley, 1982.

LESLY, PHILIP. "Analysis, Planning and Programming." Chapter 17 in *Lesly's Public Relations Handbook.* 4th ed. Chicago, IL: Probus, 1991.

LONDGREN, RICHARD E. *Communication by Objectives.* Englewood Cliffs, N.J.: Prentice Hall, 1983. An application of MBO to communications.

MARSTON, JOHN. "A Formula for Successful Public Relations Practices." Chapter 9 in *Modern Public Relations.* New York: McGraw-Hill, 1979. Describes the RACE formula, a variation of the four-step process.

HARRELL, ALLEN T. and NORMAN A. NAGER. *Management by Objectives.* New York: Longman, 1984. See Chapter 3.

NEWSON, DOUG PHD., ALAN SCOTT PHD, and JUDY VAN SLYKE TURK PHD. "PR—What and Why?" Chapter 1 in *This is PR: The Realities of Public Relations.* 4th ed. Belmont, Calif.: Wadsworth, 1989.

OTT, RICHARD. *Creating Demand.* Homewood, IL: Business One Irwin, 1991.

PAVLIK, JOHN V. *Public Relations: What Research Tells Us.* Newbery Port, Calif.: Sage, 1987.

pr reporter 36 (September 27, October 18, 1993). Two part report on twenty-ninth annual survey of significant trends in the structure, stature, and functional activities as seen by practitioners.

The Public Relations Body of Knowledge. New York: PRSA, 1993. See section IV for abstracts dealing with the "Public Relations Process."

SHOCKLEY-ZALABAK, PAMELA. *Fundamentals of Organizational Communication.* 2nd ed. White Plains, N.Y.: Longman, 1988.

"Twelve Trends That Are Steering Public Relations Practice." *pr reporter* 36 (March 15, 1993)

WALSH, FRANK. *Public Relations and the Law.* Sarasota, F.L.: Institute for Public Relations Research and Education, 1988.

PROBLEM 2 PUTTING THE PR PROCESS TO WORK

You're two years out of Bell College, with a major in journalism and an emphasis in public relations. You're working for State Capital Public Relations, Inc. Your main account, so far, is Mothers Against Drunk Driving (MADD) statewide. It's been a breeze. There is not much money to spend, but the people are nice to work with. There's a lot of talk, some publicity, and some publications for mailers, but not much action.

One day, your contact, the director at MADD, calls up and says that their project—"tie a red ribbon on your car door or antenna"—during the Christmas holiday period didn't go over very well for their relatively new chapter in Munsea. The director is mystified. There was generous local media publicity; plenty of ribbons, posters, and bumper stickers were made available in stores, banks, and public buildings; there was a timely mailing to thousands of homes, with a ribbon and a plea for donation. "Our people down there say the project just didn't catch on," your MADD contact tells you. Then he says, "Please go down to Munsea, find out what you can, and make recommendations as to where we should go from here."

You don't mind the assignment. Munsea is a bustling city of 80,000 including Bell College, with an enrollment of 7,000 students and nationally ranked year after year in basketball. No doubt some of your Bell teachers are still at the school and some local alumni you went to school with are still in town. You already know some things about the town and the school that might be relevant. It will be interesting to pay a visit on official business.

You remember well how a basketball game at Munsea always packed the splendid field house with fans from as far away as 100 miles and that many stayed overnight to celebrate or drown their sorrow. You recall that Munsea couldn't fully control the celebrating or the drinking. In fact, when you were in school at Bell, the city council passed an ordinance prohibiting any more bars or discos within the city limits. No more than a year later, a dozen or more roadhouses and motels had sprung up on the border of town. You also recall that there was a move to impose a curfew on the nights when Bell played a home game at the field house. The owners of hotels and restaurants, several unions, and most members of the chamber of commerce were successful in getting it voted down.

THE CURRENT SITUATION

Before you leave the office for the Munsea trip, your boss fills you in about the Munsea MADD chapter. It is headed by Ima Determined, a grade school principal. She initiated a MADD chapter in Munsea after experiencing a personal tragedy at the beginning of the basketball season just six weeks ago. A male Bell student, the son of a state highway commissioner, and Ima's daughter, also a Bell student, were involved in a head-on collision with an out-of-town driver visiting for the game. It was 1:00 A.M. The commissioner's son and the driver of the other car were killed. They both had been drinking heavily. Ima's daughter survived, disfigured and crippled for life. That incident, unknown to you when it happened, made rumbles in the state legislature about curbing liquor sales during sports events and about stricter accountability for vendors of alcohol. Nothing happened. The pendulum of public attention that had swung widely toward drastic action gradually came back to normal.

In the meantime, Ima had gone into action getting a MADD chapter charter, assembling a board including such influential persons as the mayor, superintendent of schools, Mercy Hospital administrator, United Way executive director, the wives of the Bell College and Munsea National Bank presidents, and a dozen or more other people at the top of the civic pyramid. The disappointing result of the red-ribbon project over the Christmas holidays was a second blow for Ima to endure.

Your boss at the firm alerts you to expect Ima to be very subjective, even bitter, about public attitudes and behavior when it comes to drinking and driving. He expects that she will be not only subjective but demanding about corrective measures devised by State Capital Public Relations, and you as its representative. Reassure her as best you can, he says, but don't promise more than can be delivered.

Ima is demanding in a constructive way. She tells you that an anonymous donor has come up with $15,000 for you and your firm to spend figuring out why the red-ribbon campaign flopped in Munsea—despite success elsewhere—and what can be done in the two-month period between now and the Regional Basketball Tournament when Munsea will be overrun by basketball fans.

You call your home office. Your boss says to tell Ima that you've got some investigating to do, and that within two weeks you'll be back with a proposal for her, and for her board, if she wants such a meeting. In the meantime, he says, you should nose around Munsea for a couple of days to find out as much as you can that might be helpful in deciding what can be done to help Munsea, Bell, and MADD officials get reasonable control of the basketball-drinking-driving problem. Time is short, so if you want any opinion soundings done in Munsea, arrange for that while you're there. He suggests that you organize your findings into a situation analysis that can be the basis for a strategic planning session directly as soon as you return. He'll set up that meeting and another one with the MADD home-office public relations director a day or two later.

Try putting on paper exactly how you will proceed, step by step. Be as specific as you can. After all, you went to school and lived in Munsea for four years. From that experience, you could have more and better insight than outsiders into contacts, methods, and improvisations with high potential for success. After you've done that and thought it through, make a situational outline of what you'll say at the firm's meeting to lead off discussion—your initial contribution to the decision process.

- Have Madd give talks
- Talk to students about problem
- Get cooperation + support from B-Ball team
- Talk to bar owners + liquor stores to make them fully aware
- Get support from the school

- Make the red ribbon campaign very knowledgable
- Maybe have a billboard where everyone coming into town will see it.

Chapter 3

Employee Relations

The first public of any organization is its employees—the people who make it what it is. As management guru Peter Drucker reminds us, an organization is "a human community" that needs the contributions of everyone to function and be successful. Many times it appears that management does not recognize this fact. Sometimes managers act as if *they* are the organization and the others just an impediment. An interchange at the annual meeting of an auto company illuminates the truth of the matter. A shareholder asked the CEO why funds were being allocated to improve employee benefits instead of increasing dividends. "Because," he responded, "you and I don't know how to build cars, and they do!"

The situation is complicated by the fact that, in the overwhelming majority of organizations today, the managers and administrators technically are also employees. They do not own the company but merely manage it for the stockholders. Senior managers may own stock—but so may production workers, secretaries, and janitors. Managers can be hired and fired like everyone else. The true employer is the board of directors elected by the stockholders to oversee the business. In community hospitals, school districts, public interest organizations, government agencies, or membership associations, of course, there is no question of management ownership.

A DANGEROUS ATTITUDE

It is easy, and perhaps all too common, to view employees as a cost in a line-item budget determining the price of a product or service. This attitude fosters the idea that the less an organization has to pay its employees, the lower the price of the product or service, and, therefore, the more competitive the product or service can be in the marketplace.

This one-dimensional view of the labor force provided fertile soil for the tremendous growth of unions, which fought to have labor seen in a multidimensional view. Throughout the decades, unions forced their way into the smallest and largest companies. They won concessions on wages, safety, medical benefits, vacation, and retirement benefits, to mention just a few. Unions became as big as big business. Their influences are reflected in national and state laws as well as in volumes of judicial and regulatory decisions.

The 1980s, however, saw a tapering off of union influence. Union membership dropped; part of this drop is attributed to the significant population move from the unionized Northeast and Midwest to the Sunbelt, which has significantly fewer unions. The impact of foreign competition—foreign cars, for example—as well as the exporting of jobs to countries where labor is cheaper are two other trends that have an impact on the labor market.

Some corporate bankruptcies have been closely tied to labor contracts. Under bankruptcy reorganization, some of these companies have bounced back into the marketplace without union contracts and with significant cuts in wage levels as well as benefits.

Another major change in the employer-employee relationship is automation. The computer radically changes the role of the individual in the workplace. The individual now competes with the robot for a place in the assembly line; in most instances the individual will lose the contest. If the computer and the robot take on most of the heavy work in the steel mill, most of the positions on the assembly line, and much of the information gathering and dissemination usually associated with general office work, what is left for the current and future individuals who would fill those jobs?

The trend is to a downsizing of the work force and to a service-oriented economy. This movement creates major reshuffling of jobs and people, with all the emotional stress problems attendant on such upheaval and readjustment. Layoffs and restructuring of organizations also weaken the loyalty of workers—which can affect morale and productivity.

During this significant time of transition, employer-employee relations change, but they are no less critical than in the past. Indeed, most people would argue that they are now more important than ever.

BENEFITS OF EMPLOYEE PARTICIPATION

Because they are accountable to the board, the real and legal seat of power in most organizations, managers have responsibility as "the employer," and others needed to carry out the operations become "the employees." Yet if there is one significant trend in successful organizations worldwide, it is the melding of interests and heightened cooperation between management and employees. Recognition of several benefits from a united effort has brought this "workplace democracy" about:

1. As the founder of Honda Motors puts it, just as cars are gauged by horse-power, so organizations can be gauged by mindpower. If only the CEO thinks about possible improvements, there is one mindpower. If only management, maybe 100–500 mindpower. But if everyone is encouraged to think about the company and their work in it, and then make suggestions, an organization can have 20,000 or more mindpower.

2. In a highly competitive economy, the successful organizations are those that deliver customer satisfaction. But customer satisfaction depends on employee satisfaction; that is, dissatisfied employees are unlikely to satisfy customers, because their own irritations or feelings of abuse will get in the way. (The next time a retail clerk fails to give you satisfactory service, remember that he or she is probably the lowest paid, least valued, least trained worker in the store—and most likely part-time to boot. Yet the retail industry expects such employees to conduct *the* most important job, serving customers.) Success involves *everyone*—those who make the policies, those who design and produce the product or service, the sales personnel, janitors who keep the premises attractive, secretaries who answer the phone, and on and on.

3. To build trusting relationships with customers, shareholders, communities, government, and other stakeholder publics, organizations need to speak with One Clear Voice. Management cannot say one thing in official pronouncements from the ivory tower and then have employees telling another story to the people with whom they interact. Achieving one voice requires shared values, which arise when employees are encouraged to participate in organizational decision making.

The benefits of mutually satisfactory employee-employer relations are significant. There are fewer work stoppages, higher productivity, and fewer errors. Sometimes the benefits are symbolized, as when the employees of Delta Airlines gave the airline an airplane during tough economic times. In a similar case, the 480 employees of Piggly Wiggly Carolina, a Charleston, South Carolina, grocery store and distributing business, conceived and organized the $40,000 "Rig for the Pig" campaign. Ninety-eight percent of the employees participated, voluntarily contributing two days' pay. In the end, they raised $7,000 more than needed for the tractor-trailer truck they gave to the company.

PUBLIC RELATIONS' ROLE

The public relations function, providing the communications channel between employers and employee groups, is important on both sides of the relationship. Practitioners are called on to participate more or less continuously in four phases of an employee's work experience:

- **The start.** For example, recruiting programs or help wanted advertising, orientation sessions, tours, or kits of information.
- **On-the-job working conditions.** For example, employee publications, bulletin boards, suggestion systems, training meetings, morale boosters, surveys of attitudes, complaint sessions, feedback mechanisms, teleconferencing.
- **Rewards and recognitions.** For example, award programs, implementation of employee participation in civic affairs, staging of political science or economic education events, old-timers' parties, open houses, wage increases or bonuses, promotions, annual reports to employees, and so on.
- **The work stoppage or termination.** For example, communications in a strike, layoff, or boycott problem, news about benefits for retirees, a retiree publication, projects to help laid-off employees relocate, or exit interviews.

In carrying out duties related to these four phases, the public relations people are usually teamed up with the human resources department in a large organization. In small organizations, all the duties related to employee relations and communication may be vested in one functionary, Public Relations or Personnel.

No matter who is assigned the duties, the responsibility is as communicator, interpreter, and persuader **for the employer.** The duties include feedback of employee opinion and ideas as a guide to management. So public relations practices are the fulcrum of a two-way relationship-building and communication system, and therefore must earn the trust **of the employees.**[1]

RULES OF EFFECTIVE EMPLOYEE RELATIONS

Although there are a variety of tools available to accomplish employee-employer communications, three basic principles prevail as guidelines for the practitioner.

1. **Employees must be told first.** Employees should be the first to be told information affecting them and their jobs; they should be told directly by the employer. The relationship is adversely affected when employees learn from outside sources about matters that affect them. Two-way trust is jeopardized. As a practical matter, external sources cannot do as complete a job of informing

---

[1]"Will Public Relations & Human Resources Clash in the '90's? Survey Finds Trust in Management Translates into Quality: Whose Job—or both—Is It to Build Trust in Management?", *pr reporter* 32 (August 28, 1989): pp 1–2. Dick Wilmot of Wilmot Associates in San Diego, explains how employees must trust senior management in order to strive for quality. He explains with the "trust triangle" who is responsible for building trust in management.

employees as the employer can. The grapevine is one of the worst of the possible sources in the eyes of employees.

2. **Tell the bad news along with the good.** All too often, organizations exploit internal news channels to report only "good" news, usually complimentary to the employer. That practice wears thin. The tools and the messages lose credibility. Motives become suspect. Employees look to other sources, such as unions, for a more balanced, objective perspective. Revealing good and bad news, openly and candidly, builds trust, common purpose, and productivity.

3. **Ensure timeliness.** Information important to employees has the same obsolescence as news of other kinds. Getting it out fast and accurately builds dialogue and trust. Delay opens the door to sources with half-truths, distortions, and bias unfavorable to the employer. Delay is the cause of most rumors, and, once started, rumors are difficult to dislodge. The employer's task is to be the first and most reliable source for employees. To do or be otherwise puts, and keeps, an employer on the defensive with those on whom the organization depends most for its success.

4. **Employees must be informed on subjects they consider important.** Years of studying employees' views of communication within their organizations reveals specific items they want to know about—often quite different from what house editors or managements think they want to know about (or *ought* to be told). The list has changed very little during the thirty years such research has been conducted. The chart in Table 3-1 summarizes biennial studies conducted in the 1980s (and updated in the 1990s) by the Interna-

TABLE 3-1 SUBJECTS OF INTEREST TO EMPLOYEES CHANGE LITTLE

Rank	Subject	Scale (1–10, high to low)
1	Organizational plans for the future	8
2	Job advancement opportunities	7
3	Job-related "how-to" information	7
4	Productivity improvement	6
5	Personnel policies and practices	6
6	How we're doing vs. the competition	6
7	How my job fits into the organization	6
8	How external events affect my job	5
9	How profits are used	5
10	Financial results	4
11	Advertising and promotional plans	4
12	Operations outside of my department or division	4
13	Organizational stand on current issues	4
14	Personnel changes and promotions	4
15	Organizational community involvement	4
16	Human interest stories about other employees	2
17	Personal news (birthdays, anniversaries, and so on)	2

tional Association of Business Communicators and Towers, Perrin, Forster & Crosby, a consulting firm specializing in internal relations. Respondents were asked to rank operations outside of their department or division on a scale of 1 to 10 with 1 being highest.

5. **Use the media that employees trust.** The IABC-TPFC Studies also replicate others telling the sources from which workers want to receive information. In order, they are:

1. Immediate supervisor
2. Small group meetings
3. Top executives
4. Large group meetings
5. Employee handbook or other booklets
6. Orientation program
7. Regular local employee publication
8. Bulletin boards
9. Annual report to employees
10. Regular general employee publication
11. Upward communication programs
12. Audiovisual programs
13. Union
14. Mass media
15. Grapevine

Note that mass media is next to last. Also notice how far down the list employee publications fall. One preference experts predict will rise is audiovisual media, if they become more sophisticated and methods are found to make them easily accessible.

- **But the trend is strongly toward face-to-face interchanges, with managers and supervisors seen as communication links first and foremost—not only from the top down and the bottom up but also laterally (between departments and work groups). Consequently public relations departments often must coach and train supervisors and managers in interpersonal communication skills.**

When asked in the same study which were their *actual* sources, as opposed to this listing of *preferred* sources, two were far out of line. Grapevine, the number 15 preferred source, was ranked second as an actual source. Bulletin boards, number 8 in preference, in actuality ranked third.

HONESTY NOW MEANS HOLDING BACK NOTHING

Public relations counselor Bruce Harrison advises in dealing with key publics such as employees, it's not enough to just communicate honestly these days. Organizations are finding that in order to foster trust, they must be entirely open and show all evidence, a method called "transparent communication." Now organizations need to let constituents know,

- Here's how we're making the decision. Here are the facts that led us to this decision.

- Here are the options. Let's look at them together so you can help us make the decision.
- I believe I'm honest but you judge for yourself. Here are the data. What do you think?

This type of policy is the key for an organization to be considered honest in the 1990s.[2]

REFERENCES AND ADDITIONAL READINGS

BAILEY, JOHN A. and RICHARD BEVAN. "Employee Communications." Chapter 12 in *Lesly's Public Relations Handbook,* 4th ed. Chicago, IL: Probus, 1991.

BARR, STEPHEN. "Smile! You're on Corporate TV." *Communication World* 8 (Sep 1991): 28–31.

BRODY, E. W. *Communicating for Survival.* New York: Praeger, 1987.

BRODY, HERB. "Business TV Becomes Big Business." *High Technology Business,* May 1988, 26–29. Summarized by Tracey Mitchell in *Purview* no. 253, December 5, 1988. Points to burgeoning use of television in linking divisions, training staffs, and disseminating company news.

CASAREZ, NICOLE B. "Electronic Mail and Employee Relations: Why Privacy Must Be Considered." *Public Relations Quarterly* 37 (Summer 1992): 37–40.

CUTLIP, SCOTT, ALLEN H. CENTER, and GLEN M. BROOM. "Media for Internal Publics." Chapter 9 in *Effective Public Relations,* 7th ed. Englewood Cliffs, N.J.: Prentice Hall, Inc., 1994.

DAVIDS, MERYL. Labor Shortage Woes—How Practitioners Are Helping Companies Cope." *Public Relations Journal* v44 (November 1988).

DRUCKER, PETER. "The Responsible Worker." Chapter 21 in *Management: Tasks, Responsibilities, Practices,* New York: Harper and Row, 1974.

[2]*pr reporter* 35 (September 21, 1992): p 3.

EHRLICH, ELIZABETH. "A Weapon That Could Backfire in the War on AIDS." *Business Week,* November 7, 1988. Essay on implications of California referendum requiring doctors to report those carrying AIDS virus (defeated).

GILBERG, KENNETH R. "Open communications provide key to good employee relations." *Supervision* 54 (Apr 1993): 8-9.

GRUNIG, JAMES, and TODD HUNT. "Employee and Member Relations." Chapter 12 in *Managing Public Relations.* New York: CBS College Publishing, 1984.

HEFTY, ROBERT. "Employee Publications." Chapter 12 in *Lesly's Public Relations Handbook.* 4th ed. Chicago, IL: Probus, 1991.

HEFTY, ROBERT. "Public Relations and Labor Matters." Chapter 13 in *Lesly's Public Relations Handbook.* 4th ed. Chicago, IL: Probus, 1991.

MCKEAND, PATRICK J. "GM Division Builds a Classic System to Share Internal Information." *Public Relations Journal* v46 (Nov 1990): 28-32.

REUSS, CAROL, and DONN S. IRVIS. *Inside Organizational Communications.* Longman, NY: International Association of Business Communicators, 1981.

SCHLACHTMEYER, AL, and MAX CALDWELL. "Communicating Creatively in Tough Times." *Communication World* v8 (Jun/Jul 1991): 26-29.

STRENSKI, JAMES B. "Practical Communications Techniques that Work with Employees." *Public Relations Quarterly* v36 (Fall 1991): 34-35.

TERKEL, STUDS. *Working.* New York: Pantheon, 1974. Insight into worker's attitudes toward jobs.

"The Workplace and AIDS." *pr reporter* v31 (April 11, 1988). A guide to sources and information. A 36-page directory free from *Personnel Journal,* 245 Fischer Avenue, B-2, Costa Mesa, CA 92626.

AIDS in the Workplace

The realization of who can get AIDS was amplified in 1992 when basketball star Magic Johnson and famed tennis pro Arthur Ashe, who died soon after, announced that they were HIV-positive. Both cases magnified the reality of AIDS, and became a triggering event for a series of questions that everyone from parents to policy makers in organizations must face today.

For example, should students be able to attend school if they have AIDS? Can corporations treat their employees differently because they have AIDS? Should employers have a policy that includes health insurance coverage for employees who contract AIDS? Does an employer have a responsibility to do anything about AIDS awareness? Should condoms be distributed in the schools? Should AIDS education be part of the school curriculum?

Not only can AIDS happen to *anyone,* it can also affect *any* organization. What was once a latent issue has, since the 1980s, become a hot one—and organizations without a policy could find themselves in a crisis situation.

PACIFIC BELL

Pacific Bell, a Pacific Telesis Company based in San Francisco, has taken a proactive approach to the AIDS issue. It is one of the largest employers to go public with its policy and commitment.

FACTS AND STATISTICS

- According to the Department of Health and Human Services, there were 226,281 AIDS fatalities as of September 1993.
- One in 250 Americans has AIDS.
- In 1992, the National AIDS Clearinghouse reported that the states with the highest number of cases were California, with 8,515 cases per 100,000 of the population, and New York, with 8,098 cases per 100,000.
- According to Fred Hellinger, a highly notable AIDS statistician, the lifetime costs for someone diagnosed with AIDS, as of 1993, were $102,000. That is $38,000 per year. The yearly costs for someone diagnosed as HIV-positive is on the average $10,000 per year.
- Hellinger reported in *Inquiry* magazine that the total cost for treating all persons with AIDS and HIV in 1992 was $10.3 billion. The projected aggregate costs for 1995 are $15.2 billion.

PACBELL TAKES ACTION

PacBell is a communication service company with more than 57,000 employees. As early as 1983, PacBell took part in a Business Leadership Task Force Conference on AIDS along with Bank of America, Chevron, Levi Strauss (see sidebar story), Mervyn's, and AT&T. The conference resulted in a comprehensive AIDS education program for employees.

In 1985, PacBell's Health Services Department worked with the Communications Workers of America, its major labor union, to begin internal programs on AIDS. These included seminars and distribution of information about the causes and prevention of AIDS. From these informal programs, three major themes emerged:

- Employees with AIDS were worried about their lives and their jobs.
- Employees without AIDS were concerned about contracting AIDS from other employees, customers, or other people.
- Employees were concerned about friends or relatives who had AIDS or who were dying from the illness.

THE PLAN FEATURES EDUCATION

On the basis of these findings, Pacific Bell implemented a program to deal with the fears that existed by educating employees about the disease. The program included both one-way and two-way communication vehicles, such as:

- **Face-to-face speakers,** including union and management representatives who visit work locations.
- **Videotape presentation,** *An Epidemic of Fear—AIDS in the Workplace,* with companion brochure for seminars and for any employee who requests it.
- **Literature,** *AIDS Education in the Workplace.* This piece was presented to managers and answers basic questions about AIDS.
- **Periodical information** about AIDS published in the company newspaper and magazine (see Figures 3-1 and 3-2).
- **Brochures** were made available, from outside sources, with additional references employees could contact.
- **Letters,** sent to district managers informing them about AIDS education programs and services.
- **Employee Assistance Program,** which offers a workshop for managers on managing employees with life-threatening illnesses such as AIDS. The one-and-a-half hour presentation uses a videotape from the San Francisco AIDS Foundation, "The Next Step: HIV in the 90s." This tape covers topics such as fitness for duty and reasonable accommodations, attendance, privacy, and how to deal with the loss of an employee or co-worker.
- **Two-way communication** between union and management at all of their programming sessions.

ONE RESULT IS MEDICAL COVERAGE

PacBell goes beyond the 1990 federal **Americans with Disabilities Act (ADA),** which states that an employer cannot refuse to hire someone with AIDS and suggests workplace policies about disabilities. PacBell includes AIDS in its health insurance package. Company policy specifies that:

- An employee with AIDS is treated under the health plan he or she chooses from among the many plans the company offers. All of them cover care for AIDS.
- People with AIDS, depending on length of service, are eligible for disability payments up to one year, long-term disability, or pension, or some combination of the three.
- The medical department provides counseling and offers referrals to outside counselors and agencies. It also offers short-term education seminars.
- Employees with AIDS may be placed in a hospice setting.
- Prescription drugs are made available by mail.

AIDS Education—
A Corporate
Responsibility

Reprinted from

UPDATE

May 4, 1987 Volume 10, Number 17   **PACIFIC ☒ BELL**
                                                      A Pacific Telesis Company

Does AIDS Affect You?

- 1.5 to 4 million Americans are estimated to be AIDS carriers.
- An estimated 15 to 60 percent of them will die of AIDS within the next six years.
- In the next 10 years, over 100 million people will become infected.

Worldwide:
- 91 percent of reported AIDS cases are heterosexual.
- 51 percent are female.
- 80 percent are nonwhite.

Pacific Bell:
- An estimated 80 active and former employees have died of AIDS.

California:
- 8,000 total cases reported so far.
- 4,000 AIDS deaths.
- By 1991, 80 percent of the cases will occur *outside* San Francisco and Los Angeles.

United States:
- 65 percent are gay/bisexual.
- 7.5 percent are female.
- 25 percent are IV drug users.
- 59 percent are white.
- over 30,000 deaths from AIDS have been reported.

Figure 3–1 Pacific Bell strove to educate its employees by providing them with the facts in this example from a mailer/handout. (Courtesy of Pacific Bell.)

Because of medical, legal, and personnel aspects of AIDS, organizations such as PacBell have developed workplace policies—but the number of organizations not yet involved in AIDS efforts is astonishing. The National Leadership Coalition on AIDS reports that sixty-eight percent of businesses have no HIV/AIDS policy and ninety percent of businesses have no HIV/AIDS educational program.

Different People...Different Myths...Different Fears.

The Facts On AIDS

Q. What is it?
A. AIDS is a fatal disease that damages the immune system, leaving the victim susceptible to illnesses such a pneumonia, meningitis, a type of cancer called Kaposi's sarcoma, and others.

Q. What's the difference between "having AIDS" and being infected with the AIDS virus?
A. People infected with the virus may have no symptoms at all. Within a few years, one fourth to three-fourths will develop ARC (AIDS-Related Complex) and have mild to severe symptoms. One-half to three-fourths of people with ARC will develop AIDS.

Q. How is it transmitted?
A. AIDS is spread in five ways only:
 • through sexual intercourse with a person infected with the AIDS virus;
 • sharing drug needles with an infected person;
 • being injected or transfused with contaminated blood products (blood screening procedures have been in place since 1985);
 • artificial insemination from an infected donor; or

 • being born or breast-fed by a woman infected with the virus.

AIDS is *not* spread by casual contact. You *can't* get it from the common use of typewriters, telephones, tools, water fountains, chewed pencils, or toilet seats. You *can't* get it through the air, or from coughing, sneezing, kissing, insect bites, tears, sweat, or saliva. You *can't* get it from donating blood.

Q. How can I avoid getting AIDS?
A. Unless you are 100 percent sure of the complete sexual history of your partner, or have had a totally monogamous relationship for the past seven years, use a condom. Make sure any needles you use have been sterilized. If you have had any risk of exposure during the last seven years, you are encouraged to get a test for the AIDS virus. By law, all test results are confidential. For more information on safe sex practices, call the AIDS hotline.

Q. Is there a cure?
A. Not at this time.

Figure 3–2 Employees were provided with "The Facts on Aids" in order to alleviate fears and provide correct information in this company newsletter. (Courtesy of

AIDS IN THE WORKPLACE IS A PUBLIC RELATIONS PROBLEM

As one public relations newsletter put it: "Employees have fears, customers have worries about sanitation, the media has inquiries regarding AIDS—no one is better equipped to address these problems than practitioners. An internal relations educational program provides an opportunity to learn what does and does not cause

TEN PRINCIPLES
FOR THE WORKPLACE

In 1991, sixty-eight percent of businesses had no HIV/AIDS policy and ninety percent had no education programs. Pacific Bell, along with eighty other corporations including Levi Strauss, Chevron, Bank of America, and Wells Fargo Bank, took the lead in this area by adopting the Ten Principles for the Workplace of the National Leadership Coalition on AIDS.

1. People with AIDS or HIV infection are entitled to the same rights and opportunities as people with other serious or life-threatening illnesses.

2. Employment policies must, at a minimum, comply with federal, state, and local laws and regulations.

3. Employment policies should be based on the scientific and epidemiological evidence that people with AIDS or HIV infection do not pose a risk of transmission of the virus to co-workers through ordinary workplace contact.

4. The highest levels of management and union leadership should unequivocally endorse nondiscriminatory employment policies and educational programs about AIDS.

5. Employers and unions should communicate their support of these policies to workers in simple, clear, and unambiguous terms.

6. Employers should provide employees with sensitive, accurate, and up-to-date education about risk reduction in their personal lives.

7. Employers have a duty to protect the confidentiality of employees' medical information.

8. To prevent work disruption and rejection by co-workers of an employee with AIDS or HIV infection, employers and unions should undertake education for all employees before such an incident occurs and as needed thereafter.

9. Employers should not require HIV screening as part of pre-employment or general workplace physical examinations.

10. In those special occupational settings where there may be a potential risk of exposure to HIV (for example, in health care, where workers may be exposed to blood or blood products), employers should provide specific, ongoing education and training, as well as the necessary equipment, to reinforce appropriate infection control procedures and ensure that they are implemented.

AIDS, diffuse employee fears, insure customers of product safety, and demonstrate concern for the well-being of employees and their families."[1]

The simple fact is that employees filled with fear or coming to work from homes disrupted by illness will not have high morale or productivity in the majority of cases. It is therefore a sound **investment** for employers to deal with conditions from **outside** the workplace that will inevitably have an impact **inside.**

[1]*pr reporter*, March 28, 1988. pp 1-4.

LEVI STRAUSS

Like Pacific Bell, Levi Strauss & Co. has made education the focus of its approach to dealing with the AIDS issue in the workplace and in the communities it serves.

In 1982, a group of Levi Strauss employees asked for the support of senior management to distribute educational materials in the headquarters lobby area and to raise funds for a then-new disease called AIDS. They were concerned, however, that co-workers would be reluctant to ask questions or take literature. The solution started with the involvement of Robert D. Haas, CEO. He stood in the lobby along with other senior managers to hand out pamphlets—sending a clear message the company recognized the importance of the issue and was giving it full support.

TARGETING EMPLOYEES AND THE COMMUNITY

Over the years since that event, Levi Strauss has continued its commitment to AIDS education. The company has filmed two videos in its plants that feature candid interviews with employees and their families. The first was called "Talk about AIDS." The second video, "Talk about AIDS with Your Family," was the first corporate program of its kind to reach out to the community and the whole family on issues surrounding HIV and AIDS. In addition, the Levi Strauss Foundation, set up by the company, has increased its AIDS-related grants over 160 times since 1985 to AIDS education and direct assistance to those who have the disease (see Figure 3–3).

Beyond these activities, Levi Strauss hosted an AIDS **conference** and organized AIDS **agencies in plant communities.** With great success, the company also designed an **employee orientation** which includes a session on the company philosophy in regard to AIDS. As in PacBell's program, complete confidentiality for employees seeking counseling or medical assistance is an important component. The company continually works to find programs that will both teach prevention techniques for the spread of AIDS and ease the depression that often characterizes people who have already come in contact with the virus. The programs are tailored to meet the needs of employees at specific plant locations and communities.

As Haas explains, "At Levi Strauss & Co., we believe that education is the key to building, understanding and changing attitudes. We learned an important lesson as we developed our employee education programs—AIDS education must be tailored to each employee audience. What worked for our employees at our San Francisco headquarters did not work in our plant facilities."

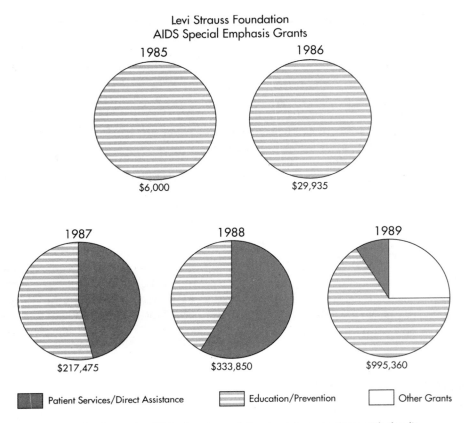

Figure 3–3 Grants for AIDS education and direct assistance to those with the disease have dramatically increased for the Levi Strauss Foundation in the past years. (Courtesy of Levi Strauss & Company.)

• Such an attitude exhibits what is meant by building relationships—which means treating persons with respect, dignity, and caring. Only with such an attitude can an organization earn the trust of its employees (or any public). And only when people have trust will they be willing to act in a way that is beneficial to the organization as well as to themselves.

QUESTIONS FOR DISCUSSION

1. PacBell cited eight vehicles for educating employees about AIDS. No mention was made of how the effectiveness of those vehicles individually or collectively would be measured so that decisions could be made about alterations

leading to greater effectiveness. What might be used as yardsticks and guidelines for such measurement of effectiveness?

2. Suppose there was an unspoken but growing resentment among many employees that PacBell policy discriminated in favor of one group (AIDS victims) without similar attention to victims of other problems such as other social diseases, harassment on the job, and unexpected layoffs. If this situation, which is primarily a personnel or human resources matter, has a functional role for public relations, what might that role be?

3. In dynamic enterprises, professionals have to be able to adapt to changing conditions, sometimes making drastic changes. Assume that you are a public relations manager for a department store, and your management has adopted a local version of the PacBell approach to AIDS. Put down on paper the alterations you'd expect to be made in your employer's policy and education program, and thus your communications about them, if and when:

   a. A medicine was developed that halted the progress of the disease in victims and blocked their ability to transmit it to others.

   b. A vaccine was found to prevent AIDS, as happened some years ago with polio.

   c. The epidemic attained such proportions that a state of national medical emergency was declared. Every citizen had to be tested. The results are made available upon request for a fee, despite legal guarantees of their privacy and civil rights.

Employee Satisfaction Leads to Customer Satisfaction

With customer satisfaction rising to the forefront of all organizational objectives, it has become increasingly important to keep employees satisfied, too. Because its employees are a company's best advocates, prudent managers pay special attention to their needs and job performance capability in order to ensure a productive, smooth-running organization.

A major study by the Wyatt Company (5,836 workers from all U.S. geographic areas, all industries, all job levels) found that only thirty percent of employees think that their organizations do a good job of involving employees in decisions that affect them. Another Wyatt study found that eighty-eight percent of executives think that employee participation is important to productivity. Clearly, both groups would like more participation. That would help employees have an awareness of decision-making processes and increase the likelihood of acceptance of ideas that come down from the top. Participation can be accomplished by implementing *face-to-face communication* programs.

BANK OF AMERICA FINDS OUT WHAT'S IN THE WAY

In 1984, in order to build a sense of direction for employees, Bank of America instituted a participative, face-to-face program that allowed managers and employees a chance to get together and discuss issues affecting the company or a particular department. An in-house survey confirmed that employees in processing areas felt stymied by obstacles in their work environment. "There had been many changes, including the centralization of a lot of our branch office functions. We sensed that employees were frustrated by old policies, bureaucracy, procedures. It became very important that management communicate (1) concern for employees' needs and (2) interest in helping them do their jobs," said Duncan Knowles, Vice-President and Director of Organizational Communication.

The Organizational Communication Department then organized the "What's In The Way" outreach program from senior management to employees. This program was designed to find and correct the problems employees were having with the infrastructure of the organization. "What's In The Way" solicited employees using three different methods:

1. **Memos.** Each person received a form asking for detailed descriptions of obstacles in the work environment. Responses such as, "Is this weekly report I do really necessary? It takes up a lot of time and I don't see its purpose," led to eradication of superfluous procedures. Employees could remain anonymous.

2. **Focus groups.** Employees were encouraged in a group setting to identify obstacles that kept them from being efficient. One focus group was able to pinpoint an inconvenient partition that inhibited the flow of information between employees. A manager was able to eliminate it, thereby making that work area more efficient.

3. **Hotline.** This allowed workers to call in and voice their concerns. Although very few employees used the hotline, the availability of it enforced management's message, that it was willing to listen to employees.[1] (See Figure 3–4.)

Another effective face-to-face program that Bank of America initiated in response to employee concerns about an upcoming merger was the "Brown Bag Program." It was a series of informal, lunchtime sessions that invited all employees to attend and eat lunch with a representative from senior management (see Figure 3–5). Before each lunch meeting, employees present would receive a briefing paper of what management would discuss. This presentation of **talking points** allowed participants to formulate questions for the question-and-answer period later. At the conclusion of the program, critique forms of the session were available for reactions and responses to the program.

"The employees were encouraged to ask honest questions, and the officers provided honest answers," said Duncan Knowles, Vice-President and Director of Organizational Communication at Bank of America. Occasionally after a meeting, an officer would actually perform work alongside the employees to really learn what resources were necessary and which were unnecessary or needed to be improved. This practice let employees know that management was willing to act on possible improvements to the system.

These successful face-to-face programs showed competency and commitment through *action,* not words. Follow-up surveys indicated that the programs improved employee job philosophy and perception of management. Anonymous questionnaires revealed that ninety-five percent of the employees felt more comfortable

---

[1]*pr reporter,* January 23, 1989.

Facing an obstacle to service?
A barrier to doing your job well?
Your senior managers want to *help*. Call the

"What's in the Way?" Hotline
BANet 624-3064

Figure 3–4 Bank of America created a hotline for its employees to call and voice their concerns. (Courtesy of Bank of America.)

about the bank's future after having been visited by an officer and seeing for themselves that the attitude the officers adopted for the programs lived on. "Officers drop in at breakfasts, for coffees, etc. with employees much more than they did before," Knowles stated.

RHÔNE-POULENC "DOES LUNCH" WITH ITS EMPLOYEES

At Rhône-Poulenc Ag Company in Raleigh, North Carolina, a similar environment also created the need for an employee relations program. Foreign ownership,

Meet Senior Management

GET TO KNOW A SENIOR MANAGER
Bring your brown bag lunch, your questions and
your suggestions to an informal discussion with

LEE PRUSSIA
CHAIRMAN OF THE BOARD

DATE: Monday, March 11th   **TIME:** 12 noon – 1 pm
PLACE: Pasadena Bankcard Center, Cafeteria, 101 S. Marengo, Pasadena
PHONE: 7-622-5500 for more information

All BAC employees are welcome

Figure 3–5 Bank of America employees had the opportunity to eat lunch with and
question senior management in these brown-bag sessions. (Courtesy of Bank of
America Center.)

changes though acquisition, and rapid growth created much internal turmoil among
the U.S.-based employees at Rhône-Poulenc, an agricultural chemical manufacturing
company. At the initiation of a newly appointed Director of Corporate Affairs and
Employee Communications, a companywide survey was taken in early 1990 to
guide management in analyzing the situation and its possible solutions.

Fact Finding

A confidential survey distributed to each of the organization's 2,602 employees across the nation indicated these problems:

- Though many employees preferred face-to-face communications with top management as their second choice for receiving information, relatively few opportunities existed for an average employee to meet with senior management.
- Employees felt that management was insensitive to their concerns and distant from their needs, therefore employees wanted more direct contact with the management and hard news of the company's future and business decisions.
- Employee morale was low because of layoffs and rumored plant closings. Environmental pressures on products led to the perception that management was not being honest and open about the issues.

The "Lunch With . . ." program was developed as an example of a more formal meeting between executives and employees. Rather than send out blanket invitations to all employees, representatives from several work units were invited to attend a luncheon with a senior officer.

An agenda and invitations were distributed to employees on a regular, rotating basis, and a summary of the discussion was compiled afterward. The groups were kept small to allow for more interchange, and representatives were encouraged to report back to their departments about the events of the meetings. Employees rated the discussions and what they thought of management's answers to questions. Most of the comments were extremely positive.

To gain credibility for the open exchange the sessions exemplified, reports on the questions and responses were carried to the entire employee audience in company newsletters. Officers reported on the sessions at executive management committee meetings; their reports resulted in quick action on problem areas revealed by the interchange.

QUESTIONS FOR DISCUSSION

1. What other formal or informal methods can you think of to initiate face-to-face contact between managers and employees? Design a face-to-face program for an organization with no budget.
2. Are face-to-face programs more important than traditional one-way communication, such as employee publications? Why?
3. Can you think of any instances where this type of program would be a bad idea? Explain your answer.

Case 3-3

Sohio's Monster Moving Day

Standard Oil Company of Ohio (whose service station marketing name is Sohio) got more than it bargained for when it had to deal with—all at once—(1) relocation to a new building, (2) a name change (to Standard Oil Company), (3) a subsequent takeover by British Petroleum, (4) another name change (to BP America), and (5) a new CEO. All of these changes occurred during a depressed state in the oil industry. There was potential for severe damage to internal relations.

As plans to move got under way, Standard Oil Company of Ohio launched a program to officially return to calling itself The Standard Oil Company, conjuring up the original Rockefeller Standard Oil legacy. The name change came about because other Standards across the United States were changing to names such as Exxon and Chevron and because people outside Ohio misread "Sohio" and took it to be Japanese. Standard Oil Company of Ohio designed a new logo, changed signs, placed corporate ads, and sent communications with the new Standard Oil Company name.

On top of this change, attitudinal surveys found low morale and apprehension about moving into the new building—even though it would be to a large, attractive structure on Cleveland's Public Square, the heart of the city.

The one situation that the company could control was the move. It was also the one that employees could use to work out their frustrations. So the move became the focus of a classic employee relations program for Standard Oil Company's 3,000 headquarters workers.

PLENTY OF PROBLEMS TO START

Because of the suffering oil market, Standard Oil was in the process of laying off employees. Job insecurity was very high. At the same time, employees were asked to relocate to a very different type of office building. Its contemporary look featured

57

Figure 3–6 Employee adjustments to a new home came at time of layoffs, a new CEO, and a change of corporate name. (Courtesy of BP America.)

many open office spaces—a drastic change for those who valued private offices. Because they had been scattered in four locations around town, the move also meant that headquarters workers would be coming together for the first time (see Figure 3–6).

The company had also embarked on a corporate art collection to enhance the open-office look. There was a lot of hostility toward this program. It had become a symbol of the company's difficulties—a misunderstood expense at a time when layoffs were occurring.

OBJECTIVES

Internal staff, aided by outside public relations counsel,[1] planned a program with four objectives.

[1]Watt, Roop & Co., of Cleveland, along with the public relations staff of Standard Oil jointly won a Public Relations Society of America (PRSA) Silver Anvil award in the International Communications-Business category for this project.

1. To reinforce belief in management's commitment and concern for the well-being of employees;
2. To inform employees about the new building and sell them on its advantages;
3. To generate pride and participation in the move, which at best would be a large and difficult task;
4. To change the employees' perceptions about the art acquisition program.

A COMPREHENSIVE PROGRAM

A variety of techniques were used to help employees gain ownership in the new building.

kept employees informed and involved

- *Video segments,* called "Added Dimensions," provided weekly updates on the new building's process and discussed art being acquired and other issues of concern. Typical features included interviews with management or follow-ups to employee events. Videos were shown in lobbies and other public spaces so employees could view them as they entered their present buildings in the morning or during their lunch hour.

- The company also began a *special newsletter* right after the groundbreaking for the new headquarters. Titled *HQ,* it focused on the advantages of the new building—items such as how the mailroom would work, the state-of-the-art phone system, and the new cafeteria.

- *Tours of a typical office mock-up* were offered. Employees were encouraged to participate with incentives and giveaways. It worked—every employee who would move to the new building took the tour. A questionnaire was administered to measure the reactions of employees before and after the tour.

- A *gala art reception* turned a trade exhibit hall into a Sohio art gallery. A total of 2,500 employees attended the wine-and-cheese opening after work and had an opportunity to talk with art consultants about pieces in the collection. The company created a brochure about the art to accompany the exhibit. The CEO made a speech.

- The *Christmas party* that year was held in the half-finished, unheated building. Three thousand employees attended. Officials felt it was a good dry run, because they learned a lot about the logistical problems of holding an open house in the building later. They found it was so spread out that they would need two-way radios for the big event. They were thus able to order forty-eight radios and hold training sessions on how to work them before the official open house was held.

- On day one in the new building, employees were met with *signage, balloons, and other welcoming symbols.* This welcome was repeated on a weekly basis as more and more employees moved in. It proved to be an effective technique.

MORE OBSTACLES ARISE

Like any program, this one needed to make adjustments to accommodate several pitfalls that occurred along the way.

The open house, originally scheduled for November, had to be postponed until March because the building was not ready. A lot of last-minute negotiating with vendors was necessary, and the finale toward which the program was building had to be postponed. Would the improving employee morale be spoiled? Then, the name change to The Standard Oil Company occurred while the event was being planned. The employee relations program had to concentrate on plugging the new name, which also meant adjusting preparatory materials for the move in midstream.

As if that weren't enough, one month before the opening of the headquarters building, there was a change in top management. British Petroleum in London bought controlling interest in Standard Oil. It ousted the then CEO and president and sent Robert Horton to head the company. This change meant starting over with a new CEO. Management change, along with the depressed oil industry and the need for austerity, increased job insecurity among employees.

Now, as the open house was planned, Standard Oil was faced with easing in acceptance of a takeover, a new culture, a lot of unknowns—as well as some job cuts and the name change. It did this through a separate but coordinated program of promoting the takeover and management change and by having Horton be very open about the reasons and about BP's belief in Standard, its assets, and its employees. Externally, Horton talked to stock analysts, public groups, and others. He helped Cleveland sort out some of its political and financial problems. Internally, he made himself very visible to employees and was very accessible, direct, and assertive in in-house interviews. And he took a large role in the building plans. He walked around and met people and built up confidence in himself during the open house and during the formal dedication that followed.

FINALLY, THE OPEN HOUSE

Standard Oil had to be careful about how to position the event: Would an expensive gala be appropriate in light of layoffs and the depressed oil industry? Public relations staff had to find a middle ground without making the party extravagant *or* skimpy.

Twelve thousand employees attended in shifts over two days. Five hundred employee volunteers helped throw the party, strategically positioned in corridors and elevators as greeters, handing out mementos and maps of the building. Twenty-six musicians played in shifts, and 160 caterers served hors d'oeuvres in shifts. Crowd consultants were hired to help manage such a large group (see Figure 3–7).

EVALUATION

An important technique utilized by the public relations professionals was ongoing evaluation—to be sure that the program was meeting its larger objectives. Performed at key intervals, this ongoing evaluation allowed necessary adjustments to be made.

Overall, employee morale greatly increased over the course of the program. Specific measures included:

1. Surveys taken after tours of the mock-up office showed that employee attitudes were changing.
2. Turnout increased with each event, from 2,500 (art reception) to 3,000 (Christmas party) to 12,000 (open house), demonstrating increased interest.
3. Good feedback from employees and positive letters to management were recorded.
4. Employees showed increasing enthusiasm over the art collection. When they were invited to pick prints from the collection for their offices, selection became heated competition. Employees were rushing down to order their

choices before someone else got them—largely a result of the successful art reception.

5. Greatly increased morale and pride were exhibited by the volunteers who helped at the open house. Beforehand, there was concern that employees wouldn't give up their weekend for such a task—but 500 did so with enthusiasm.

By reaching out to employees with a range of communications and face-to-face activities and involving employees in the events, Standard Oil overcame a collection of problems and turned what could have been a disastrous headquarters move into a step forward for everyone.

THE NEXT CHALLENGE

Standard Oil Company was not an appropriate name for British Petroleum's year-old acquisition. So, a year later, after the new building was completed, filled, and dedicated, BP changed Standard Oil's name to BP America. The switch began by unifying the company's appearance—signage, collateral pieces, everything. The public relations department had to communicate the latest change and ease the shift to BP America—creating an image that would represent BP's operations in the United States.

A major effort had to be made to explain and promote the new name internally—to the same employees who had already weathered so much change. Employee communications were the primary vehicle, while externally media placements were used. The reasoning behind using BP America was explained to the employees, while contacts such as graphic designers and others with the need to know were educated on how to use the new name and logo.

The official changeover transforming the most visual end of the business was now complete. Employees had these symbols of their "new" company: a major landmark as headquarters, a different but worldwide name, a corporate art collection they could enjoy in their own working spaces, a highly visible CEO, and all new print and marketing materials bearing the BP logo.

QUESTIONS FOR DISCUSSION

1. On the basis of the background given in this case, what other approaches or techniques might you have considered to involve employees initially?

2. What kind of long-term employee relations plan might you suggest as a follow-up to this transition? (For example, since some employees were enthusiastic volunteers at the open house, would you recommend a program that gives more opportunity for volunteerism?)

Motorola's Quest for Quality[1]

Whether it is called Total Quality Management (TQM), Continuous Quality Improvement, Customer Satisfaction, Employee Involvement, Empowerment, or some other moniker, the fact is that efforts to improve productivity and customer satisfaction are here to stay. The basic premise is that when management pushes key decision making down to frontline workers, creates work teams, and tracks quality, employees gain pride in their work and customers get better products and services.

TQM and its spin-offs are based largely on basic public relations fundamentals such as customer satisfaction, participation, and communication. But it is critical that public relations practitioners understand how the business world thinks about the quality issue—and be able to speak the language of quality in order to serve their companies and clients more effectively. Quality continues to be a core issue of the 1990s. This case discusses the efforts of Motorola's corporate public relations staff to support the company's introduction of a quality program as well as its own internal department efforts to measure and enhance quality.

TQM'S BEGINNINGS AT MOTOROLA

Motorola, a multinational manufacturer of everything from cellular telephones to semiconductors for missile-guidance systems, had enjoyed robust sales, riding the explosive growth in high-tech electronics. But, like many other U.S. companies, Motorola woke up sharply in the late 1970s to the inroads Japanese competition was making into world markets. Though Japanese brands were attracting increasing numbers of customers, Motorola didn't get serious about a response until the man-

[1]We thank Chuck Sengstock, Fellow PRSA, Director of Corporate Public Relations at Motorola Inc. for the wealth of information he provided for this case.

ager of the best-performing division in the company announced at an officers meeting, "Our quality levels really stink."

In looking for a solution, management toured factories of other companies around the world. They found Japanese plants where quality performance was a thousand times better than Motorola's. The Japanese, who had embraced the concept of total quality management (see box on TQM, names and terms), had structured their operations to achieve zero defects, on the basis of a do-it-right-the-first-time ethic. Motorola's chairman observed that "quality [is] like a religion over there. . . . It's a whole different sense of urgency." It became clear that Motorola would have to make a quantum leap in quality if it was to compete successfully with Japan and other Pacific Rim countries.

At the same time, Motorola also saw that eventually Japan would have to open up its domestic market, previously closed to most U.S. goods, or suffer serious trade consequences. Identifying Japan's competitiveness as an issue and showing that Motorola products could hold up to Japanese scrutiny became an aspect of the company's efforts to improve quality. By focusing on selling one specific product (pagers) to one company (Nippon Telephone & Telegraph), Motorola was able within a few years to open Japan's trade doors to become that company's only non-Japanese supplier. In fact at one point, Motorola was the leading supplier of pagers for Nippon Telephone & Telegraph among its three other competitors, all Japanese.

This success spawned additional successes. For example, the Japanese Space Agency was so impressed with the reliability of Motorola equipment used in NASA space shots that it specified Motorola equipment for use on many of its own space missions. Then, a Japanese national who was the first woman ever to climb Mt. Everest used a Motorola FM portable two-way radio to help guide her to the top—despite having plenty of Japanese radios to choose from. Markets in semiconductors and cellular telephones have also been opened through Motorola's efforts.

"MEETING JAPAN'S CHALLENGE"

Motorola believed that telling this story was important, not only to enhance its own reputation for quality, but also to sound a note of encouragement to other American companies whose self-confidence had been undermined by Japanese successes in consumer electronics, automobiles, steel, and a growing number of other industries. Further, by identifying the issue of opening up Japan to American manufacturers as an emerging issue, Motorola saw an opportunity to distinguish itself and ride an issue to its crest. (See Chapter 8 for a discussion of dealing with emerging issues.)

To explain its successful efforts to compete with Japan, Motorola invested in a major campaign called "Meeting Japan's Challenge." The campaign, which ran over four years, was designed to reach *opinion leaders in business and government,* particularly key executives in *customer and prospect firms* who might be actual purchasers or influence the purchase of Motorola products. As a collateral objective it also was designed to reach *investors.*

The strategy focused on dispelling the common American business notion of the Japanese as supermen—and showing how companies like Motorola were not only holding their own, but innovating and leading. The message was: America need not become a permanent weakling in foreign trade. It could compete effectively with Japan, if the rules were fair and U.S. companies had access to Japanese markets. Public opinion to the contrary, it could be a "win-win" situation. Instead of being trade enemies, Japan and the United States could become each other's customers, suppliers, and constructive competitors.

The campaign included efforts on five fronts: advertising, public relations, government relations, internal communications, and Japanese business development.

- A series of 22 advertisements ran in leading U.S. business magazines and newspapers (see Figure 3–8) with the key theme "Quality and productivity through employee participation in management."
- Editorial briefings and interviews were held with major media.
- Background papers called "Viewpoints" were developed on productivity, quality, and other topics.
- Talks given by Motorola executives at scores of forums with key audiences were followed by merchandising of vest-pocket speech reprints.
- Weekly newspapers throughout the country received preprinted news fillers on relevant topics.
- Simultaneously, the program sought to place U.S.-Japan trade issues high on the agenda of policy makers through lobbying, testimony in Congress and for Senate committees, personal visits to executives of other corporations, and direct lobbying in Japan.
- Internally, a film on "Meeting Japan's Challenge" was shown at all plants in the United States. A booklet with reprints of the ad series was distributed. Feature stories appeared in factory publications. Banners, buttons, T-shirts, and hats reading "Meet the Challenge" were distributed.

What were the results? Motorola moved from a major but self-effacing Midwestern manufacturer of technical products to a higher profile company identified as a major spokesperson on the trade issue. Audience research showed that the campaign had been instrumental in triggering changes in the American public's attitude toward the Japanese industrial complex. Ninety-one percent of journalists queried felt that Motorola was associated with quality more than any other attribute. In 1994, Motorola was named the sixth most admired company in the United States according to a *Fortune 500* report.

A more important result was that employees responded positively, developing pride and confidence in their employer as well as an understanding about what it takes to win in a tough marketplace.

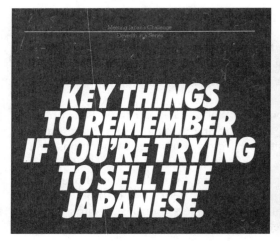

Figure 3–8 Sample advertisements from the "Meeting Japan's Challenge" series, which Motorola produced to reach opinion leaders in business and government. (Courtesy of Motorola Inc.)

WINNING THE MALCOLM BALDRIGE NATIONAL QUALITY AWARD

Motorola then decided to up the ante by going for zero defects. The company estimated that the cost of *not* having zero defects was at least $800 million a year. For the next several years, Motorola engaged in a campaign to achieve "Six Sigma," a total-quality term meaning achieving quality 99.9997 percent of the time—equivalent to just 3.4 defects per million opportunities! The goal was not to simply manufacture flawless products but to measure and eliminate defects throughout the organization—in everything from clerical output and delivery schedules to managerial decisions and production of the annual report.

To get employees excited about the concept, the company introduced another companywide education campaign that included videotapes, Six Sigma posters in every office, and a course on "Understanding Six Sigma" that was required for every employee and tailored for each division. Executive performance reviews and bonus incentives were tied to Six Sigma requirements. The result was that Motorola in 1988 won one of the first U.S. Commerce Department's brand new Malcolm Baldrige National Quality Awards, named after the former Secretary of Commerce (see Figure 3-9).

The Corporate Public Relations staff played an important role in preparing the Baldrige Award application. They collected all the information, which was essentially in technical language or quality program jargon. They rewrote the entire application to give it continuity and punch. To prepare for the possibility of winning,

Figure 3.9   Thought by many to be the Super Bowl trophy of American business, awards in three categories of industry (manufacturing, service, and small business) are made annually out of a pool of thousands of applicants. Many companies spend vast amounts of time and money completing the complicated application and preparing for a grueling site visit. Pictured here is Motorola's award. (Courtesy of Motorola, Inc.)

they developed a contingency plan that included using an outside public relations firm to help implement internal and external communications.

Soon after Motorola won, thousands of their suppliers were asked to pledge that they, too, would apply for the award within five years. Those refusing to sign the pledge were dropped from the rolls of qualified suppliers unless they did not qualify as an applicant because of size or other exclusions. Motorola's real intent was to make the Baldrige Award less a prize to be won than a *process* for inculcating excellence in a corporate culture. To help suppliers get started with quality, Motorola offers training at nominal fees in both basic and advanced quality techniques at Motorola University, the company's internal education and training center. Motorola also has a supplier certification program that ranks the supplier on the basis of total quality delivery.

"QUALITY DAY"

Though the Baldrige Award has become the country's most coveted and competitive prize, few knew about it when Motorola won. To publicize the achievement, Motorola held a "Quality Day" in 89 locations around the world, involving more than 100,000 employees. At each Quality Day event, a congressperson, senator, or governor attended, or an ambassador or foreign consul, in overseas locations. Baldrige Award flags were distributed at every plant, along with brochures, videos, speeches for plant managers, pennants, and mugs (see Figure 3-10).

APPLYING TQM TO THE PRACTICE OF PR

Each department at Motorola was given the challenge of establishing some quantitative measures to demonstrate its achievements. Total quality methodologies work for many units but are not easily assimilated into the everyday tasks of creative, often reactive, departments such as public relations and communications. They tend to work best with more production-oriented tasks such as marketing communications or product publicity (data or catalog sheets, newsletters, and product news releases). For example, the zero defects method was used by the marketing department to measure just about anything that could be quantified—errors in photography or pricing and grammar in brochures and press releases.

CYCLE TIME REDUCTION (CTR)

In cases where statistical techniques were too clumsy or required too much time and effort, or where the products or services were nonstandard and nonrepetitive, cycle time reduction was used as a measure. This concept essentially means that the

Figure 3–10 Motorola's "Quality Day" held at 89 locations around the globe helped to publicize the importance of winning one of the first Malcolm Baldrige Awards. Under the terms of the program, companies that win the award are required to promote it.

less time it takes to perform tasks the more productivity is achieved. Although it is primarily a manufacturing term, *cycle time* can be applied to many tasks.

Motorola's Patent, Copyright and Trademark Department, for example, has used the cycle time reduction process to analyze the patent applications function at Motorola and to identify ways it could be shortened. The result has been the elimination of bottlenecks and redundant approvals. Using CTR, the Law Department implemented a program for alternative dispute resolution as an option to costly litigation.

Cycle time reduction can also work in other administrative areas. For example, in 1989, it took Motorola six business days to close the books at the end of the year. A team of accountants from Corporate Finance began mapping the consolidation function and determining how to speed up the process. At the end of 1992, Motorola closed the books in four days, with less overtime than previously was used to close them in six days. The Finance Department has improved quality in its area—*and* reduced cost by $233,000 a year. This process has had an impact on accounting operations worldwide. By the end of 1992, Motorola estimated that throughout the entire company, it had saved up to $20 million a year by going from a six-day to a four-day close. The next goal was to achieve a three-day close.

THE "VALUE-ADDED YARDSTICK"

Another part of cycle time reduction is the elimination of activities that are redundant, nonessential, or do not add value. As an example, transmitting copy for a publication directly to a typesetter from a computer terminal saves at least one whole keystroking operation—thereby saving time and money as well as eliminating potential errors. In 1993, Motorola reduced quarterly report production time from 10 days to three days by using the same copy for the printed report as was used in the news release. Though using the same copy for these two vehicles may seem inappropriate, this practice has been successful in addressing the two different audiences. In addition it saves one whole approval cycle.

Complex projects or processes such as product introductions, special events, and major publications may have to be mapped or diagrammed for analysis (see Figure 3-11). This process reveals that there are many smaller tasks within the larger task, many of which are unessential or do not add value (e.g. non-essential approvals and reviews, multiple proofreadings, waiting for phone calls to be returned, waiting for meetings, waiting for a document that's stuck in someone's in-basket).

MOTOROLA AND QUALITY TODAY

Though quality has become institutionalized at Motorola, one way it keeps enthusiasm and visibility high is through an annual competition among Total Customer Satisfaction teams. In 1990, the first year of the championships, nearly 2,000 teams competed from Motorola sites throughout the world. The challenge is to take a problem the team has been dealing with and try to solve it with the target of improving either internal or external satisfaction. The final competition is judged by the company's most senior managers (CEO, president, and so on), who use specific criteria. The top 20–24 teams in the championship make presentations and compete for gold and silver medals.

WHAT TQM HAS BORROWED FROM PR

As pointed out in the introduction to this case, many of TQM's premises are based on the same principles as public relations: customer satisfaction, participation, and communication. In fact, as many organizations begin to question the value of TQM as a business management tool, public relations can help salvage TQM as it falters. Public relations can have a role in extracting the essentially valuable elements of TQM, such as facilitating continuous communication while leading employees through the typical four stages of quality programs: (1) enthusiasm, (2) frustration and discouragement, (3) exhilaration, and (4) satisfaction.

An Ernst & Young (one of the "Big-Five" accounting firms) report on Best Prac-

Press Response Procedure

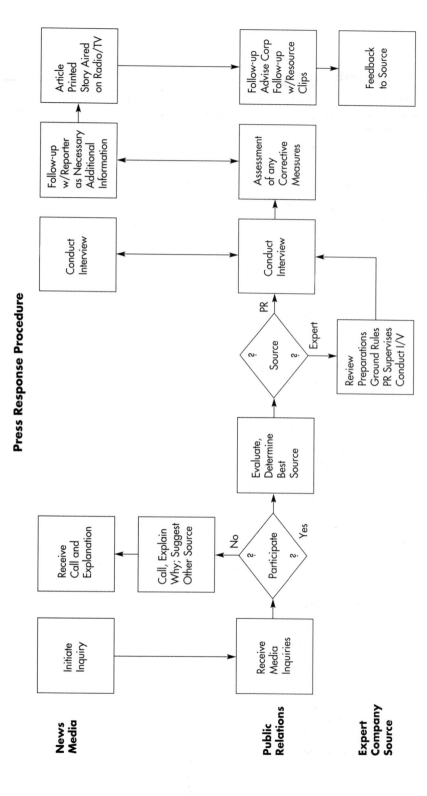

Figure 3–11 Sample mapping diagrams show how a process can be analyzed to modify or eliminate unnecessary steps. The procedure for producing and issuing a press release, for example, shows the PR director reviewing the release twice. If one review is eliminated, the process can be speeded up. A second area that can be accelerated is preparing the photo caption. Without any change, the photo caption writing and approval process can be run parallel to the news release process, ultimately saving time.

tices that affect performance regardless of the management program identified ~~three factors that have a universally significant impact on worker performance: (1) process improvement methods, (2) supplier certification programs, and (3) deploying the strategic plan.~~ Clearly, public relations has a role in building widespread understanding of and support for all three, both inside and outside the organization.

TQM PRIMER: NAMES AND TERMS

This list should suggest why internal communications is vital. In our rapidly changing world, employees and managers are continually bombarded with new approaches and new language that they *must understand* to be effective in their jobs.

> **W. Edwards Deming.** American management consultant who in the 1950s worked in Japan; his 14 points of management are considered largely responsible for Japanese industry's post–World War II recovery and rise to dominance in world markets.
>
> **Philip Crosby.** A quality guru whose Quality Colleges teach 15,000 managers around the world every year.
>
> **Joseph M. Juran.** Founder of the Juran Institute in Wilton, Connecticut, which draws more than 900 people to an annual alumni meeting at almost $1,000 a person and does a booming business in books, seminars, and videotapes in several languages.
>
> **Statistical process control (SPC).** A variety of techniques used to identify quality problems and root causes for them, such as pareto charts, histograms, and the like.
>
> **Cycle time reduction (CTR).** Efforts to reduce time spent on tasks so that the process is completed in less time.
>
> **Benchmarking.** Comparing one's own efforts against those of the best; usually done to identify best-in-class performance for a process (e.g., invoice processing, on-time delivery, manufacturing processes, supervisory communication, community relations activities).
>
> **Zero defects.** Eliminating errors, a goal of many quality programs.

PITFALLS OF TQM, OR, WHY QUALITY PROGRAMS FAIL

Though some organizations continue on the quality bandwagon, growing doubt and uncertainty are apparent. Florida Power & Light, the first non-Japanese company to win the prestigious Deming Prize, has dismantled its quality program, claiming that the bureaucracy and paperwork were detracting attention from customer service. McKinsey & Co., a management consulting firm, conducted a study of quality programs in the United States and Europe that showed that as many as two-thirds are stalling, failing, or being dropped. Numerous other studies show that quality programs have failed to have a significant impact on either reducing defects or improving competitiveness.

Though TQM's basic principles are sound, implementation is often flawed. This list of problems demonstrates how difficult—yet how vital—sophisticated employee relations programs are today.

1. **American executives have short attention spans,** and as *Newsweek* magazine reported, management plans often have the "shelf life of cottage cheese." Like many other management trends (management-by-objectives, zero-based budgeting, excellence, one-minute managing), TQM may be treated as just another managerial fad without the commitment to follow it through.

2. **Many TQM training programs are generic,** canned, or inappropriate for American industry. One size does *not* fit all.

3. **The emphasis on statistical measurement and meeting quotas** (charting, graphing, indicator reviewing) can become a "whipping boy" and divert attention from the primary focus of customer service.

4. **Oftentimes top management give TQM lip service but fail to act as role models.** Or, after their enthusiasm wanes, they delegate responsibility and soon a quality bureaucracy develops (quality director, quality council, quality department, quality committee, and so on).

5. **Middle managers can feel disenfranchised of fearful or losing their power,** which can derail efforts to enhance greater employee participation. The transformation from autocrats to "coaches" is not easy.

6. **Sometimes quality teams aren't connected** by any coordinating strategy or mechanism, creating quality islands without bridges.

7. **In many companies, rewards are still tied to the bottom line** not to quality—or individuals are rewarded, rather than the teams on which the process is based.

8. **Some organizations treat TQM as just a *program*,** doing it for marketing purposes rather than because a focus on quality is the right thing to do for customers. Quality has to be the goal, not just a slogan.

MALCOLM BALDRIGE AWARD CRITERIA

Malcolm Baldrige applicants are judged on seven criteria:

1. Leadership
2. Information and analysis
3. Strategic quality planning
4. Human resources utilization
5. Quality assurance of products and services
6. Quality results
7. Customer satisfaction

ONE SIDE-EFFECT OF TQM: DOWNSIZING

As the economy changes and organizations begin their quest for quality to stay competitive, so too changes the face of business, and therein lie the opportunities for public relations practitioners. The days of the colossal company are disappearing, and many organizations must pare down their workforce to produce *quality* work and eliminate unneeded tasks. This new trend comes under many names—downsizing, reengineering, or right-sizing.

Reengineering attempts to combine these basic things.

- Zero-based restructuring: How would we do things if we were starting this organization from scratch?

- Among the employees, it encourages cooperation instead of turfing, individual decision-making responsibility, and self-managing work teams.
- Its stimulus is the renewed drive to increase productivity. People need to work smarter not harder.
- Emphasizes keeping people broadly trained instead of narrow specialists to greater facilitate productivity.
- Takes most of the good ideas of preceding fads and gives them unified application.
- It ends up achieving the original goal of organizational redesign, QWL (Quality of Work Life).[2]

QUESTIONS FOR DISCUSSION

1. Note how much further a program like Total Quality Management goes than mere employee newsletters. Does this suggest that the need for such standard communication vehicles will diminish—maybe even die out?

2. In a zero-defects culture such as a TQM program, how do you create an atmosphere in which people feel it's ok to take risks (i.e., make mistakes) and at the same time feel the pressure to deliver perfection? What is the public relations role in resolving this conflict?

3. List all the instances in this case where public relations could have played a role, whether or not it actually did.

4. Bridging between principles and applications, which of the seven common denominators, or characteristics, to be found in almost all public relations programs (listed in Chapter 1) are clearly evident in this case? Are not evident?

[2]*pr reporter* 36 (August 23, 1993).

REFERENCES

BEER, MICHAEL, RUSSELL A. EISENSTAT, and BERT SPECTOR. "Why Change Programs Don't Produce Change." *Harvard Business Review* (November/December 1990): 158-166.

"The Cost of Quality." *Newsweek,* September 7, 1992, 48-49.

LAZA, ROBERT W., and WHEATON, PERRY L. "Recognizing the Pitfalls of Total Quality Management." *Public Utilities Fortnightly* (April 18, 1990): 000-000.

"The Post-Deming Diet: Dismantling a Quality Bureaucracy." *Training,* February, 1991, 41-43.

PR reporter 34 (June 24, 1991). Lead story critiquing TQM for number crunching rather than people empowering.

PR reporter 34 (August 26, 1991). Lead story discussing how, while customer service is the top quality concern, PR hasn't defined a clear role for itself in these efforts.

PR reporter 34 (December 16, 1991): 3. PR's role in culture change.

ROHAN, THOMAS M. "New Crisis in Quality." *Industry Week,* October 15, 1990, 11-14.

"The Role of Public Relations in Quality-Improvement Programs." Seminar reprint from PRSA Corporate Section, Technology Section, and Pittsburgh Chapter.

SCHAAF, DICK. "Is Quality Dead?" *Quality,* a special report from *Training,* May 1993, 7-11.

SKUTSKI, KARL J. "Conducting a Total Quality Communications Audit." *Public Relations Journal,* April 1992, 20-32.

ZEMKE, RON. "Bashing the Baldrige." *Training,* February 1991, 29-39.

ZIELINSKI, DAVE. "The Hidden Human Costs of Total Quality." *Business Ethics,* May/June 1992, 24-27.

Where Profit Comes First:
A New Management Style?

In the tough economic times of the 1990s it is hard not to constantly be looking at the bottom line. Every expenditure, every employee's salary, every penny spent must be justified. However, some companies can take this focus on the bottom line to an extreme, concentrating so hard on finances that the employees that enable them to exist and be profitable are treated like interchangeable parts.

One example of this trend appears to be illustrated by Cabletron Systems, Inc., headquartered in Rochester, New Hampshire, develops software to tie desktop computers into office networks. The company has been growing ever since it was started in 1983; sales have increased over sixteen-fold, and it now achieves annual sales of over $500 million.

Cabletron was begun by two men, S. Robert Levine and Craig R. Benson, serving as CEO and chairman, respectively. Their management style is different, to say the least. After an impassioned talk to sales recruits, Levine reportedly plunged a combat knife into a huge beach ball with the name of its closest competitor written on it, yelling "Let's get 'em." Their operating style is similarly unorthodox. (See Figure 3-12). Yet this style has been applauded by many stock analysts for its bold, hard-charging way of getting things done.

DIFFERENT VIEW FOR EMPLOYEES

Although this management style has seemed to work for Cabletron in the past few years, many employees do not like the Levine and Benson style of management. As one former salesman describes it, "The philosophy was management by intimidation

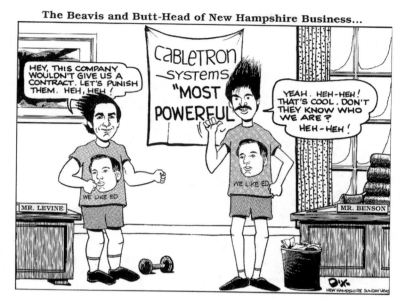

The Beavis and Butt-Head of New Hampshire Business...

Figure 3–12 The business practices of Benson and Levine were editorialized and parodied in many New Hampshire newspapers. (The "We Like Ed" T-shirts refer to a gubernatorial candidate, Ed Dupont, whom Benson and Levine had supported by writing questionable fundraising letters.) (Courtesy of New Hampshire Sunday News.)

and fear."[1] Other employees have stated that working at Cabletron was a pressure-cooker situation, "You never knew if it would be your last day." Still other management techniques are in question. For instance, when employees at Cabletron are fired, they usually don't know about it (while everyone else does), are given a box and one hour to empty out their desks, have their badges cut up in front of everyone, and are escorted out of the building.

Could Cabletron's financial success be an indication of a new type of employee relations that will set a trend for the 1990s? Instead of creating a positive work environment, an atmosphere of intimidation is created. However, as recent research suggests, quality of work life (QWL) is a major factor in workers' definitions of success and in their decisions to take or leave jobs. QWL includes having job autonomy, control over work schedules, supportive work relationships with supervisors and co-workers, and an environment that accommodates personal and family needs.[2]

[1]John Wilke, "Corporate Misfits Who Run Cabletron Play a Rough Game," *Wall Street Journal*, April 9, 1993: 1.

[2]From a study by Families and Work Institute (NYC) as reported in *pr reporter* 36 (October 4, 1993): 1–2.

QUESTIONABLE TACTICS

The antics of Levine and Benson don't stop with employee relations. When Cabletron was not awarded a contract to network the computers of the First NH chain of banks, their displeasure with the outcome was translated into direct and unfriendly action. They decided to withdraw the company's payroll accounts, plus the ATM machines installed in Cabletron buildings, and encouraged all employees in an internal memo to withdraw any accounts they had with First NH banks.

As one analyst commenting on the incident put it, "I'm aligned with Cabletron's philosophy—if they don't want to be our customer, why should we be theirs? . . . I see the whole world going this way," said Paul Johnson of First Boston Corp. Says another industry analyst, William Becklean, with Tucker Anthony Day, "[T]hey are clearly very aggressive. Maybe people are offended by some sales tactics. . . . My only concern is the extent to which this perception affects the company's ability to deliver results."[3] Apparently stock market workers agree with such tactics.

But that's just part of this weird story. Only six months before this controversy surfaced, Cabletron had been a customer of Fleet Bank (with which it did secure a computer networking contract). When it became known that First NH was in the market for a networking contract, Cabletron cleared out its accounts at Fleet and moved to First NH. How's that for company loyalty?

An interesting line of study would be to examine how Cabletron's approach to employee relations affects its bottom line in the future.

QUESTIONS FOR DISCUSSION

1. Compare and contrast the employee relations of Cabletron with that of another company that is known for its positive relations. Can you find a difference in employee productivity or QWL? Explain your answer.

2. Do owners and managers have the right to treat badly those employees who don't measure up? List the pros and cons of such behavior.

3. What protections do employees have from capricious managerial decisions? Which agencies of organizations are "on the side of" workers?

[3]Tom Fahey, "Economic Warfare," *New Hampshire Sunday News*, January 23, 1994: 1

PROBLEM 3 WHAT PRICE "GOOD" EMPLOYEE RELATIONS?

The Safeplay, Inc., has competed in the sports and recreation equipment market for more than twenty-five years. The market is hotly contested.

One of the programs for employee morale and productivity long used by Safeplay has been the retention of former athletes of national repute on its payroll at each of its five manufacturing plants. Although the athletes are part of the personnel department staff, they are made available by the public relations department for news interviews, for the conduct of sports clinics at schools, and to sit on committees for newsworthy civic events.

One of the Safeplay plants is located in Westward, a city of 20,000 located on the outskirts of a metropolitan city. This plant, with an average of 900 employees, specializes in leather items such as baseball gloves, golf gloves, basketballs, footballs, soccer balls, and leather carrying bags for sports clothing.

This plant has a former professional baseball star on the payroll as an assistant personnel manager. He is good copy on occasion, can speak with authority about the products, and directs a recreation program for employees.

A TOLERANT ATTITUDE

At Safeplay plants and in sales offices, there is some pilferage of products by insiders. There is a policy on record that any employee removing company property from the premises without authorization is subject to dismissal. So far this policy has never been invoked where products are concerned. The unspoken attitude of management is much the same as exists in many consumer product companies, particularly those that make food, confections, or inexpensive clothing items. It is tolerant, treats it quietly as a minor cost written into the price of products, and looks the other way rather than confront employees, with possible repercussions if someone is falsely accused. Put another way, management reluctantly concludes that the cost of a baseball mitt taken home in a lunch pail or paper bag to a kid on occasion is not high if employee turnover is low and working enthusiasm is high.

As a means of trying to discourage pilferage, Safeplay offers employees a nice discount on any products they buy from the store in the personnel office, and, on the tenth birthday of any employee's child, the employee can select any product priced under $20 and take it home free.

TOLERANCE ABUSED

Recently, however, the "mysterious disappearance" of sports items has gone beyond the boundaries of normal pilferage and management tolerance. Whole containers of items in the stockroom and in the shipping area have disappeared. Inventory records have apparently been doctored.

Obviously distressed, the home office has sent in a private detective agency. The agency's preliminary investigation and analysis are disturbing. It appears that there is an organized thievery ring involving as many as twenty-five of the Westward plant's employees. It appears, also, that the former athletic star on the payroll is somehow involved, but to what extent is not clear. Someone, not yet identified, on the inside deals with an outside "fence," and someone else on the inside, not yet identified, handles the payoff to all the cooperating employees. Some of the involved employees are members of the union, and some are in office "white-collar" jobs.

THE DECISION PROCESS

At an executive decision-making meeting, you, as director of public relations, have been called in, along with the director of personnel and a company lawyer from the home office. The three of you have been asked to assess the repercussions if the town's police are called in and legal action is taken. You are asked to offer any other resolution that would "better serve the interests of all involved."

The lawyer says that as soon as an airtight case can be accumulated, including photographs and eyewitness accounts of products being removed, being transported to a "fence," and an actual money transaction completed, he favors appropriate law enforcement action and legal redress against those involved.

The personnel manager prefers, he says, to bring charges only against the leader or leaders inside and all those involved on the outside. He prefers to handle the cooperating employees individually, possibly allowing some sort of plea bargaining to hold on the payroll the ones the company considers of real value. He feels this approach will adequately frighten all employees, halt the activity, and avoid having to replace some trained and competent employees.

It is your turn to speak, using whatever notes you have taken while the others stated their positions. What is your view, taking into account the impact not only on internal relations, but on other publics directly or indirectly involved—including families of employees involved, neighbors and the community generally, local law enforcement, news media in the trade, the Westward community, and shareholders of Safeplay, Inc.? Are there others?

What actions, and in what sequence, would you propose and why?

How would you deal with the recommendations of the lawyer and the personnel manager without setting up an adversary situation?

Chapter 4

Community Relations

A neighborhood, town, city, or state is obviously a human community. Like organizations, they require positive interrelationships among all members in order to function smoothly and efficiently. Because a company, hospital, school, or other organization would have difficulty operating effectively in a community that is disrupted or inefficient, it is necessary for them to accept the responsibility of corporate citizenship.

Put another way, all human communities require the mutual trust engendered by positive public relationships in order to function in a reasonable manner. A community is not merely a collection of people who share a locality and its facilities. A community is a social organism made up of all the interactions among the residents and the organizations with which they identify. As a social organism, a community can take pride in its scenery or in its high school basketball team; it can be factionalized on the basis of who lives on which side of the railroad tracks, or who is well-off or poor; it can be a heterogeneous collection of suburban residents drawn together only by a common desire to escape living within a metropolitan area.

Traditionally, employers have tended to regard their relationships with home communities as being extensions of their employee relations. The idea was that employees who were treated decently would go into the home communities singing the praises of their employer. In this traditional viewpoint, employers felt that their dollar payroll, their local tax payments, the occasional loan of a facility for a meeting, and the annual contribution to the United Way pretty well discharged their community obligations. Their attitude seemed to say, "Look what we are giving. Jobs, taxes, meeting facilities, and charitable donations." Employers who held this view tended to assume that with little more than a snap of their fingers they would be provided the practical necessities for efficient operations: streets, sewers, water lines, power and telephone, police and fire services, recreational areas, health care centers, schools, shopping centers, residential areas, cultural and religious facilities, and all the rest. The viewpoint tended to say, "These are what we are entitled to in return for what we give. The community owes us these."

This attitude has changed. Employers now know that they must have more than a general concern for the efficiency and adequacy of community services for themselves and for their employees. They have learned that they must become involved in specific community decisions and actions concerning fiscal policies; honesty in public offices; attracting new businesses and holding older ones; planning for the future; generating the enthusiasm of volunteers in charitable, cultural, fellowship, educational, recreational, business, and patriotic endeavors and that, in general they must apply the collective talents of the organization to the community in which it operates. The combination of these concerns involves having representatives in the policy-making structure of the community, sometimes directly and openly, sometimes behind the scenes.

- Community relations, as a public relations function, is an institution's planned, active, and continuing participation within a community to maintain and enhance its environment—to the benefit of the institution, its employees and stakeholders, and the larger community.[1]

COMMUNITY ISSUES

Community relations (CR) work is a dynamic aspect of public relations. If there were no other reason, the changing physical and social makeup of communities would make it so, but there are many other contributing factors. Among them, few people stay in the communities where they are born. Families move not once, but several times. Community communications programs must deal with this constant turnover of residents. Also, employers move. Sometimes they move from a congested central city area to a suburb. When they move, both areas are disrupted. A manufacturer may move a headquarters or a manufacturing facility from one city to another, mortally wounding the economy of one and perhaps starting a boom in the other. Branches of businesses and institutions are opened in areas of growing population and closed in areas that are shrinking or that are poorly managed. A new interstate highway bypasses a community formerly dependent on tourists and traveling traffic for its trade. Undesirable elements get control of government in a community. A community also undergoes change when there is a movement for reform or rehabilitation.

Almost all the needs of a community as a desirable place to live and work can be put into ten categories:

---

[1]Wilbur J. Peak, "Community Relations," in *Lesly's Public Relations Handbook* (Chicago: Probus, 1991), 117.

1. Work for everyone who desires it.
2. The prospect of growth and new opportunities.
3. Adequate competitive commercial enterprises.
4. Competent municipal government with modern police, fire, highway, and other services.
5. Educational, cultural, religious, and recreational pursuits.
6. Appropriate housing and public services.
7. Provision for helping those least able to help themselves.
8. Availability of legal, medical, and other professional services.
9. Pride and loyalty.
10. A good reputation in the area and beyond.

THE ROLE OF PUBLIC RELATIONS

Public relations work of a basic nature is involved in at least these areas of an organization's community relationships:

1. Planning and conducting open houses, or tours.
2. Planning and helping to implement special events such as ground breaking or dedication of new facilities, change in location, anniversaries, reunions, conventions or exhibitions.
3. Preparing publications for distribution to resident groups.
4. Representing the organization in all sorts of volunteer activities, including fund drives.
5. Preparing advertising or position papers aimed at residents or local government.
6. Counseling management on contributions of employees as volunteer workers or board members; arranging for use of facilities and equipment by community groups.
7. Functioning as the organization's intermediary with local governmental, civic, educational, and ad hoc groups concerned with reform, social problems, and celebrations.
8. Issuing news of interest to the community and providing top officials of the organizations with information on the status of community relations.
9. Managing the contributions function—giving donations if a corporation, raising funds if a not-for-profit organization.

With the dynamics of change mentioned earlier, less and less work of a public relations nature is concerned with "routine." More and more work deals with the

CAN COMMUNITY RELATIONS BE THE CORE OF PR PROGRAMMING?

Yes, community relations can be the core of public relations programming because it sets the tone of what an organization stands for. Not in words (rhetoric) but in actions (behavior). Today, how organizations conduct themselves in the communities where they do business is driven by two factors that make it more than just "getting the house in order":

1. **Instant communication,** encompassing burgeoning information networks that go far beyond news media data gathering. It has the capacity to capture and transmit home behavior far and wide.
2. **Global competition and the "global village"** have created interest in such information, at least by competitors, activist agencies, and others who have reason to broadcast it.

Three strategic levels need to be planned:

1. Defensive: guarding against **negative** acts, or acts of omission.
2. Proactive: being a leader in **positive** acts that appeal to key publics.
3. Maintenance: finding ways to **retain** relationships with publics not currently key—but still able to influence a company's reputation by forthright expression of their perceptions of it.

This approach is far different from "doing some nice things for the community." Assigning community relations to indifferent or inexperienced staffers because it's "easy" no longer suffices—and of course misses the centrality of community relations today.

Successful Community Relations Is Planned, Organized, and Systematized

In community programs there should be five considerations:

1. **Targeting**
   - Which *groups* in the community must be targeted
   - In order to motivate the *behaviors* needed?
   - What specific *activities* will achieve this motivation?
   - What *information* must be gathered and assessed before starting?
2. **Participate or own**
   If your reputation needs improving, working on projects with accepted partners can use their reputation to pull yours up; if yours is good, projects you can own offer more benefits and visibility.
3. **Here versus there**
   Should a program be based within the organization, or should it be an outside program?
4. **"Official" versus employee volunteer activities**
   If the latter, how will the organization get credit?
5. **Reaching opinion leaders**
   What design will assure that this critical goal is met?

*Two Types or Levels
of Programming Emerge*

Standard community relations involves basic, arm's-length, "good corporate citizen" activities that reach out, invite in, create awareness, let facilities be used:

1. **Membership network,** assigning "official" representatives to all important community groups.
2. **Speakers bureau,** placing talks to key groups on topics vital to the organization.
3. **Make facilities available.**
4. **Open houses,** visitations, tours.
5. **Programs around holidays.**
6. **Service on boards** of directors.
7. **Take part** in public events and back "must-support" causes.

The second level of community relations involves becoming part of the fabric of the community by placing people throughout its planning and decision-making networks:

1. **Ambassador or constituency relations** programs.
2. Hold regular **opinion leader briefings** or idea exchanges.

3. Set up local **community relations advisory boards.**
4. **Employee volunteer programs.**
5. **Community research,** jointly with a college perhaps.
6. **Social projects** that tackle the real community needs as seen by your key publics.
7. **Make expertise available.**

Neither list is exhaustive, but the two suggest the differences in the types. In most cases some of both levels are useful.

Other Considerations

Employee volunteerism has so many serendipitous benefits that it raises the issue of **spouse, family, and retiree** participation. Those organizations that do involve them generally report expanded impact and a widening network.

Feedback databanks may be the biggest opportunity—capturing what is heard and observed from opinion leaders and community members in a formal way. Use of databanks is *really* listening to the community, for invaluable information—which is instantly actionable through community relations programs.

unusual: controversies between factions in the community, activism on social issues, calamity or crisis, and governmental regulations as they affect the local community or as they are echoed in local ordinances affecting an organization.[2]

[2]For sudden and drastic change in local relationships, see news accounts of the oil spill of the Exxon tanker *Valdez* in Alaska in March 1989.

REFERENCES AND ADDITIONAL READINGS

ARNSTEIN, CAREN. "How Companies can Rebuild Credibility and Trust." *Public Relations Journal* 50 (April 1994): 28-29.

BRION, DENIS J. *Essential Industry and the NIMBY Phenomenon.* Westport, CT: Quorum, 1991.

Can Community Relations be the *Core* of Public Relations? *pr reporter* 36 (July 19, 1993): 1-2.

Corporate Community Relations Newsletter, 9 (September 1994). The Center for Corporate Community Relations at Boston College.

CHYNOWETH, EMMA, et al. "Responsible Care: Listening to Communities—What do they want to Know?" *Chemical Week* v153 (December 8, 1993): 68-69.

CUTLIP, SCOTT M., ALLEN H. CENTER, and GLEN M. BROOM. "Corporate Philanthropy." Chapter 14 in *Effective Public Relations.* 7th ed. Englewood Cliffs, N.J.: Prentice Hall, 1994.

FRANK, HELMUT J., and JOHN J. SCHANZ. *The Economics of the Energy Problem.* Joint Council on Economic Education, 1212 Avenue of the Americas, New York, N.Y. 10022. Pamphlet.

HUNTER, FLOYD. *Community Power Structures.* Chapel Hill, N.C.: University of North Carolina Press, 1953. A Community Relations Classic.

HUSSEY, JOHN F. "Community Relations," in *Experts in Action Inside Public Relations,* 2nd ed., eds. Bill Cantor & Chester Burger (White Plains, N.Y.: Longman, Inc., 1989): 115-125.

KRUCKEBERG, DEAN and KENNETH STARCK. *Public Relations & Community: A Reconstructed Theory.* Westport, CT: Greenwood, 1988.

LERBINGER, OTTO, and NATHANIEL N. SPERBER. "Community Relations." Chapter 6 in *Manager's Public Relations Handbook.* Reading, Mass.: Addison-Wesley, 1982.

LUNDBORG, LOUIS B. *Public Relations in the Local Community.* New York: Harper and Row, 1950. Continues to be definitive. By the public relations staffer who advanced to CEO of Bank of America.

Making Community Relations Pay Off: Tools & Strategies. Washington, D.C.: *Public Affairs Council,* 1988. Tells how companies are meeting the test of effective community relations.

MCDERMITT, DAVID. "The 10 Commandments of Community Relations." *World Wastes* 36 (September 1993): 48-51.

O'BRIEN, PAUL C. "Changing Expectations of Community Relations." *Executive Speeches* 8 (Oct/Nov 1993): 33-36.

pr reporter v35 (April 13, 1992): 3 Explains how inviting the public inside your operations is an effective and unexpected way to deal with community relations.

The Public Relations Body of Knowledge. New York: PRSA, 1993. See Section V.2 for abstracts dealing with "Community Relations."

RICH, DOROTHY. "Business Partnerships with Families." *Business Horizons* 36 (Sep/Oct 1993): 24-28.

SKOLNIK, RAYNA. "Rebuilding Trust." *Public Relations Journal* 49 (September 1993): 29-32.

A Continental Community Relations Challenge: Toronto Dominion Bank

Banking is an industry that can greatly benefit from positive community relations. No matter how widespread the banking corporation is, consumer banking takes place at the branch level—banking's "front-line." Face-to-face relationships, familiarity with the community and its people, and a reputation for trust and approachability are assets on a bank's balance sheet.

Toronto Dominion Bank, whose nearly 1,000 branches span 4,000 miles across Canada, wanted to increase its profile in local areas. It looked for a way to encourage branch managers to get more involved in their communities and to show that the bank could give something back to the community.

This goal presented a double challenge. The program would have to be effective in small towns as well as in large metropolitan areas like Toronto. It would also need to be consistently implemented by branch managers with varying personalities and managerial styles.

How could the bank develop a program that represented the company's **One Clear Voice,** was easy enough for branch managers to carry out, *and* was flexible enough to adapt to the needs of the diverse communities served?

AN IDEA DEVELOPS

The plan developed by Toronto Dominion's community relations manager involved local branches, high schools, and community services. The plan focused on a Student Volunteer Award (SVA) that would be given to high school students doing volunteer work in their communities. A 1989 study of 301 14–17 year-old teenagers showed that fifty-eight percent of those surveyed volunteer an average of 3.9 hours a week.[1] Though there are many opportunities for outstanding scholars and athletes to earn well-deserved recognition in their high schools, there are far fewer acknowledgments for students who give their time and talents to help others.

The program would also reach parents and build local support for the services that make communities a better place to live.

PROGRAM BENEFITS EVERYONE IN COMMUNITY

By acting as a bridge between the bank branch, students, and the community as a whole, the program offered benefits for all of its publics:

1. **Students** were recognized for their contributions, met new people, improved their leadership and interpersonal skills, and developed new talents.
2. The **community** gained improved services, a rekindled interest in volunteerism, and an increased understanding of the students' and the community's quality of life.
3. **Schools** appreciated having an external sponsor for a volunteer program that few—if any—schools had.
4. **Bank employees**—many of them parents of local high school students—improved morale and increased their pride in the bank's support of the community.
5. Each **bank branch** heightened its presence in the community, generated goodwill toward the parent bank, strengthened customer loyalty, and developed positive relationships with community leaders.

HOW THE AWARD PROGRAM WORKS

Anyone in the community—parents, teachers, fellow students, bank employees, and community organizations—can nominate a candidate for an SVA. Any student who gives service to the community without pay or school credit is eligible. Examples include: Candy Stripers, nursing home volunteers, coaches, community theater actors, tutors, day care volunteers, YMCA assistants, camp counselors, choir singers, church workers, and others.

Nominations are reviewed by a committee of students who select the winners. Winners are announced monthly or bimonthly. They are awarded an engraved trophy and are featured in a newspaper article (see Figure 4-1). At the end of the school year, all winners are honored at a testimonial dinner.

---

[1]From a survey by Gallup for the independent sector, as cited in *pr reporter* 33 (December 10, 1990): 4.

Figure 4-1 Newspaper articles featured photographs and the accomplishments of winning students. (Courtesy of Toronto Dominion Bank.)

SETTING UP A LOCAL AWARD PROGRAM

The SVA program was designed to be simple, relatively inexpensive, and minimally time-consuming. These are often critical attributes of successful public relations projects.

To simplify the program and make certain that there was **consistency** between branches, Toronto Dominion's Public Affairs Department created a program packet. The kit contained everything a branch manager needed to know about setting up a local SVA program (see Figure 4–2).

The action steps included:

1. **Selecting the community.** Suggested criteria included a community
   a. large enough to have student volunteer facilities;
   b. where the bank had one or more branches;
   c. with at least one high school;
   d. where no similar award existed.
2. **Inviting a local newspaper to co-sponsor.** Because publicity is so important to the program, *media participation is the key.* In exchange for co-sponsoring the SVA program, the local newspaper was encouraged to:

Figure 4–2 This comprehensive how-to kit simplified the process of setting up the SVA program. (Courtesy of Toronto Domininion Bank.)

a. publish articles before the awards were presented in order to build community awareness;

b. publish a photo story on the winner;

c. interview a local branch manager, school principal, nominator, and fellow student for additional stories.

3. **Meeting with local school administrators to explain the program.**

4. **Holding a joint meeting with all parties involved to work out the details.** A meeting with the branch manager, school principal, editor, and school board representative should be held to work out nomination deadlines and award presentation dates. All should be urged to stress the importance of community support and involvement.

5. **Presenting the program at a school board meeting.** This meeting is an opportunity to get the board's stamp of approval and public endorsement.

6. **Holding a bank branch staff meeting** to explain the program and its benefits. It is important for employees to be able to answer customer questions and to freely promote the program in the community.

7. **Issuing news releases** that announce the program through the media.

8. **Holding a "kick-off" dinner** with the board of education, school superintendent and faculty, the mayor, the media, and last year's winners.

9. **Distributing brochures with nomination forms.** These were hand-delivered to local officials, opinion leaders, service clubs, and the media. High school students delivered them and explained the program to local merchants. Stores, hospitals, nursing homes, and other community service facilities were asked to display the brochure.

10. **Ordering trophies** that students could keep. Bank branches were encouraged to display the trophy in their windows for a few weeks before the nomination deadline.

11. **Selecting a winner.** The nomination committee selects a winner and notifies the school principal. The branch manager and paper editor are also notified. The actual winner, however, is not told until the trophy is engraved and ready for presentation.

12. **Issuing a news release or article** with a photo of the winner receiving the trophy from the branch manager and the paper editor.

13. **Holding a congratulatory dinner** in honor of the SVA volunteer winner.

Toronto Dominion Bank's initiative in creating a program that develops community relationships spawned a corporate volunteer program called "The National Volunteer Activity Program," which deepens the company presence in the community and satisfies the needs of employees (see Case 4–6 on corporate volunteerism).

The corporate volunteer program is coordinated by a "National Volunteer Council" to ensure consistency in company endeavors.

SUMMARY

Logistics and vastness of territory aside, Toronto Dominion Bank demonstrates that local community relations are built on human relations. By focusing this program on a person-to-person, face-to-face level, it reduced the anonymity of the giant banking institution to the activity of one person meeting—and helping—another.

QUESTIONS FOR DISCUSSION

1. Beyond this case, what are some of the other problems, situations, or issues that would provide community relations opportunities for multibranch financial institutions? Why would these matters be particularly relevant to the business of banking?

2. What could be done to improve Toronto Dominion's plan designed to involve employees more directly in the student volunteer awards program?

3. Of the four steps in the public relations process, does one seem to be omitted or given less attention than others in the Toronto Dominion campaign?

4. This case illustrates that a program such as Toronto Dominion's benefits several groups or important publics in the community. If you (as a practitioner on the job) were asked to document this program on a formal or results basis, in seeking a renewed budget, what measurement techniques might you use?

Chemical Industry Takes Responsibility for Community Concerns

TRADE ASSOCIATION TAKES THE INITIATIVE

The Chemical Manufacturers Association (CMA) is the trade group for the chemical industry. Currently it has 185 members representing ninety percent of the industrial chemical productive capacity in the United States. Dues are based on a percentage of a company's chemical sales.

Chemical companies must be constantly innovative to remain competitive in today's global marketplace. Like most trade associations, CMA helps members stay abreast of issues and techniques. It provides assistance in complying with laws and regulations. CMA also offers **leadership training** and **task force groups** to de-

---

The public has legitimate concerns that we are just beginning to adequately address. We must recognize that the public wants no pollution. It wants no environmental damage and no unsafe products. Responsible Care[R1] represents a significant step in the right direction by the chemical industry. (Nicholas L. Reding, Executive Vice President of Environment, Safety, Health and Manufacturing, Monsanto)

We have said all along that we are not asking the public to *trust* us. We are asking everyone to *track* us, to monitor our performance and make suggestions that will help us improve. (Fred Webber, President, Chemical Manufacturers Association)

---

[1]Responsible Care[R] is a copyright of the Chemical Manufacturers Association.

velop skills and knowledge in the managerial, legislative, technical, and communications areas.

As public awareness of environmental health and safety issues has increased over the past few decades, the chemical industry has been scrutinized by activists, regulators, and consumers more closely than ever before. As environmentalists make louder protests, legislators respond with more stringent regulations.

Under SARA (Superfund Amendments and Reauthorization Act), also known as the Emergency Planning and Community Right-to-Know Act, chemical manufacturers and other businesses are required to inform employees and the community about the nature and hazards of the materials with which they work.[2]

As pressures from legislation mounted and NIMBYists[3] began paying closer attention to environmental issues in their communities, the chemical industry realized that it needed to reach beyond one-way communication of its side of the story. It needed to do three things:

1. *Listen to and recognize the perceptions and fears* of the public, especially neighbors of chemical plants.
2. *Own up to performance problems.*
3. *Take action* to correct existing problems and address perceptions.

ASSOCIATION RESPONSE TO PUBLIC CONCERNS: RESPONSIBLE CARE[R]

CMA created a program in the United States called *Responsible Care[R]: A Public Commitment* in 1988 (see Figure 4-3). It was modeled after a Canadian Chemical Producers Association program. Responsible Care[R] couples environmental, health, and safety improvements in individual plants with invitations for industry and public scrutiny. Thus, an integral part of the Responsible Care[R] program has been the creation of **six Codes of Management Practices** (see Figure 4-4). These codes established priorities for curbing emissions. CMA places reduction of emissions, reduction of the waste that facilities generate, and sound management of remaining releases and wastes at the top of its priorities.

According to Richard Doyle, vice-president of Responsible Care[R] at CMA,

> Responsible Care[R] calls for continuous improvement by the chemical industry in health, safety, and environmental performance. Responsible Care[R] is not a quick fix or an overnight cure. It is not a public relations program. It is an ongoing process, and a call for action. . . . Its ultimate goal remains to *create a dialogue with constituents in order to educate and obtain input into how the chemical industry can most effectively improve its performance in a manner that is responsive to the public. [Emphasis added.]*

[2]Bernard J. Nebel, *Environmental Science.* (Englewood Cliffs, N.J.: Prentice Hall, 1990), 290.
[3]Not *In My Back* Yard.

Figure 4-3 Shown here is the symbol of Responsible Care[R]. (Courtesy of CMA.)

Responsible Care[R] is *proactive public relations.* Rather than waiting for an accident to occur, or the public to become fearful or upset, it actively *invites* people to learn which chemicals are produced at a plant, how the plant is operated, and what protective measures are in place should an accident occur.

1. **Community Awareness and Emergency Response Code (CAER)**
   to reduce potential harm to the employees and the public in an emergency as well as bring the chemical industry and communities together
2. **Pollution Prevention Code**
   to improve the industry's ability to protect people and the environment by generating less waste and minimizing emissions
3. **Process Safety Code**
   to prevent fire, explosions, and accidental chemical releases
4. **Distribution Code**
   to reduce employee and public risks from the shipment of chemicals
5. **Employee Health and Safety Code**
   to maximize worker protection and accident prevention, through training and communications
6. **Product Stewardship Code**
   to ensure that the design, development, manufacture, transport, use and disposal of chemical products is done safely and without environmental damage

Figure 4–4   The six Codes of Management Practices put the guiding principles to use in practical application. (Reprinted Courtesy of CMA.)

Studies have shown that *fear* of an unknown event is more **powerful** than an actual *bad occurrence*. In a study of a group known to have latent tendencies for developing Huntington's disease, the majority of those whose genetic tests showed they would most likely develop this incurable malady felt that knowing was **beneficial.** "Better to know than be always wondering." Those that knew they were likely to get the disease reported their quality of life and psychological health was better than those for whom testing was inconclusive.

This holds true for knowing and communicating about chemical risks as well. Most people can handle truth better than being left in doubt. Open communication shows respect for people by treating them like responsible adults. However, the Huntington study also indicates that all people do not react the same when learning of risks. About 10% had trouble adjusting to the news, even when it was good, i.e. they would probably not develop the disease. Apparently for some, just handling the change or believing the test is accurate was more impactful than the relief. As always, no rule fits everyone.[4]

[4]*pr reporter* 36 (May 3, 1993): 2-3.

CMA set **five primary goals for Responsible Care^R:**

1. Improve chemical processes.
2. Enhance practices and procedures.
3. Reduce every kind of waste.
4. Heighten public scrutiny and input.
5. Create and maintain reliable communication and dialogue.

CMA member companies adhere to a list of ten guiding prinicples about safe plant operations and proper public communications. (Reprinted courtesy of CMA.)

1. To recognize and respond to community concerns about chemicals and our operations.
2. To develop and produce chemicals that can be manufactured, transported, used, and disposed of safely.
3. To make health, safety, and environmental considerations a priority in our planning for all existing and new products and processes.
4. To report promptly to officials, employees, customers, and the public, information on chemical-related health or environmental hazards and to recommend protective measures.
5. To counsel customers on the safe use, transportation, and disposal of chemical products.
6. To operate our plants and facilities in a manner that protects the environment and the health and safety of our employees and the public.
7. To extend knowledge by conducting or supporting research on the health, safety, and environmental effects of our products, processes, and waste materials.
8. To work with others to resolve problems created by past handling and disposal of hazardous substances.
9. To participate with government and others in creating responsible laws, regulations, and standards to safeguard the community, workplace, and environment.
10. To promote the principles and practices of Responsible Care^R by sharing experiences and offering assistance to others who produce, handle, use, transport, or dispose of chemicals.

Figure 4-5 CMA member companies adhere to a list of ten guiding principles about safe plant operations and proper public communications. (Reprinted courtesy of CMA.)

The Responsible Care^R program has centered on ten guiding principles (see Figure 4-5). These principles are based on CMA's 1983 policy statement on health, safety, and the environment and on the principles of the Canadian Chemical Producers Association's program.

CMA'S TARGET AUDIENCES

CMA's goal for the Responsible Care^R program is to continuously advance the level of chemical industry performance, demonstrating commitment to a better, safer world. They have targeted this message to:

- The chemical industry
- Teachers and students
- Employees
- Federal and state officials
- The media
- The general public
- Plant neighbors
- Local and national interest groups
- Company shareholders

BUILDING PUBLIC RELATIONSHIPS

Activities to Reach External Audiences

CMA members use a combination of one-way and two-way communication activities to invite external publics to communicate with their local plants. One-way efforts include:

- **Advertisements** (see Figure 4-6), featuring an 800 number for members of the public to call and get information or schedule a plant tour.
- **Brochures** featuring ways to make your home safe for children.
- **National television advertisements** that emphasize the responsible way in which the company is run, instead of what it manufactures.
- **Annual reports** that target the business community by emphasizing the Responsible Care member's improvements achieved through the program.

Two-way efforts include:

- **Community Advisory Panels (CAPs),** which are groups of citizens with diverse backgrounds and feelings toward the chemical industry. CAPs are sponsored by local chemical plants and encouraged to voice community concerns with industry representatives. Well-run CAPs provide dialogue between the plant and the community. To date, chemical manufacturers now sponsor over 200 CAPs in thirty-four states with great success. One example is Exxon's program, "Neighborhood Nights," which invites community members to the plant

It also occurs to you that you don't have the foggiest idea how to go about finding out.

Well, we can't say we blame you. Over the years, our industry hasn't exactly been noted for open doors, much less open dialogue.

But recently, the member companies of The Chemical Manufacturers Association have taken some crucial steps towards changing that. Through an effort called Responsible Care.®

> **You're driving by that chemical plant, just like you do every day, when one of your kids asks you what they make in there and you answer that you're not really sure and it occurs to you that you probably should be.**

Many of us, for example, are now regularly holding community meetings. Which give the people who live near our plants an opportunity to tell us about their fears and concerns. And to ask questions of the people who actually run the plant, day in and day out.

Others are offering tours to anyone interested in a firsthand look at the way we make, handle and dispose of chemicals. Because, ultimately, the best way to answer your questions about what goes on behind the walls of our plants is to show you what goes on behind the walls of our plants.

We're opening the lines of communication in other ways. In some cases, quite literally. Call **1-800-624-4321** and we'll tell you how you can find out what your local chemical company is making. We'll also send you our **Responsible Care® Brochure**, which details other ways we're working to keep you informed.

So that the next time you're driving by that chemical plant, like you do every day, and one of your kids asks you what they make in there, you can tell him.

The Chemical Manufacturers Association.
We want you to know.

Figure 4–6   This sample ad was run in many plant communities to promote the 1-800 phone number of CMA. (Courtesy of CMA.)

for a tour and supper and provides child care for the families with children. Any questions that the community members have are addressed in a question and answer session.

- **Inviting state legislators and local and national activist leaders to speak at association meetings** and sending CMA delegates or scientists to meetings of environmental groups.

Activities to Change Behavior of CMA Members

To maintain CMA membership, companies must make an ongoing effort to implement Responsible Care[R] guiding principles and codes of management practice. More than 1,000 executives and managers have attended CMA workshops on implementing the codes for Responsible Care[R]. Many have found creative ways to reach their new objectives. For example, some have tied **managerial bonuses** to achieved objectives. Others use **peer pressure of recognition** to motivate and support the Responsible Care[R] initiative.

As codes are implemented, CMA requires every company to report its progress along the way. CMA expects to have **all of the management practices in place at member companies by the late 1990s.**

EVALUATION: EXTERNAL PUBLICS

The National Association of Public Environmental Communicators commended Responsible Care[R] for its one-way and two-way communication vehicles. Participation studies show that, although comparatively few individuals use the 800 number, awareness of the invitation to call helps build public assurance about nearby plants and the chemical industry.

EVALUATION: INTERNAL PUBLICS

Reductions in Chemical Emission

CMA members reported that total releases (occurring when a chemical is discharged into the land, air, or water) declined from more than 2 billion pounds in 1987 to about 1.35 billion pounds in 1989 to about 880 million pounds in 1990. Air releases dropped more than twenty-two percent. Water releases were cut by sixty-two percent, and chemicals sent to landfills were reduced by seventy-four percent. Underground injection of chemicals was cut by forty percent.

Transfers (when wastes are shipped from plants to other locations for disposal, recycling, incineration, or other treatment) declined from 483 million pounds to 325 million pounds between 1987 and 1990. Transfers to publicly owned wastewater treatment facilities declined by twenty-two percent. Transfers to landfills were down by sixty-three percent, and transfers to other facilities were down thirty percent.

Self-Evaluation

The CMA Responsible Care[R] initiative includes a member self-evaluation process. Member companies are required to furnish CMA with an annual report of their progress in implementing the Codes of Management Practices. CMA members have shown significant gains in Process Safety, Distribution, Community Awareness, and Emergency Response.

Although these results show improvements, CMA recognizes the fact that company self-evaluations are subject to challenges of credibility. CMA is now identifying code measurement systems that meet objective public scrutiny.

This case demonstrates the trend of public relations programs to begin with *responsible action* by organizations, with public relations practitioners playing a key role in *design and strategy.* The *communications activities* then follow to gain recognition for the responsible action.

QUESTIONS FOR DISCUSSION

1. Richard Doyle, CMA vice-president of Responsible Care[R] said that the initiative "is not a public relations program." What did he intend to convey? He said Responsible Care[R] is a performance improvement initiative and that CMA's members are striving for public input into this process. What do you think he meant, and how can this goal best be achieved? Do you think the community advisory panels in neighborhoods around facilities are beneficial?

2. To what extent can a voluntary performance improvement initiative by private industry forestall government legislation and regulation on environmental matters? Explain your position.

3. What else could CMA do to attain higher credibility for its Responsible Care[R] initiative with:
   - The public
   - Its own members
   - Associated industries
   - Legislators and regulators
   - Activist groups

4. How could it measure an increase or decrease in credibility?

5. List other industries whose products or operations engender fear. What steps are you aware of that each is taking to allay public apprehension? How does the chemical industry's Responsible Care[R] initiative compare with what these other industries are doing?

6. Imagine yourself living across the street from a chemical plant. List all the feelings you can think of that you might have about the plant—positive, negative, or neutral. What specific actions would representatives from the plant need to take to address your feelings?

7. Draft a letter from a chemical plant manager to those living near the plant announcing introduction of the Responsible Care[R] initiative.

Medical Service Provides Community Service

Hospitals across the nation are recognizing the changing needs of their communities and are taking action. Health is currently the subject of most interest to Americans, according to research findings. Awareness of and concern about health issues have been aroused throughout the nation. Thus, the need for accessible information in layperson's terms is paramount. Many hospitals recognize a responsibility on their part to provide for this need.

MEDICAL CHANGES IN THE TWENTIETH CENTURY

Startling medical advances have characterized our era. All of medicine has gone through wrenching changes—miraculous medicines, organ transplants, and unbelievable plastic surgery. But the changes in hospitals have been especially difficult because hospitals are most publicly accessible. Marketing became the focus in the 1980s as hospitals hawked their wares like retailers. Day surgery replaced long hospital stays for many surgical procedures.

In addition, competition emerged as health maintenance organizations (HMOs) provided care for a guaranteed monthly payment and reformers campaigned relentlessly against the bankrupting cost of health care—for individual families with members struck by disease and for the nation, where one in seven dollars of the gross domestic product was devoted to health care.

Medical goals switched from preparing people to deal with little-understood diseases that struck unexpectedly to helping people adopt healthy lifestyles. This major change posed problems for patients and health care professionals. It put the emphasis on public education. People had to participate in their health care needs—and they had to change unhealthy but deep-seated lifestyles.

U.S. hospitals, tradition-bound institutions with long resistance to modern management practices, suddenly found themselves wracked by change within and facing competition and confusion without. The challenge was to reach out and build strong relationships with the community in a way that positioned a hospital to keep the flow of patients it needed to survive financially.

HEALTH-LINE

Successful adaptation of a telephone service enabled two hospitals to meet the new competitive challenge. This service provides answers to those who call with health-related questions on a wide variety of medical conditions. Callers can hear audio-tapes that provide general information about these subjects. Health-Line provides valuable information to employees, patients, students, community members—anyone with a need to know. Health-Line was devised in 1970 at the University of Wisconsin. Hospitals, clinics, universities, colleges, and businesses may purchase the start-up system and tailor it to their own audiences. Alexandria Hospital in Virginia did just that when it introduced its own version of Health-Line to the community in 1981.

Health-Line is very successful. Alexandria Hospital and its affiliate, Reston Hospital, increase visibility within the community and build community relations. Providing easy access to health-related information assists in health promotion, helps callers recognize symptoms or illness, prepares patients for hospital procedures, and, most important, it builds confidence in the hospitals, which draws patients.

HEALTH-LINE UPDATE

Health-Line operates out of the hospital's public relations department. The program initially had little room for growth because of bureaucracy and fear of breaking tradition. As a result, the telephone service was allocated to a volunteer community service organization called First Call (see Figure 4–7). First Call is the leading hospital-affiliated physician referral service for Alexandria Hospital and Reston Hospital Center. First Call focuses Health-Line and continually tries to make Health-Line easier for callers to use. Its objective:

> To help those who are sick gain information and obtain a doctor's appointment if needed. If only a couple of people call a day, it's worth it.

EXTERNAL POSITIVE OUTCOMES

Questions Are Answered Twenty-Four Hours a Day

Volunteers and automated systems field the questions of callers to the proper audio-tape twenty-four hours a day. Volunteers add a personal touch by thanking the

Figure 4–7   First Call also provides a physician referral service. (Courtesy of First Call.)

caller and often giving phone numbers for additional information. As of January 1992, First Call brought Health-Line into a physician-referral program that serves both hospitals. Now callers can make an appointment with a doctor for the next day. The referral service and the audiotapes serve as a complete tool for the caller (see Figure 4–8).

Figure 4–8 Health-Line offers information regarding medical problems. (Courtesy of First Call.)

Anonymity Is Preserved

Although volunteers are making one-on-one contact, no information is divulged about their personal identity. Callers may speak without fearing that their identity will be revealed.

Tapes Are Short and Simple

A real effort is made to present the information in layperson's terms. Medical terms are defined, and explanations are easy to understand. Tapes average six to eight minutes each, depending on the complexity of the topic. As of January 1992, First Call had upgraded Health-Line's tapes and trailer (the welcoming message to the caller). There are currently 325 tapes covering a wide variety of medical conditions.

Every Tape Is Reviewed by Alexandria's Medical Experts

Physicians listen to all tapes to ensure their validity, and in some cases they rewrite scripts. All tapes are reviewed periodically to keep them current with medical findings.

MAKING THE SYSTEM WORK

There are four main techniques used to make the system work.

- **Opening of the service was endorsed by opinion leaders.** U.S. Senator John Warner, Congressman Stanford E. Perris, and Alexandria Mayor Charles E.

In 1992, Alexandria Hospital had all of its audiotapes redone to include a new trailer directing callers to either the hospital's Physician Referral Service or the Emergency Department. The trailer is:

Health-Line is part of First Call, the area's leading physician-referral service, offered to you as a free public service by Alexandria Hospital and Reston Hospital Center. If you need medical attention, we recommend that you contact your family physician. If you do not have one, we would like to help you find one that best meets your needs. Please call us at 845–4848, 8 A.M. until 8 P.M., Monday through Friday. If you feel you need to be seen today, in most cases we are able to arrange an appointment for you that same day or within twenty-four hours. If your condition requires urgent attention, we recommend that you contact or go to the Emergency Department at Alexandria Hospital or Reston Hospital Center immediately. Thank you for calling, and we look forward to serving you again.

Tapes asked for the most:

- Genital herpes and cold sores
- Hiatal hernia
- Lyme disease
- Menopause
- Premenstrual syndrome
- Sinusitis
- Lupus

- Venereal warts and sexually transmitted disease
- Women's urinary tract infections

Other popular subjects:

- Breast cancer self-examination
- Cancer of the prostate
- Nutrition during pregnancy

Bealtley, Jr., were all present at the opening of Health-Line. The first tape was broadcast through the use of an amplifying system to a group of local citizens and hospital employees.

- **Tape of the Month feature.** Alexandria Hospital and Reston Hospital Center tie into ongoing health promotions, such as National Heart Week, by publicizing a relevant tape of the month. For example, the tape "Living with Hayfever," featured in June 1992, was widely requested.
- **Working with community groups to promote Health-Line.** Alexandria Hospital and Reston Hospital Center work with such groups as the American Heart Association, local clubs, and the Welcome Wagon as a means of spreading the message of the availability of this health care service.
- **Listing in telephone book.** Health-Line is in the phone book for quick and easy reference. Public service announcements on broadcast media, as well as advertising, are also used to promote the service.

INTERNAL POSITIVE OUTCOMES

Health-Line's internal publics consist of volunteers and operators who run the program from 8 A.M. to 8 P.M. (see Figure 4–9). They are given a lot of responsibility and are vital to the program. Volunteers go out on speaking engagements, set up and

In today's world of intense overcommunication and nonstop hype and promotion, research shows that people want to be *served not sold.* Health-Line is a soft-sell method to demonstrate through action that an organization cares about *serving* the community. Today, that is often the most effective *selling* method.

Figure 4–9   Volunteer Estaleah Baker handles a Health-Line call, one of 30,000 that come in annually. (Photo courtesy of J. W. Harchick, photographer.)

manage exhibits at shopping malls, and place brochures in public places to promote the program. "By giving them a significant part in the development of the program, they do not feel like all they are doing is plugging information in."[1]

The Program Is a Research Tool for Hospitals

Health-Line works as a great survey instrument. Although anonymity is preserved, it is possible to determine the sex of the caller, age, zip code, and where the caller learned about using Health-Line. At the beginning of January 1992, Health-Line began to keep all such data on computer. Automatic counters tally the number of times each tape is run. This information enables the hospital to identify major trends by area and to gear its education and medical programs to these expressed needs. This research tool helps volunteers decide which tapes to make available during the automated shift (no human interaction) from 8 P.M. to 8 A.M. During these evening and nighttime hours there are limited numbers of tapes available to the caller.

[1] *pr reporter*, April 1984.

Obstacles

One of the initial obstacles was the resistance of the medical staff. Alexandria Hospital overcame that resistance by involving the physicians. Physicians ended up supporting the program after realizing that they could benefit from Health-Line's referral system.

It was important to position Health-Line as an information source rather than a self-diagnosis tool or substitute for physicians. One way of showing physicians how the program would benefit them was to involve doctors in the review process of the audio tapes to ensure medical validity.

Physicians remain active supporters of the program by helping to distribute brochures with their names preprinted on them. They also rewrite tape scripts to keep them current with evolving medical science.

Evaluation

The program currently helps 400 to 600 people each month. The director of First Call, Jean Lowe, is planning new publicity campaigns for Health-Line. Lowe is also working to develop support and use of the program by other hospital departments. First Call is developing other services:

- Tapes made for doctors to prepare patients for procedures being done at the hospital.
- A tape on cardio catherization, a test for blockages, which prepares the patient emotionally and physically for the procedure.

According to Lowe, "It's like walking into a foreign country when walking into a hospital . . . and Health-Line could prepare them for it."

This one simple program implemented by one-to-one contacts has made First Call known in its area as the information and referral source on health topics. It has helped countless people as well as the community's doctors. In an area of hospital competitiveness, Health-Line, a modest-cost program, has demonstrated that serving the community is not only valuable in itself, but an excellent way to serve yourself.

DANBURY HOSPITAL'S SLIGHTLY DIFFERENT MEDICAL SERVICE

Today people want health information badly enough to work for answers. Citizens increasingly were turning to the medical library at Danbury Hospital, Danbury, Connecticut, for information. More often than not, these inquisitive consumers came up empty-handed in their own search because they could not decipher the medical jargon. Nonetheless, they kept trying. In addition, Danbury Public Library attests that twenty-five percent of the questions it is asked are medical questions.

CALLING-IN EQUALS REACHING OUT TO CUSTOMERS

800 numbers aren't just for ordering a set of knives or CDs or calling to get the low-down on medical questions. The corporate world also has caught on to the idea of establishing an 800 number to let its community of customers know that any question they have about their products is of importance to the company.

General Electric established the GE Answer Center in 1981 to be a twenty-four-hour-a-day resource for its customers. Customers can call and receive advice on the use of GE products on a broad range of subjects, including some that are unique, to say the least. For example, the call line has received inquiries from people asking whether it is appropriate to store a mink coat in the freezer, whether it is safe to drink water out of a dehumidifier, and if the racks in a GE refrigerator could double as a barbecue grill. People ask the craziest questions—but public relations personnel must be prepared to answer them.

More than 200 representatives work at the Answer Center, responding to consumers' questions personally. At their fingertips is a computer database of nearly a million and a half answers to questions concerning GE's 8,500 products in 120 product lines. *Four million customers a year take advantage of this service.*

Thanks to the easy access of such services as GE's Answer Center, huge corporations can respond to consumer queries as promptly as a small business can.[2]

Danbury Hospital acknowledged the need and desire of people to have access to medical research that they can understand. So in 1991, the hospital decided to use the concept of Problems Turned to Opportunities (PTO) to improve consumer health information in the Danbury area.

Background

The idea of a consumer health library had been batted around Danbury Hospital for years, but finding the resources and space within the hospital was difficult. Most hospital medical libraries recognize that there is a problem. Patients and patients' families make their way to the medical library to find out about diseases and therapies only to be thwarted by the difficulty of decoding medical journals. Students from colleges and even high schools attempted to use the medical library at Danbury Hospital. They realized that they would need more schooling to use a hospital library. Why couldn't they simply go to their public library? Because of budget cuts and the recession, college and public libraries were hard pressed to meet the demands of these clients.

[2]From a GE publication, *Business Briefings* (undated).

Solution

Danbury Hospital took a problem and turned it into an opportunity through a joint project with a local organization—the Danbury Public Library.

Funding

The hospital's Genesis Fund issued a $15,000 grant for the first year of the project and has allocated $10,000 each year thereafter. The Genesis Fund was set up a few years ago to fund projects that for some reason could not be funded through regular budgetary channels—a sort of "good idea fund."

Motivations

According to Danbury Hospital's librarian, Michael Schott, citizens need to obtain medical information that they can understand. Schott reports that sixty-five percent of the Consumer Health Information Center patrons use the center because "the doctor told me I have this." Schott explains that when a doctor has to give a patient bad news, the doctor will try to educate the patient, but often the patient blanks out when facing reality. Patients, more often than not, want to research the diagnosis when they are mentally and physically ready. After the research, they are able to ask their doctor questions that probably did not come to mind when they initially were given the news.

At the Public Library

According to George Pawlush, the hospital's vice-president for community affairs, the medical reference center at the Danbury Public Library is built around a user-friendly CD-ROM consumer health database supplemented with videotapes, pamphlets, and the library's existing book and magazine collection. Says Pawlush, "We were fortunate that Information Access, producer of a CD-ROM magazine index, happened to be introducing a new Health Reference Center just as we were putting our plans together." The Reference Center is specialized; it includes not only journal and magazine citations, but full-text articles, pamphlets, and even consumer health books. The index includes 130 core sources in health-related articles from more than 3,000 journals and magazines. If more in-depth information is needed, the researcher may use a fax machine that connects the public library with the hospital library.

In addition to the articles available there is a twelve-videotape series produced by the American College of Physicians. It was donated by a local physician. A portion of the series was made in Danbury and features one of the hospital's staff physicians.

Publicity

Danbury Hospital announced the creation of the Consumer Health Information Center at an area librarians' luncheon in conjunction with National Library Week. The Danbury *News Times* and two local radio stations covered the event. The CEO of Danbury Hospital, the director of the Public Library, and others spoke with the press. The program gave the hospital excellent exposure, and the library's stock as a valuable public institution went up as well.

Outcomes

According to Pawlush and Schott, reaction to the Reference Center has been excellent. The center currently receives six to eight requests a day. As an end result, patrons of the Reference Center at Danbury Public Library are going to Danbury Hospital for medical care. Pawlush believes that giving consumers the best possible medical information helps them make better-quality choices—which in many cases leads them to Danbury Hospital.

QUESTIONS FOR DISCUSSION

1. What is CD-ROM, the basis for Danbury Hospital's public information service? How will it and other emerging technologies affect consumers who are seeking information and organizations who supply it?

2. In your opinion, is Alexandria Hospital's telephone information service apt to be more widely used, or less, than Danbury Hospital's library service? Why? List the advantages and disadvantages of each.

3. Doctors became supporters of Health-Line when they realized it could be a source of patient referrals. How can public relations techniques assist professionals such as physicians, dentists, lawyers, engineers, and architects to increase their practices? Outline a program for a law firm.

The Struggle for Nuclear Power

One of the most challenging public relations positions since the 1970s has been working for an electric utility with a nuclear plant—such as Seabrook Station, which became a national symbol of the nuclear power debate in the 1970s and 1980s. Located in Seabrook, New Hampshire, forty miles north of Boston (see Figure 4–10), it was built on New Hampshire's seventeen-mile North Atlantic coastline in an extensive salt marsh area. During the prolonged construction and licensing process, Public Service Company of New Hampshire (PSNH)—the original owner—encountered persistent opposition from various sources.

- Initially, opposition came from environmentalists who were concerned about the potential impact a "once-through" water cooling system would have on ocean temperature. Among other issues, they were worried about possible irreparable damage that warming ocean waters would have on the biological populations in and under those waters.
- As plant construction progressed, a broader section of the community became increasingly concerned about the safety of the reactor and the proposed evacuation plans.
- The cost of the plant and its possible effect on the region's electricity rates

Maybe the first sign of problems for Seabrook Station occurred when the proposal to build came before various official boards. The illustrated model showed the containment unit, with a proposed height of 250 feet, mostly hidden from view by trees. But redwoods don't grow in New England!

Figure 4–10 Seabrook Station, located near the seacoast in Seabrook, New Hampshire. (Courtesy of Seabrook Station.)

sparked additional opposition. Increased power costs were perceived as an obstacle blocking industrial development and the prosperity of northern New England.

- Some citizens protested the plant because they doubted New Hampshire's *need* for a new power source.

Seabrook Station encountered delays as activists started demonstrating. The opposition intervened in the Nuclear Regulatory Commission's (NRC) adjudicatory review boards. The legal case was led by the Seacoast Anti-Pollution League (SAPL), while other grassroots activists spearheaded by The Clamshell Alliance led protests. The Clamshell used grassroots organizing, group decision making, and affinity networking against public or private projects felt to be disruptive to an area. Its activities ranged from peaceful demonstrations to forceful attempts at site occupation with mass arrests.

After nearly eighteen years of licensing, construction, and regulatory review, Seabrook Station began regular full-power operation on August 19, 1990. "We realize that we may never be able to satisfy the core group of people who do not support nuclear power," says Seabrook communications counsel Richard Winn, "but we do not ignore them either." Through the years Seabrook Station has become more sensitive to the needs and concerns of its publics. According to Winn, Seabrook has been doing something that a nuclear power plant does not have to do—that is, focusing on "the sorts of things that don't make electricity"—such as community relations, public education, and environmental information.

THE OPPOSITION

The Audubon Society opposed Seabrook Station before safety became an issue— before Three Mile Island. Its concern was environmental. When Seabrook changed the design of its cooling systems in order to prevent interference with the ocean, Audubon withdrew its opposition.

After the Three Mile Island and Chernobyl accidents, safety became the main concern of opposition. Seabrook opponents did include many gate-bashers, the form of opposition that comes to mind where nuclear power is concerned. But many other activists sought a different route to get their message heard. Issues of opposition ranged from complete rejection of nuclear power to the location of Seabrook Station.

The Clamshell Alliance, one of the most visible opposing organizations, went door to door in towns affected by Seabrook Station to gather support for protest. They also staged large, nonviolent and occasionally somewhat violent demonstrations.

Some **real estate agencies and banks** were opposed to Seabrook. Individuals in these fields joined other activist groups. In general, they were opposed to the possible drop in real estate value.

The Seacoast Anti-Pollution League (SAPL), a small group of dedicated volunteers, legally pursued Seabrook's perceived lack of safety. Their purpose at that time was "to work toward the deferral of the proposed nuclear plant at Seabrook."[1] Members, in conjunction with their attorney, Robert Backus, worked through the NRC's judicial system to improve the evacuation plan. SAPL believed that the initial plan was not adequate to meet the needs of the neighboring communities. Indeed, only three roads—all two-lane—lead away from the beach area adjacent to the plant, where on a summer Sunday as many as 100,000 people sometimes congregated for swimming and other beach activities.

Now that Seabrook is on line, SAPL strategies still emphasize the risks associated with living near a nuclear power plant. SAPL works in coordination with the

---

[1]Henry F. Bedford, *Seabrook Station.* (Amherst: University of Massachusetts Press, 1990), 67.

Massachusetts-based Citizens within a 10-Mile Radius (C-10) to monitor the levels of background radiation to see if any additional radiation is being emitted from Seabrook Station. Their efforts are directed toward discovering if there is a correlation between increased levels of radiation and increased health problems in the area.

SAPL members often visit local schools to speak about the dangers of nuclear power, and they set up question-and-answer booths at university fairs and other events. SAPL also responds to NRC regulation changes distributed by the Nuclear Information and Resource Service. Members receive newsletters encouraging them to write letters to the editors of local newspapers in an effort to notify people about how these regulatory changes affect the general public. To this day, some dedicate their lives to opposing nuclear power.

FINANCIAL TROUBLES PLAGUE SEABROOK

As a result of the mounting costs of Seabrook, PSNH was forced into bankruptcy. The company became financially strained when New Hampshire legislators passed the CWIP (Construction Work In Progress) law, which forbade the utility from including the cost of the plant's construction in consumer electric rates until the power was turned on. This law delayed the economic burden on New Hampshire citizens but added to the utility's interest costs on millions borrowed to finance construction.

Construction ceased temporarily in 1984. Then New Hampshire Yankee (NHY), a division of PSNH, took over the project and with the Seabrook Joint Owners[2] (other power companies with an interest in the plant) reaffirmed determination to complete Seabrook. People from PSNH were moved into top positions at New Hampshire Yankee.

DEVELOPING STRATEGIES

NHY's community relations team focused on Seabrook's publics in the seacoast area (see box). The public relations team initially used reactive programming to address the opposition's concerns and to resolve cognitive dissonance.[3] They used one-way and two-way communication techniques to address these goals.

---

[2]Seabrook was jointly owned by a large number of companies with PSNH holding the largest percentage of ownerhip.

[3]The theory of cognitive dissonance, first put forth by Leon Festinger in 1947, suggests a human desire for consistency between what people know and what they do. Any conflict creates a disturbance. See Glen M. Broom, Allen H. Center, and Scott M. Cutlip, *Effective Public Relations*, 6th ed. (Englewood Cliffs, N.J.: Prentice Hall, 1985), 159.

IDENTIFYING THE SEABROOK PUBLICS

The Seabrook communications staff identified important publics for Seabrook.

Internal Publics

- All Seabrook Station employees who live in communities around the plant site.
- Employees who do not live in the area.

External Publics

- Massachusetts and New Hampshire residents living both inside and outside the Emergency Planning Zone.

- Local and national news media.
- The financial community.

Seabrook community relations staff in the twenty-three New Hampshire and Massachusetts towns target public and private schools, day-care facilities, police and fire departments, local officials and opinion leaders, local media, advocacy groups, large (over fifty employees) and small businesses, chambers of commerce, network organizations such as the Lions and Rotary clubs and the local United Way, and citizens living within the twenty-two-mile radius.

One-Way Techniques

1. NHY created a series of hard-hitting ads featuring Seabrook employees offering words of reassurance (see Figure 4-11).
2. A "safety kit" consisting of information on Seabrook, waste management, radiation, and safety systems was distributed.
3. NHY circulated *Energy,* a community-targeted newsletter, between 1988 and 1989 to all publics in the emergency area. The articles focused on issues related to energy.

Two-Way Techniques

1. In 1986, NHY formally invited the surrounding community to tour the nuclear plant. More than 7,000 people from the surrounding New Hampshire and Massachusetts communities attended this event.
2. Seabrook Station's Science and Nature Center (see Figure 4-12) allows viewers to explore nature and science simultaneously. The center displays information about electrical generation and contains an ocean aquarium 260 feet below sea level. More than 30,000 people visit the center annually.
3. According to NRC regulations, the state must inform the public in the twenty-three affected towns about emergency and safety procedures. NHY took this

Geryl Jasinski, Quality Assurance Engineer At Seabrook Station, On Her Job And Her Commitment To Safety.

Figure 4–11 Example of ads featuring a NHY employee and "The Lesson of Chernobyl." (Courtesy of Seabrook Station.)

one-way task and made it into a two-way strategy. Public relations staff created a calendar decorated with photographs of the seacoast and mailed copies to all homes in the area. The calendars include public notification information, including which radio stations broadcast emergency bulletins and instructions. Employees hand-delivered calendars to approximately 4,000 of the 7,000 small businesses in the area. Public issues specialist Kathleen Lewis reported that only two percent of those businesses rejected the information.

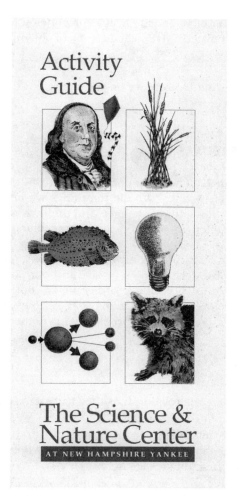

Figure 4–12 A brochure of the Science and Nature Center. (Courtesy of Seabrook Station.)

Seabrook did encounter some heated public opposition to the evacuation plan, and that attracted a lot of media attention. Some schools were unhappy with the proposed evacuation plans because teachers would be required to stay with their classes even though their instinct would be to rush to their own families. These perceptions of the proposed evacuation plan's shortcomings forced many towns to reject the emergency procedures.

4. NHY communicators representing Seabrook met with school superintendents and business executives to educate them about emergency planning. They also developed relationships with Massachusetts emergency medical squads and fire departments.

5. NHY communications approached the media proactively. If a siren that had

nothing to do with Seabrook sounded off in a surrounding town or if a rumor about Seabrook was circulated, NHY called the media before the media called them.

These efforts helped Seabrook Station achieve on-line status. NHY won its contested case before the NRC's adjudicatory boards.

THE NEED FOR PROACTIVE MEASURES

Seabrook public relations teams did not stop once the plant was on line. As communications counsel Richard Winn wrote, "We did the things we needed to do to get our license according to the rules and regulations. And then we went a step farther to be proactive and adopt a policy of 'management of expectations' for our community relations efforts."

Seabrook utilized strategy to build one-on-one relationships. Now that the plant was up and running, those relationships needed to be maintained. According to Seabrook research, the greatest percentage of people are not definitively for or against nuclear power. Therefore, public relations staff believes it is vital that the public feels comfortable about contacting Seabrook whenever there is a concern.

REINFORCING RELATIONSHIPS

NHY took measures to reinforce the relationships they had established.

1. NHY continued to send out an Emergency Plan Information Calendar to all of its external publics. The calendar consists of thirty-three pages of emergency planning and safety information (see Figure 4–13).
2. The Science and Nature Center was made accessible for school and community-based field trips. The center provides hands-on exhibits featuring energy and the environment and the Owascoag Nature Trail—approximately one mile of preserved woods and marshlands with a variety of plants and animals.
3. NHY established a local hotline for citizens in surrounding communities to call and inquire about specific problems and concerns.

FOCUSING ON THE COMMUNITY

In 1991, New Hampshire Yankee employees and volunteers participated in several community-oriented events and activities. The community relations department initiated at least one new program encouraging community involvement each quarter.

Figure 4–13 The Emergency Plan Information Calendar. (Courtesy of Seabrook Station.)

1. NHY employees participated in the Lion's Camp Pride, a summer camp facility offering educational and recreational overnight programs to children with special needs. Volunteers installed docks, stained and painted buildings, cleaned and set up bunkhouses.

2. NHY participated in the seacoast's Seafood Festival. Employees raised money at the event by selling popcorn and donated all proceeds to My Greatest Dream, an organization that benefits terminally ill children.

3. Volunteers participated in Coastweeks, a nationwide celebration of the nation's coastal areas. NHY cleaned up Hampton Beach, a New Hampshire state park about two miles from the Seabrook plant.

4. NHY donated time and building materials to Action Cove Playground, an inno-

vative playground in West Newbury, Massachusetts. The children's area was designed for explorative and imaginative play.

5. NHY founded a local Project Homefront, an effort assisting families whose relatives were called to serve in the Persian Gulf War. A total of 163 volunteers offered services and assistance in transportation; auto, electrical, and plumbing repair; carpentry; and babysitting. NHY employees also donated $1,135 to this project.

Other community endeavors aided organizations such as Wish Upon a Star, which provides anonymous Christmas gifts to needy children, and the Girl Scouts of America. According to Martha Netsch, Director of Communications for the Swiftwater Girl Scout Council, the Girl Scouts frequently visit Seabrook Station's Science and Nature Center, work with staff on scout education programs about solutions to today's energy problems, and recognize the Science and Nature Center as support for young women interested in mathematics, science, and technology.

Seabrook encourages employees to become involved in local civic organizations and in local government. As of 1991, many were on town and city boards, volunteer emergency medical squads and fire departments; Rotary, Lions, and Kiwanis clubs; or were active in school organizations. Every year employees serve as judges at local science fairs.

NORTH ATLANTIC UPDATE

In 1992, control of Seabrook was bought by Connecticut-based Northeast Utilities—which earlier took over bankrupt PSNH. One of its subsidiaries, North Atlantic Energy Corporation, owns 35.6% of its stock and sees to the daily operation of the plant. From a business perspective, Seabrook Station was recognized as Business of the Year 1991 by *Business New Hampshire Magazine.*

Activist groups, however, continue to exist, though most are now peaceful in their approach. According to SAPL's Joan and Charles Pratt, both SAPL and C-10 work as watchdogs; their mission is to make sure that Seabrook complies with NRC regulations. The Citizens Radiological Monitoring Network acts as a support group that focuses on how to live with potential hazards. Its goals are to monitor every air and water emission from Seabrook, to hold Seabrook socially accountable for every emission, and to expect a responsible attitude from the station itself. All these awareness groups keep a close eye on Seabrook.

Despite the controversial issues, Seabrook employees, for the most part, maintain professional relationships with activist groups. There are still a small number of people opposing the plant who remain very reserved and refuse to speak to anyone who works at Seabrook Station. The plant's community relations department believes it is in their best interest to deal cooperatively with these groups. North At-

HISTORY OF SEABROOK STATION

1960s

- Plans for a nuclear plant in New Hampshire developed.

1972

- Two-unit power plant proposed for Seabrook, New Hampshire.

1973

- Application for construction permit filed. Concerns about environment arise.

1977

- The Clamshell Alliance and others form and mount protests; 1400 people are arrested.

1978

- Peaceful demonstration on site is suggested to "The Clam" by an area public relations counselor, Isobel Parke, as more effective than another protest; 30,000 people attend an energy fair on plant grounds. No one is arrested.

1979

- Three Mile Island incident causes Seabrook to reconsider its design. Safety features and more emergency planning are added. Activists express concern through demonstrations.
- Interest rates skyrocket. Construction delayed because of financing difficulties.
- CWIP (Construction Work In Progress) law passed; causes more financial strain.

1984

- Changeover period. New Hampshire Yankee, a division of PSNH, takes over in June to manage completion of construction, licensing, and operation of the plant.

- Construction is temporarily suspended for three months.

1986

- Election year. Candidates' success depended on whether they were for or against Seabrook.
- Paul McEachern, Democrat, defeated by incumbent Republican governor John Sununu, over the CWIP issue.
- Construction of plant completed (July 31).
- Nuclear Regulatory Commission issues license for testing of reactor.
- Chernobyl disaster in USSR.
- More safety concerns and activist demonstrations.
- Massachusetts Governor Michael Dukakis, representing the six Massachusetts towns near Seabrook, pulls his state's support and vows to fight the plant's opening.

1988

- January, Public Service Company of New Hampshire (PSNH) files Chapter 11 bankruptcy.
- Atomic Safety and Licensing Board, an arm of NRC, approves state of New Hampshire's emergency response plan for the towns surrounding Seabrook.

1990

- NRC issues full-power operating license in March, and power is generated for the first time in May. Power level reaches 100 percent in July.

1991

- U.S. Court of Appeals rejects appeal of the NRC's decision to issue an operating license in January.

- Massachusetts Governor William Weld directs state officials to begin cooperative emergency planning with New Hampshire Yankee in March.
- U.S. Supreme Court lets the lower court's decision stand to uphold the

NRC's licensing of Seabrook Station in October.

1992

- PSNH is acquired by Northeast Utilities. Seabrook operates at 77.9 percent of generating capacity for the year.

lantic Energy Corporation has grown ever more sensitive to the concerns of all involved publics.

North Atlantic has also recognized the future problems associated with the Seabrook plant's ultimate decommissioning, spent fuel rod disposal, and radiological emissions risk correlations. The company says it plans to deal with these issues in the same "honest, proactive way we've dealt with everything since NHY was formed."

EVALUATION

Has Seabrook Station prevailed in the court of public opinion? Its community relations department has been effective in establishing relationships with the community, yet they have not changed the public's opinions about nuclear power. According to Winn, "more than half of Seabrook Station's publics are not for or against nuclear power . . . they are unsure." Yet Winn notes that, once the plant was licensed, these relationships are not something North Atlantic *had* to establish even though its product, nuclear power, continues to arouse uneasy feelings.

But he concludes: "After the battle over Seabrook, the big lesson is that you can't just comply with licensing requirements. You've got to win and maintain your license with good communications and community relations as well." Depending on its efficiency *and* its public relations, Seabrook could win or lose a lot of support from those publics who are still unsure about nuclear power. Over the twenty to forty year operating cycle for a nuclear plant, the role of sound public relations will remain vital.

QUESTIONS FOR DISCUSSION

1. What responsibilities does a business have to the community, if any?
2. Should a business that produces a controversial product or service have obligations that surpass legal and regulatory mandates? Why or why not? Does your answer depend on whether the product (or production of the product) is potentially hazardous or lethal to the environment or humans?

3. Seabrook offers an informational phone line for communities and employees to call whenever questions or concerns arise. This phone line accommodates the local towns surrounding Seabrook Station. Do you think this phone line would be more effective if it were a national 800 number, thus making it available to all U.S. residents? Why or why not?

4. Develop some strategies that could strengthen the messages or effectiveness of the remaining opposition.

5. Develop some proactive and reactive strategies that Seabrook will need when decommissioning the plant, disposing of the spent fuel rods, and if the radiological emission risk correlations show that the plant has become dangerous.

Nuclear Waste Goes Down the Drain

Every day people all across the country choose to do things that have a certain degree of risk—crossing the street, driving a car, flying in an airplane, bungee jumping, or eating foods they know do not constitute good nutrition.

What happens, though, when *someone else* controls the risks *we* face? Do we ask our friend to pull the car over so we can get out? Never fly unless we pilot the plane? What happens if an organization wants to take a risk in a community, such as dumping low-level nuclear waste, even if it may be smaller than the risks we take in everyday life?

More and more, organizations are facing strident opposition to their plans from groups and coalitions opposed to taking on more risk. Grassroots environmental concerns have fostered attitudes such as Not In My Back Yard (NIMBY) and Not On Planet Earth (NOPE) to limit any sort of activities viewed as at all risky. Yet, in many cases, organizations need to assume some risk in order to run their business, produce products, adhere to government standards, or make a profit.

Risk management deals with explaining and persuading a risk-averse public to allow the execution of necessary actions that may carry some risk (see Figure 4-14). But risk communication is more than explanation or persuasion. It must be process-oriented to allow interaction between the opposing groups—the public, proponents, experts, and regulatory officials—and allow each to identify the true issues at stake from its perspective. Only then can the average citizen form an intelligent judgment.

IS RISK COMMUNICATION A DIFFERENT BALL GAME?

As technology has changed, so have the type and amount of risks we face. Public reaction to risk can be varied, depending on each individual's mind-set and experi-

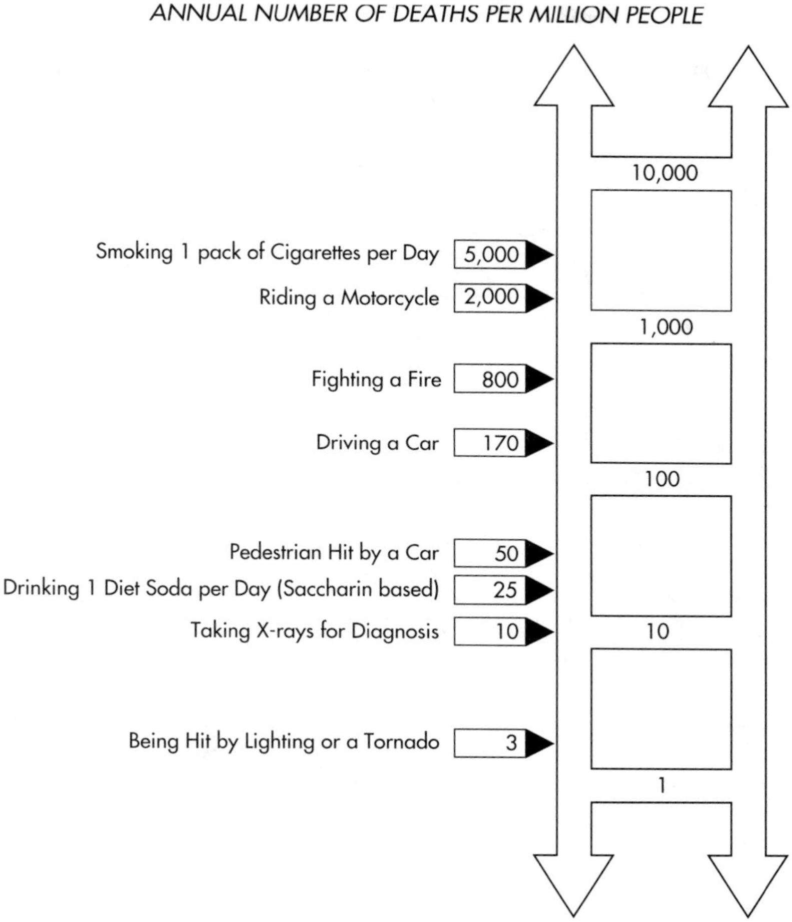

ANNUAL NUMBER OF DEATHS PER MILLION PEOPLE

Smoking 1 pack of Cigarettes per Day	5,000
Riding a Motorcycle	2,000
Fighting a Fire	800
Driving a Car	170
Pedestrian Hit by a Car	50
Drinking 1 Diet Soda per Day (Saccharin based)	25
Taking X-rays for Diagnosis	10
Being Hit by Lighting or a Tornado	3

Scale markings: 10,000 / 1,000 / 100 / 10 / 1

Source: Adapted from Schultz, W.,G. McClelland, B. Hurd, and J. Smith (1986), *Improving Accuracy and Reducing Costs of Environmental Benefits Assessment.* Vol. IV. Boulder: University of Colorado, Center for Economic Analysis.

WARNING! USE OF DATA IN THIS FIGURE FOR RISK COMPARISON PURPOSES CAN SEVERELY DAMAGE YOUR CREDIBILITY (SEE TEXT).

Figure 4–14 One tactic used by risk communicators has been to make risk comparisons in order to communicate the extent of the risk. But making quantitative risk comparisons with voluntary risk has proved illogical and damaging to the organizations who employ this tactic. Demonstrating it visually is more effective. (Courtesy of the Chemical Manufacturers Association. From Vincent T. Covello, Peter M. Sandman, and Paul Slovic, *Risk Communication, Risk Statistics and Risk Comparisons: A Manual for Plant Managers* [Washington, D.C.: CMA, 1988].)

ences. Each person perceives risk in his or her own personal context and with his or her own established biases for or against that risk.

In 1983, the National Research Council (NRC) completed a study on managing risk, leading to a report entitled *Risk Assessment in the Federal Government: Managing the Process*. Raised in this study was the realization that with risk management comes a new kind of communication, risk communication. The NRC chartered a committee, the Risk Perception and Communication Committee, to research how to communicate risks effectively to the public. The committee found that explaining risks in a logical manner was not effective for convincing a risk-averse public that the risks were nothing to worry about. People evaluate risks contextually, and their *perception* of that risk motivates their behavior.

ONE EXAMPLE

For many years, the city of Albuquerque, New Mexico, had an ordinance forbidding anyone—except hospitals and radiation treatment clinics—from disposing of low-level radioactive wastes in the city's sewer system. Low-level radioactive waste covers anything that may have been contaminated by radioactive materials, such as equipment, clothing, tools, and so on.

In 1991, Sandia National Laboratories (a facility of the Department of Energy, DOE) and Inhalation Toxicology Research Institute (ITRI) petitioned the city to dispose of their waste in the city sewer systems, as the hospitals were already allowed to do. Sandia initially made the proposal because it wanted to dump 50,000 gallons of low-level radioactive water (used to shield nuclear reactor fuel rods) into the sewer system. Radiation experts assured Albuquerque residents that the risk was minimal and their tap water had more natural or "background" radiation in it than the wastewater did.[1]

An amendment to change the city's sewer-use ordinance was put before the city council. The change would have allowed anyone licensed to use radioactive material to dump low-level radioactive waste into the sewers. Though more organizations would be allowed to dump, more stringent limits would be set on how radioactive the waste could be. They would be able to dump waste at only one-tenth the radioactivity standards established by the Nuclear Regulatory Commission.

After investigating, the city council found that its ordinance or any amendment to an ordinance regarding discharging radioactive wastewater does not fall under its jurisdiction. These regulations are set by the federal government, through the Nuclear Regulatory Commission and DOE. Thus Sandia as a federal laboratory could ignore the city ordinance and dump anyway—that is, if its managers thought this

---

[1]Background radiation is naturally occurring radiation that accounts for more than half of the radiation we are exposed to. It is generated from cosmic rays, naturally occurring elements such as uranium, and radioactive chemicals in the body.

was acceptable public relations policy. They did not, however, so the issue went to public debate.

A VOCAL OPPOSITION

Citizen opposition was immediate and outspoken. A group named People's Emergency Response Committee (PERC) began to organize. PERC was formed a year before the emergence of this issue, when those involved first became aware of Mayor Louis Saavedra's attempt to change the city's sewer-use ordinance. It is an ad hoc coalition of citizens' organizations made up of Hospital and Healthcare Workers Union 1199, Citizens for Alternatives to Radioactive Dumping, the South West Organizing Project, New Mexico Public Interest Research Group, the Albuquerque Center for Peace and Justice, Sierra Club, and the Labor Committee for Peace and Justice.

PERC immediately established its position with four fundamental statements:

- No other industries including Sandia National Laboratories should be allowed to dump radioactive wastes in the sewers.
- The existing Albuquerque sewer ordinance should be strengthened to control and monitor the radioactive wastes being dumped by hospitals and other medical treatment facilities.
- The DOE and private industries must develop long-range plans for dealing with their radioactive waste. These plans should not include dumping in the sewers as an option.
- All plans must include strategies on how these companies and the DOE will reduce the *generation* of radioactive waste in the first place.

Representatives of the group were at the first hearing regarding the change. They were concerned that the issue was more than obtaining permission to dump 50,000 gallons of waste. They saw it as a ploy to allow any business in the future to rid itself of radioactive waste. Concerns were raised about the water's path. Would it enter the Rio Grande and then affect towns downstream from Albuquerque? This was not a risk that the citizens of Albuquerque and the surrounding towns were prepared to take, PERC felt.

PERC'S TACTICS

One communication tactic that PERC utilized was to publish a newsletter entitled *Radioactive Pipeline* to establish its position. Its focus was on the risks that residents perceived: that this could be contaminator of Albuquerque and that there was no telling if Sandia and the others could be trusted. This newsletter helped PERC get its message out to make people aware of the situation. The newsletters and flyers PERC distributed urged the citizens of Albuquerque and surrounding areas to take action and voice their concerns at community and city council meetings. Postcard campaigns were mounted by distributing preprinted cards so that citizens could easily send them to local city councilors expressing opposition to this ordinance. A petition drive was started, gathering more than 7,000 signatures.

OBSTACLES FOR SANDIA

Media coverage was not helpful for Sandia, either. While officials were explaining how safe the water was in one article, other articles in the newspaper indicated some of Sandia's sewer violations and mismanagement of radioactive materials by DOE.

City council meetings were packed with citizens who came to voice their outrage. Sandia arranged for two radiation experts to speak in an attempt to reassure people of their physical safety, but this expertise did not address the underlying issues that made up a major part of this controversy.

- Many Americans have a **lack of trust** for the federal government and those organizations that are a part of it. When or if stories concerning federal mismanagement and secret nuclear tests are uncovered, the public will remember them later.
- The effects of radioactive wastes are not completely understood. Some effects will not be apparent for a very long time, and this **uncertainty** is difficult for anyone to deal with.
- Many people already have **biases** against anything nuclear, especially if it is near where they live.
- Albuquerque residents were concerned with what this initial dumping would mean for the **future.** They were asking themselves, What else would be dumped, and how often would it happen?

THE SANDIA SIDE OF IT

Sandia's public affairs department did make an attempt to educate the public about this risk to try and allay public fears about radiation and radioactive materials. Some of their activities included:

- Organizing some of the public meetings to create the opportunity for citizens to voice their concerns and get questions answered.
- Reaching out to public officials and leaders who showed opposition to the proposal to give them the facts of the issue.

PR MESSAGES SET RISK PERCEPTIONS, AND RISK IS EVERYWHERE

All communications have become risk communications. Therefore, the rules for dealing with hazardous waste and cancer fears should be applied to every communication—to employees, shareholders, stakeholders, and customers, and surely to regulators, government entities, and the body politic.

Why? Because today publics are interested in two things: What can you do *for* me? And what, if I'm not careful, might you do *to* me? That second query—people's natural skepticism raised to new levels by today's troubled economy and quality-of-life—adds a risk perspective to every message or appeal.

Influencing People's Perception of Risk

Risk communication is proactive. Its goal is to improve knowledge and change perceptions, attitudes, and behaviors of the target public, write Leandro Batista and Dulcie Straughan, of the University of North Carolina at Chapel Hill.[2] They note, however, that changing risk perception—a necessary step for behavior change—is complicated. It can be:

1. *Objective* (product of research, statistics, experimental studies, surveys, probabilistic risk analysis), or
2. *Subjective* (how those without expert or inside knowledge interpret the research or the situation—which is based on their values and particular levels of experience and knowledge).

Thus experts and lay people build different mental models that lead them to interpret risk activities differently. One does it objectively, the other subjectively.

Format of the Message

The format of the risk message forms the risk perception. For example, radon and asbestos have a twenty-five-fold difference in *actual* risk to the population, but generate only a slight difference in *perceived* threat. The inaccuracy of people's perceptions of the relative risks of radon and asbestos can be explained by the similarity of the format of messages conveying the risks involved. Regardless of the actual content of the message, the idea that is usually conveyed is that "this is a technical area that you probably won't understand, but there is a *danger here*." In other words, people will have similar responses to messages that are expressed in similar formats, even though the information may be different. Public relations teams can apply their knowledge of this aspect of human nature to formulate effective messages in a systematic way.

1. Each risk has its own identity (or risk perception), which is a specific combination of subjective risk factors (see box), or, as Neil Weinstein and Peter Sandman call them, "Outrage Factors."[3]

[2]"Dimensions Influencing Risk Perception: The Case of Lung Diseases." Unpublished paper, n.d.

[3]Neil D. Weinstein and Peter M. Sandman, "Predicting Homeowner Mitigation Responses to Radon Test Data," *Journal of Social Issues* 48 (1992).

SUBJECTIVE RISK FACTORS

Less Risky	More Risky
voluntary	involuntary
familiar	unfamiliar
controllable	uncontrollable
controlled by self	controlled by others
fair	unfair
not memorable	memorable
not dreaded	dreaded
chronic	acute
diffused in time and space	focused in time and space
natural	artificial

2. Some combination of these outrage factors leads people to be more upset about hazard X than hazard Y.

3. Not all factors are relevant for all risks, and there is no trade-off among factors—scoring high on one factor will not compensate for a low score on another (the noncompensatory model). Factors are either on or off in the overall perception of that risk.

4. Therefore, it's important to understand the underlying dimensions that affect the perception of a particular risk—how the outrage factors combine to form a risk perception.

5. Messages should not be formulated until these underlying dimensions are understood.

A final concept to keep in mind is the one that governs the decision-making process: With health or environmental risks, people will modify their behavior if a highly threatening situation exists (or is perceived to exist). Thus a *minimum standard*, or *threshold*, is set for risk acceptability. If a risk is greater than the threshold, action occurs; otherwise the status quo is preferred. In all probability, this concept is as true for risks of being overcharged, getting fired, or losing on investments as it is for nuclear discharges.

Peter Sandman's formula for identifying risk has become widely used by public relations practitioners: HAZARD + OUTRAGE = RISK PERCEPTION.[4]

- Making public affairs people available for any and all questions that the public had about the issue.
- Arranging for television interviews with radiation experts to disseminate to the public the facts of radiation.

CAN THERE EVER BE AGREEMENT?

On November 5, 1991, the Albuquerque City Council voted against the proposal to change the city ordinance. The council then formed a study committee to review important questions about radioactive dumping and offer recommendations in six

[4]Peter Sandman, *Responding to Community Outrage: Strategies for Effective Risk Communication* (Fairfax, Va.: American Industrial Hygiene Association, 1993).

months. Two years and two research studies later, the city council finally consented to the disposal of the wastewater in the sewer system.

For Sandia National Laboratories, the task of disposing of its waste became an ordeal. A simple task of applying for a permit had become an extended three-year controversy.

For all affected organizations, the question remains: What will we do with our low-level radioactive waste? What is often overlooked is the benefits that nuclear science offers. Do we abolish nuclear science altogether? NIMBYists demand that disposal not be done where they live. Where else, then? Will there ever be an acceptable alternative? For public relations practitioners, the challenge of communicated risk will only become greater as technology advances.

QUESTIONS FOR DISCUSSION

1. If you were a public relations practitioner working at a local hospital that was dumping low-level radioactive waste into the sewers, what would you have counseled management to do during the Sandia attempt to gain authorization to dump its waste? Why would you recommend that?

2. Would it have been possible to convince the citizens of Albuquerque to allow the dumping of radioactive waste in the sewers? Why do you believe this? What tactics could Sandia have used to allay the fears of the public?

3. Why was PERC successful in gathering so much public support? What did it do differently than Sandia?

Case 4-6

Volunteer Programs Improve the Quality of Life

Since the 1980s, organizational social responsibility has gained emphasis in public relations. Support has grown for an important and necessary link between companies and the communities—local, national, and global—in which they do business. Employees are also becoming more socially aware, as evidenced by the number of corporate volunteer programs created within the decade. This emphasis on social responsibility is in response not only to the needs of the community, but also to the needs of the organization *and* the individual needs of employees. Brewing companies, hospitals, and manufacturers, for example, all have adapted to the more socially conscious, modern world by creating the volunteer programs described here—to demonstrate through behavior, not words, their sense of good citizenship to all publics associated with the organization.

ADOLPH COORS BREWING COMPANY

Aware that its employees wanted to participate in programs to help the community, Adolph Coors Brewing Company started a "quality-of-life" program. Its goal was to strengthen internal and external loyalty through personal interaction among employees while serving their communities. Called Volunteers In Community Enrichment (V.I.C.E.), the program began in 1985 with a volunteer group of employees and their spouses. It is managed by a board of employees. Coors employees suggest ways in which they can volunteer in communities; an employee-run board of advisers reviews the suggestions and publishes those selected in a monthly activity

Corporate volunteer programs are beneficial to organizations because of their effect on employees. According to a study by the Conference Board in the spring of 1993, eighty percent of 454 executives agree that volunteer programs improve employee retention and enhance training, and ninety percent felt that volunteer programs build teamwork skills, improve morale, and attract better employees.[1]

The importance of these factors in attracting and retaining quality employees has allowed volunteer programs to survive and thrive through restructuring and downsizing. Respondents agree that in uncertain times, people have a greater need to do something meaningful.

If either internal or external publics are affected by a poor or strained quality of life, the organization suffers as well as the community. Further, volunteer programs are skill builders. By becoming involved in the improvement of society, both the organization and its employees improve.

guide.[2] (See Figure 4–15.) Groups of volunteers then conduct the programs, with assistance from the V.I.C.E. leadership. This program demonstrates Coors's commitment to the betterment of the community and to improving the quality of employees' lives.

The V.I.C.E. mission is to

enrich the quality of life in the local community through Coors volunteer involvement; to build quality relationships with our communities; and to enhance the company's image and ability to market its products.

This quality-of-life program has enhanced two-way communication between the company and its employees. Of 6,900 employees at Coors's central location in Golden, Colorado, 4,700 are active volunteers. Project leaders work with twenty people on logistics, coordinating a project for 150 to 200 volunteers. The V.I.C.E. Squad effort may be a bottom-up perspective on service, but the company's commitment to the program starts with upper management.

The V.I.C.E. squad benefits the company and the well-being of the community in several ways:

[1] *pr reporter,* May 10, 1993. Vol. 36, p. 3.

[2] Toronto Dominion Bank's (see Case 4-1) "National Volunteer Council," established in 1990 to meet the employees' renewed interest in traditional family values and volunteerism, also publishes a monthly list of volunteer opportunities for employees. In this case, the list offers suggestions for individuals to act upon. This encouragement enhances the bank's profile in the community, urges the employees to become active in their communities, and fosters a team spirit throughout the bank branches through community involvement.

Figure 4–15 The Coors V.I.C.E./A.D.V.I.C.E. Monthly Activity Guides allow employees to pick a project that interests them. (Courtesy of Coors Brewing Company.)

1. **Outreach.** Volunteers often involve family members or friends in other states. This attitude reflects positively on company reputation over a wide area.
2. **Loyalty.** The volunteers are like one large family.
3. **Skills training.** As a result of the community work, volunteers are uncovering latent skills and talents (for example, knitting, crocheting, performing, and helping others in their community). Organizing and managing projects also builds valuable job skills.

Volunteers can be found in every corner of the company. According to Rosa Bunn, developer of the program, "Their backgrounds differ and their work schedules vary. They range in age from 19 to 90. . . . But all share one common belief—that they can make a difference. . . . V.I.C.E. has helped build a stronger community . . . members have grown from the experience of giving something of priceless value—the gift of themselves."[3] (See Figure 4–16.)

The idea of a volunteer program began as a class assignment for Bunn and grew into such a successful reality that other companies wanted to jump on the bandwagon. The demand was so great, Coors started a consulting business to show others how to begin on the path of successful corporate volunteerism.

This innovative V.I.C.E. program took on a life of its own, spurring the creation of A.D.V.I.C.E. (Additional Duties Volunteers In Community Enrichment) for retired employees. Later, excitement for the concept lead to formation of Friends of Coors—a volunteer group of local individuals *not employed by Coors.* Other corporations and businesses throughout the nation have created programs modeled after Coors's V.I.C.E. Squad.

The V.I.C.E. program is successful because it:

- **Promotes cooperation.** Instead of giving the one-way transaction of a straight cash donation, a volunteer can select and participate in an activity that has personal and community importance.
- **Encourages creativity** on the part of the volunteers, a refreshing change for most employees.
- **Boosts the morale and pride** of employees by conveying a positive sense of the organization's values.
- **Increases productivity** because a team spirit is developed in an atmosphere of cooperative achievement outside the workplace, which can translate into on-the-job teaming.
- **Is cost-efficient,** a way for Coors to make a tangible contribution to the community beyond a standard cash donation. The time, skill, and knowledge of volunteers become the company's community investments.

---

[3]We thank Sophie Page, volunteer program specialist at Adolph Coors Co., for the wealth of information supplied for this case.

Figure 4–16   Members of the V.I.C.E. Squad Patricia Nelson and Susan Linze read to second graders at Thomson Elementary School in Arvada, Colorado. (Courtesy of Coors Brewing Company.)

- **Increases the company's positive visibility.** An act of charity captures more grapevine and media interest than the announcement of monetary contributions.
- **Is participative,** a way for employees to take action that will help their company survive and prosper in very competitive times.

V.I.C.E. Squad members have participated in a variety of programs such as a Christmas-time nursing home "adoption" effort: 120 V.I.C.E. volunteers gave 1,261 homemade lap robes to the residents on Christmas Day, 1987.[4] V.I.C.E. has also helped with a corporate fund-raising workshop for the 4-H Club and a harvesting ef-

---

[4]Coors supplied the yarn, but volunteers and their families in a twelve-state region helped. Ruth Bethrens, "Companies and Communities Share Healthy Causes," *Business and Health,* September 1988, 30–35.

fort to aid the Western Colorado fruit growers when their usual labor source of migrant workers became unavailable. They continually show dedicated involvement with the Colorado Special Olympics.

Recently the combined recycling efforts of both the V.I.C.E. and A.D.V.I.C.E. squads made it possible to provide 144 "Deputy Hugs" Teddy Bears to the Jefferson County Sheriff's Department. These bears ride along in patrol cars and comfort frightened young victims.

There is a Coors V.I.C.E. Squad kazoo band, clown troupe, parading "Umbrella" Drill Team, choral group, and veteran's group to keep morale high among the volunteers and the communities in which they perform (see Figure 4-17).

BUTTERWORTH GOOD NEIGHBORS PROGRAM

In 1989, Butterworth Hospital, located in Grand Rapids, Michigan, established, for purposes similar to those of Coors, the Butterworth Good Neighbors[5] program, a division of Butterworth Hospital Volunteer Services. Because of changing economic conditions and the curtailing of governmental social programs in the late 1980s, the neighborhoods surrounding Butterworth Hospital began to show patterns of decay, which contributed to conflicts between the hospital and those neighborhoods. The hospital recognized the need to care for the well-being of its neighbors and initiated a program that would strive to improve the quality of life for those living in the neighborhoods surrounding the hospital.

A Good Neighbors Steering Committee, created by Dorothy Munson, the director of volunteer services, was established to identify and assess neighborhood needs and which individuals would qualify for assistance from the program. The committee's other responsibilities include coordinating crew leaders on work days and obtaining necessary supplies to complete a project. The steering committee is composed of many types of hospital staff, local citizens, representatives from neighborhood associations, and others.

Initially, 240 volunteers were recruited from hospital staff and volunteers, other community service organizations, and individual community members from all over the city. To date, more than 500 volunteers from all walks of life participate in the program.

Through this program, Butterworth Good Neighbors has completed more than 475 service projects, investing more than 4,000 hours of volunteer service to fulfill the unmet needs of those neighborhoods. Projects have ranged from painting

---

[5]The idea of calling it "Good Neighbors" came from Jerry Fitzhenry, an accredited member of the Public Relations Society of America. "It immediately reflects the goals and philosophy of the program," he said, "in a way that everyone can understand." We thank him for the information he provided for this case.

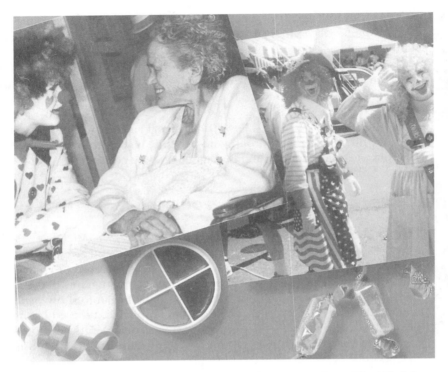

Figure 4–17   These members of the V.I.C.E. clown troupe, Bows (Cheri Tjarks), Precious (Ginger McLin), and Bashful (Debbi Murphy), spread cheer to all at V.I.C.E./A.D.V.I.C.E. projects. (Courtesy of Coors Brewing Company.)

homes, cleaning yards, and making home repairs, to doing chores for the elderly and low-income families with special needs. Some memorable projects have been:

- Donating gifts and participating in a neighborhood Christmas party for more than 500 needy children from two local schools, for the past four years (see Figure 4-18).
- Participating in three communitywide "Paint Sprees," in which homes of needy families get a new coat of paint.
- Collecting donations for the Neighborhood Food and Clothing Bank. To date more than 125,000 items have been donated.
- Organizing "Adopt a Family," an ongoing program matching hospital departments, volunteers, and community groups with needy people.
- Donating discarded hospital linens and blankets.
- Sponsoring "Operation Warm Clothing" for neighbors of all ages.

Figure 4-18 These volunteers of the Butterworth Good Neighbors Program helped to make the annual Christmas Event at a local school a great success. (Courtesy of Butterworth Hospital.)

In addition, the success of the Butterworth Good Neighbors program has encouraged Butterworth Hospital to become involved with other local programs. These include the local adult education program, and a "Partnership in Education" endeavor that encourages the development of job skills for neighborhood residents.

The benefits of the Butterworth Good Neighbors program are many, the hospital believes, including:

- Building relationships to allow ongoing communication and planning on issues affecting the community, the neighborhood, the hospital, and city government.
- Encouraging stabilization of at-risk downtown city neighborhoods by offering a better quality of life for the residents and the greater community.
- Developing other positive programs, such as job and life training for entry-level workers.
- Reemphasizing the importance of center city vitality.
- Increasing awareness of the interrelationships between those who live and work in the downtown area and greater sensitivity to the issues and needs concerning all groups.
- Generating positive encouragement and a "helping hand" to break out of a cycle of poverty and despair.
- Cultivating a greater awareness of the impact each individual can have on the quality of life in the community.

One reason that the Butterworth Good Neighbors program is successful is that it did not originally set out to change public opinion, but to create *positive relationships* with the neighborhoods adjacent to the hospital. As those positive relationships were established, a climate of favorable public opinion was created. Frictions that had once caused conflict between the hospital and nearby neighborhoods were greatly reduced. Each group now feels a greater sense of *interdependence* because of the increased attitude of cooperation.

The program earned the HAVE (Hospital Award for Volunteer Excellence) in 1991. "It was a great honor to receive the award," said Dorothy Munson in a 1991 interview with the hospital's *Network* newsletter. "It validated the fact that our efforts are on target. We had wanted to create a partnership between our neighbors and the hospital family that was mutually beneficial. I feel that we are succeeding."

THE VOLUNTEER CONNECTION

General Mills Corporation has long been known for its dedication to community enrichment. The General Mills Foundation has continually supported education, health and social action, and arts and culture. In addition, the General Mills Volunteer Connection bridges the financial contribution gap with corporate volunteerism; employees and retirees are encouraged to volunteer in the community (see Figure 4–19).

The Volunteer Connection mission is to

encourage volunteerism by matching employee and retiree talents and interest with community needs.

The Volunteer Connection (VC) was established in 1982 as an offspring of the company's corporate policy statement: "to act as a socially responsible corporation to support worthwhile civic and community projects and organizations. General Mills encourages all employees to serve their communities with personal time and talent."

VC is directed by an advisory board of employee volunteers and a corporate staff coordinator. It has a network of area coordinators whose responsibility is to increase awareness of volunteer opportunities among co-workers and retirees.

One sample volunteer opportunity is VC partnerships with several schools to support student achievement, attendance, and healthy lifestyles. Another is a collaborative project with Senior Resources of Minneapolis called "Adopt-a-Highrise." This program involves Hamilton Manor, an independent-living residence for seniors and disabled adults. General Mills employees offer the residents a variety of social events, assistance with rent credit application, and companionship. Some popular activities include holiday theme parties, ice cream socials, birthday parties, barbecues, and bingo games. Volunteers also bring their talents, food, decorations, and themselves to these activities.

The success of these corporate programs illustrates that organizations and the communities in which they do business are inexorably linked. Entities such as Adolph Coors, Butterworth Hospital, and General Mills use the talents and resources of their employees to satisfy the needs of their communities. Their contribution is in

Figure 4–19   General Mills volunteers work together with Habitat for Humanity to provide low-cost housing to those in need. (Courtesy of General Mills Corporation.)

action, not only money. These programs encourage positive relationships with the public. But they are not just for the creation of goodwill. They help to inspire the loyalty of employees and result in a more productive human resource.

QUESTIONS FOR DISCUSSION

1. Employee volunteer programs enable corporations to maintain or increase positive relations with the public and with their employees. Can you think of any other action-oriented projects that would help to create positive feedback from the community and employees of a corporation?

2. Many organizations' volunteer programs die after the initial spurt of employee participation. What can the organization do internally to maintain a high level of employee participation?

3. The creation and implementation of a corporate volunteer program *sounds* as if it will have a positive effect on community relations. How can a practitioner *measure* the results achieved in the community from one of these programs?

PROBLEM 4-A HELPING ISN'T ALWAYS EASY

You are a member of a civic organization that has 300 members locally and is the local chapter of a national organization. Most of the membership is well educated and falls into the middle- and upper-income brackets. The local organization has a reputation of civic involvement—working for better schools, increased voter registration, and equal rights for minorities and women.

About eighteen months ago, the executive committee made a presentation to the organization on illiteracy in your city. Studies show that twenty-five percent of the adult population is "functionally illiterate." By the year 1995, the number of functional illiterates is projected to reach more than one-third of the population. Although the problem is spread throughout the population, the percentage of minorities in this group is high.

Soon after the executive committee's presentation, the organization votes to establish a literacy council for adults in the city. The primary function of the council is to solicit and train volunteers to act as tutors and match these persons with individuals wanting to learn to read and write. The organization is able to get rather heavy news coverage of the council and public service announcements about the need for tutors and students. Despite the coverage, very few persons have volunteered to tutor, and even fewer persons have wanted the service.

Because of your expertise as a communicator, the organization has asked you to become involved in this program. Your review of the program indicates that the problem is really as bad as stated. There is a general agreement among individuals that something has to be done, but no one is quite sure what. Your organization sets an objective of obtaining and training fifty volunteer tutors and matching these with fifty students in the next six months.

As a well-trained public relations professional you recognize that your organization has fallen into the trap of believing that widespread and positive publicity will influence behavior. You agree to help the cause but stipulate that research is essential to discover why the program hasn't taken off.

Describe how you will design and budget (in time and money) a research program to give you the information necessary to implement a successful recruiting program for students and tutors.

PROBLEM 4-B ADJUSTING TO A CHANGE IN COMMAND

For ten years, George Loyal has been a one-person public relations department at Siwash, a college of 3,500 students in Ohio. They have been ten good years in terms of George's working conditions. There has been plenty of publicity material to pump out, and there has been cooperation on the part of news media.

A main factor assisting George has been the attitude of the Siwash president. He takes an open stance publicly. He is articulate, handsome, personable. He has been effective in attracting quality faculty, activating alumni support, and adding notable trustees who have been important in raising funds and making sure that Siwash is favorably regarded by legislators in the state capital.

But all these good things seem to have come to an end. The president was struck down by a massive heart attack and suddenly passed away. The trustees moved quickly to name a successor, who turned out to be a senior member of the Siwash faculty. He is a professor of anthropology, a scholar who is well published, quiet, and nonpublic.

The new president, in the month since his selection, has not told George in so many words that he is not going to be active in alumni affairs, visible at sports events, or ready to talk with news media when they want him to. But he spends most of his time closeted with a few of the older faculty members. His secretary seems to feel that her job is to protect him from intrusions or outside visitors. He has not sent for George or sent him a memo about any specific job to do or any change in his responsibilities.

George's work has almost come to a standstill except for routine news releases. He frankly is not sure where he stands. The cooperative relationship he has had with news media seems to be threatened. The director of alumni relations is as baffled as he is. Two trustees have quietly indicated that they are stepping aside rather than stand for reelection when the time comes. The local sports editor has tipped George off that the newspaper's managing editor plans to ask for a meeting with the new president soon if he doesn't "come out of his shell."

The question before George is, What options does he have in trying to preserve the gains in public relations attained during the past ten years?

1. What would be the most effective way of establishing a proactive relationship with the new president?
2. What would be your overall strategy for maintaining the college's relationships with its important stakeholders?
3. Given the personality of the new president, what role would you allot to him in maintaining the college's reputation?
4. How would you gain support for this strategy?

Chapter 5

Investor Relations

One aspect of financial affairs that increasingly affects the national mood is U.S. investors' evaluations of the corporations in which they have invested. The major measurements are dollar sales volume, profit, the increase or decrease in interest or dividends paid, and whether the price of the stock or bond has increased or decreased from the original purchase price. Other factors include the rank of the company among competitors in its field and what percentage of dividends are paid in comparison with the purchase price.

Experts in the financial world who make a living, and sometimes a fortune, by analyzing and trading equities for themselves and for customers have to be aware of changing conditions in the money supply, raw material prices, international monetary affairs, national economies around the world, and much more. They use sophisticated measurement tools such as stock market trend lines, a company's management capabilities, debt to asset ratio, and several others.

In addition, there is the element of government finance—borrowings by the Treasury Department, municipalities, or state agencies in the form of bonds or debentures.

Today, with stock market news and international monetary or economic status constantly reported and talked about, public relations practitioners also must keep abreast of these topics.

THE PUBLICLY OWNED CORPORATION CONCEPTUALIZED

In the U.S. business system, as an *ideal,* the publicly owned corporation's mission, performance, and behavior represent the consent granted, and the consensus of views held, by all those who have a stake in its financial success. This concept would embrace shareholders, employees and their pension fund, community neighbors, suppliers, and certainly customers. On the sidelines, appropriately, would be those associations and governmental agencies designated to encourage, oversee, referee, or discipline in the name of all taxpayers, or the voters. In this idealization, publicly owned corporations might be seen as instruments of a people's capitalism. In actuality, such a concept is simplistic.

A publicly owned business is created and managed to be competitive with others that sell the same product or service. In order to get started at all, there must be capital or credit and a product or service for which a market is perceived or waiting to be created. Prudent use of capital and skill in producing and marketing the product or service become the province of a small group that manages the enterprise day by day. Survival comes first. Beyond that, growth, diversification, and expansion make up goals that fuel ambition and drive all participants on the payroll. Profit, what's left over after all expenses are paid, makes everything else possible.

Given these realities, it is simply not possible for all those who have a stake in the outcome of an enterprise to take an active part in a forum for major decisions or as links in the decision process. Apart from being largely inaccessible, the stakeholders of a publicly owned corporation are too diverse in their self-interests and in their views of what a business should do, except for a few public issues such as quality of environment, to rally and force action. Given the realities, it should not be surprising that profit, and the power it brings, frequently leads to excesses, abuses, and corruption. These bring investigation, prosecution where indicated, and regulatory measures to preclude recurrence, in the name of the ultimate public interest.

REALITY HAS A LONG HISTORY

Corporations are not ordained by Mother Nature but are a creation of the state. Until the early 1800s, someone starting a business had no "corporate shield" but put all his or her assets at risk. If the business failed, the owner was personally responsible for all debts to the point of personal bankruptcy. Because this situation discouraged the formation of new business, laws were enacted allowing for the formation of **corporations**—business entities in which shareholders risk only the amount of their investment.

What the state creates it can regulate. Regulatory measures started a long time ago. In addition to regulations in interstate commerce mandated by the U.S. Constitution, the federal government began to institute more stringent controls over business. In 1890, the Sherman Antitrust Act was passed, aimed at concentration or monopoly within several industries. This act was supplemented by the Clayton Act in 1914, and in the same year, the Federal Trade Commission Act set up a mechanism to keep channels of interstate trade open to competition. The 1929 stock market crash and the Great Depression of the 1930s stimulated legislative and regulatory actions in the investment area. First was the Securities Act of 1933, requiring a corporation to publish a prospectus (a preliminary printed statement that describes an enterprise and is distributed to prospective investors) when it prepares to sell securities to the public. Then came the Securities Exchange Act of 1934, creating the Securities and Exchange Commission (SEC) and dealing with the conflict of interest involved when a corporate official reaps personal financial gain on information not known to the public. Rule 10b-5 in 1942 tightened up the act, prohibiting fraudulent and deceptive practices in the purchase or sale of securities.

THE MATURING OF FINANCIAL PUBLIC RELATIONS

In spite of the Teapot Dome scandal and other problems stemming from overcontrol of many economic areas by the so-called Robber Barons, financial public relations didn't spring up in the 1920s. Publicity specialists such as Ivy Lee and Ed Bernays were called in at that time for their expertise.

Financial relations in the 1930s was recognized by employers as a useful communications element, but secondary to the publicity and special events that supported marketing efforts as the economy struggled out of the depression. It gained no ground in the pecking order and earned no particular voice in the decision process during World War II, when the corporate focus was on employee morale to achieve the productivity necessary to arm the Allies and on War Bond sales to finance the effort. After the war, with so much pent-up consumer demand to be satisfied, it was hard not to be successful and keep stockholders satisfied, so financial relations specialists were not needed.

A financial relations breakthrough came in the 1960s, in a classic situation of insider trading, where a single news release was deemed by a court to be the critical factor in whether the investing public had been misled (see Case 5-1). Out of the case came in the determination by the SEC, the N.Y. Stock Exchange, and corporate officials that financial communications were important and could create or obviate legal liabilities for the corporation. Shingles labeled "Financial Public Relations" appeared by the thousands. Qualified practitioners began to sit in on the financial decision-making process of their corporations.

AT THIS JUNCTURE

Corporate growth has become almost a religion in U.S. industry. The means of getting to heaven has involved huge investment in research and technology, diversification of products and services, acquisitions, mergers, conglomeration, and multinationalization. From these actions has come an increasing concentration of corporate ownership among a few thousand very wealthy individuals, investment funds, and banking and insurance interests, both U.S. and foreign. Boards of directors of huge corporations more and more have been woven in a crisscross pattern of a few thousand individuals whose views of the system are similar and whose posture is dependably reactive when the system comes under criticism of any kind.

In the 1970s and into the 1980s, conditions were not reassuring for the small investor or average wage earner. Inflation helped wages but hurt buying power. Borrowed money for car or home was at high interest rates, mortgaging the future. Available jobs for traditional functions shrank as corporations went abroad for cheap labor and automation displaced people. Savings decreased or disappeared for a great many.

In the latter 1980s, conditions were ripe for the rich to get richer and for the high-rolling risk takers and arbitrageurs to find market manipulation and insider trading irresistible. The mood seemed to be that "anything goes if you don't get caught." Each new rumor of a corporate raid, takeover, issuance of junk bonds, or bit of privileged information spurred speculation.[1]

Black Monday came in October of 1987. It was a rude awakening as the market's Dow Jones average plummeted some 500 points, taking with it some of Wall Street's big dealers. In the wake, a Tender Offer Reform Act was proposed as an amendment to the Securities Exchange Act of 1934. Too little, too late.[2]

Things quieted down, but not completely or permanently. In 1988, another case made financial headlines when a young trainee in Morgan Stanley's mergers and acquisitions department was alleged to have fed material information to a wealthy Hong Kong customer, who then traded on that information, garnering $19 million in gains. Then for the next several months it seemed each week brought a new Wall street scandal, making the names of such men as Michael Milken and Ivan Boesky infamous.

AN ENVIRONMENT OF STRONG VIEWS

Financial relations presents a worthy challenge to the practitioner. As prime audiences, you have millions of *small investors* generally resentful of who can "control"

---

[1]Elliot D. Lee, "Takeover Predators Now Share the Prey," *Wall Street Journal,* April 29, 1988. Article lists takeover activity at the time, including Campeau Corp. buying Federated Stores for $6.6 billion and GE acquiring Roper Corp. from Whirlpool. William Celis, "Low Stock Prices Spur Takeover Flurry," *Wall Street Journal,* March 1, 1988, revealed six takeover transactions in a single day, totaling $5.4 billion in assets. Among those involved were Homestake Mining, Media General Inc., and USG Corp. A chart showed total value of transactions increasing from $10 billion the first two months of 1987 to $28 billion in the same period of 1988.

[2]George Getschow and Bryan Burrough, "Pickens, Acting Bitter, Finds Takeover Game Isn't Much Fun Now," *Wall Street Journal,* April 5, 1988. Detailed profile of Texas oil man T. Boone Pickens, who said in 1983 he wanted to take over Gulf Oil Corp; later decided not to go ahead, but made a $518 million pretax profit when speculators bid up the price of Gulf stock on the basis of his intent. In 1988, he is weary and bitter, lashing out at investment bankers, advisers, local and national news media, and many others.

the market (such as pension funds, mutual funds, and other money managers) and *leaders of publicly owned corporations,* who can make decisions that are helpful or harmful, choosing short-term expedients or long-haul public interest. Then there are the *regulators*—and the ever-inquiring *media, economists,* and *legislators,* who can make and change the rules.

The positive views small investors have of the corporate world stem in part from good news such as dividends or appreciation in the value of their investments, bullish forecasts by corporate and investment spokespersons, and profiles of company leaders portraying them as intelligent, honest, and planning for future success.

Their negative views are formed in part by information in proxy statements about lavish executive salaries, bonuses, and stock options not based on the health or performance of the corporation. Investors read news items about costly indulgences such as private aircraft, executive dining rooms, limousines, club memberships, junkets, all in the name of incentives or customer relations, that are recovered in higher prices for the products or services. And they are not reassured when such free-spending corporations, unable to compete with foreign products, run to the government for protection.

As for the views of large investors, directors chosen to direct the corporations at the top and the people hired to manage the businesses, they constitute a relatively small audience with some deeply ingrained convictions in common. They claim that the system works well. Criticism or threats of regulation tend to harden their positions and to render spokespersons less flexible rather than more open and accessible. When challenged, this posture provides an example of the *artificial censorship principle.* At times, unwelcome criticism or questions concerning economic matters are labeled as expressing an unacceptable political viewpoint—thus the strategy or tactic of *changing the issue.*

- The role of the corporate financial relations specialist or consultant tends to be that of *interpreter and mediator* between the prime audiences. He or she usually comes on as a moderate or neutral in economic and political philosophy. The position requires skill and objectivity in representing the average investor, the middle-class unsophisticated citizen, while representing private enterprise and conservative views publicly.

Among the intervenors financial relations must take into account are the financial news media, those who run and support nonprofit institutions such as education, and those charged with making and enforcing the securities laws.

THE SPECIFICS OF THE FUNCTION

The financial public relations role can be summarized as:

- Communications strategy appropriate to management goals in investor relations.

A LANGUAGE OF ITS OWN

A generation ago, practitioners had to learn new financial semantics. Terms such as *privileged information, conflict of interest, insider trading, timely and adequate disclosure, due diligence,* and *a material fact* became part of communications as well as legal language.

Over the past few years, financial affairs have had a new infusion. Practitioners need to understand *arbitrage* and *arbs, junk bonds, Payment in kind (PIK), green mail, raiders, programmed trading,* and *hostile takeover,* among a constantly emerging new lingo on the Street.

- Preparation of public literature, including reports required by law and establishing press contacts.
- Managing relationships with the financial community, including analyst meetings, tours or visits, and so on.

Among the specific situations posing communications problems and requirements are:

1. A company goes public, splits its stock, or arranges added financing.
2. A corporation wishes to make a tender offer to acquire another corporation, to merge with another corporation, or to head off or oppose an unwanted offer. An acquisition or merger may result in a change of identity such as name, logo, headquarters location, or ownership.
3. A timely announcement is needed for significant new products, services, expansion, or acquisition, which might affect the price of the company's stock.
4. Periodic reports of financial results are issued, including an annual report.
5. Arrangements are required for meetings with shareholders and analysts and for public reports of proceedings, including the annual meeting—and, in some enlightened corporations, an employee annual meeting.
6. Special literature is required, dealing with a corporation's philosophy, policies, and objectives; its history or anniversary; its scope, "identity," or "culture." Any of these may also be the subject of advertising.

REFERENCES AND ADDITIONAL READINGS

BERKELEY, ALAN J. "Stand by for Change: The Future of Investor Relations." Address at University of Texas, April 30, 1987. Synopsis in *pr reporter* 30 (August 17, 1987).

BERLE, A. A. JR. *Power Without Property.* New York: Harcourt, Brace and World, 1959. A classic book.

CHENEY, RICHARD. "What Should We Do About Takeovers?" *tips & tactics, pr reporter* 25 (supplement, April 6, 1987).

CUTLIP, SCOTT M., ALLEN H. CENTER, and GLEN M. BROOM. "The Practice: Business and Industry." Chapter 14 in *Effective Public Relations.* 7th ed. Englewood Cliffs, N.J.: Prentice Hall, 1994.

DOBRZYNSKI, JUDITH H. "The Lessons of the RJR Free-for-All." *Business Week,* December 19, 1988. Raises and answers questions about the battle for RJR Nabisco.

"Four Barometers Analysts Apply in Measuring Management Performance." *Investor Relations Update,* October-November 1992: p 15. Summary in *Purview, pr reporter* 36 (supplement, February 15, 1993).

HOLLIDAY, KAREN KAHLER. "Understanding Investor Relations." *Bank Marketing* 24 (August 1992): 22-25.

LEEDS, MARK B. and BRUCE W. FRASER. "Why Wall Street Matters." *Management Review* 82 (September 1993): 23-26.

LEES, DAVID. "A strategy that pays dividends." *Management Today,* March 1994: 5.

LERBINGER, OTTO, and NATHANIEL N. SPERBER. "Financial Relations." Chapter 7 in *Manager's Public Relations Handbook.* Reading, Mass.: Addison-Wesley, 1982.

METZ, TIM. *Black Monday: The Catastrophe of October 19, 1987 . . . and Beyond.* New York: William Morrow, 1988. A chronology of the stock market drop of 500 points and theory concerning the mystery of it.

MILLER, EUGENE. "Financial Public Relations I: Basic Planning and Programs." Chapter 11 in *Lesly's Public Relations Handbook.* 4th ed. Chicago, IL: Probus, 1991.

MOORE, PHILIP. "Ciba takes investors into account." *Euromoney,* September 1993: pp 37-38.

The National Investor Relations Institute offers a wealth of information, including *IR Update,* a monthly publication. National Investors Relations Institute, 2000 L St. NW, Ste. 701, Washington DC 20036. Phone: 202/861-0630.

The Public Relations Body of Knowledge. New York: PRSA, 1993. See section V.3 for abstracts dealing with "Financial and Investor Relations."

SEELY, MICHAEL W. "Hit the Financial Bull's Eye with Well-Aimed IR Programs." *Corporate Cashflow* v14 (July 1993): 26-30.

A Classic: On Wall Street, Inside Information Is Profitable

For nearly thirty years after the enactment of the Securities Exchange Act in 1934 prohibiting manipulation and deception in the financial world, the role of public relations in stock transactions was not taken seriously by corporate management and the relevant sectors of the Securities Exchange Commission (SEC). As a result of a landmark court case involving Texas Gulf Sulphur Company, the role of public relations changed drastically.[1] This case is definitive in understanding some of the problems and requisites in the performance of financial relations.

- At the heart of the case was a single news release drafted by a public relations consultant and the vice-president of Texas Gulf. The manner in which the

Section 10 of the 1934 Securities Exchange Act, and Rule 10b5 promulgated by the SEC in 1942, state that persons may not "make any untrue statement of material fact or . . . omit to state a material fact" that would have the effect of misleading in connection with the purchase or sale of any security.

A precondition would be that a person did, in fact, possess information whose disclosure or nondisclosure could have an effect on the value of a security. Thus, "insider" information, the disclosure of such information, and the purchase or sale of securities are mutually involved. Private gain is implicit.

[1]The name was subsequently changed to Texasgulf; the company was acquired by Elf Aquitaine Inc., a French corporation with $1.7 billion in sales. In 1986, Elf Aquitaine listed Texasgulf Chemicals and Texasgulf Minerals and Metals among its seven divisions.

news was released to the media raised questions of whether the content was deceptive.

PRECEDENTS

Until 1942, inside trading, or using private information, had not been outlawed. In fact, this device helped create many personal fortunes. It was said that advance information of the Duke of Wellington's victory at Waterloo was a key to the Rothschild wealth, and in the United States early news that the War of 1812 was coming to an end enabled John Jacob Astor to reap an enormous financial harvest. During the industrial development of the United States, advance information concerning the allocation of railroad rights fed the growth of some real estate fortunes. Discoveries of raw materials, whether coal, iron, or oil, were traditionally hushed and even hidden from all but a few people for investment, and having inside knowledge to gain an advantage in stock trading was generally regarded as "the way the chips fell."

Questions of integrity or ethics went largely unasked publicly until the Sherman Antitrust Act was passed in 1890. Even after the Securities Exchange Act was passed in 1934 and rule 10b-5 was made public, the laws were not enforced and went untested for two decades. Exceptions were instances of such blatant abuse that disapproval came even from corporate executives for whom insider trading was regarded as nothing more than a smart, low-risk move or a reward for their past efforts.

THE TEXAS GULF SULPHUR CASE

The Texas Gulf Sulphur (TGS) scenario started with some late 1950's exploratory activities for minerals in eastern Canada.[2] Aerial, geophysical surveys over a large

---

[2]The narrative and facts that follow were gleaned from some of the same sources that formed public opinion during the period when the events in this case took place. Among the sources are a complete text of the court's opinion in the U.S. Court of Appeals for the Second Circuit, No. 296, September term 1966 SEC v. TGS, 446 F.2d p. 1301 (2nd cir 1966); an article by John Brooks, "Annals of Finance: A Reasonable Amount of Time," in *New Yorker* magazine, November 9, 1968 (and from a critique of the John Brooks piece provided by TGS public relations consultant William H. Dinsmore); *Wall Street Journal* articles, "Big Boards Expands, Tightens Standards on Timely Disclosure of Corporate News" (July 18, 1968), "Texas Gulf Ruled to Lack Due Diligence in Minerals Case" (February 9, 1970), "Rise Detected in Use of Inside Information to Make Stock Profits" (October 31, 1972), "Most Executives Say They Won't Give Insider Data to Analysts" (August 16, 1968), "New Structures Prompt Firms to Revise Policies on Disclosure of News" (October 9, 1968), and "Rules on Disclosure Don't Bar Exclusive Interview, Cohen Says" (October 9, 1968); and "No Comment—A Victim of Disclosure," the *New York Times* (August 25, 1968). Also helpful was an analysis provided to officers of Motorola, Inc., by its legal counsel, entitled "Corporate Information Releases." We also drew on several references in issues of the *Public Relations Journal, PR News, pr reporter,* and other business and professional publications. An appeals brief for the defendants was requested of attorneys but was not received.

expanse of land were made until potential drill sites were selected. The people who participated in the surveys included:

- **Richard D. Mollison,** a mining engineer and later a vice-president of Texas Gulf Sulphur (TGS).
- **Walter Holyk,** a Texas Gulf geologist.
- **Richard H. Clayton,** an electrical engineer and geophysicist.
- **Kenneth H. Darke,** a geologist.

They selected a segment of marshland near Timmins, Ontario, that showed sufficient promise to indicate a survey on the ground. This land was not owned by TGS. One of the first problems was to get title or drilling rights, via an option from the owners. Contact with the owner of part of the desired area was first made in 1961.

Eventually, in mid-1963, some land was acquired and drilling began in November. On visual inspection, the sample—obtained by diamond core drilling—seemed to contain sulphides of copper and zinc.

On Sunday, November 12, 1963, Darke telephoned his boss, Walter Holyk, at his home in Connecticut with an optimistic report. Holyk called his boss, Richard D. Mollison, nearby in Old Greenwich, and later that evening called Dr. Charles F. Fogarty, TGS executive vice-president, also nearby in Rye, New York. Holyk, Mollison, and Fogarty subsequently went to the site—called the Kidd 55 tract—to see for themselves. The group concluded that the core was indeed promising and should be shipped to Utah for chemical assay.

A LID ON THE INFORMATION

Pending the results, they wanted the acquisition program for other desired land in the area to proceed as quickly as possible. They knew obtaining rights might be difficult. To facilitate matters, TGS president Claude O. Stephens instructed the group to keep the unconfirmed results a secret . . . even to other officers, directors, and employees of the company. **Following traditional prospecting camouflage customs, the first hole was marked and concealed, and another one,** *barren,* **was drilled and left in sight.**

CALENDAR OF EVENTS: 1963–64

- November. Seven TGS employees were the "keepers" of significant information. In the same month drilling began, and Fogarty, Clayton, Mollison, and Mrs. Holyk bought TGS stock totaling 2,050 shares at $17–$18 a share.

- December. The chemical assays of the test core came back, largely confirming the TGS estimate of copper and zinc content, as well as discovering a silver content. TGS scheduled the resumption of drilling in March.
- January–February. Inside informers and those they gave "tips" to owned 8,235 shares. At this point there were also 12,300 calls (options to buy a specified amount of stock at a fixed price) to buy TGS stock.
- February. The company issued stock options to twenty-six of its officers and other employees, five of whom were the insiders on Kidd 55. The option committee and the company's board of directors had not been made aware of the find.
- March 31. The company resumed drilling.

After further drilling of three more holes by April 10, there was evidence of a body of commercially minable ore. (The accuracy of the estimate later came into contention between SEC experts and TGS officials).

LEAKS AND RUMORS

By this time, there had been enough activity at the Kidd site that rumors of a possible major ore strike were circulating in Canada. A press item on February 27, in the *Northern Miner,* reported rumors of Texas Gulf's "obtaining some fat ore indications" from its work north of Timmins. On March 31, Texas Gulf invited the publication to visit and see the exposed, barren site for itself, and a date was set for April 20. Then on April 9, the *Toronto Daily Star* and the *Globe and Mail* carried stories. The *Globe and Mail* headline read, "Wild Speculation Spree on TGS: Gigantic Copper Strike Rumored." The phone lines and the conference rooms at TGS headquarters, 200 Park Avenue, New York, were busy on April 10. According to John Brooks, writing later in the *New Yorker* magazine,

> President Stephens was sufficiently concerned about the rumors to seek advice from one of his most trusted associates, Thomas S. Lamont, senior member of the Texas Gulf board . . . and bearer of a name long venerated on Wall Street. Stephens asked what Lamont thought ought to be done about the "exaggerated" reports.
> "As long as they stay in the Canadian press," Lamont replied, "I think you might be able to live with them." However, he added, if they should reach the papers in the United States, it might be well to give the press an announcement that would set the record straight and avoid undue gyrations in the stock market.[3]

[3]J. Brooks, "Business Adventures," New York: Weybright and Talley Division, David McKay. Originally published in "Annals of Finance," *New Yorker* magazine, November 9, 1968.

PUBLIC RELATIONS CALLED IN

The stories in Canada were picked up and printed on Saturday, April 11, by such U.S. media as the *New York Times* and the *New York Herald Tribune,* with the rumor of a major copper strike. Robert Carroll, a Doremus & Co. public relations consultant, helped Dr. Fogarty, the executive vice-president, draft a news release over the weekend, and it was released at 3:00 P.M. on Sunday, April 12, to appear in Monday morning's papers.

THE PRESS RELEASE: APRIL 12, 1964

NEW YORK—The following statement was made today by Dr. Charles F. Fogarty, executive vice-president of Texas Gulf Sulphur Company, in regard to the company's drilling operations near Timmins, Ontario, Canada. Dr. Fogarty said:

During the past few days, the exploration activities of Texas Gulf Sulphur in the area of Timmins, Ontario, have been widely reported in the press, coupled with rumors of a substantial copper discovery there. These reports exaggerate the scale of operations, and mention plans and statistics of size and grade of ore that are without factual basis and have evidently originated by speculation of people not connected with TGS.

The facts are as follows. TGS has been exploring in the Timmins area for six years as part of its overall search in Canada and elsewhere for various minerals—lead, copper, zinc, etc. During the course of this work, in Timmins as well as in eastern Canada, TGS has conducted exploration entirely on its own, without the participation by others. Numerous prospects have been investigated by geophysical means and a large number of selected ones have been core-drilled. These cores are sent to the United States for assay and detailed examination as a matter of routine and on advice of expert Canadian legal counsel. No inferences as to grade can be drawn from this procedure.

Most of the areas drilled in Eastern Canada have revealed either barren pyrite or graphite without value; a few have resulted in discoveries of small or marginal sulfide ore bodies.

Recent drilling on one property near Timmins has led to preliminary indications that more drilling would be required for proper evaluation of this prospect. The drilling done to date has not been conclusive, but the statements made by many outside quarters are unreliable and include information and figures that are not available to TGS.

The work done to date has not been sufficient to reach definite conclusions and any statement as to size and grade of ore would be premature and possibly misleading. When we have progressed to the point where reasonable and logical conclusions can be made, TGS will issue a definite statement to its stockholders and to the public in order to clarify the Timmins project.[4]

---

[4]From the appeals court opinion, SEC v. TGS, 446 F.2d, 1301 (2nd cir 1966).

NEWS MEDIA AND STOCK MARKET REACT

The Monday *New York Herald Tribune,* an important financial medium, headlining its story, "Copper Rumor Deflated," quoted passages from the TGS press release and hedged on the optimism in its earlier story out of Canada.

On the New York Stock Exchange, TGS stock price on April 13 ranged between $30\frac{1}{8}$ and 32, closing at $30\frac{7}{8}$. When compared with an $18 high in November, the $30 price represented a sixty-five percent rise in five months. Meanwhile, the internal, nonpublic reports from Timmins became so rosy that an official announcement confirming a major ore strike was readied for April 16.

There was a problem in the synchronization of communications. A reporter for the *Northern Miner,* a Canadian trade journal, had interviewed Mollison, Holyk, and Darke and had prepared an article confirming a 10-million-ton strike for publication in his April 16 issue. The story, submitted to Mollison, was returned to the reporter, unamended, on April 15. Separately, a statement drafted substantially by Mollison was given to the Ontario minister of mines for release on the air in Canada at 11:00 P.M. on the fifteenth, but was not released until 9:40 on the sixteenth. Also, separately, in the United States an official statement announcing a strike of at least 25 million tons ($2\frac{1}{2}$ times the Canadian trade-journal story) was read to the financial press in New York from 10:00 to 10:15 A.M. on April 16, following at 9:00 A.M. directors' meeting. The news showed up on the Dow Jones tape at 10:54 and on Merrill Lynch's private wire twenty-five minutes earlier at 10:29, another peculiar circumstance.

THE TRIAL AND APPEALS

An SEC complaint indicated that company executives had used privileged information to trade in the company's stock before the information had been disclosed publicly. In May, the complaint was argued before Judge Dudley B. Bonsal of the Southern District Court at Foley Square, New York. He ruled in favor of all the defendants except David M. Crawford and Richard H. Clayton, who had engaged in TGS stock purchase after the first press release on April 12 and before the second one, on April 16, was public knowledge.

The lower-court judge dismissed the case against the defendants who had purchased stock prior to the evening of April 9, on the grounds that information they possessed was not "material," that their purchases or tips to others were educated guesses or hunches, and that executives should be encouraged to own shares in their own company. As for trading by insiders following the April 16 directors' meeting, and whether they had waited a "reasonable time" for the disclosure to become public knowledge, the judge decided the controlling factor was the time at which the release was handed to the press, not when it appeared on the Dow Jones stock market tape.

PUBLIC RELATIONS INVOLVEMENT

The trial court judge gave a big lift to the public relations profession because a public relations consultant had been involved. The judge decided that *because corporate executives had sought the advice of public relations counsel, they had exercised reasonable business judgment.*

As for the news release itself, a major point of contention in the hearings was whether it was encouraging or discouraging to investors. A Canadian mining-security specialist said that they had had a Dow Jones (broad tape) report that TGS "didn't have anything basically." A Midwest Stock Exchange specialist in TGS was "concerned about his long position in the stock" after reading the release. TGS defense attorneys contended that the financial media had been at fault in not publishing the full text of the controversial release. The trial court stated only, "While in retrospect, the press release may appear gloomy or incomplete, that does not make it misleading or deceptive on the basis of the facts then known."

THE COMPLAINT MOVED UP THE COURT LADDER

The SEC appealed all dismissals, and the case was argued in the court of appeals. In essence, the appellate decision reversed the lower court's findings on the important issues, except for the convictions of Crawford and Clayton, which were affirmed.

The case was remanded to Judge Bonsal of the lower court for the "appropriate remedies." He:

- Ruled that Texas Gulf Sulphur Co. and its executives failed to exercise "due diligence" in the April 12 news release.
- Ordered certain defendants to turn over to TGS profits made by trading on inside information.
- Issued injunctions against Crawford and Clayton, barring them from further purchases or sales based on "undisclosed" information.
- Denied a request by the SEC that TGS, as a corporation, be enjoined from issuing false, misleading, or inadequate information, pointing out that there was no "reasonable likelihood of further violations."
- Because there was no "reasonable likelihood," did not issue injunctions against Darke, who had left the company; Holyk, chief geologist; Huntington, a TGS attorney; Fogarty, then president of TGS; and Mollison, a vice-president.
- Noted that Coates, a director, had paid $26,250 in an approved settlement, including $9,675 said to be profits to several "tippees," and that Crawford returned "at his cost" the stock he purchased.
- Assessed paybacks of $41,795 from Darke personally and $48,404 for his

"tippees," $35,663 from Holyk, $20,010 from Clayton, and $2,300 from Huntington.[5]

SOME OF THE ECHOES

In the immediate wake of the TGS settlement, several predictable measures were taken to avoid a repetition. Publicly owned corporations reexamined their practices of disclosing financial information to be sure they were in compliance. The New York Stock Exchange expanded its policies regarding timely disclosure and issued new pages for its company manual.

Financial news media, somewhat defensively, placed responsibility for the published information on the corporate sources of such information without permitting those sources to control what was published. While insisting on the media's right to edit financial releases according to the news values perceived in them, some comments by financial editors suggested that corporate practitioners constituted obstacles rather than facilitators in getting out all the relevant facts.

Corporate financial relations people, for their part, undertook with notable success to exercise a more important and outspoken role in corporate decisions regarding the "what, when, and how" of significant information to be released publicly via press or controlled media. This meant a seat in management councils for financial relations people when decisions were made regarding whether a particular item of information was newsworthy and whether it was capable of influencing the value of the corporation's shares in the stock market. This also meant attendance at meetings with groups of analysts where material information might inadvertently be introduced, calling for immediate broad disclosure.

New counseling shingles were hung out, with the words "Financial Public Relations." The trade literature abounded with analyses of the risks and requirements implied by the TGS case.

A SUBJECT THAT WOULD NOT QUIT

Despite effects by the SEC and the stock exchanges[6] and disciplinary procedures by corporations, the temptation for individuals to make a profit on secret or "privileged" information continued to be too great for some individuals. Incidents in-

[5]Extracted from the opinion rendered in 65 Civ. 1182 by Judge Dudley J. Bonsal, United States District Court, Southern District of New York, February 6, 1970.

[6]See Robert W. Taft, Hill and Knowlton, "New Disclosure Rules: More Public Information," *Public Relations Journal,* April 1972, and "Disclosure: What A Year," in the April 1973 issue. Taft and H&K have provided definitive service to the calling in their periodically updated *SEC Reporting Requirements*. Also available, Cutlip, Center, and Broom, *Effective Public Relations,* 6th ed. (Englewood Cliffs, N.J.: Prentice Hall, 1985), 688.

volved executives in many large national corporations such as ITT, Faberge, Liggett and Myers, Bausch and Lomb, Occidental, Penn Central, and Stirling Homex, and touched some smaller ones, too, such as Rheingold and Carl's Jr. restaurants.

Inevitably, insider trading allegations would include public relations professionals alerting the calling to its vulnerability. In one episode an SEC complaint aimed at Pig 'n Whistle Corp. named the firm's former counsel, Financial Relations Board, as the defendant.

The **Public Relations Society of America (PRSA)** reviewed and strengthened its Code of Professional Standards, a document that then dealt almost entirely with relationships between members of the society and employers or clients, not with behavior outside those relationships.

A few years later, the head of a Detroit consulting firm was under SEC investigation for alleged insider trading in the stock of a client company. After the SEC filed formal charges, the matter was settled with a "consent decree" (an accused, without admitting or denying charges, agrees, henceforth, not to do what was alleged). This episode was magnified within journalistic professional circles, partly because the individual under investigation had assumed the presidency of PRSA; subsequently he resigned office. The embarrassed society had to reshuffle topside.[7] As a result, PRSA now has a stronger Code of Ethics and disclosure requirements for officers and committee members.

ON WALL STREET, THE WORST WAS YET TO COME

In the 1970s, instances of insider trading did not headline the economic news. Public attention was fastened more on unemployment, continued inflation, and rising interest rates. Government kept business under the gun on those matters. In the 1980s, government sought to rev up business as the best way to slow the rate of inflation, put more people on payrolls, and bring down interest rates. In the good times that resulted, mergers and acquisitions in the name of "efficiency" and "international competition" became the order of the day. Yuppies were in. "Get-while-the-getting-is-good" was in. The stock market was ripe for excesses if not illegalities. Speculators and manipulators did not let the opportunity get away. As one bit of evidence, there were more than fifty prosecutions under the provisions of Rule 10b in the 1980s.

In one of them. W. C. Clark, a lawyer, was convicted of fraud, tax evasion, and lying to regulators about insider trading conspiracy. That made sizeable news partly because he had used *Wall Street Journal* stories for some of his information. In 1985, Dennis B. Levine, a managing director of Drexel Burnham Lambert, was charged with using insider information to make more than $12 million illegally over a period of years, found guilty, and sentenced to two years. He implicated Ivan

---

[7]The incident involved Anthony Franco, in 1985.

AN OFFICIAL INTERPRETATION OF THE CODE AS IT APPLIES TO FINANCIAL PUBLIC RELATIONS

This interpretation of the Society Code as it applies to financial public relations was originally adopted in 1963 and amended in 1972, 1977, 1983, and 1988 by action of the PRSA Board of Directors. "Financial public relations" is defined as "that area of public relations which relates to the dissemination of information that affects the understanding of stockholders and investors generally concerning the financial position and prospects of a company, and includes among its objectives the improvement of relations between corporations and their stockholders." The interpretation was prepared in 1963 by the society's Financial Relations Committee, working with the Securities and Exchange Commission and with the advice of the society's legal counsel. It is rooted directly in the Code with the full force of the Code behind it, and a violation of any of the following paragraphs is subject to the same procedures and penalties as violation of the Code.

1. It is the responsibility of PRSA members who practice financial public relations to be thoroughly familiar with and understand the rules and regulations of the SEC and the laws it administers, as well as other laws, rules, and regulations affecting financial public relations, and to act in accordance with their letter and spirit. In carrying out this responsibility, members shall also seek legal counsel, when appropriate, on matters concerning financial public relations.

2. Members shall adhere to the general policy of making full and timely disclosure of corporate information on behalf of clients or employers. The information disclosed shall be accurate, clear and understandable. The purpose of such disclosure is to provide the investing public with all material information affecting security values or influencing investment decisions. In complying with the duty of full and timely disclosure, members shall present all material facts, including those adverse to the company. They shall exercise care to ascertain the facts and to disseminate only information they believe to be accurate. They shall not knowingly omit information, the omission of which might make a release false or misleading. Under no circumstances shall members participate in any activity designed to mislead or manipulate the price of a company's securities.

3. Members shall publicly disclose or release information promptly so as to avoid the possibility of any use of the information by any insider or third party. To that end, members shall make every effort to comply with the spirit and intent of the timely disclosure policies of the stock exchanges, NASD, and the SEC. Material information shall be made available on an equal basis.

4. Members shall not disclose confidential information the disclosure of which might be adverse to a valid corporate purpose or interest and whose disclosure is not required by the timely disclosure provisions of the law. During any such period of

nondisclosure members shall not directly or indirectly (a) communicate the confidential information to any other person or (b) buy or sell or in any other way deal in the company's securities where the confidential information may materially affect the market for the security when disclosed. Material information shall be disclosed publicly as soon as its confidential status has terminated or the requirement of timely disclosure takes effect.

5. During the registration period, members shall not engage in practices designed to precondition the market for such securities. During registration, the issuance of forecasts, projections, predictions about sales and earnings, or opinions concerning security values or other aspects of the future performance of the company shall be in accordance with current SEC regulations and statements of policy. In the case of companies whose securities are publicly held, the normal flow of factual information to shareholders and the investing public shall continue during the registration period.

6. Where members have any reason to doubt that projections have an adequate basis in fact, they shall satisfy themselves as to the adequacy of the projections prior to disseminating them.

7. Acting in concert with clients or employers, members shall act promptly to correct false or misleading information or rumors concerning clients' or employers' securities or business whenever they have reason to believe such information or rumors are materially affecting investor attitudes.

8. Members shall not issue descriptive materials designed or written in such a fashion as to appear to be contrary to fact, an independent third-party endorsement, or recommendation of a company or security. Whenever members issue material for clients or employers, either in their own names or in the names of someone other than the clients or employers, they shall disclose in large type and in a prominent position on the face of the material the source of such material and the existence of the issuer's client or employer relationship.

9. Members shall not use inside information for personal gain. However, this is not intended to prohibit members from making bona fide investments in their company's or client's securities insofar as they can make such investments without the benefit of material inside information.

10. Members shall not accept compensation that would place them in a position of conflict with their duty to a client, employer, or the investing public. Members shall not accept stock options from clients or employers nor accept securities as compensation at a price below market price except as part of an overall plan for corporate employees.

11. Members shall act so as to maintain the integrity of channels of public communication. They shall not pay or permit to be paid to any publication or other communications medium any consideration in exchange for publicizing a company, except through clearly recognizable paid advertising.

12. Members shall in general be guided by the PRSA Declaration of Principles and the Code of Professional Standards for the Practice of Public Relations of which this is an official interpretation.

Boesky, a prominent arbitrageur—one who buys and sells securities simultaneously in order to profit from price fluctuations—who admitted that the insider trading world had grown to staggering size. Boesky then tagged Martin Siegal, a former Kidder Peabody executive, who, in turn, named Richard Freeman, head of arbitrage at prestigious Goldman Sachs, Richard Wigdon, a vice-president at Kidder, and Timothy Tabor, a former Kidder officer. It was like a line of dominoes falling over.[8]

In 1987, Kidder Peabody agreed to pay $25 million to settle government charges. Ivan Boesky agreed to plead guilty to conspiracy, to pay back $100 million of his ill-gotten gains to the government, and to continue spilling information about many of those who had played loose with other people's money. Much of Wall Street went into a crouch waiting to hear whose names were called.

As for Boesky's punishment, Judge Morris Lasker, reputed to be lenient in matters that "after all, are only money," commended Boesky's cooperation, gave him a three-year sentence, and in light of the $100 million he had already paid to the government, waived his fine of $250,000 and then set him free on bail. Boesky did serve the full three years of his term. However, his troubles did not end with his parole from jail. Boesky faced another lawsuit in 1992 and settled out of court for $50 million with Maxus Energy Corp., a company Boesky had bilked out of millions by his insider trading.

The doings and ordeal of junk bond king Michael Milken were yet to come. His illegal use of this high-risk financial instrument had—like most Wall Street crimes—cost investors millions of dollars while he and his clients made billions. By any definition, such activities do not promote positive relations in society—and are therefore of concern to the public relations profession.

RELEVANCE TO PR PRACTICE

With the dollar stakes involved in the stock market so large today as to seem almost fictional, the day-by-day practice of public relations may seem remote or unrelated. It is neither.

Every large corporation, bank, brokerage firm, charitable foundation and other financial institution has public relations counsel or staff. The professionals providing counsel and implementing the communications involved in financial affairs can

---

[8]For synopsis, Richard B. Stolley, "The Ordeal of Bob Freeman," *Fortune,* May 25, 1987, 66–72. For Ivan Boesky summary, Associated Press story "Boesky Pleads Guilty to Violating Securities Laws," April 24, 1987.

qualify legally as "insiders." They can be found guilty, as individuals, of knowingly releasing financial information that is false, deceptive, or misleading or of trading on privileged information. In court cases, it has been evident that financial relations practitioners are not in the clear by pleading "I only did (or said) what the client told me to." Practitioners must make reasonable efforts to verify facts disseminated. "Hold harmless" clauses no longer constitute a shield.

The PRSA Code of Professional Standards for members specifically provides an interpretation as applied to financial public relations. It places the burden on practitioners for understanding the rules and regulations of the SEC and the laws it administers and acting in accord with them. Tenets cover full and timely disclosure, confidentiality, improper compensation or gain, and the integrity of public communication.

QUESTIONS FOR DISCUSSION

1. Drawing on the information in the case, and having the benefit of knowing how it all came out, what should the public relations executive have counseled TGS officers to do differently, or to communicate publicly, at some point before TGS executives were found to be trading in the stock?

2. Apart from the TGS case, try a different situation. Suppose that a weekly financial magazine column "Tips and Rumors" regularly got into some people's hands a day before each issue of the magazine came out, and some of the stocks mentioned were suddenly traded heavily and run up in price. Suppose also, it turned out that a clerical person in the magazine's public relations department privately had been giving an advance rough draft of the column as a favor to a friend at a brokerage firm. Neither that clerk nor the friend at a brokerage firm traded or made any profit. As you understand SEC's Rule 10b, who is legally liable? Put another way, where does common sense tell you the responsibility for the privacy of material facts belongs?

3. Objectively, was the initial TGS news release about the ore strike at Timmins misleading on the basis of what was known *at the time the news was released?* Or did it go only as far as a cautious, prudent management was willing to go for fear of overstating and getting in trouble for that? Or, what else does your objective evaluation say might have been the determining consideration?

4. A reputation for being honest in economic matters, civil in social relations, and honorable in character has long been said to be a precious and fragile possession. And the reputation of communications people is generally perceived by critics and supporters alike as being a reflection of those they serve and associate with. If we accept both premises, how can we stay clean and honorable, earn a good living, and advance in a career when we are cast in an atmosphere that many moralists, historians, intellectuals, journalists, and some government officials, describe as a "moral morass"?

A Classic: Nader Takes on General Motors

THE OPPONENTS

A small group challenging a company such as General Motors (GM) sets up a bantamweight-heavyweight, David and Goliath situation. Not only is GM a Goliath in sales and earnings, but in 1987 it had more than 315 million shares of stock around the world in the hands of some 830,000 shareholders. The company takes in more money every year than all but a handful of sovereign nations!

Without doubt, the majority of shares were in the hands of a few hundred shareholders and their representatives who held views similar to corporate management's. Rounding up a majority of opinion opposing GM management on any business issue seemed unrealistic.

But not to Ralph Nader and his associates, the challengers in this case. "The Nader group versus GM" is a classic example of minority shareholders expression. The group owned only twelve shares of General Motors stock but sought to induce modifications in the corporation's management policies.

THE NADER PAST WITH GM

Nader had a prior experience tangling with GM in 1965. He had written a book, *Unsafe at Any Speed*,[1] which criticizes the auto industry in general, and in particular denounced the early Corvair autos built by GM.

At that time, GM's legal department ran an investigation on Nader that focused on his private life. To Nader this was a form of harassment invading his right to privacy. Nader brought suit. The company settled out of court for $425,000 and GM's

---

[1]Ralph Nader, *Unsafe at Any Speed* (New York: Grossman, 1965).

167

board chairman apologized for the harassment. Nader said the money would be used to establish a "continuing legal monitoring of General Motors' activities in the safety, pollution, and consumer relations area."

Shortly before the settlement, Nader created an organization of young lawyers called the Project on Corporate Responsibility. Ralph Nader, the spokesman, announced at a Washington press conference that the project's efforts would be directed at "the establishment of enduring access to corporate information, effective

THE POWER OF A SHAREHOLDER

The shareholders of a corporation collectively own it. In theory, they are collectively "the boss" and should have a voice in policy making and an active part in the decision-making process. Shareholders express their independent decisions most often through their votes on matters submitted to them. Votes are allocated on the basis of one vote for each share owned, *not* one vote for each shareholder.

In actual practice, the directors and top management of a corporation (who may also own shares) have the authority to run the corporation the way they feel will best benefit shareholders collectively. They must also look after the other publics, such as customers and employees, on whom the corporation depends for its success. A shareholder with a few shares feels powerless. The only choices minority shareholders have are to write complaint letters, accept whatever decisions are made, or sell their shares. Minority shareholders historically have rarely raised questions or expressed discourse. Consequently, most corporate annual meetings have traditionally been formal, scripted, cut-and-dry, rubber-stamp affairs.

There Have Been Exceptions

There are, however, some perennial critics who make a point to attend meetings and raise questions. On occasion, individuals in positions to speak for many small shareholders, and persons owning large blocks of stock who share a different viewpoint than the management, have banded together and spoken with a single voice. Small shareholders try to change a policy or attitude by making a proposal for inclusion in the proxy statement. This statement is voted upon at the annual shareholders' meeting.

Whether the proposal is adopted or not, small shareholders have alerted the corporate management and the financial news media (the media are usually present at the major company annual meetings) to their opinions and perhaps attracted others who share common views. Examples of questions raised have been environmental and safety issues, overextended salaries for corporate management, and minority employment. The outcomes of these efforts are considered a gain for those who represent the small shareholders in the same sense that the expression of a minority viewpoint in a Supreme Court decision is a gain for the losing side. Winners can't ignore the existence of the minority view.

voice for affected social and individual interests, and thorough remedy against unjust treatment."

THE NADER-SIDE STRATEGY

In 1970, Nader took on GM again, this time to make changes regarding General Motors' investor relations.

In conjunction with formation of Project on Corporate Responsibility, the Nader group announced "Campaign GM," which would "seek to persuade GM's shareholders to demand stronger 'public interest' efforts by GM, such as reducing air and water pollution and making safer cars." Campaign GM, the announcement said, was going to seek public and private support, climaxing at GM's annual meeting of shareholders with three proposals offered as resolutions:

- **Proposal number 1** would add three public representatives to GM's twenty-four-member board: The campaign's candidates were to be the former consumer adviser to a U.S. president, a Pulitzer Prize-winning biologist and member of a President's Advisory Committee on Environmental Quality, and a minister who was then a Democratic party committeeman from the District of Columbia.
- **Proposal number 2** would create a Committee for Corporate Responsibility, with representatives from the company and from conservationist, union, civil rights, consumer, and religious groups.
- **Proposal number 3** would deal with the amending of the company's corporate character to specify public interest requirements.

In addition, Campaign GM created six additional proposals included in the proxy sent to shareholders before the meeting.

The Securities and Exchange Commission (SEC), on inquiry from GM, decided that seven of the total of nine proposals could be omitted from the proxy statement and that the project's Campaign GM should amend one of the two remaining proposals to make it suitable for its inclusion. The surviving proposals were for expansion of the board of directors and establishment of a Committee for Corporate Responsibility. Nonetheless, the campaign's strategy called for rousing the support of institutional investors and their constituents. Nader appealed to shareholders as "citizens and consumers, victims of water pollution, congested and inefficient transportation, and rocketing repair bills for shoddy workmanship."[2]

---

[2] In preparing this case study, and again in preparing the revision, we wrote to Mr. Nader, asking for information that would tell the "Nader side of the story." Both invitations went unanswered, even though it was made clear that the information was wanted for classroom use.

THE GM-SIDE STRATEGY

The GM vice-president for public relations wrote during the months between the project's Campaign GM proposals and the annual meeting:

> February and March were extremely busy months for us. As the days passed, it became obvious that the Project was having little trouble getting all the media coverage it wanted. For us, there was the question of whether we should fight the Project at every point or whether the better course was to "play it cool" and not increase the opportunities for rebuttal headlines. In the end, our response could be characterized as walking the middle ground—answering all the charges but avoiding response which would provide a further forum.
>
> The spring saw the first Earth Day and the first teach-ins on the environment. Seminars and discussions at high schools and colleges throughout the nation focused attention on environmental problems. General Motors sent speakers to 116 of these teach-ins. . . .
>
> The Project attempted to capitalize on this college environmental movement in order to generate attention and support for its cause. It tried to form students into pressure groups to force the universities to back the Project and vote endowment shares against GM management. Generally, its efforts failed.
>
> Amid all this public controversy and discussion, the owners of our business, the stockholders, were taking the challenge rather calmly. Only 264 letters, or twelve percent of the 2,200 comments received prior to the annual meeting, dealt with one or both of the Project's two proposals. This surprised us, because we thought the publicity which had been given the Project's activities would generate a greater stockholder response.
>
> While our stockholders weren't strongly motivated to write us about the proposals, they did write in far greater numbers for tickets to the annual meeting. We received 3,500 requests for tickets.[3]

THE ANNUAL MEETING

The meeting itself, starting at 2:00 P.M., went on for more than six hours, with the GM chairman presiding. In the course of the meeting, contrary to precedent, some sixty-seven shareholders and proxy holders spoke. (See Figure 5–1.)

Before that happened, a motion picture was shown depicting how the company was meeting some of its social responsibilities. (This film subsequently went into the company's film catalog, and in its first three years was shown 11,348 times to an estimated total audience of 337,938.)

The prepared remarks by the chairman covered the deaths of a GM executive and a United Auto Workers (UAW) top official; retirement of two directors; intro-

---

[3]Anthony DeLorenzo, "Round Three," also from speeches to public relations professionals and corporate secretaries.

Figure 5–1 A packed house for annual meeting of shareholders in world's largest industrial corporation the year campaign GM began. Courtesy of General Motors.

duction of twenty directors present; the trend of sales and earnings, influences on them, and problems ahead; the matter of social responsibility and GM activities in that area; introduction of the film; and introduction of the proposals in the proxy statement.[4]

Of the five proposals on the agenda, the first one, the selection of independent public accountants, was overwhelmingly ratified. The other four—to limit executive compensation, to provide cumulative voting in the election of directors, to establish a responsibility committee, and to increase the number of directors—were defeated by massive majorities. The last two of these were the proposals of the Project.

The chairman made a closing statement pledging socially responsible conduct by the corporation. At a press conference immediately afterward, he was asked whether he thought GM had achieved a "victory." His response was, "I don't think we won a victory. I think we won a vote of confidence from our shareholders. I

[4]Extracted from *Report of the 62nd General Motors Stockholders' Meeting,* a company booklet.

think we could lose that vote of confidence very quickly unless we respond in the way our shareholders expect us to—and that's what we intend to do."

IN THE WAKE OF THE MEETING: ROUND ONE

One move came within two months. A five-member Public Policy Committee was formed as a permanent standing committee of the board to "inquire into all phases of the corporation's operations that relate to public policy and recommend actions to the full Board." On the committee at the outset were the chairman of the Mellon National Bank and a trustee of Carnegie-Mellon University; the chairman of the corporation of Massachusetts Institute of Technology; the chairman of Allied Chemical Corporation and former Secretary of Commerce; the trustee of Meharry Medical College; and the president of Marshall Field, who was also a trustee of Northwestern University.

At the beginning of the next year, the board elected the first African American to membership—the originator of the Opportunities Industrialization Centers of America. In April, a professor of mechanical engineering at the University of California (an expert in thermodynamics and air pollution) was hired as vice-president for environmental activities, to coordinate work in automobile safety, emissions, product assurance, and industrial air and water pollution control.

Spurred by the Public Policy Committee, a Science Advisory Committee, chaired by a Nobel Prize winner, was formed to assist in technological and scientific matters involving basic and applied research.

SHIFT IN STRATEGY

According to the vice-president, after evaluation GM's public relations people decided to return to and review the second step in the process, strategic planning. After review, they felt sure Campaign GM would hammer away at the responsibility theme. They decided to swing from their reactive "cool-it" tactics to a proactive advocacy.

Implementing a proactive approach, the company's news relations section stepped up the number of interviews by financial, popular, and trade media with senior GM officials. There was an all-day conference at the GM Proving Ground for newspaper publishers. This event was repeated for prominent educators and representatives of foundations and investment institutions. The range of subjects was wide, even getting into such sticky problem areas as abandoned cars.

These meetings, important in themselves, additionally provided the substance for a booklet to shareholders, employees, and business and community leaders. Concurrently, there was no letup in communications efforts; television shorts were shown, as just one example. The company's next annual report contained a report of progress in areas of social concern.

THE NEXT ANNUAL MEETING: ROUND TWO

Campaign GM, in round two at the next year's annual meeting, offered three proposals:

- **Proposal number 1** termed "stockholder democracy," would permit the listing of shareholder nominees for the board in the company's proxy.
- **Proposal number 2** on "constituent democracy," sought board positions for representatives of employees, auto dealers, and consumers.
- **Proposal number 3** on "disclosure," would require disclosure of policies, activities, and expenditures in the areas of pollution, safety, and minority hiring in the annual report.

All three proposals were put into the proxy statement by GM, and the corporation's opposition to all three was clearly stated, not because of their cost, but because they would "do more harm than good."

Those hoping for fireworks at the meeting were disappointed. The project's proposals were overwhelmingly defeated by majorities of more than ninety-five percent.

How Public Relations Became an Issue

Regarding the GM public relations function, one shareholder proposed to nominate a public relations counselor to serve on the board of directors. This item on the agenda was reported in the postmeeting report in these words:

> The Chairman said that General Motors has its own public relations staff and utilizes outside consultants in this area. He also said that directors were chosen for general as well as specialized abilities and it would not be in the best interests of the Corporation to reserve board memberships for persons identified with particular occupations or professions. A stockholder supported the proposal, saying such a director would be able to assist in meeting public relations problems. A proxy-holder recommended a woman as public relations counselor and said for too many years GM has been interested only in dividends, to the exclusion of other considerations. The chairman replied that General Motors has been concerned with many other aspects of society and business. A stockholder said the need for a public relations counselor or director at all corporations, including GM, should be obvious.

The vote on this proposal was 95.73 percent opposed and 4.27 percent in favor.

Questions raised at the meeting generally ran the same course as those the previous year. They were pleasantly received and answered with courtesy and patience. The most emotion-laden issue proved to be a proposal from the Episcopal Church to discontinue GM's operations in South Africa. The black GM director spoke for the proposal, the first time in the corporation's experience that a director had publicly opposed the announced position of the board.

ROUND THREE

The project was back at it a third year. Meantime, GM again stepped up its proactive efforts to take its position out publicly to the working, buying, investing, and voting public. Speeches, magazines, and newspaper advertising and network television were used.

In an extensive magazine article, the vice-president for public relations raised what he termed, from GM's standpoint, a basic question: "What is the Project really trying to do?" He cited GM's answer in a booklet sent to shareholders. "The Project is using General Motors as a means through which it can challenge the entire system of corporate management in the United States."

A spokesman for the Nader group, Susan L. Gross, explained the selection of GM this way: "We haven't chosen GM because it is all bad, but because it epitomized all corporations. And we have found that if you can get GM to change, other corporations will follow."

The GM vice-president for public relations termed the project a "time-consuming distraction from a basic reevaluation of goals and responsibilities which has been under way for several years."[5] Regarding the criticisms and reacting to them, he said:

> The real danger is that through misinformation or a reluctance to tell our side of the story, our political system will overreact to the critics' charges. Some critics of business exaggerate, misquote and make statements which are flatly and purposely misleading. Businessmen are not venal, money-grubbing villains who each day do their best to deceive and cheat the consumer. On the other hand, we can't complain if people hold that view of us if we don't try to tell our side of the story.

The vice-president quoted from the chairman's address to GM's divisional and central office public relations people:

> At various times in the history of General Motors, different staffs have been called upon to make vital contributions to our company. Today it is you public relations men [sic] who are being tested.

[5]This and other quotations cited are from the speech "Round Three" presented by Anthony De-Lorenzo, vice-president for public relations at the time.

GM public relations has more visibly and aggressively taken the corporation's human side to its constituency in controlled media and messages.

AT THE MARKETPLACE

In mid-1988, GM decided to use a combination of marketing and public relations pizzazz in a campaign to regain its image as the invincible leader on top of the world auto industry. The campaign was launched with a lavish exhibit called "GM Teamwork & Technology—For Today and Tomorrow," staged in New York's Waldorf Astoria, and coupled with eight-page inserts in magazines such as *Reader's Digest*, at a cost of $20 million. Streamlined design, getaway speed, power, and luxurious fittings were their evidences of image and leadership.

AS FOR CORPORATE STATESMANSHIP . . .

The company's 1993 Public Interest Report devoted twenty-six pages to internal matters considered to be in the public interest, ten pages about its programs to foster community relationships, three pages about GM's role in the economy, and three pages about its efforts in minority activities. The chairman's overview stressed the need that GM has to be competitive by "maintaining the highest standards of corporate responsibility in products, services, and processes, and in our relationships with stakeholders and communities" (see Figure 5-2).[6]

A MANIFESTATION OF SERIOUS PROBLEMS

Financial news media reported bold billion-dollar strokes by GM in 1985, including purchases of Hughes Aircraft and Electronic Data Systems, Ross Perot's company. In 1986, the *Washington Journalism Review* said GM had "the best corporate public relations staff in the nation." Since then, it hasn't looked that way to a great many employees, neighbors, shareholder representatives, and news media.

There have been plant closings and shifts of plants to rural communities. A confrontation with Perot ended in a $700 million buyout and a suit by some critical shareholders. During a period of decreases in sales, profit, and market share, executives received bonuses but workers received no profit sharing. Financial media reported that the company was preparing to select a new president. Shareholders received a letter from Chairman Roger Smith defending his record.

At an annual meeting, Ralph Nader called for Smith's resignation. Also at an annual meeting, Smith was heckled by some unhappy shareholders, and a couple of

[6]*GM Public Interest Report* is available to students and others on request. GM Corp. General Motors Bldg. 3044 West Grand Blvd. Detroit, MI 48202.

"FOCUSED ON IMPROVING COMPETITIVENESS

we recognize that this process must include maintaining the highest standards of corporate responsibility in our products, services and processes, and in our relationships with our stakeholders and the communities where we live and work."

GENERAL MOTORS 23RD ANNUAL PUBLIC INTEREST REPORT

Figure 5–2. The 1993 *Public Interest Report.* (Courtesy of General Motors.)

months later he was booed by disgruntled workers during a plant tour. *Automotive* magazine blasted him for his op-ed article in the *Wall Street Journal* calling for judicial restraint by the Supreme Court. He appeared to one major newspaper as "rapidly becoming the Rodney Dangerfield of the domestic automobile industry."

    Problems breed problems. In 1988, GM joined other domestic auto makers in seeking to restrict imports of Japanese pickup trucks, a ploy that would inevitably increase the price of U.S. pickups, according to qualified observers who cited the fifty percent increase in U.S. new car prices over a three-year period after Japanese imports were restricted in 1981.

The proxy sent to shareholders in 1988 contained information that critics might have felt was more concerned with the interests of GM executives than with public interest. It listed nine director nominees who had received a $20,000 fee and $750 additional for each meeting attended, yet held no more than 500 shares of GM stock. As for Chairman Smith, his salary was $867,000. During 1987 he had exercised options on stock worth $513,121 and had been granted options to buy 23,000 more shares. At retirement, unless things changed, he stood to receive $500,000 or more annual retirement benefit. To a small GM investor seeing the flood of Japanese cars, an hourly worker laid off, or a tradesman borrowing money for a pickup truck, life in the boardroom might seem out of touch.

Among the nine proposals or resolutions submitted by shareholders to be voted on were a few from religious organizations holding stock. They, variously, dealt critically with GM's activities in South Africa and Northern Ireland, and in doing defense and space program work. No proposal was identified with Nader's group.[7]

BRINGING A CONTINUING STORY UP TO DATE

In succeeding years, groups with which Ralph Nader has been associated have kept tabs on GM. From GM's standpoint, that should not have been all bad, because the corporation has had repeated opportunities to tell its story with a wide audience paying attention.

At one point, GM and Nader were on the same side. The Center for Auto Safety (a Nader spin-off) felt that the Environmental Protection Agency was favoring Chrysler and Ford because they were not in the same financial shape as GM.

Nader and GM differed over a housing issue regarding the Poletown renovation (a district in Detroit) and reconstruction including a Cadillac plant. Nader joined a citizens group in opposition. At the time, GM reverted to its "cool-it" stance and froze in it by refraining from comment. Not long after, Nader was reported to be working on a book forecast as "a revealing look at corporate power."

Ralph Nader was named among "The 100 Most Important Americans of the 20th Century" in the fall 1990 issue of *Life* magazine. According to *Life,* Nader "is a crusader who became backseat driver for a nation." Twenty-eight years after publication of *Unsafe at Any Speed,* there are safety standards and air bags in cars. Nader has fathered legislation from the Freedom of Information Act to the Safe Drinking Water Act. He has also headed federal agencies such as Occupational Safety and

---

[7]Update material drawn from GM annual report covering 1987, financial reports and proxy statement in 1988, and facts contained in *Wall Street Journal* index of news stories for recent years.

Health Administration and the Consumer Product Safety Commission. He has inspired people to act on their rights. "Many a tenacious idealist is called a Ralph Nader, symbol of the citizen's right to know."[8]

IS THERE A FUTURE FOR PEOPLE LIKE NADER?

In recent times "libel mania" is on top of corporate watchdog's minds more than ever. Lawsuits known as SLAPPs—strategic lawsuits against public participation—are being used against consumers and others who criticize a company's products or actions. Who are these consumers? They are civil and environmental groups objecting to development projects in their neighborhoods and state parks, activists working against air pollution, citizens who criticize their local school board or town council members, and individuals who write letters to the editor opposing a new factory or housing facility.

Corporate Reasoning

In July 1991, the *Wall Street Journal* quoted Kevin M. Reynolds as he spoke for corporations in liability cases. Reynolds, a partner in a Des Moines, Iowa, law firm stated: "Your freedom of speech stops at the point where you libel or defame our product. . . . With the economy in a recession, companies are finding themselves in a very competitive atmosphere and they are more sensitive about libel than they used to be."

A study at the University of Denver Law School found that approximately 2,000 SLAPPs were filed between 1989–1991. The success rates of these lawsuits have not been high. Many are thrown out of court, some are settled out of court, some stay on the books indefinitely without out resolution.

Speaking Against SLAPPs

John V. R. Bull is the assistant to the editor for the *Philadelphia Inquirer.* On Columbus Day, 1991, he gave an interesting speech to the College Club of Sharon, Sharon, Pennsylvania. The speech, entitled "Freedom of Speech: Can it Survive?" focused on how the Naders of America may think twice before speaking out. Bull believes that the motivation on behalf of corporations filing SLAPPs is more than monetary compensation for damages.

> There is not a doubt in my own mind that the intent of these lawsuits is not to recover financial damages but to stifle public opposition! At the moment, it is not safe for us as citizens to criticize our fellow countrymen and women, Corporate America or even our governing officials without having to worry about being sued for slander or libel. Now we have to think twice, sometimes three or four times, before speaking our mind.

[8]*Life*, Fall 1990: 19.

Bull pointed out that there is a double standard as far as SLAPPs are concerned because most public officials are immune from being sued for anything they say, write, or do while exercising their right as an official.

In essence here is the situation:

- Members of Congress are immune from libel or slander suits under Article I, Section 6, of the U.S. Constitution.
- Members of the federal judiciary are immune under the doctrine of judiciary immunity, or case law.
  - Federal agencies are also immune from libel or slander prosecution by Act of Congress.
- All states have constitutional, statutory, or judicially mandated immunity for judges.

Most states also give legislators immunity and give public officials "executive privilege," thus shielding them from lawsuits for actions taken in the performance of their public duties. Depending on the state, these protections can go right down to the township level. In Pennsylvania, for instance, district attorneys are protected from slander or libel suits, even when they hold a public press conference.[9]

Hard Hit SLAPPs

Robert McDonald, a North Carolina resident, wrote to then president-elect Ronald Reagan, stating that a former judge who was under consideration for U.S. Attorney General did not have the character or competence for the position. The former judge sued for $1 million and won.

Mrs. Beverly Fehnel, a housewife from Bethlehem, Pennsylvania, was brought to court for writing a letter to the editor after she became angry at her local government when she read in the *Bethlehem Globe Times* that an influential real estate developer brought in a circus for profit-making purposes without a zoning permit. She wrote a letter to the editor because she had spent months trying to get a zoning permit so that she could open a gift shop in the same area as the circus. The *Globe Times* and Fehnel won the case after a lengthy deposition process and a three-day trial.

In Long Island, New York, a Policeman's Benevolent Association proclaimed that it would file suit against every citizen filing a misconduct complaint that the Police Department's Civilian Review Board found to be unsubstantiated. This review board routinely dismissed ninety-five percent of the citizen complaints received. The number of complaints dropped drastically after this threat of mass libel and slander actions.

Freedom of Speech

John Bull believes that we have turned "a precious right, Freedom of Speech, over to lawyers who with their qualifying, quibbling, and squabbling are pricing it right out of existence. There was, you see, a very

---

[9]Taken from John V. R. Bull, "Freedom of Speech: Can It Survive?" *Vital Speeches* 58 (December 1, 1991).

good reason why our founding fathers went back to the Constitution only four years after it was written and added the First Amendment. Now 215 years later, the babble . . . threatens to grow quieter and quieter."

What do you say to that?

QUESTIONS FOR DISCUSSION

1. Considering what you know about GM and about Ralph Nader, and what you read in this case study, what, if any, reform or change in GM attitudes toward its public responsibilities would you credit to the activities of the Nader group? If there are some, would you conclude that small investors do have a say in the policies and decisions of corporate management, or was the Nader campaign an aberration? Should small investors have any more say than is represented by the small size (number of shares) of their holdings measured against the size of the holdings held by investment trusts, foundations, and wealthy people, including GM officers and directors?

2. There is an ancient concept, *noblesse oblige,* holding that those of noble birth, wealth, or power have a moral obligation to act with honor, honesty, and generosity, the inherent elements of leadership. Does it follow that General Motors, one of the world's largest and perhaps most powerful corporations, in its decisions, uses of power, and gestures of charity, sets the standards of character for all lesser corporations, whether it chooses to do so or not? If you think it does, how is GM doing as a true leader in the public interest?

3. GM's 1993 Public Interest Report covering 1992, a forty-eight page booklet, devotes ten pages to philanthropic activities, three pages to programs for minorities and women, and one page of statistics to Equal Employment Opportunity data. Under philanthropy, GM donated $58 million. That was about 1.6 percent as much as its net income. The biggest beneficiary was education, getting $36 million, $22 million was given to other beneficiaries such as; health and welfare, cultural organizations, urban development and community action, United Way, cancer research awards, and the National Concerto Competition. The Equal Employment Opportunity tables showed that total GM employment had gone down from 382,498 in 1991 to 365,877 in 1987. Do you think that GM would be benefited by seeking broad public disclosure of its social responsibility activities, or would the corporation be better served by quietly "cooling-it," as was done in dealing with Ralph Nader?

4. A black eye on almost all large corporations is negative public reaction to the lavish salaries, bonuses, stock options, perks, and golden umbrellas given to management, in good times or bad, whether line workers are being laid off,

jobs are going abroad, or assets being sold off. Do you think such executive rewards can be justified on the basis that some rock singers, professional athletes, film and television entertainers, and network anchorpersons also reap a golden harvest? What approach would you suggest to this real-world problem with which corporate professional people have to wrestle?

Case 5-3

A City Divided:
SDG&E Takeover

In a society where organizations must recognize the interest of stakeholders as well as stockholders, investor relations often goes far beyond stock issues and earnings reports. This abbreviated case shows how public many topics once reserved only for stockholders have become.

The late 1980s left California in a serious recession. The real estate and banking industries suffered miserably, thanks to falling property values and the S&L scandals. Southern California Edison, a power utility headquartered in Rosemead, a suburb of Los Angeles, experienced financial difficulties and was a victim of a depressed economy. The population growth of Los Angeles had begun to slow, but San Diego, served by San Diego Gas & Electric, was the fourth largest growing city in the United States. Edison, the larger of the two utilities, licked its chops at the thought of eating SDG&E for dinner in a hostile takeover.

On July 26, 1988, Edison pounced on SDG&E with a hostile takeover bid of $2.03 billion in Edison stock. SDG&E officials initially resisted the offer, continued to reject the augmented bids of $2.1 billion and $2.15 billion, and eventually asked the state to stop the Edison takeover attempt. Suddenly on November 30, SDG&E directors turned enemies into allies and embraced an Edison proposal of $2.5 billion.

City officials and civic leaders of San Diego were unnerved. Mayor Maureen O'Connor and several civic leaders challenged the merger. There was even discussion of a municipal takeover of SDG&E. SDG&E dropped out of the Greater San Diego Chamber of Commerce. Two board members at SDG&E resigned in protest of the merger. Rumors circulated that SDG&E officials were being offered positions by Edison, and a poll revealed that San Diegans opposed the Edison/SDG&E merger by a two to one margin.

GROUPS PROMOTING THE MERGER

Three groups were promoting the merger.

1. San Diegans for the Merger, a grassroots organization funded by Southern California Edison, was an "impartial" front group composed of stockholders and SDG&E employees (current and former) who felt that the merger would improve stock value. San Diegans for the Merger distributed literature and held informational meetings.
2. Southern California Edison.
3. Members of management and the board of directors at San Diego Gas & Electric.

GROUPS OPPOSING THE MERGER

Four groups opposed the merger

1. The Coalition for Local Control (CFLC), a diverse organization representing business interests, environmental and consumer issues, and organized labor concerns, was created in early 1989 when the president of The Greater San Diego Chamber of Commerce, Lee Grissom, persuaded Gordon Luce of Great American Bank to form a merger opposition committee from both public and private sectors. The CFLC was funded by contributions from concerned citizens and vehemently opposed the merger. Subsequently, the group launched a public relations campaign against it.[1]
2. San Diego Mayor Maureen O'Connor, the spearhead of the opposition, gained more respect than she had previously enjoyed by defending the independence of SDG&E. She was a major spokesperson against the proposed merger.
3. City Attorney John Witt and his legal staff.
4. The majority of employees at San Diego Gas & Electric.

THE COALITION FOR LOCAL CONTROL

The CFLC was headed by executive director Bob Hudson, who coordinated the talents and skills of a diverse group of people to unite against Edison. This coalition was formed "to convince the majority of the PUC [Public Utility Commission] mem-

---

[1]We thank Nuffer, Smith, Tucker, Inc., public relations counsel, for the information provided for this case.

bers [three of five] to rule against the merger through a groundswell of opposition."[2]

A BROAD-SPECTRUM COALITION BROUGHT TOGETHER UNLIKELY BEDFELLOWS

The conservation coordinator of the San Diego chapter of the Sierra Club, the business manager of the International Brotherhood of Electrical Workers #465, a mayor from the nearby city of Chula Vista, the executive director of the Utility Consumers Action Network, a public relations professional, and many others worked together to represent San Diego in a fight for the control of SDG&E. They adopted a vision statement that was accepted by the entire coalition by June 19, 1989.

> If we are successful San Diego would have preserved its quality of life and controlled its own destiny.
>
> - SDG&E will remain healthy, local, and investor-owned.
> - SDG&E will be supporting the community with civic leadership and philanthropic support.
> - SDG&E will provide economic vitality and responsiveness to the community.
> - SDG&E will enhance its record of effective management.
> - SDG&E rates will continue to be competitive with other Southern California utilities.

KEY MESSAGES FROM SOUTHERN CALIFORNIA EDISON

In its struggle against the mayor and the CFLC, Edison argued that:

1. The merger would prove cost-effective by eliminating duplicative functions (e.g., billing departments, public relations departments, and so on).
2. The community would benefit from price advantages, namely a promised ten percent rate reduction.
3. The environment would be saved because SDG&E and Edison wouldn't need to invest in and construct new power facilities.
4. The merger would benefit shareholders, who would partake of the savings.

---

[2]For setting rates and ruling on other issues, the PUC is often the agency that decides whether something is in the best interest of the public.

KEY MESSAGES FROM CFLC

CFLC countered with their own arguments:

1. A relocation of the utility's central headquarters to Rosemead would create a loss of corporate presence in San Diego. The city had just lost Pacific Southwest Airlines corporation, and there was speculation that another loss could psychologically damage San Diego's independence.
2. Downsizing and transfers in both companies could sacrifice between 1,000 and 1,600 jobs.
3. The pollution level of Los Angeles could increase even further.
4. The magnitude of the combined utilities would be reminiscent of the 1930s, when utility trusts had to be broken up.

BOTH SIDES TAKE ACTION

Edison and its front organizations spent more than $2.2 million on advertising and publicity campaigns, pamphlets and flyers. (Legal fees brought the total Southern California Edison expenditure close to $100 million.) San Diego and the CFLC spent their far smaller budget (approximately $80,000) on a different public relations strategy—reaching the decision makers by focusing on third-party advocates who had influence with the PUC.

The CFLC distributed its own facts refuting the claims made by Edison. Its activities began by assessing receptivity to the CFLC mission of the publics that influence the Public Utility Commission (the PUC commissioners, PUC staff, the governor and legislators, the media, and grassroots support) (see Figure 5-3). The role of the mayor as a prominent spokesperson in this campaign increased media attention on the issue and brought the story out of the business section into the general news pages. Predictably, it had a similar effect on the grapevine and coffee-break discussion.

THE RESULTS

On May 8, 1991, after a three-year battle, the PUC unanimously denied Edison's proposed merger with SDG&E. After several investigations by state and federal authorities, it was determined that the merger would not benefit San Diegans through lower pollution and electric rates.

An overwhelming percentage of the public opposed the merger because of the media and public relations efforts by the mayor and the CFLC. The Greater San Diego Chamber of Commerce welcomed the SDG&E utility back to the Chamber in

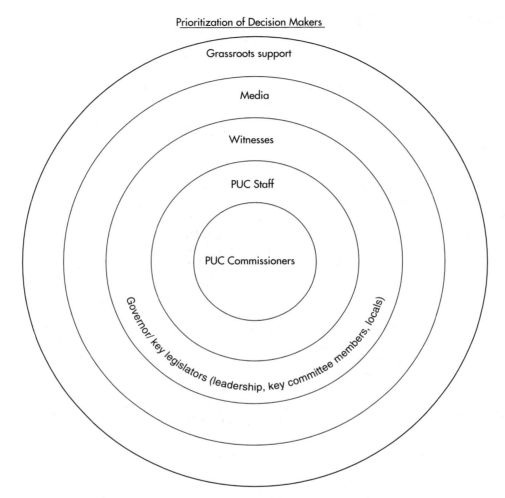

Figure 5–3 The CFLC devised its strategy by prioritizing which decision makers would be most receptive to its message. (Courtesy of CFLC.)

Figure 5–4   The CFLC "working group" celebrates its victory for the citizens of San Diego after a 32-month fight against the merger. (Courtesy of CFLC.)

a sincere effort to begin the healing process for themselves, the utility, and the San Diego community (see Figure 5–4).

QUESTIONS FOR DISCUSSION

1. Was it fair to SGD&E stockholders, who might have benefited financially by selling their stock in the proposed takeover, for other parties to intervene? Why or why not?

2. Make a point-by-point case, pro or con, on a situation in which people who own no shares in a company nonetheless have a voice in its destiny. Justify your position with comparative examples in other areas of public policy.

3. Compare the key messages from CFLC and Edison. How are they dissimilar or similar? What is the specific strategy behind each of the messages? What publics might find each appealing or persuasive?

4. How was the public served in this case?

5. How ethical was Edison's decision to fund San Diegans for the Merger?

The Seamless Web: How Relations with Other Publics Affects Investor Relations

Whether a publicly held corporation is trying to sell clothing, automobiles, houses, or homemade sausage, it needs three essential ingredients for success: quality products, quality staff, and a high profile as a quality investment. If one of the three is lacking, the entire organization is affected.

A corporation needs investors—persons willing to invest healthy sums of money and ideas to support growth. In order to attract and keep them, investor relations is a key function. Bob Evans Farms, Inc., uses a quality approach to investor relations. The bottom line is always quality—quality products, quality employee relations, quality consumer relations, and quality investor relations—because, after all, stockholders invest in all of these items.

HISTORY OF BOB EVANS FARMS, INC.

Bob Evans started this company in 1946 as a small, twenty-four-hour restaurant. As the business grew, Evans invited company guests to his farm in Rio Grande, Ohio, to

---

BOB EVANS FARMS, INC., MISSION STATEMENT

"To provide quality products and services to meet our customers' needs, allowing us to prosper as a business and to provide a reasonable return for our stockholders."

---

acquaint them with the company's deep farm heritage. Over the years the quality of sausage Mr. Evans could buy was declining so he began his own sausage company for the restaurant. The *Sausage Shop* became the basis for a corporation now operated by 18,000 employees, which includes nearly 270 full-service, family restaurants in sixteen states and distributes food products to twenty-three states.

MARK FOR CHANGE

Today Bob Evans Farms (BEF) connotes success, but its achievements came only after the mid-1980s. At that time the company's performance was sluggish. Earnings were down, and stock was lacking. According to Mary Cusick, vice-president for corporate communications, strategic planning was not used effectively if at all.[1] Executives decided that the center of these problems, the stagnancy of the organization, needed to be researched and tackled. Why wasn't the corporation progressing?

A Quality Committee was established in January, 1992, to address this question. "We're approaching quality with a committee that includes (1) operations people (employees working in the restaurant with responsibility for handling customers); (2) marketing (they put together menus and new product development); and (3) headquarters via the customer relations department," Cusick said. *This is a total quality approach to consumer relations*—which pays off with other publics, particularly investors.

ATTITUDES AFFECT BEHAVIORS

Consumers

Bob Evans Farms conducted research with one external audience, its restaurant customers, and found that people perceived it as a fattening, sausage-producing, breakfast business. This perception disturbed company executives because they had already upgraded the menus to include more salads, oil-free dressings, and other lighter options. In this health-conscious society, consumers did not perceive this change. Sales did not increase—and stock prices adjusted accordingly.

Management, Employees, and Investors

BEF's internal research found that management, employees, and investors were directly affected by BEF's lack of strategic planning. Employee job performance was affected by a lack of communication and information. Investors felt the brunt of this

---

[1]We thank Mary Cusick, vice-president for corporate communications at Bob Evans Farms, for the information provided for this case.

communication gap as well. As a result, management decided that *employees and investors needed better communication* regarding all aspects of the business.

THE NEED FOR CHANGE

In the summer of 1990, Bob Evans Farms, Inc., was internally restructured and its goals were redefined. Management used a quality approach to incorporate good communication between consumers, investors, and employees because the satisfaction of those audiences affected all aspects of the business. Its goals were to become:

1. More effective in product development.
2. More responsive to customer needs and concerns.
3. More aggressive in terms of acquisitions.
4. More entrepreneurial to retain investors, customers, and employees.

THE EXTERNAL PUBLIC: THE PERCEPTION PROBLEM

Executives worked together and implemented an "involved strategic planning process—bringing things such as changing consumer needs to the forefront," explains Cusick. The company started with consumer relations because customer perceptions were at the heart of the problem—BEF's products were not being purchased, investors would pull out, employees would lose their jobs, and the business would fail.

Through various research methods including customer surveys and strategy meetings, BEF executives set several goals and objectives for the company:

1. Upgrading facilities throughout the system. The upgrade included expanding standing room for those waiting for tables, relocating restrooms to the front of the restaurant, increasing nonsmoking areas, increasing grill lines for extra capacity and efficiency, improving the carry-out section and upgrading the dining room.
2. Implementing a point-of-sale computer system to enhance the ability to collect information on buying patterns and consumer behavior.
3. Changing consumers' perceptions about what food is healthy. The company participated in a nationwide program called Pork Promotion Grants. This program tried to change the perception that pork is unhealthy. Bob Evans Farms also set up an informal educational technique by placing a demonstration table in grocery stores. Spokespeople talked with consumers and tried to convince them that pork is much leaner than it used to be and that there are new, health-conscious ways to cook pork (see Figure 5–5).

Figure 5–5 Bob Evans Farm distributes pamphlets that let the public know a little bit more about it and healthy recipes that use its main product, sausage. (Courtesy of Bob Evans Farms, Inc.)

4. Adding seasonal dinner specials and refrigerated deli salads to the menu in order to further reinforce the new focus on value, nutrition, and taste.

THE INTERNAL PUBLICS: THE EMPLOYEE SATISFACTION PROBLEM

Corporate communications set up new ways to improve communications with employees. Bob Evans Farm's communications team recognized the detrimental effects of "word of mouth." Executives had to better inform the midlevel managers so that these supervisors could serve as a reference for others. They could answer and clarify questions that employees might have. To do this, Corporate Communications created:

1. *The Almanac,* a video news magazine, which gives managers updated news on all aspects of the company.
2. A quarterly magazine containing all kinds of information from survey results to forthcoming events.
3. A publication called *The Roundup,* distributed to all employees six times a year. This publication includes tabulated comments good and bad, from consumers.
4. A monthly management newsletter informing the management team about business details so that they can answer customer and stockholder questions.
5. Availability of an employee stock option plan, dividend reimbursements, and stocks as incentives and rewards. The idea is that if employees own part of the company, they will value it and support its initiatives.

TARGETING INVESTOR PROBLEMS

Bob Evans Farms also realized that it needed better communication between investors and the business. The corporation now:

1. Continues to send quarterly and annual reports to investors.
2. Relies more on the Ohio business press. Many stockholders live in and near its Ohio headquarters. Ohio papers and other consumer media in that area have written many feature stories about BEF. All stockholders, including "Gentleman Farmers"—investors who own a square foot of company property—receive up-to-date correspondence that might affect their view of the business.
3. Sends samples of new products to stockholders in order to survey their opinions.
4. Invites all stockholders to attend restaurant openings and other special events. In particular, investors are encouraged to spend a day on Bob Evans Farm for the annual stockholder's meeting. At the meeting, they have the opportunity to taste old and new products, see minidisplays of new restaurants, reunite with old friends, and enjoy the beautiful August weather outdoors on the farm. It isn't a typical stockholders' meeting in the city where only a couple of hundred people attend. Cusick feels it is unique because typically about 16,000 people attend (see Figure 5-6).
5. Promotes stock through speaking engagements to financial analysts and other institutional investors.

Figure 5–6 The Bob Evans Farms annual stockholders' meeting held at Bob Evans Farm in Rio Grande, Ohio. (Courtesy of Bob Evans Farms, Inc.)

EVALUATION

In 1991, the company reached a milestone when it surpassed $500 million in net sales, a ten percent increase from 1990. Stock value is high despite the down economy. According to Mary Cusick, the organization had 24,000 stockholders as of November, 1992. Approximately ninety percent are individual owners, forty percent are residents of Ohio. Bob Evans Farms recognizes the key to a company's survival—the whole is only as good as the sum of its parts.

QUESTIONS FOR DISCUSSION

1. What other strategies can you suggest to maintain current investor satisfaction and encourage new investment in Bob Evans Farms, Inc.?
2. Review the actions taken by management to address the external and internal publics problems. What have they got to do with *investor* relations? What effect might they have on investors, if any?
3. List elements of investor relations that will be different for a company such as BEF—a smaller, locally held company with mainly individual investors—than for a giant creature of Wall Street. Which do you think presents the greater challenge for its public relations practitioners?

PROBLEM 5-A CAN AN ANNUAL REPORT PLEASE EVERYONE?

Preparation of the annual report for a publicly owned corporation is probably the most frustrating, if not the most difficult, communications literary task generally assigned to the corporate communications staff. This statement is true whether the job is handled internally or with the aid of outside counsel.

As the "report card" of management to those who own the company as shareholders, and to those in the financial community who can influence others for or against owning shares, it is an ultrasensitive and personal document. In many cases it is an ego trip, for the head of the firm, for the top financial officer, or for officers hoping one day to become CEO.

The top official, when the company has had a good year, competitively and in operating results, may want a lavish four-color booklet. The senior financial officer may prefer one color or two colors (the second being silver or gold), demonstrating prudence as well as success. The heads of operating divisions, wanting to broaden the circulation to customers and prospects, may want lavish product or service pictures, particularly of the products or services of their particular division or subsidiary. The director of personnel will probably want pictures showing how happy the employees are at their jobs. Systems analysts will want their latest cost-reducing equipment shown. If the corporation is international in scope, the export department will want to emphasize "hands across the seas."

So it goes. Shareholders who may receive dividends of $1 per share of stock may receive an annual report that costs $1 to $2 per copy to prepare, not counting the time put in on it by executives and members of the communications staff. In many corporations, thinking about the next year's report starts as soon as one year's annual report has come out and has been distributed, there has been some feedback, and the annual meeting of shareholders has taken place. Given the high vanity quotient involved; the diversity of views within a corporation; the inherent "competition" for attention, recognition, and prominence among corporate divisions; and possibly financial results that are not the best, public relations has its work cut out for it.

The need is for persuasion, compromise, and reconciliation. See how you would go about this task. Select a corporation and acquire an annual report. Assume that you have to plan for the next one.

1. What questions will you ask and what research will you do before you start your basic strategic plan for the report?
2. Your research indicates the desirability of some major changes in the content and design of the report. Draw up a formal outline of your approach, including:

- Overall theme in words and graphics (with your rationale).
- Table of contents indicating obligatory information.
- Preliminary concepts for cover and layout.
- Photography needs or other visual techniques, with costs.
- Printing costs, including number of copies.
- A timetable with deadlines.

3. How will you suggest reducing the cycle time required to produce the annual report?

PROBLEM 5-B HERE COMES THAT MAN NADER, AGAIN

The article shown in Figure 5-7 appeared in the national newspaper *USA Today*.

You are newly hired, a business school graduate with an emphasis in public relations, in the shareholder relations section of a department in one of the ten companies named in the news story. (Take your choice.)

After the story appeared, there were a few well-chosen expletives expressed in your company regarding the parenthood of Nader and his associates, but there was no request from senior financial officers or top management that any responsive or reciprocal action be taken. Your immediate boss asked nothing of you, and the vice-president for public relations made no request of him. The position of your employer, apparently, is much the same as the "cool-it" posture of GM when Nader's Campaign GM was on. There is a new development, however.

A letter has come in, addressed to Director of Shareholder Relations. The letter includes these passages:

> My husband was a successful businessman. His success is the reason I am able to live comfortably on my investments, one of which is ownership of 1,000 shares of your stock. I might say that I own more of your stock than some of the people on your board of directors.
>
> Having more of my money invested in your stock than some of your directors who get paid fees concerns me somewhat. But my major concern is that you do things that invite attention and distrust because they appear unethical, illegal, short-sighted, or just plain greedy, and contrary to what investors and consumers are entitled to expect. Isn't this a legitimate basis for questioning the standards of conduct for your executives? Isn't this a legitimate reason to question the justification for the huge salaries, bonuses, and stock options you give yourselves?
>
> I know I have the alternative of removing my funds from the company and investing them elsewhere. The news article, however, suggests that the standards you set for your conduct, and your performance, are typical of all big business. That leaves me

Ralph Nader's group nominates 10 companies for Hall of Shame

They won't tell you, so we will.

They are 10 major USA companies, and what they won't tell you is they've been named to the 1983 Corporate Hall of Shame.

For outstanding achievement in "unethical conduct, narrowness of vision, lack of foresight, and unwaveringly steady focus on the short-term bottom line," Ralph Nader and the Corporate Accountability Group bring you:

■ Dow Chemical Co.: Refused to settle charges brought by Vietnam veterans claiming Agent Orange injuries.

■ Eli Lilly and Co: Said it acted "responsibly and ethically" when marketing arthritis drug Oraflex in the USA, although the public already knew that Lilly knew of Oraflex-related deaths overseas.

■ FMC Corp.: Led a nationwide effort to enact laws curtailing victims' rights to just compensation for injuries inflicted by defective products.

■ General Motors Corp.: Lobbied to defeat auto safety standards requiring USA automakers to put airbags or passive belts in all autos by last fall.

■ General Public Utilities Corp.: Pushed for federal OK to restart nuclear generators at Three Mile Island just after GPU's operating unit was indicted on charges of falsifying 1979 safety-test results at TMI.

■ Manville Corp.: Used the bankruptcy process to avert financial responsibilty for asbestos-related injury claims.

■ Mellon Bank: Loaned millions of dollars to Japanese steel makers while foreclosing on USA steel company loans.

■ The Nestle Co. Inc.: Ignored the World Health Organization by aggressively marketing infant formula in the Third World.

■ Sperry Corp.: Overcharged the Air Force $325,000 for missile guidance work.

■ Upjohn Co.: Continued to campaign for government approval of Depo-Provera — a suspected carcinogenic contraceptive the company wants to market in the USA.

How 'bout a big hand for the winners.

Figure 5–7 Ralph Nader's group nominates ten companies for hall of shame. (Reprinted with permission of *USA Today.*)

no place to go except to foreign businesses, or to government with demands that they regulate you more strictly, or take over your industry and run it for the benefit of everyone. Frankly, your speeches complaining about regulation leave me a bit cold.

Isn't it high time that you businessmen took the lead in self-discipline so that government and everybody else have real leadership to follow?

This letter has been passed down the line, and it stops with you. The note of instruction on it reads: "We may get a bundle of letters pretty much like this one. Upstairs [the president's office] they want a reply, to be signed by the president. Let's see what you can come up with."

1. What will you do before you fire up your word processor to write the letter?
2. Write a draft of the letter with a cover sheet explaining to the president the rationale for your approach.

Chapter 6

Consumer Relations

"Who are the three most important publics?" asks an old trick question. The answer is "Customers, customers, and customers." If you don't succeed in attracting and then building continuing relationships with them, you'll be out of business and nothing else will matter.

During the rise of marketing as a cure-all in the mid-1980s, this view frequently prevailed in corporations. Hospitals, universities, public agencies, and even churches adopted marketing as a response to the increasing competition for people's interest and dollars. On balance, the marketing revolution was helpful to many organizations—particularly large or very successful companies, which had often forgotten that it is the customer who pays the bill, and to not-for-profit entities, who often treated users of services as a nuisance to their routine, rather than the reason for their existence.

Ironically, while this trend reestablished a key point of public relations philosophy, it sometimes pushed public relations departments into a secondary role to marketing. A much debated point has been whether public relations is a part of marketing or vice versa or whether they are both essential strategic services and thus equal factors.

The question has become prominent because marketing has become a part of organizations that have not traditionally used marketing concepts. Hospitals in particular began marketing their "products" in an effort to gain their share of the health care market. Their patients began making it clear they did not want to be *sold* health care, and hospitals retreated—putting the function back into perspective.

Marketing and public relations share some fundamental concepts. These include analyzing market opportunities (research), selecting target markets (publics), developing a marketing mix (communication and action plan), and managing the marketing effort (evaluation).

The sharing of these concepts illustrates the close working relationship of the two fields. However, public relations and marketing are two different fields. *pr reporter* illustrated the differences, stating that public relations as a strategy does four things marketing cannot do:

> Public relations is concerned about internal relations and publics.
>
> Public relations cares about noncustomer external publics and the environment in which the organization operates.
>
> Public relations operates on the policies of human nature (what makes the individual tick), whereas marketing focuses on consumer behavior (purchasing and economics, often expressed in number-crunching research).
>
> Public relations may work to stabilize or change public opinion in areas other than products.[1]

In the 1990s, the functions have come close together, as demonstrated by the dominant customer relations strategy: relationship marketing. As the name suggests, this approach adopts public relations principles such as personalized, one-on-one dialogue regarding marketing of products and services.

The buyer-seller relationship concerns every public relations department and every public relations counselor. Ideally, their role is to help create conditions of understanding so that the objectives of sellers can be attained by satisfying needs of consumers. As a landmark conference between public relations and marketing leaders concluded,[2] public relations must both help motivate purchases *and* create a hospitable environment for the organization to sell product and services.

HISTORICAL BACKGROUND

Starting in the late 1940s, following an almost universal base of hardship during the Great Depression, consumer "wants" were for material possessions, labor saving, convenience, ease, and luxury. To producers and sellers, these were seen as consumer "needs." In the succeeding decades of increasing prosperity and affluence, it followed that if a product or service could be sold, it "deserved" to be sold. If a desire for it could be induced, it was what the people "wanted." Wants translated with adept interpretation into needs. A Hula Hoop, a Frisbee, a pair of jogging shoes became "needs" for wholesome recreation or health.

For product and service sellers, the 1950s were happy times, as they were for marketing, promotion, advertising, and publicity people. The economy was based and dependent on increasing consumption. Trading in one's car annually, building a summer home, discarding clothes for each fashion change, engaging in fads, buying on time with credit cards, maintaining a big mortgage, stocking a basement with ap-

---

[1]*pr reporter* (January 2, 1984.): 27. p. 3.

[2]"A Challenge to the Calling: Public Relations Colloquium 1989" held at San Diego State University on January 24, 1989, sponsored by Nuffer Smith & Tucker.

pliances, using hair tonics and electric shavers—these were "marks of distinction." Buying was promoted as though it were patriotic. Communications served these times well, especially when television came on the scene to give printed and audio media rough competition.

In this set of conditions, it was inevitable that sellers would stretch the boundaries of quality, service, and safety in products and services. They would exceed the limits of truth and accuracy in their claims and would abuse the privilege of using the public media. On occasion, through inadequate concern for quality, they would kill and injure some people and alienate many others.[3]

The first significant government restraint in the 1960s came in the Kefauver-Harris Drug Act in 1962. Through the decade, other federal laws were passed, involving abuses in packaging, labeling, product safety, drugs, and truth in lending. Early in the game, Ralph Nader showed up with his *Unsafe at Any Speed* (see Case 5-2). Regulatory agencies became more active and aggressive.[4] A presidential assistant was appointed to represent and help protect the consumer. A tough adversary relationship was established for business.

Meanwhile, business approaches to the consumer were shifting. "Share of mind" superseded "share of market" for many national product advertisers. Programs spoke more about "benefits" and "value." Publicists were engaged more in concepts to sell "an idea," "industrial statesmanship," "a good company to do business with," the "philosophy" or the "personality" rather than the sheer pleasure of owning the product or enjoying the service.

In public relations programming, there was an increasing shift to use of public service hitched to marketing. Recipes were provided for home economists; commemorative events were tied to products; dinosaur models went on exhibit; cars were tested by the loan of one to each family in a small town; a blimp roamed over public events, aiding national telecasts. The introduction of a new line of sports equipment endorsed by a celebrated athlete might be accompanied by a personal appearance. On tour, the athlete might sign autographs in stores, be interviewed by local writers on controversial sports subjects, be photographed at bedside in children's hospitals or wards, and conduct free clinics on sportsmanship at a local school.

- Today this approach has become the rule: People want to be *served* not sold.

Further business response to growing consumer protectionism and advocacy came in the activation of ombudspersons, 800 numbers, understandable warranty statements, devices for improved listenership and response, calls to customers to

---

[3]For further insight, see Earl W. Kintner, *A Primer on the Law of Deceptive Practices* (New York: Macmillan, 1971).

[4]Early cases of Federal Trade Commission intervention and decision concern Carter's Little Liver Pills in the 1950s and Geritol in the 1960s. There are many others more recent.

check satisfaction after purchase, quick settlement of injury claims, and product recalls. This attitude gave even more importance to public relations and its implementation, but it did not stop all the abuses. Television commercials were louder by several decibels than entertainment broadcasts. Among the largest advertisers were makers of products that were the most profitable but among the least necessary to human survival or uplift—cosmetics, liquor, and tobacco, to name a few. Going into the 1970s, consumer disenchantment with sellers, their wares, and their words expressed itself, as more and more awareness of the alternatives and here and there a boycott.

In 1970, Federal Communications Commission (FCC) Commissioner Nicholas Johnson raised and answered his own question of alternatives. "How can we make life in the corporate state more livable and more human?" His personal approach was to plan an "ideal day." In it he found fundamental elements to be love, beauty, contemplation of some kind, personal analysis, creative expression, contact with nature, and some participation in the support of one's life. He included such measures as riding a bicycle; throwing away expendable things in the house; and using bicarbonate of soda for toothpaste, gargle, mouthwash, burn ointment, stomach settler, room freshener, fire extinguisher, refrigerator cleaner, children's clay, and baking powder—at less than twenty-five cents a box.

He jotted down his thoughts on the basic elements of life. One of his observations was that "when people live their lives in ways that take them too far from these basic truths, they begin to show up in the rising statistics indicating social disintegration, crimes of violence, alcoholism, drug addiction, suicide, mental illness and so forth."[5]

THE LINK BETWEEN REPUTATION AND MARKETING

In the 1980s, a new rash of crises shared the front page; they involved violence, drugs, greed, pollution, and lack of integrity. Business has adjusted to this situation. Advertising and publicity talk about reforestation, human dignity, education, rehabilitation, and "caring." Projects and speeches focus on safety, health, and the minority, neglected, and handicapped groups in society.

There are other problems. Conglomeration and divestiture tarnish traditional identities. What happens when Armour, not only a prestigious name on a pound of bacon but a landmark at the Chicago stockyards and a family intertwined for generations in the culture and society of the city, is swallowed into a bus company, also with a well-known name, Greyhound? Or when Twinkies becomes a product of International Telephone and Telegraph? Or when the Bell System disappears and spawns Nynex, U.S. West, and Sprint, among others?

Multinationalism is another matter. Does anything significant happen in con-

[5]Nicholas Johnson, "Test Pattern for Living," *Saturday Review,* May 29, 1971.

sumer relationships when a company that has proclaimed its "loyal American heritage" goes abroad to manufacture because wages are lower?

THE ROLE OF PUBLIC RELATIONS

Technically, both marketing and public relations support the *sales* function. "Nothing happens until a sale is made," says an old bromide. The difference is that marketing is totally engrossed in selling, whereas public relations is more holistic. It supports sales to customers, but also is concerned with relationships with all other stakeholders of the organization.

Originally, public relations supported sales almost exclusively through media publicity, promotional events, and consumer information programs. The objective was to make people:

1. Aware of the product or service in the first place.
2. Knowledgeable about the benefits and advantages of the particular product or service.
3. Constantly reminded and reinforced in favorable feelings toward the product or service.

Such activity ties in with advertising and authenticates product claims. Media used are newspapers, magazines, radio, television, features, photos, planned events, sponsorship of sports or musical activities, and many other venues for promotion. These are one-way communication vehicles touting the name and claims of the product or service.

Although the emphasis on marketing pushed some public relations departments back to this role, the changing conditions of the marketplace also brought forth several new activities such as:

1. Forming user groups (as computer makers did) or customer service departments (as some auto makers and utilities did) to personally build customer loyalty.
2. Adopting customer satisfaction programs in which the entire organization is focused on delivering not just a product or service but also the quality and personal interactions consumers expect when making a purchase (as retailers, utilities, and brand manufacturers did).
3. Concentrating the publicity and promotion activities on taking customers away from competitors (which the beer and cigarette makers state as their primary reason for publicity and advertising).
4. Protecting the reputation of the product or service, and of the organization, in a period of consumer activism, government regulation, competitive predation, global marketing, and similar conditions that bring a continual bevy of public issues to bear on every organization and industry.

REFERENCES AND ADDITIONAL READINGS

AAKER, DAVID A. *Managing Brand Equity.* New York: Free Press, 1991.

BROOM, GLEN M. and KERRY TUCKER. Marketing Public Relations: An Essential Double Helix." *Public Relations Journal* v45 (November 1993): 39–40.

CRISPELL, DIANE. "What's in a brand?" *American Demographics* 15 (May 1993): 26–32.

CUTLIP, SCOTT M., ALLEN H. CENTER, and GLEN M. BROOM. "Consumer Affairs and the 'Marketing Mix'." Chapter 14 in *Effective Public Relations.* 7th ed. Englewood Cliffs, N.J.: Prentice Hall, 1994.

DAVIDSON, KENNETH M. "How to Improve Business Relationships." *Journal of Business Strategy* 14 (May/June 1993): 13–15.

DEGEN, CLARA, ed *Communicators' Guide to Marketing.* New York: Longman, 1990.

FELTON, JOHN A. "Consumer Affairs and Consumerism." Chapter 16 in *Lesly's Public Relations Handbook.* 4th ed. Chicago, IL: Probus, 1990.

FEEMAN, LAURIE. "Direct Contact Key to Building Brands." *Advertising Age* 64 (October 25, 1993): S2.

HARDESTY, MONICA J. "Information Tactics and the Maintenance of Asymmetry in Physician-Patient Relationships," D. R. Maines and C. J. Couch, eds, *Communication and Social Structure*, Springfield, IL: Charles C. Thomas, 1988, 39–58.

Harns, Thomas L. *The Marketer's Guide to Public Relations.* New York: John Wiley & Sons, Inc., 1993.

The International Customer Service Association (ICSA) has a variety of materials related to the understanding of the total quality service process and encouraging professional dialogue in the achievement of customer satisfaction. For more information, write to ICSA, 401 N. Michigan Ave., Chicago, IL 60611-4267.

KOTLER, PHILIP. *Principles of Marketing.* 2nd ed. Englewood Cliffs, N.J.: Prentice Hall, 1983.

LERBINGER, OTTO, and NATHANIEL N. SPERBER. "Consumer Affairs." Chapter 4 in *Manager's Public Relations Handbook.* Reading, Mass.: Addison-Wesley, 1982.

MAZUR, LAURA. "A Consuming Ambition." *Marketing* (January 13, 1994), 23–24.

MCMANUS, JOHN. "Disaster Lessons Learned: Customer's Lifetime Value." *Brandweek* v35 (January 24, 1994): 16.

MURPHY, JOHN M. *Brand Strategy.* Englewood Cliffs, N.J.: Prentice Hall, 1990.

OTT, RICHARD. *Creating Demand.* Homewood, IL: Business One Irwin, 1991.

The Public Relations Body of Knowledge. New York: PRSA, 1993. See section V.6 for abstracts dealing with "Marketing, Marketing Support and Consumer Relations."

pr reporter March 21, 1994. Elements on making your organization customer-friendly.

RICH, JUDITH. "Public Relations and Marketing." Chapter 14 in *Lesly's Public Relations Handbook.* 4th ed. Chicago, IL: Probus, 1990.

SANFORD, DAVID, and RALPH NADER, et al. *Hot War on the Consumer.* New York: Pitman, 1969.

WILCOX, DENNIS L., PHILLIP H. AULT, and WARREN K. AGEE. *Public Relations Strategy and Tactics.* 3rd ed. New York: HarperCollins, 1992. See chapter 14.

ZANDE, IRMA and RICHARD LEONARD. *Targeting the Trend-Setting Consumer.* Homewood, IL: Business One Irwin, 1991.

Case 6–1

The Changing Kingdom
of Coors

Times change. Organizations change in structure, in the products or services they provide, in their scope, in the values projected by their leaders, and in the public impression they wish to convey. Sometimes change is evolutionary, as with organizations committed to clothing fashions, automobile design, or nutritional and health values. Sometimes change is sudden or drastic, as in bankruptcy, change of owners, or a catastrophic event.

The public relations function, by whatever name, is an agent for change within an organization. Two-way interpretation of the organization's relationship to the greater public good, and the use of two-way communications to adjust an organization to the publics on which it depends for success or failure, can be expected to change over time in form and emphasis. The necessity for interpretive input and output, and for reconciliation of public and private interests, never goes out of style.

Change and adjustment characterize the dynamics of almost any organization, large or small, local or national, competitive or nonprofit, private or governmental. Making adjustments to changing conditions will constitute part of every practitioner's career regardless of the organizations served. For our classic example of a company's adaptation to change, we turn again to the Adolph Coors Brewing Company, (see Case 4-6), a consumer-oriented organization with a philosophical mind of its own. Its basic product is widely known and consumed.

A MAVERICK AMONG BREWERS

For many years Coors operated contrary to some of the most widely accepted textbook ideas about what constitutes success in financing and running a business and in marketing its products. The differences were enough to raise some eyebrows—and some envy—within the beer industry, and in business circles generally, not to

204

IMAGE VERSUS REPUTATION

An *image* is false, not real. Consider a snapshot, which is an image of the person photographed and not the person. *Reputations* are based on experience with a product, service, or company—or the expression of trusted comrades. Which would you rather have—a good image, or a good reputation?

mention the consternation caused among politicians whose approach to public issues was generally moderate and safe. Coors, as a company and a family, was outspoken. The prognosis by qualified analysts was not optimistic. Yet few products in America can claim the mystique of Coors beer. Demand was so great that until the "Beer Wars" of the late 1970s—when marketing came into the staid industry in a big way—Coors actually had to ration its beer to wholesalers. Travelers to states where it was sold brought it home in their luggage as treasured contraband. A popular movie, *Smokey and the Bandit,* was about a trucker illegally bootlegging a whole trailer of Coors into a state where the company did not distribute its products.

THE COORS STORY FROM THE BEGINNING

The original Adolph Coors—a quiet, private man—was born in Rhenish Prussia in 1847. He was taken to Westphalia and at the age of fifteen was apprenticed as a bookkeeper. Five years later, he left and worked for breweries in Berlin and Kassel. Orphaned, he set out for the United States in 1868. He worked off his passage in Baltimore, went to Chicago and worked first on the Illinois-Michigan Canal. Later he became a brewery foreman in nearby Naperville, Illinois. In 1872, at twenty-five, he was attracted to Denver, where he entered business, bottling wines and beer. Before the year was out, he sold that business. He and Jacob Schueler purchased a brewery site in Golden, Colorado, in the Rocky Mountain foothills a few miles west of Denver. The brewery was opened in 1873, three years before Colorado joined the Union.

Times were lean from 1917 to 1933 partly because of prohibition and the Depression but the company survived by producing malt and other items. When prohibition was repealed, Coors was ready.

Adolph Coors, Sr., died in 1929, but family management continued. By 1958, Adolph Coors III had become chairman of Adolph Coors Brewing Company and its subsidiary, Coors Porcelain. In 1960, however, Adolph III died at the hands of a kidnapper. His brother William, second son of Adolph, Jr., and president of Coors, took command. His brother Joseph headed the Coors Porcelain Company. By this time, Coors had become the fourth largest U.S. brewer.

SUCCESS IS WHAT YOU MAKE IT

Some characteristics set Coors apart from other family businesses:

1. Coors had been a regional company, limiting its sales to eleven states. The brewers ahead of it were national in their distribution. Thus, for Coors to attain fourth rank nationally, its acceptance in those eleven states had to be phenomenal, running as high as forty percent of the market.

2. A barrel of beer weighs more than 260 pounds. Nearly 11 million barrels, traveling an average distance of 900 miles each, add up to a lot of transportation expense. Still, Coors had one brewery, the world's largest, in Golden, rather than several closer to major market areas.

3. In attaining its size, the company had refused to borrow money. Growth had been financed out of earnings.

4. Coors production was remarkably integrated vertically; the firm built most of its own packaging, brewing, and malting equipment and produced its own beer cans. It also operated a major transportation company to move its beer to market and a small railroad to move items around its extensive plant site.

5. Coors's management style was informal, to the point that employees called the president by his first name. Bill Coors resembled a professional football coach in the off-season, working with cuffed shirtsleeves in a spartan office that contained an extra desk for his brother Joe. Their clerical assistance came from a secretarial pool.

6. Employee tenure was long, with attitudes generally characterized by pride and loyalty, in a family spirit. Supervisory employees didn't "go to work at Coors," they were "with" Coors. Executives were "Coors executives," almost as if indentured. Salaries were good, "for the locality." There were not some of the usual fringes such as bonuses associated with profitability. Promotion from within was the policy. All eleven members of the company's board were full-time employees. The use of outside experts tended to be avoided.

7. The company hewed to its own value standards and spoke its mind in public issues. Coors family values—austerity, dedication to hard work, honesty, pride in the best-quality product possible, and a rugged individualism that valued highly personal and corporate prerogatives—had been handed down from generation to generation. Sometimes, however, these values led to misunderstandings and accusations.[1]

---

[1]On one occasion, the FTC had charged Coors with some heavy-handed sales techniques when they refused to sell draft beer to bars unless they carried it exclusively and in insisting that wholesalers not cut prices. Referring to this episode, *Fortune* magazine said, "Bill Coors is astonished that anyone would challenge his control over his product, and he vows to fight all the way to the Supreme Court." Later, the FTC ruled that the company had "illegally restrained competition." At that time, Bill Coors put his position to a *Wall Street Journal* reporter this way: "If we have to, we'll take over distribution ourselves, and Coors will become the biggest beer distributor in the world."

8. When it came to the use of communications for marketing, Coors admitted that its Coors Banquet Beer was "the most expensively brewed beer in the world" and felt that this fact kept the demand greater than the supply without shouting about it. Its advertising had been "less than $1 a barrel," or a fraction of what major competitors spent. Here again, the do-it-yourself philosophy prevailed. An in-house staff prepared what ads and promotional pieces were used.

COORS PRESS AND PUBLIC RELATIONS

Coors's public relations was inhibited by a tight-lipped, reactive attitude where financial or competitive information was involved. Because the company was family-owned and sought no outside funding, there was no need for management to reveal these matters and no self-interest benefit. The few investors to whom an accounting had to be made could, theoretically, gather for dinner at Bill's or Joe's house.

The policies of promoting from within and avoiding the use of outside experts tended to eliminate publicity or public relations projects that might have the objective of attracting executive recruits. The employment of thousands in Golden, coupled with the Coors family's civic and charitable contributions in the Golden-Denver area, left little for public relations professionals to deal with in community relations.

In public affairs and on public issues, the brothers were both "the corporation" and the "corporate view." They need not wait for a consensus, nor need they use indirect channels in addressing the community, the trade, or local or federal officials.

In product marketing, with one product, the publicity thrust was to enhance the mystique of success. Elements of production were mountain spring water, Moravian barley, Californian and Southern rice, modern brewing equipment, shipment under refrigeration, and the resulting light pilsner brew.

By putting all this together, or perhaps by a process of elimination, the public relations function could properly have been called the "public service information function," performed if, as, and when requested.

A SHIFT OF TACTICS IN THE MAKING

By the mid-1970s, there was good reason to conclude that Coors had better make some changes in attitudes and tactics or go down the competitive tube. Events had hit Coors like a series of jabs to the face and body. Among them:

1. A union boycott starting with a strike had harmful echoes due to contentions that Coors discriminated against African-Americans, Hispanics, and females in employment.

2. Anheuser-Busch, by aggressive marketing, had cut deeply into Coors's domination of some major markets such as California. Other brewers responded to Budweiser's and Miller's bold marketing—and the "Beer Wars" were on. Initially, Coors declined to join in, which resulted in loss of market share.

3. Light, lower-calorie beer had caught on, and Coors had no entry in the field.

4. Coors had come up with a punch-top can opener that gave customers more problems than the familiar flip-top openers of competitors.

5. The trend was to fewer brewers, mainly national in scope, as local beers fell by the wayside.

6. Anticipating inheritance tax requirements, the company had to go public, raising the possibility of outside shareholder voices in its decision-making process. All voting stock, however, remained with the family.

7. Some of management's right-wing views, expressed mainly by President Joe Coors (a member of Ronald Reagan's "kitchen cabinet"), and widely reported in the news, were of no help in broadening public support in the consumer market.

SYMPTOMS OF A TURNABOUT BECOME VEHICLES

Led by public relations and marketing departments, several significant actions were taken to reverse the business downslide and bid for broad public support. A lengthy *Wall Street Journal* article put it this way:

> The company has embarked on an elaborate image-building campaign, running nostalgic ads about corporate history and messages beamed at ethnic minorities, homosexuals, union members, women's rights activists and others who may be harboring ill will against Coors.
>
> The campaign also includes a telecommunications course for Coors executives—traditionally distrustful of the media—who are subjected to intense baiting by communicators stimulating "obnoxious reporters." The notion is to condition the managers to project charm, humility and control for real interviews.[2]

Another tactic was the disarming public admission of past arrogance, articulated by the new generation of Coors management, Jeff, then president of operations, and Peter, then president of marketing and administration.

On the product front, Coors introduced a low-calorie light beer. An outside advertising agency was retained, and a budget of some $87 million was allocated for advertising and promotion. It has since grown to over $200 million.

---

[2]John Huey, "Men at Coors Beer Find the Old Ways Don't Work Anymore," *Wall Street Journal,* January 19, 1979.

This new approach encouraged the company to become more involved on the public relations front. Candor and visibility replaced "no comment" and low profile. Coors was out in the open competitively, and on the record publicly.[3]

A Corporate Public Affairs Division took shape. Its charter, publicly stated, was to

> appraise employee, public and government attitudes, problems and opportunities . . . initiate and improve programs developing an economic, social and political climate which will assist [in operating] profitably, thereby enabling employees and community neighbors to work, enjoy life, and prosper.

Implementation of the charter in the form of charitable contributions and donations, as one example, was explained in a booklet (see Figure 6-1).

Coors's ultimate objective was linked to public relations—*to building, or rebuilding, relationships that would let its products speak for themselves in the marketplace.* For public relations staff, the goal was "removing the political litmus test" that seemed to surround all the company's actions. The focus was on the boycott.[4] As with any program seeking to attain a turnaround of 180 degrees, there were bound to be some communications hitches along the way.

THE BOYCOTTS

The first boycott started in 1960 when the Coors family donated a helicopter to the Denver Police Department, which was under criticism (as were many white majority city police departments) for allegedly trying to keep minorities in the ghettos. For a variety of reasons, Coors employees voted to decertify their union. In 1977 the AFL-CIO called for a boycott of Coors products supposedly because of the company's practice of using lie detector tests in employee investigations and hiring. Several contractual issues were mentioned as well—because the unions wanted to regain their position at the company. This boycott ended in 1987 when labor agreed to stop it if Coors would hold a union certification election. (Workers voted not to have a union.)

In 1984, Chairman Bill Coors seemed to put a blemish on some of the views that they had worked so hard to change. Speaking off the cuff in a speech at a semi-

---

[3]By 1984, outside counseling services used had included Manning, Selvage and Lee, Carl Byoir and Associates; The Johnston Group; and Jackson Jackson & Wagner.

[4]Of special interest, in 1983 Coors welcomed the CBS *60 Minutes* program to look into allegations of bias toward unions and minorities long plaguing the company. Host Mike Wallace found the charges against the company basically untrue. Public relations director Shirley Richards and her staff had shown how to defang the tiger by openness and absolute candor.

Making an Impact On Illiteracy—One Person At A Time. If not for the Los Angeles Urban League Milken Family Literacy Center, Ralph Lee might very well be unemployed today. The 39 year-old Los Angeles native initially read at the 3.5 grade level, but thanks to his tutors at the Center, he now reads at the 7th grade level and was able to qualify for a full-time maintenance job at the Los Angeles Free Clinic. Lee looks forward to taking math and English classes at a junior college and is interested in writing poetry, things he never imagined he would be able to do.

Literacy tutor Liz Moseley listens as student Ralph Lee reads during sessions at the Los Angeles Urban League Literacy Center.

The Center's counselor began work with Lee by determining what he wanted to get out of the class. "I just wanted to learn how to read," says Lee, who attends tutoring sessions at least twice weekly. Having grown up in a large family, he recalls a sense of becoming lost in the crowd during his early teens, both at home and at school.

Lee works on a one-to-one basis with his volunteer tutors and has nothing but praise and appreciation for them. Liz Moseley is one of his tutors and has worked with Ralph Lee for about a year. Upon moving from San Francisco to Los Angeles in 1980, she found herself without family or community ties. "Helping others is something so basic to me. It is so easy to give," says Moseley, who began by working with children. Moseley says it is gratifying to see her students develop more self-confidence in the supportive environment offered by the Center.

Moseley is described by Literacy Coordinator LaVone Barnett as one of a number of consistent, core volunteers who gives her time and has been instrumental in planning and implementing special programs and activities for the classroom. She has volunteered over a hundred hours, and donates class supplies and materials to assist her learners.

Moseley is also involved in a mentoring program at a local junior high, and is a member of the Los Angeles Chapter of Young Black Professionals, for whom she produces a newsletter each month.

Both Lee and Moseley were honored for their achievements when Coors hosted them and their guests at the 19th Annual Whitney M. Young, Jr. Award Dinner. The two were joined by Dale Blow, who entered the program in 1990 as an elementary student learner. Dale is now in junior high school and has improved his reading and math levels by two full grades.

The Literacy Center, through funding from corporate sponsors such as Coors, provides services in reading, math, writing, listening and problem solving to disadvantaged youth and adults. Since opening its doors, the center has helped more than 800 students·improve their reading skills.

Figure 6–1 Coors's community giving program has flourished and expanded, addressing many community needs. (Courtesy of Coors Brewing Company.)

nar of the minority Business Development Center in Denver, Coors said that Africa's economic problems stemmed from a lack of intellectual capacity. This comment caused a furor in some quarters and reenergized the boycott. Coors sued the *Rocky Mountain News* because the headline that made the charges was not supported by facts in the story itself. (An out-of-court settlement resulted.)

Many distributors and marketers felt the boycott was thwarting their best efforts. Historically, however, product boycotts are rarely effective. Company research found that very few beer consumers were even aware of the boycott. Even those who knew about it were seldom persuaded to avoid the product, except in certain union areas where anti-Coors activities made the brand socially unacceptable. Fewer than four percent of retail accounts were refusing to sell the brand.

Furthermore, among those who were brand avoiders, the labor issues were much less often the reason than were the allegations of discriminatory practices against minorities. The AFL-CIO made these issues the centerpiece of its campaign, and though Coors and its workers strongly denied the accusations, they had some effect in the African-American and Hispanic communities, which are important markets for beer.

Still, sales were rising. Coors moved into new states successfully despite AFL-CIO activity to discredit them there. (By 1989, the company served all fifty states plus several foreign markets.) Public relations counsel concluded: "The boycott is not working in the marketplace, but it is very successful in the headquarters at Golden, Colorado." Stronger efforts were called for.

THE NEW APPROACH PAYS OFF

The sequential phases of disarming critics, going public, and reaching out for the national market had major punctuation marks:[5]

1. Coors signed a National Agreement with a Coalition of Hispanic Organizations, giving assurances of employment, training for management roles, increased number of Hispanic distributorships, increased use of Hispanic vendors and services, and a minimum of $500,000 annually to be spent in public service programs in the Hispanic community.

2. Earlier, Coors had entered into a National Incentive Covenant with the National Black Economic Development Coalition with much the same assurances and objectives. In both cases, company actions were linked to assistance in its marketing efforts from the other party—quid pro quo.

---

[5]Typical of the openness in present-day public relations at Coors, we were supplied a generous bundle of current information to update this case. There were no questions designed to make sure we were a "friendly" medium and no defensive ruse such as "we'll be glad to check your case study for accuracy." We are indebted to Marvin "Swede" Johnson, Vice-President of Corporate Communications for the information provided for this case.

3. The company undertook diversification into gas and oil exploration, snack foods, transportation, and occupational health.

4. New products included Coors Extra Gold, George Killian's Irish Red Ale, and Herman Joseph's Original Draft.

5. Plans were announced for the creation of a second brewery, located in the Shenandoah Valley of Virginia (see Figure 6-2) which began operations in 1987. The company added another brewery in 1990, which is located in Memphis, Tennessee.

6. An annual report displayed a statement of corporate philosophy. It was titled "Our Values" and summarized as "Quality in all we do and are." This became the theme of communication efforts.

7. Coors's V.I.C.E. Squad volunteer program (Volunteers In Community Enrichment) was recognized as a model for linking employees, retirees, and their families with community needs. So well received was the activity that a new adjunct group was established for people who had no connection with the company (see Case 4-6).

Figure 6–2   The Shenandoah Valley brewery at Elkton. (Courtesy of Adolph Coors Brewing Company.)

8. Coors' Wellness Program, created in 1981 by Bill Coors, was honored in 1992 with the C. Everett Koop National Health Award for commitment to health and wellness as a priority for employees.

9. The 10-millionth visitor took the company's highly personalized plant tour in May 1988.

10. In 1987, Coors became the first brewer to target women specifically in full-page magazine ads (see Figure 6–3). A major women's program that increased awareness about breast cancer won awards and showed that allegations of bias were unfounded (see Figure 6–4).

There was more. The year 1987 was a busy on in Coors's public affairs. Joe Coors took a turn as a witness in the Iran-Contra Congressional hearings and testified that he had contributed $65,000 to Colonel North's supply operation for the Nicaraguan rebels (or freedom fighters, if you prefer). Finally, the AFL-CIO was per-

PERSONALITY, VIEWS, AND PRODUCTS

A recurrent question in organizational public relationships is the extent to which the personality (abrasive or charming), the political affiliation (liberal, moderate, or conservative), or the views on controversial issues (such as birth control, privacy, and the public's right to know) influence consumer purchase decisions. Do they or don't they?

Domino's Pizza experienced a boycott similar to Coors's. The National Organization of Women (NOW) claimed that Domino's CEO Tom Monaghan discriminates against women, by funding programs that attempt to eliminate reproductive choices. This allegation arose when Monaghan donated $50,000 to a Michigan ballot measure outlawing tax-funded abortions. NOW spokeswoman Madeline Han-sen emphasized awareness as the focus of the boycott. "We're not telling people not to buy his pizza, but we are telling them where their money goes when they do."[6] In response to this charge, Domino's defense was that Monaghan's donation was a personal contribution.

In every locality, there are prominent, outspoken individuals whose conduct of their businesses, views on public issues, and displays of personality and character constitute mixed, if not confused, public images. It would be helpful to their public relations counsel to know whether, and under what circumstances, their expressions and actions unrelated to business adversely influence customer purchases of their products or services. Research among customers, noncustomers, and critics might provide a clue.[7]

---

[6]*pr reporter,* May 29, 1989, Vol. 32. pp 2 and 3.

[7]Refer to Case 9-4, Dayton Hudson, for further study.

Figure 6–3 Settings for women in Coors ads suggest energy and activity, not necessarily sensuality or submissiveness. (Courtesy of Adolph Coors Brewing Company.)

I never shower alone.

And neither should you. Because simply by hanging this free card in your shower, you could save your own life.

You see, this shower card will show you how to do monthly breast self exam-ination. And remind you to do it. This is vitally impor-tant. Because even though 1 in 10 women will develop breast cancer, 90% of those cancers are controllable if detected early.

So send for your free Coors/High Priority Shower Card today. Then put it in your shower and use it. And if you're over 35, ask your doctor about getting a mammogram. Because in the fight against cancer, we're not alone.

HIGH PRIORITY
Breast Cancer Research/Information Network
of the AMC Cancer Research Center

Coors

© 1987 Adolph Coors Company, Golden, Colorado 80401
Brewer of Fine Quality Beers Since 1873

For your free Coors/High Priority Shower Card, send this coupon to the AMC Cancer Research Center at: Shower Card, Box 1987, Denver, CO 80201.

NAME

ADDRESS

CITY   STATE   ZIP

One card per coupon. Offer good while supplies last.

Do it

Cher, High Priority
Charter Member

Figure 6–4 Coors's breast cancer awareness program, High Priority, encouraged women to do monthly breast self-examinations. (Courtesy of Adolph Coors Brewing Company.)

suaded to call off its ten-year boycott in negotiations, led by Peter Coors, based on carefully crafted public relations strategy that has served to deter any follow-up na-tional boycotts to date. Joe Coors, Sr., announced near year end that he was plan-ning to step down from day-to-day operations. He remained within earshot as vice-chairman, while his brother Bill remained as chairman. But actual management

Figure 6–5 Still a no-necktie management dress code. The Coors family members active in management are, from the left, Jeff, Joe, Joe Jr., Bill, and Pete. (Courtesy of Adolph Coors Brewing Company.)

passed to the new team of Peter and Jeff (both sons of Joe). Joe Jr. began moving up into top ranks (see Figure 6-5).

These new faces have been well received, and under their management the company has prospered despite a bad economy and a flat beer market. Coors is now the third largest brewer in the United States. Not too bad for a company some predicted a few years earlier would fail when it was targeted for the longest-running boycott in recent history.

QUESTIONS FOR DISCUSSION

1. List all the reasons you can think of why a company's reputation, or its executives', influence the sale of its products or services. Then list all the reasons why it does not. Do you conclude that when people reach for a Coors they are thinking of the company's reputation—or merely concerned with quenching their thirst? Or both?

2. Some companies, such as Coors and Ford, have the founding family's name on the door. What discipline does this identity demand from members of the family, especially in terms of public relationships? What problems might be created for public relations staff? Overall, is this situation an advantage or a disadvantage in operating the enterprise successfully?

3. What types of reactive strategies could have been developed by Domino's in response to NOW's allegations of discrimination? What proactive strategies would help prevent future crises?

4. Can a prominent businessperson, whose fortune came from the business, distinguish "personal" actions from those of the company? Why or why not?

The Hamburger Wars

As John Kenneth Galbraith observed in *The Affluent Society,* consumer "wants" are culturally developed. They are aggressively nurtured and promoted by those who produce products and services to sell.

Marketing is the main link between production and consumption. Under the marketing umbrella, advertising and sales promotion events reinforced and extended by publicity, form a merchandising triad.

Sometimes the competition becomes so intense that grenades are lobbed back and forth in the form of claims and counterclaims. Sometimes they go beyond exaggeration to the point where truthfulness, even fairness, may become subject to question, as often happens when new or small competitors seek to enter or dramatically increase their share of a market dominated by one supplier. It can happen when a major marketer displays a vulnerability by becoming complacent or by "milking" the marketplace. It can happen when competition tightens and there just isn't enough business for everybody to make a profit. Some may become desperate.

When competition is so fierce that the benefits to consumers become questionable, government, as a referee, may intervene. In consumer affairs this job generally falls to the Federal Trade Commission (FTC).

In these "wars of words," consumers rarely consider that they will ultimately pay for it all—the costs of selling increase but the value of the product or service does not. These costs eventually are recovered by marketers, usually in the form of higher prices.

It might have been one or a combination of circumstances that led competitors and observers, such as financial analysts, to forecast that the fast-food market was approaching a point of saturation in the 1980s. There was not going to be enough business to go around. Obviously, there would have to be some changes in market share—and there could be casualties along the way.

THE CONTESTANTS

This particular consumer-targeted battle of words started in the mid 1980s. It involved McDonald's, then with about 7,000 fast-food outlets, Burger King, with about 3,000, and Wendy's, with over 2,000. Watching on the sidelines were other fast-food businesses, such as Hardees, Big Boy, Denny's, Pizza Hut, Kentucky Fried Chicken, and Taco Bell.

The three major competitors got tangled up in a comparative advertising war started with a shot by Burger King. Advertising claims, rebuttals, and counterclaims flowed in news releases and occasionally in public statements. Eventually the argument was thrown into the lawsuit arena. Fast foods then constituted an estimated $35 billion business in the United States. McDonald's had well over $7 billion, or twenty percent of the market, Burger King did $2.3 billion, and Wendy's $1.4 billion. All could afford national advertising and a prolonged media campaign. Interestingly, the three companies were headquartered in widely separated locations—Chicago, Miami and Ohio.

THE GAUNTLET

The fast-food industry paid attention when Burger King launched what turned out to be a $19 million network television commercial blitz. The question-and-answer style campaign raised queries as to which was better, a griddle-cooked hamburger like McDonald's or a flame-broiled Burger King's burger. Embodied in the advertising message was that McDonald's hamburgers were not only "greasy," but smaller as well (see Figures 6–6 and 6–7).

McDonald's brought suit against Burger King. The charge was "deceptive" advertising. As for Burger King's "consumer research," the basis of the claims, McDonald's countered that the market surveys had been commissioned by Burger King and were therefore to be viewed as suspicious. There were questions whether Burger King hamburgers were kept warm in steam containers after flame broiling, then reheated in a microwave before serving. Thus, if McDonald's could be accused of being "greasy," Burger King could be labeled "soggy."

WENDY'S DEALS ITSELF A HAND

Whether envious of its competitors' free publicity or sensing a marketing opportunity, Wendy's entered the fray with a $25 million suit claiming that Burger King's ads were "false" and "misleading." Wendy's pointed out that both McDonald's and Burger King's hamburgers were prepared from frozen meat, whereas its hamburgers were prepared from fresh meat. To strengthen its position, especially in the court of

NEWS FROM:

BURGER KING CORPORATION
7360 North Kendall Drive, Miami, Florida 33156
Telephone (305) 596-7011

**BURGER
KING**

Contact: Release:

     John Weir   Immediate
     Burger King Communications
     (305) 596-7320

BURGER KING GOES AHEAD WITH COMPARATIVE ADS

    MIAMI, September 27th...Burger King Corporation has launched its
national advertising campaign telling consumers the Burger King® Whopper®
sandwich beat McDonald's® "Big Mac®" and the Wendy's® "Single" in
independent taste tests, according to Kyle Craig, Senior Vice President-
Director of Marketing for Burger King.

    The campaign began as lawyers for McDonald's Corporation moved to
block the campaign in federal court in Miami.

    "Lawyers on both sides met with Federal Court Judge Eugene Spellman
today to discuss the information McDonald's is demanding" said Mr.
Craig. "We are confident that the research upon which our campaign is
based will stand judicial scrutiny. All of our testing was conducted by
independent research organizations and the results were exhaustively
reviewed before we decided to go ahead with the new commercials.

    "The fact that number one was stung to action even before the
campaign was launched reflects a great deal of sensitivity to our basic

Figure 6–6 A sample of the several news releases sent from Burger King's corporate headquarters. (Courtesy of Burger King.)

Kyle Craig (center) with his "MacMarketing Team" (l-r) John Weir, Greg Thomas, Mike McCaffrey, Nick Castaldo, Scott Stubble and Shannon Maxwell.

New Switch Ad Campaign Stirs "Battle of Burgers"

The MacDonald's of Norwalk, CT can't bear the shame. Two parents, three kids and one dog are all disguised in phony glasses, bulbous noses and bushy eyebrows and mustaches.

It's not a scene from a Woody Allen movie, it's Burger King® advertising at its finest.

The namesake MacDonald's, says the ad, are embarrassed by their new-found preference for Burger King. "We can't show our faces anywhere anymore," the mother says sheepishly.

But by commercial's end, the mood changes to utter jubilation as the family advises viewers to switch over to Burger King.

The commercial is part of the new Switch campaign which began on September 12.

And by September 13, many restaurants were already feeling the impact.

The reason? Among other things, the campaign:

• Reinforces our product superiority.
• Generates intense involvement and excitement.
• Reinforces the Whopper® sandwich as our flagship product.

In short, Switch brings together Projects BOB and BIB.

It lets everyone know Burger King launched and won the Battle of the Burgers.

And it lets your customers know that millions have switched to Burger King.

More Will Switch

Even the competitors' most diehard followers will find it hard to keep from switching during October 17-23.

That's because National Switch Week will give your customers 7 full days to "cash in" any competitor's coupon or one they've made themselves for a free BOGO Whopper® sandwich.

"Depositing coupons in the Switch Display Bin and displaying the bin near the Counter or a high visibility area will show customers the switch is on," says Larry Kohler, EVP-Operations.

"And by paying careful attention to the basics of QSC&V, we can get millions more to switch permanently," he added.

Heaviest Ad Campaign Ever

Switch is the heaviest advertising blitz ever for Burger King.

Network TV spots alone will reach 95% of all Americans 14 times on average. Spot TV, radio and print will double the impact, according to Nick Castaldo, Group Director of Advertising and Promotion.

In all, 2,400 network GRPs will be aired. That's nearly twice the air time of Project BOB and four times that of Project BIB.

This means Switch will probably be seen by more people than Projects BOB and BIB combined.

Initial Response Great

Early reports from key markets show sales are up since the new ads began airing.

Plus, the media is again fanning the fires of the Battle of the Burgers, giving us millions of dollars in free publicity.

An example was Kyle Craig appearing on Good Morning America.

"It seems like those who didn't switch during Projects BOB and BIB are trying us now," say Division VPs Bruce Craig, Jay Darling and Bill de Laet.

And all agree. Once they try us, they'll switch for good!

PAGE THREE

Figure 6–7 Articles in Burger King's franchise newsletter *Dialogue BK* updating the employees on the burger war and how Burger King is winning. (Courtesy of Burger King.)

public opinion, Wendy's called for a national hamburger "taste test" (see Figure 6-8).

SETTLEMENT OUT OF COURT

Courtroom dramas highlighting controversial advertising, misleading public statements, confusing warranties, and faulty product or service claims can drag on for years. Though often dream cases for lawyers, public interest is generally short-lived. The three were aware of this and wisely chose to get out when they could—but only after each had made its points via all the publicity it could get!

A great many consumers probably found it all to be a lot of trouble over nothing. Their decision on which hamburger to eat—or whether to eat them at all— might be related to such matters as the proximity of outlets, price, specials, parking, peer acceptance, reduced-fat diets, or a host of other factors. But the three competitors were very serious. Within three months, without any true resolution of claims, Burger King, McDonald's, and Wendy's reached an uneasy truce. As for the lawsuits, they simply allowed them to lapse and agreed to phase out comparative advertising.

As part of the truce, the three contestants agreed little would be said publicly about the cessation of hostilities. But secrets were too good to keep. Burger King, having enjoyed a spurt in sales, claimed a victory publicly. Meanwhile, Wendy's came up with a hot advertising campaign featuring diminutive Clara Peller demanding "Where's the Beef?" This line eventually was used in the 1988 presidential campaign, when one candidate challenged another in a national debate. It sparked the political headline "Where's the beef?" that was later reinterpreted back into Wendy's promotional and publicity vehicles. Wendy's got a lot of mileage out of that one, and it helped increase sales for a time.

In this situation, the amount of public attention, the message absorption, and the responses loosely fit the **diffusion process model.**

1. There was enough rock throwing to stimulate public **awareness** beyond normal commercial enthusiasm.
2. Curious consumers were receptive to **news and information.**
3. No doubt, there were customers who **tried the product.**
4. Some of those may have **evaluated it on a comparative basis.**
5. Sales gains for underdogs could be interpreted as **adoption.**
6. Further claims serve as a **reinforcement.**

FOR IMMEDIATE RELEASE   CONTACT: DENNY LYNCH
JUNE 3, 1983   (614) 764-3413

                    "UNDERDOGS" ALWAYS WIN

(Dublin, Ohio) -- David had to contend with Goliath, Hercules
with a lion. Dorothy battled the Wicked Witch of the North.
And, Little Jack fought a giant on a beanstalk.

They are all familiar stories of legends and fairytales...the
"bully" threatens the "underdog", but the "underdog" always
triumphs.

Fairytales can come true in the "real" world, too. Take Wendy's
International, Inc., for example. Started in 1969, the hamburger
restaurant chain has grown to 2,500 restaurants and had annual
sales last year of $1.6 billion. That's because Wendy's, like
David and Hercules, knows how to go head to head with the
competition and outsmart them.

All these "underdogs" have something in common: they are
better than the "bullies." David had his wits; Dorothy had
heart, courage and a brain. Wendy's Old Fashioned Hamburgers
Restaurants have quality...quality that the competition cannot
match.

WENDY'S GRILLS COMPETITION

And now, in its most aggressive and competitive advertising
campaign, Wendy's is taking on McDonald's and Burger King
by dramatizing how its quality food and service "knock the
competition dead," said William M. Welter, Wendy's Senior
Vice President of Marketing.

Wendy's new ads, which begin June 13 on network television,
portray in a hard-hitting and humorous way, how its competition's
customers become "victims," Welter explained. The ads
also emphasize the basic operational differences between Wendy's
and the competition.

Unlike "those other hamburger places," Wendy's uses fresh, not
frozen beef; offers its customers a choice of toppings; and
serves its hamburgers hot off the grill.

Figure 6–8 A sample Wendy's news release during the hamburger war. Wendy's positioned
itself as the underdog and winner. (Courtesy of Wendy's.)

WHAT CAME OF IT ALL?

By 1988, McDonald's (7,200 outlets, 60 billion hamburgers) had advanced its share of the market to about thirty-six percent.

Burger King (5,950 outlets), after enjoying a sales gain from the war of words, peaked at 17.4 percent until 1986, when it undertook a multimillion dollar ad campaign that flopped dismally. News media reported that as a result, a shakeup was expected in which the Burger King unit would be spun off from its parent company, Pillsbury. That didn't happen. Pillsbury was taken over by United Kingdom-based Grand Metropolitan PLC. New ownership reviewed the $200 million Burger King communications budget, largely spent for media advertising and publicity support.

Wendy's (3,000 outlets) found "Where's the beef?" to be a success of short duration. It became tainted when Clara Peller did a commercial for Campbell's Prego Plus Spaghetti sauce saying, "I've found it." Wendy's was riled, and lawsuits were threatened. Subsequently, Clara passed away.

A NEW FOCUS

All three burger chains have since experienced growth. By 1990, McDonald's boasted over 12,000 outlets (including one in Moscow) and over 80,000 billion burgers sold. By the beginning of 1993 Burger King and Wendy's claimed over 7,000 and 3,900 outlets, respectively. The worldwide fast-food market continues to grow.

Since the rough-and-tumble campaigns of the 1980s, fast-food companies have shifted energies to more positive tactics. Emphasis on positive qualities of the company itself, lifestyle attributes, and customer satisfaction promises continued growth. For example:

- McDonald's and Burger King have introduced untraditional "fast-foods" such as pizza, skinless chicken, Italian dinner selections, even a catfish sandwich— searching for a winner.
- With miniature "Burger Buddies," Burger King found a new way to serve a familiar product—or rather, stole the idea long used by White Castle.
- To address health concerns associated with fast food, McDonald's rolled out the McLean Deluxe, a lower-fat burger partially composed of seaweed.
- Several chains have begun emphasizing breakfast in an attempt to create a new niche and provide new customer service.

For all the new activity, however, the companies are not above an old-fashioned price war—with McDonald's slashing hamburgers prices to fifty-nine cents and Wendy's heavily promoting its value meal packages. In all such marketing moves, public relations tactics are critical to success.

For instance, the restaurants themselves are becoming more user-friendly. Burger King test marketed special drive-through windows equipped with two-way monitors and considered an in-store television network. McDonald's experimented with a chain of indoor playgrounds called "Leaps and Bounds" and is designing architecturally unique and "theme" stores.

Fast-food companies are also taking on broader social issues in response to changing customer needs. In a highly publicized move, McDonald's abandoned most polystyrene packaging and has tested recycling in stores to address environmental concerns of consumers and critics. Nutritional information and information on the origin of McDonald's beef (ensuring that cattle were not fed on land that was once rain forest) is now available—on recycled paper, of course. Wendy's has also developed more environmentally sound packaging and practices. The plan is to reduce nonfood solid waste by ten percent and to recycle at least twenty-five percent

OTHER MARKETING BATTLES

The hamburger war of words is not unique. Cereal manufacturers once staged a public debate whether the "natural" Kellogg's raisin bran is more "natural" than Post's competitive brand. The importance of this debate to consumers may be unclear but not to Kellogg's, who entered suit for $100 million against Post. Another public battle involved pain killers—Tylenol versus Advil versus Anacin, with aspirin positioned off to one side. Aspirin did, however, receive a short-lived competitive advantage following reports that it reduced heart attack risk—until the Food and Drug Administration (FDA) prohibited use of that claim in advertising.

More recently, Coca-Cola and Pepsi-Cola have been engaged in a battle dubbed the "Cola Wars." The positioning of these similar products began with aggressive price slashing, but it has expanded into competition based on lifestyle—each positioning itself as the choice of the nineties. Pepsi's slogan "You Got the Right One Baby. Uh-Huh!" weighed in heavily against Coke's "It's the Real Thing." Subsequent slogans by each company are squarely aimed at the competitor's customers.

The war of words regarding product claims has become so heated that the government has threatened to get involved. The fight for the environmentally conscious "green" consumer has spurred battle cries such as "earth friendly" and "biodegradable" that can be viewed as suspicious at best. Similar conflicts have arisen in the quest for health-conscious consumers using such ill-defined claims as "lite" or "light' and "lower fat." New labeling requirements in 1993 seem only to have stimulated copywriters to find new euphemisms.

Finally, a classic war-of-words has a winner and no loser. Miller Lite's deftly created debate whether their beer is "Less Filling" or "Tastes Great" sometimes escaped the bounds of advertising and was heard shouted in the bleachers of rowdy sports events.

of the rest by 1994 (a goal that had not yet been met by the time of this writing, mid-1994).

The battlefields have clearly shifted in the War of the Hamburgers. Adversarial tactics and media sniping have matured to positive customer service as a basis for competition. With this new focus, the real winners will be both companies and customers.

Still, many people are convinced that the Burger Wars—and maybe most such battles—are collisions purposefully concocted by the participants to capture public attention. What do you think?

QUESTIONS FOR DISCUSSION

1. The structure of most huge consumer products companies situates the advertising function several decks down from top management, remote from corporate policy formation. The public relations function more often is located with direct reporting or easy access to top officials. Also, CEOs are generally more inclined to participate personally in what goes into the media as news reflecting a company's policy or conduct than in paid advertising about a product. Does this situation suggest a public relations role or responsibility that goes beyond "marketing public relations"? If so, what is this role, and how is it different from merely publicizing in marketing campaigns those events that have news value?

2. The Federal Trade Commission is the principle watchdog with authority to act when practices are deemed contrary to consumer interests or illegal. It provides guidelines for truthful advertising. Would you say the wars of words cited in this case abridge any such guidelines, or are they simply a tiny aspect of the marketplace functioning as the final arbiter?

3. If you were the director of public relations for Burger King, would you have proposed any strategy, tactics, or approach different from comparative advertising over broiled versus fried, and so on? If so, what might that have been?

4. The chapter introduction cites some newer activities, beyond publicity, such as forming user and customer satisfaction groups and protecting the reputation of the product or service. Would advertising that tends to poke fun at a product or service negate or work at cross-purposes with serious-minded communications activities? If so, what should public relations staff do about it?

5. If publicity wars are planned in advance by the supposedly warring participants, is this planning ethical? Is it honest? Is there a difference between what is ethical and what is honest?

A Classic: Tylenol Rides It Out and Gains a Legacy

The Tylenol tragedy, Johnson & Johnson's responsive reaction, the product's reissue and comeback, and the nation's applause, add up to a classic case study of how a corporate crisis can be dealt with using effective public relations strategy.

This story has been told in a variety of special and public media. It has been interpreted for its merits in the practice of management, marketing, and public relations, and for the blend of what is admirable in all three.[1]

In 1982, some Tylenol capsules, laced with cyanide, were discovered to be the cause of seven persons' deaths in the Chicago area. It was discovered that the packages had been tampered with, and the cyanide added by a person, or persons, unknown. In 1994, the crime remains unsolved. All supplies of the product in stores nationwide were pulled off the shelves by the parent company, Johnson & Johnson, at a cost exceeding $50 million. After due time and investigation, the product was reissued in tamper-resistant containers, and a sealed package of capsules was offered free to consumers who had discarded the suspect supplies in their possession. The company became a champion of tamper-resistant consumer product packaging.

In the echoing events, Tylenol recovered more than the share of market it had held before the tragedy. The company gained in credibility, public trust, and esteem. The Food and Drug Administration of the Department of Health and Human Services (HHS) tightened its regulations regarding packaging (see Figure 6-9).

---

[1]For accounts that address these issues further refer to *pr reporter,* February 13, 1983; *Public Relations Journal,* March 1983; *Public Relations Review,* Fall 1983; "The Tylenol Comeback," Johnson & Johnson, undated booklet; "Tylenol's Rebound," *Los Angeles Times,* September 25, 1983; "Tylenol Deaths Still a Mystery," Associated Press, September 26, 1983; "Tylenol's Miracle Comeback," *Time,* October 17, 1983.

federal register

Friday
November 5, 1982

Part IV

Department of Health and Human Services

Food and Drug Administration

Tamper-Resistant Packaging
Requirements; Certain Over-the-Counter
Human Drugs and Cosmetic Products;
Contact Lens Solutions and Tablets; Final
Rules

Figure 6–9   Tylenol case leads to federal regulation on tamper-resistant packaging. (Courtesy of The Food and Drug Administration)

PRACTICAL REALITIES

It is relevant here to set "what-if" questions aside in favor of a realistic situation analysis. Why was it that Johnson & Johnson, specifically, was able to weather this storm—indeed, to turn adversity into gain? Among the factors that appear instrumental:

1. The company benefited from a long history of success and service in a field of "beneficial" and "worthwhile" health care products.
2. The company took pride in its public visibility and its reputation for integrity.
3. The company benefited by having had a strong founder who believed that "the corporation should be socially responsible, with responsibilities to society that went far beyond the usual sales and profit motives."[2] High ethical standards were set in place early on to be continued as a tradition or as a legacy.
4. There was a credo, a "For this we stand" on paper, on which succeeding generations of executives have built and interpreted in terms of changing times and challenges. The credo was brought out during this episode for the world to see (see Figure 6-10).
5. In its relations with employees, neighbors, investors, customers, and government agencies, there was a candor consistent with competitive and financial security. Company spokespeople—including the CEO—showed leadership and authority.
6. There was a recognition of the public interest and its legitimate representation by news media. Information, whether good or bad, was forthcoming as rapidly as it developed (see Figure 6-11).
7. The corporate public relations function was part of management, participating in the decision process and in the implementation when communication was involved.
8. There were mechanisms for feedback from constituent publics, and a high value was placed on public input.

These virtues, some of which derived from the company's history, graced the behavior of Johnson & Johnson in its emergency. This is not to say that their behavior was without agonizing, great risk, or debates within the management task force set up to make decisions (see Figure 6-12).

---

[2]Lee W Baker, *The Credibility Factor* (Homewood, Ill.: Business One Irwin, 1993), 54.

Our Credo

We believe our first responsibility is to the doctors, nurses and patients,
to mothers and all others who use our products and services.
In meeting their needs everything we do must be of high quality.
We must constantly strive to reduce our costs
in order to maintain reasonable prices.
Customers' orders must be serviced promptly and accurately.
Our suppliers and distributors must have an opportunity
to make a fair profit.

We are responsible to our employees,
the men and women who work with us throughout the world.
Everyone must be considered as an individual.
We must respect their dignity and recognize their merit.
They must have a sense of security in their jobs.
Compensation must be fair and adequate,
and working conditions clean, orderly and safe.
Employees must feel free to make suggestions and complaints.
There must be equal opportunity for employment, development
and advancement for those qualified.
We must provide competent management,
and their actions must be just and ethical.

We are responsible to the communities in which we live and work
and to the world community as well.
We must be good citizens — support good works and charities
and bear our fair share of taxes.
We must encourage civic improvements and better health and education.
We must maintain in good order
the property we are privileged to use,
protecting the environment and natural resources.

Our final responsibility is to our stockholders.
Business must make a sound profit.
We must experiment with new ideas.
Research must be carried on, innovative programs developed
and mistakes paid for.
New equipment must be purchased, new facilities provided
and new products launched.
Reserves must be created to provide for adverse times.
When we operate according to these principles,
the stockholders should realize a fair return.

Johnson & Johnson

Figure 6–10   The well-publicized credo. (Courtesy of Johnson & Johnson.)

The Tylenol comeback

NEW SAFETY SEALED!
EXTRA-STRENGTH
TYLENOL
acetaminophen CAPSULES
extra pain relief... contains no aspirin
50 Capsules-500mg each

A special report from the editors of Worldwide, a publication of Johnson & Johnson Corporate Public Relations

Figure 6–11 Employees got the word fast in company publications. This is the cover of a booklet that Tylenol published to keep employees informed about the situation. (Courtesy of Johnson & Johnson public relations.)

Figure 6–12 The corporation used news, such as this news conference, as well as ads to communicate with the public. (Courtesy of Johnson & Johnson.)

JOHNSON & JOHNSON WAS NOT ALONE

In the crisis, public attention was focused heavily on Johnson & Johnson, the parent company, which took over for its McNeil Consumer Products subsidiary, which makes and sells Tylenol. However, many other entities were involved, some in a major capacity. It is instructive to look at the public information actions of one of them, the Food and Drug Administration (FDA).

Over a period of several days the FDA's press office was busy keeping the public informed about this incident. Constant communication about this crisis characterized its behavior. It issued several updates about the initial recall of 93,000 bottles of Tylenol on September 30, 1982. In addition, it reported on the total national recall of the drug that Johnson & Johnson installed five days after the first local recall. Finally, on November 4, the FDA released its new uniform standards for nonprescription drug manufacturers in providing tamper-resistant packages. This constant flow of information helped to quell any consumer panic.

DEALING WITH A SEQUEL

Four years after the first poisoning episode, there was a recurrence. In February 1986, a stenographer in Westchester County, New York, died of cyanide poisoning from Tylenol capsules that had been purchased at an A&P store in Bronxville. Johnson & Johnson, well-prepared for the crisis, halted capsule manufacturing and offered to refund or exchange all capsules on the market for tablets or caplets. A few days after the stenographer's death, five poisoned capsules were found in a Woolworth store. Johnson & Johnson took action to withdraw Tylenol capsules entirely from the market at a cost of $180 million, which covered "inventory handling and disposal, *and communication expenses* to reassure consumers of the safety of non-capsule Tylenol." The action fitted the public image of Johnson & Johnson, and the news media coverage was positive.

By the late 1980s, competition in the pain-easing medicine business returned to normal. Entries such as Advil (American Home Products), Ecotrin (Smith Kline), Bufferin (Bristol Myers), Anacin (Whitehall), Panadol (Sterling), and some others, matched and countermatched each other's claims in consumer media advertising and publicity to get a bigger piece of the very large and profitable market. If the tragic incident befalling Tylenol was a negative for the product, that didn't show in a 1986 poll of consumers about the same time as the second incident. Some seventy-six percent of those queried said they thought the company had done enough to ensure that its products were not tampered with. Apparently, much of the public had come to realize that isolated acts of violence and terrorism cannot be totally avoided.

THE PUBLIC MATTERED

The importance of corporate responsibility to the public is illustrated vividly by the Tylenol crisis. Although the company did not specifically have a plan before to deal with crises such as this one, its commitment to the credo "the first responsibility is to the customer" helped Johnson & Johnson to bounce back and contain the tragedy without sacrificing credibility. "Johnson & Johnson developed and geared activities to protect and communicate with its customers, to react to their fears, and provide what consumers needed."[3] A study conducted by Johnson & Johnson emphasized the importance of recognizing a responsibility to the public and maintain-

---

[3]Eileen Murray and Saundra Shohen, "Lessons from the Tylenol Tragedy on Surviving a Corporate Crisis," *Medical Marketing and Media,* February 1992.

ing positive public relationships. Companies that gave special attention to the public and their needs enhanced their profitability.[4]

James Burke, then chairman stated, "I think the lesson in the Tylenol experience . . . is that we as business men and women have extraordinary leverage with our most important asset—*goodwill*—the goodwill of the public. *If* we make sure our enterprises are managed in terms of *their obligations to society,* that is also the best way to defend this democratic capitalistic system that means so much to all of us."[5]

ALMOST ABOVE IT ALL

Regaining its competitive lead was not the only positive result for Johnson & Johnson. In 1986, the Council on Economic Priorities gave the company its "American Corporate Conscience Award" while pinning Dishonorable Mention on four other well-known corporations. Playing a few of its accumulated chips, Johnson & Johnson themed its annual report for 1986, "Managing for the Long Term," and in 1987 followed with "Strategies for Growth," beyond the record $8 billion attained that year. As a public relations exclamation point then-public relations vice president Lawrence Foster authored a book titled, *A Company That Cares,* honoring the company on its hundreth anniversary. In addition, Johnson & Johnson established itself as the world's largest and most comprehensive manufacturer of health care products in 1991 by attaining almost $12.5 billion in sales. Momentum, it would seem, applies in the marketplace as well as on the athletic field.

QUESTIONS FOR DISCUSSION

1. Business is said to be a game of hardball most of the time, and competitive success requires that the cards be played close to the chest. The pharmaceutical business is no exception. How, then, can you defend Johnson & Johnson's traditional adherence to a "do-gooder" credo written by its founder or the open and candid way the company went about dealing with the problems posed by a small number of poisoned Tylenol capsules in Chicago?

2. Tylenol is a product of the McNeil Consumer Products wing of Johnson & Johnson. When the deaths occurred, the parent organization moved in and took over both responsibility and spokesmanship. What are the pros and cons

---

[4]*pr reporter* (February 6, 1984): 3 vol. 27.
[5]Ibid.

to that strategy as far as the CEO and the communications people in McNeil are concerned? What about the news media?

3. Although the functions of marketing and public relations are often confused as one and the same, or as part of each other, what do you see as distinguishing one from the other? Use this case as an example.

4. Which of the following conclusions do you feel can properly be drawn on the basis of your personal familiarity with the Tylenol incident?

    a. The episode (diminishes/enhances) Johnson & Johnson's claim to competitive leadership in its industry.

    b. The episode illustrates that marketing and public relations are (much the same/different) in values and priorities.

    c. The episode shows that having a sterling character can (help/hinder) the bottom line.

    d. Public relations (has/does not have) a significant voice in the decision process during a crisis when big money is at stake.

Putting on a New Face

Goodwill Industries stores were once known as places to send old clothes to be mended by handicapped people and then sold at low prices to poor people. That image was ripe for change when the popularity of vintage clothing, tattered and faded blue jeans, baggy trousers, and other individualistic styles such as the "urban" or "street" look and "grunge" caught on. Shopping at thrift stores, an absolute necessity for some, became a chic and smart alternative for both trendsetters and followers. Goodwill was ready to make the changes to serve both old and new publics.

A STORE IN TEXAS

This case portrays how Goodwill Industries of Texas responded in 1990 to the opportunity to reinvent itself in terms of facilities, "image," and marketing. A major remodeling tripled the store size and added such fine touches as lighting, carpeting, fixtures, and a paint job. A redesigned "Smiling G" logo adorned several windows, and a sign in front proclaimed an extensive line of "Clothing, Electric Appliances, Furniture, and Books" (see Figure 6-13). Neighborhood Training Centers were developed to meet changing needs of customers, conveniently bringing services and operations together.

Goodwill officials conducted research to determine how best to reach and serve customers. Customer profiles were drawn, including buying habits in six of their stores. They found:

- Three-quarters of customers were between the ages of eighteen and forty-nine.
- Fifty-seven percent were of European decent, twenty-one percent were Hispanic, nineteen percent were African American.

Figure 6–13 The widely recognized Goodwill logo. (Courtesy of Goodwill Industries of Austin.)

- The item most customers shopped for was women's clothing—sixty-nine percent. More than half shopped for kitchen items, books, small electrical appliances, or furniture.
- Goodwill customers also shopped in similar second-hand thrift establishments—Salvation Army and St. Vincent de Paul stores—and visited garage sales.
- Almost half of Goodwill shoppers visited a Goodwill store once week.
- The majority of shoppers reported friends and word-of-mouth as a primary source of shopping information. Newspapers were also a highly rated source of shopping information.
- A substantial number of shoppers came from two zip code areas within the city and from zip code areas outside the city limits.
- Seventy-two percent of Goodwill shoppers were female.
- Fifty-three percent had an annual household income of $15,000 or less.

STRATEGY

The Grand Reopening was based on the theme "Look Again," urging individuals to take another look—to reexamine and readjust attitudes about used-goods shopping at Goodwill stores. Funds were allocated to cover newspaper and radio advertising and publicity. The "Look Again" theme was supported by eye-catching visuals and spunky copy to appeal to new target groups. Because of budget limitations and time constraints, the entire campaign was scheduled for three days—beginning on Thurs-

day and ending on Saturday (Grand Reopening Day). Included in the three-day celebration were:

- A preview party featuring a professionally produced fashion show of Goodwill
  clothing (invitees were sent dark glasses to wear if they might be embarrassed
  to be seen in a Goodwill store). (See Figure 6–14.)
- A feature story and color photo touting reopening day bargains.
- Ads on five consecutive pages of the weekend activities section of the local
  newspaper urged the public to "Look Again."

The results exceeded expectations in turnout and in record sales. Other stores
benefited too. At the core of the Goodwill effort were recognition of changing
needs and styles, the use of graphic identification, the creation of special events tied
to the times, and the visual symbols of change.

ONE STEP FURTHER

Goodwill has not rested on its successes. In an effort to go beyond image and marketing, Goodwill Industries created its first Neighborhood Training Centers (NTCs),
which represented an effort to build stronger relationships with the community and
to better serve customers. The NTCs are aimed at bringing services and operations
together. The center is conveniently located and functions as an all-in-one facility.
Donations are received at a drive-through area, prepared, then displayed in the retail
store. A job training and an information area help customers prepare for and find
jobs. Goodwill has gone a step further than targeting a new customer—instead of
abandoning traditional customers, Goodwill is helping them to reflect the characteristics of its *new* target customers (see Figure 6–15).

The project received community support, with many community leaders attending ground-breaking ceremonies. Several large corporations provided financial
support for the project.

NEW SURVEY RESULTS

Goodwill's efforts are paying off. Although the majority of shoppers are still women
ages eighteen to fifty, and women's clothing remains the most popular items, currently

- Sixty-nine percent of shoppers are of European decent, nineteen percent are
  Hispanic, ten percent are African-American, and two percent are "other,"
  which more accurately reflects local demographics.
- 70 percent have a household income **over** $20,000.

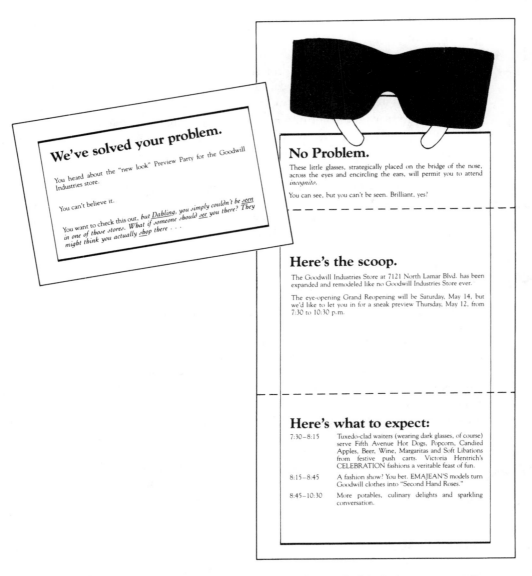

We've solved your problem.

You heard about the "new look" Preview Party for the Goodwill Industries store.

You can't believe it.

You want to check this out, *but Dahling, you simply couldn't be seen in one of those stores. What if someone should see you there? They might think you actually shop there . . .*

No Problem.

These little glasses, strategically placed on the bridge of the nose, across the eyes and encircling the ears, will permit you to attend *incognito*.

You can see, but you can't be seen. Brilliant, yes?

Here's the scoop.

The Goodwill Industries Store at 7121 North Lamar Blvd. has been expanded and remodeled like no Goodwill Industries Store ever.

The eye-opening Grand Reopening will be Saturday, May 14, but we'd like to let you in for a sneak preview Thursday, May 12, from 7:30 to 10:30 p.m.

Here's what to expect:

7:30–8:15	Tuxedo-clad waiters (wearing dark glasses, of course) serve Fifth Avenue Hot Dogs, Popcorn, Candied Apples, Beer, Wine, Margaritas and Soft Libations from festive push carts. Victoria Hentrich's CELEBRATION fashions a veritable feast of fun.
8:15–8:45	A fashion show? You bet. EMAJEAN'S models turn Goodwill clothes into "Second Hand Roses."
8:45–10:30	More potables, culinary delights and sparkling conversation.

Figure 6–14 Creativity sparked the preview party invitations. Each invitation was personally addressed and stamped. The cover let the reader know what was happening, but also set the scene for the inside of the invitation. (Courtesy of Goodwill Industries of Austin.)

Figure 6–15 The "Look Again" theme poster that was given to each customer during grand reopening day. The style of the poster and the models were also used in advertisements. (Courtesy of Goodwill Industries of Austin.)

GOODWILL'S SALES

1989—up 5.2 percent
1990—up 12.9 percent
1991—up 16.6 percent

- The University of Texas students voted Goodwill Stores best retail store in Austin—a clear sign the new audience was reached.
- Revenues are up from almost $5 million in 1989 to nearly $6 million in 1991—a 20 percent increase.
- Goodwill NTC job training has helped find employment for trainees at places like 3M, Wal-Mart, Marriott Hotels—even the IRS.

THE PREOCCUPATION WITH SYMBOLISM

As marketing techniques are becoming more sophisticated, they increasingly reach into our private lives. This is happening at a time when, because of new technology, new media outlets are virtually exploding into existence. We are being constantly barraged by a flood of information, (thousands per day), urging us to buy, to do, or to think something. That same technology—TV remote tuners, "low-flow" communication outlets such as VCRs and pay-tv channels, and caller ID devices—are giving us ways to tune out (the wastepaper basket is still the best answer to direct, or "junk," mail). This selective attention to communication messages we all exhibit makes it essential for organizations to break through the clamor and clutter. A simple, clear, strategically designed graphic identification or symbol has the best chance of doing this.

AND NOW ... TO BROADEN THE PERSPECTIVE

Symbols and Logos

The concept of graphic design is as old as cave paintings that tell stories of bison and wooly mammoth. Throughout the centuries, widespread illiteracy made it necessary to communicate with means other than the written word. Visual symbols such as government seals, coats-of-arms, and pictograms—a symbolic lock for a locksmith, a shoe for a cobbler—served as a primary means of visual communication. Today symbols and logos can be a rallying point, pulling organizations together and affirming certain ideals in the minds of target publics.

*Factors in Creating
Graphic Symbols*

- Does it fit with the overall mission, objectives and goals of the organization?
- Will it be an integral part of the complete communications program?
- Does it in reflect the dominant theme or message?
- Does it command attention?
- What connatations are associated with it—are there underlying meanings?
- Where does the eye look first?
- Is it memorable?

Changes in names, logos, slogans, locations, decor, and other basic identifications have been hard-pressed to match the pace of large enterprises in expanding, conglomerating, and internationalizing.

A name change may reflect a merger, acquisition, downsizing or "rightsizing," spin-offs, sales of assets, or a shift in corporate strategy. With over 31,000 mergers or acquisitions alone between 1980 and 1990 it is clear there is a lot of potential change. Generally speaking, a name change occurs when a name no longer correctly identifies an organization's primary mission or focus.

Ownership of shapes can be even more powerful than a logo. Our vote for three of the greatest trademarks goes to these companies, which have achieved shape identity.

1. Target Stores, whose bull's-eye is so strong it is often used alone (without the name) in store signage and ads.
2. Shell owns the shape that is its name.
3. Sunoco goes a step further. Its diamond is pierced by an arrow that points toward the service station being signaled.

Changes in graphic identification happen in all types of organizations for a variety of reasons. As reported in *pr reporter*, the Amos Tuck School of Business Administration at Dartmouth developed a new symbol as part of a marketing program to sharpen the school's identity. "Up With People" designed a logo to "communicate our educational component without looking too formal, our entertainment aspects without looking too Hollywood, and work well in Europe, Japan, Mexico, or the U.S."—no small task. American Electric Power needed a new symbol that would link its' seven regional operating companies while still reflecting local roots. The Aid Association for Lutherans associated its initials with a statement of purpose, and a statement to help employees rededicate themselves. American Hotel and Motel Association updated and unified its logo when it moved to Washington, D.C. The investment management firm, Scudder, Stevens, and Clark shortened its signature to "Scudder" and tied it to a contemporary version of its' pilot symbol (see Figure 6–16).

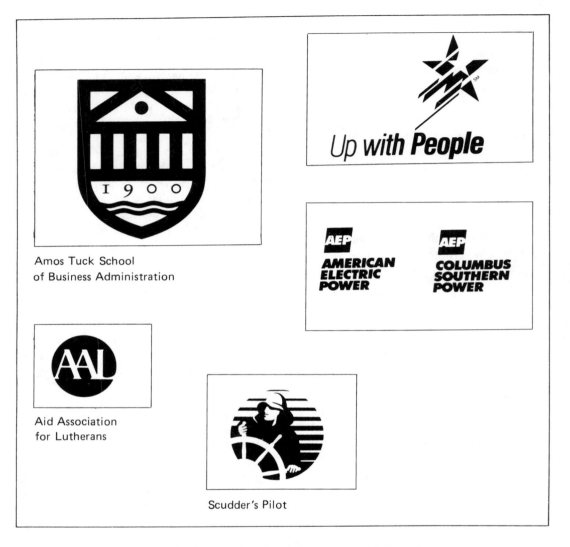

Figure 6–16. Logos can identify the company without words.

NOT ALL GRAPHIC SYMBOLS MAKE SENSE

There is more to creating an effective organizational symbol than a pen, artist, and drawing board. In many cases artists and designers don't take the time or have the business acumen to find out what really makes the organization tick or what makes it distinctive. An attractive graphic design which has no bearing on the organization's operating strategy or mission just adds to the clutter. This can be dangerous, because it can give the erroneous impression that the company is following a well-charted path. Current trends indicate that organizations are beginning to take a different approach—a planned design process based on sound investigation. Graphic psychology is the term that best describes this approach. It involves investigation of the organization mission, structure, and goals; application of graphic theory; and, finally, testing with key audiences.[1]

Greg Kolligan of Selame Design offers five qualities that will help assure that a graphic identification can be distinguished from the noise and clutter.

1. **Simple** in form, not contrived.
2. **Strong** signal value. People don't read, they see an image, and it registers. Color and simple elements are important.
3. **Memorable.** It shouldn't look like ten other things. The simpler, the more memorable.
4. **Protectable.** Create design elements that discourage look-alikes.
5. **Workable** in all sizes—from business card to fifty-foot outdoor sign—and on all types of communication vehicles. You can't design in a vacuum and then apply the design to see how it looks.

QUESTIONS FOR DISCUSSION

1. An accepted maxim is that clarity, simplicity, and symbolism all have direct and measureable effects on message acceptance by mass audiences. Symbols of newness and modernity come across in the new Goodwill logo. Where, if anywhere in their renaissance program, do you detect increased degrees of simplicity and clarity?

2. Among the numerous forms of graphic identification and slogans, what ones can you recall that make use of a distinctive shape? A particular color, or combinations of colors? A nickname? An animated figure or dynamic object? Other memorable formats for immediate identity?

3. What connection, if any, has the five-phase diffusion process (see Case 6-2) with the program of Goodwill to change its public image?

4. What are some examples of organizational identification that demonstrate the maxim "a suggested action as part of a message is more likely to be accepted than a message by itself"? Start with, "Don't leave home without it," Name how one that whets the consumer's appetite? One that reassures the audience? One that promises a delayed benefit?

[1]*Channels,* a supplement, to *pr reporter,* 30, No. 3, (March 1988): 1 & 2.

5. What symbols and identifications of your school strike you as most important from a public image standpoint? By what criteria do you consider them the most important? How could the relative importance of those and other symbols and identifications be measured? Assume that you wanted to do that as the basis for a proposal to administration telling how to capitalize on certain symbols and identifications.

Customer Satisfaction: How Wal-Mart and L. L. Bean Translated It from Buzzword to Behavior

Customer satisfaction has become a buzzword of the 1990s. With competition between businesses increasing every day, more organizations are looking to distinguish themselves by professing that they offer unsurpassed customer service. Ultimately, they are focusing on how they can build a long-term relationship with customers that will keep existing customers loyal and attract new customers.

The result: Customer satisfaction has a direct impact on an organization's bottom line, both from the view of *increased productivity* (an organization's opportu-

INTERNAL AUDIENCE (EMPLOYEES) ARE KEY TO EXTERNAL RESULTS WITH CUSTOMERS

The best way to achieve customer satisfaction is to make sure that employees—ambassadors of your organization who are closest to your customers—have been properly trained to serve customers and adhere to the philosophy that the customer comes first.

A survey by CitiCorp of seventeen companies known for excellent service showed that service *training costs for frontline employees, managers, and executives aver-* *aged one to two percent of sales.* According to Jack Pyle of Peak Performance Associates, **vertical cross-training** (employees' learning jobs above and below their own level) and **horizontal cross-training** (employees' learning other jobs at their level) greatly contribute to customer satisfaction.

According to Pyle, these training strategies allow job switching and create better understanding of how the organization operates. They also help employees more easily solve customer problems, and they increase employee self-esteem.

THE CUSTOMER SATISFACTION MODEL

Jackson Jackson & Wagner's four-step customer satisfaction model speaks to the need to define customer satisfaction internally, then *conduct customer research* to come to a consensus on a definition *that includes customer feedback.* It is then important to develop an *action plan* addressing the revised definition—and build in a mechanism for ongoing evaluation.

Phase I: Designing a Draft Model Internally

1. **Department training and preparation.** Hold a session with the department staff to outline the purpose of the customer satisfaction program, background, and related theory to create understanding and acceptance of the process.
2. **Prioritize lists of internal and external customers.**
3. **Develop a profile of a satisfied customer.** Identify specific behaviors, actions, and reactions.

Steps 1–3 set benchmarks for research with customers and departmental goal setting.

4. **Identify obstacles to delivering customer satisfaction.** This step empowers staff by considering areas for change in the process and in attitudes that may be needed to deliver customer satisfaction.

The end Product of Phase I is a draft model of what constitutes customer satisfaction from the viewpoint of *those who must deliver it.*

Phase II: Customer Review of the Draft Model

Conduct research with a representative group of customers to critique and correct the model developed in Phase I and identify the current status of customer satisfaction. This research can be achieved via *focus groups* or *brief survey research,* via telephone interviews made by staff.

This phase is an opportunity to *identify the status of customer satisfaction* and let customers critique the staff's model, thereby drafting *their* model of a satisfied customer.

The end products of Phase II are a model of what satisfies customers designed by those customers themselves and a baseline of data against which to measure progress.

Phase III: Staff Designs an Operations Process That Will Carry out the Model

Department sessions are held to:

1. **Present the results of the model** as adjusted by customer panels and research.
2. **Design an action plan for "closing the gap"** between the model (ideal) and current status (reality).
3. **Work through steps** in implementing the plan and follow up to assure successful use by all staff.

The end product of Phase III is a *staff-designed* step-by-step action plan linking operational procedures and staff behaviors to delivering customer satisfaction.

Phase IV: Ongoing Evaluation of Performance

1. **Replicate research** (entire study, or just pieces) to measure improvements

in customer satisfaction levels over time.

2. **Staff reviews model** to determine achievability and update action plans to reflect new goals.

---

nity to become a least-cost producer when employees are running the show smoothly) and an *established good reputation,* which is the best marketing tool you can have.

WAL-MART: A COMMITMENT TO CUSTOMERS

In 1962, the first Wal-Mart Discount City was opened in Rogers, Arkansas, by Sam and Bud Walton. Three decades later, their commitment to customers has paid off. The company now operates over 2,000 Wal-Mart stores, warehouse-style Sam's clubs, and Hypermart USAs (combinations of groceries and general merchandise, which include a variety of fast-food and service shops to create "one-stop shopping" for the customer) (see Figure 6–17).

Much of that success can be attributed to the company's founder and chairman, Sam Walton, and his forward-thinking philosophies on the treatment of two key constituencies—employees and customers.

Guiding Principles Focus on Customers

What is the secret of Wal-Mart's success? The three basic principles that have guided the company since its founding are aimed at *customers or publics that directly influence customers.*

- **Principle 1:** *Provide Value and Service for Customers.* Wal-mart's pledge is to always offer quality merchandise at the lowest prices. Because they claim to offer consistently low prices—and have successfully communicated that perception to consumers—they don't have to spend as many dollars on advertising circulars as competitors. That cost savings is passed on to the customer.
- **Principle 2:** *Partnershp with Associates.* Employees, or "associates," are con-

Figure 6–17   One of the many Wal-Marts in the United States, located in Somersworth, New Hampshire (Photo courtesy of Jenna Wilson.)

sidered part of the team at Wal-Mart. They enjoy a family environment and a chance to participate in every way, from making suggestions to posing as fashion models for circulars. They have a personal stake in the store's success, because employees benefit financially through Wal-Mart's profit-sharing plan.

- **Principle 3:** *Commitment to Communities.* Each store has a community-involvement project. The dollars they raise on a local level are matched by the Wal-Mart Foundation. Associates are encouraged to participate in campaigns for the United Way, Children's Miracle Network, and other causes—once again emphasizing a "caring and sharing" attitude. Foundation dollars are also available to qualifying industrial and economic development programs. Wal-Mart knows it is in the company's best interest for stores to operate in communities that have a strong economic base.

Doing Something about the Issues That Affect the Community

The issue of foreign competition taking business away from the United States, resulting in the loss of American jobs, was of concern to Wal-Mart and its customers. Their "Buy American" program was launched in 1985 with the goal of converting from foreign sources to American manufacturers. It was a cooperative effort between retailers and domestic manufacturers to reestablish a competitive position in the price and quality of American-made goods in the marketplace.

We want to ALWAYS have the best customer service. We want to ALWAYS have the best prices every day. Our commitment to the customer is ALWAYS—in everything we do. (David Glass, Wal-Mart President and CEO)

The People Greeter program is a unique form of customer service that was implemented in 1983, on the suggestion of an associate. At every store, there is an associate greeting and welcoming customers and offering assistance if any is needed. As a customer once said, "They treat you like they want you to be here."

Since 1985, Wal-Mart says it has converted or retained almost $2 billion in purchases that could have been placed for production offshore. This figure translates into 40,000 direct American jobs and 30,000 related jobs, according to company calculations.

In 1989, Wal-Mart took on another cause important to its constituents—improving the environment. They challenged their manufacturing partners to improve products and packaging. They used recycled paper for stationery and provided an outlet for customers to recycle goods, including an automobile battery-recovery program to ensure proper disposal.

Looking Ahead to Continue to Provide Top Service

Often a pioneer in technology, Wal-Mart is constantly looking for ways to improve products and services. They were the first retail chain to be equipped with scanner cash registers in all facilities. Today, each store is tied into the Bentonville, Arkansas, home office by computer for easy communication and quick replenishment of supplies.

A new program, VideOcart network, serves two purposes—promotion and research. One thousand electronic shopping cart displays flashing promotional messages change as consumers go through the store. VideOcart also tracks where the customer is going—providing important information on shopping patterns and consumer buying habits.

L. L. BEAN: NOTHING IS MORE IMPORTANT THAN A SATISFIED CUSTOMER

When Leon Leonwood Bean founded the now-famous L. L. Bean in 1912, he may not have realized that his "golden rule" would lead to a catalog, retail, and manufacturing success story that would result in more than $743 million in annual sales in 1992 (see Figure 6–18).

Figure 6–18   "L. L." Bean demonstrates to a customer the benefits of his Maine hunting shoe, the product that got it all started for him over eighty years ago. (Courtesy of L. L. Bean, Inc.)

His golden rule was, "Sell good merchandise at a reasonable profit, treat your customers like human beings, and they'll always come back for more." With its Freeport, Maine, stores open twenty-four a day, seven days a week, and offering customers a 100 percent satisfaction guarantee on merchandise whether purchased there or by mail order, L. L. Bean is often acknowledged for the management practices that have led it to become a prime example of customer satisfaction. Two important elements of L. L. Bean's success are research and training.

Ongoing Research

As in any service-based organization, listening to constituents is key. L. L. Bean's many mechanisms for keeping in touch with customers include:

- **Feedback form,** printed on recycled paper and signed by Leon Gorman, president, requesting suggestions and ideas for improvement (see Figure 6–19).

Please share your comments with us.

To our valued customer,

Your comments on our service and products are always welcome. We'd like to hear from you if you have suggestions or ideas to help us do a better job. If you need more space, please use the back of this form.

TIME AND DATE OF YOUR VISIT

Thank you, Leon A. Gorman
President, L.L.Bean

(Mr. Mrs.
Miss Ms.)
NAME

ADDRESS   APT. #

CITY   STATE   ZIP
(   )
AREA CODE   PHONE

Printed on recycled paper.

L.L.Bean®
For the outdoors inside each of us

Figure 6–19 Customer feedback is one of the many ways that L. L. Bean strives for customer satisfaction. (Courtesy of L. L. Bean, Inc.)

- **Market surveys** that provide a demographic profile of customers. As a result, the company has developed twenty-two different catalogs that are tightly targeted to fit the customer profiles.
- **Toll-free customer service number,** separate from the number to call for ordering merchandise, for instant two-way feedback and service.
- **Heavy focus on customer research, surveys, panels, and focus groups.**

"We try to get a lot closer to customers and be as responsive as we possibly can," notes Gorman.[1]

- **Internal test marketing.** "We try to get out as much as we can at Bean, and do the same things that our customers are doing, use our own products so that we have a better idea of how they're performing. We can identify better with our customers' experiences and needs."[2] Employees and owners are encouraged to give feedback just as customers are.

Training and the Internal Customer Concept

L. L. Bean's search for "total quality" is continual. Last year, over 3,000 people attended two or three days of "total quality" training. Employees are taught from day one the concept of "internal customers" as an important part of the corporate culture.

According to Gorman, "The internal customer concept means that each of us identifies who we deal with in our responsibility areas, and who are the customers for whatever we do. And it's getting together with your customers one-on-one and just discussing what they really need from you, and what they're not getting that they should be getting, and how to better serve their interests."[3]

This concept highlights the need for *internal customers to work together effectively* before *external customers can be effectively served.*

QUESTIONS FOR DISCUSSION

1. The policies and programs that Wal-Mart and L. L. Bean employ are management decisions. What is the role of public relations in them, if any? Why are these cases included in a public relations book?

2. Apply the customer satisfaction model to a real or hypothetical situation. Why does such "modeling" of how a public, such as customers, might feel, think, or behave have value in public relations practice?

3. Every department store once had greeters, known as floorwalkers. Part of their job was to move around the store and offer assistance to anyone who might need it. Today only Wal-Mart continues the practice. What public relations concepts are embodied in the idea?

---

[1] Eric Moody, "L.L. Bean, Inc.: Beyond the Maine Hunting Shoe", *Southern Maine Business Digest,* August 1991, 00.

[2] Ibid.

[3] Ibid.

PROBLEM 6A WINE BAR NEEDS POSITIONING

"Berry's" is a wine bar in a southwestern U.S. city of 400,000. In fact, it is the only full-fledged wine bar in the city. While many other bars serve wine, none specialize in fine wines of the United States and Europe as Berry's does. The fact that it is the only wine bar in the city is its problem. Although the city has ample well-educated, middle-income people, wine has not developed a following as it has in some larger cities. Because no other wine bars are available, wine drinkers have become used to ordering wine at regular bars rather than at "specialty shop" wine bars.

Berry's location is good—downtown near some fine hotels and in an area that is being revitalized, further emphasizing the upscale image. The interior is pleasant and has wine vaults for persons who want to store their wine there and have it available whenever they come into the bar. All of these vaults have been rented.

The wine bar has been open for only six months. It has a good lunch business, but needs a better evening business (especially during the week).

The total budget for creating new business is only $11,000. Mr. Berry comes to you because he knows you have just opened your own communications firm. He says, "I know it's not a lot of money, but it's a lot for my business. I can't afford to just buy ads—what do you suggest?"

Consider what type of research you would use to determine how to manage customer satisfaction—how to attract new customers and how to retain the loyalty of existing ones.

On the basis of your research, prepare a one-year strategic marketing plan that prioritizes your publics and uses a mix of one-way and two-way communication activities with evaluation methods built in. Provide a budget that allocates the $11,000 between research and customer relation activities.

Finally, what issues should Berry's be speaking out on, considering the enormity of alcoholism and driving-while-intoxicated problems, so much in the news today? Think about how to position Berry's as a socially responsible drinking establishment.

PROBLEM 6B GOOD INTENTIONS, BAD RESULT

Earlier this year, when you graduated from college, you were fortunate. You had a job waiting for you at Bart's Cartmart Inc., the largest distributor of motorized vehicles and accessories in Amarillo. The firm's slogan is, "Speed Up with Us!" Bart (Cartwright), the owner, happens to be your father. That saves having to work your way up. Besides, you've already helped out summers, when you weren't using one of the products playing golf, cruising off-road, or mowing the lawn.

This job has great promise. You're an only child, and your Dad has long had in mind that you would be taking over the business some day. In preparation, you majored in marketing, minored in public relations, and took several elective courses, including one in business law.

To start you out full-time, your Dad put you in charge of customer relations. It has been fun and challenging. This first year, you've devised a follow-up program in which you or an assistant called on each customer a week or so before the warranty period for the product purchased expired. You asked whether anything was needed by the customer that you could supply within warranty. Customers praised and liked that attention. And you've had Bart's Cartmart sponsor the winners' awards in one of the major competitive events at the annual Stock Breeders' Exhibition (motor vehicles as well as plaques and ribbons, of course).

This week, the Annual Harvest Festival is on, and acting on a request from the committee running it, you have loaned six used golf carts for the festival events.

Your father has been most tolerant about your activities. He obviously wants you to enjoy your job and to relish growing with the company. At the same time, Bart is no softie. He came off a farm and up in business the hard way. He knows what he wants and is determined to get it. At times he can be tough, if he feels he has to, and even dictatorial. That's where things stood until this morning.

When you got to work, you were handed a morning newspaper by the receptionist. In it there was a story about a twelve-year-old boy, the son of a local farmer and Harvest Festival official, who was driving one of your carts around late yesterday afternoon for fun. Something happened, and the cart tipped over on his leg, mangling it, with possible permanent damage. The kid, in the hospital, told his parents, and they told the newspaper reporter, that he "didn't know what happened." He was "just going along fine," when he felt a bump and he couldn't turn the steering wheel. Next thing he knew, the cart was headed for a big harvest machine. He tried to turn the wheel, but it wouldn't work. Next thing he knew, he was jammed between the cart and the machine. The newspaper carried a head shot of the boy. He was cute. The story indicated that the cart had been borrowed from Bart's Cartmart.

You sought out your father immediately. He said he'd gotten a call from the newspaper late in the evening, but there was no reason to disturb you. He had called the boy's father and mother, with whom he was acquainted, to express concern and sympathy. They were very upset. When he'd mentioned to them that these heavy carts weren't really made for handling by little kids, the father had made some critical remarks about lending out used carts that might have something wrong with them.

"I don't like it," your father said to you. "People don't react reasonably when their own flesh and blood is involved. I doubt we've heard the last of it." You asked him what you could do. Should you send someone in the shop with a trailer to bring the cart back and have it inspected, send the boy a book to read, arrange to retrieve all the loaned carts, or what? "We shouldn't touch that cart," your father said, "not until I can talk to our lawyer. Just sit tight for a few hours, and we'll know where this thing is going."

Within the hour, a lawyer called the company to identify himself as representing the injured boy and his family, to say he'd requested that local authorities "impound" the cart, and to indicate that he would want to talk with Bart soon. Also, within the hour, your father had talked with the company's lawyer, the agent of the firm handling the company's insurance, and with a person at the police department who said they would hold the cart. Your father's lawyer, he said, would be talking with the legal department of Rundo, the manufacturer of the carts.

Before the day was over, you and your father talked again in some detail. "This is the kind of thing you dread in a business like this," he told you. "And with so damn many ambulance-chasing lawyers around, good intentions and fair dealings don't always come out the way you had in mind. With the newspeople looking for things to blow up into headlines, I can see this thing heating up into a court case and a local issue where people who should be minding their own business stick their noses into ours and choose up sides."

You assure your father that the good intentions in loaning the carts will come out in the end and that if you're open with the newspeople they'll be fair in whatever they write or say. He says, "We'll see. If you have any ideas as this thing goes along, come tell me. I'll welcome them. But don't go off half-cocked talking with others in the newspaper, the Festival Committee, or the next door neighbors. Come see me first."

Obviously, you are anxious to help, to apply what you learned in four years, and to retain the conviction that if you treat others fairly, that's what you get in return.

Given the four-step planning process, and the aforementioned events, what might you set as your objective, your strategy, and your main tactics in helping resolve the problem before it boils over into the community and into a courtroom? What might you recommend to your father regarding the do's and don't's of customer and community relations in the future, and communications about those relations?

Chapter 7

Media Relations

The biggest misunderstanding in public relations concerns the mass media: what its role and power really are in modern society and how important media relations is in building effective public relationships.

A few practitioners still go to the extreme of *equating* public relations with publicity. So, unfortunately, do some managers. Others find contemporary journalism so unbalanced in its emphases and its audiences so fractioned that, except in unusual circumstances, they prefer to avoid the media. Fortunately, many scholarly studies have given us an objective look from which to devise workable strategies. They find that:

1. **Media influence is cumulative and long-term.** A single news report, even if covered by media across the country, or an item in a single medium, even if it's the evening news, usually causes little if any behavior or attitude change. But when many media cover a subject over the years, perhaps expressing a viewpoint on the topic, whole generations can be influenced. For example, most of us have no personal experience whatsoever with communism, yet we strongly oppose it—because all our lives it has been a subject of derision in our media.

2. **The main power of the media is to make us aware**—of products, services, companies, ideas—and to provide information about them. By itself, awareness rarely moves us to action or even shapes an opinion. But as a first step in the decision-making process, it is vital: If we don't know something exists, we can't do anything about it. Scholars call this the *agenda-setting role of the media.* (See Fig 7-1)

3. **The media concentrate on reporting bad news**—the errors, accidents, and scandals of human society. As an early American political figure said, "In a

Figure 7–1 Even members of the media, such as the creator of this popular cartoon, recognize the changes that have occurred in news gathering and dissemination. Reprinted with permission from *Universal Press Syndicate*. All rights reserved. Calvin and Hobbes copyright 1994 Watterson.

republic based upon public opinion, it is necessary to excite a spirit of in-quiry—to furnish public men with information of their errors."[1] Today, this statement is true not only of elected officials but of all executives and all or-ganizations. As educator Scott Cutlip says, "There are no private organizations today, even if they are totally owned by one or a few persons—because all must abide by the rule of public consent." But research shows we prefer to hear about bad news, rather than good news, by a factor of seven to one. In their own marketing interest, then, it follows that the media would feature bad news. It's what their customers demand.

Clearly the challenge is to create relationships with journalists and media fig-ures—as with *all* publics—that will permit them to rely on our organizations when we are the focus of interest. If reporters and editors have learned that they can trust an organization and its public relations staff, they are likely to report on the informa-tion of which we need to make our publics aware and give us a fair chance, or at least balanced reportage, when we're on the hot seat.

Though the generalized relationship between journalists and practitioners may forever be characterized as adversarial, we must remember that the two professions share one basic tenet—the First Amendment—and in pursuit of protecting this li-cense, we are united.

WORKING WITH MEDIA PEOPLE

An important part of the practitioner's job often is working with the media. This re-lationship depends on practitioners' providing information that newspeople con-sider to be of public interest—is it newsworthy?

A close and friendly working relationship is relatively easy between small or lo-

---

That word *media* still puzzles. It is plural: Newspapers in Cincinnati are the local print *media*, but the Cincinnati Post is a *medium*. Yet we often use this plural word as a collective noun and so treat it as if it were singular. How often do we read "me-dia is" rather than "media are"? Further complicating the lexicon of public relations is that *all* communication forms are also called media. Technically, we ought to dif-ferentiate between the *news* media or *mass* media—radio, television, newspapers—and *communication* media—newsletters, group meetings, speeches, letters, videos, and so on. This chapter deals with the for-mer.

---

[1]William Plummer, U.S. Senator, several times governor of New Hampshire and historian, in an ar-ticle titled "To the People," published widely, May 23, 1820.

cal organizations and the community, trade or professional media. In such situations, and there are many thousands of them, the media have small staffs and need "free" news-gathering help. Public relations practitioners provide it.

Personalized, mutually supportive relationships have become extremely difficult, however, between the mass media and the giant enterprises and institutions. Both entities tend more and more to conglomeration and automation, as the former bends to exposé journalism and the latter turns to controlled advocacy—and as animosity grows between the private and public sectors.[2]

The old image of "press relations" with a publicity- seeking "flack" wining and dining an underpaid newsperson is passé. Most major media have ethics codes that prohibit their journalists from accepting favors. The notion that it is helpful to have a buddy or a relative as a reporter, columnist, editor, publisher, news director, or producer is no longer always true. It can be suspect or even function as a handicap—particularly as media ethics codes become more common.

THE FUNDAMENTALS

Stripped down to basics, the mission of the news media is to inform audiences quickly, accurately, and fully on matters in which audiences express an interest and on matters that affect them significantly, whether or not the audiences have expressed interest, or are even aware.

In simple terms, the mission of the public relations function is to build working relationships with an organization's publics. When appropriate, doing so may require making use of news media when viewpoints or activities are newsworthy.

Along with the opportunity and capability possessed by journalists and public relations practitioners to shape public opinion go the obligations of truth and accuracy, under the law. A high degree of ethical responsibility involving moral standards and integrity is implicit in serving the ultimate best interests of the public.

The freedom of the news media to inform the public and to interpret information without bias is assured by the First Amendment to the Constitution. Abuse of that freedom could lead to loss of credibility with the audience, loss of revenue from advertisers, and public censure. Thus, while news prerogatives are jealously guarded, journalistic education and practices emphasize self-discipline. News media, owned privately and operating competitively for profit, are admittedly careful. When they interject their own views, they are expected to label them as "editorial," "opinion," "analysis," "commentary," and so on.

The public relations function comes under the freedom of speech provision in the First Amendment. Practitioners have the choice of telling their story in paid

---

[2]Ben H. Bagdikian, "Conglomerate Media? It's Already Happened," *San Diego Union,* February 4, 1979. Some twenty corporations own most of the daily papers in the United States; twenty corporations control fifty-two percent of all periodical sales; three networks and the ten largest sponsors of prime-time programming control access to two-thirds of the television audience.

space or time or offering it as news, subject to editing or rejection by the media. The penalties for abuse of free speech rights by a private organization can be loss of supportive constituents such as shareholders, employees, neighbors, customers, members, or donors, as the case might be. Then, too, there is monitoring by the FCC, FTC, and other federal agencies, as well as professional and trade societies. Within the professional practice of public relations, the penalties can be censure or expulsion by the Public Relations Society of America (see Preface) or exposure by the news media. The penalties to the individual practitioner for being "clever" in manipulating facts, being "devious" in dealings with journalists, being "unavailable" when sought by the media, or being "unauthorized as the spokesperson" for an employer can be reaped in loss of credibility and integrity in the eyes of the media and consequently loss of some functional value to the employer. The sword has an edge on both sides of the blade.

A DIFFICULT, DELICATE TASK

The practitioner serves two masters. One is the employer. The other is the public interest. Often, the news media stand between the two. The practitioner travels a precarious and rather thin line. The employer wants his or her best foot put forward in public. There are bound to be times when public exposure can be damaging to a campaign, a product, or a reputation. At these times, employers would prefer no publicity. Then there are times when the truthful and accurate response to a press inquiry is simply not known (the facts have not been ascertained). And other times when an organization's policies, or legal or competitive considerations, give precedence to its "privacy" over the "public's right to know." At such times, the forbearance of the media is desired—but rarely forthcoming.

If a practitioner is not able to handle the flow of information so that favorable news is covered and adverse news is avoided, or at least treated fairly, the practical value of the practitioner to the employer is somewhat limited. But—practitioners must make it clear to employers and clients that they cannot control the media.

GUIDELINES THAT HAVE SURVIVED

Although, as we said earlier, it is risky to draw generalizations about media relations, a number of guidelines are widely followed.

1. Start with a sound working knowledge of the methods and the technology involved in gathering potential news, in evaluating it, in processing it editorially, and in putting it into the best format and mode for newsprint, magazine, and broadcast electronic media. Be able to fit into the process.
2. Be sure that the employer has a designated spokesperson available on short notice. It may be you.

3. Have spokespeople be as candid as possible in response to inquiries—within the limits of obvious competitive and national security and of compassionate consideration for those hurt by the news.

4. Play the percentages, as in a long successful partnership, taking the instances of bad news in stride with a record of good news coverage achieved.

5. Continuously educate and train employers and spokespeople on how to handle themselves when in contact with news media.

6. Generate good news situations as a track record to offset instances of undesired news. Do not simply wait defensively for bad news.

7. Advocate an employer's views on public issues among the organization's natural constituencies and in the news media receptive to them.

8. Expect the unexpected and be prepared for it. In particular, have a crisis or disaster plan.

REFERENCES AND ADDITIONAL READINGS

CUTLIP, SCOTT M., ALLEN H. CENTER, and GLEN M. BROOM. "Media Relations." Chapter 9 in *Effective Public Relations,* 7th ed. Englewood Cliffs, N.J.: Prentice Hall, 1994.

DILENSCHNEIDER, ROBERT L. "Use Ingenuity in Media Relations." *Public Relations Quarterly* v37 (Summer 1992): 13–15.

EVANS, FRED J. *Managing the Media: Proactive Strategy for Better Business & Press Relations.* Westport, CT: Greenwood, 1987.

The Foundation for American Communications (FACS) is an organization that seeks to improve mutual understanding between major American institutions and the news media. For more information write, Foundation for American Communications, 3800 Barham Blvd., Ste. 409, Los Angeles, Calif. 90068.

The Freedom Forum Media Studies Center offers a variety of programs and publications exploring the field of mass communication and technological change. For more information write; The Freedom Forum Media Studies Center, Columbia University, 2950 Broadway, New York, N.Y. 10027.

GLYNN, CARROLL J., and ROBERT E. OSTMAN. "Public Opinion About Public Opinion." *Journalism Quarterly* 65 (Summer 1988): 299–306.

GREENBURG, KEITH ELLIOT. "Radio News Releases Make the Hit Parade." *Public Relations Journal* v48 (July 1992): 6.

GRUNIG, JAMES E., and TODD HUNT. *Managing Public Relations.* New York: Holt, Rinehart and Winston, 1984. See chaps 11, 19, 20, 21, 22.

LERBINGER, OTTO, and NATHANIEL N. SPERBER. "Media Relations." Chapter 3 in *Manager's Public Relations Handbook.* Reading, Mass.: Addison-Wesley, 1982.

LESLY, PHILIP. "Publicity in TV and Radio." Chapter 25 in *Lesly's Public Relations Handbook.* 4th ed. Chicago, IL: Probus Publishing, 1991.

LUKASZWESKI, JIM. *Influencing Public Attitudes.* Leesburg, Virginia: Issue Action Publications, 1993.

MARQUIS, SIMON. "Media Speak: Mutual Respect Fosters Healthy Media Relations." *Marketing.* (December 9, 1993): 21

MUNDY, ALICIA. "Is the Press Any Match for Powerhouse PR?" *Business and Society Review.* (Fall 1993): 34–40.

NEWSOM, DOUG, ALAN SCOTT, and JUDY VAN SLYKE TURK. "Communication Channels," and "Working with the Media." Chapters 6 and 10 in *This Is PR: The Realities of Public Relations.* 4th ed. Belmont, Calif.: Wadsworth, 1989.

POWELL, JODY. *The Other Side of the Story.* New York: William Morrow, 1984. Media seen by a presidential press secretary.

Purview, pr reporter (supplement April 4, 1994). The "new aggressiveness" in media relations; public relations learns new tricks.

RAFE, STEPHEN C. *Mastering the News Media Interview.* New York: HarperCollins, 1991.

RALEY, NANCY and LAURA CARTER, eds. *The New Guide to Effective Media Relations,* Washington, D.C., Council for Advancement and Support of Education, 1988.

REARDON, KATHLEEN K. and EVERETT M. ROGERS. "Interpersonal Versus Mass Media Communication: A False Dichotomy," *Human Communication Research* 15 (2) (Winter 1988): 284–303.

REILLY, ROBERT T. "Publicity." Chapter 6 in *Public Relations in Action.* 2nd ed. Englewood Cliffs, N.J.: Prentice Hall, 1988.

SHOEMAKER, PAMELA J., ed., *Communication Campaign About Drugs: Government, Media, and the Public,* Hillsdale, NJ: Lawrence Erlbaum Associates, 1989.

"Technology Transforms Media Relations Work." *Public Relations Journal* 49 (November 1993): 38–40.

The Public Relations Body of Knowledge. New York: PRSA, 1993. See section V.1 for abstracts dealing with "Media Relations, Including Crisis Management."

TRAHAN, JOSEPH III. "Building Media Relations During a Crisis." *tips & tactics. pr reporter* (supplement, December 14, 1992). Lessons learned from Hurricane Andrew.

TRAHAN, JOSEPH III. "Media Relations in the Eye of the Storm." *Public Relations Quarterly* 38 (Summer 1993): 31–32.

TUCKER, KERRY, and DORIS DERELIAN. *Public Relations Writing: A Planned Approach for Creating Results.* Englewood Cliffs, N.J.: Prentice Hall, 1989.

TUCKER, KERRY, et al. "Managing issues acts as bridge to strategic planning." *Public Relations Journal* v38 (Fall 1993): 41–42.

VAN LEUVEN, JAMES K. and MICHAEL D. SLATER. "How Publics, Public Relations, and the Media Shape the Public Opinion Process." *Public Relations Research Annual,* Vol. 3, Larissa A. Grunig and James E. Grunig, eds., Hillsdale, NJ: Lawrence Erlbaum Associates, 1991: 165–178.

WALSH, FRANK. *Public Relations Writer in a Computer Age.* Englewood Cliffs, N.J.: Prentice Hall, 1986.

NASSP: News Media as a Feedback Source

Thoughts about education reform abide in the minds of teachers, principals, and politicians because of the many challenges that exist in our school systems. But one essential question persists: What lies behind these education challenges? In an effort to find out and at the same time build relationships with its publics and the media, the National Association of Secondary School Principals (NASSP) investigated.

THE PROBLEMS OUR EDUCATION SYSTEM FACES

Many American students lack the resources and the motivation to score higher than their European and Asian peers on assessment tests. Yet Americans have not found a solution. These lower scores could affect the future of American business—American businesses might fall behind countries that are more competitive because their work force is better trained.

Schools are also filled with social and cultural problems. Many students are unmotivated, wrapped up in drug and alcohol problems, trapped by poverty, angry and uninterested in coping with everyday life at school. Many skip school or cheat on tests and assignments. Controversy over whose responsibility it is to teach sex education takes priority in many schools across the nation. Many other problem exist. The question is: Who will solve them, and how? Teachers were underpaid for years, and many came to feel that with minimum pay they should not have to do more than teach. In an effort to answer these questions, educational organizations, the state and federal governments, teachers and parents are looking for solutions—and many are finding some.

NASSP TAKES ACTION

NASSP's research found that one of the major problems embedded in our education system is communication between parents and secondary school principals. NASSP is an organization of 43,000 high school and middle school educators, making it the nation's largest school leadership organization. Its membership includes principals, assistant principals, assistant superintendents, deans of students, and college and university professors. Its focus is on professional development, as well as promoting the interests of education in Congress and conducting research on issues critical to middle and high schools. Its vision statement reads:

> In a profoundly changing global society, schools must be responsive to the needs and aspirations of an increasingly diverse student population. Principals, as the educational leaders, are essential to ensure the successful flow of change. They must be the primary agents of change for effective learning and teaching.
>
> NASSP, as the pre-eminent organization for middle level and high school administrators, will assert itself locally, nationally, and internationally in addressing school quality and the professional leadership needs of school administrators. In setting the educational agenda for the twenty-first century, NASSP will assist principals and other school leaders in improving the conditions under which schools are organized for effective teaching and learning.

One survey, conducted by Roy R. Nasstrom, found that principals are not perceived as instructional leaders and that many dislike contact with parents. The survey found further that these principals need to understand the value of discussing school issues with parents and other community members, because parental contact is the "major source of dissatisfaction" among secondary school principals.

With these problems in mind, NASSP decided to set up a telephone hotline at its 1989 annual meeting in New Orleans to give principals an opportunity to talk to parents from around the nation. In setting up this hotline, NASSP decided to achieve four goals:

1. To disseminate information about schools.
2. To position principals and assistant principals as knowledgeable instructional leaders.
3. To strengthen principals' knowledge about problems in the school system and make them aware of the concerns that members of the school community have about these problems.
4. To strengthen NASSP's positive relationship with *USA Today,* an important national medium for NASSP's long-term public relations program.

NASSP STUDIES ITS PUBLICS, PLANS ACTIVITIES

In order for the hotline to succeed, NASSP needed a plan. To begin the process, it first determined its publics. These included:

1. **Potential volunteers** to answer the phone (made up of the best-quality principals, personally invited, and who were attending the convention).
2. **Interested members of the public** who needed information and would ask questions.
3. *USA Today* **staff** with whom NASSP needed to maintain a reputation of credibility.

NASSP's first test was to find enough volunteers—108 principals and assistant principals—to answer the phone for the four-day period at the annual meeting. This goal became a priority because without volunteers other goals could not be achieved.

To ensure that the overall goals would be met, NASSP determined its immediate objectives:

1. Provide volunteer principals with a news release format to promote the event with news media in their communities.
2. Have at least ninety percent of the principals indicate after the project that they enjoyed the experience.
3. Have at least one of the state affiliates consider replicating the hotline as a state project.
4. Receive at least 1,000 phone calls during the four-day period.
5. Receive news coverage on the project for the four-day period that would encourage people to call.
6. Receive coverage in at least one-third of the ninety-one Gannett newspapers (parent company of *USA Today* and the largest newspaper chain).
7. Have members of the *USA Today* staff in some observable fashion indicate their pleasure with this hotline after its completion.
8. Have *USA Today* seriously consider conducting a second education hotline at the 1990 NASSP convention.

NASSP believed working closely with *USA Today* would be key to making the hotline a success. One advantage NASSP had in the beginning was that *USA Today* was making education a priority in selecting stories. However, a problem could have arisen had *USA Today* decided to do the hotline with another educational organization that also was having an annual meeting at the same time as NASSP. From a media relations angle, therefore, suggesting the idea to them was a risk.

HOMEWORK IS ASSIGNED

To accomplish its goals, NASSP undertook the following activities:

1. Wrote a pitch letter for use when soliciting principals to participate and to assure that all potential volunteers received the same information.
2. Contacted each volunteer individually to ascertain his or her commitment to the project.
3. Developed a schedule of volunteers who agreed to participate.
4. Sent letters to all volunteers, with background materials to help them handle questions about subjects that were anticipated as high interest. It also expressed the organization's appreciation and reminded them of their day and times to answer the hotline.
5. Attached reminders to every volunteer's convention registration badge to ensure that the volunteers wouldn't forget their time commitment.
6. Prepared and published articles in the daily convention newspaper, including a list of principals and assistant principals who volunteered to answer phones. This measure served as a reminder and as recognition of the volunteers.
7. Distributed a national news release to approximately 780 news outlets throughout the country. In addition, it published an article in the NASSP *NewsLeader,* a monthly newsletter for members.
8. Sent thank-you letters and a postsurvey form to all volunteers to evaluate the success of the hotline and to learn what concerns callers voiced to the volunteers.
9. Sent letters to volunteers' superintendents recognizing the principals for their efforts.
10. Sent postproject news releases to all NASSP state-affiliate newsletters.

NASSP AND USA TODAY RECEIVE AN "A" FOR A SUCCESSFUL PROGRAM

More than 1,500 people (500 more than projected) called from throughout the United States. Principals gained valuable insights to problems that secondary schools are facing and also provided some helpful answers to concerned parents, grandparents, and students.

Volunteers learned about the problems within our education system from an external perspective. They had an opportunity to offer suggestions for improvement, as well as answer the questions of those people who called the hotline. The volunteers discovered new approaches for handling educational problems, gained insights on concerns of community members, and returned to their state and local schools with ideas for making programs more sensitive to public concerns.

Budgeted at less than $500, plus staff time, the program achieved most of its goals and objectives. The total number of volunteers exceeded 108 principals, which was the original goal. News coverage could have reached 22,898,169 potential newspaper readers. Two *USA Today* staff members most closely involved wrote letters commending the project and indicating an interest in doing the hotline in subsequent years. *USA Today* not only replicated the hotline for two more years, but it also added two telephones and a fifth day to the event for the second and third years (see Figure 7-2). Budget cuts prevented *USA Today* from doing it a fourth year, but the newspaper plans to repeat it in future years.

In the words of Lew Armistead, director of public relations for NASSP: as he told the authors

There are very few instances where people can be moved to action through use of newspapers. At best, newspaper coverage makes people aware of a concern. This program goes beyond that. It involves newspapers in a real public relations effort. This program provides a way for people to get answers to their questions so they can take

Figure 7–2 The hotline was run for the third year in 1991. (Copyright 1991, *USA Today*. Reprinted with permission.)

action in their local communities. Typically, newspapers are one-way mass media vehicles. But this program turns *USA Today* into a two-way communication vehicle.

QUESTIONS FOR DISCUSSION

1. Can you think of other one-way communication vehicles that may be turned into a two-way communication vehicle as the NASSP did with *USA Today?* How could the NASSP have utilized them in order to accomplish their plans? Devise a strategy to explain.

2. Was NASSP corrupting the integrity of channels of communication by cosponsoring this event with *USA Today?* How could a *USA Today* reporter remain objective and write a balanced story about this program?

3. If you were the director of public relations for NASSP, how would you advise a principal who was featured in a national news article for his participation on the hotline but was later criticized by local parents for his inaccessibility? They claim he can't be reached on the phone and seldom returns their calls. Would you give him the same advice if he was the president-elect of NASSP?

Alar and PR: Getting to the Core of the Apple Problem

This is the story of the fall and rise of the American apple industry in 1989. The case was precipitated by a forceful public relations and publicity campaign that brought discredit and disfavor to apples and apple products. The ensuing problem was met by an equally forceful rebuttal campaign with the result that, today, apples are being consumed in normal fashion.[1]

This case will examine both "campaigns" and look at the role public relations techniques played in this national controversy.

THE SITUATION

Apples have been part of a healthful diet for centuries. An apple a day kept the doctor away. An apple for the teacher was appreciated, even if apple-polishing students were not. A favorite person was "the apple of my eye," and being "as American as apple pie" was as patriotic as one could get.

That's why the nation was shocked to hear, in February 1989, that people (especially small children) eating apples were jeopardizing their health. What had happened to change the shiny cure-all to a carcinogen? Alar and PR; *60 Minutes,* and the national media.

Since 1968, apple growers had used a chemical called daminozide (trademark Alar) to slow the ripening process and retain the red color. However, in 1985, scientists reported Alar and its residue, UDMH, could cause cancer in animals. Many

---

[1]This case study was developed by Steven Rub, a student at the University of Central Florida, under the direction of Frank Stansberry, APR and Manager of Guest Affairs at Coca-Cola USA who also teaches at UCF. The authors thank them for their contribution to this case studies book.

growers stopped using Alar at that time[2] and in 1986 a self-designated public interest group called the Natural Resources Defense Council (NRDC) began a study of pesticides and resultant risks to preschool children.[3] (See Figures 7–3 and 7–4.)

The Environmental Protection Agency (EPA) began a regulatory process to consider banning the pesticide and, in early February 1989, announced that the process was being sped up, possibly as a result of efforts by NRDC. There was no rise in consumer awareness of Alar- related problems at the time.[4]

On February 26, however, the CBS show *60 Minutes* aired a segment entitled "A Is for Apple," which characterized the risk, especially to preschoolers, of getting cancer from eating apples and apple products as "intolerable."[5] It based the report on a white paper from NRDC, "Intolerable Risk: Pesticides in Our Children's Food."

NRDC followed the CBS report with a major news conference in Washington, D.C., the next day, augmented by regional news conferences in a dozen cities around the country.[6] In short, a major publicity effort had begun.

National awareness of the "danger" of eating apples rose from virtually nil at the first of the month to ninety-five percent at the end of the month, as all news media jumped ont his journalistically enticing story.

Faced with that type of public awareness and concern, the members of the International Apple Institute voluntarily stopped using Alar on their crops.[7] In June, Uniroyal, make of Alar, announced plans to discontinue sales of the pesticide in the United States.[8]

Meanwhile, apple growers began to fight back. Spurred by the Washington State Apple Commission, the industry hired the public relations firm Hill & Knowlton (H&K), to mount the counterattack. H&K had been monitoring public opinion since before the first volley from NRDC. Its research showed that "purchase intent" for apples had gone into a "deep decline."

In its report, "The Alar Scare: Rebuilding Apple Consumption During the Alar Crisis," H&K noted that the media blitz from Alar's critics "led to a widespread panic, and a firestorm of negative reporting on the safety of apples. Moms across America began dumping apple juice down the drain. Cancer hotlines were deluged by calls from anxious parents. The message they were getting everywhere was 'don't feed your kids apples, its not worth the risk.'"

The strategy for gaining back the lost confidence was threefold—to get the facts about the safety of apples to worried consumers; to discredit the NRDC report

[2]"Apples without Alar." *Newsweek,* October 30, 1989, 86.

[3]"Intolerable Risk: Pesticides in Our Children's Food," a report by the Natural Resources Defense Council, February 27, 1989.

[4]"The Alar Scare: Rebuilding Apple Consumption During the Alar Crisis," a report by Hill & Knowlton (undated.)

[5]*60 Minutes:* Transcript "A Is for Apple," broadcast February 26, 1989.

[6]*Wall Street Journal,* October 3, 1989, an op-ed article on the Alar issue.

[7]*New York Times,* May 16, 1989, 1, 19.

[8]*New York Times,* June 30, 1989, 1, 11.

**Intolerable Risk:
Pesticides in our Children's Food**

Summary

**A Report by the
Natural Resources Defense Council**

February 27, 1989

Figure 7–3 The NRDC published a 141-page report in 1989 that examined the types and amounts of pesticides that are in foods. (Courtesy of the NRDC.)

as "bad science," and to get key sources (government regulatory bodies, scientists, the medical community) to reaffirm apples' wholesomeness and nutritional benefits.

The plan worked; by fall 1989, per capita consumption of apples had returned to an all-time high, a trend that continues today.

THE FACTS

The facts about Alar and apples are pretty clear. Alar is a plant growth inhibitor. Without Alar, apple growers will have to pick the crop four to six days earlier, before the apples drop. Thus, some varieties may go to market a little "green" and may lack perfect visual appeal. Shelf-life may also be affected.

Alar, as one of many products produced by Uniroyal, contributed only $4.6

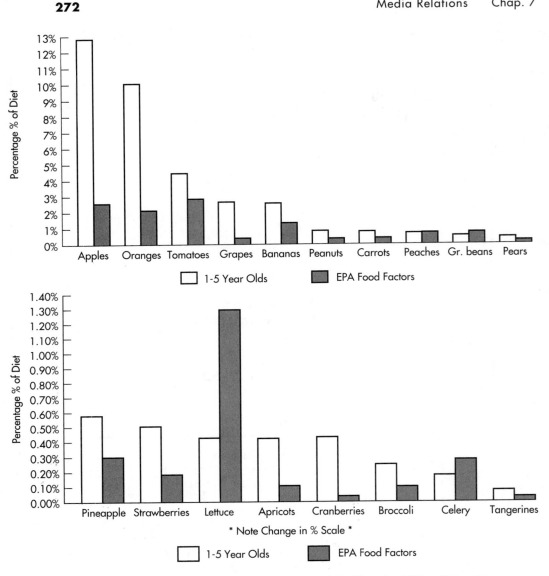

NOTE: Current preschooler consumption estimates were derived from the CSFII — *Nationwide Food Consumption Survey: Continuing Survey of Food Intakes by Individuals, Women 19–50 Years and Their Children 1–5 Years, 6 Waves,* 1985, and are average intakes of all forms (*i.e.* raw and processed) of each produce type for all children included in the 1985 Nationwide Food Consumption Survey. Food Factors were obtained from EPA, Toxicology Branch, Revised Average Food Factors, May 1, 1978.

Figure 7–4   The report of NRDC examined pesticide intakes by children and noted the large consumption of apples by children. (Courtesy of the NRDC.)

million in sales at the time of the controversy, which accounted for about six-tenths of one percent of Uniroyal's total sales. It was not a major player in the overall sales picture.

Before 1985, about 35 percent of all "eating" apples were treated with Alar, including most red apples and some Golden Delicious. By 1989, the industry estimates of Alar usage were between five and fifteen percent.[9] Most growers stopped using Alar after EPA investigations in 1985.[10]

Risk factors from Alar-tainted apples are less clear. In a table released by NRDC as part of the "Intolerable Risk" report, apples fell at the midpoint of twenty-six fruits and vegetables rated by frequency of detectable levels of pesticides. Strawberries were ranked first (sixty-three percent with detectable levels). Apples and spinach (twenty-nine percent) were in the middle, and corn and bananas (one percent) were at the bottom.

Uniroyal continually said its pesticide was safe as used. Support for this position was widespread and broad-based. Canadian health officials noted pesticide residues only one-thirtieth of safety levels and commented that a child would have to eat 250,000 apples a day for Alar residues to impose a threat to health.[11]

In England, British health officials saw "no risk to consumers," noting that an infant would have to consume 150 times a normal amount to reach even a "no effect" level of UDMH.[12]

Even Consumer's Union, through its publication *Consumer Reports,* said, "Apples treated with Alar are not necessarily unsafe to eat, since daminozide itself has not been firmly shown to cause cancer."[13] Later, in a letter to the editor of another consumer's magazine, *Consumer's Research,* the editors of *Consumer Reports* acknowledged, "The statements that 'Apples are safe to eat,' and that 'The EPA should ban Alar' sound contradictory, but they are not." *Consumer Reports* further said that current data suggest that Alar, per se, probably is not a carcinogen, but that its breakdown product, UDMH, probably is.

Thus, the risk is associated more directly with processed apple products than with raw apples (UDMH is released when apples are heated or otherwise processed). *Consumer Reports* saw the risk if UDMH levels rose to forty-five parts per million and said, "While large enough to justify EPA regulatory concern, . . . there is no need for public panic over a risk this size."[14]

The federal agencies, EPA, Food and Drug Administration (FDA), and the U.S. Department of Agriculture, agreed to issue a joint statement on March 16, 1989,

[9]"Where the Daminozide Is," *Science News,* June 14, 1985, 169.

[10]"Law & Legislation," *Newsweek,* February 13, 1989, 65.

[11]"An Apple-Spray Scare," *Macleans,* March 20, 1989, N-8.

[12]"Upsetting the Apple Spray Cart," *Chemistry and Industry,* January 1, 1990, 2.

[13]"Bad Apples," *Consumer Reports,* May 1989, 287.

[14]*Consumer's Research,* July 1989, 28. Letter from editors of *Consumer Reports* in response to article, "Does Everything Cause Cancer?"

which said, "The federal government believes that it is safe for Americans to eat apples."[15]

Mothers and Others (a spin-off group from NRDC) said in a "fact sheet" that "chances are very slight that an individual child will get cancer from consuming apples or apple products," even when Alar was in use.[16] (See Figure 7–5). And *Consumer Reports,* in a sidebar to its "Bad Apples" story,[17] tested forty-four brands of apple juice for daminozide levels and found only four (all regional brands unique to the New York area) unacceptable.

UDMH, however, continued to pose a problem. *Consumer Reports* said, "The likely carcinogen is UDMH, which appears when juice from daminozide-treated apples is cooked to produce the concentrate from which commercial juice is made."

This perception of danger, dramatized by major new outlets, was what caused the public to panic. The impact on apple growers was immediate and substantial. Apple growers lost an estimated \$100–\$150 million on the 1988 crop, which was being sold at the time. Most of this economic impact was felt in Washington State, where growers lost between \$100 and \$140 million on that year's crop. Washington supplies sixty percent of the fresh, or "eating," apples consumed in the United States.[18]

Apple juice sales in 1989 fell as much as twenty-two percent at one point and finished the year down about fourteen percent,[19] while overall apple sales were down twenty percent for the year.[20]

THE PUBLIC PERCEPTION

The facts notwithstanding, the public was not buying apples. The media images of danger were too clear. For example, the *60 Minutes* story that kicked off the scare was entitled "A Is for Apple," but it showed a skull and crossbones superimposed over a shiny red apple. The *Consumer Reports* story carried the title "Bad Apples."

Urged and directed by NRDC, actress Meryl Streep took to the airwaves and popular magazines to say she was "furious" to discover that two of her children's favorite foods, apples and strawberries, might be hazardous to their health because of Alar.[21] *Newsweek* entitled its report "EPA Is Looking for a Few Bad Apples."

The result was what publicist David Fenton described as "a sea of change in

---

[15]"Fruit Fights," *Wall Street Journal,* March 17, 1989, A-14.

[16]Mothers and Others, "Fact Sheet: Alar," undated.

[17]"Apple Juice: A Long Way from the Tree," *Consumer Reports,* May 1989, 293.

[18]Reuters; "Agencies: Alar Scare Nearly Over," *Orlando Sentinel,* November 4, 1989, 12.

[19]A. C. Neilsen and Co. report to Florida Citrus Commission, October 1989.

[20]"Avery's Uniroyal Ends Alar Sales in U.S.; Apple Product Imports Still Worry Critics," *Wall Street Journal,* June 5, 1989, B3.

[21]"Ms. Streep Goes to Washington to Stop a Bitter Harvest," *People Magazine,* March 20, 1989, 50.

Mothers & Others

for a livable planet

40 West 20th Street, 11th floor • New York, New York 10011

phone: 212-727-4474 • fax: 212-675-6481

Fact sheet: Alar

Mothers & Others is frequently asked about Alar, the chemical that was removed from the market in 1989 after a campaign by Mothers & Others and the Natural Resources Defense Council to call attention to problems of pesticides in children's food. Here, we address some of the facts and myths surrounding this controversial chemical.

Our children are safer with Alar off the market. In 1989, public pressure led the manufacturer of Alar (which was used on apple crops to control growth and enhance apples' red color) to take the product off the market. The U.S. Environmental Protection Agency (EPA) later banned Alar for use on food products—*years after the agency first acknowledged the chemical's potential to cause cancer.* After concluding its review of the scientific data in 1992, the agency reiterated that Alar and its "breakdown" product, UDMH, should be classified as "probable human carcinogens," and that long-term exposure to Alar posed unacceptable risks to public health. (UDMH was formed when apples containing residues of Alar were processed into things like applesauce and apple juice.) Children eat significantly more apples and apple products, relative to their body weight, than adults do, and therefore received relatively greater exposure to Alar/UDMH. What's more, because their physiological systems are still developing, children are usually more susceptible than adults to the toxic effects of a contaminant. So children were *even more at risk* from exposure to Alar and UDMH than the general public—and are better off with Alar off the market.

There is NO truth to the claim that a child would have to eat 28,000 pounds of apples a day to be at risk from Alar. The chemical industry makes this claim based on high doses of UDMH fed to laboratory animals. Animals are routinely tested at very high doses, and a majority of the scientific community endorses the high dose method as a valid basis for regulating human exposure to chemicals, rather than waiting for actual proof of carcinogenicity in humans. However, the *human* risk from Alar was not based on the assumption that children would ingest an equal amount of UDMH as lab animals—risks to people are always figured on real exposure levels. In the case of Alar, exposure estimates were based on actual pesticide residue levels found on apples and on actual consumption data for pre-schoolers, which the USDA says is one ounce of raw apple and two ounces of apple juice per day.

Figure 7–5 Mother and Others distributed a specific fact sheet about the Alar chemical. (Courtesy of Mothers and Others.)

public opinion." The *Wall Street Journal* reported that "apples and apple juice have been going down garbage disposals all across the country." The school boards of New York City, Los Angeles, and Chicago, among others, banned apples from the lunch programs. (Fenton later said that effect was one not recommended by NRDC.)

The NRDC report highlighted the risk to children, who, because of their size and tendency to eat more fresh fruit than adults, seemed more at risk. "Children ingest so many apples for their size," Fenton said, "that the legal federal standard is unsafe." Reuters reported "Many consumers and school lunchrooms stopped buying apples," after hearing or seeing the report. "The negative messages about the safety of Alar and apples left the public unsure about what to believe," the Hill & Knowlton report said. "This lead to a startling decline in intent to purchase apples."

The public was faced with cognitive dissonance—wanting to believe that apples were healthful, yet besieged by messages that apples would cause cancer. "The scare, though short-lived, was nearly everywhere," reports Lee Baker in his book *The Credibility Factor.*[22] People phoned the International Apple Institutes to see if apple juice should be disposed of in a toxic waste site!

Merchants, too, were worried. "Customer reaction to the program [*60 Minutes*] was explosive, prompting many retailers to proclaim they would no longer sell Alar-treated apples or apple products." The International Apple Institute said at the time that consumers' concerns about the health effects of Alar had probably cost apple growers more than $100 million, a figure that proved to be conservative.

Competitors, however, were delighted. A representative of the A. C. Neilson Company, reported to the Florida Citrus Commission that "lingering effects of the Alar scare," in 1989 helped orange juice widen its lead over apple juice as the fruit beverage of choice in American homes.

THE PUBLIC RELATIONS PROBLEM

Although the facts about apples and Alar were weighed heavily in favor of the industry, the emotions were all negative. Raw apples, even those treated with Alar, were not hazardous to health. UDMH, the suspected carcinogen, appeared only when apples were processed or otherwise subjected to heat.

The bulk of the communication, however, targeted apples and Alar in general—*without regard to the secondary role of UDMH*. Perception had been shaped in a way that left apples—all apples—tainted by association with the pesticide. Changing that perception was the challenge of the industry and its public relations counsel.

---

[22]Lee Baker, *The Credibility Factor*, (Homewood, Ill.: Business One Irwin, 1993) 120–127.

THE PUBLIC RELATIONS IMPACT

Public relations techniques created the problem for the apple growers and proces-sors, and public relations techniques helped get them back on their feet. David Fen-ton, public relations counsel to NRDC, outlined his program in a lengthy memo. In his memo, Fenton said that the situation was created "because of a carefully planned media campaign," based on NRDC's report "Intolerable Risk." Participation by ac-tress Meryl Streep "was an essential element."

Fenton said that the goal of his campaign was to "create so many repetitions of NRDC's message that average American consumers could not avoid hearing it. The idea was for the story to achieve a life of its own, and to continue for weeks and months to affect policy and consumer habits." This goal, Fenton says, was met. "A modest investment by NRDC repaid itself many-fold in tremendous media exposure and substantial, immediate revenue for further pesticide work." Other revenue-producing elements of the program were "self-published book sales . . . and a 900 phone number."

The timing of the campaign was to grant *60 Minutes* an exclusive "break," then to hold the Washington and satellite press conferences the following day. The *60 Minutes* broadcast moved the needle of public awareness to forty-five percent, while subsequent coverage moved it to nearly ninety-five percent. (But both numbers are highly questionable; for initial exposure to reach forty-five percent of *any* public, to say nothing of the food-consuming public, is virtually im-possible. The total audience for *60 Minutes* proved to be a tiny fraction of this group.)

Fenton played the "Streep" card a week later fanning the flames. Her group, Mothers and Others for Pesticide Limits, would lobby citizens to seek changes in pesticide laws and ask for pesticide-free products at retail outlets. Other celebrities joined the bandwagon as the story gained momentum. Schools began dropping ap-ples from the menu; retail stores began rejecting Alar-tainted fruit. Alar was with-drawn from the market and the EPA, USDA, and FDA issued statements saying that apples were safe.

The media relations work done by Fenton and NRDC was thorough. In breadth and depth, the coverage generated and the resultant outcry met Fenton's goals. In fact, the media took the story so strongly that, to some, the coverage be-came advocacy rather than reporting of factual information or news. This is often the case in contemporary journalism, as audiences and advertising decline and cov-erage becomes more and more sensational in an attempt to recapture them.

At a Smithsonian Institution conference for environmentalists and writers, Charles Alexander, science editor of *Time Magazine,* said, "I would freely admit that, on this issue, we have crossed a boundary from news reporting to advocacy." Later, David Brooks, editorial writer for the *Wall Street Journal,* wrote, "somehow the idea has gotten around that the environment isn't just a normal political issue, but a quasi-religious crusade. As a result, public discussion of the environment has been about as rigorous as one expects from a jihad. . . . The reporters who became advocates seem to think they are doing the environment a favor."[23]

Andrea Mitchell of NBC said, "Clearly, the networks have made that decision now, where you'd have to call it advocacy."[24] "Usually, it takes a significant natural disaster to create this much sustained news attention for an environmental problem," Fenton wrote in his memo. "We believe this experience proves there are ways to raise public awareness for the purpose of moving Congress and policy makers."

THE APPLE GROWERS RESPOND

Apple growers would probably characterize the Alar scare as an "unnatural disaster." According to Hill & Knowlton, the producers of *60 Minutes* had promised the apple industry a "balanced look at the pesticide issue," but what occurred was later characterized by the *Wall Street Journal* as "fright wig treatment of Alar." Apples, not Alar, took the center stage.

With overnight telephone surveys, H&K followed the decline in apples' reputation. The public wanted to be assured that apples were safe before sales could rebound. What industry leaders hoped could be a low-profile response shifted into a higher gear: The truth would be the chief weapon.

While Washington State apples were hardest hit, and those growers would be the principal financial backer of the defense effort, it was decided that a national organization should represent the industry. Therefore, the International Apple Institute was identified as the nominal leader for the program funded by the Washington Apple Commission.

The strategy was threefold: (1) to get the facts out about apples' safety (and to separate apples from Alar); (2) to discredit the NRDC research as being based on old, discredited data; and (3) to get key influencers—government, scientific, medical—to stand up for the safety and nutritional benefits of apples and apple products.

Key publics were (1) governmental agencies, (2) industry insiders including growers, (3) the food industry including retailers and wholesalers, (4) the medical and scientific community, (5) schools, and (6) the news media.

The results were good. Consumer awareness of the Alar "danger" remained high, but by the third week of March 1989 (less than one month after the first *60 Minutes* broadcast) the decline in intent to purchase had reversed.

Sales bottomed out and began a slow climb upward until, by early May, shipments were "setting seasonal highs." By fall, per capita consumption of apples hit an all-time high and today the average American is eating twenty-two pounds of fresh apples a year—a thirty-year high.

---

[23]"Alar PR," *Chemtech,* May 1989, 264.
[24]Ibid.

QUESTIONS FOR DISCUSSION

1. To carry out its work, a public interest organization such as NRDC must maintain a staff of administrators, scientists and researchers, lawyers, public relations practitioners and others—as either employees or consultants. Because NRDC has no products or services to sell, in the usual sense, funds must be raised through memberships, contributions, and events to cover its budget. To what extent might this consideration influence the preparation, release, and promotion of a highly visible, controversial report such as the one on Alar? Do you think that the public that is the target of such campaigns—which are carried on by all public interest organizations as an important part of their *illusions*—is aware of this possible self-interest? If the public should be aware, whose responsibility is it to make them so?

2. Why would the public listen to an obvious nonexpert such as Meryl Streep on a scientific topic like this? Critics of such celebrity involvement in issues called her a "Hollywood toxicologist." Are you aware of any similar incidents?

3. Among its target publics, Hill & Knowlton listed the news media. Are the media a *public?* Or a communications *vehicle?* What are the strategy implications of according them status as a public?

4. Does David Fenton's campaign for NRDC raise any ethical issues? Check the PRSA code in the Preface.

5. Is it possible that the attention focused on apples by the Alar scare played a part in the fact that Americans are now consuming the fruit in record numbers? Attempt to make a case for the position that it did.

Case 7-3

Nightmare in Newfoundland

In its December 23, 1985 issue, *Newsweek* gave multipage coverage to the story of a military disaster.

> The chartered DC-8 was almost as old as many passengers it carried; a 1969 plane bringing American soldiers home for Christmas after six months of peacekeeping duty in the Sinai desert.
>
> The refueling stop at the remote Gander, Newfoundland, airport took about an hour, enough time for a leg stretch or a dash into the gift shop for one of the Christmas toys later found amid the wreckage.
>
> The plane taxied to runway 22, then took off for Fort Campbell, Kentucky, in a predawn mix of snow and freezing drizzle. It flew for less than half a mile. "There was a flash . . . then an explosion," said Judy Parsons, who saw the plane from her company's parking lot. The DC-8 crashed into a wooded area, strewing bodies and debris for three-quarters of a mile.
>
> "Everything was black, charred," said Terry Harvey, a Coast Guardsman on the scene. "Even the snow was gone—melted. It was just like there had been a forest fire."
>
> At Fort Campbell the post gymnasium had been decked with banners, and a brass band was ready to welcome the peacekeepers home. As family members gathered at the gym, many had already heard the grim morning news flashes. They listened in quiet desperation as Brigade Commander Col. John Herrling confirmed their worst fears: There were no apparent survivors among the 248 soldiers and eight crew members aboard the Arrow Air charter jet. "This is the deepest and most heartfelt tragedy of my time in the Army," said Maj. Gen. Burton D. Patrick, the post and division commander, as the tightly knit community braced to comprehend the worst disaster to hit the proud elite 101st Airborne Division, known as The Screaming Eagles.

Disaster . . . a disaster in which there are lives lost, people to blame, families in shock, and a well-known, highly visible organization to which the media and the world can turn for information. So it was for the military public affairs officers when their nightmare in Newfoundland began early on the morning of December 12, 1985.[1] (See Figure 7-6.)

GANDER, NEWFOUNDLAND

Under the auspices of the Canadian government, the Gander airport had its own emergency response program and plan for disasters like this. However, the local Transport Canada public affairs officer (PAO)[2] was away in St. John's, an hour's flying time to the east. The regional PAO was two-hour's flying time away in Halifax. The crash, which had taken place early in the morning of December 12, 1985, had no coordinating official on the scene until 11:00 A.M.

The disaster plan, which had been exercised numerous times earlier, involved many agencies. By the time the public affairs officers arrived, the following steps had been taken automatically:

1. The base commander, as part of the emergency command team, immediately activated the base disaster plan.
2. Upwards of 300 members of the Canadian forces were sent out in support of activities at the airport.
3. The site itself, as far as the crash was concerned, was controlled by the Royal Canadian Mounted Police, another component of the emergency command team.

MEDIA ONSLAUGHT AS RUMORS ABOUND

Since responsibility for the crash site was held by the Royal Canadian Mounted Police, reports were given by them in the beginning. They were able to release quick, accurate information that a crash had occurred. They also allowed a local media team to go in very early for still photo and video footage, which was to be pooled.[3]

---

[1]We are indebted to Defense Information School, Fort Benjamin Harrison, Indiana, for providing detailed background on this case.

[2]Military and U.S. government public relations practitioners are, by regulation, called public affairs officers. Prior to 1980, most were titled public information officers (PIO). That term was felt to be too restrictive, considering their actual responsibilities. Both titles reflect a longstanding misunderstanding by some elected officials, who feel that government agencies shouldn't engage in "PR"—even though nearly all have professional public relations departments.

[3]When circumstances do not allow exposing all media to a site or an event, a few reporters and cameramen are chosen to go—on the understanding that what they see, learn, or film will be available to all media, or "pooled."

RADIO — TV
DEFENSE DIALOG

————— RADIO TV REPORTS INC. WASH., D.C., SUMMARIES NOT TO BE QUOTED —————

TUESDAY, DECEMBER 17, 1985 (BROADCASTS OF MONDAY, DEC. 16, 1985)

SUMMARY OF NETWORK NEWS IN THIS ISSUE

FORT CAMPBELL MEMORIAL SERVICES: Services were held at Fort
Campbell, Kentucky for those members of the 101st Airborne
Division who were killed in last week's crash of a chartered DC-8
at Gander, Newfoundland. President Reagan eulogized the dead
soldiers and consoled their families. Reports by Rebecca Chase,
ABC; Chris Wallace, NBC; Lesley Stahl, CBS.

INVESTIGATION OF GANDER CRASH: The cause of the DC-8 crash at
Gander remains undetermined. Canadian officials say the flight
data recorder indicated the plane had more than enough speed to
take off. There is some speculation that failure of the pilot to
have the plane de-iced may have contributed to the accident.
Reports by Stone Phillips and Bettina Gregory, ABC; Steve
Delaney, NBC; Peter Van Sant, CBS.

U.S. MILITARY'S USE OF CHARTER PLANES: There has been some
criticism of the use of charter planes to transport U.S. servicemen. Military officials say it would not be cost-effective to
purchase a fleet of aircraft that would duplicate commercial
planes that already exist and that have been pledged for use in
time of emergency or war. Report by Lem Tucker, CBS.

SOVIET REACTION TO SDI: The Soviet Union says that it would be
capable of defeating any space-based defense system the U.S.
might deploy, and could do so at a fraction of the cost any such
system would cost. Report by Dan Rather, CBS.

PREPARED BY THE AIR FORCE (SAF/AA) AS EXECUTIVE AGENT FOR THE DEPARTMENT OF DEFENSE TO BRING TO THE
ATTENTION OF KEY DOD PERSONNEL MATTERS WITHIN THEIR OFFICIAL RESPONSIBILITIES.
For information regarding this publication call Harry Zubkoff (SAF/AA), 695-2884

Figure 7–6   News summaries, good news and bad, are part of the military public affairs office's services. (Courtesy of Air Force, SAF/AA.)

However, it soon became evident that the increasing number of media on site was going to hamper securing of the site, protection of the remains, and the search for survivors.

The First Canadian Forces PAO arrived about 11:00 A.M., followed by a colleague at 4:00 P.M. Once they arrived, all media relations from the Gander site were handled by Canadian government representatives. As such, they were not able to answer questions on any topics except the crash itself.

More than 150 media ultimately descended on the site—including many who had been there since early in the day. With 150 reporters with deadlines to meet hanging around, concern began to grow when only limited information was released.

Under the international civil aviation code, when a crash occurs in a member country, that country assumes responsibility for determining the cause of the crash and conducting an investigation. In this case, the Canadian Aviation Safety Board (CASB) was the responsible agency. There was considerable delay in getting CASB staff to the scene because of aircraft problems. By the time they arrived, the media were concerned that they were not getting any information—so there was a tremendous amount of speculation as to what had happened.

Another problem was knowing and responding to *what was being reported elsewhere.* What could the PAOs on site confirm, what could they not confirm? Then the focus of media interest switched to the actual cause of the crash—was the aircraft de-iced or was it not? What were the weather conditions?

PROBLEMS OF MEDIA CONTAINMENT

With 150 or more anxious, impatient reporters and photographers demanding confirmation of rumors and answers to questions not yet answerable, other problems arose:

- **Perimeter security.** In search of footage and stills of the scene, media were trying to breach the perimeter, driving down the highway at night with lights out, getting into spaces within the airport that were in fact secured areas—off limits.

- **Numbers of requests.** Given the vast number of media requests and inquiries, the arranging of pool coverage, finding accurate information about soldiers on board, determining how many females were among them, and so on—many other details had to be left unanswered. Some queries were passed along to the Pentagon. A gag order was originally put on Maj. Gen. John Crosby, whom the Pentagon sent to Gander to oversee the events. The media became quite hostile when it was apparent that they were to get no feedback from the general. This hostility was relieved only when the Pentagon was persuaded to rescind the gag order.

- **Coordination with other locations.** Events related to the disaster were taking place at two other key locations—the Pentagon in Washington, and Fort Campbell, Kentucky. Information released in one location was immediately checked for confirmation in another, adding to the PAO-media interaction.
- **Which branch of the service?** Since this was a plane crash, many reporters and others assumed it was the Air Force. In fact, the plane was chartered from a commercial airline by the Army. Because both the Army and Air Force are units of the Department of Defense, many initial inquiries were directed to it.

WASHINGTON, D.C.

It was at the Department of the Army's regular 7:20 A.M. staff meeting when word first came in that a plane had gone down somewhere in Canada—and there might be American soldiers aboard. The first written report received on the incident contained many errors, not the least of which was that they were not sure of the name of the airline and the number of persons on board.

Since media inquiries first went to the Pentagon, the Defense Department public affairs office put out the first series of news releases. As it was realized that this was a matter for the Department of the Army, inquiries came there also. The Army had several goals for communications:

1. Provide accurate information as quickly as possible.
2. Allow no family members to learn about their loved one over the radio but contact them through the Casualty Notification Team before the name was released.
3. Protect the families from additional pain by handling the information that was released very carefully.
4. Represent the Army with dignity.

The first step was to dispatch a team immediately to the scene headed by Major General Crosby, the assistant chief of staff for personnel. It was deemed important to have a senior Army representative on the scene—yet there was concern for protocol: Should we be putting our general on the ground on Canadian soil? The Army was concerned they'd be sending the wrong signal, that they didn't think Canada could do the job.

General Crosby was accompanied by a Washington PAO, Colonel Miguel "Mike" Monteverde, coordinator of the Army's response to the tragedy. He explained, "If we're going to put a general on the ground, everybody knows you'd better have a public affairs officer with him for obvious reasons."

MORE COMMUNICATION PROBLEMS ARISE

Unfortunately, the Army's communication goals were impeded by other complicating circumstances:

- **Family notification versus release of names to the media.** In keeping with one of its goals—notification before release of names—the Army sent its casualty notification teams across the country. The system was that, once the family was notified, a report would be sent back to the casualty center of the Army Personnel Center before the name was released to the press.

  However, this carefully orchestrated system was impeded by media and circumstances alike. "A survivors' assistance officer would reach a family member, notify them, and for reasons that are not still completely clear, would call the local newspaper or television station," Monteverde explains. "So then you had a reporter coming back to the Pentagon right away saying, 'I understand that Johnny Jones was on that plane, can you confirm that.' In the meantime, we had not received word back from the survivors assistance office that the loop had been closed. We had to play dummy."

  Not only was the pressure for release of names heavy from the media; so too, were the inquiries from parents whose sons or daughters were members of the 101st Airborne division, or any airborne division, or the Army in general. "We were besieged by anybody who had a relative who thought, in the remotest possibility, that they might have been on that plane," Monteverde said.

- **Dover Air Force Base in Delaware scheduled as homecoming scene.** Having learned a lesson from the bombing of the Beirut embassy two years earlier, the Army went to work to prepare its Dover mortuary as soon as possible.[4] Public affairs officers were sent to Dover to organize ceremonies for the arrival of the bodies, which was to follow a presidential visit to Fort Campbell for a memorial service. An honor guard of 120 soldiers went to Newfoundland to accompany the bodies to Dover. The Dover activities added a fourth location for media coverage.

- **General Crosby and the media at Gander.** Washington's knowledge of what was going on at Gander was extremely limited. Not only was Washington unaware of the number of reporters gathered there, but also that the information the Pentagon distributed wasn't being conveyed to those in charge at Gander. When the plea came through for removal of General Crosby's gag order,

---

[4]The mortuary was established during the Vietnam War to receive the bodies of those killed in action. It has subsequently been used for other large-scale disasters. As a rule, bodies are identified and prepared for shipment to survivors, with funerals taking place in the hometown of the deceased. In all, the Department of Defense reports that 21,693 Vietnam War dead left Dover in flag-draped metal coffins.

Washington realized the magnitude of the Gander situation and gave permission for him to speak. That began to ease the pressure.

THE ARMY'S SOLUTION

In order to alleviate the communication problems both internally and externally, the Army implemented these strategies:

- **Publications of 800 numbers.** For casualty center and family assistance, CNN television began to run these toll free numbers, which were then widely published in the media. These helped alleviate the pressure of the calls coming directly to the Pentagon. The casualty center went on twenty-four-hour operation in order to respond to families who were concerned about members being on that aircraft.
- **Crisis Response Team implemented.** Able to move into action within twenty-four hours of any crisis, the team was set up for the communication of information from the operational channels to all internal staff as to what was going on with the crash recovery. They supplied:
  1. Twenty-four-hour-a-day coverage.
  2. Twice-daily briefings—7:00 A.M. and 5:00 P.M.—for the secretary of defense and chief of staff, to update them on all aspects of the crash and particularly the media coverage.
  3. Written public affairs situation reports twice daily for the first ten days.
  4. Full reports and assessments of what was being reported on each television network (an officer was assigned full-time to watching television and copying down his or her assessment of coverage); these reports were ultimately used in preparing extensive information books on everything that had been reported on the crash up to the time the president went to Fort Campbell for the ceremony.

"Not only were we spending time answering media questions, we also devoted a great deal of time and resources reporting internally to the Army staff what was going on. I would say two-thirds of our effort were devoted to the public press and one-third devoted internally to the Army," surmised Monteverde.

FORT CAMPBELL, KENTUCKY

"I didn't know that anybody else existed those few days except me," said Major Jim Glisberg, PAO for the 101st. "I got a call at my house saying 'Better watch CNN—looks like it might be our aircraft that crashed.' Fifteen minutes later I got another call saying 'Get to work now, it *is* ours.'"

Fort Campbell had been undergoing preparations for the returning soldiers. A press conference had been scheduled, and homecoming activities were planned. "We already had the press conference set up for that day for the family members and the returning soldiers, so I knew the press had already been alerted. I also knew, since CNN was carrying the story, it wouldn't be long before the press was at my office."

Immediate arrangements were made for use of the base media room. The space had been set aside months before for instances of this type, and everybody on PA staff understands how to get it operational quickly. "We had forty-five minutes to set one up before the press were there. Within two hours I had about forty press. By the end of the day, I had anywhere between 75 to 100. We had ten telephone hook-ups—it *seemed* to be adequate," said Glisberg.

ESTABLISHING MEDIA RULES

Certain guidelines were established by Glisberg for management of information:

1. All press *had* to be escorted by a public affairs official on, off, and around the base. (Security at the base required this rule at all times.)
2. All press updates would be given in the media room to everyone at the same time.
3. There would be no exclusives.
4. They would honor requests from only the media that were within the parameters listed above.

SPOKESPERSON CREDIBILITY AND MESSAGE STRATEGY

Setting the mood for the press and the nation was a key objective of all the military communications. The commander of the 101st was utilized as the most credible spokesperson. Messages centered around his *concern for the soldiers and for their families.*

"I think the one thing I learned at DINFOS (Defense Information School), more than anything else, was to find something positive in whatever disaster or tragedy you have and link on to it. The only thing I could think of was supporting the families and how the Army could do that. That was what we keyed on—and that's what we continued to key on during the entire affair," reported Glisberg.

HINDSIGHT EVALUATION

1. With three scenes of action—Washington, Gander, and Kentucky—organizational problems complicated the already difficult situation. A single point of information release could have controlled possible confusion.

2. Media were on site long before officials arrived. This situation may have been uncontrollable given the location and time of the crash.

3. International agreements designated the Canadians to run the show at first and handle all press inquiries. They did a fine job of telling what they knew—but most data had to come from the Army.

4. There was confusion in numbers and names of soldiers on the plane. There was no real roster to work from. Clearly, that situation could have been planned for.

5. An unexpected presidential visit went smoothly partly because of the effectiveness of the presidential advance team.

LESSONS LEARNED

- Be prepared to handle media from around the world in an international situation.
- Be prepared to staff a media center and have personnel allocated and trained for that.
- Chronicle your releases and update them. Provide updates very regularly — hour by hour if possible. Remember, as new media arrive they need to be brought up to speed quickly.
- Have a media room available, and able to be set up at a moment's notice.
- Consider beforehand the dilemma of releasing names before relatives are notified.

The Gander Crash was the U.S. Army's worst peacetime disaster. It happened in the year with the most air-crash deaths in history. The military PAOs' handling of the affair make it a textbook case; we could fill this book with a log of all that was done, from press conferences for the commanding general and chief of staff to appearances by Glisberg on the *Today* show. The results of this media relations activity, despite all the obstacles, can be summarized in one sentence:

Coverage and feedback (such as letters to the editor and calls to the Army) were almost entirely positive, centering on the military's concern for the families of victims and the great sorrow felt by all who wear, or have worn, the uniform.

What criticism there was dealt with the political decision to use a charter airline, rather than military aircraft, to bring home soldiers who had served in a peace-keeping mission halfway around the globe.

WHAT HAS BECOME OF THE GANDER PROBE?

There is some speculation of mismanagement during the investigation of the crash. The Canadian Aviation Safety Board found that the cause of the tragedy was an ice coating on the wings. However, four people out of the nine-member CASB disagreed with their own report and strongly felt that an explosion may have caused the crash.

Two terrorist groups, Sons of Zion and Islamic Jihad, each claimed responsibility for the crash. A witness whose testimony was not heard by the CASB reported that the plane exploded before it hit the ground.

These incidents sparked a congressional investigation led by Representative Robin Tallon. According to the *Washington Post,* the report notes that the CASB chief investigator, George Seidlein, was removed from the investigation because he "was not good at public relations."[5] Seidlein commented that he was not asked to review the final report because of his disapproval of the icing theory and the assumption that he was unlikely to convince the other board members of his views.

The report also attacked the FBI's excuse for leaving Gander before completely investigating because the Canadians were on top of things. Despite a quick examination, the Bureau made an immense, censored report about the crash. The congressional report did accept the story that the Army played only the small role of identifying the bodies of the servicemen, despite documents that imply a more investigative purpose.

The actual cause of the flight's tragedy is still unknown. Clearly there is unattended business from a public relations, as well as operational, viewpoint.

QUESTIONS FOR DISCUSSION

1. Much of the confusion and turmoil was caused by the number of sites, people, and events surrounding the crash. Another contributing factor was the uncertainty of who was the primary audience and what messages were to be communicated. You are the public affairs officer in charge. Identify your target audiences in priority order. Spell out the specific message for each. Consider carefully whether the media should be a target audience.

2. In a disaster situation, what should be the objectives of public relations activity? List them in priority order. Were these objectives evident in this case?

3. As a principle of good public relationships, silence or "no comment" are about the worst choices a practitioner can make when confronted with a legitimate

---

[5]Jack Anderson and Dale Van Atta, "Unfinished Business: Gander Crash Probe," *Washington Post,* November 29, 1990, B13.

media inquiry. Still, in real-life situations, aspects such as privacy rights, protection from harm or self-incrimination, compassion for victims, or the survival of a business, sometimes take precedence over the public's right to know. Are there ways of handling these situations without losing credibility as an authoritative source of information? Cite examples.

The Lights Go Back on at an Electric Utility

As public relations has changed and grown over the years, the way of relating to important publics has changed and gained new possibilities. In the past, people who wanted to get their message out to a broad public relied on the news media as a channel. This method of conveying information worked efficiently when the institution and the news media had a friendly relationship. Influenced by television, the role of the media is now slanted more toward entertainment values. This means that much of news is filtered by news media that are looking for the scandalous or controversial story. Worse, in some instances the media may not only put a subject on the public agenda, they may assume an adversarial role as prosecuting counsel in the attempt to influence public policy.

In pursuit of the juicy story, the media can focus excruciatingly closely on every problem that any organization may experience, magnifying those problems' intensity, and thereby influencing publics' negative perceptions of the situation. As *Newsweek* magazine stated, "No scandal, no story."[1]

Lapses of judgment and mistakes by management are not uncommon. Unforeseen crises occur. If a well-known or highly visible organization has problems, it will undoubtedly be the focus of media attention. Whether public response is positive or negative is often determined by how the organization deals with damaging information and reacts to media coverage.

This case concerns a utility company toward which some of the media adopted an adversarial role, based on their perceptions of the company's policies and management. As a result, problems were compounded and the company faired poorly in the court of public opinion. But new media strategies then enabled the utility to begin regaining public confidence.

---

[1]From a speech by Frank Stansberry, Manager, Guest Affairs at Epcot Center for Walt Disney World and Coca-Cola USA; "PR Stands for Personal Relations."

THE PNM STORY—AS GLEANED FROM PUBLIC MEDIA

Public Service Company of New Mexico (PNM) is a gas, electric, and water utility company, headquartered in Albuquerque. PNM, along with other utilities in the Southwest, encountered severe financial problems in the late 1980s, caused in part by diversification in nonutility ventures and investment in a nuclear plant. PNM's seventy years of public relations began to erode under constant scrutiny of print media, customers, critics, and regulators. Some felt that diversification had diverted the company's attention away from its primary utility business. Others were concerned that its highly paid officers had lost touch with the community.

Diversification efforts initiated by the company largely failed or were unprofitable. By the early 1990s, the company divested itself of most of its nonutility ventures. Scrutiny continued on how the company exited its diversification efforts, and accusations abounded (later found inaccurate but played out in the press) that the utility had spent money to prop up those failed ventures. Doing so would have been a violation of state law, so naturally reporters found it an inviting story line.

During the go-go 1980s, when expansion and "maximizing assets" were the themes, many utilities (and other companies) got into the same situation as PNM. Of course, local ratepayers don't care what's happening elsewhere. They are quite rightly concerned with the stability of their utility and their power costs.

An attempt to restructure the electric portion of the utility was opposed by a great portion of the public. They feared that this restructuring would increase rates and lessen public control over the utility. The company then dropped the plan. In late 1988, the company cut almost 800 jobs and eliminated $29 million a year in salaries and benefits. With this action came a continued barrage of media investigation into the company's management. Reporters focused on public proxies and filings — reporting that top officials were receiving six-digit salaries and a multiple number of benefits. This news apparently increased negative perceptions. In addition, twenty-four executives had negotiated lump-sum severances (called by the press "golden parachutes"), which would become payable if the utility was merged with or acquired by another company. These benefits were similar to those in place at other utilities and were never received by any executive. But the *Albuquerque Journal* editorialized the following:

PNM's Real Priorities

The management team at Public Service Company of New Mexico has shown over the years that when it comes to a crunch between the interests of shareholders and the interests of ratepayers, management's loyalties lie with the shareholders. But when it comes to the interest of management and those of the stockholders, it is the stockholders who come in a distinct second. Recent disclosures of princely severance pay options for the denizens of PNM's executive suite in the event of a change in corporate control make this chillingly clear.

A takeover of PNM or a merger with another utility might be viewed as a financial salvation by long-suffering stockholders, who have seen the value of their investment crash in recent years. But even though major miscalculations by management were a primary cause of PNM's present financial difficulties, the PNM board of directors has provided that management will be paid—handsomely—before the control of the firm could pass to any other entity. PNM president and chairman Jerry Geist would be entitled to a cool $1 million in severance pay if he were to lose his job as a result of PNM being merged with or acquired by another company. Some twenty-three other top executives would be entitled to severance checks of 2.5 times their annual earnings in the event of a change in control. Shareholders would have to pay the wages of the PNM management team for $2\frac{1}{2}$ years past when they were ousted, should that come to pass. It is clear PNM's board of directors is infinitely more concerned with the welfare of its management team—putative employees of the board—than it is with the welfare of its stockholders. It is difficult to see any benefit to PNM shareholders—much less ratepayers—in this carefree encumbering of the scarce assets of a financially strapped company that still cannot predict when it might reinstitute its common stock dividend.

The bottom line priorities of the men who have controlled New Mexico's largest utility for decades are exposed for all to see.[2]

Later in 1988, PNM made a request to the state Public Service Commission (PSC) to have ratepayers pay the leases and operating cost portion of PNM's share of the Palo Verde nuclear generating station, located in neighboring Arizona. The PSC approved it, but reduced rates by $2.8 million. The media continued to scrutinize this decision, focusing on future needs of customers. According to the press, customers would be paying for an investment in power they did not need. The stories ignored such factors as possible sales of surplus energy to other states, which would reduce rates. Little was said about such processes, and much was said about the rates.

One device media used to evaluate PNM was to compare local electric rates with those of other cities. The rate comparisons pushed some in the city of Albuquerque to look for alternative service. One method considered was through bidding of the franchise. In New Mexico, a franchise is a "right-of-way" agreement to distribute power and not a license to do business. Amidst continued press coverage, the city amended its charter to require the awarding of its electric service right-of-way franchise to the lowest bidder. Some argued that this was possible because the city might "own the lines that sit on public rights of way." Those critics claimed that a "friendly lawsuit" would settle the issue. PNM filed the lawsuit, stating that the system it had built and maintained was not for sale. But the judge threw out the suit claiming it was not "ripe," because no one had actually tried to take the lines from PNM.

Such controversy was regularly played out in the media. Taking approximately $410 million in losses (over a three-year period) and halt of dividend payments led to PNM stock dropping from $37 dollars a share in 1986 to $8 in 1989. This fall in value created more legal difficulties for the company as shareholders sued for al-

---

[2]*Albuquerque Journal,* April 3, 1990, A6.

leged misrepresentation of the company's assets and inflation of stock prices. Allegations were levied that the company had let its diversification efforts continue for an extra year and company officials had not been candid about the financial status of the company. At least three class-action suits were filed. The company settled these lawsuits, without admitting liability, for $35 million. The company was in dire straits; its financial situation was critical. In three years many constituencies had become alienated, including both customers and shareholders.

PROBLEMS IN MEDIA RELATIONS

Our analysis of a huge file of clippings from the many years it was under attack by press and critics shows that PNM's situation presented it with multiple public relations problems. They might be described as follows:

TONE QUALITY OF MESSAGE COUNTS

Given this difficult situation, PNM compounded its public communication problems by the perceived "tone of voice" it employed in its messages. Despite the company's obvious deficiencies, PNM seemed to adopt the stance in its public communications that it was unequivocally right in its decisions. Inevitably this attitude alienated its publics.

Gerard Fisher and Joyce DeHann, from the Center for Organization Development in Rochester, New York, offer a frame of reference that describes four levels of communication to test what type of message an organization or individual is sending to others.

- **Interdependence.** These messages say, "I am learning and friendly; others are learning and friendly." The sender has the attitude that there are usually no right or wrong answers. Growing, developing, and changing are possible only when the parties depend on each other and work together.

- **Independence.** These messages indicate, "I am right and friendly; others are right and friendly." The sender sends the message that other people have points of view, too. Others may or may not be right, but we will do it our way and they can do it their way.

- **Dependence.** These messages say, "I am right and friendly; others are wrong and misguided." The sender believes that he or she has the truth and other people will find it out when they have the benefit of his or her superior background, experience, and decision-making capabilities.

- **Negative relationship.** These messages say, "I am right and friendly; others are wrong and hostile." The sender believes that he or she has the truth and those who disagree are stupid. He or she will get angry, yell, and attempt to use authority or punishment until others agree.

1. **Relations with the media seemed to be conducted in a haphazard fashion.** Whatever its intent, PNM projected an arrogant, "so-what" attitude. In behaving this way, an organization ignores one of the fundamental functions of the media—their *agenda-setting role.* Because of its perceived arrogant attitude, PNM was seldom successful in getting the news media to put current damaging stories into focus against the long-term background of its serious financial problems. (PNM public relations tried hard to keep reporters and editors up to speed. But issues arose quickly, and a small media relations department was severely tested.)

2. It seemed that PNM **did not have a proactive policy for disclosing bad news,** and often the media used investigative reporting to unearth negative information, causing the company to look even worse. Issues that could have been handled quickly with accurate, consistent information were often dragged out for years in the newspapers with accusations flying back and forth. (PNM tried to be proactive, but once caught in a media blitz, it is very difficult to get some reporters to listen objectively, according to Rick Brinneman, company spokesperson.)

3. **PNM usually tended to react defensively** to media attacks or refused to comment at all as facts became available. For example, to defend itself from an *Albuquerque Tribune* editorial that detailed its position on the company's restructuring plan, PNM wrote a rebuttal in the form of a quiz for the consumer. Each question and answer was specifically worded in either a positive or negative tone of voice that implied the right answer (too obviously the PNM version). (See Figure 7-7.) The attitude presented in this quiz alienated readers and *gave the Tribune more ammunition to continue its negative coverage.* (On major topics, such as lawsuits or when dividends would be restored, the company *couldn't* comment—making it further vulnerable.)

4. **PNM did not seem to have a consistent spokesperson policy.** Consequently reporters could talk at random to numerous officials who may have had no experience in media relations, no facts about a particular situation, and no clear idea of the corporate stand on a particular issue. This situation created the image of buck passing and drowned any One Clear Voice for PNM. As a result, the public perceived that there was no clear leadership and that PNM had something to hide. (PNM did have a designated spokesperson, but also tried to provide reporters access to the people with the most knowledge. The result was a constant shift in who was quoted as source.)

5. **PNM appeared to espouse the attitude that it had no obligation to consider the concerns of the public** and was answerable only to the Public Utility Commission and its shareholders. This attitude ignored the fact that it had a major responsibility toward its customers, who ultimately decide PNM's financial feasibility. This seemingly cavalier attitude also served to inflame public opinion against the company. (Brinneman notes this was decidedly not

Figure 7-7 This quiz only served to alienate PNM's publics further. (Courtesy of Public Service Company of New Mexico.)

PNM's intent, illustrating how the tone of messages can become altered in the heat of negative media coverage.)

PNM CHANGED

Beginning in 1989, PNM took some management and public relations actions:

- The President and CEO, Jerry Geist, along with other top executives, who were often portrayed in the media as responsible for leading the utility to financial ruin, retired. Geist's replacement, John Ackerman, known as a direct and forthright manager, began working to restore public and employee confidence in the company's course. Positive news coverage followed this change.

- Some management decisions included continuing to sell off all its nonutility assets to "get back to basics."
- The office of CEO and board chairperson position were separated.
- A rate freeze for three years (1991–1994) was instituted, and the company filed for a $30 million rate reduction.
- PNM embraced a philosophy to be as open as possible.
- PNM filed suit against some of its former executives over certain retirement benefits. (This lawsuit was settled without going to court.)

PROACTIVE EXTERNAL COMMUNICATIONS CAMPAIGN

As it changed its performance, PNM sought recognition for its new approach. Its initial idea was a video that focused on how dedicated it was to quality customer service. As it does before launching any communications campaign, PNM conducted some research on focus groups of customers. From the research, PNM found that the customers wanted to hear about the issues the company faced, instead of a video of self-proclaiming virtues.

In response, PNM launched the "Straight from the Heart Campaign." Here are some of the external communication messages and actions it took in order to regain credibility:

- Initiated an **ad campaign** that admitted "We know we've made some mistakes in the past . . .", which invited consumer criticism, while committing to better management practices in the future. The ads clearly stated that customers were not footing the bill for them.
- Set up a **"Listening Line"** that continues to this day for customers to call and tell how the company could improve the way it does business. At the start, executives, including the CEO, took turns fielding questions and concerns.
- The **theme** throughout this campaign was, "We're listening at Public *Service* Company. For a change." (Note the emphasized word.) This statement kept things positive and forward-looking while clearly admitting mistakes.
- Made **follow-up calls** to customers who needed service and repairs, to be sure they were made satisfactorily.
- Conducted **on-going research** to test response to initial changes. From this research PNM found that the public wanted to believe it but needed some proof with action—words and rhetoric are not as believable as behavior.
- Answered customers' initial responses with a **five-point action program.**

The theme was "Meeting *your* needs as *you* see them is the real key to *our* future."

- Focused more **attention on environmental issues.** Local newspapers carried ads that spoke of PNM's dedication to the Clean Air Act and how its facilities have met and exceeded these new regulations for over ten years. These ads emphasized the **interdependence** that PNM has with the citizens of New Mexico in attaining these environmental goals.
- In addition, PNM continued **emphasizing ways to conserve electricity** and help consumers save money.

WHAT'S AHEAD FOR PNM

The financial future of PNM is not yet bright. The company still struggles to make up for the losses from its failed diversification efforts and investments in its generating plants. Some customers still believe that their electric rates are higher than those of comparable communities. In addition, in early 1993 the company had to cut staff even further and 500 nonunion workers left in a voluntary severance program. In mid-1994 its stock was not close to pre-1988 levels and was selling at about $13 a share. The company had not restored stock dividends. A new president has been selected, and John Ackerman remains chairman of the board. And media continue to report both "good" and "bad" occurrences.

But there is light on the horizon. PNM has clearly moderated its projected attitude and now offers a voice of mutual cooperation in addressing the public's concerns. As part of this program it is now speaking directly to involved publics and not forced to rely on the media as interpreter (see Figure 7–8).

The benefit of learning to speak directly to its concerned publics is more positive (or at least balanced) news coverage. PNM's efforts to consider customer satisfaction issues has moderated the anger that provided a platform for the *Albuquerque Journal's* harmful coverage and editorializing. As company spokesperson Rick Brinneman explained in the *Albuquerque Journal* in March of 1993,

> We're going to be talking with the public, asking them to help us think through some of the tougher questions, like disposing of assets, combining services, retail wheeling [a term that describes an option for customers to choose their electric provider] and other issues that face the company, because we believe we're not going to be able to solve them alone.

PNM's change in attitude and in customer-focused behavior was reflected in the fairer coverage it began receiving in editorials. (Note the journalist's typical misunderstanding of the public relations function in the final sentence.)

PNM: We'll Try Harder

If setting a corporate plan of action is the first step to regaining the confidence of ratepayer and stockholder alike, Public Service Company of New Mexico made a giant step forward in the redefinition of its mission and objectives announced last week.

Go ahead and take your best shot. Because we're ready to listen. We're starting to change the way Public Service Company works.

We've set up a special telephone "Listening Line" and we want to hear from you. What you think we've done wrong. What we're doing right. How we can regain your trust. And best serve you in the future.

You Can Help Turn Our Company Around With Just A Little Push.

It isn't a matter of fretting over the past. We've already begun the process of changing for the better. With a three-year freeze on rates. And actions by our Board of Directors to put our entire company's house in order.

At the same time, we're looking for new ways to improve. And that starts with some listening and understanding. Which is why our managers (not some paid telephone service) will be ready to hear your comments when you call in.

What kind of suggestions are we looking for? The possibilities are as limitless as New Mexico's wide open skies.

Talk to us about our rates. As it is, we're currently about a penny above the national average and less expensive than 18 other New Mexico utilities. Beyond holding rates stable through 1993 what more can we do to add value to your energy dollar? *We're hoping a lot of people will call it as they see it.*

How about our service? Are we there when you need us? Do our neighborhood offices help? If you have problems, do our people respond swiftly?

What about diversification? We're staying in the utility business, everything else is being sold. Now, we're only concerned with the main job — providing you with highly reliable energy on demand.

The point is clear. It's taken us 10 years to get where we are in the public eye. Now we're ready to head in a better direction.

So, go ahead and tell it like it is. Call 761-6070 in Albuquerque, outside of Albuquerque 1-800-339-2704 for our telephone "Listening Line." Call weekdays between 7:30 a.m. and 7:30 p.m. You never know where the little push you give us today could take us tomorrow.

We're Listening At Public Service Company. For A Change.

Figure 7–8 PNM created a "Listening Line" for customers to voice their concerns directly to the company about the issues that were of concern. Then PNM responded to their feedback in this ad. (Courtesy of Public Service Company of New Mexico.)

"Our company's mission is to be the energy supplier of choice in New Mexico and regional markets," said PNM president and chief executive John Ackerman. Since the Albuquerque city charter mandates a choice on the basis of price for the next Albuquerque franchise, the path to being Albuquerque's supplier of choice is clear.

The statement of objective promises no rate increase requests for three years, with the company profitability to be improved by market expansion and cost containment. For inventors, reinstating a sustainable dividend is the top goal set.

The statements go on to spell out obligations to employees and the community —as well as those to ratepayers and stockholders. The goals and objectives are stated in simple unambiguous language.

Of course, the proof is in the doing, and not in the mere promulgation of a new plan—but the tone and flavor of PNM's new plan suggest the company is committed to real process, not just public relations.[3]

[3]*Albuquerque Journal*, January 20, 1991, B2.

THE NEW MEDIA RELATIONS

As the focus of news media has changed from one of news provider to one of entertainer, the way for organizations to relate to media sources has changed as well. Research has shown that media coverage has a far greater chance of being harmful—because people like reportage of bad news over good news by seven to one.

Media's demonstrable value is in creating **awareness** and in **reinforcement** for those who already believe the message. The key to relating with the public today via media is being able to distinguish between the two types of contemporary media: reportorial and access.

The **reportorial** medium is telling a story through a reporter and an editor. Unfortunately, many present-day journalists would like to go beyond being a *medium* in getting stories out and be *mediators* of issues—forcing contending camps to fight it out in their pages or on their programs. This "gatekeeper" phenomenon can seriously distort public perception of an issue.

A more effective strategy is to go around the reportorial media to the **access** media: putting an organization's spokesperson directly in front of the audience to avoid the news media's interpretative filter. Some types of access media include:

- Television host   Radiomercials
  and call-in shows
- Television   Public affairs
  advertorials   panels
- Radio talk   Advertorials in
  shows   print media

These media allow the person or organization to speak for themselves—and add an element of fairness (or at least what the public believes is fair) to the proceedings.

Someone who used this strategy to reach directly to the people was President Bill Clinton. He fielded questions directly from voters on "Larry King Live," appeared on the *Arsenio Hall Show* to play the saxophone, and spoke directly to the young people in specials that appeared on MTV during the 1992 election. As *U.S. News and World Report* put it "Great politicians learn to deliver their messages through the media of the day."

QUESTIONS FOR DISCUSSION

1. According to the Fisher and DeHann model of communication levels (see the box on tone quality), what message was PNM sending to the media? What message got through to the public after media interpretation? What could PNM have done differently to change that message? Then, what message did the company start sending after it altered its approach?

2. You are the public relations director of a utility that needs to increase rates in order to cover costs for delivering future service. Devise a plan to introduce

this increase to the public with the minimum amount of negative public reaction. Is there an alternative to going through the media? If so, include your alternative in the plan.

3. What are some examples of good and bad media relations in crisis situations occurring right now?

4. Are there times not to be proactive with the media? If so, why?

5. How can you turn down the request for a media interview with the least likelihood of alienating a reporter?

A Classic: Building Media Relationships That Pay

In the late 1970s the domestic car industry was threatened by the rash of imports that flooded the country. The imports were fuel-efficient and better built than many American cars. These qualities, coupled with the economy that was hard hit by a suffocating recession, served to jeopardize the very existence of the three top U.S. auto makers. Chrysler was one car manufacturer that decided to fight back—but did not expect the media problems that would come along with the fight.

Chrysler Motors had several problems at once. Its cars did not appeal to many buyers and its sales lagged behind those of the two major competitors in the United States, Ford and General Motors. In 1978, the corporation was listed in *Fortune* as the year's "biggest loser," selling the "wrong kind of cars for the wrong kinds of buyers."

SITUATION ANALYSIS

Fortune magazine described Chrysler's problems in this way:

1. The demographics of Chrysler product owners showed that they were more conservative, older, blue-collar people less inclined to buy cars loaded with options, and people who got hurt first in an economic downturn.
2. Product engineering dominated the planning and marketing of cars.
3. Auto designs were considered "stodgy."
4. The corporation was on the move to non-automotive ventures around the world, many of which were not profitable.

5. Government regulations on mileage, safety, and emissions were things with which all manufacturers had to contend.[1]

Just at this downturn, Chrysler executives decided to launch a new product, the Dodge Omni, and its twin, the Plymouth Horizon. They were the company's first venture into the subcompact car line and also the first medium-priced cars with front-wheel drive manufactured in the United States.

The new products were introduced to the news media in two phases: The "long lead" preview for writers and editors of monthly magazines was held at the Chrysler proving grounds in Chelsea, Michigan. The "short lead" preview for daily newspapers, weekly news magazines, and radio and television stations was conducted in San Diego.

News kits timed for simultaneous release with the short lead preview were sent to all major U.S. daily and weekly papers, minority papers, and dealers.

Radio cassette actualities, featuring top sales executives and special feed from the preview site, were offered to all radio stations. Television networks were offered footage with and without sound, and a television crew was available on site for stations requesting special material.

The crucial part of the introduction, however, was the test driving of the Omni and Horizon by the reporters and editors present at the short lead preview. Approximately forty-three of them drove the cars from the proving grounds to their home cities.

Chrysler received extensive and glowing coverage from the news media. The News Analysis Institute, a Pittsburgh-based company hired by Chrysler, reported the publication of 904 news stories, totaling 16,646 column inches in newspapers with a combined total circulation of over 137 million. News/Sport Radio Network reported 12,888 radio broadcasts of the story to 136,022,600 potential listeners. About seventy-eight television stations reported that they had aired stories and visuals to an average audience of 18,448,000. Glowing reports came from the automotive publications:

> *Auto Week:* Hell of a nice car. Got a lot of favorable attention on the highway, especially from the foreign car guys. It's just what you need. Well worth waiting for.
>
> *Car and Driver:* Fine little car.
>
> *Automotive News:* It's a fine car, beautiful. Even at top speeds I was getting 31 mpg. Car handled fine.
>
> *Auto World:* I was impressed. At 70, it handled beautifully. We averaged 31 mpg at the higher speeds. It's a beautiful little car.
>
> *Motor Trend,* a magazine for automobile enthusiasts, gave the cars its "Car of the Year" endorsement.
>
> *Fortune* magazine reported that the cars had "scored well in the marketplace."

[1]*Fortune,* June 19, 1978, 55.

CRISIS HITS SIX MONTHS LATER

On a Tuesday, six months after the introduction of the cars, Chrysler was conducting another of its long lead previews at its Chelsea proving grounds. Fifty-four monthly magazine editors and photographers from such diverse publications as *Hot Rod, Medical Economics,* and *Vogue* attended.

The entire public relations department was geared toward building a responsive two-way relationship with the news representatives. They coordinated product seminars, set up interviews, ensured that the writers were involved with ride and drive programs, and arranged models and props for special photographs.

Consumer Reports, a monthly product testing and rating magazine, turned down Chrysler's invitation to the long lead preview, even though one of its reporters had attended a preview from another automobile manufacturer the week earlier.

Sometime in the afternoon that Tuesday, a reporter from the *Washington Post* called a Chrysler public relations executive: "I would like to get Chrysler's reaction to Consumers Union's finding your Omni/Horizon car unacceptable." (See Figure 7–9) The question hit like a bombshell. The reporter insisted that the charge was true; having heard it from a reliable source within Consumers Union. He also said Consumers Union would hold press conferences to announce their findings the following day, in New York and Washington D.C. By late that afternoon, Consumers

Figure 7–9 Photo from *Consumer Reports;* The new Chrysler cars are branded as "not acceptable," although earlier the cars had been rated very highly by the persons who had used the car. (Courtesy of Consumer Reports.)

Union confirmed that the press conferences would be held, but refused Chrysler admission.

CONSUMERS UNION'S CHARGES AGAINST CHRYSLER

Consumers Union's charges against Chrysler had been related to a test procedure that the Union said was performed routinely at auto proving grounds to check a car's directional stability: "ability to center itself and return to its original course when it is deflected abruptly from a straight path." The test is made by driving at steady "expressway" speed, turning the steering wheel sharply to one side and then letting go of the steering wheel with both hands. The Union claimed that in such tests, most cars waver from side to side only minimally before returning to a course close to the previous one.

CHRYSLER SWINGS INTO STRATEGIC ACTION

At their Chelsea proving grounds, Chrysler's engineers immediately swung into action. They recreated the Union's test procedure while a television crew filmed the entire demonstration and made quantities of tapes. Meanwhile, the Consumers Union's press conferences were about to begin in New York and Washington, D.C., the following day. That evening, some news networks had already begun to inform the public of Consumers Union's charges against Chrysler's Omni and Horizon cars. But they balanced their coverage with a discussion of the excellent sales figures for the cars and their being awarded *Motor Trend's* "Car of the Year."

Wednesday, June 14, 1978; New York: Chrysler's executive was outside the Consumers Union's press conference, allowed admission only on the insistence of the media representatives who had learned of his presence. He was then allowed to share the podium with Consumers Union representatives.

Wednesday, June 14, 1978; Washington, D.C., Chrysler's representative was denied admission to the press conference. He held his own sidewalk press conference after the Union's press conference.

In the meantime, the public relations staff were busy distributing tapes of the test demonstrations made the previous day to television news departments in New York and Washington, D.C., Chicago, and Detroit. They had also been preparing for a barrage of questions, which came soon enough. Chrysler released statements forcefully denying the Union's charges, reminding readers that it had received praise from professionals and consumers alike. The statement was distributed to most U.S. news media. A radio actuality (sound bite) of the statement was also released to network radio news syndicates and key stations in the country.

There was more. An information kit on the complex subject of steering and handling was prepared for spokespersons staffing the telephones, so that they could respond intelligently and with One Clear Voice to general and technical media questions.

That same day, after the Consumers Union's press conferences, Chrysler held their own news conference at the Chelsea proving grounds. Detroit and network television and radio reporters, print journalists and the long lead preview magazine writers were all present. Here again, the Union's test maneuvers were demonstrated. It was crucial to showing that the Union's test was extreme and in no way related to real driving situations. In fact, one writer was overheard to say: "That's comparable to jumping out the second floor of your house, breaking a leg, and then accusing the house of being unsafe."

With its sound strategic planning and its immediate response (with proof) to refute the Consumers Union charges, Chrysler was able to garner some positive media reaction, demonstrated by these editorials:

> Consumers Union, which issued its report with great public fanfare—simultaneous news conferences in New York and Washington—ought to be darn sure it knows what it's talking about. We're not at all sure it does.[2]
>
> Anybody dumb enough to do this (the test) is probably certifiable, and anybody dumb enough to believe that it proves anything about a car's road ability or handling deserves to be working for Consumers Union. CU's motives may be squeaky clean, but we think they've soiled their treasured cloak of impartiality. The Omni/Horizon is as safe as the *Consumer Reports'* charges are irresponsible.[3]

The article in *Car and Driver* was given nationwide newspaper distribution through AP and UPI. Various network radio and television newscasts aired the editorial. Numerous national trade publications including *Automotive News* and *Advertising Age* published it.

Not only the national media were informed; public relations staff also made information available to the local media via video tapes and radio actualities distributed to Chrysler's twenty-one zone offices across the country. This information was also accessible to dealers.

Chrysler left no stone unturned. They petitioned the National Highway Traffic Safety Administration (NHTSA) and its Canadian counterpart, Transport Canada, to conduct their own tests of the Omni/Horizon cars.

Within a few weeks after the Consumers Union's charges, the two government agencies came forth with their own separate conclusions: Transport Canada, represented by a consultant and recognized automotive-handling expert from the International Standards Organization and the director of roads and motor vehicle safety in the Canadian Ministry of Transport, announced that "automotive specialists from Transport Canada had found that they handled in a normal and satisfactory manner in both obstacle avoidance maneuver tests and on the handling track."

---

[2]"Unsafe or Unfair," *Washington Star*.

[3]"God Save Us from Our Protectors," *Car and Driver*.

NHTSA, after testings at both the Chelsea and Consumers Union proving grounds concluded: "No evidence of a safety problem in the stability and handling characteristics of Chrysler's subcompact Dodge Omni and Plymouth Horizon."

Chrysler recorded both government agencies' endorsement on videotape and radio actuality statements with the corporation's chief engineer and sent them air express to New York, Chicago, and Los Angeles network offices. Radio actualities from interviews with the Canadian expert and the deputy administrator of NHTSA were sent to the *Voice of America, Armed Forces Radio,* and Canadian news outlets. These statements were also distributed over newswire throughout the United States. The statements were telegraphed to all 7,500 Chrysler dealers.

WHEN PUBLIC RELATIONS SAVES THE DAY

The News Analysis Institute analyzed the news coverage after the storm had blown over. In its finding, a negative story is one in which the greater part of the copy was devoted to criticism of the cars and a positive story has the Chrysler position dominating (see Figure 7–10). The Institute's report stated:

> The results are unusual in two respects: Despite the negative nature of the event, Chrysler dominated the coverage in stories published, space, and circulation. Further, Chrysler's case was strongly stated in virtually all the unfavorable articles, and a Chrysler comment was usually introduced early in the article. Particularly effective in this respect was the executive's sidewalk conference outside Consumers Union's Washington headquarters and the placements of Chrysler's formal rebuttal. Also notable in positive news were the coverage of Chrysler's press test of Omni/Horizon and its rallying of auto writers to support its claims.

In evaluating how public relations saved the day, Frank Wylie, Chrysler's public relations executive at the time, cited two key "life-savers":

> Most of the writers in major cities had already experienced the Omni/Horizon from their preview rides and local test drives. This *firsthand experience* helped to nullify or dampen the negative effects of Consumers Union's charges. This is perhaps succinctly summarized by one free-lance writer who had attended one of Chrysler's previews: "I think your letting people drive the cars away was the smartest thing you folks have done in a long time." [Emphasis added.]

The other vital "life-saver" was the preparation made by the public relations staff to answer all queries with *One Clear Voice:*

> We tried to anticipate every question that we could in connection with the breaking news elements of the story and be prepared to handle them quickly and efficiently. We didn't want anybody hanging with overnight or weekend stories with unanswered questions.

The News Analysis Institute

955 LIBERTY AVENUE   •   PITTSBURGH, PA. 15222   •   PHONE: (412) 471-9411

Analysis of
Consumers Union Report on
Omni / Horizon Handling Problems

	Stories Published	Space Secured		Circulation
		Column Inches	Newspaper Pages	
Favorable	402	5,132	29.2	35,881,065
Unfavorable	342	4,815	27.4	22,928,866
Totals	744	9,947	56.6	58,809,931

	Pictures Published	Page-One Stories	Articles Running a Full - Page or Longer
Favorable	61	38	2
Unfavorable	68	17	-
Totals	129	55	2

	Chrysler or Product Name Used in Heading
Favorable	294
Unfavorable	224
Totals	518

Figure 7–10 Summary and analysis by the News Analysis Institute of the coverage of the Omni/Horizon, which helped Chrysler evaluate its countermedia activity. (Courtesy of News Analysis Institute.)

The best evaluation tool, however, still is the final results of the public relations strategy during this crisis. Although sales figures plummeted immediately after the Union's charges, Chrysler believes that they would have remained that way if they had not reacted immediately and forcefully to counter the charges.

What's truly revealing happened at the dealers. The total sales of the two cars broke all of Chrysler's previous new car records during their first year on the market. Dealers sold every Omni/Horizon they had and could have sold more, had they had any more to sell. In addition, the two cars were all-time Chrysler leaders in capturing owners of competitive cars by establishing a "conquest rate" of more than sixty-seven percent. Two out of every three buyers traded in another make of car for the Omni or Horizon.

In the final analysis, Chrysler's open and honest rapport and relationship with the news media combined with positive anticipatory action to the charges helped save it from an otherwise major media crisis.

WHAT'S NEW FOR CHRYSLER

As the years have passed since this media crisis, Chrysler has experienced many changes. With the making of Lee Iacocca into a living symbol of Chrysler and an upswing in sales in the mid-1980s, to the downtrend in their profits and the exit of the legendary chairman in 1992, Chrysler has had some true ups and downs. Since 1980, Chrysler has slipped from the number six automobile manufacturer in the world to number ten. Trying to revitalize sales in 1991, after ten years without introducing new models, it introduced four of them with the usual amount of media hoopla, this time without the surprise of unwarranted criticism of the cars.

QUESTIONS FOR DISCUSSION

1. During the Consumers Union flap, Chrysler dominated the news compared with its competitors. Though the reports contained some dangerous criticisms, is it possible all that this exposure actually helped the company? Explain why or why not.

2. Research has shown that the news media have limited effects on publics. How would you evaluate Chrysler's reaction to Consumers Union's charges in light of this statement?

3. What are some public relations or communications theories that you see in play in Chrysler's handling of the news media? Can you think of some other theories not, used in this case, that would have helped the sales figures for the Omni/Horizon cars to climb?

4. If you were in charge of managing this crisis, what are some strategic actions

you would keep or abandon? Explain your answer in terms of public relations principles or communications theories, or both.

5. The News Analysis Institute found that the original introductory publicity for Omni/Horizon generated "the publication of 904 news stories . . . in newspapers with the combined total circulation of over 137 million people." How many potential customers read about these new cars?

PROBLEM 7-A EMPLOYER INTERESTS AND MEDIA INTERESTS IN CONFLICT

Ted Square takes pride in his professional integrity. He has never deceived a news reporter, never offered to a "pay off" for publicity, never risked his own integrity for personal or employer gain.

Ted's boss is the owner of a multimillion dollar auto parts manufacturing firm whose foremost customer is a major auto maker. Ted's boss is a man of character. He has never pressed Ted for more publicity or a more favorable press at whatever cost. He is a realist, taking and relishing whatever favorable publicity is generated by events, but not worrying out loud about either the quantity, accuracy, or completeness of it. With his business good and growing, the owner tends toward an attitude fully supportive of Ted.

One day, the owner is shocked when his vice-president for operations confronts him and says it is time to make him a full partner. He claims that his efforts have made the business grow and prosper. The owner is in a quandary. He has been quietly preparing his son to run the business, figuring he could take over about five years hence. Meantime, there is no denying that this vice-president, acquired a few years ago from one of the Big Three auto makers, is of huge importance to the parts firm.

The owner refuses to be pressured by the vice-president. He does assure him that in time to come he will earn more and more income, and ultimately, he says, a limited partnership might be available.

The vice-president at this point reveals that he has received an offer from a prime auto parts competitor, including a partnership, and the presidency of the competitive firm. He presents his resignation to the owner on the spot.

In the hour following this shocking meeting, several events with public relations overtones take place:

1. The managers of the product design, the engineering, the manufacturing, and the marketing departments turn in their resignations. They are moving to the competitive company with the vice-president for operations.
2. All these executives have been promised a "much better deal" by the vice-president for operations.

3. Gossip is going around the office and shop that the business may have to be closed down and all employees terminated or furloughed without pay.

The owner is busy on the telephone, lining up successors for all the "defectors," and trying to reach the buyer at the large auto company customer to make sure the contract is intact and unaffected. His financial vice-president is busy calling other customers, brokers, and others to reassure them that the business is not threatened. In the meantime, Ted's department is working on statements the owner wants to make to employees, to automotive trade press editors, to the local media, and to wire service stringers.

Midway into these efforts, word is passed to Ted Square by his secretary that the local bureau chief of a financial newspaper, a long-time friend, is on the telephone. Ted has to take the call, and he hopes that it concerns some other subject. But it does not. The conversation goes this way.

"Ted, this is George. I'm up against our deadline in fifteen minutes, but we have a rumor down here that your vice-president of operations has resigned."

"Yeah, George. I've been working on a release about it. Do you want the name of the man who will succeed him?"

"Sure."

"It's Lem Jones. He has been the vice-president's right-hand man for several years. Consequently, the business will go right along."

"Thanks. I'll get this into the works. Let me have more details as fast as you know them."

That was it. George, as a trained newsman, had failed to ask Ted where the vice-president was going, or the full circumstances of his resignation. Ted, for his part, was aware of more than he told. He simply answered specific questions and minimized the importance of the events, even though he knew the story would get financial front-page coverage if he added more details.

As it developed later on that day, the financial newspaper was scooped by a local newspaper whose reporter had called the vice-president for operations personally, had gotten the name of the company he was joining, had called them, and had gotten quotable details. The local bureau chief, Ted's friend, was embarrassed. His boss in New York had chewed him out. He blamed Ted for holding back information that was newsworthy, and said, "I'll never be able to trust you again."

"I'm sorry you feel that way," Ted told him. "I had no information from the operations vice-president, or the other guys who were resigning, and no one gave me authority to speculate, or to speak for them. What I had officially from the president, I gave you. You didn't ask for anything else. If you had, I could have referred you to the operations VP."

"OK," the bureau chief said, "that's what you say now. But every time you call me, remember, I've got a long memory."

Obviously, this was something for Ted to think about. He reasoned that his obligation was first and last to his employer. He had to release information of news value for which he was the authoritative source. But he did not have to go beyond that, and particularly not if it might be harmful to his employer. The damaged relationship with the major financial newspaper was seriously worrisome.

Who was right: Ted? The bureau chief? Both? Neither? If you had been Ted, could you have handled the situation so that your employer's interests and your good media relationship with George were both protected at the time and for the future? What would you have done differently?

If your company was publicly owned, would you have acted differently when George called?

PROBLEM 7-B DEALING WITH THE MEDIA IN A STICKY SITUATION

You are the public relations director of Alger Tiberius Software Inc., an up and coming software development company. Things have been exciting in the last few days since the introduction of a new software program, Manufacturing Efficiency Revolution (MER). When integrated into the computer controls of manufacturing equipment, it will increase the efficiency of that equipment and cut production time in half. This program will revolutionize the manufacturing industry. Magazine previews of the product have been complimentary, and it looks as if the company has an instant best seller on its hands.

But bad news hits one day when your morning coffee is accompanied by a newspaper clipping from the *Local Yokel Times,* quoting Don T. Figgle, your president and CEO, who is particularly proud of the new product and has taken every opportunity to brag about its merits in the press. In an off-hand comment he makes to a reporter at a local restaurant, Figgle is quoted as saying that "this product will virtually replace about fifteen percent of the American manufacturing workforce. It cuts out about half of the unnecessary actions done in factory production."

Figgle's quote is followed by the reaction of the AFL-CIO in response to this new information about the product. Ned T. Green, official spokesman of the organization, is quoted as saying, "This new product was not presented with this information to the labor and computer industries. Efficiency gains in manufacturing were discussed but not the elimination of a sector of our workforce. AT Software in effect lied to the public about the impact this software program will have on the American workforce."

Needless to say, this turn of media coverage is unexpected and unwanted. Figgle was correct in saying that the software would revolutionize the computer and manufacturing industry but his statistics were incorrect. The product would eliminate ten percent of jobs for the manufacturing workforce but would create jobs in a different area for other workers. Those who would lose their jobs could be retrained for other areas. You arrange another press conference for Figgle to disseminate the correct statistics available to the press, but whether the jobs are cut by fifteen percent or ten percent, loss of employment is the real story for the media. They are already printing a tidal wave of stories with headlines like "Computer Cover-Up Leaves Workers High and Dry" and "AT Software Sends Workers Packing."

By the following morning, negative media coverage has not abated. Although the news media now have the right statistics, emphasis is on the ten percent of workers allegedly to be put out of work by the software. To top it off, a newly formed activist group, WACS (Workers Against Computer Software), is picketing outside of the main offices of AT Software with signs proclaiming "AT Software Trades in People for Programs." The local TV stations are all present to cover the protest and give up-to-the-minute reports.

In addition the media is out in full force and has gone to the local congressman Bill Zealot for reaction. His last election campaign was focused on creating jobs for America. Zealot, up for reelection in the fall, pledges his loyalty to the hardworking American public and vows to fight "big business pushing aside the little guy and trying to make him obsolete in the name of progress." It looks as if there may be legislative reaction against MER.

Later that afternoon you receive a call from the Computer Software Programmers Association (CSPA). Initially, they were behind this program, but with all the bad press they're getting a bit nervous. They don't want to endorse a program that will cause so much flak. Without the backing of CSPA the future of this product is going to be difficult.

It is now 9:00 P.M. and things look a bit bleak for MER and AT Software. Clearly what should have been a great announcement has become garbled by the gatekeepers. You are wondering how to get the real message out to those audiences that matter. You ask yourself:

- Who are those groups that are garbling my message?
- What other groups are likely to become involved?
- What are the likely behaviors of each group?
- How can I minimize their messages and maximize mine to the publics I would like to reach?
- Can I reach those publics without utilizing usual venues, in order to avoid media, political, and activist gatekeepers?

1. With those questions in mind, how would you go about creating a plan to reach key publics with one-on-one communication in order to stay some of the immediate damage caused by the negative reactions of those groups who have been most vocal?
2. Could AT Software have avoided this negative uproar to MER? What actions should have been taken before presenting this product to the public through the media?

Chapter 8

Public Issues and Concerns, Private Interests and Campaigns

The handling of public issues makes evident the link between public relations and the idea of democracy. For the people to be able to participate in decisions that affect their lives, those decisions must be put before them in a thorough, forceful manner. The ramifications, pro and con, of potential decisions need to be debated fully. *In the Court of Public Opinion, public relations practitioners are the attorneys.*

In this setting, an *issue* is a subject on which there are (1) two or more strongly opposing arguments, (2) emotional involvement of a large number of people, and (3) concern that the decision will have an impact on people's lives or the smooth functioning of society. Gun control, abortion, smoking policies, and the other topics in this chapter clearly meet these criteria.

When issues get out of hand—that is, cannot be settled before they become huge and threatening—they move to the category of *crisis*. A crisis is a public or organizational issue that has grown to such proportions that its ultimate resolution appears to mark a turning point. Depending on the decision, things may not be the same afterward. Chapter 9 presents several crisis cases.

While businesses, schools, hospitals, and other established organizations with sophisticated public relations policies devote substantial effort to anticipating or avoiding issues that might have a negative effect, they will also raise issues when they believe that public discussion might be beneficial. In contrast, there are many special interest groups whose major activity is to raise issues—in the American democratic tradition, in which the people ultimately decide. Because of the number of variables at play and the societal importance of public debate, dealing with issues is one of the most challenging segments of public relations.

TYPES OF ISSUES

Issues can be assigned to four categories:

- **Latent.** Just being formulated by far-thinking scholars or social activists but with sufficient apparent validity that it could become an issue sooner or later.
- **Emerging.** Starting to be written about in scholarly journals or specialty media; perhaps a special interest organization adopts the idea or a new group forms around it; early adopter opinion leaders begin to be aware; it starts to spill over to wider publics, but no coherent action plan or broad support is yet evident.
- **Hot.** A full-blown issue in current debate.
- **Fallout.** Leftover remnants from the settlement of hot issues, which can come back onto the public agenda because they have already attained visibility.

For example, Case 8–5 focuses on the effort to advance beyond war, an *emerging* issue of the late 1980s–early 1990s. People are surely aware of the peace topic. It is regularly discussed in mass media and among average citizens. What places it in the emerging category is that the idea that something practical can be done to attain peace is still not widely accepted—and perhaps most people are not even aware of the thought. Therefore, the strategy and tactics employed by the organization needed to be different from those one might use to deal with a hot issue or a latent one. Elements of all four categories are evident in many of the cases.

TARGET AUDIENCES

Most of the time, practitioners work with specified target audiences such as employees, neighbors, stockholders, members, donors, and customers, who are perceived to have self-interest reasons to support the organization. These audiences make up the organization's constituency. Contacts with them seek to reinforce, broaden, or deepen the two-way commitment. (See Figure 8–1).

THEN THERE'S THE GENERAL PUBLIC

When the term *general public* is used, it usually describes the uncommitted, often uninterested bystanders whose support or opposition might ultimately have a bearing on the outcome of a situation or issue. Because they are unaware or uninterested, members of the general public do not feel much of a stake or depth of conviction.

If a matter eventually will be on the ballot, or voted on by a legislative body, or

STAKEHOLDERS

NCR

We believe in building mutually beneficial and enduring relationships with all of our stakeholders, based on conducting business activities with integrity and respect.

SHAREHOLD

NCR

We are dedicated to creating value for our shareholders and financial communities by performing in a manner that will enhance returns on investments.

EMPLOYEES

NCR

We respect the individuality of each employee and foster an environment in which employees' creativity and productivity are encouraged, recognized, valued and rewarded.

COMMUNITI

NCR

We are committed to being caring and supportive corporate citizens within the worldwide communities in which we operate.

NCR's Mission: Create Value for Our Stakehol

CUSTOMERS

NCR

We take customer satisfaction personally: we are committed to providing superior value in our products and services on a continuing basis.

NCR's Mission: Create Value for Our Stakeholders

Figure 8–1 A semantic twist to the concept of constituency is *stakeholders*, an umbrella identification denoting every group that has a stake in this issue. (Courtesy of NCR Public Relations.)

decided in the marketplace, where people "vote with their dollars," involvement of the general public can be vital. Or, if social policy is being set, it is the general public that will decide what it will be—with or without laws to enforce it. At other times, interest in an issue will be so specialized that the general public will forgo its right to participate and leave the decision to the special interests who do care about the subject.

Therefore, the first problem faced by practitioners often is to get people interested. Sometimes individuals or organizations will seek to do this by attempting to speak for the general public. When consumer advocates began questioning the quality and price of various products or services, they took on a task that most people had often done themselves—so people were happy to have this leadership. But when religious fundamentalists claimed to speak for average citizens in demanding the removal of certain books and magazines from libraries and newsstands, the public rejected them. In both cases, these spokespersons were not elected or otherwise appointed by those for whom they undertook to speak. They were accepted or rejected by public consent. This principle is key to understanding issue debate.

When persons or organizations take stands on issues, pro or con, or neglect to do so, that is an exercise of a privilege and a prerogative in the democratic process. It is fundamental to effective public relations that this freedom of expression prevail. Without it, the individual or the organization is totally subject to the point of view of the state or of the noisy and the militant. Given freedom of expression as a basic underpinning of public relations practice, experience suggests that this concept is balanced and weighted by many adjustments. For example, the theoretical democratic process suggests that the majority rules. In reality, this does not always hold true. Quite often, a minority prevails. Less than half of eligible voters register to vote, and an even larger percentage of those who register do not vote. In almost all elections, it is a vocal, motivated, active minority who do vote, and therefore rule. Within most organizations, to use another setting, there is almost always a relative few who hold the decision-making power for the whole body politic or membership.

Three cases in particular in this chapter illustrate the concept that a general public does exist, available to be influenced, but that the perceived will of that unorganized body is carried out through small groups focusing on a particular issue or concern. One group took on the Spotted Owl as its concern. Another became an advocate for nonsmokers. Still another wanted stores to be open on Sundays.

In a slightly different context, Planned Parenthood claims to speak for the rights of women, and across the aisle the Right to Life movement offers its position on moral issues as one that has precedence over personal choice.

The uncommitted general public provides an arena (via public relations campaigns, the news media, and sometimes the courts) in which the motivations of special interest groups can be challenged by those who openly represent viewpoints or programs claiming to deserve a higher priority or to embody a higher moral purpose.

The general public and its elected representatives hold the key in the continuing controversy between the business sector and government agencies over how much regulation there should be, what kind, by whom, and with what reporting requirements and penalties.

PUBLIC SERVICE AS PREVENTIVE PUBLIC RELATIONS

Public service programs are expressions of an organization's concern for societal problems and needs. The public relations responsibility for organizations engaged in public service programs is normally as the creator and implementor. This role calls for the handling of:

- Strategy, planning, and research
- Program design
- Civic participation
- Government and educational liaison
- Meetings and events
- Media placement and relations
- Preparation of print, audio, and visual materials
- Interviews and news conferences

Some public service programs spring out of a crisis or an emergency, from criticism of an organization's doings, or from public clamor, as in the conservation of endangered species.

More and more frequently, public service programs have not waited for problems to arise. They have been devised to help head off the difficulties posed by protests, confrontations, or increased governmental regulations. Public service programs are seen as practical means of demonstrating socially responsible behavior, gaining trust for good deeds, building customer or clientele goodwill, or building working relationships with a constituency of public officials, investors, members, donors, or voters. For most successful enterprises and institutions, the attitude is that public service programs and expenditures are important to earn public approval. As a practical matter, management normally places two requisites on public service programs:

1. A program must fit logically into the mission, the objectives, the timetable, and the field of endeavor in which the organization has expertise.
2. There must be an identifiable, measurable benefit to the organization as well as to the public groups or noble purpose involved and affected.

Such strategic public service programs often call for cooperation between public relations or public affairs, human resources, marketing, and other departments.

SPECIAL INTERESTS

Citizens in a democratic society tend to band together in polarized common interest groups such as labor unions or manufacturers' associations, meat eaters or vegetarians, hunters or conservationists. People feel that collectively, on a given issue, their voices and their votes can get the attention needed to favorably influence decisions.

The United States, more than any other free nation, has become the world's prime example of what happens, both good and bad, when the democratic process is carried to an extreme. The nation has become factionalized to a point that the decision process is hobbled by a host of single-issue champions, protesters, and crusaders. On many public issues, factionalization has generated such a severe confrontation that all possible points of reconciliation have been passed.

The practice of public relations, historically and now, is deeply involved in helping factions to have their voices heard and their influences felt on behalf of their particular special interests.

In representing competing or opposing factions, practitioners face off against each other much as lawyers do in lawsuits or courts. The justification, if any is needed, is simply that each faction, in the eyes of its sponsors and its beneficiaries, holds that its view or needs do, in fact, serve the best interest of all. This freewheeling debate in the court of public opinion, or the marketplace of ideas, is exactly what Jefferson and the Founding Fathers had in mind when they created the United States as the first true democracy.

THE IMPORTANCE OF COMPROMISE

Given factionalization and confrontation, it remains for elected government in a free society to assume the roles of *referee* among contestants and *interpreter* of the greater public good.

When powerful and determined factions or special interests meet head on, the outcome is generally a reconciliation, with both sides compromising a bit. For example, in the matter of environmental protection, the upper atmospheric layer, or ozone, high above the earth filters out some of the sun's ultraviolet rays, helping assure that humans can live above ground and expose themselves to the sun. Chlorofluorocarbons (as in spray deodorant, insecticide, and detergent cans) have been identified as damaging to the ozone layer. The government, acting in the public interest and spurred by environmentalists, had to consider a ban on certain chlorofluorocarbons. Makers of products using them said, in effect, "Give us some time to switch over without loss of the market." Granted time, manufacturers set about providing nonpressurized containers for their products and advertising and promoting the desirable features of roll-ons, pump-can devices, and wipe-ons.

There has been so much of this kind of compromise in areas of social concern, from integration to equal employment opportunity, from atmospheric pollution to metropolitan area blight and roadside litter, and even sexuality, that the phrase *an era of trade-offs* has come into popular use.

THE UNFORGIVING DECADE

On the other hand, there is a tendency today toward emphasizing those issues that have become so emotional, or are so deep-seated, as to evoke almost (or actual) religious fervor in their adherents. These divisive issues seem to be tearing the social fabric and raise doubts about the future of the democratic process. Among them are abortion, assisted or legalized suicide, medical triage, sex education in the schools, other items of educational curricula, gun control, smoking, homosexuality, and civil rights for animals.

"True believers" among activists have resorted to violence—the murder of a physician at a Florida feminine health clinic—and angry protest against organizations—picketing or boycotting companies that have, or don't have, medical coverage for homosexual "spouses." These zealots can swerve an organization far off course unless public relations practitioners are sufficiently knowledgeable and influential to prevent overreaction. Because a few zealots put you in the headlines is no reason to panic, or to pander to what are often their very undemocratic, minority-opinion demands.

One result of this social warfare is what Ann Barkelew, vice president of Corporate Public Relations of Dayton Hudson Corporation (DHC), terms "The Unforgiving Decade." She notes that no matter what actions you take in the 1990s or which policies you adopt, *someone* is going to be angry enough to denounce you—loudly and publicly.

Her company discovered this principle when pickets ringed a company department store unexpectedly one day—protesting an activity the company had taken for granted. The "pro-life" picketers were angry that DHC contributed (as it had for years) to Planned Parenthood, whom the picketers consider to be promoting abortion. (Planned Parenthood says this is not true; they counsel on abortion and all other choices available to pregnant women who seek their advice.)

Because the contributions had continued for years, a way out, thought one company official, seemed to be discontinuing them—with the rationale that under any circumstance contributions should shift among various causes. But when this "solution" was announced, an even *larger* number of "pro-*choice*" picketers surrounded the store.

No matter how the issue was to be resolved, the company was going to make enemies and probably lose some customers.

One resolution would be to count heads; which group has the most supporters, so could do the most damage. But what organization wants to be in such a losing situation? So an alternative strategy is to work with the "side" that will be favored in order to gain pledges of extra business and support to make up for the lost

ISSUE ANTICIPATION TEAMS

Issue anticipation (IA) teams are working well for many organizations who wish to identify issues before they become a problem. In many organizations setting up IA teams both meets the need *and* deals with the middle management "wall." Teams usually involve managers from all ranks and departments. To keep interest high, teams report every so often to a formal "issues board" composed of senior officers. Some organizations have one team that looks at the realm of issues. Others have several teams concentrating on specific areas of concern. At its simplest, the team answers two questions: (1) What's happening out there? (2) Could it happen to us?

Benefits of Teams

- Serving on a team is an honor, which motivates the members.
- It forces them to read and observe things they previously didn't.
- Members interact with folks they might not come in contact with otherwise.
- Consensus and teamwork are essential.
- Supervising managers start to think broadly about the implications of what the organization does and sensitizes them to public relationships.
- Helps identify and train the rising stars.[1]

customers. Neither is ideal, and both keep the organization on the hot seat of being identified with a divisive issue.

ISSUE ANTICIPATION

The way to avoid issues is to see them coming and to find ways to reach accommodation before they become public and "hot." (See box.) Some say, indeed, that the real value of public relations is what *doesn't* happen! As you review the cases in this chapter, observe whether there were early warnings that might have enabled public relations practitioners to help their organizations take action to steer around the public debate that ensued.

REFERENCES AND ADDITIONAL READINGS

Alisnky, Saul D. *Rules for Radicals.* New York, N.Y.: Random House, 1972.

Aronoff, Craig and Otis Baskin. *Public Relations: The Profession and The Practice.* 3rd ed., Dubuque, IA: Wm. C. Brown, 1991.

[1] *pr reporter*, April 27, 1987.

Briode, Mace D., Herbert M. Baus, and Phillip Lesly, "Having a Voice in Politics," in *Lesly's Public Relations Handbook*. 4th ed. Chicago IL: Probus Publishing Co. 1990, ch. 7, pp. 106-115; ch. 31 "Working with Influential Groups," pp. 494-502.

Buchholz, Rogene. *Business Environment and Public Policy: Implications for Management*. Englewood Cliffs, NJ: Prentice Hall, 1989.

Coleman, Cynthia-Lou. "What Policy Makers Can Learn from Public Relations Practitioners." *Public Relations Quarterly* 34 (Winter 1989-90): 26-31.

Corporate Public Issues and Their Management offers a variety of information regarding public policy formation and issue management. For more information write: Issue Action Publications, Inc.; 207 Loudoun Street; S.E. Leesburg, Virginia 22075.

Cutlip, Scott M., Allen H. Center, and Glen M. Broom, *Effective Public Relations*, 7th ed. Englewood Cliffs, N.J.: Prentice-Hall, Inc., 1994. Chapter 6.

Ewing, Raymond P. *Managing The New Bottom Line: Issues Management for Senior Executives*. Homewood, IL: Business One Irwin, 1987.

Foundation for Public Affairs. *Public Interest Profiles*. Washington, DC: Congressional Quarterly, 1991.

Fox, J.F., "Communicating on Public Issues: a Changing Role for the CEO," *Public Relations Quarterly*, Vol. 27, Summer 1982.

Future Vision: The 1989 Most Important Trends of the 1990's. Naperville, IN: Sourcebooks, 1990.

Hammack, David and Dennis Young, eds. *Nonprofit Organizations in a Market Economy: Understanding New Roles, Issues, and Trends*. San Francisco, Calif.: Jossey Bass Publishers, 1993.

Health, Robert L. *Strategic Issues Management: How Organizations Influence & Respond to Public Interests & Policies*. San Francisco, CA: Jossey Bass, 1988.

Heath, Robert and Richard Nelson. *Issues Management*. Newbery Park, CA: Sage, 1985.

Jones, Barrie, and Howard Chase, "Managing Public Policy Issues," *Public Relations Review*, Vol. 5, No. 2, Summer 1979. A classic.

Kelley, Stanley, Jr., *Professional Public Relations and Public Power*. Baltimore: Johns Hopkins University Press, 1966. Classic study of a perennial question.

Mathews, David. *Politics for the People*. Baltimore, Maryland: University of Illinois Press, 1993.

Morrison, Catherine. *Managing Corporate Political Action Committees*. New York, NY: The Conference Board, 1986.

National Rifle Association. For pamphlets explaining the organization and its objectives and programs, 1600 Rhode Island Avenue, N.W., Washington, D.C. 20036.

Newsom, Doug, Alan Scott Ph.D., and Judy Van Slyke Turk Ph.D., *This is PR: The Realities of Public Relations*, 4th ed. Belmont, California: Wadsworth Publishing Company, 1989. Chapter 8, "Laws Affecting PR Practice," pp. 253-291.

Olasky, Marvin, "Engineering Social Change: Triumphs of Abortion Public Relations from the Thirties through the Sixties." *Public Relations Quarterly* 33 (Winter 1988-89): 21.

pr reporter, 37, No. 14, April 4, 1994. Lead article concerns value of public relations in grassroots organizing and coalition building.

Scheel, Randall L. *Maxims for the Issues Manager.* Stamford, CT: Issue Action Publications, 1991.

Stoltz, V., "Conflict PR in the Formation of Public Opinion," *Public Relations Quarterly*, Vol. 28, Spring 1983.

The Futurist: Outlook '94. Bethesda, MD: World Future Society, 1994.

The Public Relations Body of Knowledge. New York: PRSA, 1993. See section I.2 for abstracts dealing with "Ethics and Social Responsibility".

Public service programs are regularly reported in the following periodicals: *pr reporter*, PR Publishing Co., P.O. Box 600, Exeter, N.H. 03833. *PR News*, 201 Seven Locks Road #300, Potomac, M.D. 20854. *Public Relations Quarterly*, P.O. Box 311, Rhinebeck, N.Y. 12572-0311.

Values on a Collision Course

The process of obtaining lumber and wood pulp for domestic use, as well as for export, imposes a toll on the various environments in which wildlife can survive and flourish. Logging practices can threaten the existence of birds, fish, animals, and plant life. Single-minded timber practices are among the consequences of developing technologies that have resulted in the disappearance of 200 species of wildlife, and some 230 more are on endangered lists. Birds have made up a large part of the loss, as nearly eighty species have become extinct in 300 years in the United States.

The lumber industry plays a significant role in the fate of our forests and the wildlife that dwells within them. The U.S. Forest Service has been selling timber companies the rights to cut trees in old-growth forests at a rate of about 62,000 acres annually—under a directive from Congress to create jobs in timber regions. At this rate, most authorities estimate, the old-growth forests will be gone in twenty years.[1] Today, only 2.4 million acres of Pacific old-growth forest remain; a mere remnant of the 19 to 20 million acres of ancient forests that once existed in Washington and Oregon alone.[2] Old-growth forests consist not just of ancient standing trees, but of fallen trees, snags, massive decaying vegetation, and numerous resident plant and animal species, many of which live nowhere else. More than 200 species of fish and wildlife flourish in ancient forest ecosystems, and more than 1,500 species of invertebrates can inhabit a single stand of ancient forest. One tree can be home to 100 separate plant species. These forests provide habitat for as many as two dozen threatened or endangered plant and animal species.[3]

[1] Sy Montgomery, "Protective Legislation Filed," *Boston Globe*, July 6, 1992.

[2] Ibid. We thank the Wilderness Society for information provided for this case—though readers must realize this excellent public service organization does have a viewpoint on these issues.

[3] Taken from "Ancient Forests of the Pacific Northwest and the Northern Spotted Owl" provided by the Wilderness Society.

Through most of our country's history there was little or no demand for logging in the national forests. Intensive logging began during World War II and increased over the years. After thirty years of extensive logging, the National Forest Management Act was adopted in 1976 in hopes of serving both environmentalist and industrial groups. But despite increasing concern over the environment, logging sales by the Forest Service continued, as authorized by Congress.

One endangered species that survives in Pacific Northwest ancient forests is the northern spotted owl (see Figure 8–2). Because of past habitat loss from logging and development, today's population of northern spotted owls represents a small fraction of the numbers that once existed. Studies show that populations of the owl are continuing to decline.

Special interest groups that favor owl preservation, forest conservation, and timber production have found themselves head to head in the battle of "whose cause is most important." The thrust of this case study shows that *maintaining positive relationships through changing issues is difficult* and that *compromises don't necessarily result in a happy ending.* The best solution may be found in shifting the focus of the controversy to an activity that aims for a win-win resolution. It is a truism that we can't have the best of both worlds. There have to be choices and trade-offs.

The question is "Can one aspect of an issue oversimplify the issue in its entirety—therefore hindering the progress of achieving a positive resolution?"

In this particular study, the trade-off hinges on the disciplining of industrial practices. Specifically, how much restraint in normal timber logging operations is acceptable in order to help save the spotted owl, uphold the Endangered Species Act, conserve old-growth forest, and yet preserve timber industry jobs?

MORE THAN JUST OWL VERSUS LOGGING

The Wilderness Society and the lumber industry sought publicity to gain public awareness and support for their respective concerns and their solutions—both economic and environmental. These debates centered around the overruling of the Endangered Species Act that allowed logging on thirteen tracts of land designated as spotted owl habitat in the Pacific Northwest.

In 1992 the Forest Service found itself the center of attention throughout the debates. Until this time, the Forest Service was rarely faced with the challenge of negotiating with two strongly opposed viewpoints. They had maintained a good reputation for their work with communities, but were now considered the bad guy by two significant parties. Environmental groups lobbied the Forest Service to protect the spotted owl and save the old forests, and the timber industry wanted it to preserve logging jobs. Naturally, the Forest Service aimed to accomplish both, but as it was to find out, a compromise doesn't always satisfy opposing parties.

Figure 8–2   The northern spotted owl has been the centerpiece of extreme controversy in the Pacific Northwest. (Courtesy of the Wilderness Society.)

Figure 8–2 Continued

ENDANGERED SPECIES ACT BECOMES ENDANGERED

In 1973, Congress passed the Endangered Species Act (ESA). The act prohibits any-one, with a few exceptions, from killing, capturing, or harming a listed endangered species. Federal agencies must ensure that any action they authorize, fund, or carry out will not jeopardize the continued existence of any endangered or threatened species. The act calls for the creation of "Recovery Plans" that help restore endan-gered species through conservation programs. The ESA, however, was first over-ruled in 1979 when Grayrock Dam was built in Wyoming—despite the threat to whooping cranes, a listed endangered species, on the Platte River in Nebraska. Envi-ronmental groups were outraged at the prospect of changing the law in order to sat-isfy ever-increasing human technologies.

In 1992, the Endangered Species Act was overruled a second time. The origi-nal Recovery Plan was designed to rescue the spotted owl from extinction by pre-serving 5.4 million acres of ancient forest but at the estimated cost of 32,000 log-ging jobs. The subsequent Preservation Plan, upheld by the Bush administration, allowed limited timber harvests in areas in Washington and Oregon populated by the northern spotted owl. This overruling aimed to preserve 17,000 logging jobs and maintain the economy in small towns dependent upon the timber industry; it would, however, result in the eventual extinction of the owl in those areas. The de-cision aimed to halt the dispute between the environmentalists and the logging in-dustry by allowing limited timber harvests in certain old-growth forests while the government came up with a plan to protect the owl. [4]

The response to the Preservation Plan compromise was not favorable. Both parties felt cheated of their goals. The northern spotted owl would still reach ex-tinction within decades, and the timber industry would still lose logging jobs. The one group that felt satisfied with the plan were those working in certain lumber companies. Some lumber companies profited from the spotted owl controversy be-cause the curtailment of cutting raised the price of lumber and increased profits.[5]

OPPOSING PARTY STRATEGIES

To counteract opponents in these highly publicized debates, special interest groups initiated activities to gain awareness and public support for their causes.

The Wilderness Society

Founded in 1935, the Wilderness Society is the largest national conservation organi-zation devoted primarily to the protection and management issues of public lands.

[4]"High Court Backs Some Logging in Spotted Owl Areas," *Boston Globe*, March 26, 1991.

[5]Bill Richards, "Owl of All Things Help Weyerhauser Cash in on Timber," *Wall Street Journal*, June 24, 1992.

The society employs a combination of advocacy, analysis, and public education in its campaigns to improve management of America's National Parks, forests, wildlife refuges, and Bureau of Land Management lands.

One lobbying activity of the Wilderness Society during the debates included the unveiling of a series of computer-generated maps showing the heavy fragmentation of remaining ancient forest in twelve national forests of the Pacific Northwest. The maps were given to members of Congress in hopes of them using the data as the raw material to help forge a solution that would protect ancient forests and establish a sustainable regional economy. The maps showed that more than seventy-five percent of the remaining old growth found in the twelve national forests located in Oregon, Washington, and northern California is unprotected, and the remaining areas are in isolated and highly fragmented stands.[6]

Developing its thematic arguments, the Wilderness Society stated that lumber mill automation, improved labor productivity, and rising raw log exports—not the spotted owl—were the main contributors to the loss of 26,000 timber jobs since 1979. They also advised that a twenty-five percent reduction in raw log exports could provide the equivalent of between 4,500 and 5,000 U.S. timber jobs—jobs that would turn raw logs into finished products.

The Wilderness Society agrees that logging has a place, although diminished, in the future economy of the Pacific Northwest. The issue facing Congress is how to cushion an economic transition that will occur regardless of the fate of the spotted owl.

The Timber Industry

The timber industry argues that studies of old-growth forest measurements have been inconsistent. Environmental organizations and the Forest Service report that approximately 3,000 pairs of the spotted owl exist today. The timber industry, however, reports that 4,018 owl pairs and 2,047 owl singles exist for a total population of over 10,000 northern spotted owls, well above the previously quoted figures. New research shows that owl population and reproduction are not correlated with the amount of suitable habitat within the study sites and that more environmental factors are likely involved.[7]

The timber industry argues that the loss of logging jobs in the timber industry in the 1980s was due to the economic recession and not to automation. They claim that employment levels have remained fairly constant since 1983.[8]

Key arguments include that timber sales reductions will result in worker displacement, business closure, social service demands, and the many personal prob-

[6]Taken from a news release distributed by the Wilderness Society February 20, 1992.

[7]Ross Mickey, "The Northern Spotted Owl: The Rest of the Story," *Building Towards a Balanced Solution*, compiled by the Northwest Forest Resource Council, April 1993, 10.

[8]Charles Burley, "Employment and Mill Automation," Ibid, 5–6.

lems associated with unemployment.[9] Furthermore, restrictions on timber sales in the United States will only result in the logging of other forests worldwide.[10]

The U.S. Forest Service

The U.S. Forest Service is charged with maintaining national forests as a resource for the citizens of the United States. In the spotted owl controversy, it became clear that there was no longer any consensus or even tacit consent on which management programs could be developed.

To grasp the full implications of the spotted owl and timber industry debates, the Forest Service reviewed literature on the owl, heard presentations from scientists doing spotted owl research, considered the concerns of numerous interest groups, and conducted field trips in Washington, Oregon, and northern California to examine the owl's habitat. The Forest Service recognized that much of the attention directed toward the owl stems from a growing debate over managing old-growth forests on federal lands and from a concern about protecting biodiversity. They understood the larger issues, but kept to a mandate of developing a conservation strategy specifically for the spotted owl.

The U.S. Forest Task Force developed a conservation strategy. The outcome was a mapped network of Habitat Conservation Areas (HCAs) that would ensure a viable, well-distributed population of owls. Wherever possible, each HCA would contain a minimum of twenty pairs of owls with a maximum twelve-mile distance between HCAs. Logging and other forestry activities would cease within HCAs.

Though each interest group hoped that the Forest Service would support its cause, the Forest Service saw its role as an attempt to *maintain positive relationships* between the parties.

SEEKING CONSENSUS

On April 2, 1993, President Clinton held a Forest Conference in Portland, Oregon, to break the gridlock over federal forest management that had created confusion and controversy in the Pacific Northwest and northern California. The conference aimed to achieve economic diversification and new economic opportunities in the region.

The Forest Conference called for a plan that recognized both the importance of the timber industry to the economy of the northwest and the need to preserve old-growth forests as an irreplaceable part of our national heritage.

---

[9]Robert Lee, "Effects of Federal Timber Sales Reductions on Workers, Families, Communities, and Social Service," Ibid, 1.

[10]Con Schallau, "Global Implications of Timber Supply Restrictions," Ibid, 8.

Five principles gave guidelines to the three committees organized to put the plan together:

1. Remember the human and economic dimensions of the problem.
2. Protect the long-term health of our forests, wildlife, and waterways.
3. Make all efforts scientifically sound, ecologically credible, and legally responsible.
4. Produce predictable and sustainable levels of timber sales and nontimber resources that will not degrade or destroy the environment.
5. End the gridlock within all branches of the federal government and insist on collaboration not confrontation.

A NEW PLAN

The outcome of the conference, the Northwest Forest Protection Plan, calls for reducing timber harvests in the Pacific Northwest to an average of 1.2 billion board-feet annually for ten years. This value is approximately seventy-five percent less than the industry's harvest throughout the late 1980s. Restrictions would be placed on timber cutting around spotted owl nests on private lands. Logging would be limited in protected reserves established on federal lands.

Anticipating a loss of 6,000 timber industry jobs, a five-year, $1.2 billion economic assistance package was designed to create 8,000 jobs and provide retraining opportunities. And finally, the plan asks Congress to encourage more domestic milling by eliminating a tax subsidy for timber companies that export raw logs.

The plan also calls for new methods of forestry. "New forestry" sets out to turn younger stands of trees into forests that look more like old growth in hopes of increasing habitat for old-growth species. Loggers practicing new forestry set out to reshape the woods, taking out the uniformity by randomly cutting trees to create meadows for wild grasses and leaving the downed trees to rot to promote ground vegetation.

CONTINUED OPPOSITION

Despite these efforts to appease the opposing parties, the Forest Protection Plan didn't receive favorable response. Environmentalists recognize the plan as a positive first step, but argued in favor of the creation of permanent reserves on 8.6 million acres in three states. Environmental scientists say that new forestry won't work because forest systems contain complex details of biological, physical, and chemical processes that cannot be reproduced by humans.

The timber industry wants the administration to permit higher harvests over the next few years. The target of 1.2 billion board-feet will be a substantial loss, resulting in higher lumber prices, a slowdown in home purchases due to greater costs, and a stalled economic recovery. Those in the timber industry also disagree with new forestry because it doesn't allow for logging. It is *no forestry*.

SHIFTING THE FOCUS

Despite the opposition, the Forest Protection Plan is attempting to solve the spotted owl controversy in the context of a broader strategy. It has *shifted the debate* from the protection of individual owls to the preservation of an ecosystem for various species. It recognizes that a long-term management plan for natural resources in the public domain can no longer be based on a single set of values but must take into account a broad diversity of national interests.

QUESTIONS FOR DISCUSSION

1. The strategy of the Clinton administration was to shift the focus of the controversy from owl protection to the preservation of ecosystems for various species. Will this decision provide a long-term solution to the issue? Or will environmentalists and timber industry employees never reach a satisfying compromise? List the reasons either may result.

2. The Endangered Species Act appears to be easily overruled when economics takes a front seat on an issue. What would be the best way in terms of strategy and communications vehicles to go about revitalizing the act to deter future overrulings?

3. The introduction to this chapter offers four categories of public issues: latent, emerging, hot, and fallout. Where does wildlife preservation fit? How about endangered species? If not in the same category, why not?

4. Take the position of the environmental coalition, the timber industry, the Forest Service, or the Clinton administration and prepare a plan for communicating and gaining support for its messages and solutions.

Reproductive Rights and the Abortion Issue

Abortion has ridden a high wave of debate and challenge ever since it was legalized in 1973 by the famous Supreme Court case *Roe v. Wade*. In the early 1990s the battle cries were heard once again as new laws were being proposed to restrict the *Roe v. Wade* ruling. In the summer of 1992, the nine justices on the Supreme Court were faced with a decision that could severely limit abortion rights and possibly overturn this precedential case, making abortion illegal again. So-called right-to-life groups and pro-choice groups stepped up their efforts to sway public opinion.

EXACTLY WHAT ARE THEY FIGHTING FOR?

With the legal decision of *Roe v. Wade* came a struggle in the Court of Public Opinion. Is there any hope for resolution of this issue? More than likely no. The two sides cannot even agree on what issue they are fighting over. On the pro-choice end of things women are fighting for the right of individual liberty and jurisdiction over their bodies. On the pro-life side are fetal life and the issue of murder. The division is great and possibly unbridgeable. Abortion has become a test of democratic decision making itself. Yet it is far from a new topic. It began eight decades ago with one woman's concerted efforts.

MARGARET SANGER'S CRUSADE

The eighty-year effort of what we know today as Planned Parenthood International is an incredible story. Like many crusades, this movement started with one person of conviction and dedication: Margaret Sanger was born in 1883, the sixth child of eleven in a Corning, New York, family. Sanger, a frail, red-headed nurse, came to her rebellion at midlife, married, the mother of three, and taking the cure for tuberculosis (see Figure 8–3).

Working as a nurse on New York's Lower East Side, she was shocked at the circumstances of poverty and degradation surrounding countless attempts at self-induced abortion and the arrival of unwanted babies. Her actual decision to devote her life to changing these circumstances for the better came when she experienced the pleadings of a woman for help, and the death of a woman who had tried to abort her own pregnancy.

Sanger realized the immensity of the undertaking and the overpowering odds against her. To begin with, there was on the books the old Comstock Law of 1873 that made the distribution of contraceptive information a federal offense. Lurking in the wings was the sacred dogma of the Catholic Church. If these weren't enough, most people living in poverty, who needed help the most, had survival, not morality, or even education, as the highest priority in their lives.

Giving Birth to a Crusade

The launching of Margaret Sanger's personal crusade came in the form of several articles in *The Call*, then a leading radical paper, titled "What Every Woman Should

Figure 8–3   Margaret Sanger, founder and crusader. (Courtesy of The Sophia Smith Collection, Women's History Archive, Smith College, Northampton, Mass. 01063.)

Know" and "What Every Girl Should Know" with the theme of emancipating women, via contraception, from sexual servitude.

That was in 1912. Sanger gave a name to her proposition: "birth control." Her philosophic approach was remarkably simple: *Every child born should be wanted by parents who are prepared to care for that child.* Otherwise, conception should be prevented. At the time, topics such as sexual relations and reproduction, or such personal matters as venereal disease, hernia, menstruation, or a spastic offspring, were not freely discussed. Margaret Sanger's initial problem was how to rally support for changing public attitudes on a matter that grown men would not discuss because the open discussion of it was regarded by most people as immoral. Worse, many influential people who might have helped her saw the birth control crusade as simply another aspect of the women's rights movement, which was itself very controversial.

Margaret Sanger could not wait for resolution of the unwanted-child problem as a rider on the political issue of suffrage for women. She decided to do her homework, and to that end, with her husband and three children, went to France, where family planning was an accepted part of life. There she queried doctors, midwives, druggists, and a great many women, collecting formulas, techniques, and devices.

On her return, she established a publication, *The Woman Rebel*, in which she attacked the Comstock Law. *Her strategy was to test the law by breaking it. The Woman Rebel* was promptly banned from the mails, and Sanger was threatened with a prison term and a $5,000 fine. She continued defiantly. The magazine became a best seller overnight.

The next move was the preparation of a pamphlet, *Family Limitation*, with undistributed quantities stored in various large cities for release *at the strategically right time*. When she was arraigned for *The Woman Rebel*, she fled to Canada and then to England; when she was three days out at sea, she wired her associates to distribute 100,000 copies of the pamphlet. Before long, that publication was translated into thirteen languages.

Her flight to England was not to avoid the trial that would test the Comstock Law. Rather, the world events that were leading toward war made the timing seem wrong to Sanger.

This second tour of Europe, without her family, enabled her to study birth control practices in detail. She visited the world's first birth control clinic in Amsterdam and was coached in contraceptive techniques. (She personally thought that use of the diaphragm was the best practical approach.) During the sojourn abroad, she also came to perceive her own crusade more clearly and objectively in its relationship to a nation's overall health and economic well-being.

When she rejoined her children in New York, ready to face trial, she found that the public attitude had shifted noticeably in her favor. The term *birth control* had caught on. Her husband had become something of a hero for having served a thirty-day jail term after being tricked into a violation of the Comstock Law. Comstock himself had died; the government had backed off, and now Sanger was free of the threat of imprisonment.

The Comstock Law, however, still had not had its courtroom test.

Sanger embarked on a lecture tour, then returned to establish, in a deprived section of Brooklyn, the first birth control clinic in this country. She found that, with the Comstock Law still on the books, no doctor wanted to run the clinic and expose his professional neck. So Sanger, with her sister and a friend, ran it. Within ten days, they were arrested and carted off to jail. While free on bail, they reopened the clinic, were arrested again, and served thirty days in jail (see Figure 8–4).

When the case was subsequently brought to the court of appeals, the judge upheld the conviction but interpreted the law broadly to mean that a doctor could give contraceptive advice to a married woman if it was of benefit to her health.

Sanger took her courtroom triumph back on the road in a series of lectures and ran into some opposition that had previously been publicly silent—the Catholic Church. One zealous archbishop induced the New York police to close down one of her meetings. This action proved to be a stroke of good fortune for Sanger, because the press interpreted the action as a breach of freedom of speech and came to her defense—despite prior descriptions of her by some papers as a "fanatic" and a "crackpot."

The headlines were largely favorable to the crusade. In the ensuing debate, according to accounts published later, the archbishop argued that birth control violated the laws of nature, and Sanger responded that celibacy for nuns and priests did the same.

This did not mean the end of opposition or any substantial long-term change in convictions about sexual relations and morality, for these had been deeply ingrained for centuries. Symptomatically, young men still hesitated to buy condoms, or "rubbers," as they were commonly called, from a female clerk in a drugstore. Purchases were made surreptitiously, in whispers, and the products carefully concealed from those, such as parents, who would disapprove because of the implication of

Figure 8–4 Sanger and sister under arrest in 1916. (Courtesy of Planned Parenthood Federation of America.)

prospective immoral conduct. Sexual relations involving the educated and affluent that resulted in venereal disease or in pregnancy among unmarried women, which might have been avoided by the use of condoms, were cause for the shaming of a whole family, even of a whole neighborhood.

Four years after she started, Margaret Sanger's campaign indisputably had the aura of a movement with the potential of a social revolution.

The Maturing of an International Movement

Important punctuations of the birth control crusade came at the structural and public affairs levels. The Voluntary Parenthood League had been organized while Sanger was in France, by a group interested mainly in the suffragette and feminist movement. Subsequently, birth control leagues were started in several cities and unified as the National Birth Control League—shortly after, changed to the American Birth Control League—with Sanger as its president and with its own publication (see Figure 8-5). Then the Clinical Research Bureau opened. Scores of birth control clinics were opened. Distinguished doctors gave endorsement and counsel. Respected citizens of wealth and influence supported the activities openly and enthusiastically. Over the years, events gave increasing strength to the movement.

- 1935   Radio censorship of birth control was ended by NBC.
- 1936   The U.S. Circuit Court of Appeals ruled that physicians could distribute through the mails material "for the purpose of saving life or promoting the well-being of their patients."
- 1937   The American Medical Association endorsed birth control.
- 1942   The U.S. Public Health Service adopted a policy of giving requests from state health offices for financial support of birth control the same consideration and support given other state medical programs.
- 1950   President Eisenhower became honorary chairman of Planned Parenthood and the first of many presidents, including John Kennedy, a Catholic, to endorse and aid the program.
- 1960   The first contraceptive pill was introduced. One of its three developers is a Catholic, Dr. John Roch, showing how far professional and public attitudes had moved.
- 1966   The American Nurses Association recognized family planning education as part of the nurse's professional responsibility.
- 1967   Social Security amendments created a family planning project grants program and gave a mandate to state welfare departments for service to those of extremely low income.
- 1967   The United Nations Fund for Population Activities was established in response to resolutions in the General Assembly and the Economic and Social Council.

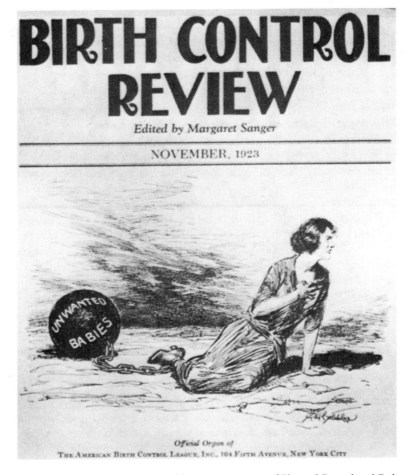

Figure 8–5   The official house publication. (Courtesy of Planned Parenthood Federation of America.)

- 1970   Congress adopted the Family Planning Services and Population Research Act.
- 1973   The Supreme Court ruled that abortion is a matter to be decided between a woman and her doctor in the well-publicized *Roe v. Wade* case.
- 1976   Congress enacted the Hyde Amendment, cutting off federal (Medicaid) funds for abortions for poor women.
- 1981   President Reagan opposed abortion and asked that the 1973 ruling be overturned.
- 1992   President Bush comes under fire during the election for his endorse-

ment of the "gag rule," which prohibited staff (including doctors) in clinics receiving public funds from even discussing the abortion option. Bill Clinton runs on a pro-choice platform and ascends to the presidency after twelve years of Republican politics.

Along the way, the American Birth Control League had changed its name to the Planned Parenthood Federation of America (PPFA). In the meantime, world population trends had become an important concern to governments. Many argue that starvation and poverty can never be conquered so long as population is increasing so rapidly, particularly in Third World nations. Sharing in this global concern the PPFA helped found the International Planned Parenthood Federation, under the dual leadership of Margaret Sanger and Lady Rama Rau of India.[1]

The Goals

Apart from contending with organized opposition, PPFA formulated a number of goals:

- Meet the unmet family planning needs among individuals who cannot afford them.
- Reduce unwanted pregnancies and births among teenagers.
- Preserve and ensure access to safe, legal abortion services and counseling for all women, regardless of age or ability to pay.
- Advance research in human reproduction.
- Reduce the unmet need for fertility regulations around the world.

Continuity and Leadership

Margaret Sanger, as rebel, missionary, and spokeswoman, did not let a false vanity get in the way of the crusade. When her efforts gained the momentum of a bandwagon, she was swept along in it. Over the years, she became almost eclipsed by the movement she had created. Whether this was good and wise is arguable. Some feel it would have been better if she had become the central dominant figure in the crusade, with a public image of heroic proportions comparable with that of Carrie Nation, Florence Nightingale, Gloria Steinem, Davy Crockett, Louis Pasteur, Martin Luther King, or Jonas Salk. We might in this study be dealing with the "Margaret Sanger Parenthood Plan," or perhaps "sangerization" (like pasteurization) or "the Sanger method" (like the Salk vaccine).

Never robust, Sanger worked tirelessly until her health dictated a move to Arizona, and rest. She died in 1965 at age eighty-two.

---

[1]A worthy subject for further study or a thesis is the effort and effectiveness of the United Nations Fund for Population Activities. Background material available 220 East 42nd St., New York, N.Y. 10017.

ON THE OTHER SIDE OF THE ISSUE

The decision of the Supreme Court in 1973 guaranteed the right of a woman to end pregnancy up to the point at which the fetus was potentially able to live outside the womb. With this decision, the issue shifted. The posture of Catholic and other conservative religious dogma and the natural resistance of many poor and illiterate people had constituted a significant opposition and a political force to be reckoned with. After the court's decision, organized anti-abortion, and pro-life groups joined importantly in the opposition.

Counterforces Gain Strength

The philosophy of pro-life groups has been that "all human life is precious and equally deserving of protection under the law. The philosophy embraces the human right of the preborn child to live at any time after conception."[2]

Initially, the pro-life groups sought to overturn the Supreme Court ruling, and then turned attention to the inhibiting of federal grants for abortions. There was some headway with Congress. An amendment to a Health, Education, and Welfare bill prohibited use of HEW funds except when the life of the mother would be endangered if the pregnancy continued.

Initially, the pro-life groups were not organized or marshaled into a dominant movement as Planned Parenthood was. As a result, several groups had to concentrate on "catch-up" efforts to identify a constituency. Publicity was the most readily available vehicle in the public arena. One of the impressive and unusual pieces of publicity was a special edition of the *National Right to Life News* reproducing an exhaustive series of articles in the *Chicago Sun Times* on "The Abortion Profiteers." One of the special events has been an annual March for Life in Washington, duplicated in several major cities. Another event has been the convention of the National Right to Life movement (see Figure 8–6).

Among the vehicles in pro-life programs are:

- Counseling hotlines
- Speakers bureaus
- Informational videotapes
- Slide shows
- Annual banquets

[2]See Robert M. Byrn, "An American Tragedy: The Supreme Court on Abortion," *Fordham Law Review*, May 1973. See also John Lippis, *The Challenge to Be Pro-Life*, a booklet, National Right to Life Committee, 419 7th Street, N.W., Suite 500, Washington, D.C. 20004. See also *Choose Life*, a booklet, Foundation for Life, 2854 Sylvania Avenue, Toledo, Ohio 43613.

Figure 8–6 Some pro-life literature has used shocking graphics to gain attention. (Courtesy of Right to Life Council, Dr. and Mrs. J. C. Wilkie and Hayes Publishing Co.)

- Volunteers trained in communications
- Pamphlets and brochures
- Espousal of Billings (rhythm) method of birth control
- Organized protests at abortion clinics

The latter, tragically, have often become violent under the influence of zealots. In addition to property damage, several people have been injured—and one clinic doctor was shot in cold blood in a Florida incident.

AN AREA FOR COMPROMISE?

Intermediaries for pro-life and pro-choice groups have sought a basis for compromise and understanding, if not total reconciliation. In the main notable occasion, the National Organization for Women (NOW) issued invitations to twenty pro-life and twenty pro-choice organizations to a joint conference on abortion. In response, the president of the National Right to Life Committee called publicly for a moratorium on abortions prior to the meeting.

When the conference convened, most of the twenty pro-choice groups had sent representatives. About half of the pro-life groups had. Others, including National Right to Life, had sent observers. Hope for meaningful dialogue on this occasion was destroyed, however, when the conference was disrupted by the dramatic and unexpected display of a five-month-old aborted fetus.

One trained observer of the conference, speculating on the future prospects, said that both sides had been friendly, conciliatory, and respectful to each other, but after the disruption, "distrust had crept in."

THE MAKINGS OF A STAND-OFF

The issue between pro-life and pro-choice groups has been increasingly narrowed to the matter of abortions. Inevitably it has taken on major legal aspects. Along with the question of prayer in schools and the separation of church and state, it has fueled political rhetoric.[3] The issue is growing more and more political—one of the first things candidates are asked about is where they stand on abortion.

There was a flurry of activity in 1983–1984, kicked off by the tenth anniversary of the Supreme Court ruling. Officials in the Department of Health and Human Services (formerly HEW) proposed that parents be notified when their daughters sought birth control devices from government-aided clinics. This proposal, dubbed the "squeal rule," was headed off or put in limbo by a federal judge. It was subsequently challenged by the American Civil Liberties Union. An amendment to the Constitution, sponsored by Sen. Orin Hatch, was defeated. Some effort was made to make the issue an aspect of the Equal Rights Amendment movement. With states and localities involved, and a national election pending in 1984, politicians were loath to come down decisively on the issue.

Meanwhile, Planned Parenthood added more and more counseling clinics, some providing referrals or abortion services. Pro-life groups, principally the Christian Action Council (Birthright) and Pearson Institute, sought to break the deadlock

---

[3]For added background on the issue, see such early articles as "Ecumenical War Over Abortion," *Time*, January 29, 1979; *A Larger Mission*, Planned Parenthood Federation, 810 Seventh Avenue, New York, N.Y. 10019; *The Right to Choose*, a reprint, Zero Population Growth, 1400 16th Street, N.W., Suite 320, Washington, D.C. 20036; "The Battle over Abortion," *Time*, April 6, 1981, a cover story, and "Holding Firm on Abortion," *Time*, June 27, 1983.

by a combination of violent and peaceful campaigns. There were incidents of clinic bombing and arson. Radical groups such as Operation Rescue orchestrated violent protests outside abortion clinics. As mentioned, a pro-life zealot killed a Florida abortionist on his way into the clinic where he worked. These extreme acts have backfired in public opinion. On the peaceful side, there was the establishment of counseling centers for pregnant women. Presumably, the help given would discourage women from having abortions as the only or preferable alternative. Pro-choice groups responded with picketing and labeling the counseling as deceptive (see Figure 8-7).

Planned Parenthood increasingly has gone to Congress or court to defend its gains. It vehemently opposed the nomination of Judge Bork to the Supreme Court, challenged the Agency for International Development for imposing conditions on the receipt of family planning funds, and brought suit against the Secretary of Health and Human Services over its eligibility for federal funds. Other challenges have been addressing state restrictions on abortion in the Supreme Court. In 1992, Pennsylvania passed a law that required women to wait twenty-four hours after requesting an abortion to have the procedure. Mississippi passed a consent law that required girls under the age of eighteen to acquire parental permission for abortions or prove to a judge that it is not in their best interest to notify their parents.

By the end of the 1980s, Planned Parenthood had 190 affiliates in the United States, serving some 2.5 million clients who made a total of nearly 4 million visits to the 816 clinic centers. Some 100,000 abortions and vasectomies were performed, but the majority received laboratory tests, diagnosis for pregnancy, and whatever counsel seemed in order for each person. Planned Parenthood operated on a budget approaching $500 million, making it the third largest international service organization after the United Nations and the Red Cross. Public relations activities were headed by a vice president for communications.

WE'RE BACK WHERE THE CASE STARTED

Although there have been 21 million known abortions performed since the Supreme Court ruling in 1973, world population still grows at a threatening pace. Every year, 95 million people are added to the world population.[4]

As in any public issue, each side is divided into factions. Some right-to-life groups have grown more zealous and radical. In some instances they have harassed abortion doctors right out of the profession; picketing the doctors' homes, blocking their way to work, tying up their telephones, and resorting to other disreputable tactics. Protests at clinics have become more aggressive, with attempts to block doors and yelling at women who enter.

---

[4]Much of the update beyond 1984 was drawn from an analytical article, "Abortion Rights: Anatomy of a Negative Campaign," by Marvin N. Olasky, *Public Relations Review*, 13 (Fall 1987).

Figure 8–7   Pro-life groups use modern techniques to make a point and to attract media attention. (Courtesy of San Diego Union-Tribune Publishing Co. Photo by John Gibbons and Joe Holly.)

In the fall of 1993, a bill was introduced into Congress that would arm the Justice Department with power to stop abortion clinic blockades and go after violent protesters. Although initial objections concerned infringing on First Amendment Rights, many pro-lifers in the Senate joined in supporting the bill, proclaiming that violence is not an appropriate manner in which to express views on such a volatile issue, no matter which way one believes.

WORLD POPULATION PROBLEMS ADD TO THE DEBATE

The relentless growth of world population threatens the well-being of the human race more than any other social problem. Incredible? Consider that in 1830 the world contained approximately 1 billion people. One hundred years later, in 1930, the world population had doubled to 2 billion. In half as much time, the next fifty years, the total approached 4.5 billion. The Population Institute projects that, if family size, life-span trends, and mortality rates are taken into account, the total will grow at about 95 million a year, which means 6 billion people on earth by the year 2000 if no additional control measures are applied.

Nearly ninety percent of the projected world population increase will occur in the developing regions—parts of Africa and Latin America, for example. These regions and pockets already contain 3 billion people, at least 200 million underfed, most of them lacking safe water or adequate health care. At least half the adult population is illiterate or otherwise unable to make a decent living. Their outlook is bleak at best. This reality tempts people in developed and prosperous areas to indulge in artificial censorship—to ignore the matter as though it doesn't affect them (see Figure 8–8).

The truth is, the problems attending rapid population growth have echoes that are planetary and deadly, not regional, and not temporary. Poverty, epidemic disease, starvation, and ignorance cannot be resolved simply by saying or gesturing, "Take this money and these medicines. Grow more food. Treat your diseases and wounds. Eat well and wisely. Study hard.

Go to church. Follow the Golden Rule. Make more jobs."

Alternatives and Conflicts

Well-qualified and nobly intentioned individuals, groups, and enterprises, including the governments of the more fortunate nations have separately and sometimes jointly sought ways to soften the consequences of too many people and too little hope. Agreement on a long-term master plan to control population growth and then implementation of that plan remain elusive.

Examined dispassionately, change in the present rate can be attained in either one of two ways: Decrease the birthrate, or increase the death rate.

Decreasing the birthrate could be done by voluntary or involuntary measures, dealing with fertility or conception. Mortality control is available by reduction of life span. As perceived as early as the 1790s by an English clergyman, Thomas Malthus, if the action were taken by humans, it would be directed at fertility, whereas nature's way would be to increase mortality.

Differences in viewpoint have not been confined to the clergy or to religious precepts. Mysticism, public policy, political expediency, and human psychology have entered into the problem. As for individual viewpoints, a person's age, ethnic background, culture, ingrained customs, urge to prove manliness or femininity, and many other factors enter into it.

This is not to say that no studies, education of the public, or efforts to achieve a

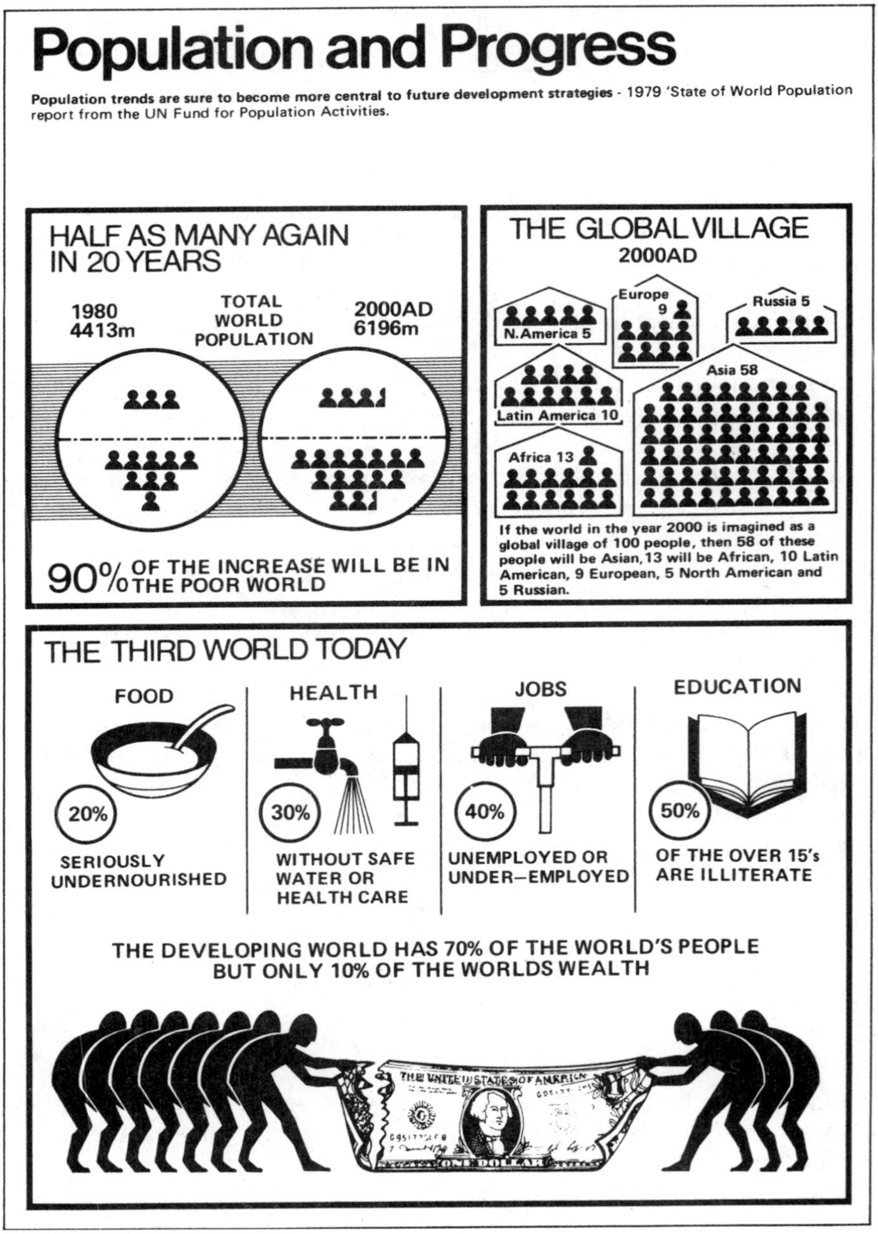

Population and Progress

Population trends are sure to become more central to future development strategies - 1979 'State of World Population report from the UN Fund for Population Activities.

HALF AS MANY AGAIN IN 20 YEARS

1980 4413m	TOTAL WORLD POPULATION	2000AD 6196m

90% OF THE INCREASE WILL BE IN THE POOR WORLD

THE GLOBAL VILLAGE

2000AD

N.America 5   Europe 9   Russia 5

Latin America 10

Africa 13

Asia 58

If the world in the year 2000 is imagined as a global village of 100 people, then 58 of these people will be Asian, 13 will be African, 10 Latin American, 9 European, 5 North American and 5 Russian.

THE THIRD WORLD TODAY

FOOD	HEALTH	JOBS	EDUCATION
20% SERIOUSLY UNDERNOURISHED	30% WITHOUT SAFE WATER OR HEALTH CARE	40% UNEMPLOYED OR UNDER-EMPLOYED	50% OF THE OVER 15's ARE ILLITERATE

THE DEVELOPING WORLD HAS 70% OF THE WORLD'S PEOPLE BUT ONLY 10% OF THE WORLDS WEALTH

Figure 8–8 The realities of population growth and distribution. (Courtesy of United Nations Fund for Population Activities. Art by Peter Sullivan.)

consensus have been attempted, or that all have failed. On the contrary. It is rather that the distance to be traveled is great, and the journey continues.

Meanwhile, the concepts and the tactics of those who seek seriously to alleviate the population problem, and the resulting controversy, merit studious attention for their precedential value to those who contemplate careers in public issue areas.

QUESTIONS FOR DISCUSSION

1. In getting her crusade started, Margaret Sanger had to rely on the printed word and limited personal contacts. There was no radio or television. Her strategy was to educate, to test laws by breaking them, and to arouse sympathy by being the underdog. If she started out today, and you were her adviser, what would you recommend as strategy, messagery, and communication vehicles?

2. If the focus is on mediating compromises in which all sides and the ultimate public good will be reasonably satisfied, what aspects of the worldwide population explosion problem do you feel could yield to trade-off during the 1990s? What might be the most effective strategy for the mediators?

3. The Right to Life movement has concentrated heavily on the rights of an unborn fetus and the question of abortion. In the process, that emphasis may tend to put the two main divisions of Christianity, Catholics and Protestants, in more of a head-to-head antagonism than is comfortable for most followers of both segments. Can you envision some points of common interest where combined effort might foster increased adjustment and reconciliation without abridging the laws or sacraments of either church? Apparently, little kids sharing a neighborhood can attain this goal, so why not adults? Consider such common interests as poverty in America amidst plenty, and the inability of 60 million Americans to read well enough to understand an explanation of the rhythm method, or to understand a map giving the location of a counseling center, or to write well enough to fill out a driver's license application? How might some avenues of common effort be tested using communications staff and volunteers?

4. Fear of contracting AIDS has been credited with the increased use of condoms, with less sexual promiscuity among single people, and with greater fidelity among married couples. Does this trend suggest that in almost all matters a threat to our physical well-being is more persuasive than an appeal to our conscience, intelligence, or character? If that is not safe ground for a generalization, what are some exceptions?

Take Your Choice—Tobacco or Health

Health issues have gone public the past several decades. Anything that may jeopardize health has come under fire. One issue that has ridden a high wave of interest and debate is the question of whether smoking endangers health—of the smoker and of those around that smoker. The extent of the role that the government plays in the tobacco industry by enacting laws and regulation has also created controversy. When does governmental regulation become an infringement on personal rights? This is not a phenomenon unique to tobacco products. Any product or service linked to a potential cause of cancer, heart disease, or any other ailment has faced increasing challenges. Ask the people who made asbestos or cyclamate sugar substitute or who operate suntanning studios.

HISTORICAL BACKGROUND

The smoking of tobacco was occurring long before Christopher Columbus arrived in the New World and brought it back to Europe. Native Americans had been smoking the plant for centuries. Not until the development of the cigarette-rolling machine in 1881, however, did smoking gain widespread usage.

From the 1870s until the 1900s, smoking and the use of tobacco in other forms were frowned on socially as objectionable masculine habits, particularly in the presence of ladies. Although this habit was merely looked down upon for men, it was totally unacceptable for women. Nevertheless, some women began smoking around the turn of the century, although many were deterred from beginning the habit by anticigarette crusades and bans. Railroad companies forbade women to smoke on trains. Several cities, including New York, has ordinances that prohibited women from smoking in public places.

348

By the 1920s, the number of women smoking had increased noticeably, and advertisers clamored to claim a share of this potentially massive market. The first advertisement showing a woman smoking appeared in 1919, but it was not until 1927 that advertising was aimed on a large scale toward women (see Figure 8–9).

In 1927, George Washington Hill, colorful and hard-driving head of the American Tobacco Company, began using the slogan "Reach for a Lucky Instead of a Sweet" to promote his Lucky Strike cigarettes. This advertisement appealed to women by indicating that they could find some sort of oral gratification and still keep their figure.

The canny Hill saw that change of societal acceptance of smoking for women needed special efforts from others to reinforce his advertising. He called in public relations counsel Edward L. Bernays for his ideas on how to increase sales among women. He also hired publicists Ivy Lee and Harry Bruno for their ideas on other problems. And he selected advertising pioneer Albert Lasker to handle his Lucky Strike advertising. Asked later why he had hired so many public relations experts, he was reported to have said "to keep my competitors from hiring them."

Bernays sought the opinion of a psychoanalyst to learn what rewards women might see in cigarettes. This was quick, inexpensive fact-finding. Dr. A. A. Brill said women most likely regarded cigarettes as symbols of freedom. Cigarettes could be

Figure 8–9 Popular vocalist Marian Hutton of the Glenn Miller band in 1941 became one of the first celebrities to appear in advertising for cigarettes. (Courtesy of *Life* magazine.)

perceived as torches of freedom, symbols protesting man's inhumanity toward women, symbols of determination to be emancipated. Moreover, he told Bernays, "Smoking is a sublimation of oral eroticism; holding a cigarette in the mouth excites the oral zones."

DRAMATIZING THE SYMBOLS

One of Bernays' projects to erode the social taboo against women smoking in public was to arrange for ten debutantes of social prominence to join the annual parade of Easter Sunday fashion finery down New York's Fifth Avenue. As they strolled, they "lighted the torches of freedom" and proceeded to walk along with cigarettes in hand. They puffed and posed for the New York newspaper photographers and reporters who had been alerted by Bernays and seized the event for front-page coverage. This one symbolic event echoed across the media nationally, breaking the ice for general acceptance of smoking in public by women.

Fifty years later, Bernays was frequently asked about his efforts to get women smoking. He would respond that in the 1920s he had no knowledge of any link between smoking and lung cancer. Had he been aware, he said, he would have refused to work for Hill.

SURGEON GENERAL GETS INTO THE ACT

As government and private research agencies learned more about carcinogenic agents, and their findings were passed on to the public by the media, opposition to smoking, regardless of sex, grew and took on organized forms under the aegis of the American Cancer Society and other groups. The lines were drawn, and the battle for public support began. On one side was the tobacco industry and those dependent on it economically. On the other were all those engaged in public health and life extension services, specifically those involved in the prevention and control of cancer.

A major event came in 1964 when the U.S. Surgeon General announced that cigarette smoking was definitely linked to cancer, and subsequently a warning message was required on any cigarette package or advertisement.

A PROGRAM FOR OPPONENTS

Even as tobacco growers were granted governmental subsidies, the Department of Health and Human Services (HHS), was distributing information about the hazards of smoking and lobbying for laws restricting the use and the advertising of cigarettes. In conjunction with the American Cancer Society, American Heart Association, and American Lung Association, the department has taken a proactive stance involving public education, regulation and research backed by higher budgets, more aggressive efforts (advocacy), and a renewed commitment by all. The main elements in the antismoking program have been:

- Asking major broadcasting networks to increase antismoking public service announcements.
- Development of education programs in schools, aimed at preventing teenagers from ever starting to smoke.
- Banning smoking originally in HHS buildings and then extending the ban to the 10,000 or more other federal buildings, local governmental structures, and eventually to most public buildings.
- Examining the federal policy on cigarette taxes (the tax, unchanged from 1951, was doubled in 1982 and is now the target of revenue raisers every time funds are needed).
- Asking insurance companies to offer premium discounts to nonsmokers.
- Ordering the Food and Drug Administration (FDA) to have drug manufacturers label products indicated by research to have higher risks for smokers, especially birth control pills.

ON THE OTHER SIDE

The natural coalition of forces for opposing efforts to control and restrict the smoking of tobacco starts with those whose livelihoods and economic well-being are tied to the raw product. This group includes growers and their employees, communities dependent on tobacco as an agricultural commodity, processors of it, and manufacturers of cigarettes and cigars. In addition, those endeavors that supply the various substances, tools, and vehicles needed—from planting and movement of goods to market to sales promotion—all have a vested interest. This large array of interests has the funding to mount effective communications programs and to lobby government officials. And of course, there also are the millions who smoke and want to continue to do so.

Organized opposition has come mainly from the Tobacco Institute, a nonprofit, noncommercial wing established by the eleven major tobacco companies in the United States in 1958. For quite a few years, the Tobacco Institute took a defensive, circle-the-wagons, reactive stance. In more recent times, the stance has become more proactive, with the core claim being that smoking is a civil liberty, a matter of free choice, a right that the government is trying to infringe upon. Its slogan has been "Freedom of choice is the best choice." Early in the 1980s, advertisements with that message appeared in national magazines with two short essays that smokers and nonsmokers can live together without need for government intervention (see Figure 8–10). This has been a continuing theme in defense of smoking.

The Institute has stated its case in the past as:

Figure 8–10   Example of Tobacco Institute approaches to creation of opportunities to tell the industry's side of the story. (Courtesy of the Tobacco Institute.)

- Tobacco smoke is not a major source of air pollution.
- People are not allergic to tobacco smoke.
- Nonsmokers in a smoke-filled room do not inhale significant amounts of smoke.
- A report by the Surgeon General states that carbon monoxide in a smoke-filled room exceeds permissible levels, but such conditions would rarely be found in real life.
- Anti-smoking efforts have increased lately, but the evidence against smoking is not increasing.
- Thorough review of the world's scientific literature indicates that smoke is not a significant health hazard to the nonsmoker.
- Common courtesy, rather than laws, should determine nonsmokers' rights (see Figure 8–11).

BATTLE AND TESTING GROUNDS

The right of each individual to decide for himself or herself has been the platform on which the tobacco interests have taken their stand against state or local proposi-

Figure 8–11 Pamphlets such as this, published by the Tobacco Institute, are guides on how to accommodate smokers and nonsmokers without legislation. (Courtesy of the Tobacco Institute.)

tions to control or restrict smoking. Today many cities have ordinances that prohibit smoking in certain public areas. Perhaps the most notable example was the passage of an ordinance by the City of San Francisco in 1983 requiring employers to provide separate areas for workers who smoke. The tobacco industry gathered 30,000 signatures on a petition, forcing the issue onto a major election ballot. The antismoking groups prevailed in the election, although the tobacco industry spent nearly ten times more on its campaign.

The battle against smoking has not only been waged by the government in passing public ordinances. Now it is also an important factor in the workplace. Over a third of the companies that make up *Fortune's* Industrial 100 have completely banned smoking inside their buildings, some going so far as to mandate no smoking even on the premises outside. Many employers will not hire smokers because of their higher health risk and greater amount of days lost from work. Comstat, the telecommunications company in Washington, D.C., has doubled the price of out-of-pocket costs for health insurance for smokers.[1] Some companies have mandated that their employees smoke neither at work nor at home. Turner Broadcasting in Atlanta has declined to hire smokers since 1988. Controversy has arisen over what control an employer can have over an employee's private life. Where do smart hiring decisions end and workplace discrimination begin? Does the right to privacy become blurred if employees participate in an activity that will raise their health costs in the future? Statistics have indicated that smoking costs the nation $65 billion per year in health care costs and lost productivity. These issues and many more difficult questions will have to be addressed in the coming years.

ISSUES THAT JUST WON'T DIE

Since the mid-1950s, the number of people over age eighteen who smoke has decreased from about fifty percent to about twenty-eight percent. Daniel Seligman, writing in *Fortune*, computes this to be an annual decline at the rate of 1.5 percent to 2 percent.

Beginning in 1981, the effect of passive smoke was magnified by more and more research findings that indicated increased risk of lung cancer in nonsmokers exposed to it, which spurred others to join in the antismoking fight. The Environmental Protection Agency has also substantiated that secondhand smoke causes cancer. These pronouncements substantially enlarged the potential constituency for organized opposition to smoking. Antismoking groups gained momentum and pushed further for legislation in regulating and restricting smoking. Then in 1992, the EPA issued its warning against secondhand smoke and its dangers to nonsmokers. Since that time many major cities such as Los Angeles and Denver have passed public antismoking laws.

Late in 1984, Congress passed a bill requiring stronger warnings of health hazards on cigarette packages. Also in the legislative arena during the mid-1980s were bills introduced by antismoking groups that prohibited advertising of tobacco products on the grounds that advertisements lure nonsmokers, especially youngsters, into tobacco use. The industry, allied with civil rights and media organizations, countered with Constitutional arguments about free speech and evidence that advertising affects brand choices among smokers but does not increase the total volume. Although the bills that required a total ban on tobacco advertising failed, new issues continue to emerge that push tobacco advertising regulation back into the legislative arena. Recent controversy about Joe Camel, the cartoon character used to advertise Camel cigarettes, and its possible appeal to adolescents and even preschoolers, has caused the industry to reexamine its position.

---

[1] "Smoked Way Out," Patricia Sellers, *Fortune*, March 22, 1993, 14.

CARTOONS AND CIGARETTES: WHO'S THE AUDIENCE?

The controversy about using cartoon characters to sell a potentially harmful product such as cigarettes became a hotly debated issue in late 1991. The *Journal of the American Medical Association* devoted an issue to studies that researched the impact of smoking and its products on society. Of interest to many antismoking groups was one study that indicated that children as young as three or four years old could recognize the character Joe Camel (see Figure 8–12), the cartoon logo for Camel cigarettes. In this study of brand recognition, the kids identified Joe Camel more than any other popular logo, such as those for NBC, Apple, and Cheerios.

From this study the researchers concluded that this type of advertising lures children to smoke by utilizing pleasing images to entice them and demanded the immediate discontinuation of the ad campaign. RJR Nabisco, the manufacturer of Camel cigarettes, countered this accusation by stating that brand recognition does not necessarily mean that the children will begin smoking and cited its own research statistics that indicate that the average age of a Camel smoker is eighteen to twenty-four. In addition, RJR Nabisco was effective in discrediting the study's main researcher, Dr. Joseph DiFranza. In court, RJR Nabisco produced evidence that indicated that DiFranza had decided he wanted to prove the detrimental effect cigarette advertising has on children *before* he conducted the study.

This controversy has further illuminated the issue of whether allowing cigarette companies to advertise their products is really a freedom of speech issue—or an opportunity to entice children to begin a harmful habit.

Figure 8–12 Joe Camel has been pummeled by critics as an enticement to convince youngsters to smoke. (Courtesy of RJR Nabisco.)

In the media coverage, when the American Medical Association got ready to call for a ban on all cigarette advertising, a major metropolitan daily newspaper editorialized that it was understandable to ban broadcast tobacco advertising in 1971 on the grounds that the airwaves are considered part of the public domain. However, the editorial contended, newsprint media are privately owned and the ban would clearly abrogate First Amendment rights. Its point: If a product is legal to sell, it should be legal to advertise. However, that editorial failed to mention that if advertising were banned from the electronic media and not newsprint media, they would stand to gain *all* the advertising dollars of the tobacco industry. The fact remains that cigarettes are the most heavily advertised products in all of the United States. Every minute, tobacco companies spend over $5,000 on advertising and promotion of their products.[2]

The levy of excise tax is another difficult issue. Antismoking groups favor increases to a point that smoking simply wouldn't be worth the dollar cost and might not be affordable to youngsters. The tobacco industry, with strong support from labor and some minority organizations, holds that excise taxes are regressive, taking a greater proportion from low-income families than from those in higher brackets.

The tobacco industry has conducted campaigns in states that propose tax hikes on cigarettes. In 1992, a Massachusetts health coalition initiated a petition that would put a proposal on the ballot to increase the tax by twenty-five cents. The petition also included that the increased revenue from the excise tax, a proposed $130 million, would be ear-marked for health education and the creation of smoking cessation programs for adults.

The Committee Against Unfair Taxes, a tobacco-industry-financed group, issued a legal challenge to the petition drive, stating that this increase in tax pinpointed only one part of the public in order to pay for these programs. Furthermore, they protested that there was no legal restriction stated in the petition that indicated exactly how the state would spend the extra revenue.

While this controversy rages on, some of the major tobacco companies have taken steps to protect their shareholders, and perhaps other stakeholders, by diversifying their product mix. As examples, Phillip Morris acquired General Foods, a $5.6 billion transaction. R.J. Reynolds put up $5 billion for Nabisco. Then in 1988 RJR Nabisco was taken over for a whopping $25 billion by Kohlberg, Kravis, Roberts Co., corporate buyout specialists, proving, if nothing else, that there was still money to be made one way or another in tobacco.

Incongruously to some analysts of the tobacco industry, the tone of its promotional literature the past few years has been aggressive (see Figure 8–13). However, many times it is seen working behind the scenes in promoting scientific research that casts doubt on the effects of smoking and championing individual rights causes to question the effectiveness of smoking laws. Then, on occasion, public statements

---

[2]Cited from a brochure from the American Lung Association, "Facts About . . . Cigarette Smoking," dated November 1990.

To the people who brought you "The Great American Smokeout," we make

THE GREAT AMERICAN CHALLENGE

We are willing to bet there isn't much cigarette smoking at American Cancer Society offices. But, according to a recent study from the National Institute for Occupational Safety and Health (NIOSH), cigarette smoke also wasn't the problem in 98 percent of 203 buildings reported to have indoor air problems.

We will pay for the testing of the air in the offices or facilities of the American Cancer Society anywhere in the U.S. Indoor air inspections resulting from worker complaints typically find viruses, fungal spores, bacteria, gases, closed fresh air ducts, and ventilation systems in need of maintenance.

We challenge the American Cancer Society to clean up the air in its "smoke free" offices.

What will the Society find in the air breathed by its employees, volunteers and guests? Nothing, if it doesn't look.

Accept our challenge. We will pick up the tab – but, we have three conditions:

1. That the testing be conducted by a certified union ventilation contractor.
2. That the test and its results be made public.
3. That the ACS act on the results and recommendations of the contractors it selects.

THE TOBACCO INSTITUTE

The executive directors of American Cancer Society chapters nationwide today have received details of how they can accept our "Great American Challenge."

Figure 8–13   Public rejoinder to the Cancer Society's Great American Smokeout promotion. (Courtesy of the Tobacco Institute.)

by spokespersons have been moderate if not conciliatory. One observer of the industry has suggested that the moderated tone reflects the vulnerability of the industry in the liability suits being brought against it.

On the antismoking side, the Coalition on Smoking OR Health (an alliance of the American Heart Association, American Lung Association, and the American Cancer Society) has increased its efforts, encouraged, no doubt, when Congress passed a law banning smoking on any domestic commercial airline flight. It didn't hurt matters for them, either, when the EPA issued its warning against secondhand smoke. They have taken this new evidence and used it to emphasize that smoking is not just an event that affects the smoker. Assistant Surgeon General John Duffy has stated that "there is no such thing as a nonsmoker in America today. As long as we have to live and work around smokers, we must accept some of the risks of smoking."[4]

The prime source of programmed antismoking activity continues to be the American Cancer Society. It directs the annual Great American Smokeout, a national event in which smokers all quit on the same day (see Problem 8-A). The Society offers a promotion guide for that event. It also has available a news media handbook, *Smoke Signals*, with a variety of ideas and instructions for groups wanting to tell the story in news outlets (see Figure 8–14).

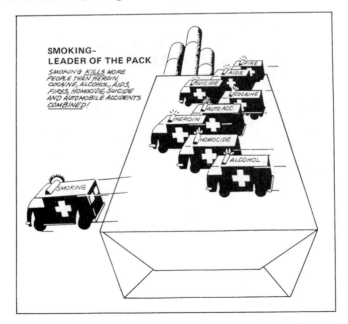

Figure 8–14 Illustration in *Smoke Signals* booklet dramatizes smoking as the major killer among dreaded causes of death. (Courtesy of the American Cancer Society.)

[4]"The Need for a Safe, Healthy, and Smoke-Free Workplace," *World Smoking and Health*, American Cancer Society, Summer 1990, 3.

In one of the most famous liability suits, Rose Cipollone brought suit against three different cigarette companies, citing them as liable for her smoking-related illness. This suit paved the way for many more cigarette maker liability lawsuits when her case was brought before the Supreme Court in 1992. Their ruling stated that cigarette manufacturers may be sued if they have allegedly deceived the public about the dangers of smoking. The industry was claiming that the warning labels on the packages were enough to shield them against any personal injury suits.

The ruling, however, does not make it easy for a smoker to prove the liability of the cigarette manufacturer. The plaintiff must "convince juries that smokers were not primarily at fault for starting and continuing their habit because they relied on industry misrepresentations."[3] The depiction of healthy people in cigarette advertisements is not enough to prove that the industry has been deceptive.

QUESTIONS FOR DISCUSSION

1. On the basis of the information in this case, your personal knowledge, and a professional, objective mind-set, which, if any, of the following conclusions might be supported by maxims of persuasion or by the strategy and tactics used on either side?

   a. The antismoking coalition and the tobacco interests have been equally effective in their communication programs.

   b. One side (which one?) has focused more on influencing behavior than opinion.

   c. The aims and actions of both sides, one side, or neither, reflect a genuine concern for public opinion and behavior over the long haul.

   d. The tobacco interests give more evidence of "issue anticipation" than the antismoking coalition.

   e. The public relations thinking and actions on both sides can be decisive factors in attaining a reasonable solution.

2. On the smoking side of the debate, there is the personal freedom to make choices in life. On the antismoking side, there is personal health. Both are strong appeals to self-interest. Are there other appeals you find significant in the contest?

3. The chapter introduction talks about stakeholders. Among the tobacco interests, stakeholders would be vehicles that carry tobacco advertising. Can you

[3]James H. Rubin, "Cigarette Makers Can be Sued," *Boston Globe*, June 25, 1992, 1–4.

think of any others? Among the no-smoking stakeholders would be insurance companies. Are there others? Does that leave anyone or any group in the middle, the neutral, or "don't care" category?

4. Are there moral and ethical considerations a practitioner should take into account before serving an employer or client involved in the tobacco, liquor, pornography, or handgun industries? Put another way, should the moral and ethical standards of a professional be essentially the same as those of his or her employer or client? Whether yes or no, can you think of a situation in which you would make an exception?

5. The issue of whether a company has the right to mandate what an employee can do in his or her spare time has been hotly debated in recent years. From the employer's viewpoint, what would be acceptable to make restrictions on and why? From the employee's viewpoint?

Guns—For Whom?
For What?

An emotionally charged controversy has long swirled around the availability, owner-ship, and use of rifles and handguns. On one side are those who are shocked by crime rates and feel that violence in many illegal forms is made convenient, if not in-duced, by gun ownership. On the opposing side are the constitutional rights to keep arms and to be secure in one's home. There are legal provisions for game hunt-ing and target shooting as sport, recreation, and employment. Somewhere in be-tween are the wildlife conservationists, the millions who must walk dark streets at night, and the millions who by nature abhor violence and killing in any form.

FACT FINDING

The Second Amendment to the Constitution of the United States (Article 2 of the Bill of Rights) stipulates "a well-regulated militia, being necessary to the security of a free State, the right of the people to keep and bear arms shall not be infringed." The interpretation and the ongoing applicability of this amendment constitute the basis for the controversy involving the personal and private ownership of guns.

Key words in the constitutional amendment appear to be *militia* and *keep and bear arms*. One dictionary defines *militia* as "all able-bodied male citizens from eighteen to forty-five, not members of the regular military forces, and legally subject to call for military duty." That is clear enough as applied to Colonial times; but what is a "militia" in modern times, when the United States has a trained stand-ing army, large Reserve and National Guard units, a Pentagon brain center, and a worldwide intelligence network, all of which are backed by an enormous nuclear capability that could be unleashed by a word of command and the pressing of a few buttons?

As for the right to bear arms, did our nation's founders intend that one needed to be a *member* of the "militia," or might he be *any able-bodied man or woman*? And do "arms" apply only to flintlock weapons of 1776, or should they include the automatic pistols, AK-47s, and other weapons of today? Such questions of definition make up only one small part of a long and many-sided debate.

Meantime, since those pioneer days, the conversion of gun usage to criminal ends has unfortunately attained disturbing proportions. According to the Senate Judiciary Committee in 1991, the death toll by criminal violence exceeds over 24,000 annually, of which nearly half are by firearms. According to FBI Uniform Crime Reports, one murder is committed in the United States every twenty-two minutes. Some fifty percent involve use of a handgun, six percent a shotgun, and four percent a rifle. Of special interest to students is the fact that about one-third of the murders happen in the twenty-to-twenty-nine age group, with seventy percent of those murders committed with firearms.

THE LEGAL CONTROLS

The old cliché, "There ought to be a law against it," seems appropriate. There have been four significant federal laws. The first one, the National Firearms Act of 1934, aimed at control of special weapons. This statute covers such firearms as sawed-off shotguns, but does not involve the pistols, revolvers, regular shotguns, and rifles commonly displayed in gun shops.

The second federal statute—the Federal Firearms Act—came four years later, in 1938. It prohibited the interstate shipment of all firearms to or by convicted felons, persons under criminal indictment, and fugitives from justice. In addition, it required manufacturers, dealers, and importers doing firearms business across state lines to have a federally issued license.

Twenty-five years later, in 1963, just a few months before President Kennedy was assassinated, a third federal statute was introduced in the Senate (S.B. 1975). It was known as the Gun Control Act. Its purposes were to ban mail-order and interstate shipment of firearms to individuals, to stop over-the-counter sales of guns to minors, to prohibit possession of guns by convicted criminals, and to bar the importation of concealable foreign handguns. This act, with some modifications from the form in which it was initially offered, was passed in 1968. Then, after years of often acrimonious debate, the Brady Bill was enacted in 1993. It is described in detail later in this case.

Local governments, meanwhile, have been free to establish certain controls of their own. All of the states and hundreds of cities and townships have done so. Many states require a license or permit for purchase of a handgun. Many states require a waiting period of a day or more between purchase and possession of a handgun, and the District of Columbia has prohibited firearm sales since 1977. There are other localized restrictions.[1]

This whole matter is complex and emotional. There are strong personal convictions and frequent flare-ups of public controversy. Hunters, hobbyists, competitive range shooters, law enforcement personnel, wildlife conservationists, gun and ammunition makers, and frightened nightshift workers, among others, hold strong convictions. The victims of armed robbery, rape at gunpoint, kidnapping, and hijacking, and the families and friends of those killed or maimed by gunshot, harbor deep emotional feelings. At times, a whole nation has been shocked with guilt.

REPRESENTING GUN OWNERS

The National Rifle Association (NRA), over 100 years old, boasts more than 2.8 million dues-paying members. It marshals and sustains resistance to restrictive firearms measures that its members feel might infringe on the Second Amendment. At the same time, it supports mandatory sentences for the misuse of a firearm in the commission of a crime (see Figure 8–15).

The objectives of the NRA extend to the use of firearms for pleasure and for protection by law-abiding citizens. The NRA describes itself as an independent, nonprofit organization. In its literature, the NRA asserts that law-abiding Americans are constitutionally entitled to the ownership and legal use of firearms. Some programs of the NRA, as it has described them, include:

- Guardianship of the Second Amendment right.
- Sponsorship of various shooting clubs and marksmanship programs.
- Initiation of civilian marksmanship programs more than 100 years ago and youth training about seventy years ago.
- Participation on a national board to promote rifle practice and to operate national rifle and pistol matches.
- Assignment by the U.S. Olympic Committee as the national governing body for competitive shooting in the United States and membership in the International Shooting Union.
- Creation of a code of ethics for hunters and the nationwide "Sighting-In Day."
- Donation source for various trophy awards.
- Origination of safety training for hunters and safety courses for firearms in the home.
- Functioning as a certifying agency for instructors, counselors, and referees.

---

[1]The particulars are available in *Published Ordinances: Firearms*, Department of the Treasury, Bureau of Alcohol, Tobacco, and Firearms. From Superintendent of Documents, N. Capitol and H Streets, Washington, D.C., 20401.

Figure 8–15 NRA poster urging greater jail sentences for crimes. (Courtesy of the National Rifle Association.)

• Total financial support for all expenses of U.S. shooting teams in international competition.

How the NRA is Financed

Total revenues available annually exceed $87 million. The major portion, more than half, comes from dues of various classes from $20 up to $1,000 for a "benefactor." Other sources are advertising, contributions to the Institute for Legislative Action, dividends and interest from invested funds, and the sale of items related to membership or gun ownership.

The NRA publishes *American Rifleman* and *American Hunter* magazines. Both accept advertising; revenues exceed $7 million annually. The NRA also has a publication for its junior members, publishes range plans and instructions, handbooks, instruction manuals, and a wide variety of pamphlets (see Figure 8-16). Free loan films are also offered.

An ancillary source of revenue has been jewelry, a book service with a catalog listing books and handbooks, and trinkets. NRA total assets are more than $56 million and include a multimillion dollar headquarters building in Washington.[2]

An Active Constituency

When it comes to rallying public support, despite Gallup polls showing that ninety percent of Americans favor federal gun control legislation, the NRA claimed as far back as twenty-five years ago the ability to produce "within seventy-two hours more than half a million letters, postcards and telegrams to members of Congress on any gun bill issue."[3] In its target constituency, starting with veterans of all wars, it specifically includes an estimated 22 million licensed hunters, 5 million members of gun clubs, and 1 million or more gun collectors, not to mention dealers and manufacturers of all kinds of equipment for hunting and target shooting.

The NRA Strategy and Tactics at Points of Controversy

When shocking incidents such as assassinations, random shootings, and gang-related violence seize the front page, public opinion swings suddenly and widely. The public often sympathizes with the families and friends of the victims, deploring the senselessness of violence, and demanding the apprehension of the perpetrator, swift and stern justice, and stricter controls of firearm ownership. Concerned citi-

---

[2]Most of the material about the NRA was gathered from information provided by Paul H. Blackman, NRA Research Coordinator, for the previous edition of this book. When asked to critique the case for this edition, Blackman accused us of extreme bias and refused to cooperate.

[3]Richard Harris, "Annals of Legislation: If You Love Your Guns," *New Yorker*, April 20, 1968.

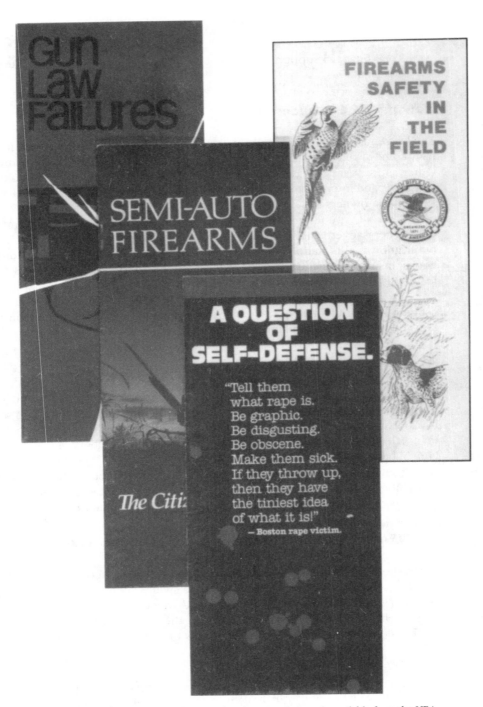

Figure 8–16 Example of the many brochures and manuals available from the NRA. (Courtesy of the National Rifle Association.)

zens write letters to editors. Law enforcement officials speak up for gun registration, regulation, and other controls.

- In the immediate aftermath of tragic episodes and public outrage, the NRA has not often taken a stance of overt rebuttal. Its strategy seems to be to lie low, knowing that the pendulum of opinion will in time return to positions held before the shocking event.

In its quiet dealings at the political or legislative level, however, the NRA has not wavered or gone silent. Its lobbying strategy for many years has emphasized that "Guns don't kill people: People kill people," implying that people rather than guns require more control, and sterner penalties for criminal use of a gun are what is really needed. Its lobbying tactics, with an amazing track record of successful opposition to restrictive legislation, have been assertive, not defensive.[4]

In its public information and education, the NRA has emphasized these points:

1. That firearms legislation would disarm the law-abiding citizen without affecting the criminal, who would ignore the legislation.
2. That if firearms were not available, some other weapon would be used by the criminal.
3. That most weapons found in criminal hands have been stolen.
4. That registration of arms might leave law-abiding citizens at the mercy of criminals, of a subversive power if it infiltrated, or of the nation's enemies if they occupied the country.

The Role of Public Relations

In the structure of NRA, governmental affairs, along with field, information, member, and fiscal services, are under the Institute for Legislative Action. Public relations and publications are among five functions set up as individual wings. In 1986, public relations for the rest of NRA was assigned to an outside firm based in Oklahoma, with a Washington, D.C., office in one of the NRA buildings.

The in-house function as described in an annual report was concentrated on publicity and advertising, plus a desktop-published biweekly legislative tabloid. The function's role was that of "communications technician" among the roles defined by Dr. Glen Broom's studies. The department's work was measured largely by quantitative media usage of news releases and three-minute radio shows. The one measurement of a qualitative aspect cited in the report was the analysis of specific news media coverage as "positive," "negative," or "balanced."

---

[4]However, the NRA's refusal to help update this case study may be a sign that it is now on the defensive.

ON THE OTHER SIDE OF THE ISSUE

The persuasive power of the NRA has given the impression in the past that those on the other side, the gun control advocates, are invisible and silent, perhaps overwhelmed or intimidated. To many neutrals or fence sitters, it might seem that the success of the NRA reflects popular public sentiment. Neither impression is complete or valid. Polls of the general public have shown that a majority of people of all ages, both sexes, in all geographic regions of the United States, favor federal legislation for control of guns, and particularly handguns—the "Saturday night specials."[5]

Gun control advocates have made these points:

1. That there are as many firearms in the United States as there are people.
2. That in most states, no license is required to purchase a handgun.
3. That the United States is the only civilized nation in the world that does not regulate the ownership of firearms.
4. That during one year there were more Americans killed by handguns in a two-day period than were killed in all of England (a country that does not allow ownership of handguns) that whole year.
5. That guns should be treated like cars—they should be registered, and the people who use them should be licensed.

One legislator echoed those sentiments in urging a complete ban on the manufacture and sale of handguns. He cited a combination of congressional fear of the NRA and big business interests behind guns for the lack of tough federal legislation.

Statistical information backing up the gun control advocates is impressive. The U.S. General Accounting Office (GAO), in a survey of crime for one full year, found that 63.8 percent of all murders, 23.6 percent of all aggravated assaults, and 42.7 percent of all robberies were committed by persons using guns. The GAO asked Congress to consider specifically the denial of a gun to a person with a criminal record and the regulation of transfers of guns from one person to another.

In the past, attempts at federal legislation have failed repeatedly, so many states and communities have exercised their local options. California, as but one example among hundreds, enacted a "use a gun, go to jail" mandatory prison sentence for crimes involving use of a gun—as well as mandating a fifteen-day waiting period to purchase a handgun. In 1989, a law banning semiautomatic assault weapons was passed by the California legislature. And in the wake of brutal shooting sprees, many state legislatures have banned the use of semiautomatic guns.

Not all local efforts at control gained popular support. In Massachusetts, voters had the opportunity of deciding whether to restrict handguns. On the one side

---

[5]Recent federal legislative efforts have concentrated on banning the manufacture and sale of "Saturday night specials," and other easily concealed handguns, supporting bans on semiautomatic weapons, and imposing penalties on owners who fail to report the theft or disappearance of a handgun.

were police officials and citizens. On the other were state and national organizations and the arms industry, including a Massachusetts manufacturer of handguns. People versus Handguns got thirty-one percent of the vote. They had to settle for raising the level of public consciousness.

There Are Grassroots Citizens' Groups

In recent years, the most vocal national citizens' lobby has been Handgun Control Inc. (HCI), successor to the National Coalition to Control Handguns. This organization has sought to attract enough contributing members to face off with the NRA in lobbying Congress for legislation, to alert its constituents to those candidates for election who favor gun controls, to report the voting records of congresswomen and men on gun issues and the amount of financial support each got from the NRA, and otherwise to provide a continuous rallying point.[6]

Handgun Control Inc. maintains a Washington, D.C., headquarters housing a Handgun Information Center. HCI has a Handgun Control Board with notables among its members. It has established regional offices in San Francisco and Minneapolis and holds an annual HCI National Conference. The chairman of HCI in 1992 was Sarah Brady, wife of former White House Press Secretary, James Brady—whose injuries in the attempted assassination of President Ronald Reagan led to the gun control law named after him. HCI communicates with its constituency in a quarterly newsletter *Washington Report*, offers a booklet, *Handgun Safety Guidelines*, and a public service announcement (PSA) on child safety, on request. It sends out periodic letters soliciting contributions (see Figures 8–17 and 8–18).

BRINGING THINGS UP TO DATE

In legislative confrontations, the NRA is a single-issue organization. Its strategy is to take an inflexible posture. Officials are convinced that to make one concession would establish a precedent and invite a nibbling away at the Second Amendment right. A new advertising approach was quite dramatic (see Figure 8–19).

However, this iron-clad stance received many blows in the late 1980s and early 1990s because of the turning tide of public opinion and the lobbying efforts of HCI and other gun control advocates, including police organizations. HCI, with the support of an impressive roster of congresspeople, concentrated its efforts on the legislative agenda. Specifically:

- A waiting period and background check (the Brady Bill, passed in 1993).
- A license-to-carry law.
- A mandatory jail sentence for using a gun to commit a crime.

[6]Much of the information about Handgun Control Inc. was drawn from materials contributed by Gwen Fitzgerald, Assistant Director of Communications. We appreciate the cooperation.

Washington Report

Published by Handgun Control, Inc., 1400 K St., N.W., Suite 500, Washington, D.C. 20005 Barbara Lautman, Editor (202) 898-0792

Vol. 13, No. 1, Spring 1987

Up Front

Chairman's Corner

By Pete Shields

As a reaction to Handgun Control, Inc.'s highly successful ad campaign featuring Sarah Brady and San Jose Police Chief Joe McNamara, the National Rifle Association has begun running a series of new print ads promoting handgun ownership

tion of Chiefs of Police, which recently passed resolutions for stronger handgun laws, has called the new ads "irresponsible" and "reprehensible." Police know that by preying on the public's fear of crime, the NRA is disregarding the safety of all Americans. We saw that all too tragically in the California freeway shootings just last summer. Easy access to loaded handguns

Sarah Brady, Rep. Feighan (L) and Sen. Metzenbaum (R) discuss the need for a national waiting period for handgun purchases at a Capitol Hill news conference.

Plastic Gun Bills Gain Momentum

Despite intense efforts by the National Rifle Association to block legislation to outlaw the sale, manufacture, and importation of plastic pistols, the measures continue to gain support among lawmakers on Capitol Hill. S.465, introduced by Senator Howard Metzenbaum (D-OH), has attracted a growing bipartisan coalition of cosponsors, including Senators Nancy Kassebaum (R-KS), Chris Dodd (D-CT), John Chafee (R-RI), Ted Kennedy (D-MA), presidential candidate Paul Simon (D-IL), and Strom Thurmond (R-SC), Ranking Republican on the Senate Judiciary Committee. A complete listing of House and Senate cosponsors of this legislation begins on page three.

Every major law enforcement organization in the country has endorsed legislation to pre-empt the flood of plastic pistols across our country. Some of the most compelling testimony on this issue came from Steven Garmon, Deputy Director of the U.S. Secret Service, which has also endorsed S.465. At a hearing before the Senate Judiciary Subcommittee on the Constitution in July, Garmon said that protection of presidential candidates would be extremely difficult if the production of plastic firearms is allowed. He also testified that the White House might even have to be closed to visitors if plastic pistols enter the marketplace.

With the production of plastic handguns likely only a year away, Daniel Hartnett, Deputy Associate Director of Law Enforcement of the Bureau of Alcohol, Tobacco and Firearms, agreed that the time to act on plastic pistols is now. Raymond Salazar, Director of Civil Aviation Security for the FAA, told the Subcommittee that it could be 2–10 years before the technology is developed and in place to detect these weapons.

Inside Washington Report

- Where Your Legislators Stand
- Law Enforcement Leader Joins HCI Staff
- Members Elect Philadelphia Attorney to HCI Board

Figure 8–17 Masthead of *Washington Report*, with chairman's letter. Handgun safety guidelines booklet inset. (Courtesy Handgun Control Inc.)

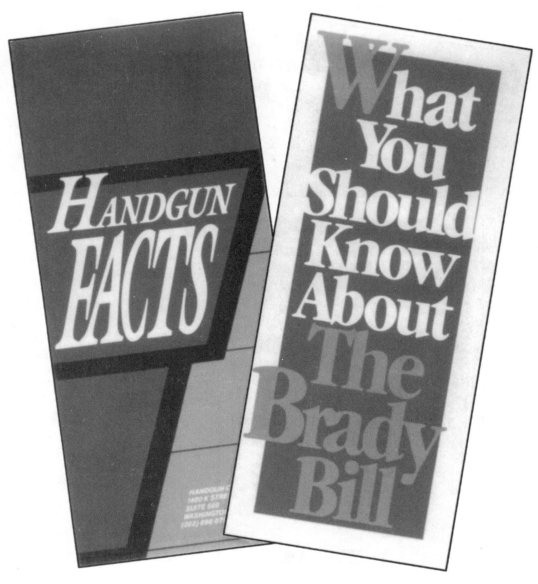

Figure 8–18 Two of the booklets made available by Handgun Control Inc. (Courtesy of Handgun Control Inc.)

Figure 8–19   Bold NRA ads make the point that crime is rampant. (Courtesy of the National Rifle Association.)

- A ban on the manufacture and sale of snub-nosed handguns.
- Restriction on the sale of UZI-type assault weapons.
- A ban on the manufacture and sale of plastic handguns (passed in 1989).

In 1987, Senator Metzenbaum and Congressman Feighan, both of Ohio, introduced the Handgun Violence Prevention Act. At the announcement press conference, standing alongside them was then HCI vice-chairman Sarah Brady. This bill was from then on dubbed the Brady Bill and required a seven-day waiting period for all handgun purchases (the bill passed in 1993 with a five-day waiting period), giving local police time to run a criminal background check.

Also in 1987, a Terrorist Firearms Prevention Act was introduced in both houses aimed at banning the manufacture and sale of plastic handguns—on the grounds they could not be detected by normal airline security checks of boarding passengers and could then be used for hijackings. Public debate over airline security was fueled when an airline employee, angry over dismissal, bypassed security checks (with a metal handgun), boarded a flight on which his former supervisor was riding, and, apparently, shot his boss and members of the crew, causing the aircraft to crash with all aboard being killed. Airline officials got tough, requiring employees to clear security checkpoints.

In 1989, and subsequent years to the present, strong feelings were stirred again by inner city youth gang wars, drive-by shootings of innocent victims, and the increasing appearance of semiautomatic assault rifles, which enable criminals to outgun police. Local bans of semiautomatic weapons were introduced and passed as the clamor for controls and restrictions increased.

Today, the National Rifle Association is not a name that every politician shrinks at hearing. More and more public support has emerged for the passage of national gun control legislation. Amid a Republican filibuster in November of 1993, the Brady Bill (now in a slightly different form than it was in 1987), passed both congressional bodies and was signed into law by President Clinton.

Though still a powerful lobby in Washington and many states, the NRA's influence has waned, evidenced by the many legislators who have run against candidates supported by the NRA and won. In addition, many more state legislatures are proposing restrictive laws for gun ownership and control. For example, Massachusetts, once extremely wary of any legislative control over arms, has proposed laws to raise the legal age for possessing a gun to twenty-one. It also has proposed its own laws to implement waiting periods to purchase a handgun.

In addition to the legislative action being taken, there is evidence that the numbers of NRA supporters have been thinning recently. In 1992, a concerted effort to recruit members was initiated in the form of an ad campaign that played upon a woman's fears of violence against women and offered a free information number. When women called for more information, they were then asked if they would like to join the NRA. On the other side, HCI's fund-raising and awareness-raising mailings continue apace.

Yet gun violence remains a major problem in the United States—although not in other First World nations. Until that situation is resolved, the gun debate is bound to continue.

QUESTIONS FOR DISCUSSION

1. The strategy of the NRA has been to oppose any legal measures that might tighten controls. The grounds are that any of these would be a foot in the door leading to demands for more such laws. As an objective communications professional, how do you feel about this "no exceptions," "no compromise," "not one inch" attitude? Has your attitude changed at all by your studies of the ultimate purpose of public relations? If so, how and why?[7]

2. For those who hold to a hard line on the gun issue (on either side) and those who hold to a hard line on birth control (either way), what similarities and differences do you find in the basis of their convictions? In their strategy and tactics?

3. Using the definitions of a public issue and a crisis given in the introduction to this chapter, which of the following would you consider issues, which crises, and which are neither?
   a. Birth control
   b. Gun control
   c. Integrity in public office
   d. Insurance rates
   e. Crime rates
   f. Drug Usage

4. Can you think of a strategy that the NRA could take in order to influence the public along its line of thinking? What strategies are they using that soften their position? That strengthen it?

5. Was the NRA's Paul Blackman right or wrong when he stated that this case is presented in a biased manner (see Footnote 2)? Give evidence for your position. This type of analysis is a regular task of public relations practitioners preparing plans and strategies.

6. How can a group with only ten to fifteen percent of the public supporting its views—which has historically been the case with the NRA—be so powerful? Why would officeholders listen to its views? What strategies do you feel enable such a minority view to prevail for so long? What must HCI and others opposed to unregulated gun ownership do to successfully make their case?

---

[7]See "Mighty Gun Lobby Loses Invincibility by Taking Hardline," Jeffrey H. Birnbaum, *Wall Street Journal*, May 24, 1988. Article suggests NRA had become too sure of itself.

The Colossal Effort to Advance Beyond War

Central America, South Africa, the Middle East—in the world of the 1980s, war dominated the headlines and the lives of millions, just as smaller conflicts are punctuating the 1990s. Even in countries like Northern Ireland, the former Yugoslavia, and others where outright conflict does not exist, the threat of war is a widespread fear. Nuclear arsenals threatened the very existence of civilization in the Cold War, and now the possibility that nuclear weapons may fall into the wrong hands is a dire fear. Yet, global peace seems an impossible goal amid such a diversity of politics, cultures, religions, and races—each clashing for its rights and share of diminishing resources.

Despite the enormity of the problem, a group in Palo Alto, California, felt in the early 1980s that with the survival of all life at stake, there was no more important task to be undertaken. Moreover, peace marches, nuclear freeze support, chilling movies such as *The Day After*, and the course of events in the Cold War had focused public attention acutely on the situation, making the time ripe to act. This case is their story—and how they used the underlying behavioral science of public relations to mount a noble humanitarian effort.

NOT JUST ANOTHER "PEACE" ORGANIZATION

Calling their effort Beyond War, the organization purposefully kept the word *peace* out of its name. Their rationale was that *peace* carries a lot of imagery, usually connoting a stereotyped group of people or an outcome devoid of conflict.

Beyond War believed that the root problem in continuing world conflict is that people think they can have a "survivable" war. Scientific and medical evidence show that this is an improbability. Beyond War saw its mission not to promote peace but to *educate*. The goal was to communicate three ideas:

1. Nuclear weapons have made all war obsolete.
2. The planet we live on is one interrelated system on which we are all dependent.
3. In order to survive, we must learn to work together to build a world beyond war.

The fundamental question was, What is the underlying thinking that has to change so that violence is no longer used to resolve conflict?

USING DIFFUSION THEORY

Beyond War's educational focus gave it a distinction among similar organizations. It also took an unusually sophisticated public relations approach in attempting to understand how an idea spreads throughout society. From a supporter familiar with the work of Everett Rogers at Stanford Research Institute, the organization tapped into one of behavioral science's most important theories: the diffusion of innovation.[1] This theory allowed them to see that, rather than worrying about trying to convince the entire population of their message, *they had to embed the idea within only a crucial five percent*. But persuading this five percent required *reaching* fifty percent of the population with their communications. Moreover, they learned that after twenty percent of the population adopts an idea, it's virtually unstoppable (see Figure 8–20).

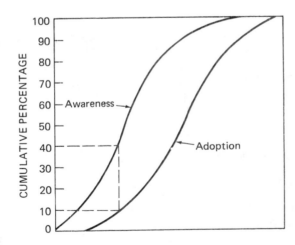

Figure 8–20   After innovation is adopted in the twenty percent range, it soars. (Courtesy of Stanford Research Institute.)

[1]E. M. Rogers, and F. F. Shoemaker, *Communication of Innovations*, (Palo Alto: Stanford Research Institute, 1971); and E. M. Rogers, *Diffusion of Innovations*, 3rd ed. (Collier MacMillan Publishers, 1983).

ADOPTION OF AN IDEA

Everett M. Rogers's work on diffusion demonstrated that the *adoption process has six stages*:

1. Attention, or awareness
2. Interest
3. Evaluation
4. Trial, or social trial
5. Adoption
6. Confirmation, or reinforcement

The *rate of adoption* is influenced by the degree to which the new idea is (1) perceived as offering an advantage over the presently held idea and (2) compatible with the individual's present beliefs. Rogers describes five classes of adopters:

1. **Innovators.** Venturesome: 2.5 percent of the population fall within this category. They are eager to try new ideas, are mobile and communicate outside of local peer networks, have the ability to grasp abstract ideas, are able to cope with the uncertainty associated with an innovation before it is widely accepted.

2. **Early adopters.** Respectable: 13.5 percent of the population. More integrated into the local social system than innovators. This group has the greatest degree of opinion leadership. Considered by many as "the individuals to check with" before using a new idea.

3. **Early majority.** Deliberate: 34 percent of the population. They adopt new ideas just before the average member of a social system. Most of their information comes from early adopters. Interact frequently with their peers but seldom hold leadership positions.

4. **Late majority.** Skeptical: 34 percent of the population. Adopt new ideas just after the average member of a social system. Can be persuaded of the utility of new ideas, but peer pressure is necessary to motivate adoption.

5. **Late adopters.** Traditional: 16 percent of the population. They are the last to adopt. Tend to be suspicious of innovations. Adoption lags far behind awareness. This resistance is entirely rational from their point of view: "If it ain't broke, don't fix it."

BLITZ THE WEST WITH COMMUNICATIONS

Beginning in California, Beyond War began to build awareness of its ideas, drawing upon an arsenal of ads, articles, films, and meetings. Public service announcements were prepared for radio and television stations. Newspaper articles were sent to hundreds of editors. A presentation was prepared for easy delivery in living rooms, offices, and worksites. As follow-up, a three-part "Orientation to a World Beyond War" was developed (see Figure 8–21).

Events of all sizes and types were sponsored—film programs, symposia, convocations—to bring more people into personal contact with Beyond War and its

Figure 8–21   A variety of educational materials and a newsletter. (Courtesy of Beyond War, 222 High St., Palo Alto, Calif. 94301.)

goals. An information brochure and monthly newsletter were developed to provide a continuing source of ideas and information. A full-page advertisement ran in major state newspapers just after the Christmas season, speaking to the sentiment of "a season of hope" and "the wish for peace, harmony, and goodwill in the world." People were encouraged to clip the ad and mail it to friends and elected officials throughout the country (see Figure 8–22).

SEVENTEEN FAMILIES SERVE AS AMBASSADORS

To broaden the movement beyond California, a full-scale education effort was introduced in fourteen other states. Word-of-mouth personal communication was essential; hence seventeen families volunteered to uproot themselves and relocate in new

Figure 8–22 Capsule-sized copy of full-page ad. (Courtesy of Beyond War.)

states where they could nurture support. Their tasks were to organize interest and orientation meetings, develop newcomers to the movement, reach area congress-people and other government officials, and find allies among previously uncommitted people in medicine, law, education, labor, and business.

Ambassador families also used their ingenuity and creativity to help gain awareness of Beyond War in less structured ways: convincing a dentist (during a visit!) to host an introductory meeting; appearing on call-in radio and television shows. One even taught a college psychology course entitled "Beyond War: The Psychology of Aggression and Conflict Resolution."

THE FASTEST GROWING STARTUP IN THE WORLD

Within two years, Beyond War had mushroomed, with 400 full-time volunteers and 15,000 part-time. The national office had forty full-time workers with sixteen phone lines and in one year processed 95,000 calls. The newsletter claimed a readership of 20,000, and over 85,000 Beyond War pins had been distributed.

BEYOND WAR AWARD PROGRAM

To recognize an individual, group, or nation making a significant contribution to building a world beyond war, the organization developed an annual award program. The crystal award sculpture, designed by Steuben Glass, shows the world's continents etched on a column. On the front surface, a half sphere deeply recessed into the crystal serves as a lens to capture the images of the continents and transform them into one unified whole (see Figure 8–23). Award winners included: Catholic Bishops of the United States (1983); International Physicians for the Prevention of Nuclear War (1984); Five Continent Peace Initiative (1985); Contadora Group (1986); and the Peace Corps (1987).

USING TECHNOLOGY TO BRIDGE WORLDS

Because diffusion theory shows person-to-person communications to be vital and programs between nations as important steps on the road to mutual trust and understanding, Beyond War took advantage of newly developing satellite technology to launch such programs. It organized the first "Spacebridge" between San Francisco and Moscow, linking audiences half-a-world away in a live, two-way presentation. During the Spacebridge, Beyond War presented its annual award to the Soviet and American co-presidents of the International Physicians for the Prevention of Nuclear War on behalf of 105,000 physicians in fifty-four countries.

Beyond War has also used electronic technology to establish downlink re-

Figure 8–23 The crystal award (inset) went to Contadora Group leaders in 1986 with the occasion seen live on two-way television by millions throughout the western hemisphere. (Courtesy of Beyond War.)

ceivers within the United States in order to telecast meetings live to volunteers in nearly 100 cities around the country.

DIALOGUE: MAKING A DECISION ABOUT WAR

Though it had the communications tools and technology to reach vast numbers, Beyond War realized that to empower the public required reaching individuals at a deeper level. On the basis of work of social analyst Daniel Yankelovich, Beyond War introduced a campaign to build informed decision making into vital efforts.

Yankelovich had pointed out the difference between *public opinion*, a casual, top-of-the-head response, and *public judgment*, based on a reasoned assessment of the situation.

He used the word *dialogue* to describe the process by which people digest an issue sufficiently to be able to make an informed judgment. Dialogue also engages the mind, creating personal involvement and launching a process of discovery essential to the learning process.

Using Yankelovich's ideas, Beyond War developed a campaign in modules to encourage deeper, more intense thinking about four issues related to then-current problems: Central America, USA-USSR, Terrorism, and National Security. The modules were designed to be released sequentially in order to heighten interest of the American public during the 1988 presidential campaign (see Figure 8–24).

The goal of the dialogue process was to provide a forum in which people could move from ambiguity and apathy to clarity and conviction. Discussion packets were prepared so that, in cities and towns across the country, people could initiate discussions.

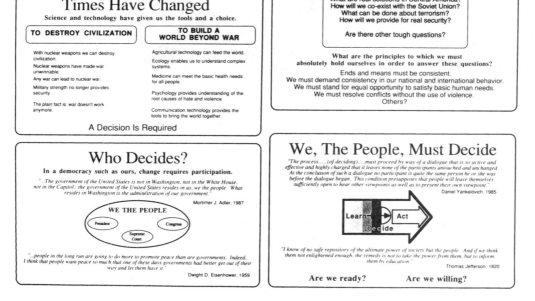

Figure 8–24   Pages from booklet *Making a Decision about War.* (Courtesy of Beyond War.)

WHAT BEYOND WAR ACCOMPLISHED

Using these research-based public relations techniques, the organization made dramatic strides from its early days in California. Thousands of people were introduced to its ideas, and citizens from countries throughout the world attended its seminars. It accomplished all this on the basis of the philosophy that each individual counts—an essential element in the public relations ethic. By developing the grassroots "power of one," the organization gathered momentum for its theme, "Working *together*, we can build a world beyond war."

WHERE BEYOND WAR STANDS TODAY

Today the fears of the 1980s have changed. Now, attention has turned from the threat of nuclear weapons and has focused on worldwide issues such as limited wars, urban violence, ozone depletion, global warming, and exhaustion of world resources. These are all threats in our society that challenge the continued existence of humankind. They are the issues that have served to emphasize the manufactured

---

TEN THOUSAND GROUPS IN UNITED STATES

Churches, schools, civic organizations, and even veterans' organizations are part of a growing "latent readiness" urging that it is time for an end to war. At latest count, there are nearly 10,000 peace groups in the United States. Public issues linked to peace have the potential to draw every type of organization into the debate. Some of these interrelated issues are:

- *Chemical warfare* influences perceptions of the danger of chemicals and toxic wastes.
- *Nuclear weapons* is concerned with nuclear power and radioactive waste issues.
- *Human rights violations* links with animal rights, ban on guns, opposition to sale of war toys, and antiviolence in movies and television.

- *Defense spending* raises debate over cuts in human resource programs, welfare, social spending such as education, repairing decaying infrastructure (highways, bridges, public buildings).
- *High-tech funding* for space weaponry jeopardizes funding of medical research and other important public needs.

Thus, the peace movement in the name of international reconciliation and human harmony will ultimately affect virtually every organization—and therefore every public relations practitioner.

nature of borders between nations and point out the importance of recognizing that we are all members of a global community living on one planet.

At the end of the Cold War, Beyond War recognized that the threats to human society had changed and began making major organizational changes to keep up with the pace of world change. Now, it works to influence those on this planet to accept their undeniable responsibilities for the global community. In order to do this it:

1. Changed its name
2. Altered its mission
3. Restructured the organization

MAKING THE CHANGES

Responding to this changing world, Beyond War became the Foundation for Global Community (FGC), a nonprofit, developmental education movement. "The name has a double meaning," said Joseph Kresse, one of FGC's executive directors. "The word *foundation* symbolizes our effort to lay the groundwork for a global community and it identifies us as an organization." They also moved from a top-down management system to a decentralized organization, permitting more autonomy locally.

Its new mission is to discover, live, and communicate what is needed to build a world that functions for the benefit of all life. The organization's goal is to convince twenty percent of the world's people by the year 2010 to commit to the long-term well-being of the global living system. FGC's strategy remains the same: tapping into the diffusion of innovation theory and creating avenues for dialogue. One recent initiative, implemented in 1993, was creating opportunity for dialogues in different areas that explored "Redefining the American Dream." As Alice Fenton, Executive Director of FGC described it, "These discussions are initiated to use as a springboard to get at what FGC is talking about, to lay the groundwork needed for a global community" (see Figure 8–25).

THE NEW CHALLENGES

The people involved in the Foundation for Global Community now face the challenge of discovering, living, and communicating to others the changes that are required in order to recognize the place the human species holds as an integral part of the living system on which it depends, such as:

- Affirming and valuing diversity
- Transforming violence into goodwill
- Transforming conflict into knowledge

Timeline

ISSUE NO. 11 SEPTEMBER/OCTOBER 1993 A bimonthly publication of the Foundation for Global Community

Redefining the American Dream

We came on the Mayflower and in the holds of slave ships. We came on jet airliners and on leaking boats. We came across oceans and across borders, by night and by day, with or without passports and papers. We came by choice or by force, in desperation and in exultation. Some very few of us came in a time so ancient that we call it prehistory. We came with our hopes and our dreams and our visions, and we have become part of the American dream.

The American dream, which has brought immigrants to our shores since before we called ourselves America. The American dream, which continues to draw waves of people from around the globe. "Life, liberty, and the pursuit of happiness." We thought we understood. But more and more of us,

continued on page 2

Figure 8–25   This issue of *Timeline*, FGC's publication, devoted itself to covering the "Redefining the American Dream" initiative. (Courtesy of Foundation for Global Community.)

- Transforming enemies into partners
- Transforming blame into responsibility
- Working in partnership with others
- Living within the carrying capacity of the earth

These goals are somewhat harder to achieve because, unlike Beyond War, FGC is now trying to change the core attitudes and beliefs that *created* problems such as war. It is a more abstract goal. FGC is working to convince others that they need to be dependent on each other in order to survive. They must sell *interdependence* in a world stuck on *independence*.

HOW TO MEET THEM

In order to accomplish its goals, FGC is working in ways that are congruent with its vision to continue the evolution of life. It is constantly developing programs that will serve to realize a global community. Some recent initiatives:

- **Earth Before Us Project.** This activity, which began in Wisconsin, is a program that strives to place a photograph of the earth in every classroom. It is accompanied by educational programs and videotapes to highlight the global focus each individual must develop. It has expanded worldwide, with over 15,000 photographs placed in schools, offices, and public buildings in thirty countries.
- **Educating the Future.** An ongoing, accredited educators' workshop in Chicago where teachers can explore ways of preparing children to be citizens of the world.
- **Middle East Task Force.** Works with prominent Israelis and Palestinians to demonstrate common ground in search for peace, promoting historical framework signed at its July conference in 1992.
- **A Better Way—Revitalizing Democracy Through Citizen Participation.** Small, local groups meet to generate creative, useful ideas that address urgent problems. These ideas—from the people—are then presented to public officials, candidates, media, and other forums.

RESTRUCTURING THE ORGANIZATION

FGC's basic premise is that global change begins with the individual; "the changes needed to achieve the vision of a just and sustainable world will not happen if left solely to governments."

When it changed its name from Beyond War, the organization decentralized, which permitted more autonomy at the local level. In addition, the organization went from having a president to having three executive directors participating in running the organization. As its literature emphasizes: "Leadership can and should come from any part of our community where there is a commitment to the vision, a willingness to risk, and the opportunity to move."

Work of the foundation is done by teams—"autonomous units, each of which develops its *own* sense of community and shared vision and is organized in a way congenial to its size and method of functioning." Day-to-day functioning of FGC runs in this manner, depending on the work of teams in order to accomplish tasks. This arrangement lays the weight of responsibility on each member of the organization, instead of just one or a handful of people. This new structure provides a way for people to take responsibility and depend on others according to expertise, interest, and time.

ANALYSIS

FGC has not reached the recognition levels that Beyond War did. Fenton attributes that partly to the fact that FGC is not committed to one concrete goal such as Beyond War was. "We lost a few people when the focus of Beyond War changed to the focus of FGC. Now, instead of focusing just on war, we are working to eliminate the base problems that create dissent among peoples." The full-time staff numbers around thirty to forty people and those involved part-time across the country number anywhere from 300 to 400 people. "Our main focus is reaching the individuals across the country," said Fenton. "Only then can we become reconnected to the global system and become a responsible species."

QUESTIONS FOR DISCUSSION

1. In addition to the diffusion process and Yankelovich's dialogue concept, what other public relations or social science theories could Beyond War have used to advance its cause?

2. Do you agree with Beyond War's reasoning in keeping the word *peace* out of its name? Is symbolism that important? Evaluate the positive and negative perceptions of the organization's original name and of its new name after reorganization.

3. What are other alternatives to Beyond War's ambassador program that would broaden the movement's awareness and build personal relationships?

4. If a show-of-hands poll revealed that a majority has been unaware of Foundation for Global Community or has limited knowledge about it, do you think that some of Gallup's "regulators" determining the absorption rate of new

ideas might help explain that? The regulators are: complexity of idea, difference from accustomed pattern, competition with prevailing ideas, susceptibility to demonstration and proof, strength of vested interests opposing, whether proposal fulfills a felt need, and frequency with which public is reminded.

5. Do you think that the organization Beyond War (now FGC) could ever be effective in eliminating war or bringing harmony to the world community? Why or why not? Do you believe it was a good or bad idea to change its name from Beyond War to Foundation for Global Community? Why or why not?

Building Support for the Centerpiece of Democracy

Though every political figure since George Washington has hailed them as the cement that holds American democracy together, probably no institution has been the topic of such continual criticism and debate as the public schools. The reasons are obvious. Education is essential in modern life, so the concern is real. What is taught influences the thought patterns of our children, and at times there are those who seek to find something subversive or distasteful in the curriculum. Despite their essential nature, schools, teachers, and boards of education have traditionally had trouble attaining financial investment and pay scales commensurate with their value. Because schools are public entities, everyone "owns" them and feels free to offer advice and even insist on a "right" way of doing things.

The 1980s saw schools excoriated from all sides. Education groups knew that the only solution was to deal head-on with the underlying cause of the criticism. They felt that this was criticism occurring because most people were taking the schools for granted. Here is one program that was strategized to counteract that attitude. Its objectives were to build the relationships necessary to get beyond criticism and to seek a cooperative stance that dealt with the real problems and issues—in other words, a program that addressed the underlying needs and values people could agree on about education and played down the disagreement on details.

A VISUAL SYMBOL TO GET ACROSS THE "BIG IDEA"

Simply stated, the question was, What should be done when the community seems to agree with the attacks on education, yet does not seem willing to help improve the programs under attack?

"Public apathy is the worst thing that can happen to your cause," said Bonnie Ellison, then president of National School Public Relations Association (NSPRA), when schools all across America found themselves facing that apathy in the mid-1980s. As expected, schools were being taken for granted. She launched a campaign as an activity to commemorate NSPRA's Golden Anniversary and to turn apathy to support by finding a "big idea" that would remind communities how basic public schools are to their way of life.[1]

But how could they come up with an idea big enough to grab people's attention when dealing with as common a topic as schools? NSPRA formed an Impact Committee of sixty public relations professionals representing every state. Edward L. Bernays, the "father of public relations," agreed to be chairman. Following his lauded strategic planning method, the first step was research—with a difference.

Rather than conducting a survey or holding focus groups, letters were sent to opinion leaders everywhere asking for fifty-word statements on (1) their assessment of the true state of education at the time and (2) what education meant to them. Hundreds of American leaders responded. The most common theme was a strong belief that public education was vital to our democracy.

The committee used the responses, and their theme, as basis for a two-day brainstorming session with NSPRA leaders from across the nation. From the session came a proposal for an education flag, The Flag of Learning and Liberty. A flag that NSPRA wanted to give to education on its fiftieth anniversary, as a visual symbol to remind the American people of their reliance on public education as the glue that holds a polyglot democracy together.

This flag, a strong, attractive, visual device, linked education (learning) to democracy (liberty). Since flags are patriotic symbols, this method of presentation strengthened the point. Flags often offer an official feeling of unity, so the message takes on an aura of being linked to formal social acceptance. Having it flown in front of schools and public buildings enhanced this official aspect. In addition, the flag could be flown by businesses, American Legion posts, or any supporter of education. It could be hung on walls in meeting rooms, hallways, or offices. High visibility of the flag was an important factor (see Figure 8–26).

Christina McFarland of Dallas, Texas, designed the flag. When asked to explain why she chose the visual elements she did, McFarland said she was seeking two: a design attractive yet simple enough to be memorable; shapes that give the feeling of "something developing" and suggest growth—as education does. Those are also the basic elements in the "big picture" project that materialized.[2]

GETTING IT USED

First came audience targeting. For this project, there were three priority publics that needed to be reached. Any other group persuaded would be an added bonus.

---

[1] *pr reporter*, Volume 28, November 4, 1985. pp. 1 & 2.

[2] National School Public Relations Association, *The Banner*, 1987, pp. 3.

**Now You Can
Fly The Flag Of
Learning And Liberty**

*Dedicated to education
everywhere, the Flag of
Learning and Liberty
symbolizes the link between
education and our democratic
society.*

Figure 8–26 The flag shown on a brochure cover has a stylized flame of red, blue, and amber fingers representing the high expectations of children, effective teaching, responsible families, and involved communities. (Courtesy of National School Public Relations Association.)

1. **The most important group was the education community.** Teachers and administrators felt under siege. School boards wondered if positive consensus between the school and the community could ever be reached. The flag served as a symbol of how vital the work they do is, and how important they are (see Figure 8–27).

2. **The next priority was the majority of citizens in the average town** who did not have children in school. These were the people who saw no benefit in supporting education because they were not parents, their kids were out of school, attended private school, or went to school in another town. Not included in most school district communication efforts, they voted against school budgets that would financially address the needed opportunities and widespread problems. Apathy was prevalent where school issues were concerned—until someone hit their ideological soft spot.

3. **Finally, parents and other supporters** needed encouragement and cheerleading. They had a vested interest in developing excellent schools but often were discouraged by the constant criticism (see Figure 8–28).

Figure 8–27   Teacher and pupils prepare to fly the flag at the Nathan Hale School, "I only regret I have but one life to lose for my country." The site is New London, Connecticut. (Courtesy of National School Public Relations Association.)

Figure 8–28   The Flag of Learning and Liberty flies over the Alamo. (Courtesy of Northside Independent School District, San Antonio, Texas.)

NSPRA members were enthusiastic about the plan. This would be an excellent vehicle to celebrate their Golden Anniversary and give to education a solid symbol that emphasized the link between education and a strong free nation. Other educational organizations—representing teachers, principals, superintendents, school board members—agreed to help. The goal of having the flag flown over every state capitol on July 4, 1985, became the start of the campaign. Then the push was to get as many schools as possible to purchase and fly the flag.

Through arduous effort, the Flag of Learning and Liberty was unfurled over the state capitols, that Independence Day in 1985. Southland Corporation, operator of 7-11 Stores, paid for designing the flag as well as the first fifty units to be used at the state capitols. Substantial media coverage resulted, followed by word-of-mouth publicity as people saw the flag and wondered what it signified.

In individual communities, acceptance was high. Schools themselves bought the flags. Principals, superintendents, and PTAs purchased them to give as gifts to their schools. Businesses flew the flag over their establishment and gave them to local schools or to the alma maters of executives or employees. In Pennsylvania, superintendents passed the flag that had flown over the state capitol on July 4 of 1985 from one school to another at ceremonies during halftime at football games. Service clubs began presenting flags to schools in their community.

ESTABLISHING A SYMBOL

Once the flag itself was launched, the next step was to make it universal across the nation. Ellison called the campaign "an involvement model—to get people involved in the future of their neighborhood public schools." Knowing about the flag—and what it stands for—was a start. Buying and using the flags came next. The complete campaign, which rolled out over several years and continues today, included:

- **Lapel pins** of the flag, to be worn by NSPRA members and school personnel, and often given to others in recognition of services to schools and in appreciation. They could be worn daily or at meetings and conferences and were a way to pique curiosity so that others would ask about the flag.

- The first **teacher in space**, Christa McAuliffe, took 200 small copies of the flag with her on the *Challenger* space shuttle, intending to donate them to schools where she spoke after her flight. Sadly, on January 28, 1986, the *Challenger* exploded after launch, killing everyone on board. One flag was retrieved after the disaster, encased in a special memorial plaque dedicated to the *Challenger* crew and presented by NASA and NSPRA.

- The **Learning and Liberty Award** was instituted, to be presented annually to select individuals whose activities epitomize the linkage between public education and a free democratic society.

- **Quotations** from well-known leaders, received in response to the research, were publicized in news media and a booklet.

- The flag was presented by American educators and business leaders to educational leaders from **other nations** such as Japan, Portugal, USSR, Italy and Israel during those American leaders' visits to the countries.

- **Constant promotion** of flag purchase and use was carried on at meetings, in personal visits, by brochures, through mailings, even a donated ad campaign presented to NSPRA by ServiceMaster Industries, which also featured the flag in its annual report, passed out lapel pins at trade shows it attended, and flies the flag daily over its headquarters.

The goal was to have the flag flying over "every school, public and private, every school district office and every educational institution in America," as Ellison phrased it, "to serve as a constant reminder and focus attention on the critical role education plays in our society."[3] Picking up the challenge in their communities, NSPRA members and other supporters of the project added these touches:

- In Illinois, the Teacher of the Year was presented a flag in ceremonies announcing the winner.

- At John Marshall High School in San Antonio, Texas, a miniature flag was mounted in a desk stand alongside the U.S. flag and the school's flag (see Figure 8–29).

- In San Jose, California, forty cross-country runners carried the flag from school to school.

- In Port Byron, New York, student government organizations and classroom representatives presented the flag to the mayor as a way to highlight school-village cooperation during Port Byron's sesquicentennial.

---

[3]*pr reporter*, volume 28, (November 4, 1985): 1–2.

Figure 8–29 The principal of John Marshall High School in San Antonio dines behind a flag threesome—U.S., school, and education's flag of Learning and Liberty, at a Parent Teachers Association founder's day banquet. (Courtesy of Northside Independent School District, San Antonio, Texas.)

- Harris County, Texas, featured the flag in full color on the cover of its 1987–1988 Academic Calendar, used by all teachers and staff.

- In Broward County, Florida, schools wove the flag into their "Catch the Spirit" emblem that kicked off at a well-promoted flag raising. The regional Wendy's fast food franchise owner did catch the spirit by providing flags to all schools and to NASA headquarters, located in that district. From this action, national and international publicity resulted, so that an annual "Catch the Spirit of Learning and Liberty" event is planned.

- San Antonio also provided evidence of the flag's popularity (with attendant media coverage): In two burglaries within six months in Edgewood Independent School District, only one item was reported missing each time—the Flag of Learning and Liberty.

- The motto of education's flag, "learning and liberty," provided the primary focal point for American Education Week in 1989 by inspiring the theme "Learning and Liberty: Our Roots and Our Future."

- The Reaching for Learning and Liberty national display, which features the actual Flag of Learning and Liberty carried on the *Challenger* by Christa McAuliffe, was created to symbolize the link between education and a strong, free nation. The granite display stands seven feet tall and is topped by a bronze sculpture of young hands reaching toward education's flag of Learning and Liberty. A replica of this display was presented to President Bush in honor of

Display Ready for National Tour

New Display Features Challenger Flag

The long-awaited national tour of NSPRA's seven-foot high display promoting learning and liberty will begin this fall. In making the announcement, President Jeanne Magmer said the timing of the tour is designed to complement the learning and liberty focus of this year's American Education Week celebration.

Details of the premiere display exhibition will be announced later this summer by incoming President Jeannie (Sissy) Henry. Meanwhile, NSPRA leaders are being asked to plan unveiling and exhibit events in each state. Henry has established a goal of unveiling the display in all 50 states during the next two years.

A Flag of Learning and Liberty carried aboard the orbiter Challenger by teacher-astronaut Christa McAuliffe is the center piece of the display. It is encased in a special plaque with photographs of the seven Challenger crew members and was presented to NSPRA by NASA at the 1987 seminar.

Swiss-born designer Hans Streich created and constructed the granite display with financial backing of The Southland Corporation. The NASA plaque is featured at eye level with details explaining the meaning of the flag appearing on the other three sides. The display is topped by a bronze sculpture of the hands of three children holding up the flag. The sculpture is the work of Deran Wright of Fort Worth, Texas.

President Magmer says the display "will be a fitting tribute to the commitment of Christa and the other astronauts, as well as a continuing reminder of the critical link between learning and liberty. It will be particularly meaningful at a time when learning and liberty is America's educational slogan."

"Hands" for President

A replica of the sculpture topping NSPRA's display has been duplicated for presentation to President Bush. Details of the ceremony will be announced at a later date. Thanks again to the generosity of The Southland Corporation, arrangements were made with Fort Worth sculptor Deran Wright to recast his "Reaching for Learning and Liberty." Mr. Wright has also assigned NSPRA all rights to his sculpture.

THE BANNER
This publication exists to keep the spirit of learning and liberty in the forefront. Its central focus is the first major symbol of the link between education and a democratic society, The Flag of Learning and Liberty. Individual issues are produced periodically by members of NSPRA's IMPACT Committee. For more information contact the National School Public Relations Association, 1501 Lee Highway, Suite 201, Arlington, VA 22209.

Figure 8–30   The Reaching for Learning and Liberty national display, another symbol that emphasizes the inexorable link between education and a free democratic society. (Courtesy of National School Public Relations Association.)

American Education Week in 1990 while the original was touring across the nation to promote learning and liberty (see Figure 8-30).

QUESTIONS FOR DISCUSSION

1. The idea for the Flag of Learning and Liberty came out of a brainstorming session. After finding out how this method works, decide whether brainstorming has widespread or limited applicability to public relations.[4]

2. What public relations disadvantages exist for organizations such as schools (or utilities or government agencies) that serve everybody in the community in one way or another? Are there also advantages?

3. Are visual communication elements, such as the flag, more or less potent than verbal ones? Why? What are the strengths and weaknesses of each?

4. What are the most important symbols and identifications of your university or college from a public relations standpoint? To be sure you are right, make a list of criteria. How could the relative importance be measured as the basis of a proposal for more public relations budget to cover projects capitalizing on those symbols?

---

[4]For a brainstorming technique useful in making presentations to prospective employers or clients, see: "Force Field Analysis: New Tool for Problem Solving," by Kerry Tucker, President, Nuffer, Smith, Tucker, in *Public Relations Journal*, 35 (July 1979).

Free the Texas Shopper!

Some behavioral scientists say that the "silent majority" can be riled up only once a decade, after prolonged and careful focus on the subject of controversy. However, this tenet may be altered when it comes to issues that hit the general public close to home. For example, shopping.

BACKGROUND

Before 1985, the state of Texas had legislation on its books called "blue laws." These blue laws were based in the Christian ideal that everyone goes to church on Sunday—or ought to—and were responsible for keeping most retail stores closed that day. Most states once had such laws, but nearly all had been repealed. Not in the Bible Belt state of Texas, however.

A coalition was formed of like-minded retailers, including Target Stores, K-Mart, and Zales, who believed it was time to do away with the blue laws. Organizations against repeal of the law were nonchain retailers, large department stores, car dealers, and especially churches.

The coalition was caught in a bind, because they knew Sunday shopping would mean greater sales but were concerned they would lose customers angered by the campaign. There was a long-standing assumption that fundamentalists, other church groups, and people living in rural areas would be against repeal, but no one knew for sure.

TIME FOR RESEARCH

The coalition decided to arm itself with data in order to know where the people of Texas really stood. A massive survey uncovered data that told them that:

- Two out of three Texans wanted the law repealed.
- Support for repeal was broad-based, including substantial support in rural areas and among fundamentalist groups.

Research was specific enough to determine *how each legislative district felt.* These data were subsequently made available to the legislators, who had to vote on repeal. Coalition representatives felt this was a very important part of their effort. When a legislator opposed the bill, evidence of support by his or her constituents was available.

CAMPAIGN PHILOSOPHY

The coalition decided to run a very straightforward, honest, open, objective kind of campaign so nobody could criticize them on those grounds. Retailers stressed their solid reputations in the communities, their support of local nonprofit agencies, their substantial business operations (representing a large share of total retail business in the state), and the large number of people employed.

Members of the coalition were accused by the opposition of being out-of-state companies, trying to change the Texas lifestyle and overturn local values.

But Target Stores' programs of social responsibility and community participation paid off. "After sixteen years," they said, "we feel as much a part of the state as others do."

MOVING THOUSANDS TO ACTION

After gathering the research and deciding on a campaign philosophy, the coalition's next task was to convert expressed support to active support. This is how it was done:

1. Newspaper ads were run that strongly advocated action (see Figure 8–31). The bold copy and strong illustration generated substantial media coverage and word-of-mouth publicity.
2. The same ad was used as a bag stuffer in coalition members' stores.
3. An 800 number was set up for people to call to obtain information. Operators gathered personal information from callers, especially their shopping habits

Figure 8–31   Ads run by coalition that echoed in media and word-of-mouth.

and location. They also read a prepared statement and requested permission to send it to each caller's legislator over that person's name. The 800 number was prominently carried in the newspaper ads and bag stuffers.

This strategy gathered 80,000 names in the coalition's databank. When the vote was being taken, if a legislator wavered, the coalition called these registered supporters and suggested they contact the legislator.

DEFUSING THE OPPOSITION

The Texas Automotive Dealers Association—effective lobbyists with a long track record of political support for candidates—was a powerful force to be up against. They did not want to open their showrooms on Sunday. The coalition needed to devise a strategy that would remove them from the equation. The bill, as it was finally adopted, excluded them. They would remain closed on Sundays. They were then standing on the sidelines, no longer in the battle.

FINAL DECISION

The Texas Senate required a two-thirds majority to have the matter put on the docket for vote. Once on the docket, it needed only a simple majority to pass. Documented research and personal contacts from people in their districts spoke loudly to legislators. The coalition expected the bill to take at least two legislative sessions to pass—but it took only one.

TESTIMONIAL TO RESEARCH AND PLANNING

The campaign lasted six months and showed how effectively public relations can influence public policy. It also showed how important public relations is to the bottom financial line; retail sales subsequently increased because of Sunday shopping. The key was fact finding, discovering that the people of Texas support Sunday openings. This knowledge put the coalition in the position of representing the will of the people. Without the research, or with different findings, an entirely different approach would have been required—with, very possibly, a different result.

BLUE LAWS UPDATE

In recent years, blue laws have faded as an issue of public concern. However, they are still debated in some states. Beer and liquor sales are limited in Massachusetts,

BLUE LAWS ADDRESS MORE THAN JUST SHOPPING

In addition to blue laws that keep stores closed on Sundays, there are other blue laws on the books. Some states still have antiadultery laws, for instance. Though ignored as archaic by law enforcement agencies, these laws have been used by some people to keep spouses in control, especially in divorce proceedings, and some people have attempted to have their spouses arrested if caught in the act of adultery.

Questions of violations of rights to privacy have arisen. But this is a relatively new "right," formulated by Supreme Court Justice Brandeis in the early years of the century. To many, the repeal of blue laws is imperative. Others would welcome more laws regulating personal conduct according to what they believe is "proper" conduct. When any specific action is taken by specific groups in either direction, emotional debate usually ensues—and you can be sure public relations counsel will be in the thick of it, ideally representing both sides so each gets its point across and the public can make an informed decision.

but not in the competing neighbor states of New Hampshire and Vermont, which is a controversial issue for some merchants and customers. Counties and municipalities in Bible Belt states are often "dry" by local ordinance even though state statutes allow the sale of liquor. On the opposite side, in 1991, Kansas car dealers proposed a new blue law to prohibit automobile sales on Sundays. This proposal caused great conflict and debate, and the bill did not pass.

QUESTIONS FOR DISCUSSION

1. Suppose research showed that about half of the key Texas population opposed Sunday sales, while half supported them. What counsel would you have given the retail group? How would you have dealt with opposing groups?

2. If you were counsel to the opposing group, what would you have suggested they do to defeat the repeal proposal?

3. Assume that your employer is moving into a new state and wants to build the type of consumer support that Target and its allies created. What types of activities would you pursue? Draw up a plan.

4. In light of Chapter 2, what are some of the considerations that go into strategic thinking leading to a plan and a program? What are some of the elements beyond media and messages? Is your response to this question reflected in your response to questions 1, 2, and 3?

Mothers Against Drunk Driving—MADD

In response to tragedy, people often reach out to others for support. Many find comfort in doing what they can to right a terrible wrong or prevent others from going through what they have gone through. Often these support groups can become a powerful and compelling voice for social change. One of the most successful and accomplished of these coalitions is Mothers Against Drunk Driving (MADD). MADD's mission is twofold: (1) to provide support for those who have experienced the tragedy of a drunk driving accident and (2) to advocate, both socially and legislatively, against the act of operating a vehicle under the influence of drugs and alcohol.

MADD was established by Candy Lightner in 1980 in response to the loss of her son in a drunk driving accident. The organization currently has over 400 chapters across the United States. Between 1984 and 1989, MADD increased its membership of supporters and volunteers by over 500 percent. That trend continues today as drunk driving increasingly is recognized as a debilitating social illness. Funding raised and spent in support of education, public awareness, victims' assistance and other programs has increased four times over (see Figure 8-32). Donations to MADD total nearly $43 million annually.

Although the incidence of fatalities in alcohol-related accidents decreased by 7.7 percent in the period between 1982 and 1990, the numbers are still staggering. In 1990, 17,366 people were killed in alcohol-related vehicle accidents.[1] Despite MADD's positive influence, there is still much to be done to change people's behavior relative to drinking and driving.

---

[1] *Fatal Accident Reporting System*, U.S. Department of Transportation, National Highway Traffic Safety Administration, 1990, 22.

HELP KEEP FAMILIES TOGETHER

This family was on their way to have a picture taken for Christmas in 1988. They were torn apart when a driver, with a blood alcohol content of .26 according to police reports, crashed into their car, killing the parents—Roy Lee and Lou Verla Adams. Their surviving children—Ronald, Daniel, Joseph, Jason and Roy, along with grandmother, Katherine, went ahead with their mother's wishes and later had this group picture taken holding a photograph of their departed parents.

Mothers Against Drunk Driving

Figure 8–32 One way that MADD has raised public awareness is by distributing brochures that tell the personal story of families or children who have been affected by drunk driving accidents. (Courtesy of MADD.)

THE PUBLICS

MADD targets several audiences, all on different sides of a drunk driving accident.

- Along with its sister organization, Students Against Drunk Driving (SADD), MADD educates *teens* (a group with a high incidence of alcohol-related accidents) against the dangers of drunk driving.
- Another focus is the *adult driver* who may become impaired after a social night out (see Figure 8-33).
- The *repeat and reckless drunk driver*—the cause of many alcohol-related deaths—is targeted in MADD's legislative efforts for harsher penalties
- MADD also supports *public service professionals*, such as police, paramedics, and physicians, who must deal with the daily consequences of one person's carelessness.
- Finally MADD maintains programs aiding family and friends who have experienced the trauma of a drunk driving accident.

GOALS AND OBJECTIVES

MADD works at the grassroots level to end the senseless deaths and crippling physical and emotional injuries caused by drunk drivers. MADD supports programs that:

1. Achieve *voluntary* liquor and beer industry support to curb alcohol advertising when television or live audiences have large percentages of those under age twenty-one. One goal is to find alternate advertisers.
2. Encourage sponsors of sporting events to limit alcohol sales too late in the event, thereby increasing the probability that fans will arrive home safely.
3. Convince Congress to add a victim's rights amendment to the U.S. Constitution—similar to the Victim's Bill of Rights in the Michigan, Florida, and Rhode Island state constitutions.

ACTIVITIES AND TACTICS

Project Red Ribbon has become one of MADD's most successful campaigns. During the holiday season, red ribbons are distributed to drivers to be tied on car antennas and mirrors (see Figure 8-34).[2] The ribbon acts as a *reminder* not to drive if they become impaired, and as a *sign of solidarity* against drunk driving. The act of tying

---

[2]Originally, they were tied on door handles to keep drunks from getting into their cars—but most present-day handles have no place to attach them.

TIPS FOR RESPONSIBLE HOSTING FROM MADD™ Mothers Against Drunk Driving

The decision to serve alcoholic beverages in your home carries with it a responsibility for the welfare of your guests. Responsible attitudes toward drinking should make us behave in such a way that we will never have to feel sorry for what happened. Remember, people don't like to admit they've had too much to drink, and may argue with you that they are sober enough to drive. Following is a list of arguments you might hear, and ways for you to respond:

"HEY, I'M NOT DRUNK!"

Share with them the penalties they'll face if arrested for drunk driving.

"I'LL JUST HAVE SOME COFFEE TO SOBER UP."

Only time sobers you up. Alcohol oxidizes at a rate of approximately one drink per hour.

"I ONLY DRANK BEER AND DIDN'T MIX DRINKS."

It doesn't matter. One 12-ounce beer, one 5-ounce glass of wine or an ounce-and-a-half of liquor contain the same amount of alcohol with the same intoxication potential.

"I LIVE REAL CLOSE, I CAN MAKE IT"

Statistics show that three out of four crashes occur within 25 miles of a person's home.

"I'VE DONE THIS A HUNDRED TIMES. I NEVER GET CAUGHT."

First, ask yourself "How did this person get invited to your party?"

Next, remind him/her there were over one million drunk driving arrests last year, over 22,000 alcohol-related crash deaths, and over 400 new tough-alcohol countermeasures passed at the state and national level.

"I NEED MY CAR."

Suggest to your guest that he/she spend the night, or call a taxi to drive him/her home. Or ask another, sober, guest to drive the intoxicated person home and have another sober guest follow with his/her car.

NEVER LET A PERSON DRIVE AWAY FROM YOUR PARTY DRUNK!

HERE ARE MORE TIPS:

If serving alcohol, always serve food. Provide seats for everyone, along with the table space to allow guests to set drinks down.

Have several jiggers at the bar so mixed drinks can be measured.

Choose a bartender of known discretion. Control the flow of alcohol – it's your home, you set the limit.

Have non-alcoholic beverages available for your guests.

If you serve an alcoholic punch, make it with a non-carbonated base.

Don't push drinks; push snacks.

Stop serving alcohol at least an hour before the party is to end.

FRIENDS DO NOT LET FRIENDS DRIVE DRUNK!

MADD
Mothers Against Drunk Driving

Figure 8–33   One way that MADD has targeted adults is by offering tip sheets for hosts of parties to facilitate a fun and safe party. (Courtesy of MADD.)

the ribbon also reminds the individuals of other preventive behaviors as well, such as calling a cab for a friend or holding his or her car keys to prevent drunk driving. The program is successful because it links a specific behavior (tying the ribbon) to a commitment against drunk driving *before* the first toast is raised, and it does this at the *point of behavior*.

- Alcohol-related deaths decreased from seventy-six per day in 1980 to sixty-four in 1989.
- According to the National Parents Resource Institute for Drug Education, beer, which is the number one drug of choice for teens, is most often consumed in vehicles.

- An independent research group found that television programs with a large percentage of under-twenty-one viewers feature a high incidence of alcohol advertisements.

More than 30 million red ribbons are distributed each year by volunteers, MADD chapters, and supporting organizations, such as 7–11 stores, across the country (see Figure 8–35). In addition to grassroots support, several companies have tied marketing efforts to the program. Welch's promoted its nonalcoholic cider in conjunction with the program. This action may or may not have boosted Welch's sales, but it did give more exposure to the MADD program—and the antidrunk driving ideal.

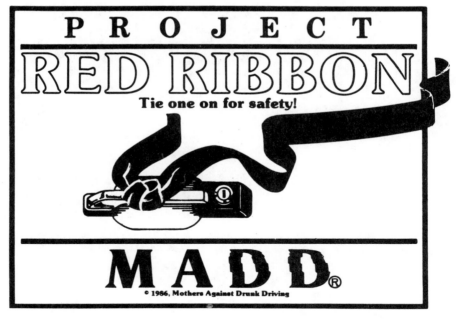

Figure 8–34 Pamphlets are distributed that create awareness of the project. (Courtesy of MADD.)

Figure 8–35   An example of the box of ribbons that MADD offered to organizations to promote Project Red Ribbon. (Courtesy of MADD.)

Since 1990 Consolidated Freightways Motorfreight, a national trucking company based in California, has been a sponsor for MADD's Project Red Ribbon. From November to January, the company ties red ribbons to its fleet of 12,000 trucks. In addition, several Project Red Ribbon kick-off events are organized by Consolidated Freightways Motorfreight employees and held at their terminals. Some companies have found that supporting a social cause boosts employee morale by adding meaning to job performance, as well as creating public goodwill.

ONE-WAY AND TWO-WAY COMMUNICATION TOOLS WHICH HELP MADD CARRY OUT ITS MISSION

1. *Support for the MADD message in television programming.* In 1988–1989, millions of Americans tuned in to their favorite television show and got a clear warning about drinking and driving—"The two don't mix." A portion of the credit goes to the Harvard School of Medicine Alcohol Project campaign, which encourages producers and writers to promote responsible drinking and designated-driver programs. MADD's national office served as script advisers.

2. *National poster contest.* More than 45,000 young people participated in the Third Annual Nationwide Poster/Essay contest aimed at preventing drunk driving. Cultural barriers were breached by including Spanish-language entries.

3. *Toll-free Victim's Assistance Crisis hotline* was established by MADD to provide support to those affected by a drunk driver's actions.

4. *Formation of Victim Impact Panels.* One hundred Victim Impact Panels were formed to serve as a forum for voicing grief, pain, and frustration associated with drunk driving accidents. These can send a powerful *emotion-laden* message to the public. Convicted drunk drivers are occasionally required to attend one of these panels as part of their sentence.

5. *Candlelight Vigils* are held to honor drunk driving victims and serve as a reminder.

6. *Crisis Response Teams* have been formed to assist families and friends of victims.

7. MADD is a strong *lobbyist for legislation for stiffer penalties* to keep the drunk driver off the road and to curb underage drinking.

8. MADD publishes *MADDvocate*, a magazine for victims and advocates.

MADD's ultimate goal is to get year-long commitment against drunk driving, not just during the holidays. There is evidence that Project Red Ribbon helps reach this goal—MADD receives requests throughout the year for replacements for worn-out ribbons.

THE OUTCOME

Coalition efforts are paying off. In addition to the 7.7 percent decrease in fatalities over ten years, the Omnibus Anti-Drug Act was passed in 1988. It is a significant victory in federal anti-DWI legislation. The enactment of the federally sponsored national minimum drinking age of twenty-one is another significant gain.

LEGISLATION: ANOTHER FORM OF PERSUASION

Years of scholarly research of public relations programming have combined to establish a four-point method for effecting mass behavior change—which is MADD's goal, of course (See box). Step 2 is enforcement, and this is where restrictive and

---

FOUR STEPS TO PUBLIC BEHAVIOR CHANGE THROUGH PR CAMPAIGNS

The work of Jim Grunig, Harold Mendelsohn, Brenda Darvin, Maxwell McCombs, and many others suggests this approach.

1. **Coalition campaign,** so that the target audience gets the feeling that everyone who counts is trying to persuade them, that it is obviously the thing to do socially. Appeals in such a campaign must follow three phases:
   - *Problem (or opportunity) recognition.* Gaining widespread understanding that the issue is an opportunity or a problem.
   - *Problem (or opportunity) personalization.* Making target audience real-

ize it involves them, they could be affected.
   - *Constraint removal.* Letting them know they can do something about it.

2. **Enforcement.** Establishing rules and laws mandating or outlawing the behavior.

3. **Engineering.** Enacting a structural change to work around the situation, for example, raising the drinking age to reduce drunk driving accidents by young drivers.

4. **Social reinforcement.** When the behavior becomes the societally accepted norm and social rewards and punishments take over the job of enforcing it.

punitive laws play their part. Thus, MADD's program must include enforcement (including punishment) to preserve the whole agenda of behavior change.

Here are some of the laws that MADD—along with a host of coalition partners, often brought together by MADD—has been successful in having enacted. MADD deserves much of the credit for one of the most remarkable behavior change efforts in recent times. Only a decade ago it was still acceptable to talk about the "drunken party" you went to over the weekend. Today, in most circles, anyone who mentioned such behavior would be scolded and possibly shunned. In large measure, this change can be traced to the catalytic leadership of Mothers Against Drunk Driving.

1. *Drunk Driving Prevention Act of 1988.* States were offered incentives in the form of highway safety fund grants for passing legislation aimed at reducing alcohol-related offenses and deaths, including a minimum twenty-one drinking age—up from eighteen in most states. The act was controversial, but eventually most states adopted the age to avoid losing federal funds.

2. *Victim's Crime Act of 1984.* This act provides compensation rights and grants for the survivors of drunk driving accidents.

3. *Alcoholic Beverage Labeling Act of 1988.* This act states that all alcoholic beverage containers bear a warning about the dangers of driving after drinking.

QUESTIONS FOR DISCUSSION

1. MADD was an organization established by one who had suffered a great tragedy because of the carelessness of a drunk driver. Today the organization has been extremely successful in exacting changes in societal attitudes against drunk driving. What does their success indicate about relationships formed when people who have suffered the same tragedy band together?

2. Can you think of another organization that was formed because of an emotion-laden circumstance? Has it been as successful as MADD? Explain your answer.

3. What other communication vehicles could MADD utilize to spread its message?

Whose Right to Know What?: AIDS and Condoms in Schools

As stated in Case 3-1, AIDS is an issue that has affected all facets of daily life. Not only corporations are taking responsibility for educating others about the disease, schools are also prime places for distributing information about AIDS and how to prevent it. And here is where the issue intensifies: Do schools have the authority to pass out condoms or install condom machines as preventive measures for students? At what age is this explicit education appropriate for teens? Will providing teens with condoms actually influence them to practice safer sex or just encourage them to become sexually active sooner?[1]

A NEW TWIST ON AN OLD ISSUE

For years the controversy raged in many school districts of whether sex education is appropriate. Opponents stated that a subject such as sex should be taught only at home in order to pass on the morals held by the family. Advocates of sex education argued that sex often is something not discussed by the family until *after* teens have already engaged in sexual intercourse.

Then a disease that can be transmitted sexually and is fatal to those who contract it entered the picture. Education and availability of condoms could be the only

---

[1] One interesting discussion of this issue is an informal paper by the Department of Education dated January 1988. Called "Will 'Safe Sex' Education Effectively Combat AIDS?" it responds to questions and comments on the "safe sex" approach to educating young people about AIDS prevention. The paper argues that "safe sex" education will not effectively combat AIDS because it emphasizes engaging in sexual intercourse and diminishes the fact that abstinence is "the only true weapon" against the AIDS epidemic.

preventive medicine that adolescents have against the fatal disease. And so began the controversy of AIDS education and condom distribution in schools.

Here the line grows cloudy of what is appropriate for the government and schools to do in order to educate young people and others (see Figures 8–36 and 8–37). It is important for officials to spread new and pertinent information in protecting the population from AIDS. However, does promoting this form of protection and encouraging young people to use condoms encroach on "parental rights" to instill in their children their own standards and morals? In early spring of 1992, this issue surfaced at a seacoast town in New Hampshire, as it has at many high schools across the country.

HISTORY

One hot topic in the fall of 1991 was the announcement of Magic Johnson's retirement after discovering he was HIV-positive. For the first time, a prominent sports figure who was obviously heterosexual had contracted the disease. This announcement affected many young people who had felt that AIDS could not happen to them. They began to examine their sexual behaviors with this new reminder of their mortality.

The Portsmouth High School newspaper, *The Paper Clip*, conducted a sex survey in the spring of 1992 and found that over half of the PHS student population was sexually active. This survey spotlighted the frequency with which teens were engaging in sexual activity.

One statistic from the survey revealed that only twelve percent of males surveyed (against seventeen percent nationwide) used contraceptive devices during sexual intercourse. From these statistics it was obvious that condoms were not a

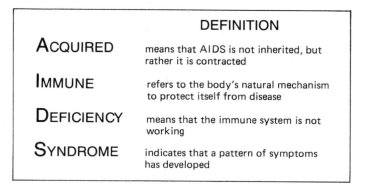

	DEFINITION
ACQUIRED	means that AIDS is not inherited, but rather it is contracted
IMMUNE	refers to the body's natural mechanism to protect itself from disease
DEFICIENCY	means that the immune system is not working
SYNDROME	indicates that a pattern of symptoms has developed

Figure 8–36 This short definition clarifies and explains the AIDS virus. (From "AIDS Update," Department of Health and Rehabilitation Services, Tallahassee, Florida, 1985.)

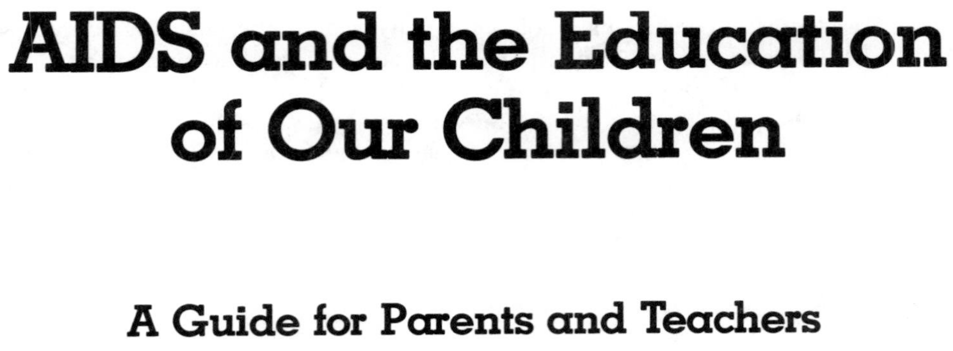

AIDS and the Education of Our Children

A Guide for Parents and Teachers

Figure 8–37   The Department of Education offers materials to facilitate AIDS education in schools. (Courtesy of the Department of Education.)

widely used form of contraception. Condoms are the only available barrier against many sexually transmitted diseases, including AIDS.

Publication of the survey coincided with a rally by ACT-UP (AIDS Coalition To Unleash Power), an AIDS-awareness group. These events and extended controversy in the community and media spurred school officials to investigate the possibility of integrating condom distribution into a comprehensive community health education program.

The issue became known to the school board when a representative of the teachers' association presented a letter that asked them to consider condom distribution. The school board devised a plan to help *collectively* decide this volatile issue. They formed a community-based committee, the Community Health Education Committee, made up of some school board members, the school nurse, parents, members of the general community, and clergy.

According to Dr. Nathan Greenberg,[2] school superintendent, the school board chose this broad range of people to serve on the committee because they wanted a balance of opinions. Bob Lister, Portsmouth High School's vice-principal, was chosen as committee chairman because of his facilitation skills. This committee worked for seven months to research the topic. In the midst of that research, they decided to expand the scope of the inquiry beyond a condom issue to a community health education issue.

PUBLICS INVOLVED

Investigating this possibility involved many publics in the decision process:

1. The teens that attended school at PHS
2. Their parents

[2]We thank Dr. Greenberg for the information, time, and cooperation he gave for this case.

3. Teachers and the school administration
4. The school board
5. Concerned members of the community

All key publics involved had many difficult issues to sort out, such as:

- Perceptions of the school overstepping bounds
- The role of parental rights in this issue
- Religious convictions involved in the issue
- Whether providing condoms was really a way to protect these teens from this fatal disease

A COMMUNITY DIVIDED COMES TO A HESITANT CONSENSUS

The issue rode a high wave of debate among members of the community. Initially, the community was evenly divided for and against condom distribution in the high school.

How did a community so divided on a volatile issue come to an agreement? According to Greenberg, the committee was "a great idea" because it allowed the decision to be made with the input and feedback of all involved. Throughout the entire process, the school board solicited large amounts of community and parental feedback through public forums. As community interchange increased, more information became available, and opinions of some community members and those on the committee began to change. Another helpful approach was that they looked at health issues as a whole, and the focus of the committee's report wasn't just on condoms.

When the committee finally made its recommendation, it was to distribute the condoms in the high school as part of a "comprehensive K–12 school health program, overseen by a full-time certified Health Education Director."[3] It was then up to the school board to decide what policy and action to take. The board voted five to four to allow condom distribution at PHS, the first school in the state to do so.

The next month, Greenberg recommended to the school board how condoms were to be distributed to students. In the spirit that this issue had been decided, the school board made an arrangement to please many of those constituents who did not want their children to receive condoms. Parents who did not want their children to obtain condoms from the nurse could write and forbid it. Also, students would have to go through an initial counseling session with the school nurse to talk about different birth control options (including abstinence), real benefits and problems of using a condom, and how to use them.

[3]Michelle Adam, "Health Education Is Gaining Importance," *Portsmouth Herald*, November 19, 1992, pp. 1–A6.

This method of change in a community, group, or organization is known as "The Co-Authorship Principle." When people are permitted to participate in creating the change . . . not merely being told to change . . . when they are invited to give their ideas about what concerns them . . . when they are given the freedom to criticize and say what they think ought to be done to improve the situation, they will be more receptive to new ideas.

MEDIA RULES ESTABLISHED EARLY HELP PUBLICS TO MAKE DECISION COLLECTIVELY

Media rules established by the school board at the beginning were a factor in making a positive experience of this issue discussion. The following actions were helpful in gaining the school board fair play in news media without having the situation develop into the emotional argument it could have become:

- Early on the school board had appointed Bob Lister as spokesman for the committee to speak in One Clear Voice to the media; all questions went through him.
- After the school board vote was taken, it tried to funnel questions through the board chairman.
- The school board always tried to keep the decision process open to the public and its scrutiny.
- The discussions and community forums never got to a personal level; they were very issue-oriented.
- Those involved handled it in a responsible way; there were no US versus THEM attitudes, and in the entire procedure, the major concerns that people had were addressed effectively.

SUCCESS OF PROGRAM TO DATE

Since the decision to make condoms available was made in February 1993, about seventy parents have written, requesting that their children not receive them. On the other hand, many young people at Portsmouth High School are using the option of going to the school nurse, who reports that they have been asking intelligent questions about the issues involved. As of December 1993, about eighty students had come to get information. Most of them were in grades 9–10.

COLLECTIVE DECISION MAKING CAN HELP AVOID THE STORM OF DEBATE

New studies concerning how decisions are made confirm the notion that relationships are the process through which individuals form opinions about issues. People learn primarily through their interactions with other people—not through the media. The public teaches itself through interactive dialogue—a dialogue that is exploratory and deliberative, with people testing their ideas rather than taking positions and trying to score points. Here are nine pivotal factors of decision making[4]:

1. People want to make connections between issues.

2. The lens through which people view issues is personal context.

3. People want coherent information, the whole story—which they often feel eludes them.

4. People *want* room for ambivalence.

5. The presence of emotion—including fear, anger, sadness, happiness—is essential if people are to form and sustain relationships with public concerns.

6. Facts are unimportant: People are looking at *authenticity* when measuring whether a statement is true or credible.

7. People want positives not negatives—a sense of possibility.

8. Media, politicians, special interests have only limited roles (as diffusion process and other models have long held).

9. People come together to talk and act on public concerns in little-noticed meeting places—churches, synagogues, neighborhood councils, and schools.

QUESTIONS FOR DISCUSSION

1. Issues such as condom distribution have been hotly debated and seem never to get resolved. What are the motivating behaviors behind this particular type of issue that make them so hard to resolve? Name some other current issues of this type.

2. If you were a school communicator trying to initiate a condom distribution policy in your school, how would you go about it?

3. Portsmouth High School and the city's school system do not at this time have a public relations officer on staff. Yet sophisticated public relations decisions were made. If you were the public relations person for these schools, what, if anything, might you have added to the decisions, the process, and the outcomes?

[4]Cited from a study by the Kettering Foundation (1993). Kettering Foundation, *Meaningful Chaos*, (Dayton, OH, 1993).

PROBLEM 8-A SMOKEOUT CAN BE HOT POTATO

You are a first-year employee at W. L. Fixit Associates, a public relations firm in Piedmont, North Carolina, a city of 40,000 people that has long thrived on tobacco growing and manufacturing. Mr. Fixit started the agency ten years earlier after handling communications for the local Chamber of Commerce. He is well known and knows everybody important in the region.

You're doing well. You've just been advanced to Associate Account Executive and assigned the Piedmont General Hospital as your very own client. Among other clients of the agency are a nearby college, a large resort hotel, a new downtown shopping mall, and the United Way.

At the hospital, you're helping them deal with complaints about the high costs of health care, as well as promoting greater use of a new day-care adjunct, annual fund-raising campaign, and employee morale.

One day in August, the Fixit senior account executive comes into your office and says, "You're about to get your first sticky wicket to handle." He tells you that the United Way has committed to implement the "Great American Smokeout" annual event of the American Cancer Society and has asked the Fixit agency to implement it with all their clients. Mr. Fixit feels that the agency could duck out by pleading a conflict of interest, but in a public health issue like this that would do the agency more harm than coming up with a plan that has a chance of keeping everybody happy.

Your supervisor tells you: "It will be your job to come up with a catchy, contagious one-day event at Piedmont General." He hands you a packet that explains the Smokeout concept of affecting smokers' behavior, suggests ways to get the cooperation of various organizations, tie in local public health officials and other community leaders, attract the media, instruct those in the facilities how to prepare, make it a fun event, recognize and reward those who abstain for a day, and measure the success. The packet includes examples such as the organization that gave out survival kits including chewing gum and candy, another that put baskets of apples all around, another that set up smokeaters in designated smoke areas, another that removed cigarette vending machines on Smokeout Day, and another that sent a congratulatory letter from the president to each smoker employee who reported successfully abstaining on Smokeout Day. There was more. The event whetted your appetite. Then the account supervisor threw the curve.

"This is no piece of cake," he said. "Your hospital's largest contributor is the tobacco company over in Winston. There's a wing named for their founder, Colonel Piedmont. Also, have you noticed that the Piedmont's administrator is a chain smoker? That's why all the major committee meetings are held out on the penthouse roof in good weather. You've got to come up with an event that makes us look good enough to nonsmokers and the United Way without doing damage to our relationship with the hospital administration. Maybe you can persuade them there is a trade-off for them. As for smokers and the tobacco industry around here, don't do anything that could cause permanent alienation. Mr. Fixit wouldn't mind landing a tobacco account someday, and tobacco companies are branching out more and more into food products."

He added, "Mull it over. If you can't involve both sides working with each other, at least figure out a project in which neither's ox is gored so badly they have to fight back. Put your ideas down on paper with a reasonable objective; keep in mind that United Way isn't a big-spending account; list what's new and newsworthy about your event, and explain what you have built into the plan to protect against seriously riling the tobacco people, including Colonel Piedmont's family, who made their millions on tobacco. Give me a call in ten days and we'll take a look together at what you've come up with."

As you start thinking about a solution to this situation, you remember that the basis of a successful message strategy

- Emphasizes the benefit statement
- Avoids stiffening the resistance
- Asks for a willing suspension of disbelief

With this in mind, what further background research will you do before you start defining the objectives and activities of your program? Who will you talk to, what concerns do you anticipate, and how will you deal with them?

Using the feedback from this research, define the objectives of your program and describe and explain how the proposed activities will support your communications strategy; include some means of measuring the success in obtaining your objectives.

Do you see any ethical issues that might arise in handling this situation? If you do, how would you deal with them?

PROBLEM 8-B REFEREEING A NEW KIND OF GAME

After earning three letters for sports at Louisiana State University, you were sidelined by a knee injury that kept you out of the professional draft. Fortunately, your journalism/public relations major helped you land a good job with Dorino, Marion public relations agency. The firm does some work for professional sports teams and suppliers and has good connections in the state capital. They also have a reputation for public service assistance to nonprofit organizations. You like it at Dorino, Marion. They like you.

The main account you personally handle is the subcommittee of the Mardi

Gras, which brings in celebrities for the annual event. Your work tends to be seasonal except for periodic planning meetings, some out-of-town contacts, and some correspondence. So you have considerable spare time.

That situation changed suddenly one day, when the agency was approached to take on the public relations problems arising from the actions of Brother Omans, the charismatic, activist minister of the local Bible-For-Everybody Church. It seems that Omans, with the active support of a doctor who wrote an antiabortion book, has challenged the activities of the local Birth Control Institute Inc., an affiliate of Planned Parenthood International. They are known to perform and arrange abortions.

Brother Omans has notified the institute by mail that they are "committing murders" and that they risk "harsh judgment" in which "proper penalties can be imposed." He has led a picketing group, some of whose members went beyond passing out pamphlets to shouting at clients heading into the institute.

Mrs. Safeway, head of the institute, has gone to the police for protection. The police say that the pickets do not trespass as long as they stay on the sidewalk, that they have rights of assembly, and freedom of speech. If and when Brother Omans or his constituents break any law, they will be apprehended.

Mrs. Safeway is concerned that this reactive attitude may allow further escalation of potential violence. She therefore approaches Dorino, Marion to ask for advice in seeking a more proactive approach to the situation.

You are assigned the task of analyzing the situation and coming up with a proactive approach as a public service of your agency. You know that Louisiana favors restricting abortion rights and probably would, if it were legal, forbid any abortions except in very narrow circumstances.

To get your facts straight, even before you go to see Mrs. Safeway, you talk to a member of the local media with whom you went to school. He tells you that Brother Omans set up shop locally about eight years ago. A profile the newspaper did on him shows that he has had quite a career. At one time he was a circus barker hailing originally from San Antonio, Texas, traveled through the southern Bible Belt, became a minister, and then moved to New Orleans. If he had anything in his background of moral turpitude, or arrests, there is nothing about it in the newspaper morgue.

From other sources, you find that in the past eight years, Brother Omans, from the pulpit, has taken on or opposed witches, homosexuals, pornography, X-rated movies, the "mercy death" of a ninety-three-year old comatose man, Mormon missionaries in general, and any woman who goes into politics specifically.

Armed with this information, you go to see Mrs. Safeway at the Birth Control Institute. She's scared. There have been so many instances of bombing or arson at Planned Parenthood clinics, she can envision some of Brother Omans's constituents making her place a target. She has notified the Planned Parenthood national office. She has read their Clinic Defense Manual and notified the appropriate offices in New Orleans of her concern. She hopes you can do something to calm the situation down, not antagonize Brother Omans, his doctor supporter, or his followers. She appreciates that your agency has agreed to take on this project as a public service. You respect her professionalism but recognize that some of her actions have themselves been adversarial.

TIME TO FISH OR CUT BAIT

Back at your office, you talk it over with your boss. You agree that there are such strong feelings on both sides that it would be tough to marshal enough neutral public opinion to induce a reconciliation without at the same time rousing special interests with strong bias toward a confrontation or worse.

"This looks like one of those situations calling for a brainstorming session at the agency, bringing together representatives of groups with a stake in peaceful co-existence, and no ax to grind, on abortion," your boss says. "Maybe we can get a strategic plan out of the session. If not, it will put Brother Omans on notice that some important people are watching him, and it may reassure Mrs. Safeway she isn't about to be bombed."

Your boss instructs you to make up an invitation list of about fifteen organizations, starting with city hall, the police department, and the county medical society, a brief statement of the meeting's purpose, and a tentative agenda for the meeting. "When you get those done, let me have a look," your boss says.

1. Before you start on this project, what issues affecting other members of the firm and the firm's reputation in the community might you want to discuss with your supervisor? How would you suggest dealing with them?
2. Do you agree with the suggestion that the invitations list should include city hall and the police department? If so, why? If not, on what basis would you suggest omitting them?
3. Would you include Mrs. Safeway or Brother Omans or both in this initial meeting? What could be the positive and negative results of having them there?
4. What would be your list, the statement to invitees, and the agenda?
5. What would be your recommendation in alerting or not alerting the media and dealing with the possibility of a premature leak?

Chapter 9

Crisis Management

Because a true crisis is a turning point, after which things may change drastically, an organization not prepared to deal with crisis is constantly at risk. Even sudden emergencies of crisis proportion can be anticipated—if not avoided—so risk management, issue anticipation, and crisis communication programs have become an important part of public relations technology.

Despite this sophistication in the work, the term *crisis management* does not imply that an organization or its public relations staff can *manage* external influences. What can—and must—be managed is the *response*. This depends on the practitioner's thorough understanding of three things:

1. The **public and political environment** in which the crisis is occurring.
2. The **culture and inner workings of the organization** facing the crisis.
3. **Human nature**—how will the persons and groups involved most likely react to the crisis itself, to attempts to alleviate it, and to various communications?

HUMAN NATURE

When people are subjected to great emotional stress, their normally self-controlled behavior tends to become irrational and unpredictable. Their reactions turn down the steps of Maslow's hierarchy of human needs. At the bottom, of course, are a person's physical needs. One step above are a person's safety needs. When people feel that physical needs and safety needs are threatened, they are prone to panic. In panic, people's baser instincts for survival take command.

These phenomena become immediately apparent in such catastrophic circumstances as fires, floods, explosions, and tornadoes. The same pattern emerges, with less severity, in noncatastrophic situations such as a scarcity of gasoline or coffee, a spate of crime in a community, or even a standing-room-only crowd at a public event. The symptoms of potential panic and the concern for self are there. Similarly, sensations approaching panic may invade us when it appears that we may miss a departing airflight, may lose a dear friend, find ourselves unexpectedly deprived of light in our home at night, or must walk a dark street to our parked car.

THE ROLE OF COMMUNICATIONS

People tend to get reassurance concerning their physical well-being and safety largely from believable information that pierces through the uncertainty, the rumors, and the gossip. Human nature, fortunately, has a toughness about it, enabling most people to handle substantial bad news or physical danger by making adjustments. Knowing the alternatives, we make the best of a bad deal. But we find it very difficult to cope for long periods with the uncertainties that come from not being informed or not trusting the information, whether the threat to us is as vital and near as a local rumor of a toxic chemical leak or as remote and impersonal as a drop in the Dow Jones stock market average.

Not every crisis is of the "instant" variety. Some crises develop over a period of time—days, weeks, even months. Nevertheless, these events are just as much a crisis as those that are fast-breaking. But the consequences for managing a crisis, for keeping credible communication flowing, are intensified when the situation drags out. In any case, the public expects the leaders of organizations to act with total honesty and sensitivity during and after a crisis.

MEDIA INFLUENCE

The interpretation of public events affecting our lives falls heavily on the news media. News prerogatives and privileges are legally assured by the First Amendment to the U.S. Constitution. Abuses of these rights surface most often when fierce competition among the media makes a competitive advantage more important or urgent than simple truth and accuracy in the public interest.

In recent years, few would argue that news media have been responsible carriers of information needed by citizens; most would say they have concentrated on scandals and titillating trivialities that provided public entertainment. This perception must be taken clearly into account when planning crisis strategy.

Similarly, the obligation of public relations toward the public interest is sometimes submerged or subverted by the desire to attain the special competitive interests of employers or clients.

A classic example of news media importance in alleviating uncertainty and preventing panic, or fostering the causes of panic, was the Three Mile Island nuclear plant accident in 1979. The onslaught of newspeople from literally all over the world was a new experience for the few thousand residents of the area. They were accustomed to the presence of the nuclear plant but not to the swarm of reporters and photographers seeking to outdo each other in shock-inducing coverage under the pressure of news deadlines. Some news media, notwithstanding the temptations, did not yield to the competitive advantage that might have come from purveying rumors and gossip of dire predictions. Others clearly did.

For the power company and the Nuclear Regulatory Commission, this was an experience for which there were no precise precedential guidelines, no rules. Their early silence was lamentable. However, an admission that they did not know what was happening might have been even worse.[1]

Under the circumstances, local panic was averted more by what President Carter's visit communicated *symbolically* than by any *information* issued by the company or nuclear authorities or by any suggestions, analyses, or complaints on the part of news media.

After the problem had been brought under control and an evaluation was conducted in an unemotional environment, testimony brought out that it was the lack of information that distressed neighbors and local officials most of all. Lacking trustworthy information, humans tend to assume the worst. Trust must precede information.

The ability to communicate trustworthy information, whether directly or via news media, is a measure of a practitioner's effectiveness or ineffectiveness. In unexpected situations of disaster, crisis, or emergency, the news media and the practice of public relations have had their finest examples of public service and their most severe episodes of failure and ineptitude. The cases in this chapter illustrate this point.

FUNDAMENTAL GUIDELINES

There are some guidelines that continue to help organizations handle crisis communication situations. Among them are:

1. Anticipate the unexpected. There are few events that cannot be anticipated. You might not know when they will happen, but an organization can anticipate a fire, a flood, a strike, a fatal accident on the job, a robbery, and many other unexpected events.

---

[1]Rear Admiral David M. Cooney, former Chief of Information, Department of the Navy, makes the point that "in the early stages of a crisis situation, you don't tell people things you don't know or aren't sure of. . . . You never involve yourself in conjecture . . . because the chances are that you are going to be wrong. A crisis situation breaks down to certain questions. What happened? Why did it happen? What are you going to do to keep it from happening again? What is the overall impact on the people who are involved and their dependents?" He recommends, "Be organized always to handle a crisis in the next fifteen minutes."

2. Institute and practice a crisis communications plan for those events that may happen to your organization.

3. Train employees in what to do in these circumstances.

4. Have one spokesperson to the public and media during the crisis.

5. If it is a crisis affecting the public, rather than just the organization, another spokesperson or persons will also be required to keep elected officials and opinion leaders directly advised.

6. Do not speculate on the cause, the cost, or anything else. Provide information about only what is known.

REFERENCES AND ADDITIONAL READINGS

ARMBRUSTER, TIMOTHY D. "Crisis in Cleveland." *Public Relations Journal* (August 1968). Classic community crisis.

BARTON, LAWRENCE. *Crisis in Organizations.* Cincinnati, OH: Southwestern Publishing Company, 1993.

FINK, STEVEN. *Crisis Management: Planning for the Inevitable.* New York: Amacom, 1986.

JACKSON, DEBBIE. "Bayer Mobilizes Resources to Counter Crisis at Home." *Chemical Week* v152 (April 21, 1993): 24–31.

JOHNSON, DANIEL G. "Crisis Management: Forewarned is Forearmed." *Journal of Business Strategy* v14 (March/April 1993): 58–64.

LERBINGER, OTTO. "BEYOND CRISIS MANAGEMENT—ISSUES RAISED BY THREE MILE ISLAND" *Purview, pr reporter* (supplement, September 10, 1979) Discusses the articles in *Public Opinion* (June/July 1979).

LERBINGER, OTTO, and NATHANIEL N. SPERBER. *Managers Public Relations Handbook.* Reading, Mass.: Addison-Wesley, 1982. See chapters 1 and 2.

LERBINGER, OTTO. *Managing Corporate Crises.* Boston: Barrington Press, 1986.

LESLY, PHILIP. *Overcoming Opposition.* Englewood Cliffs, N.J.: Prentice Hall, 1984.

MINDSZENTHY, BART J., T. A. G. WATSON, and WILLIAM J. KOCH. *No Surprises: The Crisis Management System.* Toronto: Bedford House Communication, 1988.

NAGELSCHMIDT, JOSEPH, ed. *The Public Affairs Handbook.* New York: Amacom, 1982. Several leading public relations practitioners and corporate executives share their experiences on all aspects of issues and crises.

pr reporter v31 (June 27, 1988). Lead article emphasizes challenge to influence behavior and induce action by supertargeting, focused appeals, rather than broadsides to shape attitude or opinion. Cites Dayton Hudson's thwarting of a takeover attempt covered by Case 9-4 in this chapter.

pr reporter v36 (May 10, 1993). United Way case: Answer to a Good Crisis Plan is Prior Work on the Basics.

ROSNOW, RALPH L. "Rumor as Communication: A Contextualist Approach." *Journal of Communication* 38 (Winter 1988): 12–28.

Schoeny, Heather. "Koala Springs International's Product Recall." *Public Relations Quarterly* v36 (Winter 1991–92): pp 25–26.

Shell, Adam. "At City Hall, Every Day's a Crisis." *Public Relations Journal* v48 (February 1992): p. 7.

Shell, Adam ed., "Communicating Foreign Crises; Panel Debates Best Approach," Public Relations Journal, 50 (February, 1994):4.

Snyder, Leonard. "An Anniversary Review and Critique: The Tylenol Crisis." *Public Relations Review* 9 (Fall 1983): 24–34.

The Public Relations Body of Knowledge. New York: PRSA, 1993. See section V.1 for abstracts dealing with "Media Relations, Including Crisis Management."

Tiller, Michael J. "Is Your Disaster Plan Effective?" *Management Review* v83 (April 1994): p. 57.

See "Investigative Reporter Says Candor and Immediate Answers Not Always Necessary, Even in Crisis Communication." *pr reporter* v22 (October 8, 1979). Cites views of Les Whitten, senior reporter on Jack Anderson's staff.

Four classic programs worthy of investigation: The handling of employee news when a company president and four employees were killed in an air crash, Southern Company Services, P.O. Box 720071, Atlanta, Ga. 30346; a disaster plan by Johns-Manville, in *pr reporter,* June 18, 1979; closing an oil refinery in a small town, Amoco Company, P.O. Box 5077, Atlanta, Ga. 30302, ask for PR manual *Communications During an Emergency;* oil spill off Santa Barbara, Calif. and see "Effects of the Santa Barbara Blowout," *U.S. News and World Report,* February 8, 1971.

Beer and Cookies: Rumor and Reality

The risk of product tampering—whether it be real or rumored—is enough to cause any organization great concern today. Few products are completely safe from attempts to sabotage. Organizations at risk can be as diverse as a brewery and the Girl Scouts. Unless careful public relations planning is done and quick and decisive responses are made, an organization can be dramatically affected in the future.

BIG-SELLING BEER; DAMAGING RUMORS

Popular Corona Extra from Mexico was fast becoming the number one imported beer in the United States when, in mid-1987, a false rumor that the product was contaminated with urine threatened to take the fizz out of sales. The rumor, which was immediately traced to the wholesaler of a competing brand, spread throughout the South and Northwest before the importer, Barton Beers of Chicago, could stop it.

Barton had no previously prepared crisis plan—in fact, Barton had no public relations department—yet the company lawyer and sales vice-president were successful in spiking the rumor by assembling a crisis team to take action.

1. *The first step was to try to stem the rumor at its source* by obtaining the competing wholesaler's oral commitment to have employees stop spreading the rumor. Concurrently, the retailer that first reported the rumor was contacted with the facts in an effort to prevent the rumor from spreading to consumers.

2. One week after first knowledge of the rumor, *sales teams went into the marketplace to deal with the problem at the retail level.* Armed with fact

sheets and other data, they contacted retailers through mail and personal visits. This action helped prove that the rumor had no foundation. It also evoked confidence in Corona and Barton Beers for their speedy and direct response.

3. Corona *filed suit against the rumor-spreading wholesaler, not for damages, but to obtain a public apology.* Reprints of the apology were sent to all retailers as further evidence that the rumor was false.

4. Corona chose *not to deal with the rumor at the consumer level to avoid feeding the fire.*

THE BAD NEWS KEEPS ON COMING

Product tampering scares can be one of the most difficult risk-management issues to handle. In the summer of 1993, Pepsi-Cola Company was faced by reports of hypodermic needles found in its cola cans. Though the accusations were later found to be false, that didn't keep Pepsi from losing a share of its consumers who belonged to the "why risk it" crowd.

The public relations newsletter *pr reporter* describes this type of situation as a "lose-now, lose-later" issue. Regular consumers of the product will stay away in the present. In addition, any time the incident is brought up at a later date, the company loses, because of the unfavorable *mental image* that is created every time it's brought into people's consciousness.

Luckily, there are some strategic actions to take that may limit the damage of product-tampering rumors or reality.

- **Get the tampering incident behind you A.S.A.P.** Research shows that the more people discuss a threatening issue the more the threat becomes real. Pepsi took this rule into account in its July 4 television ads. They said "thank you" to the public without indicating what the viewer was being thanked for. This tactic does not rehash the incident or inform those consumers who weren't aware.

- **Try to make the incident forgettable.** Negative symbols that stay in the mind of the consumer can do long-term damage.

- **Credibility begins in daily operational quality.** Although the hypodermic needle incident was not from company manufacturing, nuts and bolts were later found in soft drink cans, proving that the company could have taken more quality control precautions.[1]

- **The main rule to follow is to expect the unexpected.** Always be prepared with a plan to minimize the damage when a potentially critical issue arises.

---

[1]*pr reporter*, July 12, 1993.

Halt of the credibility for the rumor—if not the rumor itself—was aided by widespread favorable news coverage. Yet the rumor had been unleashed among unsuspecting bartenders and waitresses, and they unwittingly continued to fan the flame. As a result, two months later, the *Los Angeles Times* called the company to confirm or deny an added rumor that the state of California had embargoed sale of Corona. The resulting *Times* interview with the leader of the crisis team became the turning point. Corona knew it had to deal directly with the beer-drinking public, despite the possible side effect of further spreading the rumor.

"One of the things we did was devise a positioning for our rebuttal," Fred Mardell, Barton legal counsel and executive vice-president of corporate development, said. "It wasn't enough to say the rumor wasn't true; we also reported our suspicion that the rumor had been started by a competitor for the express purpose of damaging the Corona brand." The distributor that started the rumor had ample motivation. Its Heineken brand, long the leading import, was being challenged overnight by upstart Corona, which had entered the U.S. market only six years earlier.

Coordinated with the favorable coverage given by the *Times* and syndicated papers, was a four-and-a-half minute satellite videocast. Prepared for television stations (it ultimately reached over 200 media outlets), the videocast featured a question-and-answer format and footage of the Mexican brewery to confirm cleanliness of facilities and purity of product. "Not surprisingly, the greatest impact on sales was felt in those areas where the rumor had its earliest publication and which were least affected by the kind of favorable media attention eventually received," Mardell reported when the threat had passed.

COOKIE TAMPERING THREATENS GIRL SCOUT SURVIVAL

Across the country headlines blazed, "Girl Scout Cookies Tainted." After years of community service, the Girl Scouts of America became the subject of suspicion and confusion during a rash of alleged cookie tamperings. The public, astounded and frightened, refused to buy the cookies, cutting off the major source of income for the Girl Scouts. The organization's credibility was not only in question, the children it served were discouraged and confused, and troops across the nation lost hundreds of thousands of dollars (see Figure 9–1).

Even though the alleged tamperings were scattered across the country, Chicagoans weren't taking any chances, and sales in Chicago came to a sudden halt. (Remember, Chicago was the site of the Tylenol tamperings; see Case 6–3). The Chicago Girl Scout Council had expected cookie sales to net $800,000, nearly half of the agency's operating budget. The financial crisis would cause immediate cuts in handicapped and urban programs, counseling, and other important services and ac-

Figure 9–1   Delivery time for Girl Scout cookies starts out locally with helping to unload the truck. (Courtesy of Martha Netsch, Swift Water Girl Scout Council, Inc., Manchester, New Hampshire.)

tivities. With the situation worsening, the agency hired public relations counsel and went to work to stop the damage.

Objectives and Action

The first order of business was to set the objectives of the campaign. They arrived at three:

1. Diffuse public fear.
2. Present the Chicago Girl Scout Council as a forward-looking, united group.
3. Enlist community sympathy and support for a new fund-raising effort to re-cover lost funds from the canceled sales.

Information or publicity alone cannot as a rule motivate decisions or behavior. But public relations counsel felt that where a preexisting behavior or loyalty was disrupted by an unexpected occurrence, publicity could heal the wound. Immediately, press materials were prepared explaining the details of the crisis. The press kit contained a fact sheet and news release covering many key details:

- What the Council was doing to ensure that no bakery supplying the cookies was in fact negligent.
- The ongoing investigation by the FBI and others to determine the source of the tamperings (the accusations of tampering were later found to be false).
- The effect of the crisis on the Council and the girls it serves.
- Announcement of the new program developed to offset losses from annual cookie sales.

Campaign for Community Support

Designed to rally businesses and individuals around the Council, the Chicago Girl Scout Challenge asked for contributions from the metropolitan area. It emphasized its 27,000 members, most of whom lived in the inner city, and how Girl Scouts had served the city for sixty-one years. The campaign sought to raise half of the $392,000 deficit the Council foresaw as a result of the rumor of tampering.

Board members of the Council—all representing large Chicago businesses—were the first to be asked for donations. The announcement of these donations, the largest at $5,000 from Continental Bank, was to be made at a news conference.

Emergency media training sessions were arranged for the president of the Council, a volunteer who had to lead the press conference and field media questions but was inexperienced in dealing with the press.

Knowing that the media might be tough, the Council left nothing at the press conference to chance. The Council president took the opportunity, after stating the Council's position on the tampering, to talk about positive Council work—special urban outreach and career development projects and its work with handicapped girls. The news conference ended with presentation of the checks and announcement of other pledges to the fund.

Media's focus was successfully turned to the positive aspect of the fund-raiser and away from the cookie tampering. Coverage emphasized the Council president's outrage at the past weeks' events and their effect on the little girls of Chicago. Local newspapers not only published daily features about Girl Scout programs, but both dailies also announced their own fund drives—along with other local businesses—to help raise money from readers.

Campaign results were highly successful. Nearly ninety percent of the lost revenues were collected through the fund drive—more than twice what was expected. Chicago Girl Scouts were saved from disaster by astute public relations.

Some Advice for Others

The Girl Scouts' director of communication subsequently offered advice to other professionals who might confront a similar problem.

1. Confine the story to the locale of the incident.
2. Put the situation in perspective, for example, "For more than fifty years we've been selling quality, safe cookies."
3. Give consistent message with limited number of spokespersons (for greatest credibility).
4. Avoid comparisons. Don't give people the opportunity to link your incident with a worse one.
5. Limit statements to facts. Don't speculate. Don't guess.
6. Limit exposure. Answer all questions, but try not to do it piece by piece.
7. Hold the line. Institute levels of defense. Have a spokesperson who can quote management and truthfully say, "I don't know—I'll get back to you." If the crisis escalates, then you'll have a higher authority with more credibility to come forward.[2]

QUESTIONS FOR DISCUSSION

1. Were any ingredients in planning and crisis management missing from Corona's initial response to the problem? How would these ingredients have helped the situation?
2. How do you feel about legal counsel also being Corona's public relations counsel? What problems or opportunities do you see in such an arrangement?
3. Corona's strategy called for stemming the rumors at their source, communicating face to face with the offenders, and entering into litigation. Would it have

---

[2]Rhoda Pauley, Director of Communication, Girl Scouts of America, in *pr reporter*, November 24, 1986.

been better, in the final analysis, to deal with it at the consumer level, possibly gaining public sympathy and widespread publicity?

4. What principles of communication theory does the seven-point advice offered by the Girl Scouts' director of communications confirm? What principles does it refute?

Case 9–2

Bhopal and Valdez: Corporate Crises of Epic Proportions

In effective handling of a critical issue, preparation and anticipation are key considerations. Managing issues means intercepting the ninety percent that are self-inflicted. Critical issues may be created in any of the following manners:

- Maintaining irresponsible policies
- Failing to monitor internal activities
- Not applying sound response strategies when faced with criticism
- Failing to allocate adequate resources and priority to anticipating issues

And, of course, sometimes crises will occur even when all possible preparations have been made.

When an issue escalates, it may become a crisis. A crisis is defined as a highly stressful struggle or conflict within an adversarial environment. It is marked by a potentially damaging turning point that could result in financial or mortal disaster—after which things will never be the same.

Effective communication is an essential part of trying to control any crisis situation. It is the responsibility of the company or organization to provide information about what is happening, the effects it will have on numerous publics, and what the company plans to do to resolve the situation. The questions most asked by the publics involved are:

1. What exactly has happened?
2. Why was information about the crisis not released sooner?
3. What could have been done to prevent it from happening?

When a crisis hits, its effects are felt throughout an organization. The atmosphere is emotionally unstable and forces those involved to react quickly and sometimes without thinking of long-term ramifications, even if there is some sort of anticipatory plan in place.

The focus of this case is the analysis of two major industrial corporations and how they anticipated and managed their crises—or, you be the judge, how they failed to do so.

BHOPAL: A NIGHTMARE FOR UNION CARBIDE

In December of 1984, Union Carbide Corporation (UCC), a chemical manufacturer, was the thirty-seventh-largest industrial organization in the United States.[1] The chain of events that occurred on December 2 and 3 in Bhopal at Union Carbide India, Ltd. (UCIL), changed the face of UCC forever.

History

UCC had formed UCIL in the 1920s for manufacturing its products there. After India gained its independence from Britain in 1947, the government began to push for greater ownership in the country's businesses.

According to J. J. Kenney, the director of federal government affairs (now retired), construction of the Bhopal plant in 1977 was controlled by the regulations of the Indian government. After UCC gave the preliminary plant designs to the government, government agencies took over the final design and construction of the Bhopal facility.[2] It was the government that approved the plant design when the facility was built.

The government wanted the plant to be as labor-intensive as possible—in order to provide needed employment—so it had not installed the computer systems in use at UCC plants in the United States to monitor operations.

By the time of the Bhopal tragedy, UCC had reduced its share of ownership to 50.9 percent, while the Indian government and private citizens owned the other 49.1 percent. Plant operations were managed solely by Indians.

The Crisis Hits

At about 11:30 P.M. on December 2, a leak in one of the valves was discovered by employees at the plant. The leak was detected after a report that the eyes of some employees were tearing from irritation. At approximately 12:15 A.M. a control room

---

[1]Our thanks to Bob Berzok, Director, Corporate Communications, at Union Carbide for providing us with a wealth of information for this case.

[2]Lee W. Baker, *The Credibility Factor,* (Homewood, Ill.: Business One Irwin, 1993), 48.

operator reported an increase in tank pressure. The tank contained liquefied methyl isocyanate (MIC), a lethal pesticide. A safety valve ruptured and released excess liquid into an adjacent tank, where a caustic soda solution should have neutralized the chemical. This neutralization did not occur.

In the case of an emergency, the safety system was supposed to flash (instantaneously light and burn) any escaping gas to prevent it from entering the outside atmosphere. This system was not operating, and forty tons of deadly gas poured into the neighboring community.

Theories as to how the leak had occurred were many and widespread. One popular theory reported extensively in the newspapers was that an employee had failed to follow correct procedures and thus started the reaction that released the MIC gas. It wasn't until one and a half years later that investigators found that an employee had sabotaged the tanks by deliberately connecting a water hose to the MIC tanks (see Figure 9-2).

Death in the Community

Many residents in the area thought UCIL manufactured *kheti ki dawai*, a harmless medicine for the crops. In reality, the chemical-turned-gas was lethal to humans because it formed liquid in the lungs of its victims. While some died in their sleep, others drowned from the liquid in their lungs while running through the streets looking for help.

Official estimates stated that 1,700 residents were killed. In addition, 3,500 were hospitalized and 75,000 were treated for injuries sustained from exposure to the gas. Death figures range from anywhere between 1,700 to 4,000. It was also estimated that 60,000 people will require long-term respiratory care. These figures earned it the designation as "the worst industrial disaster ever."[3]

Many of those killed were living in shantytowns constructed illegally near the plant. UCC had repeatedly requested that these be moved from the area. Instead of requiring the people in these illegal shantytowns to move, the Indian government changed the law to make it legal for them to be so close to the plant.

UCC Policies Broken

The magnitude of disaster at the Bhopal facility was partly attributed to the many breakdowns in its safety equipment (see Figure 9-3). The plant would poorly repair or simply shut off malfunctioning equipment. Both of these actions are serious violations of UCC policy. The following inconsistencies contributed to the conditions during the emerging crisis:

- A cooling unit was shut down months before the incident. Policy stated that this unit must remain functioning to prevent overheating.

[3]Ibid, 45.

Union Carbide and Bhopal

*Setting the
Record Straight
on
Employee Sabotage
and
Efforts to
Provide Relief*

WHAT REALLY HAPPENED AT BHOPAL? Since the tragedy in December 1984, Union Carbide Corporation's primary concern has been with providing relief and assistance to the victims, and determining how the incident happened. Generally, initial details and subsequent news reports and books have contained a great deal of erroneous information. New information uncovered during an on-going investigation has led UCC to the conclusion that the tragedy was caused by employee sabotage and that there was a cover-up afterwards by certain operators on duty that night.

Figure 9–2   Union Carbide published a brochure that illustrated its hypothesis as to how the tragedy in Bhopal happened. Shown here is "Setting the Record Straight on Employee Sabotage and Efforts to Provide Relief." (Courtesy of Union Carbide.)

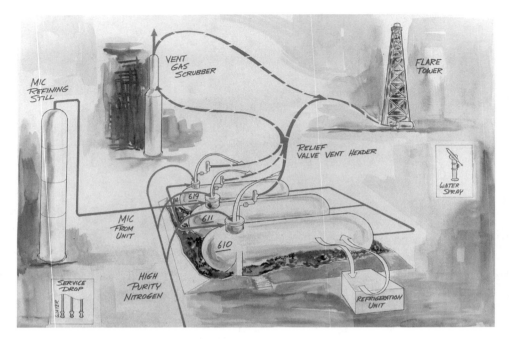

Figure 9–3   A diagram of the system setup at the UCIL plant in Bhopal. (Courtesy of Union Carbide.)

- A flare tower, designed to flash escaping gases, had been out of service for six days.
- A scrubber (an apparatus used for removing impurities from gases), which was to be continuously running, had been down for two months.
- The warning system was inadequate for the tasks that the plant was performing. There were no alarms, no employee drills, no public education, and so on.

Communications Difficulties

From the beginning, UCC encountered problems in addressing public concerns because of the physical communication difficulties it encountered.

- *In an international incident such as Bhopal, communication difficulties can be caused not only by physical boundaries but also by cultural ones.* UCC communicators in the United States from the beginning tried to be open and candid. However, UCIL officials in India were advised by legal counsel not to communicate.
- *Bhopal, a city of 750,000, had only two international telephone lines serving the city. This situation hampered any communications that were neces-*

sary. Because of this obstacle, UCC was receiving the bulk of its information from media reports.

- *The company's communication specialists who were put on this case found it extremely difficult to obtain reliable information from India.*
- *The Bhopal facility failed to educate the community.* Death could have been avoided if the citizens had been instructed to place a wet cloth over the face. Most of the deaths that occurred were the old and the young because their lungs could not withstand the poison.
- *Communications management for UCC in the United States was among last to know about the incident.* Hours after the incident, Edward Van Den Ameele, UCC press relations manager and officer on duty, received a call at 4:30 A.M. at his home from a reporter from CBS radio. The reporter was calling for a reaction to the pesticide leak. This was the first that Van Den Ameele had heard of it.
- *The plant manager of the Indian subsidiary had no background in communication, let alone crisis management.* He told a local official that "this will probably have no ill effect."

UCC Accepts Moral Responsibility

UCC did have a domestic crisis plan, but what happened in Bhopal was unimaginable for all. The initial reactions of UCC executives in the United States were humanitarian ones. Within hours of hearing the news of the chemical leak and what limited information was available, CEO Warren Anderson declared he was traveling to India to serve as the immediate supervisor of the situation and offer any assistance that the company could contribute. UCC also announced it would cease producing MIC until the cause of the explosion was known. Anderson announced that UCC would be open with the public and the media.

Unfortunately, communication was poor *in* Bhopal as well. While the Indian government had assured Anderson that he could travel safely there, when he arrived he was placed under "house" arrest for charges of "culpable homicide." In addition, he was faced with the challenge of conducting communications in an area that displayed an emotionally gripping scene.

UCC declared that it accepted moral responsibility for the tragedy. One week later, UCC offered $1 million to the Prime Minister's Relief Fund, which was accepted. Four months later it offered another $5 million in humanitarian aid to the Indian government. In this instance it was refused. UCC then offered the money to the Red Cross to disburse to those who needed it in India—and that was turned down for more than a year.

The Aftermath of Bhopal

After the Bhopal incident and the intense scrutiny and criticisms UCC received from the public and the media, the company grew cautious. Many of the company's lucrative divisions were sold off, and by 1991 the company was half the size it was before Bhopal.

UCC poured money into its safety systems and supervisory procedures, some analysts say too much, according to The *Wall Street Journal.*[4] Maintenance practices that should have taken thirty minutes began to take three or four hours to complete. Even CEO Robert D. Kennedy (replacing Anderson in 1986) concedes that the same safety levels were achieved at some of his rivals' plants, while spending a fraction of the cost incurred by UCC.

As for the legal outcome of the Bhopal tragedy, UCC settled Indian civil suits in 1989 for $470 million. The Indian courts have recommended that former CEO Anderson be extradited to India to face charges for culpable homicide. To date, the Indian government has not requested Anderson's extradition from the U.S. government.

LESSONS LEARNED FROM BHOPAL

According to Bob Berzok, director of communications at Union Carbide headquarters in Danbury, Connecticut, UCC learned four very important lessons from the Bhopal incident.[5]

1. It is important to be *open and candid* in every message prepared to deal with a situation. Attempts to shield information are immediately picked up by the public.

2. In the event of a huge crisis, *make immediate use of existing programs that are identified with the organization* and accentuate their strengths.

3. Don't forget *secondary publics.* "When you have a sudden crisis like Bhopal, two audiences people think of communicating with are press and employees. It's important to consider shareholders, government officials, and customers," advises Berzok.

4. Each crisis is different—*there is no formula for dealing with them.*

EXXON: WHEN POSITIVE ACTIONS DON'T RESULT IN POSITIVE PERCEPTIONS[6]

On March 24, 1989, the Exxon *Valdez* struck Bligh Reef in Prince William Sound, releasing 11 million gallons of crude oil (one-fifth of its cargo) into the sea.[7] This in-

---

[4]"Wounded Giant: Union Carbide Offers Some Sober Lessons in Crisis Management," *Wall Street Journal,* January 28, 1992.

[5]*pr reporter,* April 23, 1990.

[6]This section of Case 9–2 was developed from a case study authored by two University of Florida students, Fred Forlano and Greg Lorenz, under the direction of Frank Stansberry, Manager of Guest Affairs for Coca-Cola U.S.A. at Epcot Center.

[7]Lee W. Baker, *The Credibility Factor* (Homewood, Ill.: Business One Irwin, 1993): 38.

FACTORS TO CONSIDER WHEN DEVELOPING A CRISIS COMMUNICATION PLAN

- Develop a crisis communication plan in advance to handle any situation; determine exactly how key publics will be instructed of what to do in case of an emergency.

- Conduct research to discover information that is not readily available.

- Insist that all company operations be monitored regularly. A crisis that results because of operational failure without these preparations will surely cause the company to lose credibility.

cident created a crisis of epic proportions for Exxon. The mission was to clean 1,300 miles of shoreline, approximately fifteen percent of the area's 9,000 miles of shoreline, and restore the area to its original condition. In 1992, after the completion of successful and extensive clean-up efforts, a federal on-scene coordinator (the U.S. Coast Guard) declared the clean-up complete saying, "Further shoreline treatment would provide no net benefit to the environment." The State of Alaska confirmed these findings. However, the damage for Exxon did not end with the termination of clean-up efforts. What was the real problem?

Perceptions, Not Facts. Actions, Not Words.

While it was only the thirty-fourth largest oil spill at that time, it goes on record as one that people will remember the most. In one study, the Exxon *Valdez* remains one of the most remembered corporate crises.[8] Environmentalists have perceived it as limitless in damage even though there are few remaining signs of the spill. Many have characterized the accident as civilization once again trouncing on nature in order to reap the benefits of its limited resources and associate it with the deaths of many birds, otters, and other aquatic life.

In reality, the Alaskan food chain has survived (see Figure 9–4). Pink salmon harvests set records in 1990 and 1991. Tourism has rebounded strongly and so have Exxon's profits. It appears that the only thing severely damaged was the company's reputation. Those that remember it perceive a disaster that was poorly handled by Exxon.

---

[8]*pr reporter,* July 12, 1993.

Figure 9–4 Exxon published a series of reports about the aftermath of the *Valdez* oil spill and its effect on Prince William Sound and the Gulf of Alaska. Shown here is a report entitled "Three Years After" from October 1992. (Courtesy of Exxon Company, U.S.A.)

How Did These Perceptions Develop?

Today, the spill has been cleaned up and Exxon is thriving as it was previously, but the residual effects of the ordeal linger.

From the beginning, Exxon concentrated on emphasizing clean-up efforts rather than addressing the public perception that it didn't do enough, soon enough (see Figure 9-5). This emphasis was apparent from the moment that CEO Lawrence G. Rawl entered the picture. Unfavorable media comparisons were made of Rawl with the positive images of James Burke of Johnson & Johnson and his handling of the Tylenol incident (see Case 6-3). He was characterized as opposed to serving as a spokesperson, or even publicly showing interest, because he remained in New York until two days after the spill. When he finally entered the scene, he presented himself as rigid and aggressive, not bowing to the groups that opposed him or to the

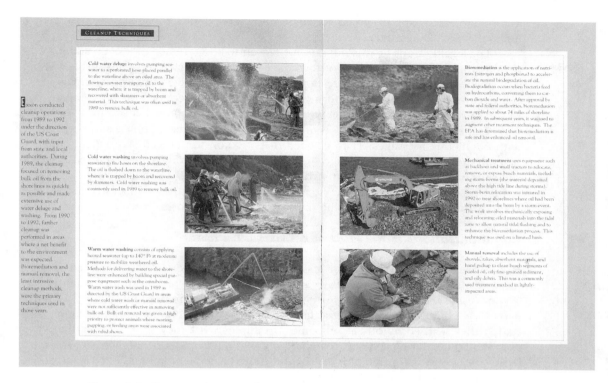

Exxon conducted cleanup operations from 1989 to 1992 under the direction of the US Coast Guard, with input from state and local authorities. During 1989, the cleanup focused on removing bulk oil from the shorelines as quickly as possible and made extensive use of water deluge and washing. From 1990 to 1992, further cleanup was performed in areas where a net benefit to the environment was expected. Bioremediation and manual removal, the least intrusive cleanup methods, were the primary techniques used in those years.

Cold water deluge involves pumping seawater to a perforated hose placed parallel to the waterline above an oiled area. The flowing seawater transports oil to the waterline, where it is trapped by boom and recovered with skimmers or absorbent material. This technique was often used in 1989 to remove bulk oil.

Cold water washing involves pumping seawater to fire hoses on the shoreline. The oil is flushed down to the waterline, where it is trapped by boom and recovered by skimmers. Cold water washing was commonly used in 1989 to remove bulk oil.

Warm water washing consists of applying heated seawater (up to 140° F) at moderate pressure to mobilize weathered oil. Methods for delivering water to the shoreline were enhanced by building special purpose equipment such as the omniboom. Warm water wash was used in 1989 as directed by the US Coast Guard in areas where cold water wash or manual removal were not sufficiently effective in removing bulk oil. Bulk oil removal was given a high priority to protect animals whose nesting, pupping, or feeding areas were associated with oiled shores.

Bioremediation is the application of nutrients (nitrogen and phosphorus) to accelerate the natural biodegradation of oil. Biodegradation occurs when bacteria feed on hydrocarbons, converting them to carbon dioxide and water. After approval by state and federal authorities, bioremediation was applied to about 74 miles of shoreline in 1989. In subsequent years, it was used to augment other treatment techniques. The EPA has determined that bioremediation is safe and has enhanced oil removal.

Mechanical treatment uses equipment such as backhoes and small tractors to relocate, remove, or expose beach materials, including storm-berms (the material deposited above the high tide line during storms). Storm-berm relocation was initiated in 1990 to treat shorelines where oil had been deposited into the berm by a storm event. The work involves mechanically exposing and relocating oiled materials into the tidal zone to allow natural tidal flushing and to enhance the bioremediation process. This technique was used on a limited basis.

Manual removal includes the use of shovels, rakes, absorbent materials, and hand pickup to clean beach segments of pooled oil, oily fine-grained sediment, and oily debris. This was a commonly used treatment method in lightly-impacted areas.

Figure 9–5 Exxon used many techniques in order to clean up the shoreline along Prince William Sound in Alaska. (Courtesy of Exxon Company, U.S.A.)

media. His inflexibility may have cost him opportunities to seek positive relationships with the various publics.[9]

When Exxon designated a location for a crisis center, the company created another situation that conflicted with its goals. It staffed the media center in Port of Valdez. Information was often slow in coming, and communication lines to Port of Valdez became jammed with information inquiries from media. It was also hard for management in New York to get information.

Another problem hampering Exxon's credibility was that it did not address how the public was perceiving the spill and its effects. It focused primarily on the *facts* concerning clean-up efforts and let *impressions* about long-term effects on the region form on their own. These facts consisted of dollar amounts, size of work force, and stories about the confusion they had to overcome to begin the process.

[9]When Rawl was asked later why he did not become more of a force in the crisis communications, Rawl replied that "his first instinct was to head to Alaska . . . but he was swayed by his colleagues' arguments that he would 'just get in the way'." From *The Credibility Factor,* 41.

The public, knee deep in "green issues," found no reassurance that Alaska's vast natural regions would recover.

For legal reasons, it was difficult for Exxon to show remorse or even admit to the environmental ramifications of the crisis. It did not realize the significance of visual images and the emotional response they evoked. Media images of animals in distress were displayed often and increased negative perceptions of the company. Exxon's credibility and reputation were being strongly questioned at this time.

Exxon's full-page apology ads on April 3, 1989, were badly timed and plagued with conflicting messages. They claimed that, "Exxon has moved swiftly and competently to minimize" the damage. In the *same* papers, front pages reported how slowly the company had been in starting the clean-up, with a specific list of unflattering reasons why. The actual "we're sorry statement" appeared in the last paragraph, vastly minimizing readership in today's sound-bite world.[10]

Communications Is the Hub of a Crisis Situation

Exxon became the scapegoat for all environmental causes. CEO Rawl served as a prime example of stereotypical negative perceptions of the corporate executive. Topics discussed in the media portrayed Exxon as being money-focused and inhuman. How could a company so vast have such poor crisis communication planning? Hadn't they learned by other companies' examples what they should do and how they should act during a crisis? Remembering that hindsight is 20/20, here are some basic communication principles that Exxon should have kept in mind before and after the *Valdez* ran aground.

- Develop a plan that will construct a positive image. Or at least try not to create a situation that will put you two steps back.
- Exxon could have spent more time emphasizing the personal commitment being made, rather than the processes involved and the $2.5 billion spent on clean-up.
- Conduct media research to discover the realities of opinions conveyed to the public. Are the messages strong, or do they have gaps that you can fill with your own information? Whose side is the media on? What are they saying to whom? Where are they getting their information, and is it accurate? In addition, conducting gap research (gap research measures the gap between reality and expectations of an audience) with publics would have been fruitful.
- Attempt to establish credibility by being honest and personable with the public. If Rawl was not an effective spokesperson, he could have been replaced with someone who had the training and experience. The faces and images the public saw on television were the ones that are associated with Exxon.

---

[10]*pr reporter*, April 17, 1989.

Much like UCC in the Bhopal case, Exxon needed to make certain that all information was accurate, consistent, and complete. Cases like this illustrate why candor is the best policy. Reveal what is being done and why. Convey what is known and when it became known. Don't let the media find out for themselves. Exxon did not follow these basic guidelines when clean-up efforts halted for the winter in September of 1989. Rather than telling the public that because of weather limitations, clean-up would prove fruitless, Exxon simply discontinued efforts for the season. Clean-up continued until the federal on-scene coordinator and state declared it complete in 1992, but the public did not completely understand the clean-up process. They needed someone to explain it to them, and *it could have been Exxon.*

When it comes to the source of communication, make certain that the spokesperson is qualified, with proper crisis communication training. Shooting from the hip should be avoided, and a clear message should be sent at all times. Providing the image of sympathy and remorse, complemented with sincerity, may have saved Exxon's reputation and, in turn, made the future seem brighter for all the parties involved.

A plan that defines all necessary contacts and a proposed sequence of events could have been developed. A spill of any variety would involve the media, state and local governments, environmental groups, and internal and external publics. The support of employees is crucial. At a time when it is difficult to reach the spokesperson, the media often will create its own in a security guard or a technician.

The clean-up effort was not effectively coordinated with the efforts of all groups involved. No one knew what each group should do or when. Observers felt that both of these aspects should have been considered and put into the crisis plan as well. Even if a plan was not in place, as soon as the smoke cleared Exxon could have been initiating the coordination of communications and development of a strategy and plan with all pertinent groups.

A better understanding of how the media works in relation to delivering a prescribed message to different publics would also have been beneficial. As mentioned earlier, the public can and will sympathize with helpless animals. A good portion of media attention was given to oil-covered birds vividly depicted on television and in magazines. Even journalists said at the time that it would have been more sensible for Exxon to divert this attention by devising *proactive* programs the media could focus on. Since hard news sells, a program of hard-hitting environmental programs and principles could have been implemented. This strategy could have made the media a channel for communicating to the public that Exxon was aware of and cares about the environment and its inhabitants.

LESSONS LEARNED

Issue anticipation is the key to averting many crises. Some top management advisers insist that positive leadership is the only way to develop positive relationships. They believe that to think negatively would not be consistent with their goals or beneficial to the company. Exxon and UCC learned that even very large companies have malleable reputations that can change in an instant.

As indicated earlier, the principle that ninety percent of all crises are self-inflicted seems evident in these two cases. After receiving reports from the Bhopal facility that everything was in order, UCC could have conducted regular inspections to confirm the statements presented. Simply relying on reports received from the plant obviously was not enough. If those inspections had been done, the company may have avoided the serious magnitude of the incident, prevented some of the deaths and injuries, saved legal fees and fines, and maintained a positive reputation. A proactive plan focusing on safety measures and policies covering topics such as community relations, internal responsibility, and inspection requirements could have saved UCC from its own near demise and lost reputation. The public relations staff therefore has a stake and a role in monitoring operations.

Exxon also was forced to realize that perceptions control reputation. In relation to other oil companies, Exxon's clean-up and spill control plan was reportedly top-of-the-line. However, by communicating specifics about the clean-up process, rather than the effects the spill would have on the environment, the company was not addressing the issues of concern. Displaying emotion and remorse for the outcome could have created a positive image of Exxon in the public's eye.

The hard lesson learned by both is that *anticipation,* while it may not prevent a crisis, certainly makes the road a little less bumpy. Ignoring possible situations that may occur, be they positive or negative, can lead to reputation and relationship disruptions that continue for years. An organization must be forward-thinking in order to survive in our volatile world.

QUESTIONS FOR DISCUSSION

1. As indicated from the Bhopal disaster, Union Carbide India, Ltd., did nothing to prepare the community for any potential hazard that could have and did occur. What are some proactive actions or programs that UCC could have implemented in order to avoid the fatal tragedy that occurred? What is the public relations role in them, if any?

2. As evidenced by the Exxon case, perceptions speak louder than the actual facts. Can you think of anything more that Exxon could have done to avoid this public relations disaster and salvage its soiled reputation? Can you think of any proactive measures Exxon should take now to repair battered relationships with publics still disgruntled with the company?

3. Exxon received a blow to its reputation from the *Valdez* oil spill, but is profits really weren't hurt. Does its financial muscle and lack of real competition in the oil market move it beyond control of the Court of Public Opinion? Why do you think this?

4. Compare Bhopal with Responsible Care (Case 4–2). What part do you think the differing cultures and governments in the United States and India played in the Bhopal tragedy?

5. From all appearances, it seems that UCC was innocent of any direct causes of the Bhopal tragedy. Yet the company was all but destroyed by it. Did public opinion actually cause this near destruction? Might it have been caused by company overreaction or feelings of guilt? If not these, then what were the causes?

Building Grassroots Support to Avoid Bankruptcy

The difficulties of nuclear power, opposition groups, cost overruns, construction problems, charges of fiscal mismanagement, and litigation: That was the scenario facing Consumers Power Company (Jackson, Michigan). It was on the brink of bankruptcy and in a swirl of controversy. Management had to make tough decisions—and fast.

BACKGROUND

In 1967, Consumers Power announced plans to begin construction of the Midland nuclear power plant, designed to provide both electricity and to process steam to a nearby Dow Chemical Company plant. After almost two decades or problems, Consumers Power (CP) canceled the plant. CP and Dow fought each other over who was at fault and for how much.

The plant was a drain on CP: It reported a net loss of $270 million in 1985. Budgets were cut; employees were laid off; stock sold at one-fifth its book value; and dividends weren't paid on common stock. The Midland plant represented forty-five percent of the company's assets.

VIEWS OF THE CEO

Chairman William McCormick said:

> When I accepted the CEO position at Consumers Power, I found that the company had many major attributes which should have prevented it from approaching the brink of bankruptcy. Its operations were sound. Its employees were skilled. Its markets were

good. The company had the finest safety record in the industry. It stood number two in fossil plant efficiency. It had the fewest number of employees per customer of any major utility that produces its own power.

For a number of years, the company had been ineffective in telling the story of its importance to Michigan and the state's future economic growth. Nor had it been successful in building media, political, and business community support for its needs.

In both areas, the company had the capability and the professional resources to do the communications job, but its management—embroiled in a nuclear construction program—had been totally occupied on the brick and mortar objective of completing Midland. There was little time for anything else.

There was a need for substantive change in the way the company was run. It needed to be synchronized with the environment in which it operated. We would need to enter the real world of public policy and exercise our rights to communicate and influence its development if Consumers Power was to survive. It would be a new experience for many.[1]

THE PROBLEM

Consumers Power saw two basic problems:

1. The need to resolve the Midland crisis and the technical issues surrounding it.
2. Communications. The company had to make its case with key publics throughout Michigan.

OPTIONS STUDY

The company undertook an options study to examine alternatives for the Midland plant. Among the options available were:

- Abandon Midland and purchase power outside Michigan.
- Convert to a coal-fired plant.
- Complete Midland as a nuclear plant.
- Convert to a natural gas combined-cycle plant.

The options researched became the benchmark for the overall communications strategy. Among the findings:

1. Although the company was viewed negatively, employees were highly regarded. When it came to reliability and good service, the company consistently received high ratings.

---

[1]American Gas Association, *AGA Monthly*, (August 1987): 14–17.

2. A work force spread throughout Michigan offered a tremendous resource to reach publics at all levels.

THE SOLUTION

In January 1987, CP and Dow announced a new partnership to convert a portion of the Midland plant to a natural gas–fueled, combined-cycle cogeneration facility (*Cogeneration* refers to the production of two different forms of energy—electricity and steam—from the same fuel.) (See Figure 9-6.)

Figure 9–6   Brochure explaining the Cogeneration Venture featured close-up of interior and, on the back, the identities of the partners. (Courtesy of Consumers Power.)

GETTING SUPPORT

CP relied on its employees to build grassroots support for the conversion proposal. They were encouraged to make one-on-one contact with friends, neighbors, local government, and business leaders. But the company had an obstacle to overcome: raising employees' low morale. The approach selected was to (1) reach, (2) inform, (3) motivate, and (4) support them in their grassroots efforts.

To kick off the program, CP prepared a twenty-minute videotape, presented to all 10,000 employees at seven regional meetings. It unveiled the tools available and the objectives. The presentation attempted to get across these points:

1. Here's our problem and what we're trying to do about it.
2. Here are the messages we think are important to convey.
3. Here are the tools we've developed to do the job.
4. Here's how you can help.

EMPLOYEE COMMUNICATION SURVEY

An employee communication survey measured the effectiveness of existing communications and determined how well-informed the employees were about the campaign. It also provided a baseline for follow-up research.

Simultaneously, CP established a new communications department, combining government and public affairs. The company also prepared and put into effect its plan, whose goals were:

1. Prepare the public to be receptive to whichever option was ultimately proposed.
2. Build support for the recommended option.

In addition to employees, a *team of twelve upper-level executives targeted leaders at the state level*—the governor, leading businesspersons, creditors, vendors, civic leaders, large customers, and editorial boards.

COMMUNICATION TOOLS

To highlight their contributions to Michigan's economy, CP chose "Powering Michigan's Progress" as the unifying theme for the grassroots campaign. Among other communications tools used were:

1. *Chairman's Briefing Book* for top executives. It focused on CP's contribution and importance to the state's economy and on problems that might arise from a forecast shortage of generating power.

2. *"Slim Jim"*, a condensed version of the briefing book. This was distributed to all 10,000 employees. It contained the same arguments in simpler terms and provided tips on helping employees structure their presentations to business, civic, and labor leaders.

3. *Employee communications vehicles were reduced to two new formats,* each with ongoing updates on the campaign: *Progress,* a monthly magazine mailed to workers' homes, thus reaching the whole family, and *CPWeekly,* a newspaper distributed at work (see Figure 9–7).

4. The new *slogan,* "Powering Michigan's Progress," was permanently added to the company logo. In addition, it was placed on stationery, trucks, and buildings to serve as a constant reminder of CP's mission in the state.

5. *Aggressive approach with the media,* through editorial board meetings and constant updates, kept the issue in the forefront of state news.

"We could not have implemented this campaign without all the willing arms, legs, and voices of our employees. When you have 10,000 employees spreading the good word, it is an extremely powerful force. Any political candidate would give his right arm for just half of that support," said Rick Matteson, director of publications and executive communications, when we interviewed him for this case. "The most effective aspect of the program was our 'hat in hand' approach. Over the course of twenty years, we had reached a defensive 'circle-the-wagons attitude' which had managed to antagonize virtually everyone. The turning point in public opinion came when they realized we had changed—had become more open and really tried to build a relationship."

OUTCOMES

1. *Public approval was eventually won for the natural gas alternative.* The campaign was spurred by more than 500 resolutions of support from key groups throughout the state and by 250 editorials urging the public not to prejudge the options study. John Clark, senior vice-president of communications, reported, when we interviewed him:

Utility companies are positioned better than most other kinds of private businesses to have substantial political impact through the judicious use of their workforce in the field. It was the depth of public support and the involvement of employees at all levels—from the CEO and senior officers to our district people throughout the state of Michigan—that most impressed the state's political leaders and enabled us to go forward.

2. *Financial recovery.* Standard & Poor's raised its rating of the company's mortgage bonds to investment grade. Common stock had the highest increase in

Figure 9–7 Employee communications included *Progress,* a monthly magazine mailed to homes for family reading, *CPWeekly,* a tabloid distributed at work, and a briefing book for all 10,000 employees (shown here is the *"Slim Jim"* condensed version). (Courtesy of Consumers Power.)

value among utilities listed on the New York Stock Exchange for 1986, and the seventeenth highest increase in value overall.

3. *Improved employee morale and communications.* Clark concluded that:

> We showed employees you can be successful in dealing with controversial subjects even with a skeptical customer base. The challenge now is to maintain the momentum. We have created high expectations. They now expect to hear regularly from management and to be meaningfully involved in the company's efforts to stay ahead of the game. We are finding that we have to scramble to meet this need, but *it's a nice problem to have.*

CONSUMERS POWER TODAY

Unfortunately for Consumers Power, financial troubles have created communication problems with constituents. In 1991, trying to recoup losses form the failed Midland Plant, Consumers Power attempted to raise electric rates by eleven percent to cover the $2.1 billion the company had lost. The Michigan Public Service Commission ruled that Consumers could not raise its electric rates and instead must lower them by 2.3 percent. In response to this rate case ruling, CP cut 500 white-collar jobs. In addition, the state regulators ordered CP to cut its electric rates another $28.1 million a year because the utility would not commit to spending more to improve service.

One interesting line of study would be to examine how Consumers Power's management handles its relations with the Public Service Commission and the rest of its constituents in the future.

QUESTIONS FOR DISCUSSION

1. Employees now expect to hear regularly from management and to be meaningfully involved in decision making. How can management sustain this commitment?

2. In what ways can Consumers Power maintain—and strengthen—the grassroots support it earned in this campaign when other issues or crises face the company?

3. Although, as pointed out in Chapter 1, public relations projects might variously seek change by motivating new behavior, reinforcing existing positive behavior, or modifying negative behavior, this project seeks to do all three at the same time. What other public relations projects can you think of that also try to do all three things?

4. What do you think happened in recent times to CP's philosophy of grassroots support?

Established Relationships
Save a Landmark Company

Of all the crises that can strike an organization, probably none is as threatening as a hostile takeover attempt. Sometimes one company wants to acquire a competitor or a firm that will add new markets or products. Often the raider has neither the intention nor the capability of operating the company. The objective is to obtain its asset value by selling off the company in pieces. In most takeovers, some dismembering, layoffs, or budget cutting must be done in order for the raider to pay off debt incurred to purchase the target company.

The final decision whether to allow a takeover rests with the stockholders. In an earlier time, they were largely individuals whose purpose in investing was to earn dividends and hope the stock would appreciate in value so they could sell it at a gain for their retirement. Such "little investors" in our era have been replaced by giant investment funds managed by shrewd professionals with sophisticated computer programs to guide their decisions. They work for mutual funds, pension funds, and other large-volume investors with billions of dollars that they must "keep working" for the benefit of their shareholders or members.

Under pressure to "grow" a pension fund's assets as large as possible, so that it will be able to meet commitments to retirees, investment managers "play the market," searing for maximum profits while guarding against any possible loss. As a result, their decisions can be ruthless. The slightest downturn in a company's fortunes may cause some investment managers to quickly sell large blocks of its stock.

On the other hand, when it appears that a stock may rise, they will buy large amounts and do what they can to keep the stock price going up. In recent times, one of the best ways to make a "killing" has been to accumulate the stock of a company targeted for takeover. Invariably, the price of acquiring the company is at a high premium over the normal trading value or actual worth of its stock. Price per share may rise fifty percent or even more during the bidding battle among rivals vying to take over the company, as each makes a tender offer to the stockholders at increasingly higher prices. It is really an auction, with each stockholder free to sell shares to the bidder of choice.

Faced with an unfriendly takeover, management and the board of directors must first decide whether it is in the present shareholders' best interests to sell. The best management teams and directors will also take into account the effect on stakeholders as well as stockholders, including employees and the community. If the raider is after asset value, planning to break up the company, they may conclude that operating the company will give better long-term value to shareholders, while selling it off piecemeal provides merely a one-time gain.

Then management must devise a defense to thwart the raider. By and large, such defenses are the *product of public relations*. In some cases, this means trying to convince the stockholders not to sell their shares to the raiders. In the case that follows, it meant persuading state legislators to pass new laws that make it difficult for raiders to accomplish their aims.

A PREMIER COMPANY

Dayton Hudson Corporation (DHC), headquartered in Minneapolis, *is one of the five largest retailers in America, with sales of over $18 billion annually.* It is also one of those rare companies that, almost from its inception, has been an innovator and leader. This is how James Shannon described DHC in the Minneapolis *Star and Tribune* at the time of its takeover troubles:

> In the 1880's and early 1890's, George Draper Dayton was a banker in Worthington, Minn. In that capacity he began to buy real estate in Minneapolis. In 1895 the original Westminster Presbyterian Church at the corner of 7th and Nicollet in Minneapolis burned to the ground. Because of the economic panic of 1893, the vacant lot (really an empty hole) at that site went unsold for more than a year. At the urging of his Minneapolis business conferees, Dayton in 1895 bought the land and constructed the store that today is the keystone of the Dayton Hudson retail chain.
>
> Known originally as the Dayton Co., and privately owned by the family of George Draper Dayton, the company went public in 1967. Now known as the Dayton Hudson Corp., its 1986 sales exceeded $9 billion. By 1993 Dayton Hudson Corporation had expanded to 33 states and operated 892 stores, including Target, Mervyn's, Dayton Hudson, Lechmere, and Marshall Field's, the famous Chicago-based department stores. It has 34,000 employees in Minnesota.
>
> Ever since the company was privately owned by the Dayton family it has given five percent of its annual pretax profits to worthy causes in communities where it has a significant presence. In 1986 it contributed $20,718,500 to the arts and to social-service programs nationwide, half of them in Minnesota.
>
> In a community nationally known for its corporate support of the arts, social services, and education, the Dayton Hudson Corp. is the flagship for dozens of other pub-

licly and privately held corporations committed to the proposition that a successful company has an obligation to be a good corporate citizen. In 1984 the University of California School of Business Administration named Dayton Hudson "the best managed company in America." As the first recipient of the Vanguard Award (for corporate social responsibility), Dayton Hudson was cited for its "unusual dynamism . . . entrepreneurial zeal . . . and its uncompromising ethical standards."

The company's 1983 Management Perspectives program, a participatory activity that attempted to identify and pass along for future use its corporate culture and values, determined that DHC's goal was to "be premier in all we do."

THE RAID BEGINS SUSPENSEFULLY

In mid-June 1987, after several weeks of unusually heavy trading in its stock, Dayton Hudson learned that it was the target of an unfriendly takeover. But who was the raider? Writers in the *Wall Street Journal* and other media speculated it was this one, then that one—but the company didn't know for sure. Rumors of a takeover attempt—and the escalating stock price that inevitably accompanies it—resulted in an extremely dangerous situation: Within a three-week period, nearly thirty percent of DHC's stock changed hands, making the situation so fluid that someone could have taken control of the company at any time.

As a company statement put it issued via press release, "That means thirty percent of our stock is owned by people who have had it less than fifteen days. They could care less about our customers, our employees or our communities. We have every reason to believe those shares moved from stable institutional investors to speculators, short-term investors and what are called arbitrageurs [a person working in a brokerage firm who trades in stock on speculation]."

Under Securities and Exchange Commission (SEC) regulations, whenever a stockholder accumulates five percent of any company's stock, it must report the fact. However, through various tactics, the purchaser may take as long as a year before making the report. Realizing the danger, management began taking steps to defend the company. In addition to usual activities, such as having investor relations staff scrutinize activity in the stock and media relations staff monitor news coverage, special steps were taken:

- CEO Kenneth Macke sent a memo to all corporate staff warning them not to speculate or comment on the situation, since that could fuel rumors (and the stock price); he also reminded them that the official spokesperson for the corporation was its vice-president of public relations (VP-PR), Ann Barkelew.
- A task force was assembled to study what others had done in such situations, investigate all available data about the most likely raiders, and review new laws passed by some states to deal with hostile takeovers; included were rep-

resentatives from public relations, investor relations, public affairs, law, and outside consulting firms.

- On the morning of June 17, 1987, Macke set a meeting of the crisis team for 2:00 P.M. Its members were himself as CEO, the president and COO (Chief Operating Officer), the CFO (Chief Financial Officer), the general counsel, and the VP-PR. The objective was to determine action and timing "assuming I receive the five percent letter" today. Specific agenda items included: What actions are required? What actions are recommended? Will we have a press release and, if so, what will it say? Who will notify all concerned parties?

As speculation about a takeover and a possible raider swirled around the company, Barkelew fell back on established policy to handle the hundreds of media, stock market, and other inquiries. She reported to Macke: "I continue to stand on our corporate policy of no comments on rumors or speculation of this nature . . . and, except for the rumors, we know of no reason for the fluctuations in our stock price or trading volume."

SEVEN DAYS IN JUNE

The task force established the objective: "To build support for a special legislative session to enact tougher anti-takeover laws that would provide greater protection for all Minnesota-incorporated public companies." June 18, the day after the action and timing meeting, Macke requested and got a meeting with Governor Rudy Perpich. He briefed the governor at three o'clock on the situation—using a script and briefing paper prepared by public relations—and asked him to call a special legislative session to pass the new law.

Considering that the regular session of the legislature had ended only recently, and that special sessions are costly and unpopular, this was a bold move. It meant that the governor and legislative leaders had to be completely convinced of the severity of DHC's situation—and of the possibility that it could happen to other Minnesota concerns. This, in turn, meant that public relations and allied departments had to generate massive amounts of materials in an exceedingly short period.

When Macke went to meet Perpich, much of this material was already in his hands, thanks to late night and weekend work by public relations staff and its consulting firms.

At eight o'clock that evening, Governor Perpich met with legislative leaders to rally support for the special session. He told the press afterward, "We will not act hastily but we will not hesitate to act to protect a good Minnesota company that provides about 34,000 jobs to Minnesotans." The news conference was held at 10:30 P.M., prompted, reported the *Star and Tribune* by leaks about an imminent takeover bid.

The next day, June 19, the raider communicated its intention to seek control of DHC. This action prompted two events: (1) June 20 news reports spread the fact widely and gave emphasis to another fact, that the suitor, Dart Group Corp. of Landover, Maryland, "had already attempted hostile takeovers of six other retailing firms," as the *St. Paul Pioneer Press* reported. (2) The company launched an intensive effort to win the public, other corporations, and legislators to its side. That day alone these events were staged:

- Macke met with editors in the morning, then appeared on a public affairs television show in the evening.
- In the afternoon he met with business and community leaders at DHC headquarters.
- A letter to the company's 34,000 employees in the state, over Macke's signature, asked for their active help "to support our state legislators in enacting tougher anti-takeover laws that will provide us and other Minnesota companies protection from stock market raids and other abusive tactics."
- Dayton Hudson Foundation called 200 community and arts organization leaders to a meeting at the Children's Theatre, where audience members urged the crowd to write or call their legislators and the governor, in order to protect the $9 million the company provided through its foundation that year to nonprofit groups in Minnesota.
- General Mills, Honeywell, and other prominent companies headquartered in the state issued supporting statements to the legislature and the media, as did the Minnesota Business Partnership, comprising chief executives of seventy-five of the state's largest companies.
- Backgrounders, question-and-answer pieces, in-depth discussions of the pros and cons of the legislation, data on Dart (including an unflattering *Fortune* article depicting it as a predatory outfit whose operating practices took advantage of suppliers and customers), and other material was widely distributed. The material brought forth substantial editorial support from state media in the days following.

Meanwhile, standby advertisements were prepared, ready to run if public opinion shifted against the special session. One pictured Dayton's Department Store's Christmas teddy bear, used for several years as a holiday premium and known as Santabear, with the caption "Who'll get custody?" A shopping bag stuffer was entitled, "A special session to keep Minnesota a special place." Even a glossary of terms used in takeovers was developed, explaining words and phrases such as *arbitrageur, white knight,* and similar jargon.

Survey research was undertaken both as a planning guide and, when results proved favorable, as a lobbying tool. Telephone interviews were conducted over the weekend in order to have information available when the decision about calling a special session was being made (see Figure 9–8).

Minnesota Resident Attitudes Toward a Special Session of the Legislature That Would Consider Changing Minnesota Law to Make Hostile Takeovers More Difficult

Question: "The Governor has announced that he may call a one day special session of the legislature that would consider changing Minnesota law to make hostile takeovers of Minnesota companies more difficult. Which of the following statements best describes your feelings toward a special session to change the Minnesota law?"

	All Residents	Sex		Place of Residence		Political Affiliation		
		Male	Female	Seven County Metro	Out-of-state	Demo-crat	Repub-lican	Inde-pendent
I'm in favor of changing the law to protect Dayton Hudson from a hostile takeover	7%	6%	7%	6%	8%	6%	6%	6%
I'm in favor of changing the law to make hostile takeovers more difficult as long as the law applies to all Minnesota corporations, not just Dayton Hudson.	78	76	81	82	72	85	77	79
I'm not in favor of a special session to consider changing the law.	12	15	9	10	15	6	15	12
Don't know	3	3	3	2	5	3	2	3
TOTAL	100%	100%	100%	100%	100%	100%	100%	100%
Number of Respondents	(772)	(384)	(388)	(515)	(257)	(222)	(158)	(346)

Figure 9–8   The results from the telephone interviews. (Courtesy of Dayton Hudson Corporation.)

THE PEOPLE AND THEIR ELECTED OFFICIALS DECIDE

As the week of June 22 began, DHC representatives visited cities and towns across the state seeking support. An employee rally was held. And massive media coverage continued. On Tuesday, key legislative committees met to hear testimony, including Macke's (see Figure 9-9). It appeared that sentiment was favorable toward the anti-takeover law and the special session necessary to enact it. But for quick action, enough votes must be available to suspend the rules—rarely an easy proposition. Some committee members were not convinced, feeling that too much protection of current management could be as harmful in some cases as unfriendly takeovers.

As Governor Perpich considered whether to call the session, a freak occurrence brought yet more attention to Dayton Hudson's stock. A Cincinnati investment manager and member of a prominent family made a bid for DHC shares at a higher price than Dart was offering. After frantic trading, plus efforts to identify the validity of the offer, the New York Stock Exchange halted trading in DHC shares for

Figure 9–9 Dayton Hudson Corp. leader Kenneth Macke, left, addresses special legislative hearing. Next to him is Representative Wayne Simoneau. (Courtesy of St. Paul Pioneer Press & Dispatch, Mark Morson, photographer.)

two hours. In the end, the bid turned out to be bogus—another public relations challenge management had to contend with, and at the worst possible time.

Wednesday night, the governor called a one-day special session for the next day. He had insisted that House and Senate leaders reach agreement. After the usual compromises and political posturing, plus adding some features of their own to the bill, they told Perpich they were read to go into session.

When the vote came on Thursday, June 25, the House passed it 120 to 5, the Senate 57 to 0. The governor signed it into law that evening. The *Pioneer Press* lead next morning told the story:

> The prospect of a department store chain rallying a state government to save it from a corporate raider, doing it all over seven days in June and with barely a whisper of opposition, would probably be seen as long odds by folks from other states.
>
> Dayton Hudson Corp. accomplished that in Minnesota Thursday with stunning swiftness by cashing in on customer goodwill built up over decades, the clout of 34,000 employees, a small army of top state lobbyists and the assistance of groups that have received millions of dollars in contributions.
>
> By any yardstick it was a boggling show of clout.

Thus ended one of the swiftest crisis responses ever witnessed. In spite of (or perhaps because of) the severity of the case, within a seven-day period Dayton Hudson was able to plan, execute, and succeed in a hostile takeover defense—thus becoming the only major takeover target to escape unscathed until that time. But the work wasn't over for public relations staff.

SAYING THANK YOU

Illustrating the attitude that built positive public relationships for the company over many years and enabled it to orchestrate such a rapid response to crisis, DHC put as much creativity and energy into expressing appreciation to its supporter as it had into the campaign. Some highlights:

- Life-size Santabears, wearing "There's no place like home. Thanks Minnesota" sandwich boards, greeted downtown visitors (see Figure 9–10).
- Employees signed a giant "Thanks Minnesota" banner, which was then placed in Minneapolis' major downtown center for others to add their names, before being sent to the governor (see Figure 9–10).
- "Thanks Minnesota" buttons were worn by employees, after Macke appeared at an employee ice cream social and thank-you party wearing one.
- All employees received a letter from the chairman thanking them, urging them to pass their appreciation along to public officials and customers, then noting that only by redoubling efforts to make the company even better would they be truly free of raiders.
- Ads were placed, as well as publicity, and personal thank- you letters from Macke went to legislators.
- The next issue of the company's internal newsletter, *Courier*, reprinted Macke's remarks at the ice cream social, in which—by name—he thanked each headquarters employee who had taken part in the effort.

The takeover case generated 3,600 inches of newspaper coverage. *Corporate Exposure* newsletter, which tracks media coverage of companies, found Dayton Hudson in first place for the period—but also reported that the dominant tone of reportage was favorable to DHC.

After the legislation was passed, Dart Group quietly sold its holdings in Dayton Hudson.

Figure 9–10 Santabears greet visitors to the IDS Center's Crystal Court at lunchtime with a message encouraging them to sign a huge thank-you banner to Minnesota from Dayton Hudson Corp. The Minneapolis Star and Tribune recorded the public response. (News photo by Tom Sweeney, Staff Photographer.)

DHC FACES ANOTHER CRISIS

In 1991, DHC faced a new obstacle. A small group of employees at one of its Detroit-area stores voted to unionize, soliciting the United Auto Workers Union, since there was no union for retail employees. DHC contested the employees' vote to unionize and thus began the battle between the UAW and DHC. The UAW claimed DHC was antiunion. To protest the organization's refusal to unionize, the UAW organized a boycott and picketing of seventeen DHC retail stores. It was set for the three biggest shopping days of the year, the three days after Thanksgiving.

Media coverage of the planned boycott was extensive. The UAW ran ads in many local newspapers entreating the public to shop "Anyplace But Hudson's." Yet, most all of the articles portrayed the company in a positive light, as willing to work with its employees, but not through the UAW. The UAW was portrayed as extreme in some newspaper articles. Often there were quotes from employees who had supported the union at the beginning and now just wanted the UAW to leave them alone. The UAW was portrayed as bullying and out to accomplish its own agenda, instead of looking after the needs of the DHC employees.

Dealing with the Boycott

Some measures that DHC public relations staff took to effectively combat the UAW boycott:

- Company spokespeople emphasized the negative effect a successful boycott would have on the employees, the very people the UAW were trying to represent.
- Supervisors and employees were positioned at the front door, apologizing to customers for the inconvenience, offering to throw away materials UAW protesters were distributing, and offering free refreshments to shoppers.
- Along with their usual holiday sales, DHC mailed out extra savings coupons to its charge card customers.
- Managers were prepared for inquiries from the media with a list of answers to questions that might be asked.

DHC officials were often the first quoted in response to the updates on the situation, giving an air of authority to what the company said. In addition, there were specific spokespersons who responded to media inquiries. DHC spoke with One Clear Voice before and after the boycott. This combination of public relations actions helped the stores to have their most profitable Christmas season every despite the boycott.

QUESTIONS FOR DISCUSSION

1. In its various subsidiaries that operate stores across the country, Dayton Hudson has 168,000 employees. Why was it important to keep them informed of the Minnesota legislative effort? How would you have done it?

2. Dart Group Corporation had been the subject of unflattering news reports about its operations and reputation. Generally, the raider was depicted as profit-hungry and a haggler with its suppliers. How might this depiction have affected various publics in the DHC takeover attempt. How might it have affected other DHC stockholders? Legislators? Editors and reporters? Employees? Management? Communities in which the company operates? What motivations in each group would Dart's reputation have stimulated?

3. The new Minnesota law allowed corporate managements to take the effect on stakeholders as well as stockholders into account when deciding whether to accept a takeover bid. Without this provision, managements are apt to consider only whether the deal is good for shareholders. Is it fair and sound social policy for employees, customers, communities, local governments, and other stakeholders to be considered when they have purchased no stock? What investment do they have? Why should they be considered?

4. What influence on the case, if any, do you think the bogus offer had? Did it make matters worse for DHC or better?

Whose Rights
Are They?

Since the 1970s, the rights of animals in the field of medical testing and experiments has gathered momentum as an issue of passionate debate. Scientists use animals in areas such as compulsory laboratory tests of new drugs, organ implant experiments, experimental treatments for "incurable" diseases, battle injuries, and attempts to unravel the mystery of intelligence. Many animal lovers have jumped up on the speaker's box and cried "foul."

Those in favor of animal testing argue for its benefit to medical science and the human race. Sacrifices of animals are made in order to better human existence. The information gained from these experiments far outweighs the price these animals have to pay. Their view is supported by evidence that animal experimentation takes place under regulated conditions that safeguards them from unnecessary pain.

On the other side are those who feel that deliberately causing pain to any animal is not acceptable. They believe that other methods can be found to test drugs and that it is morally wrong to cause suffering to animals for human gain. To an animal rights activist both humans and animals have rights that require universal respect. They feel that taking animals out of their natural habitats is yet another example of how the human race imposes its power on the weaker wildlife of the world. They believe it is up to them to take responsibility for the well-being of these animals and to free them from the bonds of captivity and experimentation.[1]

Animal activism covers a wide range of attitudes and beliefs. Many who are in-

---

[1]For a more in-depth look into the philosophical issues of animal rights, we recommend these books: Fraser, Laura, et al. *The Animal Rights Handbook.* Los Angeles, Calif.: Living Planet Press, 1990. Singer, Peter. *Animal Liberation.* New York City: Random House, 1990. Regan, Tom. *The Case for Animal Rights.* University of CA Press, 1983. "The Animal's Agenda." A publication dealing with animal rights issues. To receive this publication write to, *The Animal's Agenda,* P.O. Box 6809, Syracuse, N.Y. 13217.

volved have differing degrees of commitment to the cause. Some may eat free-range meat or eggs, but be opposed to wearing fur; many are vegetarians; others are against raising domestic animals for any reason at all. For a small number, these beliefs are expressed in extreme acts. Those involved in the more moderate factions are beginning to question whether extreme tactics are effective in obtaining support for animal rights or just zealous acts of terrorism. Like many "cause" groups, animal rights groups are engaged in intense internal debate.

Animal activists' attacks have most often occurred at research facilities at universities across the country. If the activist attack is successful in garnering public support and sympathy it can bring large amounts of negative media attention to

---

Moderate animal rights activists have achieved many gains legislatively in the past few years. Some success stories:

- More than 100 countries have signed the Convention on International Trade in Endangered Species of Wild Fauna and Flora (CITES), a treaty that protects endangered species and outlaws their national trade. In 1989, CITES placed the elephant on the list of endangered species and approved a ban on the international trade in ivory.
- Because of a consumer boycott led by environmental and humane groups, the world's major tuna processors announced in March 1990 that they would refuse to purchase any tuna caught in purse seine nets, which are responsible for the deaths of millions of dolphins.
- In 1988, it became illegal for any ship to dump its plastic trash in U.S. oceans or navigable waters, where they may cause harm to fish and aquatic mammals.

- Because of the efforts of environmentalists, eleven states have passed laws requiring plastic six-pack carriers to be made with new degradable plastics, so that if they are thrown away or lost they will not pollute our oceans or damage the creatures living there.
- Animal activists have helped close off the markets for seals. The Canadian government announced a total ban on the commercial killing of whitecoat and blueblack seals, and the European Community banned the import of baby seal skins permanently.
- The wolf, once near extinction, is on the rebound because of environmental efforts. Recovery and reintroduction efforts are under way in the Rocky Mountains, the Southwest, and the northern Midwest.
- In response to worldwide citizen protests, virtually every country is now observing a moratorium on whale hunting.[2]

---

[2]Taken from *The Animal Rights Handbook* (Los Angeles, Calif.: Living Planet Press, 1990), 85.

Many animals rights groups have sought to change attitudes toward animals' place on the planet. As an example, they have created a "bill of rights" for animals adopted by 30,000 participants in a March for the Animals in Washington on June 10, 1990.

DECLARATION OF THE RIGHTS OF ANIMALS[3]

Whereas it is self-evident

That we share the earth with other creatures, great and small

That many of these animals experience pleasure and pain

That these animals deserve our just treatment and

That these animals are unable to speak for themselves

**We do therefore declare
that these animals**

Have the right to live free from human exploitation, whether in the name of science or sport, exhibition or service, food or fashion

Have the right to live in harmony with their nature rather than according to human desires

Have the right to live on a healthy planet

these institutions. How they deal with the crisis as it occurs makes the difference in the public's perception of an animal rights cause.

OSU AND ANIMAL RESEARCH

Oregon State University (OSU) uses animals in its biomedical, agricultural, and veterinary research departments and for student education. Both fundamental and applied studies are conducted on human, plant, and animal disease problems, nutrition and animal reproduction, and a variety of other topics.

More than 125 principal investigators at OSU conduct research programs that involve some use of animals, and at least eighty-five scientists are conducting biomedical and animal research under the centralized supervision of OSU Laboratory Animal Resources. In fiscal year 1988–89, OSU attracted $97.5 million in research funding, of which a small portion was used for research involving animals.

Excluding fish and large animals, OSU uses more than 190,000 laboratory ani-

[3]Ibid., 102.

mals each year, ninety-five percent of which are rats and mice. The other experimental animals include rabbits, guinea pigs, dogs, snails, cats, hamsters, gerbils, and frogs. Special agricultural research programs also conduct studies with dairy and beef cattle, swine, sheep, mink, llamas, horses, and poultry.

Animals that are used in experimentation are purchased from commercial vendors, supply houses, and other sources. The large animal research programs at OSU, such as those in the colleges of agricultural sciences and veterinary medicine, are largely self-sustaining by breeding testing animals from the research herds.

OSU has an Animal Care and Use Committee whose purpose is to review all proposals for research involving animals, before the application for funding or the beginning of any research. In its review each month, the committee considers the animal-handling protocols that are proposed for the animals to be used. The approval of this committee is required for any research or teaching to proceed. The committee is composed of six people, including one veterinarian, three OSU scientists who use animals in their research, one OSU faculty member who does not use animals in research, and one member from outside the university.[4]

CRISIS COMES AS AN EARLY MORNING SURPRISE

Early on the morning of June 10, 1991, Oregon State University was faced with a potentially damaging situation when animal rights activists set fire to a barn at the mink farm on campus and vandalized research offices (see Figure 9-11). None of the 1,300 mink at the farm were missing or injured, but activists destroyed research records, emptied files and broke a toilet, flooding the office and causing over $62,000 in property damage. Graffiti displaying the initials A.L.F. (Animal Liberation Federation) were painted on the office walls as well as other messages such as "This is only the beginning" and "Concentration camp for animals" (see Figure 9-12).

The first alert to the incident came at 6:00 A.M. when the News and Communications Services[5] (NCS) director of the university relations team received a phone call from the Oregon State Police. This call provided little initial information for the director to assess the situation adequately.

In addition, there were three special problems that the NCS had to overcome in terms of media relations and coordination of the event.

- The farm was at a remote location far from campus.
- Firemen and police were already at the scene when most OSU communications staff and other university people were still on their way.

[4]Taken from an "Animal Rights Background Information" sheet prepared in 1990 for the media bout OSU's animal research and practices.

[5]We thank Bob Bruce, Assistant Vice-President of University Relations at OSU, for the information he provided in assembling this case.

Figure 9–11 The remains of the barn at the mink farm after the fire. (Courtesy of Oregon State University.)

- NCS needed to contact a large number of university officials, including vice-presidents, deans, department heads, research administrators, and on-site staff. This coordination was essential to NCS's ability to disseminate the news about the fire quickly and accurately and speak with One Clear Voice to its internal and external audiences.

OSU WAS PREPARED

Since 1989, the News and Communications Services unit at OSU has had an emergency response plan in place. The objective of that plan is to delineate the university's public information responsibility and functioning in times of unusual circumstances and to assure that OSU responds quickly, accurately, and professionally in facilitating communications with the media. As part of the planning and review process, NCS staff seek ways to improve or supplement the written plan with additional materials and resources. In 1990, NCS augmented the plan with the development of a background paper on animal rights, knowing that the issue had attracted national attention. This background material could be used as a resource to inform

Figure 9–12 Michael Holland, archivist at Oregon State University, sorts through publications and records damaged by vandals in 1991. (Photo by Mark Floyd, courtesy of OSU.)

the media of the university's procedures and research activities involving the care and use of animals.

On the morning of the attack, OSU activated its emergency response plan. Its staff sought to achieve four specific objectives in dealing with media relations in this crisis situation. Those objectives were:

1. Gaining quick control of the information flow and putting NCS in a *proactive media relations position* to manage, rather than be managed by, events and circumstances.

2. Establishing the NCS as *THE credible and accurate source of information* about the event.

3. Having OSU speak with *one, consistent "voice"* in responding to both media and general public inquiries for information about the event.

4. Assuring that the *occurrence of illegal acts (arson and destruction of property) was not overshadowed* by the claims and self-serving political utterances of the animal rights activists responsible for the incident.[6]

OSU USES EMERGENCY RESPONSE PLAN

By 8:00 A.M., less than four hours after the incident, OSU had established a news management team. The team blended the talents of professionals from Agricultural Communications, the University Research Office, and NCS. It initially set about the tasks of dividing informational responsibilities and getting out an immediate notice to the media, informing them that OSU would be providing more information as soon as possible.

A team of media relations professionals was dispatched to the scene to gather information and provide on-site assistance to police and fire units. Because access to the fire scene was initially restricted, one member of the news team photographed the scene and returned quickly to the office to process the film for prints to release to those who might want them. A second member of the team established a liaison with the state police and remained at the scene to work with media who arrived on-site to report on the fire. Use of a cellular telephone provided direct contact between on-site staff and the news management team.

In the early hours after the fire was extinguished, OSU confirmed that the fire was suspected arson and that damage had allegedly been perpetrated by avowed animal rights activists. As the news management team gathered that information, it also gathered background information on the research being done at the farm and the history of the mink program at OSU. These materials were quickly assembled in a packet of information that would subsequently be made available to all media.

Shortly after OSU's initial phone calls alerting media to the incident, newspeople from around the state headed to the university campus. To help assist their need for interviews and access, the news management team identified and briefed a university spokesman, Dr. Kelvin Koong, head of animal science, and channeled requests for interviews and information to him.

In the meanwhile, the news management team continued to develop and disseminate news stories about the incident via fax and direct computer connections to Oregon newspapers and wire services. By 11:30 A.M., OSU had issued three updated versions of the story, identified the act as animal rights vandalism, and had shared the information with other Oregon universities, federal agencies and associations, and the national news media.

---

[6]These specific objectives were taken directly from a summary of events written by Bob Bruce, Assistant Vice-President of University Relations at OSU. The emphasis is ours.

OSU FOILS TERRORISTS' MEDIA STRATEGY

The Animal Liberation Federation's strategy had been to claim responsibility for their campaign against animal research. To achieve that objective, those responsible had videotaped themselves in the act of vandalizing the mink farm and delivered copies of the tape, along with a press release claiming responsibility for the act, to the Associated Press and the KATU-TV studios in Portland by midmorning. However, by the time those materials were received, the story was already known to the media because of OSU's dispatches.

Over the course of the next several days, OSU responded to inquiries from around the country. The news management team also prepared materials supporting testimony before a state legislative committee considering passage of a more stringent animal rights vandalism bill. The bill made acts of animal rights vandalism a felony rather than a misdemeanor. Following the testimony by OSU spokespersons, the bill was one of the first enacted by the 1991 Oregon Legislative Assembly.

LESSONS LEARNED

Though this crisis was not physically threatening to those involved, it could have been very threatening to the university's reputation if the media had zeroed in on the animal activists' point of view and given them sympathetic coverage. The public might have rallied behind the A.L.F.'s cause of, as they put it, saving the innocent, furry creatures from a life in captivity and premature death to feed human vanity. Instead OSU reacted quickly and focused attention on the violent and extreme acts committed by the activists that had destroyed property paid for by public funds. Subsequent news coverage was positive for the university; many editorials favored the university and its involvement in animal experimentation.

QUESTIONS FOR DISCUSSION

1. What other strategies or plan might you have used if you were head of this activist group trying to gain public support against this research institution? What are the trade-offs of going beyond legal and normally acceptable behavior?

2. The introduction to this chapter speaks of three understandings essential in managing the response to a crisis. What would be an example in which the political environment was critical? The culture and inner workings of the organization? Facets of human nature or behavior?

3. In a crisis are there significant differences (additions or eliminations) from nor-

mal gathering and analyzing of information, assisting news media and others entitled to information, providing feedback to the employer or client, and mediating among groups that might be in conflict?

4. As a public relations practitioner working for a research university or institution, do you feel that you could develop a strategy to combat animal rights activists if you believe that animal experimentation is wrong? Why or why not?

5. What are the elements essential to a successful crisis communication plan? How well did OSU utilize these elements?

PROBLEM 9 WHEN ASSOCIATES DISAGREE IN HANDLING AN EMERGENCY

Three months ago, you were hired to start a department at Reliable Steel Products Company. This is a young company with big ambitions. It is located in a medium-sized city in an area where industrial and residential building are predicted to boom. Reliable manufactures pipes, beams, rods, and other heavy parts for just about any kind of building.

After three months, your "department" consists of you and a secretary. Your outlook is bright, however. You report directly to the president, and he wants to be publicly known and highly regarded in the community and in the industry. To be of maximum help you have done your homework by checking on the reputation of Reliable around town and in the industry. In the home community, Reliable and its president are not universally known, but employees, neighbors, and the people at the Chamber of Commerce feel that Reliable is well managed, makes good products, and is a civic-minded neighbor. A few people did say that there have been a few accidents to employees; it seems a rather dangerous place to work.

One morning, when the president is on his way to the state capital, you get a call from a reporter at the local daily newspaper. He says that an ambulance driver told him a Reliable employee had been killed a few minutes earlier, when some pipes rolled off a pile while a truck was being loaded in the shipping yard. The reporter asks for details.

You tell him you will check it out at once and get back to him. You call the safety supervisor. He blows up and insists that no details be released to any outsider until all the facts can be determined, the employee's family notified, the insurance company alerted, and the company lawyers informed. He says for you to hold off until the president returns the next morning. You agree on the priority of the employee's family, but explain that you cannot prevent the newspaper from publishing anything they have gotten elsewhere, whether it is accurate or not.

The safety supervisor says to take it up with the personnel director. You call him. He says they have someone out at the employee's home now, but he agrees with the safety supervisor that situations like this have all sorts of possible problems, with a chance of backlash. He thinks an unplanned response without the president's knowledge would be dangerous. He wants no part in it.

There are a number of alternatives open to you, but not much time to choose among them. What would be the best course to follow now? Everything considered, what immediate initiatives—if any— would you take?

What further issues can be anticipated as a result of the crisis? How would you recommend dealing with them?

Chapter 10

Standards, Ethics, and Values

Regulation of human conduct by standards rather than brute force or basic biological drive is the definition of civilization. Social conduct is regulated by five factors:

- **Tradition:** How has the situation been viewed or handled in the past?
- **Public opinion:** What is currently acceptable behavior to the majority of one's peers?
- **Law:** What is permissible and what prohibited by legislation?
- **Morality:** Generally connotes a spiritual or religious prohibition; immorality is a charge usually leveled in issues on which religious teachings have concentrated.
- **Ethics:** Standards set by a profession, an organization, or oneself, based on conscience—what is right or fair to others as well as to self? (See box.)

Admittedly, these factors, as described, are attempts at pragmatic definitions for the 1990s. It would not be hard to get into an argument over the differences or the details. The point is that, however we use the words, there are forces that keep society functioning despite the strong pull of self-interest, ego, competitiveness, antisocial behavior, criminality, and other ills that could destroy it.

THE ROLE OF CONSCIENCE

The difficulty in trying to pin down ethics in terms of standards or principles of conduct is that there is so little uniformity. Short of what is legal or illegal, determination of what kinds of conduct are acceptable, in various kinds of circumstances, comes down to the individual or the group conscience. And among individuals or

ETHICS PROGRAMS
ARE BIG BUSINESS

As evidenced by the cases you are about to read in this section, organizations today are finding it imperative to establish codes of ethics—and then educate their members about them: two jobs for public relations.

Ethics training and education have become hot topics as centers such as the Josephson Institute of Ethics in California and the Ethics Resource Center in Washington, D.C., offer assistance to organizations to create ethics programs.

The Josephson Institute has trained a multitude of organizations—from Pizza Hut to the IRS to Girl Scouts of the U.S.A. At least half of all Fortune 500 companies have some sort of ethics-training program for employees. And between fifteen and twenty percent of large companies have an "ethics officer" who is in charge of creating and maintaining the company's ethics program.[1]

Is having an ethics officer just a chic way of impressing the public and demonstrating to authorities that a company is concerned with staying on the "straight and narrow," while still conducting business as usual? In some cases it may be. One study by the Center for Business Ethics at Bentley College found, when asking Fortune 1000 companies why they had estab-

lished ethics programs, that the most frequently cited answer was that the organization was facing formal charges or that it was worried about federal sentencing guidelines (this means that executives can be held criminally responsible for their company's actions). The federal sentencing guidelines, updated in November of 1991, encourage organizations to "maintain internal mechanisms for preventing, detecting and reporting criminal conduct." They also provide incentives for organizations who hire ethics officers and develop policies and programs.

What does this new emphasis on ethics mean for the practice of public relations? What many esteemed practitioners have been saying all along—without ethical behavior there is no credibility. And without credibility there is no business.

An already distrustful public is wary of the motives of business, government, and even not-for-profit agencies, as scandal after scandal surfaces about improprieties and mismanagement. A solid commitment to an ethics program by management and employees can help to gain, regain, or hold public trust and credibility.

Michael Josephson, founder of the Josephson Institute, predicts that "the ethics movement will be the '90's what the consumer movement was to the '60's."

groups having differing functional roles, the threshold of conscience can be high or low, near or far.

Consider the range of conscience or early warning sensations in a clergyman, prostitute, used-car dealer, illiterate, doctor of medicine, judge, or addicted derelict, to name but a few. Also, there are wide variations within each functional role, based

[1]Nancy K. Austin, "The New Corporate Watchdogs," *Working Woman,* January 1994.

on the personal makeup of the individual. The range of variations goes all the way from the person who feels that "anything in my own interest is right as long as I don't go to jail," to "anything that pricks my conscience is wrong, no matter what anyone else says or does."

Then, too, most people tend to prescribe for others ethical standards of conduct that they do not practice themselves.

Customs and changing times are significantly involved in ethics and standards. Gifts and favors of various kinds are accepted in many countries as part of the cost of doing, or expediting, business. U.S. businesses international in scope claim they must comply to compete. In this country, public attitude in general frowns on gifts and favors as thinly disguised forms of bribery or payoff.

As another example, the dogma and ways of groups committed to strict standards and stern discipline come under assault. Consider the pressure on the Amish people as they see the luxuries and laxity of their neighbors. Or the differing practices of orthodox and reform Jews. Or the Catholic dogma, or the "Protestant work ethic" opposing a wave of permissiveness, liberation of the young, and psychiatric forgiveness for lapses in self-discipline.

APPLICATION TO THE PRACTICE OF PUBLIC RELATIONS

Any effort to bring all of these considerations down to the practical world of public relations finds generalizations fraught with exceptions. The practice of public relations has been codified and disciplined for the 15,000 members of the Public Relations Society of American since 1950. In 1988, PRSA and its twelve sister organizations in the North American Public Relations Council adopted a uniform code of ethics (see Figure 10-1). But more than 200,000 persons are engaged in activities identifiable as public relations, most without equivalent standards or discipline.

That the public relations calling has been able to outgrow such labels as "flackery" and to rise above recurrent instances of news manipulation, coverup, sugar coating, and some cases of deliberate deceit testifies eloquently to the potential power and promise of two-way communications and positive relationship building when the skills are turned to noble purposes.

For most practitioners, the Golden Rule is seen as an ethical guide—even as a definition of public relations. If we do unto others as we would have them do unto us, harmonious public relationships will result.

THE ASPIRATIONS AND CONCEPT ARE PURE

Consider the following concept. If people would communicate more—and better—in a spirit of compromise and reconciliation, most problems in human relations would be solved. There would be understanding and peace. Lifestyle would include

CODE OF PROFESSIONAL STANDARDS
FOR THE PRACTICE OF PUBLIC RELATIONS

Public Relations Society of America

This Code was adopted by the PRSA Assembly in 1988. It replaces a Code of Ethics in force since 1950 and revised in 1954, 1959, 1963, 1977, and 1983.

Declaration of Principles

Members of the Public Relations Society of America base their professional principles on the fundamental value and dignity of the individual, holding that the free exercise of human rights, especially freedom of speech, freedom of assembly, and freedom of the press, is essential to the practice of public relations.

In serving the interests of clients and employers, we dedicate ourselves to the goals of better communication, understanding, and cooperation among the diverse individuals, groups, and institutions of society, and of equal opportunity of employment in the public relations profession.

We pledge:

To conduct ourselves professionally, with truth, accuracy, fairness, and responsibility to the public;

To improve our individual competence and advance the knowledge and proficiency of the profession through continuing research and education;

And to adhere to the articles of the Code of Professional Standards for the Practice of Public Relations as adopted by the governing Assembly of the Society.

Code of Professional Standards for the Practice of Public Relations

These articles have been adopted by the Public Relations Society of America to promote and maintain high standards of public service and ethical conduct among its members.

1. A member shall conduct his or her professional life in accord with the public interest.

2. A member shall exemplify high standards of honesty and integrity while carrying out dual obligations to a client or employer and to the democratic process.

3. A member shall deal fairly with the public, with past or present clients or employers, and with fellow practitioners, giving due respect to the ideal of free inquiry and to the opinions of others.

4. A member shall adhere to the highest standards of accuracy and truth, avoiding extravagant claims or unfair comparisons and giving credit for ideas and words borrowed from others.

5. A member shall not knowingly disseminate false or misleading information and shall act promptly to correct erroneous communications for which he or she is responsible.

6. A member shall not engage in any practice which has the purpose of corrupting the integrity of channels of communications or the processes of government.

7. A member shall be prepared to identify publicly the name of the client or employer on whose behalf any public communication is made.

8. A member shall not use any individual or organization professing to serve or represent an announced cause, or professing to be independent or unbiased, but actually serving another or undisclosed interest.

9. A member shall not guarantee the achievement of specified results beyond the member's direct control.

10. A member shall not represent conflicting or competing interests without the express consent of those concerned, given after a full disclosure of the facts.

11. A member shall not place himself or herself in a position where the member's personal interest is or may be in conflict with an obligation to an employer or client, or others, without full disclosure of such interests to all involved.

12. A member shall not accept fees, commissions, gifts or any other consideration from anyone except clients or employers for whom services are performed with their express consent, given after full disclosure of the facts.

13. A member shall scrupulously safeguard the confidences and privacy rights of present, former, and prospective clients or employers.

14. A member shall not intentionally damage the professional reputation or practice of another practitioner.

15. If a member has evidence that another member has been guilty of unethical, illegal, or unfair practices, including those in violation of this Code, the member is obligated to present the information promptly to the proper authorities of the Society for action in accordance with the procedure set forth in Article XII of the Bylaws.

16. A member called as a witness in a proceeding for enforcement of this Code is obligated to appear, unless excused for sufficient reason by the judicial panel.

17. A member shall, as soon as possible, sever relations with any organization or individual if such relationship requires conduct contrary to the articles of this Code.

Figure 10–1   Shown here is the *Code of Professional Standards for the Practice of Public Relations,* revised by PRSA in 1988. These seventeen articles apply to less than 10% of public relations practitioner. Courtesy of PRSA.

self-discipline and acceptance of responsibility, affluence with charity, possession without greed or avarice, and personal integrity under rules of law and mutual respect.

It is in this area that the public relations function has sought to fulfill its aspirations by exerting an ethical and moral force as well as technical skill and, by doing so, developing an identity and a professional discipline of its own.

It is a long road to travel, because only recently has the body of knowledge been codified; there is no single accepted academic curriculum leading to a distinct, recognized public relations doctorate, no licensing of practitioners or other public recognition of professional competence and authority.

Consequently, rather than functioning as advocates of understanding or public interest, qualified by academic discipline, practitioners have functioned generally as skilled communicators and persuaders on behalf of the organizations that employ them. Ethical standards have tended to be the reflections of the employers and clients served.

Putting it another way, the public relations voice has generally emerged publicly more as an echo of an employer's standards and interests than that of a professional discipline applied to the employer's problems. The practitioner still may come on as narrowly organizational rather than broadly professional, but this situation is changing as both employers and the profession embrace a new wave of ethics.

WHAT IS ACCEPTABLE ETHICALLY?

- Is it acceptable for food companies, in the name of nutrition and education, to provide elementary schools with educational kits prominently featuring their labels, product photographs, slogans, and product recipes?
- Is it acceptable for a county agency supported by taxpayers to spend money for a public relations firm to put out its news and promote its work?
- Is it acceptable for a utility to include in the rates to customers the cost of donations it makes to charity, for which it gets credit as being generous?
- Is it acceptable for soft drink, cereal, and other product manufacturers to shower television and movie prop people with free merchandise so that their products appear to be "standard" on television and in motion pictures?
- Is it acceptable for big businesses to preach that their growth creates jobs, when many of them have doubled in sales over a ten-year period yet their employment total remains what it was ten years ago?
- Is it acceptable for a corporation to hand out a news release at the outset of its annual meeting saying that its presentation was accorded a standing ovation?
- Is it acceptable for television networks to tie in a tire company blimp with their newscasts at sports events, giving the blimp owner free publicity?
- Is it acceptable for a public relations counselor to send a client a flattering

clipping with a note, "I knew you'd like to see this as soon as we got it," as if the counselor had something to do with generating the publicity, though actually he or she had not?

- Is it acceptable for an incumbent member of Congress to use perks of office such as staff paid by taxpayers, free mailings, pork barrel (including $25 million for grasshopper control back home) and PAC money to clobber any opposition and perpetuate himself or herself in office?
- Is it acceptable for a public relations director to tell the public a lie on a matter of no real significance if the intent is to protect the privacy or reputation of his or her boss?
- Is it acceptable to use fear in advertising to raise funds for poor people flooded out of their homes? To help cut down on the sale of tobacco? To sell a fire detection device? Insurance?
- Is it acceptable for a congressperson to accept a box of oranges from a grateful fruit grower in his district? An envelope with $20 in it? Season tickets to the Washington Redskins games? A television set? A new automobile?
- Is is acceptable to announce publicly that an official has resigned "for personal reasons" when in fact he or she was fired for the good of the organization, or at the whim of a more powerful, jealous individual?

"So what" is often the reaction after reading these ethical situations. This comment comes from two different concepts: (1) I'd never do any of those, or (2) I'd have to wait until I saw what else was involved before I decided what I would do[2]

With regard to the first concept, it would be the exceptional person who has a high standard and never goes against it. Lives are a mixture of doing exactly what we think should be done and being "flexible" where the area is more gray than black or white.

The second concept suggests situation ethics, where a person not only waits to make a decision but may make different decisions involving the same situation at different times. Ethics are often gray, but there are situations in which a person should be able to be counted on to do or not to do. Certainly your peers employers want to believe this. The Public Relations Code of Ethics sets standards we are expected to follow.

REFERENCES AND ADDITIONAL READINGS

BAKER, LEE W. *The Credibility Factor.* Homewood, IL: Business One Irwin, 1992.
BERNAYS, EDWARD L., et al. *tips & tactics, pr reporter* (supplement October 21, November 18,

---

[2]For an interesting classroom exercise classroom exercise in professional ethics, see Lynne Masel-Walters, "Playing the Game: Ethics Situations for Public Relations Courses," *Public Relations Research and Education Journal,* Vol 1 (Winter, 1984): 47–54.

and December 2, 1985). Bernays and others express divergent views on the proposal that practitioners be *licensed,* like doctors and lawyers, in a three-part series in *t&t.*

BOVET, SUSAN FRY. "The Burning Question of Ethics: The Profession Fights for Better Business Practices." *Public Relations Journal* 49 (November 1993): 24–25, 29.

BRAIN, JOHN. "Openness or Irrationality." *Public Relations Journal* v44 (December 1988). Editorial dealing with ethical questions in openness, cites cases involving Nestle, Gerber, and Johnson & Johnson.

CENTER, ALLEN H. "What About the State of the Art?" *Public Relations Journal* v32 (January 1976). A timeless discussion piece.

The *Corporate Conduct Quarterly* is a publication that addresses the improvement in the day-to-day behavior of business and its leaders and is published by the Forum for Policy Research at Rutgers. For more information write, 401 Cooper Street, Camden, NJ 08102.

CUTLIP, SCOTT, M., ALLEN M. CENTER, and GLEN M. BROOM. "Ethics and Professionalism." Chapter 5 in *Effective Public Relations.* 7th ed. Englewood Cliffs, N.J.: Prentice Hall, 1994.

FEINBERG, STUART A., and BRUCE SERLEN. "The Crisis in Business Ethics." *Corporate Accounting* (1988): 36–39.

GRUNIG, JAMES E., and TODD HUNT. *Managing Public Relations.* New York: Holt, Rinehart and Winston, 1984. See Chapters 3 and 4.

HOFFMAN, W. MICHAEL. *The Corporation, Ethics & the Environment.* Westport, CT: Quorum, 1990.

JACKSON, PATRICK, and JOHN PALUSZEK. "Demonstrating Professionalism." *Public Relations Journal* v44 (October 1988). Discusses the options available for practitioners to demonstrate their value to society.

The Josephson Institute for Ethics provides a variety of materials and training tools to prepare business for ethical issues and scenarios. For more information write, Joseph and Edna Josephson Institute of Ethics, 4640 Admiralty Way, Suite 101, Marina del Rey, Calif. 90292.

LESLY, PHILIP. *The People Factor: Managing the Human Climate.* Homewood, IL: Dow Jones-Irwin, 1974.

NEVINS, ALLAN, et al. *Public Relations Review* v4 (Fall 1978). A series of six scholarly lectures on the relationship of public relations to eras in U.S. history.

NEWSOM, DOUG, ALAN SCOTT, PhD. and JUDY VAN SLYKE TURK, PhD. "PR Ethics and Social Responsibilities." Chapter 7 in *This is PR-The Realities of Public Relations.* 4th ed. Belmont, Calif.: Wadsworth, 1989.

OLASKY, MARVIN N. "The Aborted Debate Within Public Relations: An Approach Through Kuhn's Paradigm." Chapter 4 in *Public Relations Research Annual* v1 New York: Lawrence Erlbaum, 1989.

PEARSON, RON. "Beyond Ethical Relativism in Public Relations: Coorientation, Rules and the Idea of Communication Symmetry." Chapter 3 in *Public Relations Research Annual* v1. New York: Lawrence Erlbaum, 1989.

PEARSON, RON. "Albert J. Sullivan's Theory of Public Relations Ethics." *Public Relations Review* 15 (Summer 1989): 52–61.

pr reporter (November 4, 1991). Ethics seen as a competitive advantage & a way to earn trust.

The Public Relations Body of Knowledge. New York: PRSA, 1993. See section I.2.A for abstracts dealing with Ethical Issues.

WALSH, FRANK, and PHILIP LESLY. "Considerations of Law in Public Relations." Chapter 47 in *Lesly's Public Relations Handbook.* 4th ed. Chicago, IL: Probus, 1991.

WALSH, FRANK. *Public Relations and the Law.* New York: Foundation for Public Relations Research and Education, 310 Madison Ave., New York 10017; 1988. Most recent compilation of legal issues facing the field.

WARD, GARY. *Developing and Enforcing a Code of Business Ethics.* Babylon, New York: Pilot, 1989.

WILCOX, DENNIS L., PHILLIP H. AULT, and WARREN K. AGEE. "Ethics and Professionalism." Chapter 6 in *Public Relations Strategies and Tactics.* 3rd ed. New York: HarperCollins, 1992.

Fund-Raising—A Question of Trust

Any organization, profit or nonprofit, must have credibility with its key publics. In the case of charity organizations, credibility and trust are perhaps more essential than in most. They inspire confidence from the public that their donations will be used for their intended purpose. Can this kind of credibility and trust be rebuilt once doubts about them have been raised?

BACKGROUND AND HISTORY

As a paragon in the field of charity work, the United Way provides support and important services to the community. These services include: substance abuse counseling, crisis intervention, job training and placement, disaster relief, and literacy programs—among dozens of others. Their multifaceted approach is reflected in their mission: to increase the organized capacity of people to care for one another.

Services are provided at a local level by independent, separately incorporated organizations administrated by local boards of volunteers known as the United Way. The United Way of America (UWA) is the National Service and Training Center for community-based United Ways. The national branch does not raise or appropriate money. Rather, it furnishes the community-based United Ways with marketing support, national resources, administrative and personnel programs, and computer software, and it acts as a liaison with other charities, national media and opinion leaders, and organized labor.

The first United Way (UW) was founded in 1887 in Denver, by religious leaders calling themselves "The Charity Organization Society." A year later the first "United Way" campaign raised $21,700. Regulations for charitable organizations were established within thirty years.

For a century the organization continued along a smooth road to success. In 1985, United Ways raised $2.33 billion, and the trend was toward an even greater increase in donations. By 1987, UWs numbered more than 2,300 across the country. In 1990, the United Way of America published the fifth annual environmental scan document—*What Lies Ahead: Countdown to the twenty-first Century*—and for the first time, Americans gave over $3 billion to local United Way campaigns. The organization was certainly speeding on a lucrative yellow brick road. However, it was not prepared for the potholes and detours that lay ahead in 1992.

THE CRISIS

On February 16, 1992, the *Washington Post* and *Regardies Magazine* released a story about alleged misconduct by United Way of America's longtime president, William Aramony (see Figure 10-2). After serving for 22 years, Aramony was publicly accused of wrongdoing and financial mismanagement.

The exposé examined such questionable issues as his:

- Management of the United Way of America
- Yearly salary of $463,000 including benefits

Figure 10–2 William Aramony was the center of intense public attention for his management of the United Way of America.

- Use of United Way money for travel and personal discretion (e.g., chauffeurs and expensive condominiums)
- Hiring practices: employing friends and family
- Installation of United Way "spin-off" companies such as Partnership Umbrella and United Way International, created both for profit and not for profit

THE ENSUING EVENTS

The day the exposé appeared, Senior Vice-President for Corporate Communications, Sunshine Overkamp, sent a memorandum to the chief officers and communications directors of all the local United Ways across the country. This memo included the article from the *Post,* and a number of *talking points* in an attempt to be responsive to the concerns of key audiences involved, including:

- *Contributors*
- *Volunteers*
- *Staff*
- *The public*
- *The media*

The memo also gave the numbers of telephone lines set up to handle questions. Another internal investigation was under way, at Aramony's recommendation, by outside counsel, Verner, Liipfert, Bernhard, McPherson, and Hand. The results were to be reported April 2, 1992.

In the weeks to follow, there were numerous follow-up articles in the *Washington Post,* as well as the *New York Times, USA Today, Time, Newsweek, U.S. News and World Report,* and many other publications. Overkamp distributed copies of these articles to the local United Ways across the country in an effort to keep them abreast of the situation.

The national office initially supported Aramony under the auspice of innocent until proven guilty. However, eleven days after the exposé was released, Aramony resigned as president of United Way. As Aramony announced his retirement, he apologized for his "lack of sensitivity to perceptions" about his management and spending techniques.[1]

The next day, a memo was sent to employees that Aramony's retirement took effect immediately and that no successor was chosen. The search for a new president and an investigation was announced by Chairman of the Board, John F. Akers, CEO of IBM. Kenneth W. Dam, another IBM executive, was named interim president and CEO of the United Way of America in a March 5 news release. One of the

---

[1]*Washington Post,* February 28, 1992, p. A10.

first tasks at hand was a thorough review of policies, practices, and procedures of UWA.

NATIONAL RESPONDS

On the national level, United Way of America took these actions to try to regain its credibility:

- Initiated its own investigation of Aramony's conduct.
- Updated local United Ways with breaks of new information and guides of how to respond.
- Responded immediately to the affirmation of Aramony's misconduct by forcing him to resign and finding a reputable replacement.
- Fully disclosed events to the public and the media.
- Reformed ethics policy to prevent similar situations in the future.

The national organization responded to a negative reaction by locals over the question of Aramony's continued salary and opted to discontinue it, giving him only the same coverage as other retirees under UWA's group health plan. It was busy over the next few weeks putting policy into action and trying to reassure the local chapters. Here are some examples of what they did:

- Answered questions at a *three-day annual conference for volunteer leaders* and organized a *series of "listening forums"* organized to give local representatives a chance to give input.
- *Gave local UW's seats on the board.*
- *Financially cut off United Way International from UWA and put its chief operating officer on leave.*
- *Created a fifteen-person search committee for a new chief for UWA,* stating that the members were chosen with care "to represent a diverse balanced group of individuals dedicated to the United Way and the volunteer process."
- *Interim CEO Dam initiated face-to-face communication with local United Way leaders and volunteers by visiting Connecticut to meet with them on April 21, 1992.* He answered questions and gave suggestions on how to restore credibility. Dam told them, "The public relations nightmare ultimately may serve as a springboard to redefine the organization's mission." He emphasized that the organization must be seen as more than just a fund-raising mechanism; it needed to be a builder of communities.[2]

[2]The Danbury News-Times, (April 22, 1992): 1.

Dam sent each UW a copy of the full report on the investigation and the work done to date on recommendations and closed his memo with this thought, "From this crisis, we can, working together, become stronger."

PICKING UP THE PIECES: THE LOCAL LEVEL

Once the scandal broke and Aramony resigned, the focus then turned to concentrating on regaining the public's trust in the United Way, so as not to damage the local chapters. The strategies developed in order to facilitate this difficult task differed among local United Ways. Many had their own strategies, which included:

- *Fact sheets* that positioned themselves as *not* associated with the national organization by emphasizing their autonomy (see Figure 10-3).
- *Refusing to pay national dues* until satisfied with investigations and resulting changes. (Some continue to refuse paying dues to this date, and there is evidence that this was the real reason the locals so quickly distanced themselves from national.)
- *Considered changing their name.*
- Many *circulated letters from the leaders of prominent organizations who encouraged their employees to continue supporting the local United Ways.*
- Organized *advisory panels* of key persons in the community to answer any questions and find the appropriate way to solicit them in the upcoming year.

LOCAL UNITED WAYS FILE FOR DIVORCE

A prevalent strategy was to *utilize the local media in order to distinguish between the local and national United Ways.* Here are two examples of the specific strategies some UWs implemented.

Making Lemonade Out of Lemons

The United Way of Massachusetts Bay used the Aramony Scandal to educate the public of the autonomy existing between the local organization and the national. It released the amount of money that goes toward service projects, 91.4 cents of every dollar. In addition, it asked the press to be sensitive to its plight and use headlines using "United Way of America" or "National Charity" to help people differentiate between the local and the national organization. It convinced two major papers to run full-page ads for free that spread this information. The area's number one radio station ran a campaign two times a day saying, "Thanks to the employees at x company who last year contributed *y* dollars to the United Way campaign, 3,000 people were fed a hot meal at St. Francis House." This message helped make "the connection be-

They Look Alike *but* They're <u>not</u> the Same

It's not just the *fine print*... Let's look at the facts.

FACTS:

- UNITED WAY of the NATIONAL CAPITAL AREA is your local United Way whose sole purpose is to serve *this* community. It is one of over 2,000 *local* and *autonomous* United Ways across the nation.

- Your local United Way sees that more than 90 cents out of every dollar collected goes directly to services.

FACTS:

- UNITED WAY OF AMERICA is the national trade association for local United Ways. It is not a headquarters and neither raises nor allocates any funds

- United Way of America sets no policy for local United Ways and is supported by dues of one percent from local United Ways.

Our suspended dues will go to local services.

We take our stewardship seriously. Our immediate response to this troubling controversy at the United Way of America was to <u>suspend our payment of dues</u> and call for a full and open investigation of the United Way of America and its spin-off operations.

In keeping with our dedication to serve this community, **the suspended dues payments will now be made available for increased programs and services needed in our community.**

| **Geoffrey Edwards**
Volunteer President
United Way of the
National Capital Area | **Ronald Townsend**
Chairman of
Trustees Assembly | **Burt K. Fischer**
1992 General
Campaign Chairman | **Sheldon W. Fantle**
Vice Chairman of Trustees
Assembly and Campaign
Advisory Chairman | **Delano E. Lewis**
1991 Campaign Chairman |

Figure 10–3 Many local United Ways used posters or fact sheets to demonstrate the difference between the local and the national organizations.

tween when they gave money and where it is going, how it is making an impact," explained Maureen Sullivan, director of public relations.

In addition to utilizing the local media, it maintained a policy of full disclosure and open communication by responding to every letter and call it received. It accepted invitations to meetings to further discuss the situation and urged CEO's to support the UW and to encourage their employees to do the same. Finally it planned a "Community Care Day" to gain community visibility, let donors know where the money goes, and have a positive impact on some lives.[3]

United Way of Orange County (UWOC) response was to work with the local media to get a local perspective, with all the stories coming over the wire. It did a direct mailing of fact sheets to campaign coordinators of local companies, the local board of directors, and agencies that receive money from the Orange County United Way. This mailing included a position statement from UWOC. It planned attitudinal research at some organizations that conduct United Way campaigns to survey the damage and guide future tactics. It set up forums for the public attended by the local president and chairman of the board. It ran a pilot fund-raising campaign to find out what questions people might ask to help direct the fall campaign strategies.[4]

IT'S NOT JUST THE UNITED WAY

Until the United Way scandal occurred, charities often escaped public scrutiny because they tended to be judged on whether the cause they supported was worthwhile instead of that charity's actual performance, a reality that most for-profit organizations must contend with. Nonprofit organizations are not constrained by the marketplace pressures and electoral politics that regulate big business.

United Way is not the only nonprofit organization whose finances have been scrutinized. According to an article published in the *Wall Street Journal,* the financial expenditures of affiliates of the American Cancer Society create some difficult-to-answer questions. While many of these affiliates claimed spending seventy-eight percent of their budgets on direct services to combat cancer, included in that amount was salaries and overhead, which is often up to sixty percent of the total budget.[5]

In addition, these charities often have huge cash reserves from which they are earning large amounts of interest. These cash reserves are often monies intended by donors to immediately be applied to combating cancer. Such asset holdings call into question both the fund-raising rhetoric and priorities of Cancer Society affiliates.

In the future, charities will not be given the free reign that they were given in the past. Americans now want positive proof that their money will be used for the purpose for which it was given.

[3]*pr reporter,* May 18, 1992.
[4]*New Milford Times,* June 4, 1992.
[5]*Wall Street Journal,* March 13, 1992.

WHERE THE UNITED WAY STANDS TODAY

One year after the Aramony scandal rocked the United Way of America, the future looks difficult but not so dismal. This comeback is partly attributed to the change in the structure and operation of the national organization.

- *The Board has been expanded to include members from local United Way chapters* who make up a third of the total; this board now meets four times a year instead of two times.
- *Created new volunteer oversight committees* in an effort to greater regulate the national organization.
- *Appointed Elaine Chao,* former director of the Peace Corps, as *president and CEO.*
- *Instituted a membership fee structure for local chapters that is lower* than the previous one percent of campaign requirement.
- Changed its objective to focus on *restoring confidence, instituting true accountability and quality management* and *focusing on customer* (local United Way organizations) *satisfaction.*
- Reduced salaries: banned first-class travel for UWA officials.

The fund-raising results for United Way of America were not outstanding in 1992. Donations decreased 3.3 percent compared with those collected in 1991. However, according to evaluations completed by executives at the end of their corporation's UW fund drives, this decrease has largely been attributed to the recession and corporate downsizing, not to the Aramony shake-up.[6] In addition, other fund-raising organizations have been cashing in on the employee pledging programs, a trend that was prevalent even before the scandal. One dismal fact for UWA is that *almost one-third of local chapters still continued to refuse to pay dues,* which forced the UWA to cut its staff by one-third and its budget by millions.

FUTURE VARIABLES

Questions still remain about criminal charges, with the FBI and the IRS continuing to investigate Aramony and the organization, and the possibility of legal action hanging overhead. Then remains the legal battles between Aramony and UWA. Aramony claims that UWA owes him over $5 million, including benefits owed from two special retirement funds, pay remaining from his unfinished employment contract (he was slated to retire in July 1993), and reimbursement for damages he has suffered from the UWA report that described his management spending practices unfavor-

---

[6]We thank Doris Burke, Director of Communications for United Way of Greater Manchester, New Hampshire, for the information provided for this case.

ably. At this writing, neither side is willing to settle, and it is uncertain whether Aramony will sue for the money he claims is owed to him.

A new level of awareness has been established among the public, regarding how and where charitable organizations spend their money. Because of the Aramony scandal, people will not let charitable institutions go about their business unchecked in the future. Potential donors now have an "excuse" not to give money unless charitable organizations can convince those people of their dedication to the cause for which they are raising money.

QUESTIONS FOR DISCUSSION

1. In the trend toward social responsibility in the 1990s, ethical considerations are often foremost in importance for operating an organization. Do you believe that an established ethical credo is more, less, or equally important for profit and nonprofit organizations? Why?

2. Was the UWA wrong to stand behind Aramony at the beginning of the scandal? Do you believe this stance caused further damage to the organization's credibility? Why or why not?

3. To keep a nonprofit organization running in the business world of today, managers often must adopt some of the standards of for-profit businesses. What limitations do you see for nonprofit organizations in adopting these standards and why? What advantages do you see?

4. Aside from the number of dollars campaigns bring in, what other ways can you think of to evaluate how successful local United Ways have been in distancing themselves from the national scandal?

A Classic: Baby Formula Raises Questions

In capitalist theory, the law of supply and demand and the human virtues of honesty and fairness are determinants regulating competition in the marketplace. If and when these get out of kilter, appropriate restraints or regulations can be imposed by governmental authority.

However, laxity in self-imposed standards back in the 1960s led to a number of consumer protection laws and to the growing intervention of the consumer's advocate. The advocate came in the form of either a person or an organization, acting as investigator or quality control manager, on behalf of the consuming public. Over time, nongovernmental consumer protection and advocacy have come to involve the Better Business Bureaus, *Consumer Research* and *Consumer Reports* magazines, telephone hotlines, television programs, newspaper and magazine features, newsletters, and dozens of special interest groups with their networks for investigation and communication.

COMPETITION IS THE CULPRIT

Product producers who are in business for the long haul don't set out to deliver an unsafe, fragile, or overpriced product. Occurrences when consumers are harmed or abused by gutter-level tactics and ethics are the exceptions. More often, breaches of the buyer-seller relationship stem from competitive pressures resulting in use of substandard materials; inadequate research, testing, or quality control; improper packaging; overstated claims of product benefits or capabilities; or faulty instructions. When consumer complaints pile up and a protectionist group moves in or litigation threatens, product makers go on the *defensive,* sometimes to stonewall, and other times to recall, to replace, or to refund.

MOTHERS, BABIES, AND NUTRITION

To exemplify a breached buyer-seller relationship and a consumer group moving in, we have chosen powdered infant formula as the product, and two giant producers, Nestlé, the world food colossus based in Switzerland, and Bristol-Myers, a multibillion dollar U.S. company diversified in pharmaceuticals, household products, cosmetics, and many other products.

The problem arose when powdered infant formula was distributed by these two competitors in underdeveloped areas of the world. Medical studies conducted by world health organizations found that when the product was administered it was a contributing factor in malnutrition and the cause of the diarrhea and a higher mortality rate in babies in underdeveloped countries (see Figure 10-4).

At the core of the problem was the reality that most infant formula sold in underdeveloped countries comes in powdered form, and these milk solids must be mixed with water before they are usable. According to the reports, babies frequently received contaminated milk because in many areas there is a general ignorance of hygiene, unclean water, or limited fuel for sterilizing bottles. These conditions prevented mothers from following formula preparations correctly.

Figure 10–4 Emotion-packed phot carried by *Mother Jones* dramatically shows the impact of the use of powdered formula sold in underdeveloped

HIGH COST OF POWDERED FORMULA

Moreover, according to the reports, the powdered formula was so expensive that mothers often diluted it to make it last longer. It was estimated that in Nigeria, where American-made formula was widely used, the cost of feeding a three-month-old infant with formula was approximately thirty percent of the minimum urban wage. Making matters worse, there was a sweeping shift away from breast-feeding throughout developing countries. The shift was associated with the rapid urbanization of these countries.

Critics admitted that the infant formula manufacturers were not responsible for the trend away from breast-feeding. However, faced with stagnant or declining birthrates in the developed world, the critics maintained that these companies encouraged the abandonment of breast-feeding by stepping up their sales effort in the baby-booming areas of Latin America, the Far East, Africa, and the Middle East.

Profits from baby formula sales reached new highs for some of the companies. In 1975, Bristol-Myers enjoyed a one-year record in profits largely because of formula sales. For another company, baby formula sales increased by more than thirty percent for two years in a row.[1]

ETHICAL MISCONDUCT, CLEVER MARKETING,
OR SOCIAL IRRESPONSIBILITY?

Most of the criticism of the companies focused on how they achieved their sales. In underdeveloped countries, they relied heavily on "milk nurses" or "mother craft workers" who went into hospitals, clinics, and private homes to instruct new mothers on child care and on the advantages of using the company's formula. The "nurses" wore traditional nurses' uniforms, which, the critics charged, lent a spurious air of authority to their sales appeal, and in some cases they were paid on a commission or bonus basis, adding a conflict-of-interest charge to the matter of morality.[2]

As public awareness of the controversy grew, better-known organizations became involved. The Protein Calorie Group of the United Nations issued a statement that emphasized "the critical importance of breast feeding under the sociocultural and economic conditions that prevailed in many developing countries." Later, the Twenty-Seventh World Health Assembly passed resolutions strongly recommending the encouragement of breast-feeding as the "ideal feeding in order to promote harmonious physical and mental development of children." The resolutions called for countries to "review sales and promotional activities on baby foods and to introduce

[1]*New York Times*, September 11, 1975.
[2]Ibid.

appropriate remedial measures, including advertisement codes and legislation where necessary."[3]

PUBLICITY CONTINUES FOR YEARS

The controversy continued at the publicity level four years before organizations within the United States adopted the role of consumer advocate. Perhaps the most influential advocate was the Interfaith Center on Corporate Responsibility (ICCR), a division of the National Council of Churches. The group represents fourteen major Protestant denominations and more than 150 Catholic groups. In an annual report, ICCR stated that it "exists to assist its member boards, agencies and instrumentalities to express social responsibility with their investments. Members of ICCR agree that as investors in businesses, they are also part owners and therefore have the right and obligation to monitor the social responsibilities of corporations and act where necessary to help prevent or correct corporate policy that produces social injury."[4]

CONSUMER INTEREST STRATEGY

As an initial step, ICCR members filed shareholder resolutions with U.S. baby formula manufacturers, including Bristol-Myers. Management met with ICCR members and disclaimed any responsibility for formula misuse. Despite this disclaimer, other organizations supported the resolutions. The Ford Foundation joined the other shareholders in support of the resolution-calling for a report on sales and promotional activities. The president of the Rockefeller Foundation wrote to the chairman of Bristol-Myers requesting the "publication of all relevant information to the outer limits permitted by competitive considerations."

---

[3]Other studies and reports were made both in the United States and in foreign countries. They told the same stories using different examples from different places in the world. While most of these reports went unchallenged by the producers of baby formula, one exception should be noted. An organization called Third World Action Group reprinted a report entitled *The Baby Killers.* The booklet was aimed at Nestlé and reported on infant malnutrition and the promotion of artificial feeding practices in the Third World. When the booklet was released in Switzerland, Nestlé sued for defamation. The suit made news throughout the world for two years before it was settled. In the end, Nestlé dropped three of the four defamation charges. On the fourth charge regarding the new title, *Nestlé Kills Babies,* the judge said that since it could not be shown that Nestlé directly kills infants—the mothers who prepare the formula are third-party intermediaries—the title must be defamatory. However, the judged imposed only minimal fines and asked Nestlé to "fundamentally rethink" its advertising policies.

[4]ICCR 1977 Annual Report.

TACTICS AND DEBATE

A short time later, Bristol-Myers published a nineteen-page report entitled *The Infant Formula Marketing Practices of Bristol-Myers Company in Countries Outside the United States.* ICCR called the report "an attempt to obfuscate the issue" and sought responses by experts in infant nutrition. Dr. Derrick Jelliffe, one of the early expert critics in the baby formula controversy, condemned the report as "inadequate and evasive." Within a couple of months, more than twenty ICCR members, joined by staff members of the Rockefeller and Ford foundations, met with Bristol-Myers management. The meetings changed little, and ICCR members filed another shareholder resolution with Bristol-Myers, requesting the correction of the company's report.

Four months after the ICCR resolution requesting a correction, Bristol-Myers issued a proxy statement stating that the company had been "totally responsive to the concerns [of ICCR members]" in the stockholders' resolutions. Feeling sure the proxy was inaccurate, the Sisters of the Precious Blood and ICCR members filed a lawsuit against Bristol-Myers. The suit charged Bristol-Myers with making a "misstatement" in its proxy and called for "a resolicitation of proxy votes, free from the taint of fraud." The Sisters of the Precious Blood submitted massive evidence in support of their claim, but the U.S. district judge dismissed the suit. The judge declined to rule on the accuracy of the proxy statement, saying the Sisters were not caused "irreparable harm" by the statement. The text of the decision implied that since a shareholder resolution is "precatory" or not binding on management, it is not relevant whether a company fails to tell the truth in responding to a shareholder proposal. Sometimes even the courts seem to condone or encourage ethical lapses.

SEC SUPPORTS SISTERS

The Sisters of the Precious Blood announced plans to appeal the dismissal on the grounds that the ruling "did not address the merits of the charge and makes a mockery of Securities and Exchange Commission laws requiring truth in corporate proxy statements." The Securities and Exchange Commission added pressure to Bristol-Myers when it indicated a plan to file a brief in court in favor of the Sisters if the appeal went forward. In the end, the appeal did not have to be filed because Bristol-Myers agreed to send a report to stockholders that included evidence from Third World countries, details of sales of Bristol-Myers in poverty areas, and a description of the medical problems caused by these practices. Bristol-Myers also agreed to halt the use of all consumer-oriented advertising and to withdraw milk nurses.

About the same time as the Sisters of the Precious Blood filed their lawsuit against Bristol-Myers, members of Congress began to act on the controversy. The first step was a resolution co-sponsored by twenty-nine members of Congress calling for an investigation of U.S. formula companies. A year later, an amendment to the International Development and Food Assistance Act urged the president to develop a strategy for programs of nutrition and health improvements for mothers and children, including breast-feeding. The report accompanying the House version of the amendment stated that "business involved in the manufacture, marketing or sale of infant formula have a responsibility to conduct their overseas activities in ways which do not have adverse effects on the nutritional health of people of developing nations."

Legislative involvement continued the following year as the U.S. Senate Subcommittee on Health and Scientific Research heard testimony on the infant formula controversy. Dr. James Post of Boston University stated that "for eight years, the industry's critics have borne the burden of proving that commercial marketing practices were actually contributing to infant malnutrition and morbidity. . . . From this time forward, the sellers of infant formula must bear the burden of proving that their products . . . actually serve a public purpose in the developing world." While no legislation came from the U.S. Senate, Senator Edward Kennedy did request that the World Health Organization sponsor a conference on infant formula promotion, marketing, and use.

Group action then fastened on Nestlé. However, when competition is international, what the U.S. Congress thinks or does is not always binding on foreign-based businesses. A responsive set of tactics came into play.

NESTLÉ FORMS COUNCIL

To disarm critics and defuse the issue, Nestlé led a number of large baby formula companies to form the International Council on Infant Food Industries (ICIFI). One of the major undertakings of ICIFI was the publication of a "Code of Ethics" for formula promotion. While the "Code" appeared to strengthen the position of baby formula manufacturers, it was criticized as being vague and meaningless. It was further weakened by the fact that two of the largest formula marketers, including Bristol-Myers, refused to join ICIFI.

While stockholder resolutions continued to put pressure on American companies, a new citizens' action group formed to bring pressure on Nestlé. INFACT (Infant Formula Action Coalition) began a national campaign. The Minnesota chapter initiated a boycott of Nestlé's products. The boycott became necessary, according to INFACT, because Nestlé did not change its policies on infant formula marketing techniques. INFACT made these demands of Nestlé:

1. Immediately stop all promotion of Nestlé artificial formula.
2. Stop mass media advertising of formula.
3. Stop distribution of free samples to hospitals, clinics, and homes of newborns.
4. Discontinue use of Nestlé milk nurses.
5. Stop promotion through the medical profession.

6. Prevent artificial formula from getting into the hands of people who do not have the means or facilities to use it safely.

Nestlé representatives made themselves available to groups across the United States. They met with representatives of various health advocate groups, medical professionals, and others. Nestlé's basic position stemmed from a history of manufacturing and selling formula in developing countries for more than sixty years. The root causes of infant malnutrition and mortality in the Third World, according to Nestlé, were poverty, lack of food, ignorance, and poor sanitation. Nestlé advocated breast-feeding, but stated that most Third World infants needed a supplement to mother's milk to sustain normal physical and mental growth for a period of months.

The national INFACT conference reacted to the meetings with Nestlé officials by deciding to continue the boycott. Boycott endorsements came from the Democratic Farmer-Labor Party of Minnesota and Ralph Nader. Nestlé representatives again met with action group representatives. Nothing was resolved, and the groups indicated that they would continue the boycott until Nestlé made substantial policy changes.

SPICING UP THE BOYCOTT TO BUILD A BIGGER CONSTITUENCY

To bring more attention to the boycott, action groups sponsored "Infant Formula Action Day" across the United States. The activities included a Boston Nestea[5] Party, demonstrations, leafleting, letter writing, fasts, and other public events. Later the same year, INFACT sponsored a program called "Spook Nestlé." The program urged Halloweeners not to buy or accept Nestlé candies. Leafleting at grocery stores and film showings was also part of the program (see Figure 10-5).

The list of those endorsing the boycott continued to grow. At the top of the list was the governing board of the National Council of Churches, which had facilitated earlier meetings.

The stalemate continued for more than five years. Nestlé published a list of nineteen excerpts from letters indicating support of Nestlé activities in Third World countries, but this action did not swing public opinion in its favor and end the boycott. The boycott cost Nestlé millions of dollars, yet these costs did little to actually hurt the giant corporation, which had profits in the billions during these years. What Nestlé wanted to get rid of was "the public relations nightmare." Church groups, labor unions, feminists, and other activists accused Nestlé of killing babies.

---

[5]Nestlé's brand of instant tea.

WHAT YOU CAN DO ABOUT
THE BOTTLE BABY SCANDAL

1. Boycott Nestlé. Nestlé is the largest infant-formula distributor in the Third World. A boycott of the company's products has been under way for some time in Western Europe; one in the U.S. began on July 4, 1977. Don't buy Taster's Choice/Nescafé/Nestlé Quik/Nestlé Crunch/Nestea/Libby, McNeill & Libby products (Libby's tomato juice, canned vegetables, etc.)

2. Join the campaign. As we go to press, active groups in more than a dozen American cities are working to spread the Nestlé boycott, distributing articles and a documentary film called *Bottle Babies*, speaking about the problem in churches and on talk shows, and so on. To find out how to link up with the campaign where you live, write or call:

Interfaith Center on Corporate Responsibility 475 Riverside Drive New York, NY 10027 (212) 870-2294	Third World Institute of the Newman Center 1701 University Ave. Minneapolis, MN 55414 (612) 331-3437	Earthwork 1499 Potrero Ave. San Francisco, CA 94110

3. Sound Off. Clip or copy the coupon below and send it to:

Name of Your Representative
U.S. House of Representatives
Washington, DC 20515

Name of Your Senator
U.S. Senate Office Building
Washington, DC 20510

Send a copy of your letter to:

Bristol-Myers
345 Park Ave.
New York, NY 10022

Nestlé Co., Inc.
100 Bloomingdale Road
White Plains, NY 10605

Add a note to Nestlé saying that you are boycotting its products until it stops all promotion, advertising and free-sample distribution of infant formula in the Third World, and all distribution of formula anywhere where people do not have the money or the facilities to use it safely.

- -

Dear_____:

The attached article details the growing problem of death and disease that results from aggressive infant-formula sales in the Third World. I am outraged by this practice. We need legislation that will bring it to a halt. Please inform me what you intend to do about this.

Sincerely,

_____

Figure 10–5 Boycott Nestlé was promoted in a variety of ways, including advertisements such as this one appearing in *Mother Jones*.

A CODE OF ETHICS IN PRACTICAL FORM

In the 1980s, the World Health Organization (WHO) tackled the problem by establishing the International Code of Marketing of Breastmilk Substitutes. The membership of WHO voted 118 to 1 to adopt the nonbinding code. The United States cast the one dissenting vote, claiming that restrictions called for violated the constitutional guarantees of free speech and freedom of information.

The code restricted the promotion of infant formula, prohibited the widespread practice of free formula samples to new mothers and the use of "mothercraft" nurses, a long criticized marketing aspect. Advertisements and other promotions to the general public were forbidden, as were gifts to mothers given to promote the use of breastmilk substitutes. The code also required that manufacturers discontinue use of product labels that idealized the use of infant formula. All products were to be labeled explaining the health hazards of bottle feeding.

After the passage of the code by individual governments, Nestlé changed several of its marketing practices, even in countries where the code had not formally been adopted. Despite these advances, the ICCR and the National Council of Churches found a long list of violations by Nestlé.

On its own, Nestlé released a revised set of policies designed to follow the code. The boycott continued, however, with focus on Nestlé's Tasters' Choice brand product. Several groups gathered and dumped 112,000 signatures onto the front steps of the company's headquarters in Switzerland.

A RESOLUTION OF SORTS

Just as it seemed as though the standoff would go on forever, Nestlé reached an accord with the protest groups in 1984. Bristol-Myers, Ross division of Abbott Laboratories, and Wyeth Laboratories, a unit of American Home Products, major baby formula manufacturers in the United States, also reached accords with the protesters.

Another incident with ethical overtones did not seem to rattle or deter Nestlé. In 1986, a suit hit Nestlé's Beech-Nut Nutrition Corporation and its two top executives for selling formula apple juice that was not composed of the fruit juice. The company settled that for $2 million, legal costs, and some slump in sales, not an indigestible bite out of Nestlé's billions in sales.[6] In 1988, two Beech-Nut executives,

OF ALL THE PARTICIPANTS, WHO WON WHAT?

The news coverage of the accord between Nestlé and the health advocate organizations indicated that the health advocate organizations had won the long battle. For example, an article in *Newsweek* (included a photo of a Nestlé ad with the subhead: "A Boycott That Hurt." The headline on the article stated, "Nestlé's Costly Accord." The lead in the story set the tone and clearly put the health advocate organizations in the winning position:

For the past seven years, scores of religious, women's health and public-interest groups have waged a very rough and costly boycott against the Swiss-based Nestlé company.... Last week, after spending tens of millions of dollars resisting the boycott, Nestlé finally reached the accord with the protesters.

Nestlé agreed to change four of its business practices as the basis of the accord.

1. Put information on labels.
2. Update and provide all information in literature.
3. Stop giving gifts to health officials.
4. Stop distributing samples and supplies.

[6]"What Led Beech-Nut Down the Road to Disgrace," *Business Week*, February 22, 1988. pp 124-128.

including the president, took the fall with a sentence of one year in jail and $100,000 in fines. Meantime, a *Wall Street Journal* article reported that an acquisitive-minded Nestlé, with plenty of cash, was back on the prowl paying $1.3 billion for some European food interests and bidding $4 billion for a British candy maker.[7]

AT THIS WRITING

In 1988, the International Baby Food Action Network (IBFAN) released a detailed and illustrated report on the international marketing practices of the infant food and feeding bottle industry prepared initially for the World Health Assembly. The report was titled "Still Breaking the Rules" and IBFAN continues to update this report (see Figure 10–6).[8]

A worldwide report on violations of the WHO/UNICEF International Code of Marketing of Breast-milk Substitutes.

International Baby Food Action Network (IBFAN)

Figure 10–6   The report "Still Breaking the Rules" examines all baby food makers and their compliance to the international marketing practices. (Courtesy of IBFAN and Action for Corporate Accountability.)

[7]John Marcom, Jr., "Acquisitive Nestlé, with Cash to Spare, Is Set to Continue Its Takeover Search," *Wall Street Journal,* April 28, 1988.

[8]For a copy of the report, write to IBFAN USA, c/o ACTION, 129 Church Street, New Haven, Connecticut 06510.

The report indicated that the infant foods industry, in pushing its products around the world, continued to employ methods that "endanger infant health and undermine the efforts of national policy makers, primary health care workers, consumer protection organizations and international agencies which have worked for more than a decade to encourage mothers to implement inexpensive and simple measures, including breast-feeding, to protect their babies' health and lives."

In naming offenders, the report went beyond Nestlé and Bristol-Myers. The list was far-reaching, demonstrating that the international infant food market has attracted entries from many countries, making control or discipline extremely difficult. Success in competition comes first in business whether local or worldwide.

Also in 1988, *Action News,* a publication issued by an IBFAN member named "Action For Corporate Accountability," reported that despite the code, Nestlé continued to "dump supplies of formula on hospitals" and thus gave the impression of medical endorsement for artificial baby feeding. If Nestlé persisted, the planned responsive action would be a renewal of the boycott in the United States starting on October 4, 1988, the fourth anniversary of the date the first boycott was ended.

As promised, the boycott was initiated again that year and continues in 1993. Action for Corporate Accountability spearheaded the effort against Nestlé in the United States and has focused attention on another company in this most recent boycott, American Home Products. AHP and Nestlé control about sixty-five percent of the global infant formula market and refused to succumb to ACTION's demands to end the practice of supplying their formulas free to hospitals. It began circulating a petition and collected over 50,000 names that it has presented to Nestlé to pressure it with grassroots support. To emphasize its point, ACTION sent out frequent newsletters and fact sheets to update the violations Nestlé and AHP have recently committed in marketing and selling their baby formula worldwide. To follow up the U.S. effort, boycotts were initiated against AHP, Nestlé, and local formula companies in twelve other countries from 1988 to 1990.

In 1992, the "Baby-Friendly" Hospital Initiative was issued by UNICEF and WHO. It is a global campaign to foster support for breast-feeding and an effort to end the supply of free and low-cost formula to maternity institutions. Both AHP and Nestlé agreed to the initiative and to stop suppling hospitals with free samples of their formulas. However, ACTION remained unconvinced of the formula manufacturers commitment to the initiative, citing the company's behavior of "business as usual" as an indicator of how seriously the companies are taking the proposal. Enforcing the Baby-Friendly Hospital Initiative also may be sticky, considering that "UNICEF and WHO have no power to implement this initiative globally," says ACTION's Executive Director, Dr. Idrian N. Resnick. "Only an intense campaign of consumer and media pressure will force these corporations to quit stalling and do what's right."[9]

And where is Nestlé in all this? Nestlé continued its efforts with the Interna-

---

[9]Taken from a press release issued by Action for Corporate Accountability on March 11, 1992.

tional Association of Infant Food Manufacturers (IFM) to prove its commitment to work with "international agencies, governments, non-governmental organizations, and all others concerned, to end all supplies of infant formula in developing countries except for the limited number of infants who need it." This statement, taken from a Nestlé policy update in December of 1990, suggests its continued commitment to ending free baby food supplies to hospitals of third world countries.

But once a company or organization behaves irresponsibly, it takes more than words to regain trust. Many are therefore undoubtedly asking, "Does Nestle mean it this time?"

QUESTIONS FOR DISCUSSION

1. As between the open system and the closed system, which label fit the posture of Nestlé and of IBFAN, expressed in their policies and actions? How about proactive versus reactive?

2. To change people's opinions, there are several options in strategy and tactics such as persuasion, coercion, compensation, or compulsion. Which ones among these, or others, do you see employed by various opposing groups in this case study?

3. In 1988, when IBFAN announced a plan to renew the boycott of Nestlé products, would that clearly constitute a more effective or less effective threat as stated in a Chapter 1 maxim? Might the factor of mildness or harshness depend on Nestlé management's reaction based on its marketing strategy and practices? Whether it would or not, what does that say to you about the practical application of maxims?

4. If you feel this was a matter on which the opponents could work out a reasonable resolution in the public interest, and both sides had professional counsel morally committed to reconciliation, what could have been done better or differently so that the matter wouldn't drag on for years? After you figure out your answer to this, try coming up with a resolution for the abortion issue. Are the intervening forces and stubborn issues the same?

5. Is it possible for Nestlé (and other baby formula manufacturers) to come to a definitive accord with these activist groups? What is the issue each is fighting for or against? Compare the underlying value systems of the two sides.

Ethics Woven into the Decision-Making Process

Most dictionaries define ethics as a system of moral principles. A behavioral scientist might characterize relationships as being ethical when they are mutually acceptable to the principal parties involved. For our purposes, ethical conduct should additionally be harmless to all those affected by the relationships or behavior.

Laws such as the Ethics in Government Act, rules and regulations, and codes of standards have long existed to encourage and upgrade morality and to penalize conduct that crosses the boundary or skirts around the end of legality. There are watchdog agencies such as the Better Business Bureau and the Consumer Protection Agency. Then, too, the news media do their part by digging into and exposing selected instances of questionable and scandalous behavior—as does that most basic of all media, the grapevine.

In the 1970s, a period of "anything goes," "me first," and "just don't get caught" in both private and public sectors, laxity in ethical behavior went along with sexual self-indulgence, drug and alcohol abuse, and seemingly insatiable economic appetite. Those who might have taken leadership to change the mores seemed to be busy as participants, to be waiting for the other person to take the first step, or to be resigned that nothing short of national or cultural catastrophe could do much good.[1]

Something had to give. Moving into and through the 1980s, some of those heading the nation's largest enterprises, hit by increasing instances of bad publicity and surveys showing loss of public trust, surmised that morality was part of the bottom line of good business practice. Giving leaders the benefit of sound human instincts, no doubt some sensed that beyond their business accountability, their famil-

---

[1]John A. Koten, "Moving Toward Higher Standards for American Business," *Public Relations Review,* Vol. XII, No. 12 (Fall 1986). Worthwhile background to ethics in business public relations. Story of Arthur Page and his pathfinding work as the first public relations vice-president at AT&T.

ial relations and their ultimate personal legacy of character could be at stake. Whatever the combination of considerations, many made moves to activate corrective measures and higher standards of conduct *within* their organizations—and *between* their organizations and those who could support, criticize, or condemn.[2] One of the large enterprises leading the way was McDonnell Douglas Corporation, headquartered in St. Louis, Missouri.

THE MCDONNELL DOUGLAS STORY

The company was formed by two high-principled and tough-minded men. James S. McDonnell had started a company in 1939 that later specialized in jet fighters and spacecraft. Donald W. Douglas had founded a company in 1920 that by the 1960s was concentrating on missiles and transport aircraft. They got together in 1967.

In the process of growing to $13.7 billion a year in 1992, McDonnell Douglas Corporation (MDC) became the twenty-third largest dollar volume company in the United States, the twenty-third largest employer (87,000 people), and among a handful of the largest and most elite defense contractors.[3] It is easy to envision the impact that the personal work and behavior habits and standards of MDC top officials could have on employees, suppliers, and government contacts if adequately and effectively communicated.

GENESIS OF A PROGRAM

In the general frame of the late 1970s and early 1980s, news about huge outlays for national defense was punctuated by news items of understandable concern to the taxpayer having trouble meeting his or her monthly bills. There were news reports of a $60 Navy ashtray and a toilet seat that cost $600 or more, and defense contractors were compelled to refund large sums of overcharges. Overzealous executives were fired or demoted, and ultimately the guns-for-hostages (Irangate) scandal came out. Public reaction naturally evolved as a variation of the diffusion process advancing from interest to concern, then to suspicion, and to distrust expressed in criticism (see Figure 10–7).

Against this backdrop in 1980, Sanford N. McDonnell (Sandy to employees), a nephew of the founder, became MDC chairman and CEO. It was his conviction that ethical considerations must be woven into the decision process as it moved along

---

[2]John A. Byrne, "Businesses Are Signing Up for Ethics 101," *Business Week,* February 15, 1988; Archie B. Carroll, "In Search of the Moral Manager," *Business Horizons* 30 (March 1987); Robert Chatov, "What Corporate Ethics Statements Say," *California Management Review* 22 (Summer 1980). Saul W. Gellerman, "Why 'Good' Managers Make Bad Ethical Choices," *Harvard Business Review* 86 (July 1986). All provide insight.

[3]From the "Fortune 500," *Fortune,* April 19, 1993.

Figure 10–7 To American wage earners trying to make ends meet, frequent news headings like these raw and grimy clippings from respected media did not inspire confidence or trust. Rather, the appearance of misconduct by those in high places encouraged others to look around for ways to "beat the system," "get a piece of the action," or "avoid paying the piper" at various levels in an organization.

step by step and up the levels of responsibility. Within that year, he personally initiated the McDonnell Douglas Ethics Program. The tenets were spelled out in a Business Ethics and Conduct guide subsequently placed in the hands of every employee. The program was launched with Sandy McDonnell's personal commitment to it. In June of 1990 the Business Ethics and Conduct guide was revised and updated (see Figure 10–8).

Figure 10–8 Booklet given every employee. (Shown is the version from 1990.)
(Courtesy of McDonnell Douglas.)

Over time, McDonnell also put his mark on the company with "The Five Keys to (Corporate) Self-Renewal." The keys to effective management were (1) strategic management, (2) human resource management, (3) participative management, (4) quality/productivity management, and (5) ethical decision making. (The concept went into values such as fairness and individual rights, far beyond not telling lies and not engaging in shady deals.)

PROGRAM IMPLEMENTATION

In 1983, at McDonnell's personal instigation, a study was made to determine the best course of action in establishing a corporationwide training program that would raise employees' ethical awareness and give them tools to aid in making ethical decisions. The task was assigned to the then-corporate director of human resources management.[4] She and her aides took the following steps:

- Reviewed current literature on competitor's corporate ethics programs.
- Interviewed representative managers to identify situations they encountered, and the issues raised, and surveyed employee attitudes on "fairness."
- Discussed findings with the CEO and heads of human resources, law, and corporate communications.
- Selected two outside professionals, from Harvard and Stanford, to aid in program implementation.
- Conducted an all-day meeting of nineteen top MDC managers and ethics professionals for group evaluation of ethical cases and workshop discussions.
- Designed an ethics training workshop program for employees.
- Developed a videotape and workbook (see Figures 10-9, 10-10, and 10-11.)
- Conducted all-day workshops throughout the organization.

RESULTS AND CONCLUSIONS

Over time, more than 75,000 employees underwent an eight-hour or half-day workshop seminar in a program required, eventually, for all employees (see Figure 10-12). Among tangible conclusions:

- The subject of ethics became an acceptable topic for discussion.
- The participation of Sandy McDonnell personally in the videotape sent a

---

[4]Georganne Riley MacNab. On behalf of public relations instructors and students, we are indebted to her and staff for abundant information and her cooperative attitude, enabling the detail in this study and an objective approach.

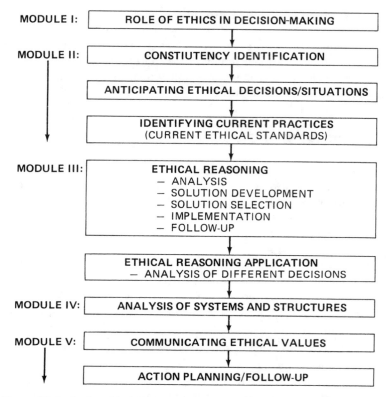

Figure 10–9 In the ethical decision-making workbook, decision making is shown as a conceptual model. (Courtesy of McDonnell Douglas and Kirk O. Hanson, Stanford University.)

strong message attesting to the importance of the ethics factor and carrying over into decision-making actions (behavior).

- The idea of identifying "constituencies" affected by decisions was new and valuable.

- The use of actual cases from employees' working experiences in such matters as a plant closing and the impact on a community, or an environmental issue, illuminated ethical issues with practical benefits.

- Employees learned that they did not have to face ethical issues by themselves.

- An ombudsperson program was established to provide an independent, "private" channel for personnel-related problems such as being asked to change the amount of time allocated to a particular contract in official records.

- Increased sense of pride in being part of an ethical organization was evident. Employees wanted to be ethical and associate with others who were.

Figure 10–10 This diagram shows employees how to identify their working constituency on the job. (Courtesy of McDonnell Douglas and Kirk O. Hanson.)

- A new policy and procedures manual for interacting with the government on pricing and contracting was prepared and issued.

AT THE INDUSTRY AND GOVERNMENT LEVELS

By 1986 the defense industry, the Pentagon, and Congress were under the gun of broad public criticism for waste and dishonesty in the procurement process. That

Figure 10–11 This shows trainees the outside constituency interested in, and affected by, company policies and decisions. (Courtesy of McDonnell Douglas and Kirk O. Hanson.)

Figure 10–12 Georganne R. MacNab, then-project director, McDonnell Douglas Institute, conducting a typical face-to-face small group Workshop of employees. The group discusses its way through the ethical decision-making book.

year, the False Claims Act Amendments gave potential whistle blowers increased incentives. Citizens could file lawsuits. Recovery would be three times the damages. Citizens were guaranteed a minimum of fifteen percent of the recovery amount plus costs and attorney fees.[5] That same year, the Defense Industry Initiatives on Business Ethics and Conduct came into being. Major contractors, including MDC, signed agreements pledging to a concept of self-governance.

Separately, MDC inaugurated a new program called the Significant Business Issues (SBI) Program, which designated specific, concrete goals of requiring actions to make the company fully competitive, such as "Reduce costs by 40 percent. Improve quality by 90 percent."

Under SBI came a walkaround management style involving three levels of management and cellular teams of engineering and manufacturing people designed to assure progress toward goals. Here, MDC began its initiation of Total Quality Management (TQM).

Assessment was done by surveys of employees and contacts with external audiences such as customers and community leaders.

LESSONS LEARNED AT MDC

According to an analysis by qualified outsiders:

1. Ethics training should not be presented as an abstract. It must be managerial, pragmatic.
2. Strong leadership is needed from the top with a constant stream of communications.
3. Ethics education needs a name appropriate to the culture of the organization.
4. Implementation must be from the top down, not the other way around.
5. Consultation with operating groups on form and content is critical.
6. Consistency of training requires a standardized format for training workshops.
7. Workshops should follow a participative process, with leaders creating an atmosphere in which sensitive and controversial issues can be raised without fear of reprisal, and substantive problem areas must be followed up by management or work teams.
8. Actions speak louder than words; managers must serve as role models at all levels.

---

[5]The pros and cons of whistle blowing make up an inviting subject for study against a backdrop of American culture historically, journalistic practices, and employer-employee relations. One current article examining the motives behind whistle blowing is "Why Whistleblowers Do It and How to Stop Them," *Pr Reporter* 35, (November 9, 1992).

A NEVER-ENDING PROCESS

Turning around a public impression requires long-term commitment and patience. Setbacks are to be expected. For example, in defense contracting there can be a gap of several years between the time a contract is awarded, a government accounting office finds an apparent error, failure or malfeasance, an investigation is conducted, and a final conclusion or settlement is reached. News media might find only the accounting office action and the settlement years later worth reporting. At both times public impression is negative. Meanwhile a contractor may have a spotless record.

Uninvolved readers of news items may scan only the headline or lead paragraph of business doings, mentally note that here is another instance of hanky-panky in business and government, and turn to comics, sports, or entertainment.

A track record of exemplary conduct builds slowly. It requires constant tending. An honorable reputation is both precious and fragile. Opponents or competitors are rearmed by infractions.

THE PROGRAM AT MDC PUT TO THE TEST OF TIME

Beyond top management's commitment, MDC's employees were enrolled as partners. From this core of many thousands whose livelihoods were tied to MDC, the concept of ethics in the decision process logically radiated outward in the words and attitudes expressed by employees to their families, neighbors, merchants in the stores, and among the personnel of customer and supplier organizations encountered in the course of work. Common sense says that myriad MDC suppliers, and many customers, wanting to foster a good relationship with the company, would rethink, tighten, and restate their own standards of conduct. Other stakeholders would take note. The progress MDC made in ethical dealings would find its way to the Pentagon, to other major defense contractors, and to members of Congress. There would be a combination multiplier and amplifier at work.

The inherent risk, of course, is that somewhere along the line the process might be thwarted and the appearance of misconduct exposed, possibly setting MDC back in public trust and credibility farther than it was before the program.

MILITARY-INDUSTRIAL FIASCO

Something like that happened in the military-industrial complex, triggered by the public announcement in 1988 of investigations by the Navy, the FBI, and the Justice Department, revealing wiretap evidence of rampant bribery, fraud, and kickbacks in defense contracting. Some 75 to 100 defense contractors, and contracts totaling in tens of billions of dollars, were involved. Among the contractors named in the news was McDonnell Douglas.

News accounts explained that professional business consultants, some of them former Pentagon people, paid present Pentagon personnel nominal sums in the hundreds of dollars for information about contract specifications, then sold those bits of information for $50,000 or more to contractors who would be helped by the information in shaping their bids for contracts.

In the front-page stories that ran in June of 1988, little was said by participants or public authorities about whether honesty or ethical conduct should have a different or higher value when taxpayer money, the nation's security, or personal patriotism were at stake. Rather, President Reagan said tolerantly that some corruption is "understandable" in an enterprise as big as the Defense Department. A contractor spokesperson said, "If everybody else is doing it, why shouldn't I?" A member of the establishment said that corruption is a "way of life" in the defense business.

WHERE THE MDC ETHICS PROGRAM STANDS TODAY

With the many management changes that McDonnell Douglas faced in the late 1980s, it was questionable as to what direction the ethics program would be traveling.[6] However, as of late 1993 the ethics program is alive and well and constantly developing, according to a fact sheet distributed by MDC.[7]

Its ethics program is part of its TQM initiative, constantly developing and being honed for improvements. Now the program consists of three essential areas of activity: communication, education, and enforcement.

Communication

Some recent developments in the channels in which MDC carries its ethics message:

- Presentation of ethics topics in the Chairman's quarterly video message to all employees, entitled "90 Days."
- Surveys of employees that include specific ethics questions and will be conducted regularly throughout the corporation.

---

[6]See "The Odd Couple at McDonnell Douglas," a profile by Colin Leinster in which Sandy McDonnell, instigator of the "ethics in decision-making" program, handed the CEO baton to his cousin, John McDonnell, son of the founder. *Fortune* magazine, June 22, 1987. John McDonnell steps up to chairman, and Herald A. Johnston becomes president. Moves affected several other officers, ostensibly to "maximize effectiveness and to strengthen efficiency." Nothing was said about ethics.

[7]Our thanks to John Strickland, Vice President Corporate Ethics and Ombudsman at MDC, for providing updated information for this case.

Education

The Ethical Decision-Making Course, first developed in 1985, is now mandatory for all employees. Every employee will go through training after the first six months at MDC.

As part of its TQM improvement process, MDC created a task team made up primarily of human resource representatives to begin the development of a new training model for the corporation, in early 1992. The model created in 1985, though a valuable foundation for an ethics training model, needed to be revamped because it was not designed to address the evolving needs of a broad and diverse workforce. Some of the levels that the new training model would address are:

- Compulsory refresher training for all employees.
- Specific, specialized training for certain disciplines.
- Extended ethics training for management and supervision.

Some of the new features of the ethics training model as currently planned, include:

- Development of a three-hour college course by Webster University and MDC that addresses MDC's Code of Ethics and Standards of Business Conduct, combining also ethics philosophy and case studies in ethics. This course is available for college credit in both baccalaureate and graduate degree programs.
- MDC joined forces with other defense contractors such as Honeywell, Boeing, and IBM in a Management Training Consortium to convert compliance training courses originally developed by GE Aerospace to general use throughout the defense industry. Some of the specific subjects the courses will address are: truth in negotiations, procurement integrity, and the Drug-Free Workplace Act.

Enforcement

The third aspect of the ethics training model is enforcement. Its primary purpose is to see that MDC's Code of Ethics and Standards of Business Conduct is adhered to. Some venues for enforcement have been:

- A Corporate Responsibility Committee that monitors the MDC ethics and compliance programs.
- An MDC Ethics Council, which oversees the administration of ethics communication and training programs throughout the corporation.
- Administering an annual Conflict of Interest census that requires completion by all management and employees engaged in contracting, marketing, or purchasing decisions.

- An employee hotline to provide a means for reporting ethics concerns and issues.

- Top management working closely with the Defense Industry Initiative Working Group and Steering Committee to facilitate exchange of data to measure the effectiveness of MDC's ethics program.

QUESTIONS FOR DISCUSSION

1. A communication maxim points out that in times of crisis, sensitivity to leadership is heightened. True, but with unsavory practices (and people) prevalent in high places everywhere, leadership in business and government cannot be very reassuring to the average middle-income taxpayer. What can you say about the judgment, if not integrity or credibility, of leadership? Does leadership proceed more from personal example or from organizational policies and pronouncements? Does it start with those making up the bulk of an organizational family or with those in power at the top? Could you come up with a half-dozen or so criteria for anyone or any major organization seeking to be seen as providing credible leadership in the ultimate public interest, whether in a crisis mode or not?

2. Another maxim holds that credibility and trust increase when an original message is reinforced by succeeding events. (Weather forecasters know this all too well.) Turn this maxim around: If succeeding events fail to reinforce an original message, or in fact disprove it, the course of the original message and the implications of the message are disbelieved. (A prediction of fair weather turns out to be rain four days straight.) How would you say McDonnell Douglas, other large contractors, Pentagon authorities, and many elected officials claiming to serve the public interest have been faring, judged by either maxim?

3. In most large organizations, the public relations function is positioned somewhere between "where the buck stops" and "do what you're told and don't argue." The impact of practitioners on improving the standards of ethics and integrity where needed depends heavily on the practitioner's own character, standards, and human relations skills. Short of resigning when a policy or decision can't be tolerated by a practitioner, what would you say would be the best way to go about being a force for morality or necessary reform, and staying on the payroll at the same time?

4. If you give a group of advanced students a list of situations that involve ethical dilemmas, the students will not all agree on what are acceptable responses and what are not. A good example is the list in the chapter introduction, "What Is Acceptable Ethically?" How can this disparity exist when all students, like yourself, are mature and well-intentioned, honed by some of the same academic courses, and theoretically headed for similar professional careers?

Disarming the Critics and Making Friends

The public relations profession has regularly been given special attention in the news media, usually in a negative way. Much of the denigration has been earned and deserved by practitioners whose entire repertoire is relentless pursuit of media, or who try to cut deals in the back room out of the public eye. In addition, some employers and clients want the benefits of effective relationships without acknowledging the value of public relations practitioners in such tangible ways as an officership and the paycheck that goes with it. This situation is changing as more and more organizations get into relationship trouble with publics on which they depend and realize their need of professional guidance through it. Still, many of the larger and more self-satisfied administrations want relationship experts to do their thing behind the scenes.

These attitudes tend to be reflected in the academic values and curriculum structure of higher education in regard to public relations. While more and more university students have sought sequences, minors, or majors in public relations, administrators have puzzled over what to do about it in the curriculum. Thus, it usually ends up as one of the emphases tucked into a journalism or mass communications department, with old-line news editorial people pleased with the faculty positions, students, and funds it brings, yet looking down their noses at it. As such, for too long the public relations profession did not attract enough of the highest qualified scholars in communications and behavioral sciences willing to devote their lives to teaching a discipline that wasn't fully respected.

It comes as a welcome surprise then, when such recognition comes in tangible form out of a major corporation engaged in a serious effort to improve its own relations with the public.

DOW CHEMICAL'S REPUTATION PROBLEM

Dow Chemical has long been one of the largest and most successful corporations in its field. It has also experienced a generous share of uncomplimentary media and public attention for some of its activities. Dow made napalm and Agent Orange, chemicals useful in wartime military activities. Dow plants, literally dominating the environment of its small hometown, Midland, Michigan, emitted small amounts of dioxin, a cancer-causing agent. Top management had a run-in with neighboring Central Michigan University over a paid appearance by Jane Fonda in which she was critical of big business generally as "a new group of rulers, tyrants, who have learned to manipulate the tax laws to get away from paying their fair share." She named Dow specifically. Dow reaped adverse publicity over its operations in South Africa. Add to this that its posture was defiantly chip-on-the-shoulder, expressed on occasion by Paul Oreffice, then CEO, who, when he felt pushed, had the reputation of pushing back harder.[1]

A PROGRAM STARTS WITH FACT-FINDING

Going into the 1980s, Dow was busy telling its story to the world, mostly from a re-active posture. Director of Corporate Communications Rich Long, almost as a personal gesture of putting something back into the profession that had been good to him, had coincidentally started accepting some invitations to visit university classes. The students wanted him to talk mainly about negative things, problems plaguing corporations, such as Dow in South Africa, Union Carbide at Bhopal, or a derailed, overturned tank car spilling poisonous chlorine gas. He became something of a spokesperson for crisis management.

In 1984, not directly related to campus visits by Rich Long or others, Dow top management decided to undertake a study of public attitudes toward its approach to public policy. A twelve-member internal team representing public relations, public affairs, marketing, research, and others was formed to do the survey. Rich Long was designated its chairman. This team started by identifying six key audiences. They were:

1. Employees and plant communities
2. Media
3. Legislators

---

[1]John Bussey, "Dow Chemical Tries to Shed Tough Image and Court the Public," *Wall Street Journal,* November 20, 1987. This page-one lengthy story paints a before-and-after picture of Dow, with some of the changes linked to the styles of the former and the new CEO. Also, "Dow Chemical Wants to Be Your Friend," *New York Times,* November 22, 1987.

4. Customers
5. Academia
6. Scientific community—Dow stakeholders

They interviewed the company directors and a sample of employees and managers. Outside, they canvassed public attitudes toward Dow's environmental performance and corporate citizenship.

The findings, oversimplified, labeled Dow as an "insular and sometimes arrogant company that shunned compromise." When the dust of discussions had settled, top management had approved task force proposals for remedies over an extended period that would involve several separate programs and a budget of $75 million for implementation.

In 1988, nine programs had been launched under the Dow vice-president for government and public affairs. They were:

1. **Twenty-four-hour toll-free phone line** providing continuous access for news media.
2. **A Science Journalism Center** established and funded at the University of Missouri.
3. **A Visible Scientist Program** enabling Dow scientists to be interviewed about environmental issues.
4. **An Advocacy Group Outreach** of joint ventures with environmental and wildlife protection agencies.
5. A cadre of executives participating in a **Speakers Program** aimed at disarming and reassuring critics.
6. **A Community Relations Resource Center** to provided guidance to plant and sales managers.
7. **Public interest reports** sent to a mailing list of 60,000.
8. More than $1 million contributed annually to a **National Education Program** concerning organ transplants.
9. **National advertising** featuring a nonproduct message, "Dow Lets You Do Great Things."[2]

Since 1988, Dow has implemented programs in addition to the original nine. Included is a **Community Advisory Panel** as part of its commitment to Responsible Care (see Case 4–2), which has been established in many Dow sites across the world. Its object is to help Dow reach out and get proper feedback from the communities and allow them the opportunity to help Dow make decisions that may have an impact on them. These panels are made up of people from all walks of life, from the member of the school board to the average citizen in the community.

---

[2]Detailed description of the program is in *PR News* 43 (May 11, 1987), Case Study No. 2,095.

Recent soundings of public opinion show improvement in feelings toward Dow. A survey of business editors rated Dow's public relations effort tops among large chemical companies.

DOW'S EFFORTS HAVE REWARDS

Implementing the programs has been not only necessary, but also beneficial to all involved. Matt Davis, manager of news media relations, said, "The biggest benefit is that Dow has become a more open company and has been able to reach some of our key audiences." Dow has continued to build dialogue with these audiences, and the programs it has developed have kept Dow rolling in the right direction. The company feels that it can now have more open communications with those audiences who were adversaries previously.[3]

"I don't know if we're there yet [clear from public controversy]," explained Davis, "but we've made a tremendous amount of progress. If we ever say that we've made it, that is probably when our efforts will start to decrease. This type of initiative has to be part of the company from here on out."

According to Davis, several veteran reporters have commented about Dow's complete turnaround of reputation with the public. More than 10,000 people take tours of its plants; and the company lets reporters come in to interview and take pictures, a policy it wouldn't have dreamed of fifteen years ago.

ACTION KEY TO COMMUNITY TRUST

According to Davis, the key to positive public outreach for Dow is action and not empty promises. It is up to the company to tell its public what it plans on doing— and then doing it. If it fails, the public has every right to express disapproval. Dow has taken responsibility to find out what the public concerns are and take action per the communities' requests. As Davis explains, "If we don't continue to operate in an environmentally safe manner . . . if our products aren't handled safely . . . and if we don't conduct ourselves as a good corporate citizen, then no model of advertising is going to help the perception that people have of our company."

GETTING BACK TO EDUCATION

Coincidental with Dow's corporate program, Rich Long also had generated a personal program of his own designed to put Dow in a favorable perspective and

---

[3]Ibid.

strengthen journalism and public relations education on the pragmatic side. Again, everybody involved stood to benefit.

Some thirty or more educators with whom Long became acquainted on and off campus began periodically to find in their mail printed information helpful in the classroom and in preparing students for entry, level jobs (see Figures 10–13, and 10–14). The program continued until 1989 when it evolved into an on-request basis for speakers to come to the universities.

Why did rich Long get into this? In his words, "I wanted to give something back to public relations education. We have daily firing line experiences which can be translated into classroom discussions. Why not share our projects and results with educators? Interest in helping education coincides with some encouraging progress at Dow. If Dow gets some benefit from the service, that's fine. Ditto, if professors decide to steer some of their bright graduates our way. But there are no strings attached."[4]

CONCLUSION

Changing public perception—whether of a large corporation, or of a professional calling—almost has to start from an awareness and an acceptance *within*. Credibility with key publics comes from credible actions. Changes within an organization may involve standards, values, behavior, or style. Efforts to change must be more than cosmetic. And programs of correction require a commitment to the long haul. Single shots simply won't echo long enough to be credible or durable.[5]

---

[4] In answering our questions about the "coincidental" aid to PR education, Long disclaimed credit for invention. He wrote: "Bill Adams, while at Phillips Petroleum, really wrote the book on corporate support of pr education. When we started our mailings, we weren't aware of Bill's efforts. But, time and again, his name would come up as a standard of excellence. If imitation is the sincerest form of flattery, I guess we plead guilty." On behalf of educators, we plead that professionals in all sectors give thought to what they might do to put something back into the sourcespring and underpinnings of a career that has been good to them.

[5] Views on the absolute need for credibility in order to affect all other issues of relevance, and how to attain credibility, as expressed by new Dow CEO Frank Popoff, are summarized in *pr reporter*, (February 22, 1988). pp. 1&2

Figure 10–13   Some of the booklets supplied interested public relations educators for their students (Courtesy of Dow Corporate Communications.)

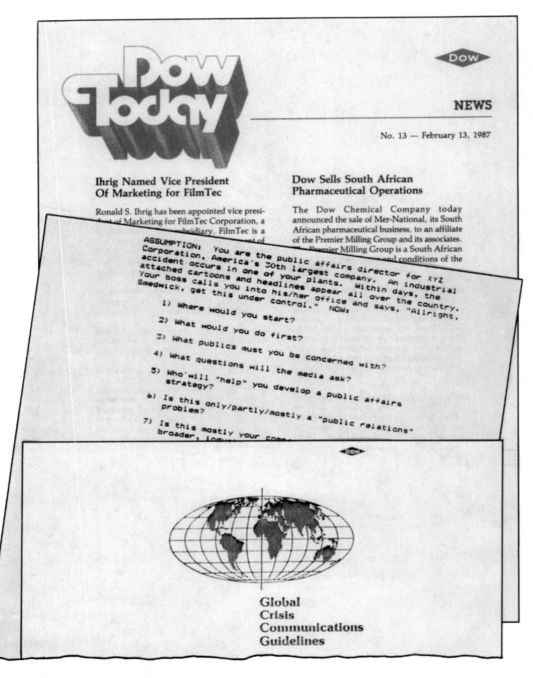

Dow Today

Dow

NEWS

No. 13 — February 13, 1987

Ihrig Named Vice President Of Marketing for FilmTec

Ronald S. Ihrig has been appointed vice president of Marketing for FilmTec Corporation, a ~~subsidiary~~. FilmTec is a ~~division~~ ...

Dow Sells South African Pharmaceutical Operations

The Dow Chemical Company today announced the sale of Mer-National, its South African pharmaceutical business, to an affiliate of the Premier Milling Group and its associates. ... Premier Milling Group is a South African ... and conditions of the

ASSUMPTION: You are the public affairs director for XYZ Corporation, America's 30th largest company. An industrial accident occurs in one of your plants. Within days, the attached cartoons and headlines appear all over the country. Your boss calls you into his/her office and says, "Allright, Smedwick, get this under control." NOW:

1) Where would you start?

2) What would you do first?

3) What publics must you be concerned with?

4) What questions will the media ask?

5) Who will "help" you develop a public affairs strategy?

6) Is this only/partly/mostly a "public relations" problem?

7) Is this mostly your comp... broader, indus...

Global Crisis Communications Guidelines

Figure 10–14 Top: Sample of one-page broadly distributed topical newsletter. Middle: PR case problem for class discussion led by teacher or Rich Long. Bottom: Guideline folder distributed to corporate communicators and others. (Courtesy of Dow Corporate Communications.)

QUESTIONS FOR DISCUSSION

1. Dow Chemical has changed from a reactive (defensive and tough) stance to a proactive stance. Dow has a new CEO. All this has been put on the public record in the *Wall Street Journal* and the *New York Times* profiles. And $75 million has been allocated for programs to communicate and implement the change. How long would you guess it will take to gain wide public awareness and confidence that Dow is really no longer "insular" or sometimes "arrogant" or unwilling to "compromise." Years? Decades? Generations?

2. Given today's cost of advertising and the kinds of programs Dow has inaugurated, in your judgement will the $75 million allocation be enough to produce measurable change in attitudes among Dow's constituent publics?

3. Beyond the nine programs set in motion by 1989, what significant additions do you feel Dow might consider in the advance and continuing planning that any such long-term commitment entails?

4. In the introduction to Chapter 8, the point is made that public service programs, whether born in crisis or simply expressing a societal concern, usually have two requirements put on them by corporate management. They must fit into the overall mission of the company. And, there must be a benefit of some kind to the company as well as to the public being served. Did Rich Long's service to journalism and public relations educators meet these requirements? If you, as a public relations practitioner would like to initiate such a program, how would you link it to your organization's objectives and the nature of the benefit?

Breast Implants and Dow Corning: Dealing with the Perception of Deception

One of the biggest headaches for manufacturers these days is the proliferation of product liability suits. Some companies are taking products off the market because of the risk of these suits, yet a goodly number of the cases are filed with reason. What would be the responsible and ethical thing to do if a product has been implicated as defective or harmful, even if some research may indicate the opposite? What can be done to make it up to those who may have been harmed or to allay the fears of those who *perceive* the product as harmful?

In the early 1990s, Dow Corning was faced with a great number of angry women when silicone-gel breast implants (manufactured by Dow Corning and several others) were indicated as a possible cause of health problems the women were experiencing. This case examines how public *perception* of Dow Corning's behavior evolved into a question of credibility for the organization.

The company *did* have an ethics policy in place since 1976 that was guiding decision making, but the public perceived that it was making business and legal decisions without addressing the ethical issues around the continued use of its breast implants.

HISTORY

The history of breast implantation in the United States is quite a long one. Since 1962, women have been paying to have doctors surgically enhance their breast size, for various reasons, through the use of silicone-gel or saline solution implants encased in silicone envelopes. Many do it for self-esteem reasons (about eighty percent), and others want reconstructive surgery after having a mastectomy due to breast cancer (about twenty percent). Almost two million women have had breast implants to date.

Silicone-gel was the choice for many women because it seemed more "lifelike" after implantation. Saline solution implants (made of salt and water) are considered less risky for the body, but women chose them less often because they did not feel as natural and sometimes made "sloshing sounds."

Until 1991, the highest perceived risk from breast implantation was in the surgical procedure itself. (Like any device implanted into the body, it may have adverse effects in a small number of patients.) However, silicone's effects on the human body's autoimmune system were not known. This branch of science had just begun to develop in the 1980s with the appearance of AIDS. An enormous amount of breast implant testing had been done in the 1950s, but when the issue arose there was a perception that there was none. Despite the amount of research that had been done, breast implants were alleged to be the possible cause of serious medical problems, including immunological disorders, arthritis, infections, reduced mammogram effectiveness, and cancer.

The possible risks of breast implants fall into two basic categories: those related directly to the breast (easy to observe) and those that may involve distant parts of the body (much harder to observe and difficult to measure).

Some of the breast-related risks are:

- Difficulty in detecting abnormalities in the breast when mammographic X-rays are done.
- Breast may harden—as a result of fibrous tissue growing around the implant— possibly causing discomfort and pain.
- Breakage of the envelope, causing the gel filling to be released.

Other risks are:

- Migration of the gel filling throughout the body (unknown effects).
- Possible cancer.
- Possible autoimmune diseases.

DOW CORNING'S ROLE

Dow Corning, jointly owned by Dow Chemical and the Corning Glass Makers, has been one of the most visible manufacturers of silicone-gel breast implants, although implants represented less than one percent of the company's sales. Dow Corning came under fire in 1991 when Marianne Hopkins, who had had implantation of silicone-gel breast implants in 1976, brought suit—claiming the product was responsible for damage to her immune system. The alleged cause was silicone leakage. With this case, many questions began to surface about implants.

One contributing factor to the uproar is that all medical devices were unregulated until 1976, fourteen years after the procedure of breast implantation had begun. There was no standard of testing and regulation to follow. Devices in use before the regulations were considered "grandfathered," which meant the manufacturers of those products were not required to provide the Food and Drug Administration (FDA) with scientific evidence of safety and effectiveness. That stipulation in the law is based on the premise that more is known about the safety of a device that has been in use for some time than about one that is newly developed. But if questions arise over time that cast any doubt about a grandfathered device's safety, the law gives the FDA the authority to go back and require that its manufacturer provide evidence to demonstrate it is safe and effective.[1]

In the 1980s, the FDA Devices Division did not have the budget or personnel to regulate adequately and had adopted a lax attitude in testing and regulating new medical devices put on the market. Finally, in April of 1991, with intensified publicity and court cases, implant manufacturers were ordered to prove that their silicone implants were safe. This regulatory action had been recommended by an FDA advisory panel a decade earlier, although it had not been enforced—a damaging fact in forming public perceptions.

CREDIBILITY PROBLEMS

Then in June of 1991, Dow Corning documents surfaced in a *Business Week* article that implied that the implant may have been rushed to market without proper medical testing. Top management was reassuring the general public of the relative safety of this product, but internal memos (created by those not aware of research taking place or past research that had been conducted) were being passed around that alleged there was awareness of animal studies that linked the implants to cancer and other illnesses. In addition, investigative reports dating back twenty-five years were brought to light indicating that implants could break or leak into patient's bodies. (Those reports had been a matter of public record, but now received attention with this new public scrutiny). The company *appeared* as if it had been covering up the reports and hiding the true facts.

At first, Dow Corning attacked investigators. This action was interpreted as a lack of concern for the public interest and prompted many to criticize the company as lacking any code of corporate ethics, concerned only with covering itself legally. The irony behind this was that the company did have an code of ethics in place.[2] Some of the initial communications actions that it implemented to allay some of the public misconceptions were:

---

[1]From "Background Information on the Possible Health Risks of Silicone Breast Implants," released by the FDA in December of 1990 and revised in February of 1991.

[2]Lee W. Baker, *The Credibility Factor.* (Homewood, Ill.: Business One Irwin, 1993), 35. An informative book emphasizing the importance of ethics in the practice of public relations by examining the mistakes and successes of organizations in varying ethical situations.

- Developed a packet of information that physicians could share with their patients that was user-friendly and explained the research conducted by Dow Corning and others about the implants (see Figure 10-15).
- Company physicians and scientists scheduled technical presentations at medical meetings to discuss the scientific implications of implants.
- Made public all proprietary information available to competitors in publicly releasing all the scientific studies used to support its Pre-Market Approval Application for the implant.
- Met directly with breast cancer support groups and representatives of other consumer groups, both for and against breast implants.

COMPANY IS DEALT PAINFUL LEGAL BLOW

Judgment in the Marianne Hopkins case was handed down in December of 1991. She was awarded $7.3 million in compensatory and punitive damages, and Dow

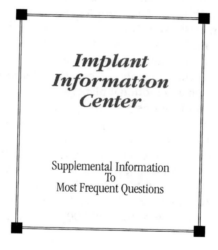

Figure 10–15 This packet of information was distributed by Dow Corning to outline all of the risks that could be possible with silicone breast implants

Corning was found to have committed fraud and malice by failing to disclose evidence from its research about the implants. With this damaging judgment, public scrutiny intensified and many questions were brought up in the media about the implants and what other information Dow Corning may have withheld. (Dow Corning is appealing this decision.)

The company was taking the hard line in dealing with this issue in the media. Dow Corning was finding it difficult to appear sympathetic to the women who did have problems without undermining its legal strategy and admitting fault. It appeared to be a classic case of legal versus public relations. And it was not helped by CEO Lawrence A. Reed, who, unfortunately, was not adept in media situations. This deficiency reduced his ability to take command of this crisis or to stay ahead of the critics. Reed's invisibility as a spokesperson confirmed the prevalent *perception* in the court of public opinion that the company was not concerned with the welfare of those who had received the implants.[3]

The task of presenting the Dow Corning "voice" to the public was passed around to many people until it rested on the shoulders of the vice-president in charge of health care, Robert T. Rylee, and others on his staff. There was no One Clear Voice responding to the public.

Reed's failure as a leader in the public eye was compared in the news media to the fumbling responses and lack of reaction from Exxon CEO Lawrence Rawl in handling the *Valdez* oil spill in 1989 (see Case 9–2). At Dow Corning, spokespeople were taking a reactive stance and focusing on the fact that there was little or no *scientific* evidence proving that the implants caused these health problems—ignoring the fact that women had gotten the implants for *emotional and cosmetic* reasons and would predictably respond on an emotional plane.

To deal with the barrage of questions from the public, Dow Corning set up an "Implant Information Hotline" in July of 1991. By the end of the year that, too, was receiving criticism from the FDA and high-profile news media coverage. Callers to the hotline were being reassured by the operators about the safety of the implants, and Dow Corning was accused of overselling their safety. The company then agreed to offer only to send printed information to callers. However, the operators of the hotlines were ultimately retrained to offer only factual information in order to allay any public misconceptions. To date, more than 50,000 women have called the hotline to obtain information.

THE FDA TAKES ACTION

On January 6, 1992, as public scrutiny intensified, FDA Commissioner David Kessler proposed a voluntary moratorium on the sale and use of silicone implants pending further investigation. Most all silicone-gel implant manufacturers complied.

[3]Kevin, McCauley, "Dow Corning Fumbles PR in Breast Implant Crisis," *O'Dwyer's PR Services Report*, 6 (March 1992). p. 1.

Dow Corning complied with the request, still claiming that the implants did not have a damaging effect on the body. However, public and media scrutiny did not abate, instead it intensified. The *Wall Street Journal* and the *New York Times* ran articles giving Dow Corning failing marks for its handling of the crisis. The rising tide of lawsuits was threatening the corporation and further thinning its already waning credibility.

The *New York Times* stated that Dow Corning failed in the court of public opinion because it was ignoring how consumers respond to health threats:

1. Even a small number of people who feel they have been mistreated by a company or received a poor product can rally enough friends and allies to have a great impact against the company involved.

2. The numbers of defective or dangerous products often turn out to be more than the company that manufactures them originally projects. With the publicity that the implants were receiving, many more complaints, both valid and invalid, were bound to surface.

3. Consumers who feel they have been deceived often become extremely upset. The information that leaked out over the years of litigation about the implants suggested that Dow Corning was trying to cover up information that may be damaging to its product without concern for the consumer.[4]

MEDIA COVERAGE INTENSIFIES PROBLEM

As the issue unfolded, Dow Corning began to track the media coverage of the controversy. While the news media were widely reporting the issue as it ensued, most of the coverage was incomplete and unbalanced (see Figure 10–16). Women were clamoring for information because of the intense media scrutiny. In order to respond to the need for information, Dow Corning took communications actions to reach out to those concerned:

- Became more responsive to the news media by distributing an 800-page book compiling memos, scientific studies, and related issues.

- Gave a grant to the American Society for Plastic and Reconstructive Surgical Nurses to collage and distribute educational materials to patients.

- Proposed a national communications registry; a collaborative effort between the FDA, consumers, health professionals, and current and former breast-

[4]Barnaby J. Feder, "Dow Corning's Failure in Public Opinion Test," *New York Times*, January 29, 1992, pp. D1 & D2.

**Total Press Coverage
Slant Percentage - Year Total 1991**

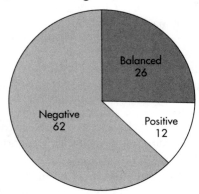

Figure 10–16 This graph illustrates the media tracking that showed an imbalance of coverage. (Courtesy of Dow Corning.)

implant manufacturers to provide periodic newsletters to breast-implant recipients.[5]

DOW CORNING RESPONDS

On February 10, 1992, Dow Corning began to take steps to repair its battered reputation. Lawrence Reed stepped down and was replaced by Keith McKennon, a former Dow Chemical executive well known for his conciliatory abilities. McKennon had helped Dow steer itself out of potentially damaging public relations situations that involved the Agent Orange defoliant used in Vietnam. McKennon's attitude was much more take-charge and less defensive, and from the start of his appointment he was the company voice concerning the issue. In the spirit of this new openness, McKennon gave almost 100 interviews on the issue.

In keeping with this new attitude, Dow Corning announced in March of 1992 its plans to get out of the breast-implant-manufacturing business. In addition, it promised to spend $10 million on research into the safety of the implants and

[5]Ralph C. Cook, Myron C. Harrison, and Robert R. LeVier, "The Breast Implant Controversy," *Arthritis and Rheumatism* 37 (February 1994). A thoughtful article examining the medical issues and communication problems of the breast implant controversy, written by three Dow Corning scientists (available from the company, Midland, Mich): 1-14.

would contribute up to $1,200 per patient (depending on financial need) to remove the silicone-gel implants. While Dow Corning still maintained that the implants were safe, it was finally taking conciliatory actions that recognized the need for further research to satisfy the concerns of the FDA and those women possibly at risk. One month later, the voluntary moratorium against silicone-gel implants was withdrawn, but breast augmentation was allowed only for breast cancer patients.

Dow Corning succeeded in removing some of the damaging attention from the information that had suddenly been brought into public view. Now the company focused on the *positive* actions it would take in order to make restitution to those women who felt they had been wronged.

REBUILDING ITS CREDIBILITY

Dow Corning has succeeded in making small gains to win back public opinion. It is funding thirty laboratory and clinical safety tests to establish the risks of the implants in the human body. Some women have been allowed to have the silicone implants if they agree to become part of a long-term study on the implants' effects. Also, a national registry of those with implants has been proposed to help monitor their health.

In September of 1993, the company announced that a global settlement had been proposed, a $4.75 billion fund for breast-implant recipients, funded by the manufacturers, suppliers, doctors, and insurance companies involved in the implant issue. It would give women the opportunity to recover money for their injuries over the course of thirty years. Dow Corning would contribute up to $2 billion to the fund over a period of thirty years. The fund would pay for checkups for women with implants, removal of the devices, and treatment of varied illnesses. Other terms of the agreement were:

- Recipients of any type of brand of breast implant would be included.
- Claimants would not be required to prove that their breast implants caused their injuries.
- Those who claimed that the breast implants had caused damage to their health would be able to exclude themselves from the general settlement and then sue individually.
- A recipient of breast implants who had sued a financially unstable company would be able to submit a claim to the fund.[6]

---

[6]"Dow Corning Nears Implant Settlement," Associated Press story, as it appeared in *Bangor Daily News*, September 10, 1993.

CONTINUED CONTROVERSY

In the wake of this financial settlement, the effects of silicone implants continues to be greatly disputed. The FDA has engaged in heated debates with the American Medical Association (AMA) about the level of risk posed by silicone breast implants. To date, the AMA has supported allowing all women the right to have breast implants once they have been informed of the risks. FDA Commissioner Kessler disagrees because he feels that physicians have not been responsible in informing women of risks. He faults physicians for using implants for thirty years without adequately discussing the risk.[7]

One irony is that, as the multibillion dollar settlement is establishment by the implant manufacturers, new evidence is emerging that shows no causal link between the implants and the autoimmune diseases allegedly caused by them. What if there is no link between the implants and the diseases they have been accused of causing? What would be the ethical thing for Dow Corning to do then? These questions pose some interesting public relations problems.

QUESTIONS FOR DISCUSSION

1. Dow Corning fumbled this crisis because it found it difficult to show concern for the recipients of breast implants while still maintaining a legal stance that endorsed the safety of the product. What could the company have done differently to keep this issue from rising to the epic proportions it did in the public arena? Could the entire issue have been avoided through appropriate communications?

2. Can a company act unethically and maintain credibility? Why or why not? Can you think of examples one way or the other?

3. Several companies manufacture implants. It is surgeons who suggest them to women and perform the operation. Yet only Dow Corning drew unfavorable public reaction. Why?

4. Whose responsibility is it to inform women who are interested in having breast implants of the risks of the procedure? Why do you believe this?

5. What are the ethical implications if it is found by scientific study in a few years that there is no known health effect of the implants? What are the implications for Dow Corning and its role in the settlement?

---

[7]Christopher Connell, "Doctors Protest Curb on Breast Implants," Associated Press story as it appeared in *Bangor Daily News*, December 1, 1993.

Political Correctness: Is It Just a Polite Way to Restrict Freedom of Speech?

Political correctness is an issue that has surged to the forefront of academic debate in the past few years. Dissent on college campuses and incidents of hate crimes have only intensified the issue. One of the main reasons it is so hotly debated is because it is such a fluid issue and because the definition of political correctness seems to be constantly changing. What does being politically correct entail exactly?

Initially the term *politically correct* "was used to identify . . . people whose politics were Left-liberal in the Reagan era, when such positions were clearly out of favor in the larger culture."[1] Now that definition is being altered, to fit the campaign of those fighting against racism, sexism, and general oppression. Although the cause seems noble enough, this preoccupation with political correctness is becoming a power struggle in many places.

POLITICAL CORRECTNESS DISPUTE AT DARTMOUTH

College campuses are some of the most fertile breeding grounds for this fanaticism with political correctness, and the institutions themselves do not always escape the battle unscathed. On the Dartmouth College campus, an incident involving political correctness rocked the community and threatened the esteemed reputation of the college.

An Upsetting Episode

On the eve of Yom Kippur, 1990, readers of the independent underground newspaper the *Dartmouth Review* were surprised to find the *Review*'s regular masthead

[1]D. Charles Whitney, and Ellen Wartella, "Media Coverage of the Political Correctness Debate," *Journal of Communication* (Spring 1992): 84.

replaced by a passage from *Mein Kampf*. This display of religious hostility was immediately identified by *Review* editors as an act of criminal sabotage, and they launched a private internal investigation to apprehend the offender. Suspicious fingers pointed at a *Review* staff writer, one of four who resigned after the incident. Although *Review* editors claimed to be ready to name the person responsible for the act, their internal investigation quickly closed, and the matter was turned over to local police.

The Consequences

Perhaps the hardest hit in this episode was the college itself, labeled by many as an institution intolerant of ethnic and religious minorities, women, and homosexual students. In an effort to separate the college from the *Review*, Dartmouth's president James O. Freedman issued a public statement accusing the *Review* of consistently attacking "blacks because they are black, women because they are women, homosexuals because they are homosexuals, and Jews because they are Jews."[2] In addition, Freedman held a Rally Against Hate a few days later, once again charging the student journalists with bigotry and racism. By focusing the blame on the *Dartmouth Review*, Freedman attempted to expose the *Review*, not the college, as the intolerant party.

Freedman Under Fire

Freedman's strategy for redeeming the school's public image was harshly criticized by Jeffrey Hart, Dartmouth professor of English. Hart claimed that President Freedman had "abused his office and ignored his moral responsibilities as an educator"[3] when he failed to contact any of the students involved or inquire into the incident before issuing his public statement. Hart also stated that although the *Review* is guilty of committing occasional breaches of taste, "it has never attacked anyone on the basis of race, only on performance."[4] Hart's rebuttal not only criticized Freedman's management of the situation, but also enhanced the negative publicity that the college received.

A Different Approach

In a separate attempt to redeem Dartmouth's image, the school's admissions department emphasized its "Take Dartmouth Home" campaign, urging students to go to their hometown high schools to encourage prospective applicants and explain that the *Dartmouth Review* was *not* the college's official newspaper. This strategy was

---

[2]Jeffrey, Hart, "Mr. Freedman's Moral Suicide," *National Review*, November 5, 1990, 23.
[3]Ibid, 22.
[4]Ibid, 23.

similar to Freedman's in that it attempted to dissociate the college from the *Dartmouth Review,* but the admissions department acted positively by employing student word-of-mouth rather than negatively by attacking the *Review* to rectify the college's image. Still, even talking face-to-face with friends can fuel the flames of an issue if they were unaware of the incident or had already forgotten it—a likely case for many people in this busy, overcommunicated age.

The Outcome

Thanks to favorable preexisting relations with the media and the efforts of some students and administration, Dartmouth came out of this incident relatively unscathed. The Anti-Defamation League investigated, and although it could not pinpoint the guilty party, it did find the *Review* at fault for creating a climate in which the *Mein Kampf* episode was considered acceptable behavior. As much as Dartmouth college won, however, it also lost. The number of black applicants diminished after the *Review* incident, and the Rockefeller Foundation rejected the school's request for money to recruit minority women professors. No efforts or strategies were strong enough to erase the fact that the Dartmouth name had been negatively associated with an act of prejudice.

JUST ASK BEAVIS AND BUTTHEAD

In the fall of 1993, the issue of speaking and acting politically correct surged to the forefront as an issue again. The video music cable channel MTV had been airing a cartoon show featuring two characters called Beavis and Butthead, who were positioned as moronic high school students with a serious interest in rock 'n' roll—among other things. Their behavior on the show was described by many as socially unacceptable. The show was deemed "disgusting" and trash by many critics, yet it gained a following among young adults and teenagers.

Beavis and Butthead were known to often exclaim on their show "Fire's cool!! Heh, heh, heh." And this is the phrase that got them in trouble. In Ohio a five-year-old boy allegedly heard this phrase on the show, found a book of matches, and started to play with them. In doing so, he burned down his house and killed his sister. Then the media uproar began. Calls came from everywhere to remove the "Beavis and Butthead Show" from the airwaves. It was deemed the cause for this tragedy and a bad influence to have on television.

Television watchdog groups asked for its removal, but MTV producers compromised by having the characters no longer make references to fire and airing the show after 10:00 P.M.

At issue in this controversy was not the tragedy that occurred, but who was at fault. Many placed the blame on Beavis and Butthead's politically incorrect behavior (those characters on the show who usually exhibit politically correct behavior are often ridiculed and awful things happen to them).

DON'T BE A BUTTHEAD

Some suggestions on how to avoid political incorrectness[5]:

- **Adopt participative dialogue and decrease one-way communication.** Cut back on use of publications and other communications "products"; use one-on-one, participative activities to communicate.

- **Make all communications *transparent*, not merely open.** Explaining the reasoning behind statements and decisions allows others to participate in the thought patterns and understand more clearly.

- **Establish a policy on what is politically correct for your organization.** This policy should be established participatively and then continually communicated, transparently.

POLITICAL CORRECTNESS VERSUS CENSORSHIP

Although these two incidents are quite separate and different, they both illustrate the fact that in today's society anyone—and everyone—is responsible for being politically correct. The hazard of penalizing media vehicles such as MTV and the *Dartmouth Review* for acting politically incorrect is that the line between what is acceptable in the media and what is not becomes dangerously fuzzy. This position now opens doors to censure others because of things they say. Does political correctness take precedence over freedom of speech? The legitimacy of political cor-

PC POLICE AT HARVARD

Stephan Thernstrom is a tenured professor at Harvard, and a preeminent scholar of the history of race relations in America. In 1987, *racist* was added to his list of titles.

Thernstrom was accused of racial insensitivity by students from his popular race relations course "Peopling of America." His offense? Thernstrom had used the word *Indians* instead of the politically correct *Native Americans*, endorsed the idea that the breakup of the black family was a cause of persistent black poverty, and as-

signed a book that mentioned that some people regard affirmative action as preferential treatment.

Thernstrom offered many explanations and objections, but the condemning students weren't buying. "It's like being called a Commie in the fifties," Thernstrom said. "Whatever explanation you offer, once accused, you're always suspect."[6] The next semester he stopped teaching the course altogether, to avoid being misquoted or misunderstood again.

[5] *Pr Reporter*, January 3, 1994. Vol. 37, No 1 pg. 1
[6] John Taylor "Are You Politically Correct?" *New York*, January 21, 1991, 34.

rectness becomes questionable when it steps on the toes of First Amendment rights—is it necessary to sacrifice one for the other?

The central preoccupation of the politically correct seems to be to make people more aware of what they say, but as a result of the PC obsession, more people are afraid to say anything at all (see Figure 10-17). Many institutions have adopted codes of conduct that punish students for deviating from politically correct speech, and Stephan Thernstrom is not the only professor to have stopped teaching controversial courses to avoid being hassled or accused of racism.

For publish relations practitioners, it is imperative to guard First Amendment rights and let people decide for themselves what is appropriate for them and what isn't. *History shows that imposing restraints on the availability of information to a free people is far more dangerous than any ideas that may be expressed in the formation they seek.*

QUESTIONS FOR DISCUSSION

1. As public relations director for MTV, what reasons can you give for defending the "Beavis and Butthead Show" even after an event such as the Ohio tragedy?
2. What would be your reaction if you were a professor like Stephan Thernstrom and you were accused of being politically incorrect? Was he right to stop teaching the class?

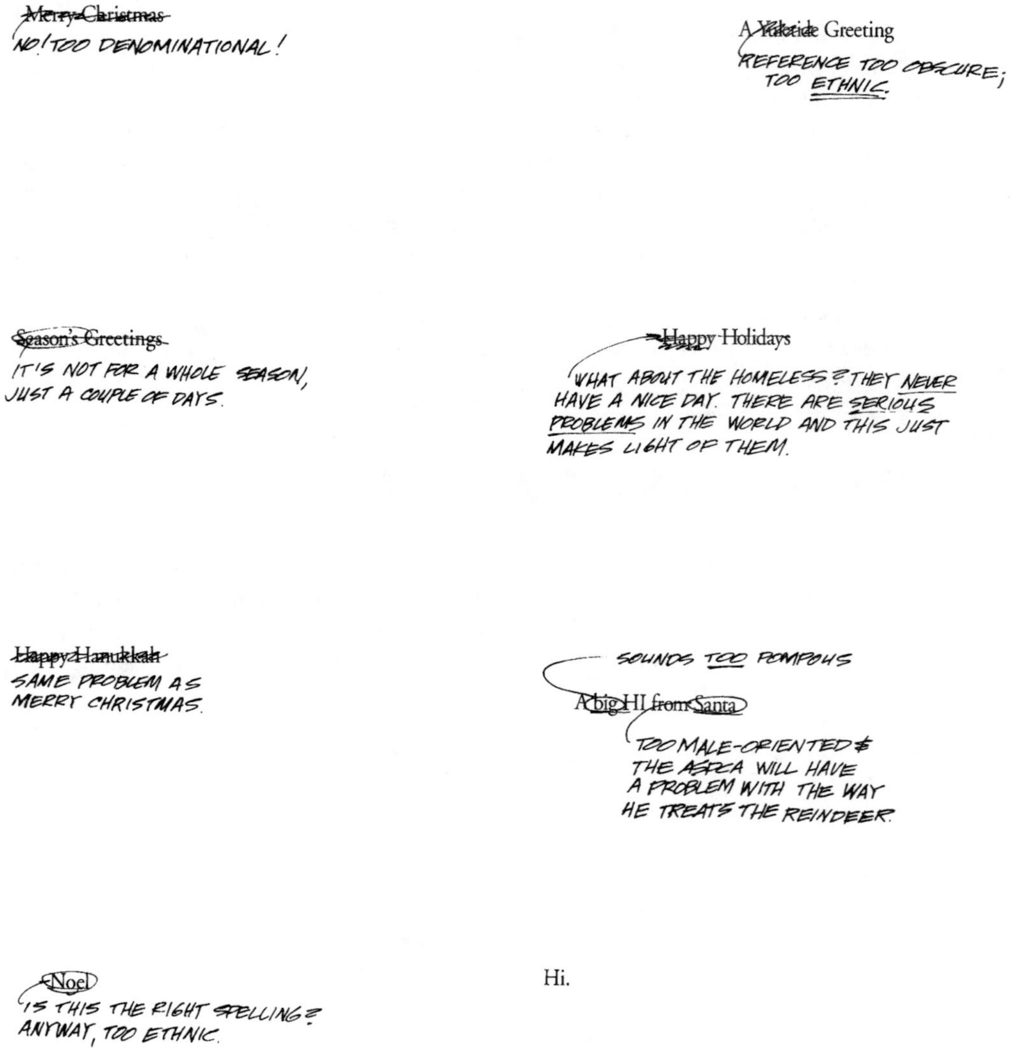

~~Merry Christmas~~
NO! TOO DENOMINATIONAL!

A ~~Yuletide~~ Greeting
REFERENCE TOO OBSCURE;
*   TOO ETHNIC.*

~~Season's Greetings~~
IT'S NOT FOR A WHOLE SEASON,
JUST A COUPLE OF DAYS.

~~Happy Holidays~~
WHAT ABOUT THE HOMELESS? THEY NEVER
HAVE A NICE DAY. THERE ARE SERIOUS
PROBLEMS IN THE WORLD AND THIS JUST
MAKES LIGHT OF THEM.

~~Happy Hanukkah~~
SAME PROBLEM AS
MERRY CHRISTMAS.

SOUNDS TOO POMPOUS
~~A big HI from Santa~~
TOO MALE-ORIENTED &
THE ASPCA WILL HAVE
A PROBLEM WITH THE WAY
HE TREATS THE REINDEER.

~~Noel~~
IS THIS THE RIGHT SPELLING?
ANYWAY, TOO ETHNIC.

Hi.

Figure 10–17 Political correctness has even affected holiday greetings, as is humorously shown in this card. (Courtesy of Duval Woglom Bruekner Partners.)

The Mammography Issue: The Effect of a Triggering Event

In 1992, 175,000 women were victims of breast cancer. Over a lifetime, an average of one in eight women will get breast cancer. In Michigan, breast cancer is the second leading cause of death among women.

As these statistics make clear, the importance of early detection of breast cancer is critical. Early detection can increase a woman's chance of living cancer-free without radical breast surgery.

Consequently, when systems and equipment used to conduct mammograms, the prime mechanism for detecting breast cancer, came under fire in Michigan in February of 1992, public concern exploded. The emotionalism of the issue added fuel to the fire and sent hospitals and other entities responsible for ensuring safe and accurate mammograms scrambling to do one of two things:

- Reassure patients and the general public that existing policies and procedures reflected the highest standards.
- Enact change to ensure that those higher standards were being met.

PRIMETIME LIVE BRINGS NATIONWIDE ATTENTION TO THE ISSUE

On February 27, 1992, ABC News *Prime Time Live*—an often sensationalizing investigative news show—took hidden cameras into clinics around the state of Michigan and interviewed several women who were victims of faulty mammograms. The program exposed the doctors who had misread mammograms as well as facilities claiming to be accredited by the ACR (American College of Radiology) when they were not.

In a follow-up segment on March 5, *Prime Time Live* reported that the ACR was taking actions against those clinics who falsely claimed accreditation. (ACR also reported receiving 500 new applications for accreditation since the February 27 show aired.) *PrimeTime* also reported that the American Cancer Society had received 50,000 calls in the last week from people with questions about where to get a good mammogram.

It was clear that *PrimeTime*'s report had escalated the public's fear—and raised their concern and mistrust of *all* entities performing or regulating mammograms.

ACCURACY OF STATE'S GRADING SYSTEM IN QUESTION

At the center of this dispute was the state of Michigan's process for grading mammography machines. Michigan's system was based on grading machines on a scale of A to F based on the "phantom test," a device that determines good or bad mammograms on the basis of the clarity of the phantom image.

Experts in the health care industry, however, had serious concerns about the validity of the state's phantom-image evaluation study and about basing a grade solely on the clarity of the image. They felt that the ACR guidelines for accreditation were much more comprehensive and valid.

THE ENVIRONMENT BEHIND THE ISSUE

The issue of mammograms and how they are regulated was already a hot one in Michigan. In 1989, legislation introduced by Representative Maxine Berman (D-Southfield) was passed, requiring annual inspection of mammography facilities. This legislation made Michigan's law governing mammography one of the most stringent in the nation. The stringency of Michigan's laws might cause the public to think—if the Michigan system has problems, what about the system in my own state?

Adding to the panic in Michigan was the fact that the Michigan Department of Health revealed that one of every six mammograms in the state flunked the state's test. Eighty percent of those that flunked were in Oakland, Macomb, and Wayne counties, putting even more pressure on the facilities in those areas to reassure patients. These areas of metro-Detroit and suburbs also had the highest geographical concentration of mammography machines in the state.

ST. JOHN HOSPITAL'S STRATEGY AND RESPONSE[1]

Two dangers loomed as possible outcomes once the *PrimeTime Live* report was aired.

[1]Our thanks to Michael E. Kairis, Media Affairs Manager and Dr. Christine Watt, Director of Mammography and Women's Imaging at St. John Hospital, for providing a wealth of information for this case.

1. The public would no longer trust Michigan-based clinics and hospitals conducting mammograms.
2. Women would lose faith in the effectiveness of mammograms and stop having them altogether.

St. John Hospital and Medical Center of Detroit conducts an average of 11,000 mammograms per year. Their machines are ACR-accredited. They have two machines, one of which received a failing grade under the state's grading system in April 1991. The machine was immediately retested in settings normally used, and passed—raising again the validity of the state's testing procedures.

The hospital public relations department's challenge was to take a proactive approach that would:

1. Reassure current patients of the high standards at St. John.
2. State St. John position on the issue.
3. Help drive the system's reform.

Here is what they did:

- Director of mammography, Dr. Christine Watt, *checked all mammograms* done in the month from when the machine received the failing grade to when it was retested, to see if any were questionable. None were.
- In a February 14 press release, they offered to *retake any patient's mammograms* free of charge.
- Dr. Watt also *responded personally* to anyone who called with a concern or a question.
- *Joined a coalition of medical physicists* representing the Great Lakes Chapter of the American Association of Physicists in Medicine (AAPM) and signed a *position paper,* along with other medical experts in the coalition, indicating the drawbacks to the grading system the state adopted.
- Joined with the Michigan Radiology Society chapter of the American College of Radiology in *indicating the drawbacks to the state's grading system.*

The hospital's public relations department also requested:

1. That the recent mammography image evaluation study be retracted.
2. An opportunity to voice concerns with the grading system at a public hearing with the Michigan Department of Public Health.

In addition, staff initiated a position paper on behalf of St. John Hospital and Medical Center that stated:

- Support for the state's interest in improving overall quality of mammographic services in Michigan.
- St. John is ACR-accredited and continues to follow ACR quality assurance programs.
- St. John is committed to patients and to making them feel safe and confident in the hospital's abilities, and therefore is concerned that the multilevel grading system is not in the best interest of hospitals or patients because it is misleading.

They also:

- Placed an editorial by Dr. Lawrence G. Wayburn, Medical Director at North Oakland Radiology Group, in the *Oakland Press.* The editorial pointed out the weaknesses of the evaluation process and the fact that when changes are made to place an institution in compliance with the system, it takes an entire year to get the letter grade changed.
- Worked through the Michigan Hospital Association to get other respected opinion leaders from the American College of Radiology and hospital presidents to write letters to the editor on the subject, pointing out the superiority of ACR accreditation to the state's grading system.
- Convinced Ellen Creager, journalist at the Detroit *Free Press,* to do an essay on her first-hand, very positive experience at St. John in which a St. John radiologist encourage her to have a follow-up exam when a suspicious abnormality appeared on her routine mammogram.

"We had good media relations in place, and we did our best to help them with their stories," said Mike Kairis, Media Affairs Manager. "We communicated what to say if the press calls to other departments to ensure we'd all be speaking with One Clear Voice."

RESULTS

After the reaction from Michigan's health care industry, the Michigan Department of Health released a statement that grades are not intended to be a reflection of the overall quality of a machine. Dr. Vernice Davis-Anthony, the State Public Health Director, sent a press release that stated that:

- The State was not convinced that the grading system used was the best and most accurate, and admitted they should have sought more input from the healthcare industry. This quote appeared:

Director Davis-Anthony also announced that the Department would convene a meeting in the near future to discuss the results of recent Department inspections of mammography facilities and to examine alternative methods of interpreting inspection results to the method of grading recently established by the Department. The grading system was used for the first time to interpret only one portion of the information from 1991 inspections of mammography facilities and may have resulted in public misunderstanding of the overall quality of some mammography programs.

• Overall, Michigan has a greater proportion of excellent quality mammography programs and machines than any other state, both because of the 1989 legislation requiring annual inspection of mammography facilities and the excellent cooperation and willingness of most facilities to make improvements when recommended by Department staff.

The state health department began issuing weekly updates on mammography centers in Michigan via a hotline staffed by the American Cancer Society to give the public up-to-date information about accredited centers and what to look for before having a mammography exam (see Figure 10–18). (As much as six months after the initial media coverage, the hotline was still fielding thirty-five to forty calls per day.)

The state noted a great number of applications to the American College of Radiology by hospitals who were not presently ACR-accredited.

PUBLIC HEARING AND TASK FORCE TO CHANGE LEGISLATION

As a result of the public hearing requested by the Great Lakes Chapter of the AAPM, the state withdrew the letter grades. It formed a task force including physicists, representatives from the American Cancer Society, the Michigan Hospital Association and others. In addition, the Food and Drug Administration will pass new federal standards, effective October 1, 1994, that require clinics to have specialized equipment and trained technicians, keep complete records of performance, and undergo annual audits.

GREATER AWARENESS LOCALLY

According to Dr. Watt, the hospital continues to average 11,000 mammograms per year via their St. John, Macomb, and Partridge Woods facilities. "The difference is that more patients ask about accreditation—the public is more discerning," she said. Since St. John has always been an accredited facility, "we haven't lost any patients. In fact, we may have increased." St. John opened a Women's Breast Imaging Center during the summer of 1993. Television stations such as Channel 50 in the Detroit area, have run Breast Cancer Awareness programs. St. John was one of several hospitals to advertise during the series.

Figure 10–18 These materials are offered by the Michigan Department of Health as well as the American Cancer Society to answer women's questions about mammography and breast cancer.

TRIGGERING NATIONAL CHANGE

The events in Michigan triggered nationwide attention to the importance of having a process to regulate the effectiveness of mammograms, and other states began their own reform. A July 1992 study by Lou Fintor, public health analyst and advise for the U.S. Department of Health and Human Services, found the following:

- As of July 1992, thirty-six percent of all mammography units in the United States had been accredited by the ACR.
- The number of states approving laws governing mammography reimbursement jumped from two percent in 1986 to eighty-six percent in 1992.
- As of July 1992, forty-two states and the District of Columbia had passed laws encouraging or requiring third-party coverage of mammography screening.
- Twenty-five states now place restrictions on radiation exposure. Thirty-two states include equipment specifications. Sixteen states mandate standards for mammography facilities. Twenty states include personnel standards.
- In October of 1994, all clinics with mammogram equipment will be required by the FDA to pass inspection, become accredited, and have the machines calibrated regularly according to the standards published by the American College of Radiology.

PUBLIC EDUCATION

As a result of the widespread attention to the mammography issue, other states are also doing more to educate the public about breast cancer and the importance of mammograms. In addition to passing a bill to establish statewide standards for mam-

---

Aided by St. John Medical Center's public relations staff, the *Grosse Pointe News* Feb. 20, 1992 ran an article featuring six key questions NCI advises to ask a provider before getting a mammogram. It typifies the type of public health education that hospital and health-related practitioners perform regularly—as a major public service.

1. Are you certified by the American College of Radiology or the American Osteopathic Board of Radiology?

2. Is your equipment certified by the state licensing board (the Michigan Department of Public Health)?

3. Is your X-ray equipment dedicated to or specifically designed for mammography exams?

4. Is your X-ray equipment calibrated regularly by a certified radiological physicist? (The NCI recommends that mammogram machines be calibrated at least once a year and checked against a standard to make sure that radiation doses and measurements are correct.)

5. Have the radiology technologists who shoot and read the mammograms taken special courses in mammography? (They should also be licensed by the state or certified by the American Registry of Radiological Technologists, the NCI says.)

6. Is mammography part of your regular practice? (The NCI suggests that a facility should perform at least ten mammograms a week.)

TECHNICAL PUBLIC RELATIONS

The accreditation program of the American College of Radiology (ACR) evaluates mammography facilities with respect to the standards listed below. Communicating and gaining professional and public understanding of technical information is a growing area of public relations practice (see Figure 10–19). This relatively simple example illustrates the challenge.

- **Radiation dose.** The average glandular dose must be measured at least annually. For examination of a 4.5 cm thick, compressed breast consisting of fifty percent glandular and fifty percent adipose tissue, the dose must not exceed 0.4 rad per exposure.
- **Equipment.** The mammography equipment must be designed especially for mammography and have a compression device and removable grid. A low-energy beam is required to produce high subject contrast, and a compression device is essential to further improve contrast, minimize radiographic scatter, produce uniform density, and reduce dose and subject motion. Molybdenum target/molybdenum filter tubes are recommended for film-screen mammography.
- **Facility quality control program.** The mammography facility must have a documented quality control program with procedure manuals, technologist's checks, and physicist's checks. Systems for reviewing outcome data, including follow-up on the disposition of positive mammograms and correlation of surgical biopsy results with mammogram reports must be established.
- **Personnel qualifications.** Physicians must be certified by the American Board of Radiology of the American Osteopathic Board of Radiology or have two months of full-time documented formal training in mammogram interpretation. Each physician should interpret or review a minimum of 480 mammograms per year and should regularly participate in mammography continuing education programs. *Radiological physicists* should be certified by the American Board of Radiology in radiological physics or diagnostic radiological physics. *Radiological technologists* must be certified by the American Registry of Radiological Technologists and/or have state licensure. They should receive continual supervision on image quality from the interpreting physicians and regularly participate in mammography continuing education programs.

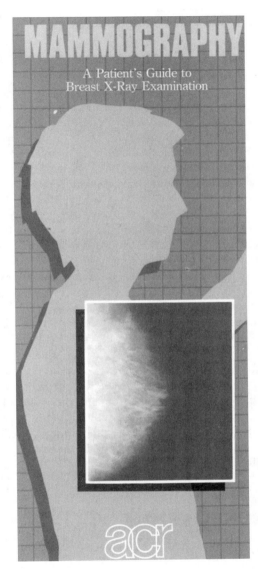

Figure 10–19 The American College of Radiology distributes printed materials to women who would like more information about mammography. (Courtesy of ACR.)

mography machines, Governor Weld of Massachusetts dedicated $3 million of the fiscal 1993 budget to breast cancer education and outreach programs.

SUMMARY

Though the initial attention to this issue was panic-driven, it has resulted in positive outcomes—both in patient awareness and legislative reform. Yet in the fall 1993, many general questions about the validity of mammograms were brought up. New research by the NCI recommended annual mammograms only for women over fifty. A debate ensued, between the National Cancer Institute, the American Cancer Society, and the National Breast Cancer Coalition about what guidelines to recommend for women from the ages of forty to forty-nine.

The debate revolves around whether women in this age bracket should get mammograms once a year or every two years. Granted, these are only guidelines and it is up to each woman to decide, but these recommendations do play a role in determining whether health insurance will cover the routine mammograms or the woman must pay for it out of pocket. The NCI later backed down from its proposal and voted to unanimously retain its original guidelines to recommend an annual screening for woman over forty. One deciding factor in the debate was a rally in Washington at the time the study came out. Members of the Breast Cancer Coalition and others presented 2.6 million signatures to the president to emphasize that breast cancer has become a national epidemic.

In this instance, as in the original furor in Michigan, *it was public relations activities, dealing with public perception, that drove supposedly scientific decisions.*

The benefits and effectiveness of mammography remain somewhat cloudy. However, one fact remains. More than 2 million women will fall victim to breast cancer in the 1990s and 400,000 of those women will die unless more research is conducted to curb this disease. Perhaps creating awareness of the need for more research is the ultimate task for public relations action.

QUESTIONS FOR DISCUSSION

1. Many changes in health care will probably result from national health care reform. What opportunities do you believe these changes will create for public relations practitioners? What ethical questions may arise in regard to mammography?

2. What other activities might St. John's Medical Center have undertaken when state authorities said publicly that one of the hospital's mammography machines had failed to meet state standards?

3. When unfairly accused, as St. John's was in this case, is it good or bad strategy

to make a big point of the unfairness? Why? Cite some public relations maxims or rules of behavioral science to support your position.

4. Exactly what was the triggering event in this case? List the behaviors it triggered, and from whom.

PROBLEM 10
WHETHER TO BLOW THE WHISTLE

You are nearing the end of your second year of employment as editor of the main publication for employees in one of the three largest not-for-profit hospitals in the county. You have a good deal. Your boss, the director of public relations, a woman of about thirty-five, listens to your ideas about the publication. You have converted it from a tabloid appearing once a month to a weekly illustrated newsletter. An audit shows that readers, including staff doctors and donors as well as employees, find it more dynamic. They like it. The only intervention you have had from your boss was near the end of your first year. At that time, she told you to follow the hospital's policy of getting three competitive printing bids annually and then to award the contract for the next year to a particular one of the three. You noted that this bid was not the lowest. Your boss explained that she preferred the quality of their work and added that the printing firm had made generous financial contributions to the hospital. At that time you followed the directions of your boss.

The future looks bright to you. And why not? You are aware that your boss has her eyes on the next job up, as director of development, a position now occupied by a woman scheduled to retire in a few years. You can see yourself succeeding your boss at that time.

Looking back, you consider your first two years to have been a period of learning the ropes and how the game goes in the hospital. During this period, the owner of the printing firm doing the newsletter has established a social relationship with your and your spouse including taking you to dinner at their country club.

You have also noticed that the printer has a close personal relationship with your boss and the hospital's director of development. You know that they receive entertainment and gifts. When the director of development decided to buy a new car, the printer sent her to a dealer where she got a fantastic discount. As for the public relations director, your boss, she was sponsored for membership in the printer's "Executives Only" tennis club.

Here you are, finishing up your second year. A few days ago, quite by coincidence, you overheard some disconcerting comments during a cocktail party. The comments indicated that your boss's husband is the brother of the printer's wife—this you didn't know. Also, your boss apparently has had some sort of financial interest in the printing firm. Your director of development's daughter, you heard, has worked at the printing firm as a typist-receptionist. Someone at the party said that she earned more than other clerical employees, including those with greater skills and experience.

Naturally, this information is upsetting to you, and, to make matters worse, this is the week the three competitive printing bids for next year's contract have come in. You have looked at them. The present printer, whom you have again been told to favor, has submitted a bid twenty percent higher than the lowest of the three.

You have every right to be upset and in a quandary. If you grant the business for the coming year, amounting to $60,000, to the highest bidder, and someone in the treasurer's office questions it, you could be in big trouble. If you tell the present printer he has to submit a second bid at a figure fifty percent lower, you will be unethical in conduct and in contravention of the hospital's stated policy. Beyond that, what if one of the other bidders found out and turned in a complaint to the consumer advocate in the state's attorney general's office? If you take the matter to your boss, you may have to confront her with what you have heard about an apparent conflict of interest on her part.

Of course, an alternative would be to go over the boss's head to the director of development. She, too, has accepted favors from the printer on a social basis. Maybe she would just as soon not get involved. On the other hand, perhaps she has been involved in helping the printer get work from other departments in the hospital. If so, where would that leave you?

Then there is the hospital administrator. If you bypass both of your superiors in the structure, you will almost surely wind up with a unhappy working situation—or be out looking for a new position.

Finally, if you do nothing, are you committed to a standard of honesty or business ethics that you cannot live with?

Everything considered, what are you going to do—specifically, in what sequence, with what goals, and what personal strategy and tactics?

Chapter 11

Career Preparation

RESOURCES ARE HANDY

College and university libraries and bookstores have selections of books and pamphlets providing career guidance information. In fact, some universities have offices that can provide you with information or set up interviews with practicing professionals.

It is not our purpose here to enlarge on those resources. You can focus on career options by researching those sources—and you should. It is as important to investigate before you start making calls, writing letters, or showing up for interviews, as it has been to do your homework before showing up in class.

Some not-so-common informational resources about public relations jobs are listed at the end of this chapter.[1]

We concentrate on straight talk about some of the unvarnished realities you will encounter as you launch yourself into a public relations career.

YOU ARE INVOLVED IN A MATCHING GAME

It has been said that many people working for a living spend their lives in jobs and in working environments in which they do not find much satisfaction. They feel constrained to stay in their job, or career track, simply because they need the paycheck to pay off student loans, house mortgage, or maintain health insurance. These

---

[1]For information on salary for various specialties within public relations, see the "Eighth Annual Salary Survey" summary covered by Nicholas J. Tortorello and Elizabeth Wilhelm in *Public Relations Journal* 49 (June 1993) pp 10–19.

people put in fifty weeks of merely fulfilling the norm, take two weeks' vacation from it, and then do it over again.

Do not get caught in that trap. Unhappy employees generally share their unhappiness and their gripes with their associates, hurting morale and lowering productivity all around. But employers do not readily fire people in whom they have invested time and money to train, simply because they are not resident cheerleaders. So, as an employer, you may put up with less performance than you want; as an employee you become content with average expectations. It is, frankly, a bad deal for both employer and employee.

COMMITMENT COUNTS

Spend whatever time and effort it takes, including false starts, trial and error, to *match yourself to a career track on which you are so enthusiastic and deeply committed that other employers will try to hire you away*. Circumstances and your nature may dictate that you change employment on occasion, as a professional entrepreneur of your particular talents. You may prefer the route of choosing one company for the long haul and, step by step, climbing the ladder there. However, downsizing and reengineering offer no guarantees of employment security. You will discover early on whether fulfillment for you personally derives from growth within a single environment, or whether you have to respond to a three-, five-, or seven-year itch for totally new surroundings and challenges. Either way, your attitude going into any and every job should be one of commitment. That is contagious. It impresses your associates and bosses. It makes you attractive to other employers.

In seeking a match-up with an employer, particularly the first one, you will be ahead of the game if you set down in writing those values and characteristics that are critical to you. As a minimum:

- Culture and character of the workplace
- Opportunity for using skills, creativity, and professional growth
- Mission and social values of the organization
- Security and support systems versus risk taking and self-direction

SOME BASIC PRINCIPLES OF JOB HUNTING

For entry-level graduates who like things neat and orderly, we have tailored this list to reflect the working environment of today[2]:

---

[2]Adapted from Leonard Corwen, "The 11 Rules of Job Hunting," *There's a Job for You* (Piscataway, N.J.: New Century Publishers, 1983).

1. Make your job search a full-time occupation; be persistent in your efforts.
2. Use your personal and professional contact network for "hidden" jobs.
3. Be confident and enthusiastic but not immoderately so.
4. Know yourself: your strengths and weaknesses.
5. Be prepared. Do advance research about the company.
6. Get objective advice on how to prepare your résumé and cover letter.
7. Keep records of interviews: Never assume that a closed door will remain that way.

JOBS—THE WORK TO BE DONE

When an employer wants to hire a public relations practitioner, the job description will contain some or all of the following categories of skills, depending on whether a specialist or a generalist is sought. The more closely your skills and experience are related to the description, the better your chances (see Figure 11–1).

1. Writing.
2. Editing.
3. Submitting newsworthy material to appropriate outlets.
4. Preparing speeches for others and giving speeches.
5. Arranging for production of printed matter, slides, films.
6. Programming campaigns and special events.
7. Supervising institutional advertising programs.
8. Preparing reports, position papers, public statements.
9. Monitoring meetings and interpreting conclusions.
10. Training spokespersons; being one.
11. Planning a budget, operating on it, accounting for the outcome.
12. Evaluating public opinion, program results, and competitive intelligence.

THE PUBLIC RELATIONS SKILL BASICS

In general, employers are looking for these basic traits or talents from a new employee:

1. Ability to write for publication or electronic media.
2. Natural enthusiasm, easy to motivate.
3. Mental maturity, a broad range of interests.
4. Ability to express thoughts effectively.

Science Public Relations Manager

National scientific organization located in midtown Manhattan seeks Science Public Relations Professional to manage its Public Information Division representing physical scientists.

Duties will include:

○ Representing the institute and its Societies in communication with mass media, government, the scientific community and the general public.

○ Participating in the development of projects that enhance scientific education.

○ Overseeing, writing, and assisting in the graphic design of print materials.

Experience in radio & TV product desired. Degree in communications, journalism, public relations preferred.

Five years or more experience in PR management, with good background in physical science necessary.

Competitive salary, as well as excellent benefits, offered. Send resume including sal. history, to:

Theresa C. Braun
Personnel Manager

BUSINESS PUBLICIST

We are looking for highly motivated professionals with a minimum of 4 years **business-business, financial** or **real estate** PR. Emphasis on **media relations** is a must. Salary commensurate with experience. Generous benefit package.

Resumes in confidence to:
CLEO PHILLIPS VP/Recruitment

MEDICAL / HEALTHCARE

Mid sized agency with prestigious client list needs pro with excellent medical and science contacts placement record. Strong writer, team player, competitive salary and benefits.

Resumes to: **Brown & Powers**

PUBLIC RELATIONS ASSISTANT

International Jewish migration agency has an opportunity for a self-starter with proven PR skills including writing, editing and media relations. Minimum 3 years related experience, excellent interpersonal skills and familiarity with production. Salary mid to high 20's, generous benefits and potential for professional development. Please send resume with salary requirements to: Personnel Dept

HIAS

DIRECTOR, PR/MEDIA

Wash. based public affairs firm seeking senior level executive to direct all PR/Media efforts including support of: grassroots, lobbying, business promotion, corp. public relations, and new business development. Ten year exp. minimum. Please send resume and salary requirements to:

PR/Media, P.O. Box 65661

ACCOUNT EXECUTIVE

Investor relations firm seeks highly organized and articulate person with excellent writing skills. Ideal candidate will have one or two years of PR or IR experience. Send resume, salary requirements and writing samples to:

Sharon Hunt, The Equity Group Inc.,

Figure 11–1 Ads from one publication give specifications. Entry-level openings are not frequently advertised. [Firm addresses deleted.] (Courtesy of PR Week and Public Relations Journal.)

5. An attractive personality, with wit or humor and poise.
6. Practical work experience gained while a student.
7. A working knowledge of the graphic arts, including desktop publishing skills.
8. Creativity in tying public relations to sales, promotion, and advertising.
9. A good feel for community relationships.

The ability to write and speak persuasively is critical in public relations. If you do not possess those abilities you might be better off to choose another field of endeavor.

Of course, there are careers concentrated on opinion research, or lobbying legislators, or raising funds for charities, or staging public events. However, research findings have to be put on paper. Lobbyists present verbal statements of position, sometimes testify at hearings, or prepare testimony for clients to deliver. Fundraising is done with written or oral appeals, whether direct mail or on a telethon. A public event, such as a postseason bowl game, never flies without dozens of written proposals, committee meetings, discussions, and the like, involving public relations or promotional people.

AUTHORITY AND ROLES

The level of authority and the assigned roles of practitioners vary from one organization to another. Roles have been categorized by research, on the basis of behavior and strategy reported by practitioners.[4] The roles are those of:

1. **Communications technician**, who prepares information for internal or external audiences.
2. **Expert prescriber**, who defines problems, devises programs, and oversees implementation.
3. **Communication facilitator**, who provides liaison, interpretation, and mediation between an organization and its publics; increasingly practitioners have been designated as authorized spokespersons for the institutions that they represent.
4. **Problem-solving process facilitator**, who consults and collaborates on matters involving diagnosis, planning, implementation, and evaluation.

The ability to help an organization adjust to its total environment is the name of the game. At its highest levels, public relations is a *management function* that deals with strategic planning, issue anticipation, and stakeholder management internally and externally.

Professionals who excel in the art and science of communications are not born that way. *Most have struggled word by word, error by error, until they have mastered such things as spelling, syntax, and adverbs.* They have studiously gained a sophisticated understanding of the mission and the values of their employ-

---

[4]Scott Cutlip, Allen H. Center, and Glen M. Broom, "Practitioners of Public Relations," Chap. 2 in *Effective Public Relations*, 7th ed. (Englewood Cliffs, N.J.: Prentice Hall, 1994): 26–55. For a more complete description of roles, see Glen M. Broom and George D. Smith, "Testing the Practitioner's Impact on Clients," *Public Relations Review* 5 (Fall 1979).

ers, whether business, government, or private welfare, and the particular language, jargon, and symbolic gestures that prevail.

Effective communication is hard work. For those qualified and committed, the work is a labor of love.

JOB PROSPECTING

Your prospect list can be made up by types of employers you prefer, corporate versus nonprofit, in-house versus outside agency, and so on. Your list can be selected from potential employers in a city or a region where you prefer to locate. Or it can be made up on the basis of the kind of work atmosphere you prefer: small organization or large; heavy on news media relations, identity advertising, or community affairs. It can be based on the scope of an organization's activities, whether local, regional, or national. It can prioritize the kind of specialization or role you seek.

Most libraries have lists of employers and their headquarters, branches, or subsidiaries in any given community. Within public relations specifically, there are two mainstay resources. One is the Public Relations Society of America's directory. Each member of the society, including faculty, has a copy. The other consists of directories put out by the publisher of Jack O'Dwyer's *Newsletter*. One directory lists public relations firms, the other, corporations.

There are also directories at local chambers of commerce, membership rosters of local chapters of PRSA, the International Association of Business Communicators, and nonaffiliated local publicity and public relations clubs. If these are not available, try the Yellow Pages of the phone book.

Beyond just making a list, job prospecting or networking means meeting professionals through activities in PRSA (Public Relations Student Society of America) and internships—going to their offices during breaks and introducing yourself, and keeping them up to date. You should begin networking as soon as possible (yes, it can be done while you are in school), because you will need more than a short time; building contacts takes a year or more. Employment agencies may be helpful, particularly in metropolitan areas. But they usually do not deal with entry-level or graduate-level jobs.

RÉSUMÉ AND COLLATERAL MATERIAL

Your résumé should contain whatever a prospective employer needs to know about you. Of course, it needs to be presented in a logical sequence for quick digestion. The following should all be included in your résumé:

- Where can you be reached by mail or phone?
- What kind of job or career are you seeking? In a shrinking world and the global village coming, are you fluent in a foreign language? Will you relocate?

- What education and training have you had that are relevant? Are you proficient in computer-word processing, opinion research analysis, photography?
- What work experience, if any, have you had that was related to your job objectives? Have you been involved in an internship? Pro-Am Fellowship? School publication? Media? Agency?
- What work experience have you had (1) that shows that you are not afraid of work or (2) that helped you pay your way through school?
- What professional student associations did you belong to during school?

Your résumé might be helped by containing something unusual that catches the prospective employer's attention, that singles you out of the pack as an "interesting person," and provides a conversational gambit for an interview. In this last category, passive or general hobbies do not qualify. For example, the fact that you enjoy spectator sports, watching television or movies, walking, or traveling are commonplace. A specific, unusual hobby or activity does qualify. For example, "Teach piano privately." This says something interesting. So does "Speak three languages fluently," or "President of Student Association," or "Member air rescue squad," "Have sold five feature stories to national magazines," "Studied abroad for a year."

Describe your activities in terms of the skills an employer needs. Such information may be along the lines of "scheduling other employees in a summer job," "closing the store," "coordinating and updating a mailing list," or "answering complaint calls."

In dealing with references, the standard listing to put on your résumé is a phrase such as, "References are available on request." For convenience and legal reasons, most prospective employers will use the telephone in following up a reference. So be sure to have a phone number available if they request it.

A portfolio is an essential tool. "The degree is not enough. We need to know what skills you have," was the point made by one employer. A portfolio with examples of your communication skills in various media demonstrates that the prospective employee has passed the test of real-world experience.

To say "an employer wants experience, but won't give me a chance to get it" is no excuse for the student who wants to be prepared for a career upon graduation. There are any number of volunteer organizations who want volunteer public relations help, and a growing number of summer internships. A student needs to demonstrate initiative to gain some of this early experience. Be selfish—if a volunteer organization will not let you write for its newsletter, news releases, or public service announcements, do not volunteer for them—look for another organization.

A portfolio should have in it a résumé and any other information about you—awards and the like—near the front. Next, samples of your published writing in school papers, commercial newspapers, magazines, and so on. The next section should contain some material on graphics, photography, and video. All of this material helps the prospective employer understand that you have good, sharp skills that you can put to work *now*.

Obviously, material for a portfolio cannot be produced overnight. Most students work one or two years collecting their work from a variety of organizations for a portfolio. Do not wait until next quarter or semester; begin now to gather material for your portfolio.

A **cover letter** can be the deciding factor in getting you an interview. It should be short and should not duplicate the résumé. It should, in the first sentence, express your interest in, or admiration for, the specific organization's mission, or products or services, or whatever else attracted you to it. Put another way, your letter should tell *why you are applying to them,* not why you are casting bait on the ocean, or why you desperately need a job. In your cover letters, the pronouns *you* and *your* are preferable to *I* and *my* in starting sentences. Practice using them. In order to be specific about the organization, you will need to do some research on the company. This research also helps in the next step—the interview.

THE MOMENT OF TRUTH

People are hired for all sorts of reasons, not all of them objective or based on merit. There is nepotism. The boss's nephew gets the job. There is the supplier-customer relationship. The daughter of a customer joins the public relations department of a major supplier. The son of the president of a cosmetics manufacturer joins the firm that serves that manufacturer. The owner of a firm hires a son or daughter and pays three times what the offspring is worth to skim off some profit and reduce taxes in the process.

An employer may be in need of a particular skill, such as that involved in the production phase of printed literature. Specialization, over general capability, will be the deciding factor in that situation.

An applicant may bring to an employer some experience in working for news media, or a broad range of media contacts. Similarly, an applicant may have connections with legislators, a political orientation, experience with a Political Action Committee (PAC), or a citizen group important to the employer. Such special considerations can weigh heavily. These are only a few of the many realities.

EVERYTHING ELSE BEING EQUAL

You should assume, in trying for public relations jobs, that you will not be the only applicant. Each applicant will probably have résumé, portfolio, and available references and will get a shot at the job. Each will probably be almost as intelligent, ambitious, well-training academically, and available as you are.

The single most prevalent deciding factor is the interview (see Figure 11–2). The interview is where it all comes together and a choice is made.

At the interview, "first impression," personal appearance, poise, compatibility, personality, attitudes, and articulation come into play. The interviewer wonders,

Figure 11–2   (Art by Gaston Lokvig. Courtesy of Women in Communications Inc.)

"Would this person fit into our scheme of things? Would this person bring us something we need? Would this person wear well, be more than worth the time and money we invest? Would this person grow, if we want that, or would this person be content in what we have to offer, if we want that?"

For your part, while projecting yourself against what you perceive the employer to need and want, putting your best foot forward, you will be getting some answers to your own questions. Would I like it here? Could I get excited about what these people say is important to them? Is there room to advance, if that is what I want? Or, considering my personal situation, is there security and safety here, if that is what I want most?

WHAT TO TALK ABOUT

Many topics, expected and unexpected, can come up in exploratory interviews. You would be ahead of the game to make notes after your first couple of interviews and to be prepared. One student reported the following questions asked by most interviewers?

- Tell me about yourself.
- Why do you think this would be a good place to work?
- What do you consider your strengths?
- Your weaknesses?
- What do you hope to be doing five years from now?
- Have you any questions you'd like to ask?
- What did you have in mind for a starting salary?
- If you got the job when could you start?

There were other questions related to the résumé and comments by the interviewers about their "employee program," what salary they generally started a "trainee" at, and some plugs for the organization's "promotion from within" policy.

AN OVERALL APPROACH

On the theory that practice makes perfect, do not go for your first interview at the place you would most like to work. Practice on a couple of places not so high on your list. If one of them offers you a job, you can take it, or ask for time to think it over, and check out your preferred choice in a hurry. There is nothing unethical about doing this. If an employer has three likely candidates, the choice is often delayed. You have the same option, carefully used.

Be honest. There are some questions an employer cannot ask by law. At the same time the interviewer may assume that the status of personal relationships may affect job performance. If the interviewer "guesses" that you will get married and move, you might lose a job opportunity. Volunteer enough information to let the interviewer know how long you expect to be in the area, or discuss professional goals that will help put your personal life in some perspective.

There is a lot to be gained by using any informal contact you may have at an organization to find out in advance about expected standards of behavior and dress for a formal interview. You can learn much about the customs and standards prevailing simply by looking around at the people and the workplace on your first visit.

In the interview, you are not expected to volunteer information that would hurt your chances. But **do not deliberately conceal something that can come back to haunt you later on.** If you are asked whether you can type, and you do it by hunt-and-peck, you are better off to say that you are not a touch typist, rather than be asked to flip off a news release or a letter for the boss late one afternoon and not get it done. If an employer asks if you can handle photography, the question is not whether you own an instamatic.

More and more employers of public relations professionals are assuming word-processing, desktop publishing, and video experience. A writing test may also be required. Again find out in advance whether a company has any special interview procedures. One type of test provides you with a one-sentence statement of fact and indicates that the person administering the test will answer questions you need answered to write the story. In fact, the person has a long list of questions and answers. Once you have finished your questions, you are provided with a word processor and given a set time to write the story.

Another writing exam lets you take the material home. Still other interviewers have wanted to know what you know about local media and placement of a particular story.

Some organizations are also requiring a personality profile of prospective employees. These provide the employer with general personality characteristics and some indication of how this kind of person would fit into the organization. Some of these personality inventories indicate level of initiative, follow-through, and detail work. Such indicators may be important to the office makeup. Regardless of what you may think of these inventories, do not try to "outguess" them. If you do not answer openly, the results may look significantly different from the way you want to be perceived.

Most interviews are open-ended. **Make sure you know what is supposed to happen next, or is not going to happen at all, before the interview ends, or you leave.** There should be a stated conclusion by the interviewer. "We'll call you," or "We're talking to some more people, and we'll get back to you." Or "There is somebody else here we'd like you to meet," or "Could you come back again next week?" or . . . "We appreciate your interest, but we are looking for someone who has a little different experience." If you do not hear a conclusion, ask for one. "Is there anything else I can supply to help you reach a decision?" or "When do you plan to make your decision?" or "Should I check back with you later?" Do not let yourself be left hanging out on the line. **If you are out of the running for the job, it is better to know that and get on to the next opportunity, rather than waste time until a long period of silence on the employer's part and worry on yours answer the question.**

Regardless of how you come out, write a note of thanks for the time and consideration given by the person who interviewed you. Doing so is good manners, but there can be more to it. Suppose that you were runner-up, and the first choice did not take the job. You're in. Also, every friend has a friend. If you made a favorable impression, the interviewer may tell a colleague at another organization that you "ran a close second." And you might get a call.

You will know that you have entered career heaven when the hours, the days, weeks, and months on a job go by so fast that you sometimes lose track of them. That is an infallible test.

REFERENCES AND ADDITIONAL READINGS

Almy, Robert E. and Vivian Harris. "Piloting Your Career Through Turbulent Economic Seas." *Communication World* v8 (December 1991): 24–26.

Bovet, Susan L. "Firms Use Internships to Test Entry-Level Job Seekers." *Public Relations Journal* v48 (September 1992): 26–28.

Brett-Elspas, Janis. "Self-Marketing for Career Success." *Public Relations Journal* v46 (March 1990): 10–11, 39.

Careers in Public Relations. Pamphlet from Public Relations Society of America. Available from PRSA, 33 Irving Place, New York, N.Y. 10003.

"Lessons Learned: What Winners Would Study Today." Public Relations Journal. October/November 1994 p. 40. An excerpt from the "Pursuing Professional Excellence" issue in which Gold Anvil Winners were asked what they would do if given the opprortunity to re-do their formal education.

Maister, David. "Why Employees and Their Needs Will Get the Emphasis in PR Departments and Firms Themselves," *pr reporter*, Vol. 32, No. 16, April 18, 1988. Analysis of talk to Counselors Academy.

Public Relations Career Directory. 5th ed. Detroit, MI.: Gale Research, 1993.

Public Relations Professional Career Guide. New York: PRSA Foundation, 1993. Booklet. The prevailing career ladder. Available from PRSA Foundation, 33 Irving Place, New York, N.Y. 10003.

Tortorello, Nicholas J. and Elizabeth Wilhelm. 8th Annual Salary Survey. Public Relations Journal (July 1993): 10–19.

Index